SOCIAL, POLITICAL, AND LEGAL PHILOSOPHY

Philosophical Issues Volume 11

Previously published volumes (which are available from Ridgeview Publishing Company, Box 686, Atascadero, CA 93423):

CONSCIOUSNESS,Volume I, 1991
RATIONALITY IN EPISTEMOLOGY, Volume II, 1992
SCIENCE AND KNOWLEDGE, Volume III, 1993
NATURALISM AND NORMATIVITY, Volume IV, 1993
TRUTH AND RATIONALITY, Volume V, 1994
CONTENT, Volume VI, 1995
PERCEPTION, Volume VII, 1996
TRUTH, Volume VIII, 1997
CONCEPTS, Volume IX, 1998

Previously published volume (which is available from Blackwell Publishers, 350 Main Street, Malden, MA 02148):

SKEPTICISM, Volume X, 2000

Forthcoming volume (which will be available from Blackwell Publishers, 350 Main Street, Malden, MA 02148):

OBJECTIVITY AND REALISM, Volume XII, 2002

SOCIAL, POLITICAL, AND LEGAL PHILOSOPHY

Philosophical Issues Volume 11

Edited by Ernest Sosa and Enrique Villanueva

Blackwell Publishers Boston MA & Oxford UK

Blackwell Publishers, Inc.
350 Main Street
Malden, MA 02148 USA

Blackwell Publishers, Ltd.
108 Cowley Road
Oxford OX4 1JF
United Kingdom

Library of Congress Cataloging-in-Publication Data has been applied for.

ISBN 0-631230-27-0

ISBN 0-631230-26-2 (P)

ISSN 1533-6077

Contents

Philosophical Issues, 11
Social, Political, and Legal Philosophy, 2001

Editorial Preface

This volume includes main papers delivered at the SOFIA conference held in Mazatlan, Mexico, December 11–14, 1999, as well as papers invited specifically for the volume. We express our gratitude to the following persons and institutions for supporting the conference: Instituto de Investigaciones Jurídicas (UNAM) and its Director, Dr. Diego Valadés Ríos; the State of Sinaloa, Mexico; and the Colegio de Sinaloa, in Sinaloa, Mexico.

Ernest Sosa and *Enrique Villanueva*
Co-Editors

PHILOSOPHICAL ISSUES, 11
Social, Political, and Legal Philosophy, 2001

"I Thought She Consented"

Marcia W. Baron

In criminal law, a mistake of fact is often an adequate defense. That is, it is recognized as a decisive reason for acquittal. Should mistakes be considered adequate defenses only when they are reasonable? Or should unreasonable mistakes also be decisive grounds for acquittal?

The question arises in connection with various offenses, and often is discussed as if the answer must be the same no matter what the crime (or, no matter what the mistake). I think this is misguided, for the issue turns in part on what it is reasonable to ask of people, and how much we ask of people if we do not allow unreasonable mistakes to exculpate will vary depending on the type of crime, and thus the type of mistake. The answer may well turn out to be that unreasonable mistakes should never be complete defenses; indeed I think that is likely. But we should not assume that, and should examine the issue with attention to the types of mistake that can arise in connection with each particular crime. In this essay I'll focus on the crime of rape. Although I'll examine arguments claiming that mistakes should not have to be reasonable to be a complete defense—or what is roughly equivalent, that negligence should never be considered an adequate mens rea—I will for the most part discuss the question in relation to rape, where the usual mistake defense is 'I thought she was consenting'.[1] Mistakes, I'll argue, are possible regarding sexual consent, and for this reason, a jury instruction on mistake defenses should sometimes be given, but only reasonable mistakes should exculpate. An unreasonable mistake is only possible if the defendant was indifferent as to whether his partner consented, or at best cared about it too little to attend to the matter and to stop if there was reason to think she wasn't consenting. An unreasonable mistake shows him to be culpable in roughly the same way that recklessness does.

I.

The issue I am addressing is a mens rea issue. There are two main components of almost any conviction: the act element, or actus reus, and the mental element, or mens rea.[2] The prosecution has to show both that the defendant committed a voluntary act (or omitted to do something that she was legally required to do) and that she acted with a state of mind that shows her to be culpable.[3]

Although the subject of my paper is a mens rea issue, the act element in rape needs to be mentioned, as well. What exactly is the act? Is it nonconsensual sex? If that is how it is defined, what the prosecution has to prove, to satisfy the actus reus element, is that the defendant voluntarily engaged in sex with the complainant (however sex is defined by the statute) and that the complainant did not consent to it. But in much of the US the prosecution has to prove something more, namely that sex was forced. It is usually part of the statute that what took place was not merely nonconsensual, but forced (and courts then struggle to determine exactly what satisfies the force requirement, other than the obvious, such as brandishing a weapon). My view is that force should not be part of the legal definition of rape, and thus that the prosecution's task, with respect to the act element, should only be to prove nonconsensual sex.[4] I won't argue for that position here, but I mention it because it bears on my position regarding mistakes.[5] One might argue that we should not have a mistake defense at all. I would be sympathetic to this position if I favored retaining the force requirement (particularly if I favored retaining it in a robust form), but if we abandon the force requirement, as I think we should, a mistake defense is warranted. (See Sect. VII.)

Three other preliminaries: I understand consent not as a mental state, akin to wanting, but more nearly as a performative, as an expression, or a manifestation of a mental state.[6] Whether one has the mental state is immaterial. So if I say 'Yes' or indicate enthusiasm in my actions, and do not in any way signal dissent, I consent even if I in fact am not at all enthusiastic—provided that the reason for saying 'Yes' is not terror or some other condition that keeps this expression from constituting consent.[7] If I say 'No,' I withhold consent, and it doesn't matter what my actual mental state is (unless it is terror). I might in fact feel sexual desire towards the person I am refusing; but that does not change the fact that I am withholding consent.

Second, although women are by no means the only people who are ever raped, I will generally use pronouns that suggest that the rapists are men and the victims are women. I think that most of what I say applies also to rapes of men, by either men or women, but I know less about such rapes and don't want to claim that what I say covers them as well. I also am not covering rapes of children, and a lot of what I say would not apply to them since what needs to be said about children and consent is quite different from what needs saying about adults and consent.

Finally, let me mention that the position I favor—that unreasonable mistakes should not be a complete defense to a rape charge—is consistent with the position that they should mitigate. One might hold that this is something that should be taken into account at sentencing. Alternatively, one might favor degrees of rape, comparable to degrees of homicide; a rape committed by someone who did not realize the woman was not consenting might be classified as "negligent rape" and would warrant a lighter sentence than a rape by someone who knew the woman was (probably) not consenting. Whether unreasonable mistakes should mitigate is beyond the scope of this paper.[8]

II.

Before I narrow the focus to the 'I thought she consented' defense, an explanation of the broader mens rea issue is in order. As noted above, the prosecution has to prove not only that the defendant committed a voluntary act (or omitted to do something that she was legally required to do) but also that she acted with a state of mind that shows her to be culpable. What state of mind should the prosecution have to prove? For some crimes, it is purpose; for others, knowledge suffices; in yet other cases, e.g., reckless homicide, it suffices to show that the defendant acted recklessly. In the language of the Model Penal Code,

> A person acts recklessly with respect to a material element of an offense when he consciously disregards a substantial and unjustifiable risk that the material element exists or will result from his conduct. The risk must be of such a nature and degree that, considering the nature and purpose of the actor's conduct and the circumstances known to him, its disregard involves a gross deviation from the standard of conduct that a law-abiding person would observe in the actor's situation.[9]

Although there is sometimes disagreement over which of the three levels of culpability just named should be required for a particular crime, there is no controversy regarding their suitability in general. All three are considered unquestionably to constitute culpability sufficient for criminal liability. By contrast, negligence, the fourth (and lowest) level of culpability listed in the Model Penal Code, is controversial. Negligence differs from recklessness primarily in not requiring that the actor consciously disregards a risk. Instead, "a person acts negligently with respect to a material element of an offense when he *should be aware* of a substantial and unjustifiable risk that the material element exists or will result from his conduct."[10] The definition also specifies that "the risk must be of such a nature and degree that the actor's failure to perceive it, considering the nature and purpose of his conduct and the circumstances known to him, involves a gross deviation from the standard of care that a reasonable person would observe in the actor's situation." I note this not because of any significant contrast to the definition of recklessness (see note 9) but because of the contrast to civil negligence: criminal negligence, unlike civil negligence, requires a *gross* deviation from the standard of reasonable care.[11]

In mounting an 'I thought she consented' defense, what the defense claims is that the mens rea has not been proven. If the mens rea required in that jurisdiction for sexual assault is recklessness, the defense can argue that the defendant did not consciously disregard the possibility that the complainant was not consenting. The following claims would, if true, show that the mens rea requirement was not met [though asserting (1c) or (2) would presumably not be good courtroom strategy]: (1) the defendant considered the possibility that she was not consenting and decided (a) that there was no risk that she wasn't; or (b) that there was, but that it was an insubstantial risk; or (c) that there was and it was substantial, but it was "justifiable";[12] (2) the defendant never gave any thought to whether the complainant was consenting or not and hence did not "consciously disregard" the risk; or (3) the defendant felt sure that the complainant was consenting and never considered—or even noticed—the possibility that she was not. As long as he did not consciously disregard the risk, the mens rea is not proven. It doesn't matter why he was unaware of the risk (or although aware, saw it to be insubstantial or justifiable). His belief that she was (probably) consenting—or failure to concern himself with the matter at all—does not have to be reasonable to negate a mens rea of recklessness.

By contrast, if negligence suffices to meet the mens rea requirement, the prosecution has an easier task. It needs only to show that the defendant *should have known* that there was a "substantial and unjustifiable" risk that she was not consenting. That he did not know (or even suspect) does not negate the mens rea. If he was not aware that she did not consent but should have been, he acted negligently.

What arguments are available to the defense to show that he did not act negligently? My interest is not in tactics that might non-rationally persuade, but in arguments that, given the MPC definitions, would show the defendant not to be legally culpable. And I am supposing here that the complaining witness did not consent and that the defendant was not aware that she didn't (and was not even aware that she might well not be consenting). Given the MPC definition of 'negligence', the defense would ideally show that a reasonable person might well not have recognized (or better still, would not have recognized either) that the complainant was not consenting or that there was a substantial risk that she wasn't consenting. (The idea is that if a reasonable person might well have recognized this, the defendant did not act culpably in failing to recognize that she wasn't consenting). Put differently, the defense aims to show that the defendant did not, in failing to be aware of the risk, deviate from "the standard of care that a reasonable person would observe" in the defendant's situation. The shorthand but somewhat misleading way of putting the point is to say that the defendant reasonably believed that she was consenting. This is what the defense aims to show. Of course, since the burden of proof is on the prosecution, the defense needs only to show that the prosecution has not proven beyond a reasonable doubt that he did not believe, on reasonable grounds, that she consented.

I said it is a "somewhat misleading" way of putting the point for the following reason. What matters isn't really that the defendant (un)reasonably believed that she was consenting, but that the defendant conducted himself (un)reasonably. Suppose he unreasonably believed that she was probably consenting, even though she had said "No, I don't want this," but that he decided to stop just in case she in fact wasn't consenting. Even though he unreasonably believed she was probably consenting, there is no negligence. So the problem, in negligence, is not exactly that one's belief is unreasonable; it has more to do with a failure to exercise due care, failure to properly attend, or to make sure that x is the case rather than just assume, or hope for the best.[13]

It is standard in US legal scholarship to treat as equivalent the positions that even unreasonable mistakes should exculpate and that negligence should not be punishable. I shall follow suit, with the caveat mentioned above. There is, however, a tendency to use 'reasonable belief' in a way that is ambiguous, and I want to avoid reproducing the ambiguity. 'Reasonable belief' is ambiguous between 'a belief that the actor held on reasonable grounds' and 'a belief for which there are reasonable grounds', where the latter leaves open the possibility that the actor's grounds for the belief were not reasonable. When I speak of 'reasonable belief' I mean that the actor's grounds were reasonable. An analogous point holds for 'reasonable mistake'.

III.

The inclusion of negligence in the MPC list of levels of culpability was controversial at the time that the MPC was drafted and remains controversial. In the view of some legal scholars, the very idea of mens rea is at odds with counting negligence among the ways to satisfy the mens rea requirement.[14] 'Mens rea', they point out, refers to a state of mind.

If at the time that I committed the offense I intended to harm the person, clearly my state of mind at that time is one that shows me to be culpable. Likewise if I knew that I was harming him but went ahead anyway. If I acted recklessly, I knew that there was a substantial and unjustifiable risk that what I was about to do would harm him, but I consciously disregarded that risk and proceeded to act in a way that, as it turned out, did harm him. Once again, I acted with a state of mind that shows me to be culpable. But what is my objectionable state of mind when I act negligently? Here it is not the case that I intend to cause harm, or know that I will (very probably) cause harm, or consciously disregard the substantial, unjustifiable risk that I'll cause harm; my fault is only that I am not aware of a risk that I should be aware of.[15] There is, it is claimed, no guilty state of mind here, no state of mind that shows me to be culpable, for not being aware of something is not a state of mind.

The problem with the argument is that it assumes that a state of mind can show one to be culpable only by what was present, not by what was absent. There is no reason to assume this (other than the fact that it generates the result desired by those putting forward the argument, namely that negligence should not count as a way to satisfy the mens rea requirement).

A related but more promising argument is that not even blame, much less punishment, is in order if the person simply does not notice these things that he should notice, the suggestion being that if this is the way he is, he probably cannot do much about it. Thus Jerome Hall asks, "Is one to be blamed because one is not normally sensitive to ordinary danger or to a duty to attend to such danger?"[16]

Now as a matter of fact, we blame people for such things all the time. If someone pitching a baseball to her child close to a play area full of children just isn't sensitive to the possibility that the ball might hit a child in the head, or if she bikes at high speed through the park, oblivious to the fact that elderly people who cannot safely leap out of the way use the same path, we blame her for failure to be aware of the danger. And we do not just blame; when she harms someone, we may punish. We hold careless people responsible for their carelessness, as when a careless driver, with no malice whatsoever, fumbles with the radio as he approaches the intersection, failing to notice that there is a traffic light, that it is red, and that there are pedestrians crossing the street. People are blamed and sometimes imprisoned for such conduct.

That people are in fact blamed and imprisoned for such conduct does not, of course, show that it is right that they are so treated. We need to ask whether it is unjust to punish people for such failures. In particular, we need to respond to the claim that careless people cannot help being careless and therefore do not deserve to be punished.

In thinking about whether a person could have acted otherwise in a given situation, we should bear in mind that we may consistently hold that once in that situation, he could not have acted otherwise, but that he could, and should, have taken measures to avoid getting into the situation. We make such judgments all the time, both blaming people and holding them criminally liable even though we do not think that once in the situation, the person could have acted differently. The very intoxicated person could not, once intoxicated, have exercised greater caution; the person who drove even though he knew he was prone to epileptic seizures (and had been told by his physician not to drive until tests showed that his medication was effective) was not able during his epileptic seizure to avoid hitting the pedestrian in the crosswalk. But both people may be held criminally liable—and I think rightly so—since they knowingly put themselves in a situation in which they would not be able to stop themselves from seriously harming others.[17]

In general, character traits do not excuse.[18] We don't say 'This person is just violent; he couldn't have kept himself from acting violently in that situation.' We might indeed believe that once in the situation, feeling very angry, he could not at that moment have acted differently. But we hold people responsible for dealing with their character flaws rather than treating them as fixed points, as forces that propel them to act this way or that and that simply have a life of their own. The violent person, the careless person, the lazy person, the impatient person—each may need to set rules for himself so that in a given situation he does not strike another or fail to attend to dangers. The careless driver may have to force himself not to change a CD or radio channel or even engage in conversation while driving; the violent or irascible person may make herself exit the scene when feeling angry. They may need to force themselves to abide by a certain standard of care and devise, ahead of time, reminders to prompt them to do so.

Jerome Hall poses the following challenge: "To my knowledge...none of the advocates of punishment for...negligence has pointed to any evidence or stated *why* he thinks that a careless person could have been careful in the situations described in the law reports."[19] Part of my task will be to figure out how mistakes regarding sexual consent can arise, and to indicate why even a "careless" person can fairly be asked to be careful in such situations. In so doing I will not be showing that no matter what the crime—no matter what it is that the person failed to be aware of, and should have been aware of—the careless person can fairly be asked to be careful; it depends on the crime and what it is that she should have been aware of. So my defense of the position that negligence should sometimes satisfy the mens rea requirement applies directly only to negligence regarding sexual consent (though some of what I say will be suggestive regarding other contexts and other crimes).

In thinking about these issues it is helpful to keep in mind the following remarks on negligence by the drafters of the Model Penal Code:

> As with recklessness, the jury is asked to perform two distinct functions. First, it is to examine the risk and the factors that are relevant to its substantiality and justifiability. In the case of negligence, these questions are asked not in terms of what the actor's perceptions actually were, but in terms of an objective view of the situation as it actually existed. Second, the jury is to make the culpability judgment, this time in terms of whether the failure of the defendant to perceive the risk justifies condemnation. Considering the nature and purpose of his conduct and the circumstances known to him, the question is whether the defendant's failure to perceive a risk involves a gross deviation from the standard of care that a reasonable person would observe in the actor's situation.[20]

Notice that the MPC drafters hold that failure to perceive a risk—even a serious risk—does not automatically suffice to establish criminal negligence. We must take into account the nature and purpose of the conduct, and ask what standard of care a reasonable person would observe in the actor's situation. More to the point, we need to ask what standard of care it is reasonable to require everyone to observe. It will be my contention that it is reasonable to require everyone to attend to whether or not their (supposed) partner is consenting to sexual intimacy, and, if there is reason to suspect that he or she is not consenting, to ask. Of course, fair warning that this is required is in order, and improved public education may very well be needed to get out the message that this is required. But that means that education is needed, not that because the education isn't offered, we should not require the conduct. The fair warning requirement is a reason to give the warning, not to abandon plans to require the conduct.

IV.

The issue I am addressing—whether a mistake should have to be reasonable to constitute a complete defense to a rape charge—came to the fore in a famous English case, *Director of Public Prosecutions v. Morgan.*[21] Mr. Morgan and three male friends were out drinking when Morgan suggested that they all go to his house and have sex with his wife. According to his co-defendants, he told them not to be surprised if she struggled and protested; this was just her way of getting turned on. They proceed, and each rapes her, while the others forcibly hold her down. Since at that time, forcing sex on one's wife did not count as rape, Morgan was not charged with rape, but he was charged with aiding and abetting the rapes by the others. The other men were charged with rape (as well as with aiding and abetting the other rapes). They argued that it was not rape, but consensual sex (despite the fact that they dragged her from where she was sleeping to another bedroom and that she screamed to her children to call the police). The trial judge said in summing up, "If the defendant believed or may have believed that Mrs. Morgan consented to him having sexual intercourse with her...he would be not guilty of the offence of rape, but such a belief must be honestly held by the defendant in the first place. He must really believe that. And, secondly, his belief must be a reasonable belief; such a belief as a reasonable man would entertain if he applied his mind and thought about the matter" (400–401). The defendants were found guilty as charged.

The Court of Appeal affirmed the conviction but had some doubts about the instructions the trial judge had given to the jury.[22] So they asked the House of Lords to address the following question: Can you properly convict someone of rape if he honestly but unreasonably believed, at the time of the alleged rape, that the woman was consenting?

Two Lords answered 'Yes'; three answered 'No'. In other words, three out of five held that if the defendant believed at the time of the alleged rape that the woman was consenting, then he cannot be guilty of rape (even if the belief was not based on reasonable grounds). But they dismissed the appeal, holding that although the judge erred in giving the jury instructions quoted above, it was a harmless error. The jurors did not believe that the appellants believed that she consented, nor, the Lords judged, would any reasonable juror, given the evidence presented at trial. So the convictions were upheld. But what was startling to many, and the reason why the case is famous, is that they ruled that an honest but unreasonable belief that the woman was consenting was an adequate defense. You could not convict someone of rape, they said, if he believed the person was consenting, no matter how unreasonable the belief.

For those who find this holding disturbing, as I do, it is helpful to try to figure out why it is disturbing. One reason is evident: it provides an easy defense to a very serious and alarmingly frequent crime.

It might be objected that it is not all that easy a defense; after all, the defendant cannot just say 'I believed she consented'. He has to convince the jurors that he really *did* believe this. The objection is somewhat misleading. The standard of proof, after all, is 'beyond a reasonable doubt'. The jury needn't believe that the defendant believed she consented; they are supposed to acquit unless they are convinced, beyond a reasonable doubt, that he did not believe that she consented. If they believe there is room for reasonable doubt—if they are not convinced, beyond a reasonable doubt, that he did not believe that she consented—they would have a duty to acquit, even if they are completely convinced that she did not consent and that there was no reasonable basis for thinking, at the time of the act, that she did.

V.

In case we were not already worried that the *Morgan* ruling makes it easy for rapists to be acquitted, Lord Cross's opinion in *Morgan* is likely to give rise to that worry. The Lords were unanimous in holding that if there was an error, it was a harmless error. As Lord Cross put it, "The jury obviously considered that the appellants' evidence as to the part played by Mrs Morgan was a pack of lies and one must assume that any other jury would take the same view of the relative credibility of the parties." But the reason Lord Cross judged that no reasonable juror could have found the defendants not guilty was *not* that it was unthinkable that they—or anyone in their situation—might really have believed that she was consenting. Lord Cross doesn't think it was unthinkable. The problem, rather, was that the defendants bungled things at their trial, changing their story, claiming not that they mistakenly thought that Daphne Morgan consented, but that she really did consent. Too bad for them that they didn't have the advice of Lord Cross at the time of their trial! Lord Cross suggests what they should have said in court: "If the appellants when they came to give evidence had said that what Mrs Morgan had said was perfectly true, that she had never at any stage given any sign that she was consenting to—let alone enjoying—the intercourse, but that they were so much influenced by what her husband had told them that they believed throughout that her manifestations of unwillingness were only play acting, then it is conceivable that a jury, on a proper direction, might have acquitted them" (353).[23] Had this been their testimony, Lord Cross would presumably have voted to overturn the conviction, believing that a reasonable juror could then have found in favor of the defendants if the jury had received proper instructions.

Still stronger evidence that *Morgan* makes it easy for rapists to get an acquittal comes from a British case that went to trial about a week after the Court of Appeal had certified to the House of Lords the question raised by the *Morgan* case. Before the Law Lords resolved the question of whether a mistaken belief that the woman was consenting has to be reasonable to be an adequate defense, Cogan was convicted of rape, and Leak, the husband of the woman Cogan raped, was convicted of aiding and abetting the rape (as well as some other charges).[24] Here is what had happened. Furious with his wife for refusing to give him money that he requested from her while he was intoxicated, Leak knocked her down and kicked her repeatedly while she was on the floor. The next day he punished her further by forcing her to have sex (in his presence) with his friend, Cogan. Both Cogan and Leak acknowledged[25] that she was sobbing while Cogan was "having sex with" her. Leak's statements made it clear that, in the words of the appellate judge, he "intended that she should be raped and that Cogan's body should provide the physical means to that end." Cogan, by contrast, claimed in his written statement that he thought she had consented. The judge explains: "The basis for his belief was what he had heard from her husband about her. The drink he had had seems to have been a reason, if not the only one, for mistaking her sobs and distress for consent." The jury found Cogan guilty of rape and found Leak guilty of aiding and abetting the rape. In response to questions from the judge (questions the judge posed in case the House of Lords ruled as it in fact did in *Morgan*), the jurors indicated that they thought that "Cogan had believed she was consenting but that he had had no reasonable grounds for such belief." This, conjoined with the *Morgan* ruling, provided a basis for the appeals. Although the appellate judges found their task with respect to Leak's appeal a challenging one—and upheld his conviction—they found Cogan's appeal easy.[26] Given the *Morgan* ruling, Cogan's conviction had to be quashed.

Cogan should lay to rest the claim, put forward in response to (and in anticipation of) upset over the Morgan ruling, that surely if the jury thinks a belief unreasonable, they are very unlikely to think that the defendant held that belief. They are less likely, to be sure; but the notion of holding a belief without holding it on unreasonable grounds is a coherent one, and the possibility that jurors will give a defendant the benefit of the doubt and judge that he may really have held the belief, though he held it unreasonably, is by no means negligible.

VI.

The Cogan case, together with Lord Cross's suggestions of what Morgan's co-defendants should have said, is some indication that the *Morgan* ruling may make it fairly easy for those who lie when they say 'I thought she consented' to get an acquittal. But that does not show that an honest but unreasonable mistake should not exculpate. After all, any defense makes it easier for the guilty to be acquitted. The question is whether the defense is needed. *Is* an injustice done if someone is convicted of rape who falsely and unreasonably believes the woman consented? If the answer is 'Yes,' then the mere fact that some rapists will be acquitted if they claim, dishonestly but persuasively, to have believed the complainant consented, will not be a weighty consideration. (We should still seek to limit the damage by giving jury instructions regarding what counts as evidence of a belief in consent, or the like, but we would allow that an unreasonable belief can be an adequate defense.) But if no injustice is done if we convict someone who honestly but unreasonably believed that the woman consented, then why not say that a mistake has to be reasonable to exculpate?

Recall Cogan. We'll all agree that if he is lying, his consent defense should not result in an acquittal. But suppose—even though it takes a good bit of imagination to do so—that he *did* think his friend's wife was consenting. Did he deserve to be acquitted?[27]

In a letter to *The London Times* concerning the Lords' ruling in *Morgan*, Glanville Williams wrote: "To convict the stupid man would be to convict him for...honest conduct which may be the best that this man can do but that does not come up to the standard of the so called reasonable man. People ought not to be punished for negligence except in some minor offences. ...It would be wrong to have a law of negligent rape."[28] As Williams sees it, the man who believes that a woman is consenting to sex with him when she is screaming for her children to call the police is simply stupid. The suggestion is that the man who believes this is not culpable. Commenting on Williams' remarks, Susan Estrich writes: "If inaccuracy or indifference to consent is 'the best that this man can do' because he lacks the capacity to act reasonably, then it might well be unjust and ineffective to punish him for it. But such men will be rare. ...More common is the case of the man who could have done better but didn't, could have paid attention, but didn't; heard her say no, or saw her tears, but decided to ignore them. Neither justice nor deterrence argues against punishing this man."[29]

Estrich's reply is on the right track, but is not satisfactory. "Such men will be rare," she says. She seems to be saying that since we'll only very occasionally punish the innocent, it is okay. That is not a position I would like to take. To reply more satisfactorily to Glanville Williams' and Jerome Hall's claims about negligence, let's consider the possibility that someone might be genuinely yet unreasonably mistaken regarding consent, and ask whether punishing such a person would be unjust.

First, a word about Glanville Williams' "stupid man." If the idea is that this man "lacks the capacity to act reasonably" (as Estrich put it), then a different defense seems to be in order, namely a diminished capacity defense (or possibly even an insanity defense). If the man lacks the capacity to act reasonably, his responsibility is called into question with respect to a wide range of conduct. But his incapacity would have no bearing on what mens rea should be required for rape (or for any other crime). Such abnormalities would never constitute a sound basis for lowering the standards to which we hold the general population. That some individuals might have an excuse in the form of a particular incapacity is not a reason for not criminalizing negligence, but only for making sure that there is a mechanism for determining whether the special excusing conditions obtain in a particular case.[30] If the stupid man (more precisely, the fact that there are stupid people) gives us reason not to criminalize negligence—not to require that mistakes be reasonable—it is not because of an incapacity of this sort.

Suppose, however, that what is meant by 'the stupid man' is someone who is not lacking in normal capacities but who nonetheless mistakenly believed that his "partner" consented. If what we are talking about is someone who really did his best yet made a mistake, through no fault of his own (except stupidity, if that counts), then perhaps there is something to Glanville Williams' worry.[31] So we need to ask: Could one get it wrong? How are mistakes about sexual consent possible? And does a requirement that a mistake be reasonable risk punishing those who really did their best to make sure that their partner was consenting?

VII.

Given how implausible most "I thought she was consenting" claims are, it may be tempting to hold that mistaken beliefs that one's (supposed) partner is consenting are actually impossible (except, of course, if the agent suffers from certain mental disorders, of a sort which would warrant an insanity or diminished capacity defense).[32] I believe that mistaken beliefs are possible and that it is possible for someone to be doing his best and be mistaken. But in those circumstances, where we think he was doing his best, we think the mistake reasonable, and think acquittal is in order. Only insofar as we judge a mistaken belief that the "partner" is consenting *reasonable* do we think that the belief should exculpate. If we judge it unreasonable, it is because we believe that the man couldn't really have believed this if he cared about whether she was consenting, and cared enough to desist if there was room for doubt. And in that situation, we judge him culpable and do not think it unjust to punish him for rape. Now, it may not be true of all unreasonable beliefs that in calling them unreasonable, we hold that the agent could not have cared much about the truth of the matter if he held this belief, but it holds here because it is so easy to take appropriate steps to find out the truth of the matter. In the cases where we think the mistaken belief was unreasonable, we think either that her lack of consent would have been obvious to anyone who cared whether she consented, or that any ambiguity could easily have been resolved had he cared. He needed only to ask her.[33]

How might one be mistaken? Hearing problems and language problems might possibly give rise to a mistaken belief that one's "partner" was consenting. The woman says 'no' repeatedly, but does not yell, and does not push the man away. He is deaf in one ear, and let's imagine that he is blind, too (or at least that she is faced away from him), since otherwise he would probably see that she is saying something to him and would, we hope, ask her what she was saying (and turn his "good" ear in her direction). Another instance might be one in which the two people do not speak the same language (literally) and are not aware of how very little of each other's languages they understand. So when she says 'no' he thinks she is saying 'yes' or something else that indicates consent. Of course all these examples are implausible because one would think that the behavior of the woman would alert the man to the fact that she is objecting to his advances. But we can imagine, especially if we bear in mind the power of wishful thinking, that for some reason this is not the case.

If you find this unimaginable, let's try another example, one concocted by David Archard.

> Jones correctly believes that there is an escaped psychopath, Brown, who has committed many appalling acts of violence. He likes to rape women, but he most likes to secure sexual compliance which is behaviourally indistinguishable from pleasurable and consensual sex. Should a woman fail convincingly to act out the part of willing partner in a mutually enjoyable sexual encounter Brown resorts to crude and brutal violence to get his way. Jones mistakenly believes that Smith is Brown and has sex with him. Smith believes that Jones really is consenting to sex with him and he certainly would not have sex with her if he thought that she was not consenting. Jones does not consent to such sex at the time, because she is in a state of terrified acquiescence. But she successfully masks such terror, and her charade of pleasured compliance is convincing—she thinks it must be if she is to prevent "Brown" from detecting her real feelings and proceeding to awful violence against her.[34]

Now there is a puzzle about Archard's example. One might wonder why, if Jones believes that Smith is Brown, the psychopath, she has chosen to spend time with him in the first place. We are to assume that Smith is a nice guy; clearly he would not have kidnapped her or broken into her apartment, so she must be with him voluntarily. So let's embellish the example by imagining that she met Smith at a party, liked him very much, and went home with him, only to suddenly "realize" that the man she was with was Brown, the escaped psychopath. Because Smith lives way out in the country, and because they drove there in his car—so that she has no transportation apart from what he could provide—and because of a violent thunderstorm, she doesn't see any way to escape. And she is too terrified to recognize an escape route if there is one. Smith initiates some physical intimacy and although he in no way forces it, she, believing this man is the escaped psychopath she has been hearing about (and being an excellent actress) feigns enthusiasm...and the rest is as Archard explained it.

Archard's example of a genuine mistake is more compelling than most precisely because it is believable that Smith would have no reason to suspect that Jones is not consenting—if we assume, as the example asks us to, that Jones is an excellent actress (even when she is terrified). Does it matter that the example is unrealistic, and that we can just barely imagine it happening? It matters a little, because the more believable it is that such things really do happen, the more important it is to make sure that the law leaves room for a defense that covers such cases. If mistakes about consent were impossible, allowing such a defense would serve no good purpose, and would only make it easier for rapists to be acquitted. However, if they are possible—albeit infrequent—it seems necessary to allow the defense (in some form).

I want to stress, however, that my position is shaped by my rejection of the force requirement. Notice that although it seems natural to say that in Archard's example we have the actus reus of rape—sex without consent—though not the mens rea, the law in most US jurisdictions says otherwise. The actus reus as Archard thinks of it (and as I think it should be) is nonconsensual sex, but in the US, force is usually a required element of rape. The actus reus is thus nonconsensual, forced sex. In the examples we've been discussing—and the one I will suggest in a few minutes, of a survivor of abuse—the element of force would not be present, so there would be no need (where force remains part of the legal definition of rape) even to consider whether the mens rea requirement is met. It could not possibly count as rape, because the element of force was absent.

So although I take it to be necessary to have a mistake defense, I probably would not if I favored retaining the force requirement.[35] A mistake defense is not needed unless a mistake is possible—a mistake which calls into question the defendant's culpability–and it is hard to imagine how someone could be mistaken as to whether his partner was consenting if he used force (either actual force or the threat of actual force) to secure her compliance.

Even without the force requirement, however, there is a significant cost to allowing the mistake defense. The number of rapists acquitted thanks to the mistake defense is very likely much larger than the number of innocent men who would have been convicted had there not been a defense. But as long as we are committed to the principle that it is far worse to convict and punish an innocent person than to acquit a guilty person, this is not a very strong argument against having a mistake defense. It is, however, a reminder that we should do all we can to limit the defense, so that it is harder for someone who has committed rape to use the defense successfully.[36]

Although it is barely believable that the scenario Archard described could actually happen, a similar scenario is, sadly, all too imaginable. We can imagine a young woman who is a survivor of chronic sexual abuse, and is so accustomed to refusal being at best pointless (and more likely dangerous, as well), so accustomed to accommodating the men who abused her, that she is unable to express her refusal—at least, unable if the initiator is at all pushy. Although he is not threatening her, she feels fear; but she is skilled at concealing it. We can imagine that she was expected as an adolescent to act as if she enjoyed or at least didn't mind it, and perhaps learned, almost as if it were just a matter of basic courtesy, that not only was she not to refuse, she was also to be "gracious" about it. A perceptive, sensitive man would hopefully pick up on signs that something is amiss, even if he has no knowledge of her history, but lack of perceptiveness is not punishable by criminal law, nor should it be, unless it is so extreme as to be evidence of a lack of concern as to whether she consents or not. A mistake surely is imaginable in this instance, and indeed in other situations where the woman is afraid that the man will kill or seriously harm her if she refuses or even seems reluctant, and makes an effort to conceal her fear and distress. If her efforts at concealment succeed, and there is nothing about the situation that should have alerted him to the possibility that she was afraid of him, it seems clear that he is not culpable, precisely because his belief that she was consenting was reasonable.

This example supports my claim that mistakes are possible, and that a reasonable mistake exculpates. The remaining task is to show that an unreasonable mistake does not exculpate.

VIII.

To support my claim that mistakes about sexual consent are possible, I provided various examples. They were all instances where we would (I think) believe that the mistake was reasonable (assuming that we think it at least a reasonable possibility both that the defendant actually believed that his "partner" was consenting, and that she in fact was not consenting). We need now to consider cases of an "honest but unreasonable mistake." These are harder to think up. To the extent that the belief seems to us unreasonable, we have doubts as to whether he really believed she was consenting. But it is crucial, if we are to address Glanville Williams' worry, to consider the possibility of an unreasonable mistake and ask whether it really is just to convict someone if he honestly believed that the complainant was consenting.

In the *Morgan* case, counsel for the appellants stressed that "There can be no crime without a tainted mind."[37] Their suggestion was that someone who makes an honest mistake lacks that taint, hence lacks the mens rea necessary for him to be guilty of a crime. The suggestion has a prima facie appeal simply because the word 'honest' carries a connotation of 'blameless'. We don't want to be swayed by the connotation, so let's bear in mind that in this context 'honest' means simply 'genuine'. Let's agree, then, that it is at least logically possible for there to be an honest, unreasonable, mistaken belief that the woman was consenting—and for it not to exculpate.

We can make use of what we already said to figure out how an unreasonable mistake might arise. Consent involves two elements: an expression, verbal or physical (or at the very least an absence of an expression of dissent), and the absence of any conditions that would keep the expression (or the absence of dissent) from constituting consent.[38] That being the case, mistaken beliefs that someone is consenting, in a sexual context, are of two types. The first is either a mistaken belief that the person did not dissent, or a mistaken belief that some expression in fact was an expression of consent. The second type of mistake is a failure to recognize the presence of conditions that keep the expression (or the lack of dissent) from constituting consent. A reasonable mistake might be possible if hearing or language problems lead to a mistake as to what the other is saying, with the result that the person is mistakenly thought to be consenting. More imaginable is a failure to be aware of conditions that keep what would normally be expressions of consent from constituting consent—in particular, fear that the initiator will kill her if she refuses to have sex with him. And this is imaginable if we suppose that the woman sought to conceal her fear and her lack of interest in sex on that occasion.

Now let's try to imagine an unreasonable mistake. We should look for unreasonable mistakes to arise in two ways: an expression or a set of behaviors on the part of the complainant is taken to constitute consent when there is no rational basis for so construing it; or, it is taken to constitute consent in conditions which keep it from doing so. In the latter scenario, the mistake is unreasonable only if the initiator *should have noticed* that such conditions obtained—or at least should have seen that there was a strong possibility that they obtained—and should have seen that those conditions kept (or might well keep) what would otherwise count as consent from constituting consent. Let's consider this type of mistake first.

We can construct an example by borrowing from a 1981 Maryland case, *Rusk*.[39] Before acquiescing to sex with Rusk, Pat asked him, "If I do what you want, will you let me go without killing me?" Now in the actual case Pat had repeatedly refused to go up to his apartment, and asked to leave after entering it (having entered it because he had pocketed her car keys and made it plain that he would not return them unless she accompanied him). But let's imagine a hypothetical case where there was no sign of dissent and this was the only indication that she was submitting out of fear, rather than consenting. If Rusk had not heard Pat's question, a reasonable mistake would be possible. If, on the other hand, he did hear her, he can't be mistaken at all. He must know she is submitting out of fear—unless he thinks that she is joking. I'll return to this possibility shortly.

But, someone might ask, what if he is just very unsophisticated philosophically—let's be blunt, what if he is just really dumb—and doesn't understand that to submit out of fear is not to consent? He hears her, he sees that she is submitting because she is afraid that he'll kill her if she refuses, but he thinks this is consent. Put differently, he doesn't think it is rape as long as she's going along with it (even if she's doing so only out of fear that he'll kill her if she doesn't). Could that count as an unreasonable mistake? And if so, should it exculpate? Maybe this is just the sort of case Glanville Williams has in mind: the man is so stupid that he doesn't understand what consent means, hence doesn't realize that if she submits out of fear, this is nonconsensual sex. Surely, Williams might say, he isn't a rapist if he doesn't understand that she isn't consenting.

In reply, let's recall first that if he has a severe cognitive deficiency, that is a reason to invoke an excusing condition in his case, but not a reason to alter our expectations for the general population. But suppose he doesn't. Should his belief that she is consenting exculpate? No—not unless we want to argue that mistakes of law should exculpate. Provided that the law gives fair warning, a belief that submission out of fear is consent should be treated as a mistake of law, and hence not as a defense. Mistakes of fact are defenses; mistakes as to the law, including any material elements such as consent, generally are not.[40] With some exceptions that need not concern us, as long as the statute spells out what rape is, it is a mistake of law if one gets it wrong.[41] And to the extent that statutes don't spell it out, as was the case in England at the time of *Morgan*, they should be revised.

We need to distinguish two questions when we ask whether it is unfair to punish someone who, genuinely believing that women who dress a certain way (etc.) are consenting, regardless of what they say, thought that the complainant was consenting. Is it fair to do this now? Would it be fair to do so once we made a serious effort to announce our policy, clarifying the notion of consent (via public service announcements on TV, and posters in such public places as driver's license testing stations and high schools)? Even if the answer to the first question is 'No'—and whether it is turns on matters I'll not explore here—the answer to the second question is 'Yes'. There is no reason to allow people to understand 'consent' for the purposes of the law just any way they like, any more than there is reason to allow people to understand 'force' or 'fraudulently' any way they like in other legal contexts.

Back to my hypothetical based on *Rusk*. What about the possibility that Rusk thought Pat was joking when she asked, "If I do what you want, will you let me go without killing me?" Is that a mistake that supports Glanville Williams' and Jerome Hall's claims regarding negligence? I don't see how it can. Either we'll judge that the mistake was reasonable because we take the facts to be that there was absolutely no sign of fear, that she seemed quite enthusiastic, and that she does seem to have an odd sense of humor; *or* we'll think that given the circumstances and the way the question was put to him, he couldn't possibly fail to see that she might very well be acquiescing only out of fear of him. He must be aware that although maybe she was joking, she might very well not have been. If he chooses just to figure that it probably is a joke, he must not really care whether she is consenting. So I don't see that the example provides a case of an unreasonable mistake that exculpates. Either it is reasonable or it is actually a case of recklessness.

It might be objected that in the latter scenario, he need not have *consciously* disregarded a substantial risk that she wasn't joking—and wasn't consenting. Maybe he just unconsciously disregarded it. Maybe it was just a case of wishful thinking, of refusing—but not consciously—to consider the obvious because one just doesn't want to recognize that it might be true.

Let's suppose this is possible. This would be a case of negligence, rather than recklessness. Is he still culpable? Yes. He is culpable for his failure to advert to the possibility that she isn't joking, and to take that possibility seriously. His is not a "mind without taint." His is not an "honest mistake" unless we regard an unconscious refusal to consider the possibility that driving 60 mph in a residential neighborhood might cause serious harm as an "honest mistake." That driving at such a speed is, besides being illegal, very dangerous, liable to cause serious harm, is something the driver must know. If the driver causes a death it would not be a plausible defense to a charge of reckless or negligent homicide to claim "I didn't know that what I was doing was dangerous." It is true that the driver might know it is dangerous but fail at the time to attend to that fact because she is so intent on getting to her destination (or caught up in testing out her new car or singing a favorite song). But we hold people responsible for attending, not merely for 'knowing'. The same holds for knowledge that people do sometimes decline opportunities to have sex, and that saying 'No' is a way of declining. It is not unreasonable to ask everyone to be aware in the relevant situations of such evident risks as the risks of driving dangerously, or of pushing ahead to sexual intercourse when one's partner shows signs of not consenting.

Failures to advert to risks are not all of a kind. Some are due to inattention to x because one is absorbed in y. I forget that I have a pot boiling on the stove because I am absorbed in reading Glanville Williams' "The Unresolved Problem of Recklessness." Or to take an example he offers in that essay, a driver, "preoccupied by business matters, throws open his car door and causes injury to a passing cyclist."[42] There is plausibility in the claim that criminal liability should not attach to such inadvertence, even if I leave the house when the pot is boiling, leading to a fire that causes the death of a sleeping houseguest.[43] (It depends on the activity. We require more attention to what one is doing when one is driving than when one is opening a car door, or cooking.) But compare this to a failure, in the modified *Rusk* case, to attend, when he hears her say, "If I do what you want, will you let me go without killing me?" to the "risk" that she is not consenting, but only acquiescing out of fear. This is not a case of inattention to x because one is engaged in y. Williams remarks, with regard to the driver who flings open the car door, "We cannot, in fact, always use that little extra circumspection that would be an absolute guarantee against accident. Life cannot be lived on these terms."[44] Jennifer Temkin replies, "But is the same to be said of the man contemplating sexual intercourse with a woman? Unlike the cyclist whose presence is unknown, she is there right next to him. Since non-consent is always a possibility, is it too much to expect him, in circumstances where the risk of this is obvious, to employ that little extra circumspection to ascertain whether consent is present? Or must we accept that he cannot be expected to lead his life like this?"[45]

I have argued that the mind of a man who fails to advert to obvious signs that the woman might not be consenting to sex is not, contrary to what was claimed in their appeal by Morgan's companions, without taint.[46] There is a taint here that we don't see in cases of mere carelessness or inadvertence, cases which seem to warrant tort liability but arguably not criminal liability.[47]

It might be argued, however, that the "taint" suffices only to establish moral culpability, not culpability for purposes of criminal law. It might be held that although there is greater culpability in acting on an unreasonable belief that one's "partner" is consenting than in opening one's car door without checking first for bicyclists, there is still insufficient culpability for criminal liability. To respond to this claim, we do well to compare negligence to the MPC mens rea levels that are regarded as beyond dispute.

Why do the other mens rea levels suffice to establish criminal liability? In the case of purpose, it is because one had as one's purpose to harm another (or steal, or whatever). In the case of knowledge and recklessness the reason is different. What establishes culpability is not that the defendant intended to harm, or intended some other wrong, but that he cared so little about not harming the person (or not having sex without the other's consent) that he proceeded with his plan, knowing that his action would in all probability cause harm (or would constitute sex without the other's consent), or that there was a risk—substantial and unjustifiable—that it would do so. What I have been suggesting is that this is exactly what happens in a case in which one has sex with another, unaware, but unreasonably so, that she does not consent. One cares too little about whether the person consents to attend to obvious indications of non-consent. Here we see the contrast between negligence (as defined by the MPC) and inattention or inadvertence, to which criminal liability does not attach. It is not the case with every instance of inadvertence or inattention that one cares too little to attend. But given the presence of the non-consenting person, and the obviousness of the signs of non-consent, it *is* the case with unreasonable mistakes regarding sexual consent. So the "taint" is sufficient to establish criminal liability, if we accept that a mens rea of recklessness or knowledge suffices to establish criminal liability.

At the start of this section I distinguished two ways one might be unreasonably mistaken in thinking that one's "partner" was consenting to sex: one mistakenly sees an expression or a set of behaviors to constitute consent when there is no rational basis for thinking it does, or one takes it to constitute consent in conditions that keep it from doing so (where he should have noticed that such conditions obtained).[48] So far we have been discussing the latter possibility. I turn now to the former. Reflection on such a mistake will, I believe, lend further support to my claim that there is no unfairness in holding that unreasonable mistakes regarding sexual consent do not exculpate.

How could someone take a set of behaviors to signify consent when there is no rational basis for so construing it? It is possible if he thinks that what she says is trumped by how she is dressed, whether she seems to be sexually attracted to him, what he thinks "women like her" really want, or really mean. It is possible if he subscribes to such views as that a woman who really did not want sex would scream and physically fight (at least so long as the man was not threatening her with violence); if she simply says 'No' clearly, firmly, repeatedly but doesn't offer vigorous physical resistance, she must be consenting.

That there is no injustice in holding such a defendant criminally responsible (assuming that there is fair warning) is evident from what we said regarding the modified *Rusk* example. The defendant must know that people do sometimes refuse sex. If he thinks that 'No' doesn't constitute a refusal if she doesn't physically fight him or if she is wearing "provocative"[49] clothing, then either this is a mistake of law and thus does not exculpate, or the law needs to be more specific, so that (with fair warning) it would then constitute a mistake of law. If he knows that 'No' does generally constitute a refusal but doesn't attend to this at the time, and instead engages in wishful thinking, he is still culpable. He is culpable in the way someone who acts recklessly is culpable if he chooses to disregard the risk and act on the basis of what he hopes might be true. Having sex with someone against his or her will is a serious matter. About this and other serious matters we may hope or believe what we like, but we must take due care, and that entails heeding the possibility that what we hope is true, in fact is not true.

What if the defendant just is not "normally sensitive" (as Jerome Hall put it) to such risks "or to a duty to attend to such danger"? Is this a reason for holding that all mistaken beliefs that the complainant was consenting excuse? Hardly. There is no reason to regard such "insensitivity" as fixed and unchangeable. By announcing that those who fail to attend to such dangers may, if they turn out to have had sex without the complainant's consent, be prosecutable for rape, we hope to make them aware of their duty. If it is suggested that some people (though not suffering from any mental disability) are constitutionally careless, a point made early on in this essay needs to be repeated: character traits alone do not excuse. We hold people responsible for dealing with their character flaws, and it is in part because it is hard to control our impulses (and hard to be careful when we tend to be careless) that we think an added incentive is needed in the form of a threat of punishment.

I have argued in this paper that although mistakes about sexual consent are possible–mistakes, that is, that one's "partner" is consenting when in fact she or he isn't—and that some such mistakes should exculpate, those not based on reasonable grounds should not exculpate. I have said very little about the standard(s) by which we should assess reasonableness, about the notion of the reasonable person, or even about whether we do better to rely on the notion of reasonableness or should instead focus on 'due care' (though this may itself implicitly involve the notion of reasonableness). These are issues I hope to address elsewhere. But I believe I have shown that there is no unfairness in holding that unreasonable mistakes regarding sexual consent should not be a complete defense to a rape charge (provided, anyway, that the standard for 'reasonableness' is not set very high).[50]

Notes

1. Technically this is a failure-of-proof defense. In a failure-of-proof defense, some element of the crime has to be negated, in this case, the mens rea. But a "true defense" constitutes a defense even if all the elements of the crime have been proved. As a matter of constitutional law, the prosecution must "shoulder the burden of *disproving* beyond a reasonable doubt a defendant's failure-of-proof claim." By contrast, legislatures "may allocate to the defendant the burden of production and the burden of persuasion regarding true defenses." Joshua Dressler, *Understanding Criminal Law*, 2d ed. (Matthew Bender, 1995), p. 182.
2. The exception to this rule is strict liability crimes, which lack the mens rea component. I should also note that some crimes have other elements as well. E.g., all homicides have a result element (viz., someone's death).
3. Exactly what mens rea has to be proven is determined by the legislature. In the US, some jurisdictions have adopted the Model Penal Code's classification (which I explain below), while others follow the traditional and very messy general intent/specific intent approach to mens rea. I will throughout this paper follow the MPC division without, of course, taking as given that negligence is rightly included by the MPC as a basis for criminal liability.
4. There are some who, while sharing my view that it is a mistake for consent and force both to be part of the definition of rape, favor dropping consent and retaining force. See Catherine MacKinnon, *Toward a Feminist Theory*

of the State (Harvard University Press, 1989) and Donald A. Dripps, "Beyond Rape: An Essay on the Difference Between the Presence of Force and the Absence of Consent," *Columbia Law Review* 92 (November 1992): 1780–1809. Both see the notion of consent to be highly problematic. For another discussion of consent that expresses grave doubts about its helpfulness, see Carole Pateman, "Women and Consent," in *The Disorder of Women: Democracy, Feminism and Political Theory* (Stanford University Press, 1989).

5. For discussions of force, see Susan Estrich, *Real Rape* (Harvard University Press, 1987); Lynne Henderson, "Rape and Responsibility," *Law and Philosophy* (1992); Kit Kinports, "Rape and Force: The Forgotten Mens Rea," *4 Buffalo Criminal Law Review* (forthcoming 2001); Joan McGregor, "Why When She Says No She Doesn't Mean Maybe and Doesn't Mean Yes: A Critical Reconstruction of Consent, Sex, and the Law," *Legal Theory* 2 (1996): 175–208; and Stephen Schulhofer, *Unwanted Sex: The Culture of Intimidation and the Failure of Law* (Harvard, 1998), in addition to the works cited in note 4, above.
6. The locus classicus for the notion of a performative is J.L. Austin, *How to Do Things with Words: The William James Lectures Delivered at Harvard University in 1955*, 2d ed. (Harvard University Press, 1975). I am indebted to Heidi Malm, "The Ontological Status of Consent and Its Implications for the Law on Rape," *Legal Theory*, vol. 2 (Winter 1997): 147–164.
7. The reason for the proviso is that terror vitiates consent. To use Austin's term, the "felicity conditions" for the performative are not met. Consent must, as the jury instructions typically put it, be "freely given." An alternative approach would deny that absence of terror, on the part of the agent, is a felicity condition (i.e., is necessary for her expression to constitute consent), holding instead that the absence of threats is. (Only serious threats, not simply "I won't go out with you any more unless..." would matter.) If one were to take that line, the Archard case below (Sect. VII) would *not* count as a case where she did not consent but he thought (and on reasonable grounds) that she did; it would instead be a case of consent. I think it makes much more sense to take absence of terror to be a felicity condition.
8. For an argument that it should not mitigate, see Anthony Duff, "Recklessness and Rape," *Liverpool Law Review* 3 (1981): 49–64 and *Intention, Agency and Criminal Liability* (Blackwell 1990), pp. 167–73.
9. Model Penal Code, 2.02. Two comments. (1) I cannot imagine any good reason for using the term 'law-abiding'. I can think of a bad reason: perhaps the idea is to ask 'Which people are the ones we know are good and should not go to jail? These, the good law-abiding citizens, mark a boundary for us: if the risk is one they would take, then the conduct cannot count as reckless for purposes of criminal liability.' I prefer to use the term 'reasonable person'. Legal scholars I've consulted tell me that they know of no reason why the MPC drafters use 'law-abiding person' in explaining recklessness and 'reasonable person' in explaining negligence, rather than use 'reasonable person' in both instances, and the MPC comments to 2.02 shed no light on this. (2) I should note that the MPC does not have legal force; it is only a blueprint, and not all states follow the MPC on mens rea. But as

Dressler observes, no aspect of the influential Model Penal Code has had greater influence on the direction of American criminal law than the section on mens rea (Dressler, p. 120).

10. Ibid., 2.02, italics added.
11. Ibid., 2.02., italics added.
12. I put 'justifiable' in quotes because I can't imagine what could possibly justify this particular risk. I am not taking issue with the MPC wording; some ends do justify taking substantial risks. Risking injury to others in order to save lives certainly is sometimes justifiable, for instance. But what could justify having sex with someone if there is a substantial risk that he or she isn't consenting?
13. See on this topic the last section of E.M. Curley, "Descartes, Spinoza and the Ethics of Belief," in *Spinoza: Essays in Interpretation*, edited by Maurice Mandelbaum and Eugene Freeman (Open Court, 1975). Discussing W.K. Clifford's "The Ethics of Belief," Curley claims that "belief 'on insufficient evidence' has moral significance principally where the belief is more or less directly connected with some action fraught with potentially serious consequences for others" (182). "What is culpable is not the belief, but acting on a belief which has not been fairly examined, in circumstances where the possible consequences of acting on the belief—and in particular, the possible consequences for other people—are so momentous" (181).
14. This paragraph develops an argument that is hinted at (and not endorsed) by George P. Fletcher in Ch. 3 of his *A Crime of Self Defense: Bernhard Goetz and the Law on Trial* (University of Chicago Press, 1988) and by Dressler in *Understanding Criminal Law*, p. 113.
15. I am developing this point by reference to harm only for reasons of simplicity. With all four levels of culpability, the risk or the object of intent or knowledge can but needn't be harm. See the quotations in Sect. II, above, from the MPC.
16. Jerome Hall, "Negligent Behavior Should be Excluded from Penal Liability," in his *Law, Social Science, and Criminal Theory*, a publication of the Comparative Criminal Law Project, Vol. 14 (Fred B. Rothman & Co., 1982), p. 254.
17. The underlying moral principle is evident in restrictions to certain defenses, for example, duress. In most states, the defense of duress is unavailable if the defendant "was at fault for being in the coercive situation." If, for example, she voluntarily joined an organization that "she knows or has reason to know is likely to subject her to coercive threats at a later time, she will not be permitted to claim the defense if that foreseeable event arises" (Dressler, p. 275). There is a similar restriction in many states on the necessity defense. See Dressler, p. 264.
18. See Aristotle, *Nicomachean Ethics*, Bk. 3, chap. 5. Curiously, Jerome Hall claims that although Aristotle "disapproved an act done in ignorance or in a state of intoxication if that condition was the result of past voluntary misconduct," he "nowhere suggested that this phase of his theory of fault should be applied to legal liability" (Hall, p. 249). But Aristotle very clearly does, not merely suggesting but asserting it. He reports that "legislators also impose corrective treatments for the ignorance itself, if the person seems to be

responsible for the ignorance." "A drunk, e.g., pays a double penalty; for the origin is in him, since he controls whether he gets drunk, and his getting drunk is responsible for his ignorance." Legislators also impose corrective treatment for "ignorance that seems to be caused by the agent's inattention; they assume it is up to him not to be ignorant, since he controls whether he pays attention." Of course Aristotle could merely be reporting that this is what is done. But a few lines later he defends the practice against the objection that "presumably his character makes him inattentive," claiming that "he is himself responsible for having this character." Quotations are from Terence Irwin's translation, 1st ed. (Hackett Publishing Co., 1984).

19. Hall, p. 260.
20. American Law Institute, *Model Penal Code and Commentaries*, Comment to 2.02 (Philadelphia, 1980), p. 241.
21. *DPP v. Morgan* (1975) 2 All ER, pp. 347–383. Subsequent page references to this case are indicated in the text.
22. I too have doubts about the jury instructions, but not about the part that was challenged. Just before the part I quoted, the judge said: "The prosecution have to prove that each defendant intended to have sexual intercourse with this woman without her consent. Not merely that he intended to have intercourse with her but that he intended to have intercourse without her consent." That is ambiguous: Is it that he intended to have intercourse with her, and did so without her consent? Or is the content of the intention to have intercourse with her without her consent? The majority of the Law Lords rejected the former reading. The latter reading, however, would enunciate a most peculiar requirement. It would mean that the prosecution had to show that if she had consented, he would not have wanted to have intercourse with her. His intention to have intercourse with her was to have intercourse with a woman he knew (or believed) to be non-consenting. Lord Hailsham acknowledges the oddity of such a requirement and tries to patch things up by claiming, "if the intention of the accused is to have intercourse nolens volens, that is recklessly and not caring whether the victim be a consenting party or not, that is equivalent on ordinary principles to an intent to do the prohibited act without the consent of the victim" (357). It would have been better either to have spelled out, in the jury instructions, that the mens rea requirement is intention to have intercourse, and that it is an affirmative defense that the accused believed, on reasonable grounds, that she was consenting, or to have said that the mens rea is intention to have intercourse, together with (at least) negligence as to whether she was consenting. The claim that the prosecution has to prove intention to have intercourse without her consent seems to have tangled up the Law Lords' thinking. See Hailsham's discussion on p. 357.
23. Lord Cross is, to be sure, not saying that a reasonable jury would have acquitted them, but only that it might have—thus meeting the standard of proof generally relied on at the appellate level. (That is, an improper jury instruction is considered harmless if and only if no reasonable juror, given a proper jury instruction, would have concluded from the evidence presented at trial that the defendant was not proven guilty beyond a reasonable doubt.)

24. *R v. Cogan* [1975] 2 All ER, pp. 1060–1063. Leak was convicted of attempted buggery and of assault occasioning actual bodily harm, in addition to aiding and abetting a rape.
25. They did so in their statements. Neither testified in court.
26. Leak argued that if Cogan was not guilty of rape, no rape occurred, and so he could not be guilty of aiding and abetting a rape. The Court of Appeal held that although Cogan was innocent of rape (because he lacked the necessary mens rea) a rape did happen, and Leak very clearly aided it.
27. This is a clumsy question to raise; given *Morgan*, there is a clear sense in which there was no choice but to overturn the conviction. Still, we can ask whether he deserved acquittal, where a negative answer would indicate not that the Court of Appeal erred, but that the *Morgan* ruling was wrong.
28. Glanville Williams, "Lords' Decision on the Law of Rape," *London Times*, May 8, 1975, at 15. Quoted in Saltzburg, Diamond, Kinports, and Morawetz, *Criminal Law: Cases and Materials,* 2d ed. (Matthew Bender & Co., 2000), p. 407.
29. Susan Estrich, "Rape," *Yale Law Journal* 95 (May 1986): 1087–1184. The quote is from p. 1104.
30. It is true that diminished capacity defenses are rare, and in many states are virtually precluded by law. But I think it would be a mistake to take that as a fixed point and adjust the mens rea for rape accordingly. Instead, we should strive to bring it about that a diminished capacity defense or some comparable defense is available.
31. There would be a great deal to Glanville Williams' worry if the standard of reasonableness were very high, as Williams claims it is. "The 'reasonable man' of the lawyer's imagining is the prudent, cautious, circumspect, anxiously calculating paragon who is held up by the judges as a model of behaviour." This is not a bad approximation to the notion of the reasonable person in tort law (though it is somewhat exaggerated), but is certainly not the notion at work in criminal law. In fact Williams acknowledges parenthetically, "at least that is the position in the law of tort." Williams, *Textbook of Criminal Law* (Stevens & Sons, 1978), p. 43. I see no reason to think that the position that mistakes must be reasonable to exculpate entails that they must be mistakes that even an exceptionally reasonable person (or, what in fact is different, an "anxiously calculating paragon") might well make. And a perusal of cases makes it very clear that the danger, if anything, lies in the opposite direction. Mistakes we can barely imagine are all too often regarded by judges and jurors as mistakes that a reasonable person might well make. *Mayberry* is a case in point. See footnote 36, below.
32. I'll quit mentioning that exception, but bear in mind that unless I indicate otherwise, I am talking about cases where the agent does not suffer from such disorders.
33. I said that if we judge a mistaken belief unreasonable, it is because we think the man could not have believed this if he cared about whether she was consenting, and cared enough to doubt if there was room for doubt. (Of course not everyone agrees; Glanville Williams does not. We'll get to his view later.) And I said that insofar as we judge such a belief unreasonable,

we think that it does not exculpate. Is this the same 'we', or a subset of those who, if they judge a mistaken belief unreasonable, do so because they think the man could not have held this belief if he cared (much) about whether she was consenting? My guess is that it is a subset. I am not sure how to explain the view that although he couldn't have cared much about whether she was consenting, his unreasonable mistake exculpates, but my guess is that (if anyone really does hold that view), the view is that as long as he cared a little, that is good enough. Their disagreement with those of us who think an unreasonable mistake does not exculpate concerns how big a deal it is if the man makes a mistake and has sex with her when she isn't consenting. In their view, I'm guessing, it just isn't all that big a deal.

34. David Archard, "The *Mens Rea* of Rape: Reasonableness and Culpable Mistakes," in *"A Most Detestable Crime": New Philosophical Essays on Rape*, edited with an Introduction by Keith Burgess-Jackson (Oxford University Press, 1999), p. 216.
35. This would depend on how 'force' is defined. If the force requirement is retained, but diluted, the mistake defense might be in order. If it is understood as "force used to overcome lack of consent," as was urged by the public defender in *State in the Interest of M.T.S.*, 609 A.2d 1266, 1269 (N.J. 1992), then no mistake defense seems to be needed. But if it is defined as it was by the Supreme Court of New Jersey in the case just mentioned, a mistake defense would be in order. They held that "physical force in excess of that inherent in the act of sexual penetration is not required for such penetration to be unlawful. The definition of 'physical force' is satisfied....if the defendant applies any amount of force against another person in the absence of what a reasonable person would believe to be affirmative and freely-given permission to the act of sexual penetration" (1277). This holding is facilitated (indeed, perhaps dictated) by New Jersey's understanding of sexual assault as a criminal battery.
36. One obvious way to limit the defense is to allow only reasonable mistakes to exculpate, but I would not want to leave the impression that this suffices. Recall the facts of *Mayberry*. The defendant had grabbed the complainant as she walked to the store, threw a bottle at her after she managed to escape, caught up with her and, when she responded negatively to his suggestion that they have sex, hit her in the chest, knocking her down, and threatened more violence if she didn't comply. The California Supreme Court overturned his rape conviction because the judge had not instructed the jury that a reasonable, good faith belief that the complainant consented is a complete defense [*People v. Mayberry*, 542 P.2d 1337 (Cal. 1975)]. It is hard to see what work 'reasonable' does if a Court holds, as the California Supreme Court apparently did, that a reasonable juror might judge that Mayberry reasonably believed that the complainant consented! More recently, however, the Court has ruled that a *Mayberry* instruction—a jury instruction to acquit if they think the defendant may have reasonably believed that she consented—should be issued only when there is some basis for thinking that the belief is reasonable. Moreover, the jury should be instructed that "reasonable mistake of fact may not be found if jury finds that...equivocal

conduct on part of victim was the product of 'force, violence, duress, menace, or fear of immediate and unlawful bodily injury,'" *People v. Williams* 841 P.2d 961, 967 (Cal. 1992). This suggests steps that can be taken to limit the defense.

Another way of limiting mistake defenses is that taken by Canada. While not requiring that a mistaken belief that the woman consented be reasonable to exculpate, Canada provides in its sexual assault statute that "'a mistake about consent is no defense if it was caused by the defendant's self-induced intoxication' or 'recklessness or wilful blindness,' or if the defendant 'did not take reasonable steps in the circumstances known to [him] at the time, to ascertain that the complainant was consenting'" (Criminal Code, R.S.C., ch. C-46, sec. 273.2). In a 1999 ruling, the Canadian Supreme Court added that "a belief that silence, passivity or ambiguous conduct constitutes consent is a mistake of law, and provides no defense...," *Queen v. Ewanchuk* (1999) 1 S.C.R. 330, 356–57.

37. Lord Edmund-Davies mentions this in his opinion in *Morgan*, p. 376. The quote is itself a reference to *R v. Tolson* (1889) 23 Q.B.D. at 180, [1886–90] All ER Rep at 33.
38. I prefer to understand consent affirmatively, as do Heidi Malm (see note 6, above), and Stephen J. Schulhofer (see note 5, above). It seems wrong for lack of resistance, verbal or physical, to suffice to constitute consent, *except* (and this is where things become tricky) in long-term relationships that are free of violence. It is certainly far from ideal for one party to be merely a passive recipient of the other's kissing and fondling, but that it is non-ideal does not make it non-consensual. But while it would be wrong for courts suddenly to treat such acts as rapes, there would, I think, be no serious loss if, after due warning, such cases were prosecutable as rapes. I do not see it as desirable to treat them as rapes, but also do not think it a strong reason against understanding consent affirmatively that it would have the implication that in theory they could be so prosecuted. It is not, after all, as if sex in which one party is passive would be illegal, only that the person initiating sex would have to make sure that the passive partner was in fact consenting, i.e., to make sure that a failure to object counted, in this situation, as consent.
39. *State v. Rusk* 424 A.2d (Md. 1981). I should note that the issue in *Rusk* was force, not whether he believed she was consenting.
40. Unlike mistakes of fact, mistakes of law almost never negate the mens rea. They do so only if the criminal statute makes awareness of the law an element of the crime, and this is very rarely the case.
41. For details, see Dressler, Ch. 13.
42. Glanville Williams, "The Unresolved Problem of Recklessness," *Legal Studies* (1988): 74–91. The quote is from p. 82.
43. Tort liability, by contrast, certainly should.
44. Williams, "Recklessness Redefined," *Cambridge Law Journal* (1981): 252–283. The quote is from pp. 271–72.
45. Jennifer Temkin, "The Limits of Reckless Rape," *Criminal Law Review* (1983): 5–16. The quote is from p. 14.

46. See also E.M. Curley, "Excusing Rape," *Philosophy and Public Affairs* 5 (1976): 325–360. Curley writes, "In these circumstances" (where the defendant's belief that she consented to sex was unreasonable) "the disposition to act on an unreasonable belief is a vice" (346).
47. If, however, the choice were between attaching criminal liability to a failure to check before opening one's car door and holding that an unreasonable belief that the woman consented is a complete defense to rape, I'd opt for the former.
48. Another possibility to consider would be a mistaken belief that the person uttered something or gestured in a way that she did not, where, had she done so, it might well have constituted consent. But I don't see that such a mistake could be judged an unreasonable mistake. Any evidence that he held the belief would also be evidence of its truth or evidence that, although it was false, it was a reasonable mistake. So if we thought he held the belief, we'd think either that it was true or that it was a reasonable mistake.
49. A telling word!
50. Earlier versions of this paper were presented at the 2000 Pacific Division APA meetings, and at the University of Miami, Northwestern University, and the University of Chicago. I am grateful to those who offered comments on those occasions, and to the following people for their written comments or helpful conversations: Kate Abramson, David Archard, John Bogart, Anthony Duff, Leslie Francis, Anita Superson, Peg Tittle, David Wasserman, and Alan Wertheimer. Special thanks are due to Kit Kinports, who not only commented on two drafts of this paper but taught me criminal law in a fabulous course that got me hooked on the subject. I would also like to acknowledge the generous support of the Center for Advanced Study at the University of Illinois at Urbana-Champaign during Fall 1999 and the hospitality of Auckland University, where I began this work in Summer 1999.

Philosophical Issues, 11
Social, Political, and Legal Philosophy, 2001

Against Constitutive Incommensurability or Buying and Selling Friends

Ruth Chang

- **Comparisons turn friends into enemies.**

—Philemon: Fragment c. 310 B.C.

- **Though we philosophers love both the truth and our friends, reverence is due to the truth first.**

—Aristotle, *Nichomachean Ethics*, Bk I

One day I meet an eccentric billionaire who, on a whim but with utmost seriousness, offers me a million dollars to end my friendship with a close friend, Eve. What should I do?

Two subsidiary questions arise. First, would a friend, in virtue of being a friend, necessarily respond to the offer in a certain way? Perhaps being a friend requires one to react to such trade-offs by refusing to make the exchange, for example. Second, are the friendship and the money comparable? Is there a 'positive' value relation, such as 'better than' or 'as good as', that holds between them, or does every such relation fail to hold and the goods thereby incomparable? Perhaps any attempt to compare the friendship and money is doomed to failure, and thus my accepting or rejecting the billionaire's offer cannot be justified in terms of the relative merits of the friendship and money. Many have thought—rightly in my view—that there can be no justified choice between incomparable alternatives. Choice between them must instead be a matter of 'feelings,' 'the will,' or the like—at any rate, beyond the reach of practical reason.[1]

It is natural to think that the second question, concerning incomparability, is more fundamental than the first, concerning actions and attitudes. For suppose a friendship and a sum of money are comparable. It would then be very odd to maintain that in order to be a friend one would have to act as if they were not or to have attitudes that conflict with the fact that they are. Why build into what it is to be a friend that one act and feel in ways that might conflict with the truth? It seems that the answer to the second question constrains the answer to the first.

Recently, however, some proponents of incomparability have suggested that it is the first question that is the more fundamental. These incomparabilists claim that an answer to the question of what actions and attitudes are necessary to be a friend determines an answer to the question of the comparability of friendship with goods such as money. Whether friendship and money can be compared is determined by the actions or attitudes required to be a friend. Without the required responses to tradeoffs between friendship and money, the good at stake is not friendship but some other kind of relationship; the required actions and attitudes are 'constitutive' of the friendship good. This approach to incomparability involves a two-step inference: first, certain actions or attitudes are constitutive of a good, and second, those constitutive responses determine the incomparability of that good with other goods. The novelty of the view is in where it locates the source of incomparability; instead of appealing to relational facts about goods with respect to certain relevant features, 'constitutive incomparabilists' see incomparability as a constitutive feature of goods themselves.

Whether there is any constitutive incomparability is of importance in matters not only of individual choice but also of broader social interest. It might be thought that not only is friendship constitutively incomparable with money, but so too are human life, individual well-being, environmental integrity, political freedoms, and so on. If this is so, it is unclear how tradeoffs between such goods should, if at all, proceed. When has the Russian government spent enough trying to save its sailors trapped in a sunken submarine? How should the Ford Motor Company evaluate competing designs for the Pinto if one design saves $100 million but involves a significantly higher probability of lost lives? Is the wealth generated from strip mining the side of a mountain comparable with the pristine beauty of that mountain? If free speech is constitutively incomparable with money, are objections to campaign finance laws based on appeals to the First Amendment misguided?

In this article, I examine the two lines of argument for constitutive incomparability, one proposed by Joseph Raz (Raz 1986) and the other by Elizabeth Anderson (Anderson 1997, 1993).[2] I shall argue that both fail; Raz's implausibly requires that a belief in incomparability is constitutive of certain goods, and Anderson's relies on a common but erroneous understanding of what the comparability of goods entails. Following both Raz and Anderson, I focus my arguments on the case of trading friendship and money, but the discussion can be generalized to any other supposed case of constitutive incomparability. While my primary aim is the modest one of showing how existing arguments for constitutive incomparability fail, I end the paper with a positive suggestion for how putative cases of constitutive incomparability should be understood. Constitutive incomparabilists have, I believe, mistaken what I shall call 'emphatic comparability' for constitutive incomparability. With an account of emphatic comparability in place, the temptation to think that there is constitutive incomparability can be more readily resisted.

1. We start with a couple of background notes. First, what I have called constitutive 'incomparability' is defended by its proponents under the label 'incommensurability.' But these thinkers take 'incommensurability' to be a synonym of 'incomparability,' and so I will take the liberty of recasting their arguments in what I think is clearer terminology. "Incomparability," in turn, should be understood in an intuitive way: two goods are incomparable if there is no positive value relation, like "better than" or "equally good," that holds between them.[3] Many philosophers add a substantive assumption to the ordinary understanding: they say that the possible positive value relations that could hold between two items are given by the trichotomy of relations 'better than,' 'worse than,' and 'equally good.' If one good is neither better than nor worse than another and if they are not equally valuable, it follows that no value relation holds between them—they are incomparable. For the purposes of this paper, we can take this widely

held substantive assumption to be correct although I have argued elsewhere that it is not (Chang, forthcoming, ch. 5).

Second, the claim that friendship and money are incomparable is a claim about the *intrinsic* value of these goods. But claims about the intrinsic value of money need to be carefully understood, for money has little or no intrinsic value, and so, strictly speaking, claims about the intrinsic value of money—the value of the paper on which money is printed, the ink used, and so on—are of no particular interest.[4] Rather, what philosophers have in mind when they compare goods like friendship and money is a comparison of the intrinsic merits of goods like friendship, on the one hand, and the intrinsic merits of what money is used for, on the other. And not any good that money can buy is included; money can be used for a wide variety of goods. I can spend a million dollars securing a life-saving operation from my mother, for example; and, in this case, the "intrinsic" value of the million dollars would be the intrinsic value of my mother's life. But constitutive incomparabilists implicitly have in mind by "money" a particular class of goods that does not include significant intrinsic goods like human life. When they urge that friendships are incomparable with money, they mean that friendships are incomparable with what we might call *mere* market goods—goods one can buy with money that are not instrumental to some significant intrinsic good such as human life, freedom, health, or friendship. Mere market goods are the commodities and services enjoyed by agents *qua* consumers; insofar as such goods are instrumental to or constitutive of significant goods like life, freedom, or friendship, they do not qualify as mere market goods. Thus, in our discussion, the term 'money' should be understood as a placeholder for mere market goods, such as a new car, luxury cruise, or fine meal. Our question, then, is whether goods like friendship are constitutively incomparable with mere market goods.

I.

2. The idea that incomparability can be a constitutive feature of goods themselves originates with Joseph Raz in *The Morality of Freedom*.[5]

Raz starts by noting that there are choice situations in which agents typically refuse to exchange one good for the other and feel indignant at the suggestion that they would be willing (346, 349). A choice between keeping friendship and getting money is paradigmatic of such situations. If offered money to give up seeing a chum, most people would refuse and would be indignant at the suggestion that they would be willing.

According to Raz, this refusal and indignation is *constitutive* of friendship; anyone who does not have these responses is incapable of being of a friend, and what she has with others is not a friendship but some other kind of relationship. Which responses are constitutive of friendship is, according to Raz, determined by "social forms"—roughly, social conventions including "shared beliefs, folklore, high culture, collectively shared metaphors and imagination, and so on" (311)—which are constitutive of the good and "determine its typical contours" (350). If, for example, Eve is depressed about her no-good boyfriend, social conventions constitutive of friendship dictate the range of responses a friend might have to her state of depression. As a friend, I might listen to her complaints with care and concern and then try to help her to decide whether to dump him. If instead I were to try to take advantage of her glum state to extract a favor, I would be responding in a way inconsistent with friendship. As Raz urges, the social conventions constitutive of friendship require friends to refuse to give up their friends for money and to be indignant at the suggestion that they would.

We should now ask, What belief about the merits of the goods underwrites such rational responses? If the responses constitutive of friendship depend on the friend's having a particular belief about the merits of friendship and money, then it follows that in order to be a friend, one must evaluate the goods in that way. As we shall see, Raz thinks the evaluation required is that the goods are incomparable. This result is then parlayed into the conclusion that the incomparability of those goods is a constitutive feature of them.

We shall assume for the sake of argument that Raz is right about the conventional nature of certain goods and that the refusal and indignation Raz identifies are constitutive of the friendship good. Our focus is on the two crucial steps of the argument: first, that in order to be a friend one must believe that friendship is incomparable with money, and second, that therefore friendship and money are constitutively incomparable.

3. Why think that friends, in virtue of being friends, must believe that friendship and money are incomparable? Although Raz is not explicit about this, his reason for thinking that they must seems to turn on an argument by elimination. To see how, we must consider what constraints the refusal and indignation impose on the underlying evaluation of the goods.

Some acts and attitudes have "symbolic significance;" they symbolically signify a particular evaluative view. The act of burning the American flag, for instance, symbolizes deep dissatisfaction with some aspect of American policy or way of life. According to Raz, the refusal and indignation constitutive of friendship symbolize "a proper appreciation of the value of [friendship]," "respect for the [friendship]," the "very high value...place[d] on having [friendships]," and "rejection of the idea that having [friendships] has a price" (348). The symbolic significance of these responses explains why a *direct* exchange of friendship for money is objectionable and an *indirect* exchange often is not. Many people willingly give up a friendship in order to take a job far away that pays more, and there is no indignation at the suggestion that they are so willing. But where the exchange of friendship for money is direct—as in the billionaire's offer—there is refusal and indignation (348–49). This difference in the acceptability of direct and indirect exchanges ramifies through all choices involving significant intrinsic goods on the one hand and mere market goods on the other. Many people would refuse to take any amount of cold cash in exchange for letting someone die, but they would be willing to spend only so much to save a sailor trapped in a sunken submarine. And although most would not take a lump sum of cash in exchange for exposure to known carcinogens, many accept a higher wage in exchange for such exposure in the workplace.

A refusal to exchange goods in direct cases has symbolic significance while a refusal in indirect cases arguably does not. As Raz writes "...the symbolic significance of the fact that one cannot trade companionship for naked money but one can for a job is that while companionship is not up for sale, it is but one ingredient in a complex pattern of life including work. It competes with those other ingredients in legitimate ways which allow individuals to strike their own balance between them. But...there are balances which indicate lack of...loyalty to the relationship. All this...is indicated by the symbolic significance of taking money for not seeing someone" (349–50). Taking money in exchange for giving up a friendship symbolizes a lack of respect for one's friend that moving far away for a higher paying job does not. Similarly refusing to make such an exchange symbolizes respect and a high regard for the friendship while refusing to move away arguably does not. (The same goes for indignation at the suggestion one would be willing to make such a trade).

Granting that refusal and indignation symbolize a high regard for friendship, we may ask, What belief about the merits of the goods makes the symbolic significance of my refusal and indignation possible? In order for my refusal and indignation (correctly) to symbolize my high regard for a friendship, it seems I must have some belief about the respective values of the friendship and the million dollars. The crucial question is, What is this belief?

4. Raz takes for granted that the belief must be about the *relative* merits of the friendship and money, for he does not consider any candidate nonrelative beliefs. Here is where the argument from elimination comes in. There seem to be only three possible beliefs one could have about the relative merits of friendship and money: that the friendship is worse than the money, that it is better, and that they are equally good. It is hard to see how a belief that the friendship is worse than the money could make possible the symbolic significance of the refusal and indignation. How could a belief that the friendship is worse ground a high regard for the friendship? A similar difficulty holds for the belief that the goods are equally valuable; how can the belief that friendship and money are equally valuable ground responses that symbolize a very high regard for friendship without symbolizing a similar regard for money?

The belief that a friendship is *better* than money seems more promising. This belief could certainly ground responses that symbolize respect and a high regard for friendship. But, as Raz argues, this belief cannot ground the high regard symbolized by refusal and indignation, because if one really believed that a friendship is better than money, then one should be perfectly willing to give up money in order to attain that friendship, and one is not so willing (347). (At $99.99, my friendship with Eve would be a bargain.) The high regard I have for friendship is symbolized, it seems, not only by my refusal to exchange friendship for money but also by my refusal to exchange money for friendship. Since I am not willing to trade what would be the worse thing—the money—for the better thing—the friendship—the belief that grounds my refusal to trade friendship for money cannot be the belief that friendship is more valuable than money. The only remaining possibility, then, is that the refusal and indignation symbolize a high regard for friendship in virtue of a belief that the goods are *incomparable*: neither is better than the other, nor are they are equally good.

If friendship and money are incomparable, friendship "has no price"—there is no way even in principle to measure the value of friendship in terms of money. The belief that friendship and money are incomparable implies that friendship is not the sort of good that can be replaced, compensated, or measured by money; and it is in virtue of the belief in incomparability that refusal and indignation symbolize a high regard for friendship. Raz goes on to suggest that the belief in incomparability *itself* symbolizes a high regard for friendship. He writes, "The most crucial fact about the kind of symbolic actions we are examining is now visible: *what has symbolic significance is the very judgment that companionship is [incomparable] with money*" (350, emphasis original). What Raz seems to have in mind is this: the belief that friendship and money are incomparable is that in virtue of which the refusal and indignation symbolize a high regard for friendship because the belief in incomparability itself symbolizes a high regard for friendship; there is a kind of 'transference' of the symbolic significance of the belief to the symbolic significance of the responses constitutive of friendship.[6]

Given that the refusal and indignation are constitutive of friendship, the belief that grounds them is also constitutive of friendship; unless one has the belief that friendship and money are incomparable, one is not capable of being a friend. As Raz explains, "[t]he capacity to have such relations involves interest in other people, empathy with them, and other psychological attributes. It also involves certain evaluative beliefs....My claim regarding [incomparability] is that belief in [incomparability] is itself a qualification for having certain relations. The attitude of mind which constitutes such a belief is analogous to attitudes such as respect for the other person, which are commonly accepted as prerequisites for a capacity for these relations" (350, 351). And, again, "[c]ertain judgments about the [in]comparability of certain options and certain attitudes to the exchangeability of options are constitutive of relations with friends, spouses, parents, etc. Only those who hold the view that friendship is neither better nor worse than money, but is simply not comparable to money or other commodities are capable of having friends" (352).[7] Therefore, Raz concludes, a belief that friendship and money are incomparable is constitutive of being a friend.

5. So much for the first step of Raz's argument. We turn to the second: How does the belief that friendship and money are incomparable determine that they are?

If the belief that friendship and money are incomparable is constitutive of friendship, then all those who are friends must have this belief. *For* friends, then, friendship and money are incomparable. But for those who are not friends, who are not, as it were, card-carrying members of the friendship institution, friendship and money may well be comparable. As Raz writes, "People who say 'For me money is more important than friends' are neither mistaken nor do they commit a wrong. They are simply incapable of having friends...So long as they are aware of the fact that [their belief disqualifies them from being friends] there is no mistake that they commit" (353). The error, then, lies not in the content of the belief that the goods can be compared but in thinking that this is so without also thinking that the belief disqualifies them from friendship. Thus there is no error in believing that friendship and money are comparable, even by those who have a full appreciation of the value of friendship and choose to pursue money instead. Since there is also no error in believing that friendship and money are incomparable, we are left with a striking result: friendship and money may be incomparable for you but comparable for me. It seems there is no 'objective' fact of the matter as to whether friendship and money are comparable. There is no point of view that is neutral between membership in the friendship institution—no 'viewpoint of reason'—from which it can be true or false that friendship and money are comparable. The question of whether they can be compared can be asked only from the point of view either of those engaged in the friendship institution (to which the reply is that they are incomparable) or of those who are not (to which the reply might be that they are comparable). Raz's conclusion that certain goods are constitutively incomparable, then, is relative to one's participation in certain goods. Because he does not think there could be any unrelativized claim of incomparability involving such goods, the relativized conclusion is the only truth there is.

6. We examine each step of Raz's argument in turn: Is a belief that friendship and money are incomparable constitutive of friendship? And if it is, does it follow that the incomparability of friendship and money is a constitutive feature of friendship?

It is hard to believe that in order to be a friend, I must believe that friendship is incomparable with money. Suppose I am faced with a choice between keeping my friendship with Eve and getting a dollar. If I judge that the friendship is worth more than a dollar, am I thereby disqualified from being Eve's friend? How can my belief that friendship is worth more than a dollar make me incapable of being a friend? Indeed, we might think that genuine friends would necessarily judge that friendship is more valuable than a dollar. Given that the value of a dollar is the value of the mere market goods one can buy for a dollar—two packs of bubble gum or a box of Cracker Jacks or a subway ride, etc.—surely a friend *could* believe that friendship is more valuable than any of these goods.

A thought experiment shows that the belief in incomparability could not plausibly be constitutive of friendship. Suppose that you have never considered, either implicitly or explicitly, the question whether friendship is comparable with money. Now someone puts the question to you. Does your answer determine whether you are a friend—whether all the relationships you have had with people that you thought were friendships were in fact some other kind of relationship? Compare the belief in incomparability with a willingness to trade a friendship for one dollar. It *is* plausible to think that your answer to the question, 'Would you be willing to trade a friendship for a dollar?' determines whether you are capable of being a friend. For if you are willing to give up a friendship for a box of Cracker Jacks, you do not know what it is to be a friend. A judgment that friendship is incomparable with money, however, is not plausibly constitutive of friendship. Indeed, one's beliefs about the comparability of friendship and money might be the result of philosophical reflection, and how could holding one philosophical view rather than another determine whether one is capable of being a friend?

Where does the argument for the claim that a belief in the incomparability of friendship and money is constitutive of friendship go wrong? There are numerous places where questions might be raised, but the core of the argument is the claim that a belief in incomparability is that in virtue of which the responses constitutive of friendship symbolize respect and high regard for friendship. There were two considerations in favor of this claim. First was the thought that the belief that friendship and money are incomparable itself symbolizes respect and high regard for friendship. Second was an implicit argument by elimination: given that some valuation of the relative merits of the goods is required to ground a refusal with symbolic significance, a belief that the goods are comparable will not do and so, by elimination, a belief that they are incomparable must be required. Both considerations, however, are subject to worry.

Start with the claim that a belief that friendship and money are incomparable symbolizes respect and high regard for friendship. There are good reasons to think that the claim is false, or if true, true in a way that saddles Raz's argument with a fallacy of equivocation. Some people no doubt believe that friendship and money are incomparable. Does their belief symbolize a very high regard for friendship? Consider other cases in which these people might think incomparability holds. They might think, to take a different example, that a career as a lawyer and one as a clarinetist are incomparable or that a limerick cannot be compared with elevator musak or that chocolate mousse cannot be compared with cheese and crackers. The belief that such goods are incomparable in these cases does not, as Raz would agree, plausibly symbolize respect and high regard for one of the goods as opposed to the other. Why then should we think that when 'incomparable' is applied to friendship and money that what is being symbolized is a high regard for friendship?

There are certain beliefs that might be mistaken for a belief in incomparability that do plausibly symbolize respect and high regard for friendship. The belief that friendship is not a mere market good, that it cannot be bought and sold like a commodity, or that it cannot be replaced, compensated or measured by money might plausibly symbolize respect and high regard for friendship. Indeed, Raz sometimes seems to treat a belief in incomparability as one of these other beliefs (347, 351, 353). But these beliefs do not entail that friendship and money are incomparable (though the converse arguably holds). Consistent with these beliefs is the thought that friendship is lexically superior to money. If no amount of money or commodities could ever be at least as good as any amount of friendship, friendship would not be any mere market good and so could not be replaced, compensated or measured by money.

A closer look at the relation of incomparability suggests that a belief that friendship and money are incomparable could not plausibly symbolize respect and high regard for friendship. Incomparability is a symmetric relation and understood literally cannot favor one good over the other. Respect and high regard for friendship, however, in some sense favors friendship over money; money is not regarded with the same reverence that friendship is. How could a perfectly symmetric relation symbolize a high regard for one good over the other? A belief that friendship and money are incomparable may entail that friendship is not measurable by money, but if it does it equally entails that money is not measurable by friendship. How can we extract from these symmetrical entailments a symbolic high regard for friendship?

There is, however, a *metaphorical* sense of incomparability that is not symmetric and that plausibly has the needed symbolic significance. In this sense, one good is 'incomparably better' than another, that is, vastly, significantly, off-the-charts better. So, for example, one might pronounce Pollini's performance of the Chopin Preludes as 'incomparable' or remark that there is 'no comparison' between a meal at Le Cirque and one at McDonalds. What one is saying is that the performance is significantly better than all or most others or that the sole soufflé au gratin is significantly better than the Fishwich with cheese. A belief that friendship and money are 'incomparable' in this metaphorical sense may indeed symbolize respect and high regard for friendship. But if this is the sense of incomparable upon which Raz's argument depends, the argument to the conclusion that friendship and money are literally incomparable suffers from equivocation.[8]

7. We have just noted that the belief that friendship is significantly better than money very plausibly symbolizes a high regard for friendship. This point raises doubt about the second consideration in favor of Raz's claim that a belief in incomparability is constitutive of friendship—the argument by elimination. Can a belief that friendship is significantly better than money do the explanatory work required? In particular, can it account for the symbolic significance of refusing to trade not only friendship for money but also money for friendship? Recall that the difficulty with this suggestion was that the belief that friendship is better than money could not explain why someone would refuse a direct trade of money in exchange for acquiring a friend. Raz himself suggests a response on behalf of comparabilists. Perhaps, Raz says, agents have the following ranking: "avoiding naked exchanges of [friendship] for money is best, having [friendship] is second best [, and] having money or other commodities is third best" (347). With this ranking, an agent would refuse to exchange friendship and money whichever good she starts with, and yet it could still be true that agents have a high regard for friendship that they do not have for money.[9]

Raz admits that the comparabilist explanation can account for the refusal to exchange friendship and money. As he writes, "[t]here is no doubt that the choices of people who have these attitudes [i.e., a very high regard for friendship] are consistent with certain ways of ranking the options" (348). Nevertheless, he continues, "My argument does not depend on denying that. My claim is the more elusive one that the rankings which are consistent with these views and treat all options as [comparable] do not represent people's *actual* valuations" (348). So, while Raz admits that a belief that friendship and money are comparable is compatible with the refusal to exchange friendship and money, and, as we have noted, can be the source of the symbolic significance of refusals, there is still the question of whether the belief represents people's actual valuations. He is concerned with actual valuations because he thinks that the merits of friendship are given by social forms which are a matter of social convention. It is people's actual valuations that will give us insight into how friendship relates to money.[10]

Raz thinks that people's actual valuations cannot be that friendship is more valuable than money because such a "preference for one option over another...would amount to a condemnation of those who forgo the possibility of friendship for money as people who act wrongly and against reason" (352). And, as he continues, "Some may take this attitude. But others (most of us, on reflection) do not. They regard such people as one regards people who neglected their musical abilities and lost their sensitivity to music in order to be better able to pursue some other goals....Their life is impoverished in certain respects, but enriched in others. Our judgment of them is no different from our judgment of people who lost their ability to form close and exclusive personal ties through joining a monastic order" (352–53).

There are two points here. First is the claim that a belief that good A is better than good B commits one to the belief that someone who chooses B over A "acts wrongly and against reason" while a belief that A and B are incomparable does not. Second is the claim that people who refuse to exchange friendship and money regard those who are willing to pursue money instead of friendship as simply missing out on one good but getting another. Since they believe pursuing mere market goods is, like pursuing friendship, one valuable activity among others, they believe that those who pursue money instead of friendship do not commit any error.

Both points can be questioned. Take the second first. Do those who refuse to exchange friendship and money really regard the pursuit of material wealth to be, like the pursuit of friendship, one valuable activity among many? If they do, they believe something false. Listening to opera instead of going to soccer games, cooking instead of learning to play the piano, hang-gliding instead of playing chess—these are plausibly cases in which one pursues one activity among many others without error; these valuable pursuits are perhaps 'on a par,' and so failure to pursue one in favor of another does not involve making a mistake of reason. But the pursuit of material wealth at the cost of pursuing personal relationships does seem to involve a mistake. Money—mere market goods—does not seem to be on a par with friendship, human life, health, freedom, and other significant intrinsic goods; it is not simply 'one good among many' but has a different status.

At the very least, there are *certain* circumstances in which pursuing money over friendship *does* involve a mistake, and this is all that is required to show that the belief Raz attributes to those who refuse to trade is false. Suppose that one has all the basic necessities of life but no personal relations and no mere market goods. Suppose too that one has an equal chance of success in making close friendships as in acquiring mere market goods. If one has a choice between pursuing friendship and pursuing the creature comforts of mere market goods, one should choose to pursue friendship. Indeed, anyone who appreciates the intrinsic values of friendship and mere market goods would in these circumstances go for friendship. This is not a case in which it would be appropriate to shrug one's shoulders and say, "to each his own," as one might do if the choice were between friendship and spiritual communion with God. Similarly, there are circumstances in which going for friendship over mere market goods might involve error. Suppose one has a maximum of deep loving relations—with a spouse, children, relatives, etc.—as well as many other significant goods—health, freedom, etc. One's life is at a full capacity for significant intrinsic goods but lacks the pleasures, enjoyments, and comforts of material wealth. In such a case, the balance of a good life arguably requires that one pursue mere market goods over friendship. Or, perhaps, because one's life is at full capacity for deep loving relationships, pursuit of friendship would be a mistake because it would involve detracting from one's deep loving relationships. In short, whether one makes a mistake of reason in pursuing one good over the other depends on what else one has in one's life. A categorical claim that those who pursue money over friendship do not make an error of reason cannot be sustained, and thus we may query Raz's insistence that those who refuse to exchange friendship for money have this false belief.

Even if people do have this false belief, Raz's attempt to connect the opposite of this belief with a belief about how friendship and money compare does not succeed. That is, Raz's first point—that a belief that A is better than B commits one to the belief that someone who chooses B over A "acts wrongly and against reason"—is open to doubt. For as Raz himself insists in the case of the belief that A and B are incomparable, the belief that A is better than B might be one not made from 'the viewpoint of reason' but from the point of view of someone participating in the relevant social form. Just as I might judge, from the viewpoint of membership in the friendship institution, that friendship is incomparable with money, I might also judge from that viewpoint that friendship is better than money. Thus, the belief that A is better than B does not necessarily entail the belief that those who choose B over A make a mistake of reason. By Raz's own lights, agents can have valuations of goods that are not required by reason but are instead relativized to their participation in certain goods. Raz thinks that the belief that certain goods are incomparable is one such valuation. The belief that one good is better than another might be another.

At any rate, Raz's argument is premised on the thought that people are indeed unwilling to make direct exchanges of money for friends. But any intuitive appeal of this thought may derive from a confusion stemming from the impossibility of buying friends. One can buy the *conditions* required for friendship. Just as one might 'buy' a child from an adoption agency and hence secure the conditions that make a loving parent-child relationship possible, so one might buy the conditions that make a friendship possible. But one cannot buy a relationship itself, off the shelf as it were. Friendships and other loving relationships develop via a genuine care and concern for the other that cannot, in the world as we know it, be instantaneously possessed after a visit to the ATM. There *is*, however, a sense in which buying friends is possible. I can make a direct purchase by striking a deal with God: Take my yacht, and, in exchange, alter the past (or future) so that X and I now (will) have a history together in which we are friends. And there are at least some circumstances in which one would (and should) be perfectly willing to strike such a bargain: if one has a friendless, lonely life and lots of mere market goods, one would be willing to swap some of those mere market goods for a new life with a friend. Moreover, many significant intrinsic goods can be bought, and people are perfectly willing to make direct purchases of those goods if given the opportunity. If I can save a human life in a direct trade for my toaster oven, I would be willing to do so.

In sum, Raz's conclusion that friends must believe that friendship and money are incomparable does not withstand scrutiny. There are good reasons to think that a belief in the incomparability of friendship and money is not constitutive of friendship—believing that friendship is worth more than a dollar does not plausibly disqualify one from being a friend. Moreover, Raz's argument that the belief in incomparability is constitutive of friendship relies either on an implausible claim about the symbolic significance of this belief or on a metaphorical understanding of 'incomparable' that saddles the argument with an equivocation. As we have seen, there is no reason to think that a belief that friendship is significantly better than money is incapable of doing the required explanatory work. Such a belief as plausibly symbolizes respect and high regard for friendship over money and could ground a refusal to give up a friendship for money and indignation at the suggestion that one would. Finally, the thought that people would be unwilling to make direct purchases of friendship for cash if they could is doubtful, and even if correct, does not support the conclusion that friendship cannot be better than money.

Supposing, for the sake of argument, that Raz's premises are correct, his conclusion would not constitute a total victory for the incomparabilist. For the truth that friendship and money are constitutively incomparable would be relativized to membership in the friendship institution and may vary from person to person, even though they are perfectly rational. This would make constitutive incomparability a mere shadow of incomparability as it is usually understood—that is, relativized to one's particular interests in certain rationally optional social forms.

II.

8. Elizabeth Anderson thinks there *is* a truth about the comparability of friendship and money from the 'viewpoint of reason': they are incomparable. But she is a pragmatist about value and so this truth is a construction of practical reason. While Raz is an eliminativist about such truths of constitutive incomparability—there are only truths relative to participation in a social form—Anderson is a reductionist—such truths reduce to truths about what there is reason to do or feel.

Anderson thinks that the value of an item is simply a matter of the practical responses—in particular practical *attitudes*, like awe, love, respect, honor and so on—towards that item that one endorses as rational to have towards that item (Anderson 1997, pp. 90–109).[11] So, for example, the beauty of a Cubist painting amounts to no more than the attitudes of awe and admiration it is rational to have towards it; there is no further question of whether such attitudes 'track the truth' about whether the painting 'really' is beautiful. As she puts it, "I reduce 'x is good' roughly to 'it is rational to value x,' where to value something is to adopt toward it a favorable attitude susceptible to rational reflection" (95). Thus whether something is valuable is wholly given by whether it is rational, or makes practical sense, to regard it with a favorable attitude.

Just as the value of an item consists in nothing more than the practical attitudes it is rational to have towards them, so too the *comparative* value of items consists in nothing more than practical attitudes we have reason to have towards them. Anderson writes,

> To determine whether two goods are [comparable], pragmatists ask what practical attitude- or action-guiding function claims of comparability can serve....This analysis implies a simple test for [incomparability]. If there is no point to comparing the overall values of two goods, the comparative value judgment about them will serve no practical function. Pragmatism says that if a value judgment serves no practical function, then it has no truth value or warrant. And if a comparative value judgment has no truth value or warrant, then the goods it compares are [incomparable]. Therefore, if there is no good reason to compare the overall values of two goods, the goods are [incomparable]. Call this the "no good reasons principle" for [incomparability] (99).

Anderson's approach to incomparability can be seen as "constitutive" because she thinks that the respect, awe, and honor it is rational to have towards certain goods is constitutive of them—they help make the goods the goods that they are—and it is in virtue of those attitudes that there is no good reason to compare them with other goods like money.

The attitudes constitutive of certain goods give rise to three ways in which there can be "no good reason" to compare them: sometimes "it is boring or pointless to compare them, other times it makes sense to leave room for the free play of nonrational motivations like whims and moods, and sometimes goods play such different roles in deliberation that attempts to compare them head to head are incoherent" (91). Even assuming that her pragmatic view of value is correct, we will see that none of these paths lead us to the incomparability she thinks there is.

9. Sometimes, it seems "silly, boring, and arbitrary" to make comparisons between items. It is silly to compare the aesthetic merits of a piece of doggerel and some subway graffiti, boring to grade seventh- and eighth-rate artworks, and arbitrary to compare a Bach concerto with a Picasso nude. There is, it seems, no practical point in judging the comparative aesthetic merits of such items, and, as Anderson urges, the project of compiling a Michelin guide to *The Ten Billion Greatest Artworks of All Time* would be the project of "philistines, snobs, and prigs, precisely those

least open to a free exploration and development of their aesthetic sensibilities" (99–100). Since we have reason not to be such people, it seems there are no practical situations reflectively endorsed by practical reason in which such comparisons have any use. And since there is no good practical reason to compare the goods, the goods are incomparable.

But is it so clear that there are no practical projects worth pursuing that could make use of comparisons that, in the abstract, seem silly, boring or even arbitrary? Suppose, for example, that I am a judge in an art contest "Now! Youth Art In New York City," and the entries include a piece of doggerel and some subway art. Surely in this case, although other considerations may be relevant as well, the aesthetic merits of the two artworks is relevant to my choice of winner, and the contest, whose purpose is, say, to encourage the flourishing of art by Manhattan youth, is not a project for "philistines, snobs or prigs." Or suppose I am on a funding committee for a charitable organization and am faced with two proposals for funding: a performance of a Bach concerto on original instruments at Carnegie Hall and temporary installation of a Picasso nude at the Museum of Modern Art. Surely one question relevant to my deliberations is, Which artwork has greater aesthetic merit?

Anderson overlooks the practical use of these comparisons because she assumes that if they are to have practical use, they must be the sole grounds for a choice. Since they can have practical import as *part* of what matters to a choice situation, by her own pragmatist lights, Anderson must conclude that the artworks are comparable. In general, I cannot think of any comparison that, although perhaps seemingly boring or silly or arbitrary if made in the abstract, could not have practical import as part of deliberations about what to choose in a particular choice situation. This conclusion has ramifications for Anderson's general pragmatic principle for incomparability: if for any comparison between two items there is always some possible choice situation in which that comparison has a practical point, the "no good reason" principle never yields a case of incomparability.

10. Perhaps, however, sometimes "it makes sense to leave room for the free play of nonrational motivations like whims and moods," and in such cases, there would be no good reason to compare the items since a rational choice can be made on the basis of nonrational considerations. So, for example, a choice between two deserts might properly be made on the basis of a whim or mood.

On this view practical reason divides choices into two types: those that require reasons to be rational and those that do not. But it is not clear how exactly this view of practical reason supports the claim that there is "no good reason" to compare items. For it does not follow from the fact that a rational choice need not be based on reasons that there is no good reason to compare the alternatives for choice. Practical reason may well *allow* me to decide between the chocolate cake and passion fruit mousse on a whim, but at the same time, I might have good reason to compare the two with respect to their nutritional content. So long as I am not rationally *required* to decide between the desserts on the basis of something that is not a reason, it is conceivable that I might have good reason to decide on the basis of a reason. If practical reason does require me to choose between the desserts on a whim, mood, or other nonrational motivation, then the attractive thought that underpins this view of practical reason, namely, that we are "free" to allow nonrational motivations to have a role in rational choice, must be abandoned.

In any case, even if there were no good reason to compare alternatives in the 'special' cases, this would constitute only a small victory for the incomparabilist. For the main interest of incomparability is in its upshots for those cases in which rational choice must be based on reasons. Many have thought that in these cases, if there is incomparability rational choice is precluded. Thus Anderson's second proposal, if sound, would succeed in establishing incomparability, but only at the cost of robbing it of its primary significance for rational choice.

11. Anderson's final suggestion as to how there can be no good reason to compare items is the most interesting and raises the basic question of what the comparability of goods involves. She says that sometimes goods play such different roles in deliberation that attempting to compare them is incoherent, and thus there is no good reason to compare the goods.

The fundamental assumption at work here is that if goods are to be comparable, they must have some value or evaluative property in common. Unfortunately, this assumption has often been mistakenly thought to entail one or more further claims. First, it has sometimes been thought that if two goods are comparable, there must be some common unit of value in terms of which they are compared. But we can compare goods even though those goods cannot be measured by a common unit of value. For example, one friendship can be Pareto better than another if it is at least as good in every aspect of friendship and better in at least one. There need be no unit of friendship in virtue of which this comparison holds. Or a friendship might be lexically superior to bubble gum; there is plausibly no common unit of value that measures both the friendship and the bubble gum, nevertheless, it is clear that the friendship is better. There are also ordinal comparisons that do not admit of any unit of measurement; a human life is more valuable than the life of a cockroach even though there is no common unit that measures the worth of both. Second, many have thought that a comparison of two goods is essentially a comparison of two *quantities* of some one value. For if a comparison of A and B presupposes that A and B bear value *V*, it seems that the comparison between them must proceed according to which has more *V*. But this is to fall into the trap of thinking that a single value can differ in its instantiations only by amount. A value can have qualitative as well as quantitative dimensions. So, for example, a Monet painting can differ in aesthetic merit from a child's finger painting not by the amount but by the quality of aesthetic merit it bears. A difference in quality of a single value can ground a claim that the Monet is aesthetically better than the finger painting. Third, it is widely thought that if comparisons are the basis for rational choice, then because there must be a shared value in terms of which the alternatives are compared, practical rationality must be a matter of *maximizing* that shared value. But perfectly compatible with the claim that comparisons are the basis for rational choice is a satisficing or even a "mean-median" view of rationality according to which it is sometimes rational to do what is not best but merely good enough or what falls within the mean or median of the available alternatives. Finally, it is often thought that if a shared value is a prerequisite of comparison and comparison is relevant to rational choice, then what one rationally ought to do is to bring about the state of affairs that is best with respect to that given value. In this way, it has been supposed that the relevance of comparisons to rational choice presupposes the truth of consequentialism. But A can be better than B in its intrinsic worth or with respect to its contribution to fulfilling one's duty quite apart from considerations of which would bring about the best consequences.

Anderson's proposal trades on all four mistaken inferences. She writes:

> Ordinary moral thought enables us to make choices in these cases without placing mother's life and friendship on a common scale and declaring one to be more valuable than the other....Instead, considerations of what we *owe* our

> mothers and our friends in different circumstances play a central role....Contrast this with the way we would have to regard mother and friends if their values were scalar. Then they would figure in principles that tell us to maximize the number or endurance of their bearers. This is to regard mother and friends as valuable only for the ways their existence improves the state of the world....Alternatively, to regard their values as scalar might be to accept a principle that tells one to adopt different degrees of the same attitude toward them. But mother is a proper object of filial love, one's friends of friendship. These forms of love differ in kind, not degree, and so mark their objects as intrinsically good in different ways, not just in different amounts....
> Thus, there are no valid practical principles that express a regard for the values of mother and friends as scalar. So we have no good reason to try to compare the values of one's mother and one's friends, or of her life and one's friendships, in terms of some common value they possess to a greater or lesser degree. These goods are therefore not [comparable]....
> [On the view that one must compare alternatives for rational choice], the sole practical role of the concept of value is to assign *weights* to goods, so that reason can choose what is weightiest or most valuable. It supposes that all values are scalar...[On an alternative view], the role of the concepts of intrinsic value is generally to assign a *status*, not a weight, to goods....The principles that express such attitudes generally take a distributive, not an aggregative or optimizing form....Thus, choices concerning those goods or their continued existence do not generally require that we rank their values on a common scale and choose the more valuable good; they require that we give each good its due. (103, emphases original).

The centerpiece of the argument is the distinction between "scalar" and "nonscalar" value. Scalar values can be measured on a "common scale" and figure in one of two types of practical principle: "principles that tell us to maximize the number or endurance of their bearers" and "principle[s] that tells[tell] one to adopt different degrees of the same attitude toward them." Nonscalar values, in contrast, are given by considerations of what we owe people in different circumstances and figure in principles of obligation that "mark their objects as intrinsically good in different ways, not just in different amounts." Scalar values assign "weights" to their bearers while nonscalar values assign "status" to their bearers, and practical deliberation involving items with weight proceeds by aggregation while deliberation involving items with status involves nonaggregative principles. Since the role in practical deliberation of scalar values is different from that of nonscalar values, it is "incoherent" to try to compare a scalar good with a nonscalar good. Thus, to revert to our familiar example, it is incoherent to compare friendship, a nonscalar good, with money, a scalar good, and therefore, by pragmatism, the goods are incomparable.

There are two arguments here. One is this: comparisons require that the goods be measurable by a common unit of value; only scalar goods can be measured by the same unit of value; therefore, it is incoherent to try to compare a scalar good with a good that cannot be measured by the same unit of value. It is worth noting that this argument does not strictly rely on her pragmatism; the putative incoherence entails the incomparability of those goods quite apart from whether it gives us no good reason to compare the goods which then in turn, via pragmatism, entails their being incomparable. The other argument supposes that comparisons can be relevant to rational choice only if rationality requires one to maximize either consequences or amount of value; but it is inappropriate to try to maximize nonscalar goods which figure in nonaggregative practical principles; and therefore there can be no practical point to comparing a nonscalar good with any other sort of good, and thus, via pragmatism, the goods are incomparable.

Both arguments depend on tacking onto the claim that items can be compared further claims that do not follow from it. In the one case, the further claim is that comparable goods must be measurable by a common unit of value, and in the other, the further claim is that for the comparison to have practical import, rational choice must be determined by principles that tell us to maximize consequences or amount of value. But as we have seen, comparability does not entail these further claims.

Once we strip away the claims Anderson attaches to the notion of comparability, we are left with no good reason for thinking that there is no good reason to compare friendships with money, for it is the further claims that do the argumentative work in establishing that there is no good reason to compare certain goods. Anderson's conclusion that there is "no good reason" then is not strictly a conclusion about comparability but rather a conclusion about the limits of comparing by a shared unit of value and the inadequacies of practical principles that tell us to maximize consequences or amount of value. Her distinction between "weight" and "status," while interesting as a thesis about practical reason, does not have the upshots for comparability she supposes.

III.

12. Raz's and Anderson's arguments, then, do not establish that goods like friendship and money are constitutively incomparable.

This is not to say, of course, that there is no such argument, but whether there is remains to be seen. In the meantime, we may note that there is a natural *comparabilist* way of thinking about how intrinsically significant goods like friendships, and mere market goods, like money, relate. For we may say that a friendship is a 'higher' good than a sum of money, which is a 'lower' good, and from this it may be thought to follow that the friendship is *better than*—or, as we shall say, *emphatically better than*—the money.

The view that a good like friendship is 'higher' than a good like money is familiar and unsurprising, but many philosophers have supposed that the terms 'higher' and 'lower' mark incomparability, not betterness (e.g., Taylor 1982, Lukes 1997, cf. Mill 1861). Indeed, in the course of arguing that friendship and money are constitutively incomparable, both Raz and Anderson themselves suggest that friendship is appropriately held in "high regard" or is of a "higher kind" than money (Raz 1986, p. 348; Anderson 1997, p. 105). It is worth noting in this regard that Anderson introduces at the end of her article what she calls "hierarchical incommensurability," cases in which "we deny that one good is more or less valuable than another precisely by insisting that it has an incomparably higher value altogether" (Anderson 1997, p. 104). Higher goods are incomparable with, not better than, lower ones: "[w]e refuse the language of 'more' or 'better'; we reject commensuration in favor of hierarchy" (Anderson 1997, p. 105). The language of 'higher' and 'lower' signals incomparability, not comparability, because she thinks comparability requires scalarity. But as we have already pointed out, a nonscalar good can be better than a scalar good—my friendship with Eve is better than a stick of bubble gum—and so scalarity is not a condition of comparability.

Granting that higher and lower goods can be comparable, how is this comparability to be understood? The distinction between higher and lower goods is a distinction concerning the *intrinsic* merits of those goods; friendship is intrinsically better than money in a way that makes it 'higher.' The standard account understands the way in which higher goods are intrinsically better in terms of lexical superiority: roughly, no 'level' of the lower good, however great, can be intrinsically better than any 'level' of the higher good, however slight. Thus friendship is a higher good and mere market goods a lower, human life is a higher good and chocolate a lower, freedom of speech a higher good and beautiful millinery a lower.

But lexical superiority, in its various possible formulations, falls prey to a fundamental intuition: a nominal token of a higher type of good can be intrinsically worse than a notable token of a lower type of good (Griffin 1977; Griffin 1986; cf. Tribe 1972).[12] Take, for example, a superficial and banal friendship I might have with the local butcher. Whenever I visit his shop, we exchange pleasantries, cheerfully inquire after each other's children, and engage in desultory conversation about the weather and the state of politics. I then take my side of beef and leave. We like each other well enough, but our pleasantries are a bit forced, and our hearts are not really in the conversation. At the same time, our relationship is clearly a friendship, though a distant one. And it has intrinsic value—although barely rewarding and somewhat uncomfortable, it would be better to have that friendship than not. Barring consideration of all extrinsic values, is this friendship better than a million dollars worth of mere market goods? It seems clear to me that it is not.

There are many other such intuitions to which the emphatic comparabilist might appeal. Are three seconds of a human life intrinsically better than a lifetime of gustatory pleasures? Is the freedom to drink cranberry juice in public intrinsically better than a billion dollars worth of mere market goods? Is a fifth-rate modernist painting intrinsically better than sexual pleasure for every person who engages in consensual sex? This is not to say that for every higher and lower type of good, there is a higher token that is worse than a lower, but it seems clear that *some* tokens of higher type goods are intrinsically worse than *some* tokens of lower type goods. It seems that lexical superiority constitutes overkill and does not capture the intended distinction between higher and lower goods. In the short space remaining, let me very briefly sketch an alternative to it.

Our use of the term "good" has so far slid back and forth between token goods and types of good. Sometimes we have referred to the incomparability of 'friendship' and 'money,' and at other times we have referred to the incomparability of a particular friendship and a particular amount of money. Of course, the distinction between tokens and types is itself problematic, but we can nonetheless work with it in a rough and intuitive way. I want to suggest that the adjectives 'higher' and 'lower' apply in the first place to token goods and only derivatively to types of goods: a type of good is a 'higher' type of good than another just in case there is a token of the first type that is a higher good than a token of the second. So if my friendship with Eve is a higher good than a million dollars, then friendship is a higher type of good than money; and likewise, given that a million dollars is a lower token good than my friendship with Eve, money is a lower type of good than friendship. It does not follow, however, that every token of money is a lower good than every token of friendship. Indeed, it may be a tendency to focus on *types* of good that explains why so many thinkers have been attracted to an account of the distinction between the higher and the lower in terms of lexical superiority. Focusing on tokens instead will, I think, naturally lead to a more finely-tuned comparabilist account of the distinction. What, then, makes one token good higher than another?

I suggest that a token good A is higher than a token good B just in case 1) A is better than B, and 2) A is better than any 'B-improvement' of B, i.e., any token of the same type as B that is at least as good as B. If both these conditions are met, I shall say A is *emphatically* better than B; A is 'emphatically' better because there is no B-improvement in B that could make A *not* better.[13] Suppose, for example, that my friendship with Eve is better than a million dollars. If, no matter how many dollars we add to the million, my friendship with Eve is better, the friendship is *emphatically better* than the million dollars and therefore a higher good than the million dollars.

Emphatic comparisons are, strictly speaking, comparisons of two *bundles* of goods—in the present case, the bundle (an existing sum of money, my close friendship with Eve) and the bundle (an additional million, no friendship with Eve). My friendship with Eve is emphatically better than the million if the first bundle is better and no 'dollar-improvement' in the second bundle could make the first bundle not better than the second. Thus emphatic comparability can be understood as a kind of 'localized' lexical superiority: the 'threshold level' of the higher good beats anything with the lesser level, no matter how much one improves the other type of good with which it is bundled. Emphatic comparability allows the possibility that some token of a higher-type good is worse than some token of a lower-type good. This possibility is important because it points to an interesting feature of the nature of values: the conceptualization of values into types does not directly track how bearers of those values compare with one another. This, in turn, allows us to see that the deep intuition at the core of incomparabilist arguments, namely that goods are incomparable in virtue of their belonging to very different types, is misguided.[14]

Notes

1. Some philosophers think that choices made on the basis of feelings, the will and the like are choices within the scope of practical reason. See e.g. Raz 1997 and Anderson 1997.
2. Anderson's account has been endorsed by others with variations that need not concern us, e.g., Sunstein 1994, Lukes 1997. For an interesting, related argument that global 'commodification' blocks certain desirable conceptions of the good, see Radin 1996.
3. I have offered a more precise definition of incomparability elsewhere (in Chang 1997): two items are incomparable with respect to a 'covering consideration' if there is no positive value relation that holds between them with respect to that covering consideration. According to this definition, it is a requirement of incomparability that it be relative to a covering consideration. However, since the arguments of the paper do not rely on this requirement, I ignore it here.
4. Some thinkers claimed that the intrinsic value of goods like friendship is incomparable with the 'use' value of money, and so the incomparability is not between two intrinsic goods but between an intrinsic and an instrumental one. See e.g., Sunstein 1997. But I believe that the best interpretation of their arguments is one in which their claims are about the intrinsic value of goods like friendship on the one hand and mere market goods that money can buy on the other.
5. The discussion of constitutive incomparability occurs on pp. 345–357, but all of chapter 13 and some of chapter 12 provide relevant background. All subsequent page references in this section of the paper are to this work. For an alternative interpretation of Raz's argument that sees constitutive incommensurability as a version of Raz's notion of exclusionary reasons, see Warner 1998. Since Raz himself does not link his notion of constitutive incomparability with his notion of exclusionary reasons, I will assume that he thinks there are two ideas here, not one. I am sympathetic, however, to Warner's focus on the latter notion which may, I believe, ultimately prove to be the more interesting one.
6. I find Raz's text especially murky on the question of how the putative belief in the incomparability of two goods relates to the symbolic significance of certain acts and attitudes constitutive of those goods. Because he insists that the belief in incomparability itself has symbolic significance, I take it that he regards the belief as grounding the refusal and indignation at least in part because it transfers its symbolic significance to the refusal and indignation. Note, however, that not all symbolic acts and attitudes must be grounded in beliefs that themselves have symbolic significance. The act of burning a flag is grounded in a belief that, for example, the nation's policy on war is despicable, but that belief need not symbolize anything. Raz must therefore think that there is something special going on in the friendship case (and all cases analogous to it). Perhaps he thinks that the belief that friendship and money are incomparable has symbolic significance in the way

that a belief that Bill Clinton did not have an affair with Monica Lewinsky symbolizes utter trust of and devotion to Clinton, or a belief that one's ten year old daughter could win an international competition for professional pianists symbolizes one's faith and pride in one's child.

7. I follow Raz in various shifts, such as between conditions on the capacity for friendship and conditions on being a friend and between token friendships and the type of good, friendship. The distinction between tokens and types will become relevant in the final part of the paper.
8. The same ambiguity between a metaphorical and literal sense applies to Raz's claim that "friendship has no price." On one reading, it is the claim that friendship is significantly better than money—friendship is priceless—and on the other it is the claim that there is no (relevant) way evaluatively to relate friendship and money—friendship is not priceable. Only on the first reading is it plausible to suppose that a belief that friendship has no price symbolizes respect and high regard for friendship.
9. This strategy of reindividuating options can also be employed to defuse the apparent problem of explaining people's choices in indirect cases. Given the ranking '1) avoiding direct exchanges 2) having friendship, and 3) having money' it may seem a mystery as to why anyone would choose to take a higher paying job at the cost of losing a friend. But if the higher paying job is not the same good as money—perhaps it is money-earned-through-job—the puzzle disappears.
10. I believe this is what Raz has in mind when he states that beliefs about the (comparative) merits of certain goods are "self-verifying" (350).
11. All further page references in this part are to this work.
12. Nominal-notable comparisons also hold among values that might all be considered 'higher' or, at any rate, not distinguished from one another in terms of status. So, for example, equality of access to good coffee is intrinsically worse than liberty of thought.
13. The account of 'higher' and 'lower' goods favored here is very close to an account of 'incommensurable values' proposed in Griffin 1986, pp. 85–89. Griffin says that types of value are incommensurable when they are "discontinuous," that is, when "enough of A outranks any amount of B," where A and B are value types. If I understand Griffin correctly, the point of appealing to "enough of A" is to fix a token of A-type value than which no token of B-type is better. There is a slight difference between "better than any token of B-type value," which is Griffin's criterion, and "better than any token of the B-type that is at least as good as the token B," which is ours. Our criterion allows that some tokens of B-type value might be incomparable with one another, and so A might not be better than every B-token. The two criteria collapse if we assume that for any tokens A and A′ of a given type, there is an A+ that is at least as good as both.
14. The first version of this paper was written many years ago for a conference in honor of Joseph Raz at Nuffield College, Oxford, and many people, including Elizabeth Anderson, John Broome, Jim Griffin, Elijah Millgram, Andrew Moore, Martha Nussbaum, Derek Parfit, Joseph Raz, Seana Shiffrin,

Cass Sunstein, Charles Taylor, and Andrew Williams, helped me with it. Almost none of that version survives here, but this paper considers the same general subject matter, and I am grateful for the help I received earlier. For useful comments on or discussion of aspects of the present version I thank Kit Fine, Derek Parfit, Fred Schick, and Richard Warner.

REFERENCES

Anderson, Elizabeth. 1993. *Value in Ethics and Economics* (Cambridge: Harvard University Press).

Anderson, Elizabeth. 1997. "Practical Reason and Incommensurable Goods," in Ruth Chang, ed., *Incommensurability, Incomparability, and Practical Reason* (Cambridge: Harvard University Press).

Chang, Ruth. 1997. "Introduction." In Ruth Chang, ed., *Incommensurability, Incomparability, and Practical Reason* (Cambridge: Harvard University Press).

Chang, Ruth. Forthcoming. *Making Comparisons Count* (New York: Routledge Dissertation Series, ed. by Robert Nozick).

Griffin, James. 1977. "Are There Incommensurable Values?" 7 *Philosophy and Public Affairs*.

Griffin, James. 1986. *Well-Being: Its Meaning, Measurement and Moral Importance* (Oxford: Clarendon Press).

Lukes, Steven. 1997. "Comparing the Incomparable: Trade-offs and Sacrifices." In Ruth Chang, ed., *Incommensurability, Incomparability, and Practical Reason* (Cambridge: Harvard University Press).

Mill, John Stuart. 1861. *Utilitarianism* (Indianapolis: Hackett Publishing).

Pildes, Richard and Elizabeth Anderson. 1990. "Slinging Arrows at Democracy: Social Choice Theory, Value Pluralism, and Democratic Politics," 90 *Columbia Law Review*.

Radin, Margaret Jane. 1996. *Contested Commodities* (Cambridge: Harvard University Press).

Raz, Joseph. 1986. *The Morality of Freedom* (Oxford: Clarendon Press).

Sunstein, Cass. 1994. "Incommensurability and Valuation in Law," 79 *Michigan Law Review*.

Sunstein, Cass. 1997. "Incommensurability and Kinds of Valuation: Some Applications in Law." In Ruth Chang, ed., *Incommensurability, Incomparability, and Practical Reason* (Cambridge: Harvard University Press).

Taylor, Charles. 1982. "The Diversity of Goods," in Amartya Sen and Bernard Williams, eds. *Utilitarianism and Beyond* (Cambridge: Cambridge University Press).

Tribe, Laurence. 1972. "Policy Science: Analysis or Ideology?" 2 *Philosophy and Public Affairs*.

Warner, Richard. 1995. "Excluding Reasons: Impossible Comparisons and the Law," 15 *Oxford Journal of Legal Studies*.

Warner, Richard. 1998. "Does Incommensurability Matter? Incommensurability and Public Policy," 146 *University of Pennsylvania Law Review*.

PHILOSOPHICAL ISSUES, 11
Social, Political, and Legal Philosophy, 2001

Law and Social Order

Russell Hardin

Introduction

There have been many debates about the relationships, if any, between law and morality: the positivists, such as John Austin (1954) and Hans Kelsen (1967) vs. virtually everyone else, especially natural law theorists; H. L. A. Hart (1958) vs. Lon Fuller (1958, 1969); Hart (1963) vs. Lord Devlin (1959); and recently Richard Posner (1999) vs. Ronald Dworkin and many others (Posner et al., 1998). Most of the debate in each case has been about the moral content of the law, often about whether there is a necessary or minimal moral content of the law. In the most recent debates, the question is whether judges and others in the legal system would be able to do their jobs better if they were educated in academic moral theory. This issue presumably turns on whether laws are thought to have a moral content or are thought to be guided by a morality external to the law or at least whether a common law or appellate judge should bring moral considerations into deciding cases, perhaps in order to bring law into line with moral views.

I wish to argue that actual legal systems in reasonably successful societies have a clear moral principle behind at least much of their law. That moral principle is mutual advantage, which, at a minimum, includes social order. There may be many laws within a general legal system that have other moral bases or that arguably have no moral basis at all. If certain laws have a moral basis, that is merely a historical fact about what motivated legislators or common law judges to give those laws their content. But the central program of law to create social order is itself commonly guided by mutual advantage. This can happen by intent of those who devise the law or it can happen through a more nearly evolutionary or quasi-common law development that is itself not under the clear control of designers with intentions. It would be perverse to say that, if there is a legal system, then it must have been designed to be mutually advantageous. But it is not so perverse to say that, if a legal system has succeeded in effecting social order, then it must substantially serve mutual advantage.

Mutual advantage, which is simply ordinal utilitarianism, is roughly Paretian. A policy serves mutual advantage if it benefits some and harms none—this is the Pareto principle in economics. At a more nearly systemic level, a legal system serves mutual advantage if, ex ante, it secures social order and the opportunity for prosperity. This is the core claim of Thomas Hobbes in his defense of rule by a sovereign with the power to secure order. Because he lacked a strategic insight that David Hume thoroughly grasped, Hobbes supposed that any sovereign must be supported without any threat of attempting reform against that sovereign's rule. He seems to have believed that order must be intentionally created and managed. Hume's insight is that we are capable of spontaneous coordination that can secure political stability even when there is no absolute power over us. Hume called such coordination over any particular matter a convention. Government helps us to organize and accomplish many things, but conventional devices help us to accomplish many other things that are not formally regulated—including, most importantly, government itself.

The content of law is commonly quite specific and it is often backed by powerful sanctions that make us comply with it. Prior to such content, however, a legal and enforcement system must be created to give the content and to back the sanctions. Hence, the explanation of the working of law in detail and the explanation of the fact of a legal system are fundamentally different. We can sensibly say that what makes a particular law right in some sense is that it is promulgated by a legal system. To say that a particular legal system is right or good, however, is essentially to say that it serves us well.[1]

If a legal system roughly meets the Pareto criterion, we can say that the system itself is efficient relative to no system at all, as Hobbes argued must be true for virtually any system that secures order. If this is a reason for having a legal system, then we might suppose that the same criterion should often apply to the details of the system, that is, to the actual content of various laws. In general, however, it is wrong to apply a systemic principle to choices under a system justified by that principle. For example, we might give a utilitarian justification for a particular public institution but not be able give a direct utilitarian justification of specific actions required of the role holders in the institution. This is the argument of John Rawls (1955) against a commonplace criticism of utilitarianism: that it can sometimes commend that officials act unjustly in order to reduce overall harms to citizens. Rawls argued that institutions that are designed to achieve utilitarian outcomes might require role behaviors that are not directly governed by a principle of utility maximization. For example, a sheriff should obey the law and should not ignore the requirements of the law in order to achieve higher utility.

Nevertheless, although it is not always correct to argue from the same principle at both the institutional and the individual level, it might be correct to defend both a particular legal system and the laws and other details of it on the grounds that they serve mutual advantage—that is to say, that they are Pareto efficient in this sense.

Before turning to issues of morality in the law, I will briefly discuss the structure of much of modern argument in the law, the two-stage structure of social and legal order, the nature of mutual advantage, and the related nature of efficiency arguments in the law. The dominant tradition of legal theory until recently has been legal positivism, which is driven by concern with definition, a concern that continues to haunt scholars today who would not wish to be labeled positivists. Prior to the positivist sidetrack into definitionalism, the focus of debate in legal theory was more nearly on explanation, about making law work. Jeremy Bentham and John Austin are transitional figures between Hobbes, who focused on making social order work, and the twentieth-century positivists, who have tied law into definitional knots.

In value theory, Hobbes was arguably the first great mutual advantage theorist and, implicitly, an ordinal utilitarian. He was only implicitly an ordinalist because the issue of cardinal, additive welfare was not well framed before Bentham, so that Hobbes had no reason to argue against it. Hobbes's mutual advantage was a grand version of efficiency at the whole-society level. In the twentieth century, efficiency in the law is more commonly a concern at the intermediate level between specific actions or choices and legal rules or laws. After a long and misconceived detour into cardinal utility theory in the nineteenth century, Vilfredo Pareto restored the focus on ordinal efficiency, which has massively influenced contemporary law and economics through the Coase theorem of Ronald Coase (1988) and, at the case level, the Hand rule of Judge Learned Hand.

Once these general theoretical issues are made clear, I will turn to various arguments about the role of morality and moral theory in the law. My general argument is that the one general moral principle in law is the background principle of mutual advantage, as in Hobbes and Coase. Moral claims that are far more explicit and more pervasive than this principle are not persuasively requisite for law to work. Indeed, one can make a claim that is nearly the opposite of the usual claim for a necessary connection between law and morality. Any legal system that is heavily infused with morality will work well only if its subjects share that morality.

I. Two-Stage Theory of Social Order

In any account other than a simplistic natural law theory, justification of law must inherently be in two stages. In the first stage, we follow mutual advantage to design and put a government and legal system in place or to make substantial changes in it; and in the second stage, we follow the dictates of the state and its legal system. Such a two-stage theory of legal justification is a commonplace in utilitarianism (Rawls 1955, Hardin 1988), in legal positivism (Hart 1961), and in constitutional theory (Hardin 1999, chap. 3) Even within a legal system, there are often institutional choices that then determine specific policies or actions. For example, we justify an action, such as establishing a legal rule, given the prior justification of the system for establishing such a rule. This is a distinction Joseph Raz and others see between making a new law and applying an existing one. This is the inherent nature of institutions that are to serve particular purposes.

Hobbes gives only a holistic justification of a legal system, and his argument does not immediately apply to particular laws. I have a reason for wanting a legal system in general, a reason I share with virtually everyone. But we do not necessarily share a common reason for choosing particular laws. Jurisprudential debates about the law or particular laws within a legal system have no status in debates about whether to have law (Fuller 1969, 138). For example, Kelsen's basic norm (Raz 1979, 122–127) must be a non-positive norm from which positive norms are derived. Indeed, constitutional principles are conventions outside or over the law. Hart's rule of recognition—a customary rule—is external to the legal system and justifies actions within that system (Hart 1961, 100–110). Fuller says praise and blame for actions of an agency (for example, such allocative agencies as the now defunct Civil Aeronautics Board) are misplaced when directed at individual agents of the agency; the praise or blame should be "directed to the aptness of the institutional design of the agency to perform the task assigned to it" (Fuller 1969, 174).

Similarly, we may characterize many of Dworkin's (1996) issues as part of his implicit two-stage theory of law. There are constitutional moments to establish general principles and institutional structures and then, under the constitution, there are quotidian or policy moments. Hart and Fuller supposed their views apply to law as such. One might often read Dworkin's views as applicable only to the US Constitution and law under it. Although his integrity of a legal system seems quite generally applicable to any legal system, freedom, liberty, and equal treatment need not be.

II. Hobbesian Social Order

I will briefly spell out Hobbes's theory of social order, because that theory is the background of subsequent discussions here. It is not important here whether my account of Hobbes is correct—those who think I have Hobbes wrong can read my account of his theory as my theory of social order. What leads to his theory are several background issues of what the world and the people in it are like. Among these are the rough equality of ability (Hobbes 1968, 183), the state of war in which we find ourselves if we have no powerful government, and the consequent uncertain payoff from investment (186) and lack of security. There are three causes of quarrel: competition, anticipation of attack (out of diffidence or fear of equality), and glory seeking (185). What makes sense in general for maintaining individual interests is peace. Passions that incline us to peace are fear of death, desire of such things as are necessary to commodious living, and a hope by our industry to obtain them (188).

Hence, our basic problem is the need for regulation of competition and exchange in daily life. Hobbes supposes that this can basically be accomplished by coordinating on a sovereign. What the sovereign oversees and what leads us to require a sovereign are interactions that are not simply matters of coordination but that involve elements of conflict, as exchange does. Hobbes understands that exchange is not of "equal values" (Hobbes 1968, 208) but benefits both ("the just value is that which they be contented to give"). Hence, exchange is superadditive in that, after completing an exchange, we are both better off. It can be represented game theoretically as a prisoner's dilemma (Hardin 1982). Because it increases value to both (or all) parties, exchange is a source or generator of value. It is not merely a libertarian issue of fulfilling my desires and yours, but of our making ourselves better off. That is why someone committed to the use of law to support morality might insist that law should not be used to govern contracts that do not, in the view of *their* morality, enhance value, as in contracts for prostitution, gambling, and so forth.

Hobbes's view of exchange is contrary to that of Aristotle and medieval Catholic doctrine, in which exchange is of supposedly equal values.[2] If exchange is of equal values, then it must be subjectively a matter of indifference, in which case it is not clear why we would bother to exchange. The value of X to me is subjective (meaning that the value I assign to it need not be the value you assign to it) because it depends, among other things, on what I already have. Moreover, Aristotelian exchange is not superadditive so that, game theoretically, it would be zerosum (or constant sum). Ordinarily, zerosum games are of pure conflict so that whatever value you gain from our interaction I must lose, while Aristotelian exchange would entail moving from one outcome with its utility values to another outcome with identical utility values for each party, with neither gains nor losses to either party.

We can say that Hobbes presents two theories, one about the creation of government and the other about the maintenance of government. Both of these are coordination theories, but the second is relevant to the real world of his and all times, while the first is essentially fictional (Hardin 1999, 145–150).

In the two-stage theory of social order, the central problem of the state of nature is that, in it, there are many potential prisoner's dilemmas. In these, there is always the possibility that one of the players will cheat the other by taking what the other has without surrendering anything in exchange. But neither the whole state of nature nor its resolution is a prisoner's dilemma; and contract cannot resolve it because there is no sovereign available there to enforce the contract. In these conditions, notions of right and wrong, justice and injustice have no place—these are qualities that relate to men in society (Hobbes 1968, 188). We need government to get us out of or to keep us out of such a disastrous state of nature.

Hobbes could not handle two problems that were urgent in his time: religious commitments and glory-seeking. Religious fanatics preferred disorder to any order that did not establish their views in power to govern the society; and (generally aristocratic) glory-seekers wanted disorder that would give them opportunity to achieve glory through combat. Hence, Hobbes's coordination on a sovereign was not strictly a mutual advantage move in his time, because it ran against what these two groups wanted.

Two centuries after Hobbes's *Leviathan*, Hume resolved a lingering problem of Hobbes's analysis, although without reference to Hobbes per se. Hume supposed that we can spontaneously coordinate for order and that we can more or less spontaneously sustain that coordination for order, so that we do not require a regime of draconian enforcement (Hardin 1993). Strangely, Hobbes himself would have had implicitly to assume that such coordination could work for the establishment of government through contracting if the social contract argument could be made to work. He also assumed that the strategic structure of social order once a government is in place is that of a coordination game (all prefer to go along with any extant government rather than to attempt to change it—if they understand the nature of the problem as Hobbes did). Hence, maintenance of a government, whether one established by contract or by imposition by a foreign power or a revolutionary party, is also sustainable by spontaneous coordination. Hobbes's overall argument for government was that it serves mutual advantage to have one and to keep one in place once it is in place.

III. Mutual Advantage and Efficiency

If social order is mutually advantageous, then by definition it strategically *coordinates* us. As Henry Hart supposes, law is a facility enabling individuals to live a satisfactory life in common (Fuller 1969: 223). The purpose is something like Hobbes's mutual advantage. In comparison to other major legal theorists, Hobbes was much more nearly a sociologist. He was concerned with what could make order work to our general benefit, both to help us survive and also to help us prosper once we survived. Note that Hobbes's device for making us prosper was a bit like the device of nuclear deterrence in our time until recently. Each side's capacity for retaliation from beyond the grave reduced the incentive of the other side to make a preemptive attack. Persons cannot have a literal capacity for retaliation from beyond the grave, but they have a near equivalent from a state that acts as their agent of retaliation.

Fuller is essentially a Hobbesian interested in what will make the law work. He is not a Hobbesian in the specific details of his sociology. In particular, he is much more sanguine about our prospects than Hobbes was. But his value theory is Hobbes's value theory: mutual advantage. He shares Hobbes's view that we need law for our own benefit. He also supposes that we cannot even live up to any moral principles we might have in a social vacuum or in a war of all against all (Hobbes 1968, 215–217; Fuller 1969, 205). Hence he is centrally concerned with the facilitative branches of the law and with the coordination function of the law (Fuller 1981).

The concern with mutual advantage is a concern with efficiency in an ordinal sense. Such efficiency is the core of ordinal utilitarianism (Hardin 1988). The idea of efficiency has had a long developmental history that is instructive for our understanding of mutual advantage in the law. We could begin an account of its rise and articulation with Hobbes. In brief, we can say that Hobbes's theory of social order and the notion of efficiency are closely tied together and the modern views of efficiency of Vilfredo Pareto and Ronald Coase complement Hobbes's view.

I will not rehearse the full history here (see Hardin 1996), but will only note highlights. A vague ordinalism reigned from Hobbes to Hume and Smith. But it was sometimes distorted by the assumption that value is in objects, so that it is objective. Jeremy Bentham assumed an objective utility in this sense and supposed that it is cardinal, so that we could add values of various objects or consumptions to obtain a measure of our total utility. Pareto broke this view completely with his metaphysical assertion that interpersonal comparison is meaningless. Since Pareto's time, utility is seen as subjective, ordinal, and not interpersonally comparable.

Contemporary discussion assumes a rough general form for the values that can be counted: they must be capable of trading for one another. There can be no absolute values included. Every value must be in a form that can be taken as more or as less depending on how it 'trades off' with other values. Hobbes, Pareto, and Coase attempt to avoid one kind of tradeoff—that between individual satisfactions. Hobbes fails for the cases of religious fanatics and aristocratic glory seekers. Pareto resolutely refuses to fail even at the cost of being radically indeterminate. Coase comes close to succeeding, although he has some difficulty for changes in rules or regimes when there are intrusive transaction costs or for changes whose effects we cannot know very well in advance.

This is the major problem for such a value theory: how to add or judge across persons. Hobbes evidently was as antipathetic to interpersonal comparisons as was Pareto later. He was concerned only with improvements to each and every person's existence, not with some additive notion of overall improvement. As noted, he also held the vision of exchange that came to dominate after Pareto. Exchange between two people is always Pareto improving if it is *voluntary*. Voluntary exchange works to mutual advantage. For example, in the 2-person static Pareto diagram, the only way to move to the frontier is through exchange, because that diagram represents the possibilities given what is already available—that is, without further production. Hobbes's view has become the modern economist's view as well as the libertarian's view.

Hobbes differed somewhat from the modern view in his concern with efficiency when there are massive knowledge constraints (for example, he supposed that, at least in his time, we could not even know of significant differences between monarchy and aristocracy or democracy). We may call this Hobbesian efficiency: It specifies merely a crude direction of improvement to mutual advantage rather than a precise direction, and it specifies only that we move some substantial distance without any claim to reach a frontier of possibilities (since we cannot know where such a frontier might be). In this, Hobbes shares the vision of John Dewey and other pragmatists. Dewey (1960) says the most that we can expect of our efforts is that they bring improvement in our state of affairs, not that they bring us to some well defined final goal. This is also Fuller's (1969, 10–12) view. We need not know the morally best state of affairs in order to judge one state better than another. "And it is on this common sense view that we build our institutions and practices" (32).

Legal positivists, such as Hart, Hobbes, and others, hold that legal duties are positive. They somehow derive from social relations of reciprocity, and so forth. We want greater welfare; we achieve it by creating institutions that regulate behavior and make it a matter of legal duty. This is what Fuller (1981; see also Fuller 1969, 9) describes elsewhere as the "coordination function of law." Law serves mutual advantage. This is analogous to the account of Hobbes given above. Fuller is concerned not with whether you and I make an exchange but with whether, if we wish to exchange or we stand to gain from doing so, the law will facilitate our doing so. Contract law, tort law, and much else are, in this sense, among the facilitative branches of the law. (Fuller argues that laws which are not facilitative but that attempt to block voluntary mutual choices, such as laws against crimes without victims, fail because their morality as law is wrong. Contrariwise, law can be very well used to enforce morality in promise-keeping or contract.)

Fuller argues that there is much we need to know that is not in the law. The law is limited in what it can include. For example, it cannot give us the meanings of the words it uses to stipulate legal requirements. Such knowledge may be conventional or "customary." For example, our knowledge of what it means to violate a relatively terse contract is likely to be customary in this sense. But we did not agree to or legislate the customary meanings—why then should they be binding? *Only because it is mutually advantageous to us that they be binding*, because there is no other way to go. *If we agree with Fuller on this issue, then we evidently must grant that there is an inherent morality of law.* But note that Fuller's general argument, as is true of Hobbes's argument, applies essentially at the whole-system level, not at the level of choosing particular laws, which are apt to have losers as well as gainers. Hence, the inherent morality is merely that of the mutual advantage of having a legal system, not of particular laws (Fuller 1969, 138).

Typically, there are numerous, often very different moves that we can make that are all efficient in comparison to the status quo. We can, therefore, choose an overall efficient organization of the society that would not be the same as the organization that would have followed from manifold moves over piecemeal matters even though every one of those moves might have been individually efficient. A legal system that is geared for efficient outcomes need not include laws that themselves would all produce efficient outcomes piecemeal. Therefore, although one might argue that the principle of efficiency in some guise should be the moral foundation for law, it does not follow that it must be the moral foundation for all particular laws. Much of the time, however, it may be the right principle despite its being only intermediary for welfare. That makes generally good sense given that law is itself only intermediary for good life.

IV. Legal Theory

Much of the modern concern with what might be called the morality of law is a residue of historical arguments for and beliefs in natural law, which is both a moral and legal theoretic tradition. Classicists recur to the arguments of Antigone and Aristotle that there is a natural law that is more or less everywhere right for every society. Catholics recur to medieval Catholic scholars who argued that there is a true law from god that we can either infer directly in specific instances of its application or in general as the background of a legal order. In the strongest natural law positions, it is supposed that individuals should follow natural law against the actual positive laws of a legal system when these conflict. Natural law theorists generally suppose there must be objectively correct moral-legal principles discoverable by reason. Legal validity is therefore merely moral validity, which is everywhere the same. Legislated law and judicial precedent might be useful in helping us to deduce what the true law is, but they have no moral weight in their own right otherwise. I will not address traditional natural law principles or claims here except in passing when addressing contemporary scholars who assert supposed principles of natural law.

There is a third position that is labeled natural law by some writers. If there is some common human nature, we might immediately suppose that efficacy requires some fit with that nature; if that common or universal nature includes normative predispositions, efficacy might even require relevant normative content in the law. De facto, this is Fuller's position, which leads him to call himself a natural law theorist. While this position is often explicit or implicit in legal theory today, the Aristotelian and Catholic visions are taken by many legal theorists to be so transparently wrong as not to require any argument.

Although he spoke of natural law, Hobbes broke with the natural law tradition, whose terminology he used only to undergird his own positive law views. He was almost Cartesian in inferring his natural laws, or "lawes of nature."[3] But his natural law arguments are very different from those of the natural law tradition. He does not say what is a priori right at all times independently of what is the positive law but only *what would be right if it were the law.* His laws of nature are laws in the sense of theorems, not of commands of a sovereign (Hobbes 1968, 217). These laws of nature include, for example, the law to perform covenants (contracts for exchange over time) made (201). They do not bind rationally—in *foro interno*—as David Gauthier (1986), Alan Gewirth (1978), and various others suppose their deduced moral laws do bind as rationally incumbent on any individual. Rather, they bind in *foro externo* (Hobbes 1968, 215), which is to say, only when they are enforced by some power external to the individual.

For Hobbes, law is not a means of securing rights. Rather, law defines positive rights, which are the only rights worth discussing. But law is a means. It is a means of securing welfare. The welfare consists in survival beyond the likely lifetime one would have without law; success in social interactions, such as exchanges, that would be virtually impossible without law; and the benefits of working for one's own interest. It is in the nature of the tasks of law that they can best be accomplished collectively. Hence, law is a collective good. But the good that comes from it is individualized and fully accountable at the level of the individuals whose welfare is served by it.

Natural law arguments are commonly brought to bear at the level of specific cases or policies, such as policies on abortion and genetic engineering. In this form of argument, they are therefore not part of a two-stage theory of law, because natural law reduces directly to the single stage of applied laws, which are supposedly knowable independently of the nature of a legal system or its institutions. That Hobbes is not a genuine natural law theorist follows immediately from the fact that he requires a two-stage theory, with the elevation of a sovereign at the first stage and the application of laws at the second stage.

We can deduce the content of laws of nature but not any motivation independent of the threat of external force to follow them. For example, the bonds of a covenant have their strength from fear of some evil consequence upon the rupture (Hobbes 1968, 192). Hence, the laws are binding only for rational reasons. A covenant not to defend ourselves is void because we cannot rationally decide to let even the state kill us (199). Our duty to the state is not one of moral obligation, but is merely that of one who is obliged by the power of the state to abide by its laws. We might call this view, which is caricatured by Hart (1961, 18–20), the "gunman theory" of law.

The big change from natural law to positive law perspectives is the positivists' rejection of any claim that there is a necessary connection between law and morality (Raz 1979, 38). Moreover, there is no substantive "natural" good as would seem to be required for natural law theories or even, arguably, for the theories of Hobbes and Fuller, although most of us would accept Hobbes's central values of survival and prosperity. The positive law view raises the *is-ought problem*, an issue in the so-called fact-value distinction that pervades discussions of law and its justification. We cannot derive an "ought" from an "is"—hence, evidently, we cannot say from the fact of law somewhere, such as the US, that there is anything right about it. This is a basic principle of positive law theorists. Hobbes makes an initial claim of value: self interest, especially in survival. One might conceive this as part of the nature of humans, in which case the value is merely functional. But one might also think it generally good that human interests be served.

Fuller (1981) is, in effect, Hobbesian here. He thinks law should serve interests, it should be facilitative. This is not a conceptual or definitional "should." Sometimes, it sounds like a moral "should," but it is only a causal "should." That is to say, law should be facilitative or it will fail to work. Fuller supposes we can conclude from the fact that law works that it must serve people's interests (facilitatively). This is a social-psychological, not a normative or conceptual, claim. Unfortunately, in populations that split into harshly conflicting groups, what is facilitative for one group may be destructive for another (consider the US; Iraq with its religious factions; some of the residual nations from the former Soviet Union; Yugoslavia; and the case that drove much of the debate between Hart and Fuller, Nazi Germany). To have moral force, Fuller's view requires a principle of universalization. Coke's objection to repugnancy (Fuller 1969, 100) is really about non-discrimination, or equal treatment. Non-discrimination is not inherently required by law. Or, if it is, then the US Constitution and the law under it, which have massively discriminated over, for example, race and gender, cannot be law.

Much of legal theory is dominated by conceptual analysis and definition with little or no attention to explanation. Austin, Kelsen, and Hart were centrally concerned with definition, with the "province of jurisprudence," the "pure theory of law," or the "concept of law." This is the core of their positivism: to define law by what people do. The focus on the definition of law raises the prior issue of deciding whether what people do in this case is law. For example, is a system that is secret from the people to whom it is applied a system of law?

Fuller was concerned not only with definition but also with explanation, with the "efficacy of a system of legal rules." Fuller (1969, 49) says Austin failed to distinguish these two matters, and this failure was the basic defect of his analysis. Hart distinguishes them occasionally, but he insists on keeping them separate and on giving his attention almost wholly to conceptual analysis. His main exception is his sociological claim that, without the voluntary cooperation of many, "the coercive power of law and government cannot be established" (Hart 1961, 201). In this respect, Fuller is much more fully Hobbesian than are the main legal positivists of the past two centuries. Indeed, as does Hobbes, Fuller focuses more generally on the social science of the law than on conceptual issues.

The differences between Fuller and Hart are that Fuller addresses the more important issue (how law can be made to work vs. Hart's concern with the definition of law) while Hart writes with much greater clarity. Fuller was a strong voice for the Hobbesian vision in our time. But his was a muddled voice, as for example when he spoke for natural law in a way that can be aptly characterized as confusing. His misconceived declaration for natural law was particularly provocative to the positivist school of contemporary legal theorists.

Part of the intellectual agenda of legal positivism has been a variant of that of logical positivism in the sciences. The chief concerns have been the separation of normative and positive considerations in explanations of the law and its workings and the careful stipulation of how we are to know when we have a case of whatever is at issue. The first of these concerns is one that most philosophers since Hume have shared and that I will generally assume. The second concern is operationist. As physicists suppose they can know what is the meaning of an electron or a meter only by stipulating how to operationalize their observation, so the legal positivists have been at great pains to give operational definitions of the central concepts of law. Unfortunately, positivists such as Austin, Kelsen, and Hart have begun with operationalization of the largest, most complex, *most inclusive social concepts*: "law" and "legal system." Modern social scientists commonly join forces with the legal positivists when they insist that we start any inquiry by first defining what we mean by "institution," "government," or "power."

Against this move, one might imagine Ernst Mach, the physicist and early logical positivist, starting with the operationalization of "nature" instead of mass or distance. But that would have been metaphysics, not physics. And it would have played little role in the life of an actual physicist concerned with real, perhaps newly discovered phenomena. Kelsen, Hart, Raz, and, to a lesser extent, Austin have been unduly concerned with the relatively metaphysical issue of what law is, the concept of law, the province of law. They are definitionalists.

Fuller (1969, 157) criticizes Hart for conceiving law entirely in terms of its formal source—for example, King Rex—rather than as a complex undertaking capable of various degrees of success. Although he was an important part of the tradition that led through Austin to Hart, Hobbes was very different. His chapters 13 through 15 in the *Leviathan* are plausibly the most richly packed justification of government and law ever written (Hobbes 1968, 183–217). The central focus of these few pages is the *sociological possibilities of law and order.* Hobbes started not from the top down with a definition of law but from the bottom up with a psychology of the person in social interactions. He shared with the positivists a relative disinterest in the content of the law. But he dramatically differed from them in his focus on its workability.

He shared none of the positivists' concern with the "identity" of law or of a system of law, with such questions as whether some particular set of institutions is a system of law. At first glance, one might think the positivists' overwhelming worry with such questions is merely analogous to the physicists' worry whether what they are seeing in their observations is the effect of an electron rather than of something else. But even a moment's thought suggests that the parallel is faintly ridiculous. For the physicist, the operational definition of an electron is useful only as part of a theory of how it works, what it does. That was Hobbes's concern with law, a concern the twentieth-century positivists have largely ignored.

The legacy of definitionalism infects the work of contemporary legal scholars who do not share the utilitarianism of Austin and Hart. For example, Joseph Raz writes of "the authority of law," by which he means its source. Hence, he is with the analytical legal positivists in his concern with who can make law. He speaks of the "set of all the pure statements referring to one legal system" (1979, 80). Mach would bridle at such metaphysics.

The core of a positivist position should be that what works works. For Kelsen, a legal system "exists if it is effective and this does not entail acceptance as morally just" (Raz 1979, 141). If Hobbes and Fuller are (positively) right about human nature, then part of what works for us is what is good for us—or at least what serves our interests. Hence, the demand that it work might require that law have some moral core. But this is a sociological debate about how we are constituted and how we are likely to react to various devices of regulation. It is an issue on which the legal theorists have had better or worse insights, but none of them is seriously concerned with sociological analysis, even though Hobbes, Austin, and others have made substantial sociological claims.

In one of the major debates over the morality of law, Devlin (1959) has an essentially sociological view about the effect of certain "immoral" practices on the stability of society and its legal system. Hence, he is interested in explaining the effectiveness of a legal system and not merely in giving its definition. But his views on legalizing homosexuality and its supposedly catastrophic effects on his society are little better than an amateur's prejudices, a relatively ignorant amateur's prejudices. Hart (1963, 50) slyly says that "it is not at all clear that for [Devlin] the statement that immorality jeopardizes or weakens society is a statement of empirical fact." Sociologists can do little more than formulate Devlin's question. They can certainly not answer it with any confidence or agreement. Fuller (1969, 133) argues that legal suppression of homosexuality will fail. A subjective assessment of the difficulties and disruptiveness of enforcing laws on homosexuality and on various vices, such as gambling, prostitution, and drinking alcoholic beverages suggest that Fuller and Hart have the better case.

V. Moral Theory in the Law

Posner and his recent critics address the question whether academic moral theory would be useful to judges in helping them rule in specific cases. Posner (1998, 1999) holds that laws cannot and should not be grounded in what he calls academic moralism. Of course, any particular law could be grounded in academic moralism, but the whole system of law could not be because no academic moral theory is adequate to the task. From the perspective of a two-stage theory of legal justification, one could ask whether moral theory can or should play a role in understanding the principles behind the law itself. The answer is clearly yes. But Posner's focus is on the role of judges dealing with specific cases, not on justifying a legal system (he is not explicit about this, but the position seems to be clear in a sense analogous to that in which Dworkin holds that certain principles are instinct in the Constitution). Understanding the general principles behind the law need commonly play no role in guiding judges in their decisions. Indeed, this is virtually an instant implication of the two-stage theory. Whereas Posner seems to keep his arguments focused on the lower level issue, some of his critics slip between the justification of the legal system itself and the justification of decisions in particular cases within the system.

Variants of academic moralism include Kantianism, virtue theory, rights theories, and utilitarianism. Kantian moral theory is so thoroughly anti-consequentialist that it arguably cannot have a major role in guiding a general legal theory, but it is regularly invoked and Kant also wrote extensively on law. Arguably, however, his moral theory does not inform his legal theory, whereas it is his moral theory that often informs contemporary claims for morality in the law. It is often brought to bear at the level of specific cases rather than at the systemic level. Utilitarianism, which is causal social science plus central concern with welfare (consequentialism), and legal positivism have had a long and close association from Jeremy Bentham and Austin through Hart. Indeed, Austin (1954) supposed that good law has a utilitarian moral basis. Virtue theory, which is usually functionalist, was for many centuries closely associated with natural law, although it is not independently associated with a major school of contemporary legal theory. There are many rights theories, including those of Dworkin, Gewirth (1978), libertarians, and others. These have been the chief alternative to utilitarian justifications in law in recent decades, although their lack of a coherent set of principles often makes them seem ad hoc. (Hart [1983] saw utilitarianism as the standard position in Anglo-American legal theory for nearly two centuries until the rights revolution after about 1970.) Their popularity may be fading. Dworkin himself has more recently argued from principles that he supposes are "instinct" in the very idea of law itself. So, for example, he argues that the idea of integrity is "instinct in the concept of law itself" (Dworkin 1996, 83).

Sometimes, particular laws are grounded in overtly moral principles, although it would often be wrong to claim that the principles are consistent from one law or body of law to another within the same legal system. Civil law commonly coordinates and makes more efficient. To a substantial extent, criminal law does as well, although superficially most observers are apt to suppose that any particular criminal statute or prohibition is itself directly moral and likely morally motivated. It is a bit too easy to reach such a conclusion in many contexts, because what is commonly outlawed is virtually defined as immoral. For example, although it is not always either morally or legally wrong to kill someone, it is legally wrong to murder someone. But this is just to say that "murder" is legally defined as wrongful killing.

Our view of what counts as wrongful killing has changed over time. Killing in a duel was once a matter of great honor in many societies in which today it would be murder. Debates about dueling were commonly about the stupidity and waste of the practice. The most effective move against it was arguably not to call it immoral but to ridicule it, because ridicule eviscerated the sense of honor that backed the convention of dueling (Hardin 1995, 98–100; Bacon 1614). Similarly, so-called crimes of passion—killing one's spouse and the spouse's paramour when caught in flagrante—have been a matter of honor in many societies, including Texas within recent memory.

Posner has three theses on the relation of academic moralism to law. These are, first, that there are no moral universals. One might ask, does this mean merely that there is no actual agreement across times and places? And one might think that this claim trades on the act versus consequences distinction. There might be no universal moral rules on rightness or wrongness of types of acts even though there might be a universal principle of judgment of consequences.

Second, much of what is of moral concern can be handled without moral theory, as in a judge's decisions. Even a casual reading of important recent decisions suggests that Posner's point here is descriptively compelling. Judges do not often invoke moral theories. However, if what is of interest is "what works," Posner must show that reading academic philosophy does not work for judges. But reading economic theory or having an economic rule of thumb (such as the Learned Hand rule) works. Why not moral theory? Economic theory is useful because it helps to handle consequences. The only major moral theory that focuses on consequences is utilitarianism, and it depends heavily on economic analysis for many issues. It is not clear that moral theories not focused on consequences have resources for assisting judges.

Finally, Posner claims that academic moralism cannot succeed, because the discourse of moral theory is interminable because indeterminate (Posner 1998, 1802).

Posner's claims may be too strong or even outrageous by some lights, but they mostly have the strength that we know what it is that we agree or disagree with. But some of the criticisms of his views are too high-blown to be very grounded—for example, those of Anthony Kronman and Martha Nussbaum (Posner et al. 1998). There are strings of words that look like sentences but that lack the content. It would be hard to say what it would take to show that they are either right or wrong. Kronman (Posner et al. 1998, 1758) says that reason "promotes the flexibility of attitude and approach that every effort of cultural preservation requires"; and he speaks of our character as a people (1763).

Critics of Posner's complaint that moral theory is of little use in the law often invoke "moral reason," as though to say that it is something other than reason tout court. For example, Kronman (Posner et al. 1998, 1764) says Posner has it backwards when he says that the role judges play leaves especially little room for *moral reason.*[4] (Posner's complaint is generally against the use of moral theory, not moral reason.) What is added when the qualifier "moral" modifies reason? We could speak of reasoning *in* a moral theory, which is presumably nothing more than reasoning that begins from moral claims and reaches conclusions from these. Or we might speak of reasoning *to* a moral theory or principle, which is clearly something more than mere reasoning because it actually generates moral principles or rules. Natural law theorists, intuitionist moral theorists, and many others, such as Gewirth (1978), have claimed to reach moral conclusions directly from reason.

The central problems or disputes of moral philosophy are cases of disagreement *between* moral theories (for example, as in the case of abortion).[5] If reason is supposed to lead us to moral principles in such cases, then it evidently fails us in the sense that it leads some of us to one set of conclusions and others to a contrary set of principles. This is Posner's complaint, that when there is a moral issue, moral theories cannot settle it for a court. He says that judges do legal reasoning, which is not much different from ordinary reasoning about nonmoral issues; rarely do they engage in moral reasoning and, when they do, it is without the help of academic moral philosophy (Posner 1998b, 1811). Hence, problems of reasoning to a moral theory or principle vitiate any claim for the use of moral reason. Indeed, one might suppose that a case could be made for a reason-value distinction that is analogous to the fact-value distinction.

Posner argues that judges don't need moral theory, indeed, that they can't make use of it (Posner 1999, 131, 141). His critics do not actually address this point with cases to show how judges can or do use moral theory successfully. He argues further that such political "innovations as republicanism, the separation of powers, the system of checks and balances, and the secularization of politics can be...detached from their philosophical aegis and evaluated without regard to philosophical principles" (Posner 1998b, 1810). He supposes that the central issue for legal scholars is how to instruct a judge and that metaphorical and vague talk about moral reason cannot do this.

VI. Concluding Remarks

We can say that law as mere principle or set of behavioral rules would have no content. Its use typically involves implicit evaluations, which must often have moral overtones. This fact may suggest that there is an even stronger connection to morality, but there need not be. Still, if law is to work it must serve people well. This is the minimal moral content of law not by definition but by causal requirement if law is to work well. Of course, one might still suppose that a legal system would work best if its subjects shared many important values.

One might suppose that we must have common values if we can see the same meanings in what are essentially vague laws. Much of our written law is in reality unwritten; the law in the books requires an understanding of the shared assumptions that enter into making and interpreting it (Fuller 1969, 232). Indeed, custom is explicitly made a standard of decision in the Uniform Commercial Code (234). Customary law helps fill the gaps that will always be perceived in any body of enacted law. But shared meanings are not shared values, as any logical positivist would have recognized from the beginning. For some objective matters in the law, the conventional understanding can be quite clear and definitive; for many more nearly subjective matters, such as quality of workmanship, the understanding may be much looser and it may be much harder to agree on what "the" convention is.

In sum, a grand principle of efficiency—overall mutual advantage from having social order—stands behind a successful legal system. A simpler principle of piecemeal efficiency might be thought derivatively to apply to particular laws. However, no such inference can be drawn from the higher order grand principle. Although efficient piecemeal moves often do lead to overall efficient states, inefficient piecemeal moves do not rule out overall efficiency. Moreover, if law is restricted to the governance of dyadic relationships, these can be piecemeal efficient even while they lead to overall inefficient outcomes. When we have done our best with dyadic moves, we may stand in need of government or other collective action to move us to a state in which we are all still better off. It is striking that the principle of efficiency—from Hobbes to contemporary law and economics—has come to stimulate a theory that is much fuller and more articulate than any alternative. Indeed, most alternatives seem to be the ad hoc creations of individual scholars.

Arguments in law and economics (Calabresi 1985; Polinsky 1989; Posner 1986) are generally relevant to considerations *at the margin of a background of general arrangements.* Hobbes addressed this background and not the marginal issues. From roughly Hume and Adam Smith forward, most discussion has been at the margin and, indeed, marginal analysis revolutionized economic theory in the late nineteenth century. John Rawls (1971) attempts to establish principles for the background of general arrangements. Henry Sidgwick (perhaps the greatest utilitarian) argued that we don't know enough to start from fundamentals, we can only talk intelligently about improvements. Oddly, Hobbes seemingly agreed in that he thought we should live with the regime of law that we already have rather than engage in revolutionary action to change it.

I have not considered any alternative moral principles for the law with anything more than passing comments here. In large part, that is because many of the critics of the mutual advantage vision and its variants do not present any alternative and do not appear to have one (see, for example, Coleman 1988; see further, Hardin 1992) or have positions that are idiosyncratic and not widely enough adopted by others to be very articulate or comprehensive (for example, Dworkin 1996). Hence, extended criticisms of other principles would be premature here. In considering any alternative, however, one might ask first: Must every philosophy of law be consequentialist? We would not have law except to achieve or have effect on something, or on various things. Hence, law is inherently consequentialist, although the consequences at issue could be quite diverse, including, for example, autonomy, welfare, and religious commitment. (Jonathan Baron [1998] makes the same claim about public policy.)

Even when law is used to enhance autonomy or religious commitments, however, it must generally also maintain social order or it cannot achieve these other goals. Social order and even more extensive mutual advantage are not much, perhaps, in comparison to an articulate moral theory, but we must almost all want them. Social order, a minimal form of mutual advantage, is a sine qua non of almost all else; and more extensive mutual advantage is the equivalent of individual welfare generalized to cover all. I can achieve prosperity best if my society achieves it in general. Of course, the occasional Mobutu can do best as a parasite on the whole society, amassing great personal wealth by impoverishing most others (at some risk of assassination or overthrow), but few of us can expect to prosper best while most others languish. Our prospects are causally connected. As noted earlier, Hobbes cogently supposed that survival and welfare are to be achieved collectively.

Raz (1986) wants liberty or autonomy to have a role in his account roughly like that of mutual advantage in the account here. He recognizes the essentially consequentialist nature of law, and therefore adopts a consequentialist principle of autonomy in the sense that he wants laws to have the effect of enhancing autonomy as measured somehow in the aggregate. As moral theories go, this one is much less well worked out than is utilitarianism, and the nature of autonomy as a value is much less articulated than is the nature of economic value theory (Hardin 1992, 382–4). Robert Nozick (1974) criticized what he called a consequentialism of rights, that is, the trading off of some rights fulfillments for others. That is, of course, a large part of what a working legal system does. Indeed, one might even claim that this is a principle reason for having a legal system. For Nozick, rights were prior to law. For legal positivists, rights are the construct of law, so that this claim is true essentially by definition in the positivist vision. In any system of law, however, it seems implausible that a complex set of rights could be applied without occasional—even frequent—need to trade one against another, either my right to X against your right to X or one kind of right versus another kind, such as the partially conflicting rights of the accused and of the victim (Posner 1999, 160; see also Hardin 1988, 117–126).

Consider an essentially sociological claim that is made in many forms by many legal theorists of quite different views. Hart (1961, 201) says that law works because of the willing compliance of most people, without which the coercive power of law and government cannot be established and the state would not have the capacity to deal with even the few miscreants. Fuller (1969, 219) says that the functioning of a legal system depends on a cooperative effort, as, for example, it obviously does in traffic regulation (220). The central sociological fact here might mislead us into thinking that somehow people share a normative commitment to the law and that it works therefore.

Fuller's example of compliance with traffic regulations highlights the central issue, which is that law coordinates us, commonly in ways that we would choose for ourselves if only we could do so without a central regulator. That there is a lot of willing obedience to the law (virtually any law or system of law anywhere) does not entail any moral commitment beyond that of a commitment to any order that coordinates us in each living his or her own life. We might happen to share some moral vision of what that life should be, as deeply religious communities commonly do, but we need not have any vision in common that goes beyond mere coordination on social order. In contemporary pluralist societies, we might share strong moral views within particular communities but not across multiple communities, all of which are sustained by a single legal system. Hart (1963, 51) supposes it an "acceptable proposition that *some* shared morality is essential to the existence of any society." He has no way to show that this is true and it seems plausible that some societies have existed without any shared morality beyond what could count as egoistic concern with coordination on social order.

Notes

1. We might quibble over legal systems that are essentially religious, such as Shariya in Islam. The arguments here do not depend on whether every legal system fits my account, but one might relatively easily characterize even an ostensibly religious system as one that serves mutual advantage for a particular society—insofar as its populace shares the religious views.
2. Aristotle's view seems to turn on seeing value as objectively inherent in the objects exchanged, not determined by the use we would make of the objects and hence their subjective worth to us. Hobbes is one of the first major thinkers to adopt the subjective theory of value, a theory that did not finally become firmly established in economic writings until the nineteenth century.
3. One could suppose that Hobbes argued from natural law because that was the going theory of law in his time. Similarly, Hume argued as though he were a virtue theorist because that was the going theory of morality in his time.
4. Kronman (1988, 1759) further says that, "just as a good habit cannot be created by reason, it cannot be undone by reason either"; and that "only reason can reconstruct the individual who no longer feels the force of an earlier, unthinking loyalty to a particular community either to that community or to any other" (1761).
5. Some might wish to say that, in the case of abortion, the disagreement is between religious and secular moral views.

REFERENCES

Austin, John. ([1832] 1954) *The Province of Jurisprudence Determined.* New York: Noonday.

Bacon, Francis. (1614) *The Charge of Sir Francis Bacon Knight, His Majesties Attourney generall, touching* Duells, *upon an information in the Star-chamber against Priest and Wright.* London; New York: Da Capo Press, facsimile reprint, 1968.

Baron, Jonathan. (1998) *Judgment Misguided: Intuition and Error in Public Decision Making.* New York: Oxford University Press.

Calabresi, Guido. (1985) *Ideals, Beliefs, Attitudes, and the Law.* Syracuse, NY: Syracuse University Press.

Coase, R. H. ([1960] 1988) "The Problem of Social Cost." In Coase, *The Firm, the Market and the Law.* Chicago: University of Chicago Press: 95–156.

Coleman, Jules L. (1988) *Markets, Morals and the Law.* Cambridge: Cambridge University Press.

Devlin, Patrick [later Lord]. (1959) *The Enforcement of Morals.* Oxford: Oxford University Press.

Dewey, John. ([1929] 1960) *The Quest for Certainty: A Study of the Relation of Knowledge and Action.* New York: G. P. Putnam's Sons.

Dworkin, Ronald. (1996) *Freedom's Law: The Moral Reading of the American Constitution.* Cambridge, MA: Harvard University Press.

Fuller, Lon L. (1958) "Positivism and Fidelity to Law." *Harvard Law Review* 71: 630–672.

______. ([1964] 1969) *The Morality of Law.* New Haven, CT: Yale University Press, revised edition.

______. (1981) "Human Interaction and the Law." In Fuller, *The Principles of Social Order*, ed. by Kenneth I. Winston. Durham, NC: Duke University Press: 211–246.

Gauthier, David. (1986) *Morals by Agreement.* Oxford: Oxford University Press.

Gewirth, Alan. (1978) *Reason and Morality.* Chicago: University of Chicago Press.

Hardin, Russell. (1982) "Exchange Theory on Strategic Bases," *Social Science Information* 2: 251–272.

______. (1988) *Morality within the Limits of Reason.* Chicago: University of Chicago Press.

______. (1991) "Hobbesian Political Order." *Political Theory* 19 (May): 156–180.

______. (1992) "The Morality of Law and Economics." *Law and Philosophy* 11 (November): 331–384.

______. (1993) "From Power to Order, From Hobbes to Hume." *Journal of Political Philosophy* 1 (March): 195–207.

______. (1996) "Magic on the Frontier: The Norm of Efficiency." *University of Pennsylvania Law Review* 144 (May): 1987–2020.

Hart, H. L. A. (1958) "Positivism and the Separation of Law and Morals." *Harvard Law Review* 71: 593–629.

______. (1961) *The Concept of Law.* Oxford: Oxford University Press.

______. (1963) *Law, Liberty and Morality.* Stanford, CA: Stanford University Press.

———. (1979) "Between Utility and Rights." In Hart, *Essays in Jurisprudence and Philosophy*. Oxford: Oxford University Press, 1983, pp. 198–222.

Hobbes, Thomas. ([1651] 1968) *Leviathan*. Harmondsworth: Penguin, ed. by C. B. Macpherson.

Hume, David. ([1739–40] 1978) *A Treatise of Human Nature*. Oxford: Oxford University Press, ed. L. A. Selby-Bigge and P. H. Nidditch, 2nd edition.

Kelsen, Hans. ([1934] 1967) *Pure Theory of Law*. Berkeley, CA: University of California Press.

Locke, John. ([1689] 1950) *A Letter Concerning Toleration*. Indianapolis, Ind.: Bobbs-Merrill.

Nozick, Robert. (1974) *Anarchy, the State, and Utopia*. New York: Basic Books.

Okun, Arthur M. (1975) *Equality and Efficiency: The Big Tradeoff*. Washington: Brookings Institution.

Polinsky, A. Mitchell. (1989) *An Introduction to Law and Economics*. Boston: Little, Brown, second edition.

Posner, Richard A. (1986) *Economic Analysis of Law*. Boston: Little, Brown, 3rd edition.

———. (1998a) "The Problematics of Moral and Legal Theory." *Harvard Law Review* 111 (May, no. 7): 1637–1717.

———. (1998b) "Reply to Critics of The Problematics of Moral and Legal Theory." *Harvard Law Review* 111 (May, no. 7): 1796–1823.

———. (1999) *The Problematics of Moral and Legal Theory*. Cambridge, MA: Harvard University Press.

Posner, Richard A., Ronald Dworkin, Charles Fried, Anthony T. Kronman, John T. Noonan, Jr., and Martha C. Nussbaum. (1998) "Symposium on Richard Posner's Oliver Wendell Holmes lectures at Harvard." *Harvard Law Review* 111 (May, no. 7): 1637–1823.

Rawls, John. (1955) "Two Concepts of Rules." *Philosophical Review* 64 (1955): 3–32.

———. (1971) *A Theory of Justice*. Cambridge, MA: Harvard University Press.

Raz, Joseph. (1979) *The Authority of Law*. Oxford: Oxford University Press.

———. (1986) *The Morality of Freedom*. Oxford: Oxford University Press.

PHILOSOPHICAL ISSUES, 11
Social, Political, and Legal Philosophy, 2001

Rapes Without Rapists: Consent and Reasonable Mistake*

Douglas N. Husak & George C. Thomas III

I: Introduction

In this paper we defend a theory about how to assess whether a mistake about consent in a criminal prosecution for rape is reasonable or unreasonable. Since the issue of rape is inherently controversial and subject to misunderstanding, we begin by clarifying the somewhat narrow focus of our article.

The most important point to emphasize is that our topic involves the criminal liability of persons who have in fact committed **acts** of rape. Suppose that the crime of rape is defined as nonconsensual sex.[1] A person who performs an act of sex without the consent of the victim has thereby committed an **act of rape**. The victim of this act has been raped. But the fact that a victim has been raped and a defendant has committed an act of rape does not resolve the question of whether this person has committed the **crime of rape**. The crime of rape requires not only that a person commit the **actus reus** of rape, but also that he do so with **mens rea**.

If this person has committed an act of rape, but lacks **mens rea** and thus has not committed the crime of rape, is he a rapist? Ordinary language is inconclusive on this point. A rapist might be defined either as someone who has committed the **act** of rape, or as someone who has committed the **crime** of rape. Suppose that we adopt the former definition, and conclude that a person who commits the act of rape but not the crime of rape is not a rapist. This definition gives rise to a paradox; it is peculiar to say that a victim has been raped, but not by a rapist.[2] Despite this linguistic oddity, the crime of rape resembles virtually every other crime in this respect. If Ben takes your coat without your permission, intending to keep it, your coat has been stolen whether or not he acted with **mens rea**. He would lack **mens rea**, for example, if he mistakenly believed that the coat was his own. In this case, he is not guilty of the crime of theft. Is Ben a thief? If not, you have been victimized by a theft that was not perpetrated by a thief. If these locutions sound too paradoxical, we can adopt the latter definition, and describe the person who acts without **mens rea** as a rapist or a thief, as long as we are careful to remember that he has not committed the **crime** of rape or theft.

The imposition of criminal liability and punishment ordinarily requires **mens rea**. The criminal law typically recognizes that persons who make reasonable mistakes of fact that rebut **mens rea** are not subject to punishment. Few courts or commentators question the proposition that a reasonable mistake of fact about consent should be a defense from liability for rape.[3] Only a handful of crimes—none of them as serious as rape—fail to recognize reasonable mistake of fact as a defense.[4] In any event, we presuppose rather than defend the widespread view that reasonable mistake of fact about consent should function as a defense from liability for rape.[5]

A defendant who admits to having engaged in an act of sex but who alleges that he made a reasonable mistake about consent in a prosecution for rape is making two separate claims that must be carefully distinguished.[6] First, he is claiming that he was **mistaken** about whether consent had been given. Mistakes, by definition, are false beliefs. Therefore, he is conceding that his belief about consent is false; he is conceding that consent had not been given.[7] Using the terminology we prefer, the defendant is admitting that he committed an act of rape and that his victim was raped. But was he **really** mistaken—or is he merely lying about his belief in an effort to evade criminal liability and punishment? In Anglo-American law, the determination of whether a defendant is telling the truth or lying about his belief has always been entrusted to juries. Any theory of reasonable mistake is of limited use to jurors who must decide whether a defendant is lying or telling the truth about his beliefs. Many (and perhaps most) criminal defendants lie; we do not contend that the question of whether a defendant is telling the truth is trivial, unimportant, or uninteresting. But this issue, however crucial, is not the central focus of our article. Suppose, then, that the jury believes that the particular defendant is telling the truth, and really was mistaken about whether the victim of his act of rape gave her consent.

The second of the two claims made by a defendant who alleges that he made a reasonable mistake about consent is that his belief was **reasonable**. However juries decide whether a defendant is telling the truth or lying, the means by which they decide whether his belief is reasonable or unreasonable is somewhat different.[8] Some beliefs are reasonable, and other beliefs are unreasonable.[9] The question of whether a belief is reasonable or unreasonable is analytically distinct from the question of whether that belief is true or false. Some true beliefs are unreasonable, while some false beliefs are reasonable. The former category—unreasonable but true beliefs—are perhaps compatible with moral blame, but not with criminal liability. If a person believes that consent to sex had been given, and his belief happens to be true, he has not committed an act of rape, no matter how unreasonable his belief may be. In this paper, we are interested only in the latter category—reasonable but false beliefs. The determination that a false belief about consent is reasonable will result in the acquittal of a person who has committed an act of rape.

In this paper we focus on the criteria by which one should decide whether a mistaken belief about consent to sex is reasonable or unreasonable. In other words, we offer a theory about the general kind of evidence that should persuade a third party to conclude that a mistaken belief about consent to sex is reasonable or unreasonable. This theory is composed of two distinct parts. First, we assert what we believe to be an uncontroversial empirical claim—consent to sex is typically given and withheld nonverbally. Second, we argue that these empirical generalizations about the means by which consent to sex is typically given or withheld should be used to assess the reasonableness of a mistake about consent. Of course, the first part of our theory can be correct even if we are mistaken about the second part. We hope, however, that our inquiry succeeds in demonstrating the relevance of empirical investigation to normative issues of criminal liability.

Our theory should prove useful to jurors who must make the difficult determination of whether a belief about consent is reasonable. In actual legal practice, jurors probably make this determination without reference to any set of guidelines that could be described as a theory.[10] When jurors are required to decide whether a mistaken belief is reasonable, they probably ask themselves whether they might have made that same mistake in the circumstances in which the defendant was placed. Our theory helps to explain why a juror might answer this question affirmatively or negatively. It provides a reason why a reasonable person would come to have a false belief about whether consent to sex had been given.

The outlines of the theory we will propose are not entirely new. In 1992, we published a paper in which we argued that social conventions are crucial in assessing the reasonableness or unreasonableness of beliefs about consent to sex.[11] That paper has attracted substantial scholarly discussion, almost all of it critical. We take this opportunity to expand, qualify, clarify, and defend our earlier thoughts about reasonable mistake and the crime of rape. In Part II, we will briefly examine the ontological nature of consent—what consent **is**. Parts III and IV introduce empirical data. In Part III, we will describe how consent to sex is typically expressed in cases in which no mistake is made. The means characteristically used to express or withhold consent help to explain how mistakes occasionally occur—as we will discuss in Part IV. In Part V, we will account for the relevance of this empirical data by developing our theory about how to distinguish reasonable from unreasonable mistakes. In Part VI, we will conclude by responding to critics who allege that our theory is unfair to women in general and to rape victims in particular.

II: The Ontology of Consent

Suppose that someone believes, correctly or incorrectly, reasonably or unreasonably, that a person has consented to sex. What is his belief **about**? It is about **consent**, of course, but what kind of thing **is** consent? This question is ontological. In this Part, we briefly discuss two contrasting views about the ontology of consent. Fortunately, we believe that our topic does not require us to identify every detail of the correct account. Although commitment about the precise nature of consent may be needed to answer questions about the criminal liability of rape defendants that we do not address,[12] it is not needed in order to defend our theory about the conditions under which mistaken beliefs about consent are reasonable or unreasonable.

What kind of thing is consent? Two broad kinds of answers have been given. According to what we call **mentalistic** conceptions, consent is wholly a state of mind. Many and perhaps most accounts either explicitly state or implicitly presuppose that consent is a mental state.[13] According to what we call **behavioristic** conceptions, on the other hand, consent is composed entirely of behavior. Defenses of behavioristic conceptions have become somewhat more prevalent recently.[14] We describe each of these conceptions as broad **kinds** of answers (rather than as particular answers) to the question because there is room for enormous disagreement within each kind about the details of the ontological nature of consent.

Needless to say, these competing conceptions of the ontological nature of consent differ radically. According to mentalistic conceptions, the behavior that conveys consent can be distinguished from consent itself. A person can consent without ever expressing consent, and a person can engage in behavior that appears to express consent without actually consenting. In these respects, consent resembles other mental states such as belief. According to behavioristic conceptions, no such distinctions can be drawn. Unless a person engages in whatever behavior expresses consent, he simply has not consented. This is because the behavior that expresses consent **is** consent.

How might we adjudicate between these two kinds of accounts?[15] This question is difficult. In our judgment, no evidence from ordinary English is likely to be dispositive—or even helpful. Linguistic locutions are too ambiguous to shed much light on the matter. In particular, the phrase "to consent" often means "to **give** consent," which surely requires behavior. But that locution may mean "to **be** consenting"—to have that which is given **by** behavior—which may be a state of mind. Ordinary language is too susceptible to differing interpretations to be helpful with this metaphysical issue.

The foremost challenge in defending a mentalistic conception is to identify the exact state of mind that consent is.[16] No inventory of the several kinds of states of mind that are widely acknowledged to exist would include consent. Therefore, if consent is a state of mind, it is likely to be reducible to other, more basic states of mind. One view is that consent is composed of beliefs and desires. But what particular pair of beliefs and desires comprise consent? No one has yet provided a satisfactory reply. This difficulty with mentalistic accounts has led some writers to infer that consent cannot consist in a state of mind at all, but must consist wholly in behavior.

This inference, however, is unwarranted; a similar difficulty infects behaviorist accounts as well. Just as defenders of mentalistic accounts have been unable to characterize the mental state that consent is alleged to be, defenders of behavioristic accounts have been unable to describe the behavior that consent is alleged to be. The fundamental challenge for defenders of a behavioristic account is as follows. For any description of behavior B, no matter how complex or disjunctive, it seems possible (indeed, it seems easy) to imagine that a person can exhibit B without actually consenting. If asked whether he consented, a person who exhibits B could sincerely answer "no." Of course, behavior B cannot **be** consent if a person can perform B without consenting. Thus we conclude that an adequate account of the ontological nature of consent cannot dispense entirely with a mental component. Consent must be at least **partly** a mental state.[17] Regardless of how he might behave, we contend that no person can consent to sex without having an intention to consent. This conclusion will prove crucial in defending our subsequent theory about the conditions under which mistakes about consent are reasonable or unreasonable.

If we are correct, why do so many theorists continue to embrace behavioristic accounts? One possible explanation is that these theorists are addressing a somewhat different issue from the ontological question we raise here.[18] Although we believe that it is impossible to identify the behavior B that **is** consent, it is relatively easy to identify the behavior that would make it reasonable for a person to **believe** that he has been given consent—and to be permitted to act accordingly. Under normal circumstances, in the absence of deception or duress, a simple "yes" would suffice for this purpose. But this only shows that people sometimes are entitled to act **as though** they have been given consent, even when consent does not actually exist.[19] The ontological question we raise in this Part is not identical to the epistemological or normative question (which we raise in Part V) of when a person reasonably believes that consent has been given. Here we ask what consent **is**, and conclude that consent must be at least partly a state of mind.

In their purest forms, behavioristic and mentalistic conceptions of consent are, of course, mutually exclusive. Consent cannot be both entirely behavior and wholly a state of mind. But the best account of consent may be some sort of hybrid that combines mentalistic and behavioristic components.[20] On all such hybrid accounts, consent does not exist in the absence of both an intention to consent and some behavior by which that intention is expressed. Fortunately, however, we need not specify all of the details of the correct account of the ontological nature of consent in order to defend our theory of when mistakes about consent are reasonable or unreasonable. We are now in a position to introduce our theory about the means by which reasonable mistakes about consent should be distinguished from those that are unreasonable.

III: How Consent is Expressed

Regardless of whether consent to sex is purely a mental state or some combination of a mental state and behavior, there can be no doubt that persons **give** their consent only by engaging in behavior by which their intention to consent is conveyed. They do this in various ways. How? On our view, the best way (indeed, the only way) to find out how persons express their consent to sex is through empirical investigation.[21] Rather than deciding **a priori** how consent to sex **must** be expressed, a more fruitful mode of inquiry is to ask persons who have expressed their consent to describe how they have succeeded in accomplishing this feat. When theorists approach this matter because of their interest in rape and its prevention, they are likely to conclude that the means by which persons manage to express their consent to sex is extraordinary and mysterious. In fact, however, persons seldom encounter a problem in expressing their intention to consent or not to consent. In Part IV we will discuss how this process occasionally misfires and gives rise to confusion and misunderstanding.

The use of empirical data to identify how consent is typically expressed has an enormous advantage over alternative devices that are not based on surveys about what persons actually do. An alternative account about how consent **must** be given is bound to generate different results from an empirical analysis. A non-empirical account will entail that some persons who insist that they have actually given their consent to sex will turn out not to have succeeded as a matter of law. Suppose, for example, that a theorist insists that consent to sex is effective only if it is conveyed linguistically.[22] Clearly, the laudable motivation for this position is to reduce the incidence of mistake and the frequency of acts of rape. But since (as we will see) fewer than half of the persons who intend to express their consent to sex do so linguistically, such a position would deny legal efficacy to the efforts of the majority of persons. Of course, the advantages of requiring a linguistic expression of consent may outweigh this disadvantage.[23] Still, any non-empirical account of how consent must be given will give rise to the problem that many efforts to express an intention to consent will be deemed inefficacious.

Not surprisingly, answers vary to the question of how persons succeed in expressing their consent to sex. Still, patterns emerge that permit a few generalizations about the answers that persons provide.[24] These generalizations include what persons do **not** do as well as what they **do**. It is important to be clear at the outset about the precise connection between the expression of an intention to consent and the generalizations we will describe. These generalizations are descriptions of behavior. As we argued above, however, consent cannot simply be reduced to behavior. If we are correct, a person can consent without conforming to the generalizations we describe, and a person can conform to the generalizations we describe without consenting. Our generalizations are derived from ordinary cases—the behavior that most persons exhibit in expressing their consent.

Consent to sex is conveyed in a variety of ways. For the purpose of exploring mistakes, however, the most significant fact—confirmed by numerous studies—is that both the initiation of sexual activity as well as the giving of consent to sexual activities is typically nonverbal.[25] In another culture, or at some future time in our culture, asking for and giving consent to sex may become exclusively verbal. But the studies of contemporary Anglo-American culture indicate that consent is more often than not requested and given without words.

A study of sex in marriage found that 60% of the subjects used nonverbal techniques to initiate sex.[26] A study of unmarried college students concluded that both men and women were more likely to use "indirect strategies to have sex"—such as body language and seduction.[27] This researcher concluded that the "popularity of indirect strategies" is "reasonable." "Men and women probably prefer indirect over direct strategies for influencing a date to have sex because these are subtle enough to be consistent with the romantic notion that sex is sought after by both parties."[28] In a Canadian study, 93% of the men initiated sexual activity non-verbally (a verbal request accompanied the nonverbal initiation in about one-third of these cases).[29] In an Australian study, almost all of the respondents employed indirect, non-verbal strategies to encourage sexual activity.[30] For example, 93% of the females encouraged sexual activity to occur by not stopping their partner, and 98% encouraged sexual activity by responding to their partner's sexual advances.[31] Only 39% of the females reported that they had **ever** made an explicit request for sex at the start. The researchers concluded that the rules for communicating about sex are "very similar for boys and girls." [32] In another Canadian study, females were less likely to use verbal consent than indirect strategies (such as failing to resist genital fondling) to "give clear signals that [they are] in agreement to sexual intercourse." [33] Indeed, "clear verbal consent" was chosen by only 26% of the women as the most important way to communicate consent to sex.

Perhaps more importantly, even **rejection** is frequently nonverbal. In many situations, persons reject sexual advances by blocking or simply not performing the unwanted activity.[34] In the second Canadian study mentioned above, 48% of the women ranked saying "no" as the most important way to communicate non-consent; another five percent listed crying, screaming, or yelling as the most important way.[35] But fully a third of the female respondents thought the most important ways to refuse consent were by indirection.[36] That category included 10% who thought the most important way to refuse consent was to be "unresponsive and passive." In the other Canadian study, 23% of the women who did not want to engage in the initiated sexual activity made no verbal refusal. Another 36% refused in ways that implied the advances might be acceptable at some other time or place (what Perper and Weis call an "incomplete rejection strategy").[37] This study contained another important finding: when the woman disagreed about the level of sexual intimacy the man requested, sexual activity nonetheless continued in 36% of the cases—at a level the woman considered acceptable.[38] Thus, even rejection can be consistent with some level of permissible sexual activity.

In light of the enormous complexity of personal relations and the popularity of indirect means to convey or withhold consent, one could hypothesize that a man might believe consent to sex has been given when a woman did not intend to convey it. Do men actually make this kind of mistake? We turn now to that question, which we treat initially as an empirical question, thus reserving judgment about whether this kind of mistake can be reasonable.

IV: Mistakes

Some commentators speak of men and women as if they were idealized types who know what they want and how to get it, and who speak clearly and listen attentively. The reality is far more complicated. Real people act for overlapping, often inchoate reasons. Sometimes we know exactly what we want, but sometimes we don't know and act (or fail to act) anyway.[39] Sometimes we say clearly what we want, but often we hope others will know what we want without our having to ask. Sometimes we listen carefully to what others say to us, but at other times we hear what we want to hear. Frequently we do what we do not want to do because we wish to benefit others.

The indirect means by which consent to sex is typically conveyed show how mistaken beliefs about consent can occur. There is substantial empirical support that men have the attitudes necessary to make a mistake about whether women are consenting. Empirical studies consistently indicate that men are more likely than women to perceive behaviors as sexual. Men are "more inclined to perceive friendly behavior by women as sexual rather than social, to define social interactions with women in sexual terms, to interpret women's behaviors as sexually expressive, and to assume that women's conduct is motivated by sexual interest or desire."[40] Men imagine that a hypothetical sexual touch from a female stranger would be pleasurable, while females say that a hypothetical sexual touch from a male stranger would not be pleasurable.[41] In sum, several studies conclude that men read more sexual content into female behavior than females intend.[42] These biological or cultural predispositions help to explain how a man could make a mistake about whether his date wants to be sexually intimate, and what level of intimacy she might desire.

This evidence is uncontroversial. But isn't the man's mistake about whether the woman wants to be sexually intimate dispelled when she indicates, by word or action, that she does not want what he thought she wanted? Of course, if the woman is clear enough—if she says "no" or removes his hand—the possibility of mistake about consent diminishes. But male misperceptions about female behavior are very strong and tend to be compounded by three cultural factors. First, as we have seen, women often reject an initiated sexual activity but permit a different type of sexual activity to continue. Thus, a man might believe that any rejection he perceives is only partial or temporary in scope. Second, men have been exposed to the cultural message that "good girls" say "no," whether they mean it or not.[43] If a man believes that a woman wants to have sex (based on his misperception of her behavior before she said "no" or removed his hand), he might view his role as insisting that sex occur so that she could have the sex she wants without feeling guilty. The "fault" for having sex would then be attributable to him.

Moreover, even though most women rarely engage in "token" resistance to sex, several studies have concluded that many women do so on some occasions. That women sometimes say "no" when they hope the man will continue reinforces the belief that women want sex more often than they say they do—a belief that can contribute to misunderstanding in the large majority of cases when they say "no" and intend for him to stop. The classic study is Muehlenhard and Hollabaugh's 1988 survey of college women, which found that 39% had engaged in token resistance to sex—they reported that they had said "no" to sex even though they had every intention to engage in sexual intercourse.[44] The frequency reported was from once to a few times. A later study by Muehlenhard and McCoy found a strikingly similar rate of 37%.[45]

These phenomena are not peculiar to women nor to the United States. A 1994 study included both men and women in Russia, Japan, and the United States.[46] The question put to over 1,500 respondents was "almost identical to that used by Muehlenhard and Hollabaugh":[47]

> Has the following ever happened to you? You were with a person who wanted to engage in sexual intercourse and you wanted to also, but for some reason you indicated that you didn't want to, although *you have every intention to and were willing to engage in sexual intercourse*. In other words, you indicated "no" and you meant "yes." Has this ever happened to you?[48]

Among U.S. female subjects, 38% answered yes, a result indistinguishable from the earlier Muehlenhard studies (39% and 37%). The result for Japanese women was also strikingly similar (37%) while 59% of the Russian females answered in the affirmative. This study suggests that engaging in token resistance to sex is not unique to the United States culture. Indeed, among the subsample of non-virgins, 70% of the Russian women answered the question in the affirmative.

Perhaps most surprisingly, *men* in all three countries reported a high rate of token resistance—47% in the U.S., 48% in Russia, and 21% in Japan. In the United States, men reported engaging in token resistance more often than women (47% to 38%). Of the

U.S. sample reporting that they had engaged in token resistance, 44% reported doing so only once, 41% reported doing so two or three times, and 15% reported a frequency of four or more times. As a percentage of the total sample, therefore, 6% of the U.S. respondents reported engaging in token resistance four or more times while 23% reported doing so more than once.[49]

This study is an important contribution to our understanding of how mistakes about consent can occur. If a substantial portion of men as well as women engage in token resistance to sex, a man who mistakes his partner's behavior as sexual might very well believe that her subsequent "no" is a token resistance like one he has used himself or had encountered previously in women. The fact that token resistance is relatively infrequent does not matter for the purpose of showing how mistakes occur. The number of times men and women use token resistance is probably less important than the number of people who have engaged in that conduct. Having engaged in token resistance oneself, even if only once or twice, makes one aware of the possibility that another person may be employing that strategy. The empirical evidence helps to show how a man can mistake real resistance for token resistance.

Complicating the issue further, both men and women engage in sex when they do not **want** to have sex—conduct that Muehlenhard and Cook call "unwanted sexual activity"[50] and Shotland and Hunter call "compliant sex."[51] The assumption made by some feminist commentators—that unwanted sex is equivalent to coerced sex[52]—cannot be true if "unwanted" and "coerced" are given their usual meanings. One may not want to go to work, to kiss an elderly relative, or to exercise, but millions of people willingly engage in these activities every day. A claim that an adult is coerced to go to work makes nonsense of the idea of coercion. Persons often voluntarily engage in activities they do not want to do at the moment.

No reason exists to exclude sex from the category of behaviors that can be both unwanted and consensual. As O'Sullivan and Allgeier conclude, "it is possible to consent freely to some type of sexual activity that is not desired or wanted—that is, to engage in unwanted but consensual sexual activity....Despite not wanting or desiring the sexual activity, an individual may be placed in a situation in which he or she freely accepts a partner's invitation for sex."[53] In the Muehlenhard and Cook survey, more men than women reported that they had engaged in unwanted sexual intercourse—"almost two thirds of the men and almost half the women."[54] Two later studies also found that many men and women engage in sex when they would rather not have done so. Shotland and Hunter found that 38% of the sample of 378 college women had engaged in "compliant sex"—saying "yes" to a date when they really did not want to have sex.[55] A 1998 survey by O'Sullivan and Allgeier found that 26% of men and 50% of women reported having engaged in unwanted sexual activity within the two-week period of the study.[56] The subjects reported a lifetime average of 11.9 occasions when they willingly engaged in unwanted sex, with an average of 2.5 partners. Within the prior year, the average was 7.8 occasions and 1.5 partners.

Unwanted sex is far from the ideal of how sex should occur. But the ideal is, apparently, far from contemporary reality. The law rarely, if ever, incorporates the ideal model of behavior as the minimum threshold to avoid criminal liability. Lying, adultery, and failure to come to the aid of others are all morally problematic but rarely subject to criminal penalties. If unwanted sex were equivalent to coerced sex, and coerced sex is defined as rape, then hundreds of thousands of women as well as men would be guilty of rape every month.[57] Surely this result is unacceptable. Perhaps more importantly, there is good reason not to translate this ideal into legal policy. If the law should function to protect sexual autonomy—as many commentators indicate—one would think that persons should be free to engage in uncoerced sex for **any** reason they choose.

The empirical picture we have painted now becomes more complete and also more complicated. Men and women usually request and give consent nonverbally (and often by acquiescence). Men and women sometimes say "no" when they intend to engage in sex. Men and women often engage in sex when they do not really want to have sex—and seem to do so with sufficient frequency that willingness to have compliant sex can be said to be part of the dating culture. In sum, men and women sometimes willingly engage in unwanted sexual activities, and sometimes say the opposite of what they mean. Thus, a man might believe that the woman who rejects his advances really wants to have sex, wants to be persuaded to want to have sex, or can be persuaded to have compliant (but consensual) sex.

In these situations, the male mistake is compounded if the woman engages in an "incomplete rejection strategy"—a technique that seeks to avoid sexual intimacy at the moment but leaves open the possibility that consent could be given at some future time.[58] As we have seen, one study indicated that 36% of all women used this strategy. A man who believes that his partner wants to have sex—or wants to want to have sex, or is willing to have sex whether she wants to have sex or not—would be likely to think that his perception is at least partially confirmed if the woman delivers her rejection in a soft or equivocal manner.

The next step in our unfolding story of mistake is the use of force by a man to overcome what he believes to be token resistance—to persuade a woman to change her mind, or to engage in compliant sex. Regardless of whether a man is mistaken that the woman wants to engage in sex, or misconstrues a soft "no" for token resistance, or believes that the rejection still permits some kind of sexual activity, how can he be so mistaken about consent that he is led to use force to get what he wants? A study by Susan Haworth-Hoeppner casts light on this question.[59] When asked whether the use of force would be justified to overcome the woman's refusal in various hypothetical dating situations, men were more than twice as likely as women to reply that force was justifiable. One situation involved a first date in which the female "allowed the male to put his arm around her or to hug her, but not to kiss her." Men were 2.3 times more likely than women to say that the man would be justified in obtaining a kiss by force.[60] More to the point for mistakes that lead to rape, subjects were asked to suppose: "while on a date with her steady boyfriend, a female allows him to engage in erotic touching below the waist and under her clothes, but then tries to stop things at that point." Men were 3.1 times more likely than women to say that the man would be justified in using force to continue.[61] Indeed, over one-third of the males in the study, and a surprising one-eighth of the women, approved of force to achieve intercourse "when a partner has a change of mind concerning intercourse."[62] Other studies have reached a similar conclusion about male and female attitudes toward coercion in dating situations.[63]

Are men who believe that some force is justified to overcome resistance simply brutes who deserve to be imprisoned? Perhaps. But we should inquire **why** men believe force would be justified. The most charitable view is that a man believes that a woman wants to go further, and that he is only "forcing" her to do what she wants to do. This man can rely on his view of the culture—"good girls" don't say "yes" but sometimes mean it—and on the incomplete rejection strategy. He hopes that the woman will become fully cooperative by the time of sexual penetration. O'Sullivan and Allgeier note that their study of unwanted sex was not designed to determine "whether the sexual activity remained unwanted throughout the sexual encounter," and conclude that future studies should test for this change in attitude.[64] It seems likely that many men who use minor force to overcome resistance at the initial stage believe that consent to penetration will be forthcoming (even if the consent is to unwanted sex).

It is difficult to imagine how minor force can accomplish the rape of a woman who resists. Moreover, if a woman resists physically at the point of penetration, it is almost impossible to believe that a man can continue to be mistaken about her consent. Perhaps some women become passive and signal their non-consent only weakly, if at all, once their initial resistance is ignored. In these cases, the man who used minor force at an earlier point could believe that, despite her lack of cooperation, the woman now wants to proceed—or is at least willing to proceed. Whether this belief is reasonable, of course, is a different question.

We have painted a picture, using empirical data, of how a man might make a mistake about whether a woman is consenting to have sex even though she has indicated her lack of consent and even though he may have used minor force to overcome her resistance. We have assumed that the man has misperceived the woman's behavior as more sexual than it was, and that the man acts in a forceful manner to get what he believes they both want, or to persuade her to engage in compliant sex. What remains to be examined, though, is the critical question: Can any of these mistakes ever be reasonable?

V: Reasonable Mistakes

Although the issues are distinct analytically, we claim that the foregoing considerations provide the key to a theory of **reasonable** belief about consent. We do not, however, propose a **general** account of reasonableness. Nor do we propose a general theory of what makes a **belief** reasonable.[65] In our judgment, even this latter question is too broad to address profitably. I believe that the earth is round, that pi is an irrational number, that George Washington crossed the Delaware, that my wife is in love with me, and that my sense organs are generally reliable. The means by which I would defend my claim that each of these beliefs is reasonable are so varied that few meaningful generalizations seem possible. The scope of our inquiry must be limited to the question of what makes a belief about a mental state reasonable. As we have argued, consent is at least partly a mental state.[66] When the reasonableness of a belief about a mental state is assessed, we claim that the empirical considerations we have described play a crucial role.

How might I defend the reasonableness of my belief that you have consented to something? Whether consent is wholly or partly a mental state, the answer can only be that I have made an inference about your mental state from your behavior, linguistic and otherwise. What makes my inference reasonable, even when it is mistaken, is that you have behaved in a way that many persons behave when they actually have that mental state. Of course, I will be able to make a more accurate inference from a broader range of behavior when I am familiar with you and your individual mannerisms and idiosyncrasies. Inferences are more likely to be mistaken when persons are relatively unfamiliar with one another—as in many dating situations. Still, empirical generalizations about behavior play a central role even when I make an inference about the mental states of persons I know very well. My belief that my wife is in love with me is unreasonable unless she behaves in the way that persons generally behave when they are in love. If she pays little attention to me, and dates other men, I may continue to believe that she loves me. But my belief is unreasonable precisely because her behavior is so contrary to how I should expect her to behave if my belief were true. Under these circumstances, it is reasonable for me to doubt (at the very least) that her love is genuine.

To understand how a person might defend his belief that someone has given his consent, consider non-sexual contexts in which consent is expressed or withheld. Suppose that a person finds $20 on a table, and puts it in his pocket instead of returning it to the person he knows to have left it there. The finder appears to have engaged in an act of theft. Suppose, however, that the finder believes the money to have been left on the table deliberately, as a gift. Suppose further that this belief is mistaken; the money was actually left inadvertently. How should we decide whether the finder's belief that he had been given a gift is reasonable or unreasonable? Empirical generalizations are crucial in answering this question. If the finder is a waiter in a restaurant and the person who placed the money on a table is one of his customers who had just finished an expensive meal, the waiter's belief that he has been given a gift is perfectly reasonable—even if it turns out to be false. The waiter's false belief is reasonable because persons who intend to leave tips usually behave in this way.

In a given society at a given time, generalizations about tipping are likely to be relatively familiar and uniform. Such generalizations are paradigms of **social conventions**. Of course, we do not pretend that the means by which consent to sex is expressed or withheld are nearly as familiar or uniform as those that apply to the context of tipping. We rely only on the empirical fact that consent to sex is frequently expressed and denied nonverbally and indirectly. **This** empirical fact, at least, is sufficiently familiar and uniform to qualify as a social convention. But nothing depends on whether it is appropriate to describe this generalization as a convention. Our point is that such generalizations are employed in both the tipping and the sexual context to defend the reasonableness of beliefs about consent.

In relying on such generalizations to assess allegations of reasonableness, we employ what is sometimes called a "totality of the circumstances" approach. We see no reason to privilege or exclude **any** material evidence of consent from consideration by the jury.[67] The active response of the participants should not be the sole basis from which evidence of consent should be derived. Because we have seen that both men and women sometimes engage in unwanted but consensual sex, a lack of enthusiasm in the activity by the participants would not, by itself, cause the defense of reasonable mistake to fail. Moreover, linguistic expressions should not be the sole evidence from which evidence of consent should be inferred. In the first place, a reasonable inference about a mental state may be made even though no words have been expressed. In addition, even when expressed, words are not always dispositive. I might reasonably believe that my wife loves me even though she explicitly denies it. I might reasonably believe that my wife is not in love with me even though she explicitly affirms it. Of course, in such cases I must be able to cite behavior that gives me good reason to doubt the truth of what she says. Clearly, however, I might succeed in citing such behavior—conduct that corroborates my belief and makes it reasonable despite linguistic evidence to the contrary. In this respect, beliefs about consent to sex are no different.

Our theory applies to a man who indulges in "wishful thinking" that his companion is consenting to have sex. Men who desire sex, we can suppose, succumb to the tendency to believe what they want to believe. Of course, the reasonableness of their belief is ultimately a jury question, and "wishful" honest beliefs come in a great variety of contexts, some more clearly unreasonable than others. It is one form of "wishful thinking" to assume that a woman who passively accepts foreplay wants to have sex. It is obviously quite another kind of "wishful thinking" to indulge the belief the defendants in *Regina v. Morgan* claimed to have—that the wife of their drinking partner was screaming and struggling because she enjoyed being forced to have sex.[68]

Again, our theory is not about when persons actually **do** consent. We have argued that consent is at least partly a mental state, and we do not claim that persons must actually have the mental states that others reasonably believe them to have. Because a person behaves in the way that persons typically behave when they are in love does not entail that they are in fact in love. Some such persons are not in love. Their behavior, however, makes reasonable someone else's belief that they are in love. Moreover, a person can actually be in love without behaving in the way that persons in love typically behave. In such an event, a belief that this person was in love would be unreasonable—even if it happened to be true. The same points apply to consent. A person who behaves in the way that persons generally behave when they consent to sex does not entail that they have in fact consented. Some such persons have not consented. Their behavior, however, makes reasonable someone else's belief that they have consented. Since that belief is reasonable, actors who hold it lack **mens rea**; they might commit a rape, but they are not rapists.

VI: Is Our Theory Unfair to Women?

Our claim that empirical generalizations should be used to decide when mistakes about consent are reasonable or unreasonable has not been warmly received. In this part we will respond to what we take to be the most forceful criticisms of our view. Many commentators have protested that our use of the data we have described is unfair to women generally and to rape victims in particular.[69] They maintain that these generalizations should not be used to decide that a mistaken belief about consent is reasonable because they are inadequate to protect women and thus need to be changed. These commentators have not tended to question the accuracy of our description of the means by which women express their intention to consent to sex. Indeed, they regard the fact that women typically express or withhold their consent to sex nonverbally to be the crux of the problem. Given the lack of clarity in the way that consent is expressed, mistakes are bound to arise, and acts of rape will be all too frequent. To prevent these acts of rape, they insist that persons should not be entitled to rely on the data we have described. Thus, many commentators "want to change social conventions by changing the law....Since in the event of an error we have a serious and irremediable harm to an individual's life, it seems reasonable for the law to intervene and force a change of social conventions."[70]

Commentators sometimes support their claim that persons should not be entitled to rely on existing conventions by allegations of how and why these conventions came to be as they are. After all, clear expressions of consent or nonconsent do not seem especially difficult. Why, then, do so many women behave in the ways we have described? If they actually intend to express their consent to sex, why do they sometimes use words and deeds that would seem to indicate their intention not to consent? And if they actually intend not to consent, why do they sometimes use words and deeds that can be misconstrued as expressions of consent? We have discussed these issues above. Some of these commentators, however, provide a different answer—an answer that alleges the pervasiveness of pernicious sexual stereotypes and gender inequality. Women behave as they do because of the expectations and attitudes of men. As long as men believe that women are undesirable if they accept sexual overtures too readily, women will continue to engage in ambiguous and misleading behaviors. Thus, the expectations and attitudes of men must be changed. Once sexual stereotypes are improved and gender equality becomes a reality, there will be no reason for women to behave so ambiguously.

There is much in this criticism with which we sympathize and agree. We concur that existing devices to express or withhold an intention to consent to sex can and should be improved. Acts of rape are too frequent, and the incidence of mistakes about consent needs to be reduced. No one can dispute that gender equality and the eradication of pernicious sexist stereotypes are highly desirable goals. It is hard not to be appalled by the current state of affairs. Still, we have not been persuaded to abandon our theory of how the reasonableness or unreasonableness of mistakes about consent should be assessed. In this part, we will hazard several replies to the charge that our theory is unfair to women.

First, we are reluctant to abandon our theory unless we are confident in the superiority of an alternative to replace it. Exactly what devices to express consent should substitute for those we have described? Although our critics are nearly unanimous in their unhappiness with existing conventions, they disagree widely about what should replace them.[71] Consent to sex must be expressed **somehow**. The objective, of course, is for the law to "provide a clear, easily manageable test for consent."[72] This goal is more easily described than achieved. At the very least, any fair evaluation of our theory should await the elaboration of the details of a competitive theory.

In fact, however, the foregoing criticism of our theory does not provide even a bare outline of a competitive theory about how to assess the reasonableness of mistakes about consent to sex. Virtually all of the focus has been on the details of various proposals to replace existing conventions of how consent to sex should be expressed. Suppose that these details have been completed and a new means to express consent to sex is agreed upon and implemented. However "clear and easily manageable" the new test for consent is made to be, mistakes are bound to occur. Mistakes may become less frequent, but they will not disappear altogether. After all, controversy surrounding mistakes provides a livelihood for lawyers even in contexts in which the law demands the clearest expressions of consent—as in the writing of wills and in the conveyance of real property, for example. Thus, a theory of when mistakes about consent are reasonable will still be needed. Fortunately, we (but almost none of our critics) have such a theory.[73] If a new (and better) device to convey or refuse consent replaces the old, we assume that the reasonableness of mistakes about consent will then be assessed relative to this new device.[74] Remarkably, then, virtually none of our critics appear to challenge our proposal to use the empirical data to assess the reasonableness or unreasonableness of mistakes about consent to sex—once existing devices are replaced by less ambiguous means to express consent and nonconsent.

Until better devices to express consent are in place, is our proposal really unfair to women? We think not. In the first place, our theory makes no prediction about how frequently women who do not consent will behave in ways that make reasonable a man's belief that they have consented. Such cases may be quite rare. Our theory simply attaches normative significance to the empirical reality that persons often express or refuse consent in indirect ways. In addition, although our theory has been interpreted primarily as a means to decide that mistakes about consent are reasonable, we should emphasize that our theory is equally helpful to decide when mistakes about consent are **un**reasonable. Many defendants who falsely but sincerely believe that consent to sex was given will be found to be criminally liable and subject to punishment by the application of our theory. They will be unable to show that their beliefs conform to generalizations about how consent is typically expressed.[75] Perhaps greater numbers of mistaken perpetrators of acts of rape will be convicted than acquitted if our theory is implemented. In any event, a theorist who lacks a theory of when mistakes are reasonable also necessarily lacks a theory of when mistakes are unreasonable. Our theory suffices for both purposes.

Moreover, we are dubious that the law **can** do much to change the means by which persons express their consent to sex.[76] We have already indicated our agreement with those commentators who insist that existing conventions should be improved. We support educational programs to help achieve this objective. But we are modest in our expectations about the effectiveness of using the criminal law to alter the way that persons do something as personal and fundamental as expressing their consent to sexual relations. Sex is perhaps the most expressive act of which humans are capable. Changing behaviors associated with acts that express the human personality is, as many have noted, very difficult.[77] One commentator contends that, because of mistake and misunderstanding, "the question for law is whether to leave matters as they stand or to intervene to clarify the convention."[78] But how exactly can the law "intervene" to "clarify the convention"? By definition, conventions are generalizations that describe how persons actually behave. A legislature could announce that the means by which persons have conventionally expressed their consent to sex is from this moment ineffective as a matter of law. But whatever the legislature may say, persons are almost certain to continue to express their consent to sex in the way that is familiar to them. Confusion is bound to result if the law fails to give legal effect to their accustomed ways of doing things. Commentators display both arrogance and naiveté in supposing that statutory change is likely to alter the way that persons relate to one another sexually.

The problems with our critics run deeper. Even if the law could change deeply embedded behaviors, there is bound to be a considerable lag between the time a law is passed and the time that conduct actually changes. What does justice require in the meantime? One commentator who endorses a change writes that "nothing is lost by imposing an affirmative duty on men to ensure that the women that they are involved with are truly consenting."[79] This comment either assumes that all men will suddenly change their behavior once the duty is imposed or ignores the felony liability of those who fail to get the message. In fact, a great deal is lost in the interval between when the new law is passed and behavior comes to correspond to it. In this time period—which could be several years or even decades—men who make mistakes about consent to sex that our theory assesses as reasonable will be convicted and punished. And these punishments no doubt will be severe, since rape is a serious crime. This strikes us as manifestly unjust.[80] Perhaps commentators are willing to convict persons who lack **mens rea** in order to achieve the objectives we have agreed are laudable. But they should not pretend that "nothing is lost" by their proposals.

Some commentators belittle these concerns about fairness to men. Stephen Schulhofer, for example, concedes that an "inconvenient fact" for rape law reformers is that "the 'no means no' claim isn't uniformly true—*even for women*." Sometimes, a man who interprets a woman's "no" as "keep trying" or "try harder," or even "get physical" will have "read her intentions...exactly right."[81] As a result, Schulhofer continues, "mistakes—even reasonable mistakes—are not impossible or even rare....And *sometimes*, in *some* settings, those mistakes will be 'reasonable,' even from the perspective of many women."[82] To this point, we concur with Schulhofer's analysis. Remarkably, however, he goes on to propose that all men who proceed with sex in the face of an explicit "no" should be convicted of a felony sex crime. After all, he continues, "we must inevitably *assign* some meaning to the word 'no.'"[83] The "assignment" that Schulhofer favors is for the law to "treat 'no' as conclusive proof of unwillingness....Once the law makes clear that it is no longer permissible to proceed to intercourse in the face of a verbal 'no,' it will be perfectly fair to punish anyone who disregards that standard."[84]

We reject Schulhofer's assessment of what is fair as well as his overall proposal. The "assignment" we prefer to the word "no" should reflect the "totality of the circumstances" approach we defended above. Words are evidence, but not conclusive proof, of intention. Schulhofer himself admits that some men who proceed with sex in the face of an explicit "no" are not mistaken about consent at all, and that some others make a mistake that is reasonable. Nonetheless, he proposes that all such men should be convicted of a felony sex crime. He contends that a requirement that "verbal objections be accepted at face value" represents a "fair allocation of risks."[85] The rationale for punishing even those men who are correct in their beliefs that the woman is consenting must be that the majority of men who proceed with sex in the face of an explicit "no" are incorrect in their belief. To protect women, all men must be precluded as a matter of law from arguing that their mistake is reasonable—even those men who are not mistaken at all.[86] This position, we think, is unfair to men.

We suspect that our theory seems unfair to women precisely because it allows men who have perpetrated acts of rape to escape criminal liability and punishment. Of course, **any** theory about the conditions under which mistakes about consent are reasonable will have this effect. It is not a special objection to our theory that it will result in the acquittal of persons who have perpetrated acts of rape but are not rapists. It is no accident that those who protest most vehemently about our use of empirical data tend to have no alternative theory of reasonable mistake to offer. Any such theory would undermine their primary objective of punishing persons who have committed acts of rape. Again, this objective is laudable. The demand for retribution against persons who have committed acts of rape is strong. Sometimes this demand is so strong that it creates reservations about acquitting persons whose mistakes are reasonable. If persons who make reasonable mistakes about consent are subject to conviction, however, rape will become a strict liability offense. We began this paper with the premise that strict liability for the crime of rape is unjust. Of course, theorists are free to propose that rape should be a strict liability crime. But they should confront the difficulties with that position directly, instead of simply ignoring the implications of rejecting reasonable mistake as a defense to rape.

In addition, we have seen no evidence that our theory will have the effect of increasing acts of rape. Some commentators seem to presuppose that the acquittal of men whose mistaken beliefs conform to existing generalizations about how consent is expressed or withheld will increase the frequency of rape. But why? How will convicting persons who commit the act of rape but lack **mens rea** lead to a decrease in the incidence of rape? Here, as elsewhere, changes in legal rules can produce deterrence only if potential criminals are made aware of the legal change. By what mechanism is this information to be disseminated? Will "word get around" that persons can no longer rely on their prior experience to form beliefs about whether a woman consents?[87] We are skeptical.[88]

The generalizations we have described are derived from the behavior of women themselves. They are identified by an empirical investigation of how women actually succeed in expressing their consent to have sex. Some have claimed that these methods to convey or withhold consent have not been created by women, but have been created by the sexist attitudes and demands of men. We do not deny that male control over women tells part of the story of how devices to convey or withhold consent came to be the way they are. But the data we discussed above suggest another explanation of the high frequency of ambiguous behaviors that persons—women **and** men—frequently exhibit in connection with sex. In contexts in which persons are uncertain of what they want, they are bound to respond to sexual overtures with ambiguous signals. No legal reform about how an intention to have sex should be expressed can hope to assist persons who are unclear about what they really desire.

Finally, many commentators indicate that the goal of rape law reform is to protect the **autonomy** of women.[89] We share this objective. The strategy sometimes employed to attain this goal, however, is frequently counterproductive. In the guise of protecting their autonomy, how can the law preclude women from expressing consent in any way they see fit? How has the autonomy of a woman been enhanced when the law denies effect to the means by which she chooses to express her intention? Attempts to answer this question, we suspect, will invoke an unduly narrow and impoverished conception of personal autonomy.[90] If we really aspire to respect autonomy, we will allow persons to express or withhold their consent to sex by whatever means they choose.

Conclusion

We make two claims about consent to sex in this paper. First, we claim that consent to sex is expressed or withheld by a set of devices that generally fail to include words. We presented empirical data to support this claim, which we believe to be widely accepted. Our second and more controversial claim is that the reasonableness or unreasonableness of a mistaken belief about consent—a belief that is at least partly about a mental state—should be assessed by reference to the devices that people actually use to express consent. We described some of the kinds of evidence that are relevant to the reasonableness of a mistake about consent to sex. While we do not know how a jury would weigh this kind of evidence against the testimony of the victim that she did not consent, we argued that juries should consider evidence of how people typically give or refuse consent to have sex. To forbid the jury from evaluating this evidence makes it more likely that a man would be guilty of the crime of rape even though his mistaken belief about consent conforms existing data about how consent to sex is expressed. We find this result to be unjust. A jury should be free to use the empirical evidence we have described to find a mistake about consent to be reasonable—to conclude that, although a woman was raped, the man is not a rapist.

NOTES

*We would like to thank Professors Joan McGregor and Donald Dripps for offering a number of very helpful suggestions—even though they disagree with much of what we say. We thank James McGovern, J.D. 2001, for his research assistance.

1. The typical rape statute in the United States has tracked the common law requirement of sex with a woman by force, without her consent and against her will. See, e.g., *State v. Rusk*, 424 A.2d 720 (Md. 1981). At least one state court has interpreted its rape statute to require only the amount of force used in the sexual penetration—which has the effect of construing the crime as non-consensual sex. See *State of New Jersey in the Interest of M.T.S.*, 609 A.2d 1266, 1278 (N.J. 1992). Some commentators have proposed novel reforms that create various categories of sexual offenses that may delete consent from their definitions. See Donald Dripps: "Beyond Rape: An Essay on the Difference Between the Presence of Force and the Absence of Consent," 92 *Columbia Law Review* 1780 (1992).
2. Some commentators have seized upon this linguistic oddity to seek to discredit the idea that even a reasonable mistake about consent can constitute a defense to rape. "When reality is split—a woman is raped but not by a rapist?—the law tends to conclude that a rape **did not happen**." Catherine MacKinnon: "Feminism, Marxism, Method, and the State," 8 *Signs* 635, 653–654 (1993) (emphasis in original).
3. See, e.g., *People v. Mayberry*, 542 P.2d 1337 (Calif. 1975) (requiring jury instruction that reasonable mistake of fact is a defense to rape); *State v. Smith*, 554 A.2d 713 (Conn. 1989) (same); Susan Estrich: "Rape," 95 *Yale Law Journal* 1087, 1102 (1985). Some commentators, however, have proposed that rape should be an offense of strict liability in some contexts. See Lynn Henderson: "Rape and Responsibility," 11 *Law and Philosophy* 127 (1992). See also Beverly Balos and Mary L. Fellows: "Guilty of the Crime of Trust: Nonstranger Rape," 75 *University of Minnesota Law Review* 599, 607 (1991). Cf. *Laseter v. State*, 684 P.2d (Alaska 1984) (requiring instruction that state must show "reckless disregard" of lack of consent). One state—Massachusetts—has apparently imposed strict liability with respect to the element of nonconsent. See *Commonwealth v. Simcock*, 575 N.E. 2d 1137 (1991). See also *People v. Hale*, 370 N.W.2d 382 (Mich. 1985) (third-degree criminal sexual conduct is strict liability offense) (alternative holding).
4. Statutory rape is a rare exception to this generalization. The continued existence of this strict liability offense in most states, despite persistent expressions of dissatisfaction from commentators, is no doubt due to the special protection the criminal law affords to minors.

5. Perhaps this plea should not be described as a "true defense." It may negate an element of the offense, and thus qualify as what some commentators have described as a "failure of proof." For a discussion of this distinction, see Paul Robinson: 1 *Criminal Law Defenses* (St. Paul: West Pub. Co., 1986), pp. 72–76. Although the distinction between "true defenses" and failures of proof is unimportant for our purposes, it may be crucial to allocate the burden of proof.
6. Most rape statutes require sexual penetration. In what follows, we will use "act of sex" or simply "sex" as short for "sexual penetration."
7. Of course, a defendant may plead in the alternative. That is, he may allege **both** that he was mistaken **and** that the victim consented. Inasmuch as he alleges a mistake, however, he is conceding that his belief is false and that consent was not actually given.
8. The two inquiries we have distinguished are clearly different. Of course, the more unreasonable the jury finds the mistake to be, the less likely it is to think that the defendant is telling the truth about whether he really made that mistake. As a result, rape defendants rarely offer mistake defenses. Defendants who can make a plausible claim of mistake can also make a plausible claim that the victim consented. See David Bryden: "Redefining Rape," 3 *Buffalo Criminal Law Review* 317, 414–415 (2000).
9. Moreover, the law assumes that judgments of reasonableness are gender-neutral. Commentators who propose to reform rape law have frequently attacked this assumption. For a discussion of the price that is paid by these attacks, see Donald Hubin and Karen Haely: "Rape and the Reasonable Man," 18 *Law and Philosophy* 113 (1999).
10. Presumably, the absence of a theory is what leads Stephen Schulhofer to remark that "a reasonableness standard gives no content to the requirement of consent and simply allows all the difficult, culturally contentious issues to be resolved case by case, behind closed doors, by police, prosecutors, and juries." See his *Unwanted Sex* (Cambridge: Harvard University Press, 1998), p. 63.
11. Douglas Husak and George C. Thomas III: "Date Rape, Social Convention, and Reasonable Mistakes," 11 *Law and Philosophy* 95 (1992).
12. Suppose that consent is wholly a mental state. If so, and that state of mind exists, then a rape has not taken place when sex occurs, even though the woman has not expressed her consent in behavior. Of course, the absence of an expression of consent would strongly indicate that a man's belief that consent had been given would not be reasonable. Still, he would not be criminally liable for rape despite his lack of reasonable belief about consent, since no rape had actually taken place. See Note 86 *infra*.
13. For a defense of this position, see Heidi Hurd: "The Moral Magic of Consent," 2 *Legal Theory* 121 (1996).
14. The following comment is typical of behaviorists: "Consent is an act rather than a state of mind. Consent is something I do rather than think or feel." David Archard: *Sexual Consent* (Boulder: Westview Press, 1998), p. 4.
15. It is possible, although unlikely, that the ontological nature of consent would differ depending on what it is to which consent is given.
16. Some commentators reject mentalistic accounts by assuming that if consent is a state of mind, it must be a state of mind of kind x. Then they proceed

to demonstrate that consent cannot be a state of mind of kind x, and believe that they have shown that consent cannot be a state of mind at all. Nathan Brett, for example, inquires into the nature of consent in medical contexts in defending a behavioristic account. He maintains that "no one believes that for a patient to consent to an operation it is only necessary that she have a certain attitude toward it." Brett's claim is true, but inconclusive in the present context. First, if consent is partly a state of mind, that state of mind surely is not a mere **attitude**. Moreover, a patient who has whatever state of mind consent is alleged to be certainly has not **given** consent to an operation. Admittedly, consent can be given only by behavior, but that does not entail that consent **is** behavior. See Nathan Brett: "Sexual Offenses and Consent," XI *Canadian Journal of Law and Jurisprudence* 69, 69 (1998).

17. Such locutions as "meeting of the minds" suggest that the same is true in contract law.
18. Alan Wertheimer defends a "performative view," according to which consent is "exclusively behavioral." He reaches this conclusion, however, by putting the ontological question aside. Instead, he asks what would permit someone (A) to have sexual relations with another (B). According to Wertheimer, "the important question is not whether consent *is*—ontologically speaking—a performative or a mental state. Rather, we begin by reminding ourselves that we are interested in consent because it renders it permissible for A to engage in sexual relations with B, and we ask 'what could do that?' From that perspective, a suitably qualified—that is, moralized—performative view is, I think, closest to the truth." See his "What Is Consent? And Is It Important?" 3 *Buffalo Criminal Law Review* 557, 568 (2000).
19. Contract theorists call this **quasi-contract**. Sometimes, people are entitled to act **as if** they have made contracts, even if they have not actually done so.
20. According to some commentators, "consent is two things: It is both a subjective decision and a social act." Emily Sherwin: "Infelicitous Sex," 2 *Legal Theory* 209, 216 (1996). It seems likely that juries often proceed in a way that informally combines both conceptions of consent. When faced with a real case, jurors probably use the behavior of the person who claims not to have consented as one way to gauge whether she is telling the truth about her mental state. Or, to the extent that jurors view consent as behavior, they probably use the victim's testimony about her mental state in gauging the truthfulness of her testimony about her behavior.
21. The empirical evidence we present is not as comprehensive as we would like. Sometimes the studies are two decades old, which makes them less useful in assessing behaviors that are likely to be evolving. Sometimes the studies occur in countries other than the United States, which makes them less useful in formulating generalizations about behaviors that are likely to be somewhat different from culture to culture. But the available evidence is sketchy, as Naomi McCormick noted in 1979: "[There is] very little empirical information about how people influence one another to have sexual intercourse or to avoid it." See Naomi B. McCormick, "Come-ons and Put-offs: Unmarried Students' Strategies for Having and Avoiding Sex," 4 *Psychology of Women Quarterly* 194, 194 (1979). What was true in 1979 is

largely true today. In our view, these difficulties point to the need for further research.

It is hard to know why so little research has been undertaken on this issue, but our personal experience might offer a clue. One of the present writers began in 1991 a long-term study of how "no" is understood in the dating context, and found the university committee on human research initially unreceptive to the project. One reviewer even questioned the utility of trying to determine what everyone already knows—that "no" means no. The project was finally approved, however, and the results are forthcoming in George C. Thomas III & David Edelman: "Consent to Have Sex: Empirical Evidence About 'No,'" 61 *University of Pittsburgh Law Review* 579 (2000).

22. Few theorists defend such a proposal. See, however, Peggy Reeves Sunday: *A Woman Scorned* (New York: Doubleday, 1996), p. 284. Among other difficulties, the suggestion that consent to sex must be expressed linguistically threatens to turn many **women** into rapists. Many contemporary rape statutes are gender-neutral. If men who consent to sex do not do so linguistically, the application of these gender-neutral statutes to women who engage in sex will have the absurd effect of making them guilty of rape.
23. The law has taken a similar approach in other contexts. Until recently, a person could sell an automobile without completing any paperwork. Eventually, the law came to require a transfer of a written title for a sale to be effective. This change frustrated the intentions of some buyers and sellers, but ultimately proved to be advantageous to both.
24. These generalizations might be described as **conventions**. Some commentators, however, believe that the means by which consent is expressed are too varied to give rise to any meaningful generalizations that can be described as conventions. See H. Malm: "The Ontological Status of Consent and Its Implications for the Law of Rape," 2 *Legal Theory* 147 (1996). But compare Archard: "[I]t would be absurd to deny that there are no sexual conventions." *Op.Cit.* Note 14, p. 31. On our view, the issue of whether these generalizations should be described as conventions is unimportant.
25. See, e.g., Sandra Byers: "Female Communication of Consent and Nonconsent to Sexual Intercourse," 5 *Journal of the New Brunswick Psychological Association* 12 (1980).
26. Mildred Brown & Alfred Auerback: "Communication Patterns in Initiation of Marital Sex," 15 *Medical Aspects of Human Sexuality* 107 (1981).
27. McCormick: *Op.Cit.* Note 21, p. 204.
28. *Id.* at 209.
29. E. Sandra Byers and Kim Lewis: "Dating Couples' Disagreements Over the Desired Level of Sexual Intimacy," 24 *Journal of Sex Research* 15, 22 (1988).
30. Doreen Rosenthal & Rachel Peart: "The Rules of the Game: Teenagers Communicating About Sex," 19 *Journal of Adolescence* 321 (1996).
31. *Id.* at 327, tbl. 4.
32. *Id.*
33. E. Sandra Byers: "Female Communication of Consent and Nonconsent to Sexual Intercourse," 5 *Journal of the New Brunswick Psychological Association* 12, 14, tbl. 1 (1980).

34. Byers and Lewis: *Op.Cit.* Note 29, p. 23, tbl. 1.
35. *Id.* at 15, tbl. 2.
36. The three indirect ways to refuse consent were to resist breast fondling (10%), to resist genital fondling (14%), and to be unresponsive and passive (10%).
37. *Id.* For a discussion of "incomplete rejection strategies," see Timothy Perper and David Weis, "Proceptive and Rejective Strategies of U.S. and Canadian Women," 23 *Journal of Sex Research* 455 (1987).
38. Byers and Lewis: *Op.Cit.* Note 29, p. 23, tbl. 3.
39. See, e.g., R. Lance Shotland & Barbara A. Hunter: "Women's 'Token Resistance' and Compliant Sexual Behaviors Are Related to Uncertain Sexual Intentions and Rape," 21 *Personality and Social Psychology* 226 (1995).
40. Susan Haworth-Hoeppner: "What's Gender Got To Do With It: Perceptions of Sexual Coercion in a University Community," 38 *Sex Roles* 757, 758 (1998).
41. *Id.* (citing Cindy Struckman-Johnson & David Struckman-Johnson: "College Men and Women's Reaction to Hypothetical Sexual Touch Varied by Initiator Gender and Coercion Level," 29 *Sex Roles* 371 (1993)).
42. See, e.g., Antonia Abbey: "Sex Differences in Attributions for Friendly Behavior: Do Males Misperceive Females' Friendliness?" 42 *Journal of Personality and Social Psychology* 830 (1982); Catherine B. Johnson, Margaret S. Stockdale & Frank E. Saal: "Persistence of Men's Misperception of Friendly Cues Across a Variety of Interpersonal Encounters," 15 *Psychology of Women Quarterly* 463 (1982).
43. See, e.g., Charlene L. Muehlenhard: "'Nice Women' Don't Say Yes and 'Real Men' Don't Say No: How Miscommunication and the Double Standard Can Cause Sexual Problems," 7 *Women and Therapy* 95 (1988).
44. Charlene L. Muehlenhard & Lisa C. Hollabaugh: "Do Women Sometimes Say No When They Mean Yes? The Prevalence and Correlates of Women's Token Resistance to Sex," 54 *Journal of Personality and Social Psychology* 872 (1988).
45. Charlene L. Muehlenhard & Marcia L. McCoy: "Double Standard/Double Bind: The Sexual Double Standard and Women's Communication about Sex," 15 *Psychology of Women* 447 (1991).
46. Susan Sprecher, Elaine Hatfield, Anthony Cortese, Elena Potapova, and Anna Levitskaya: "Token Resistance to Sexual Intercourse and Consent to Unwanted Sexual Intercourse: College Students' Dating Experiences in Three Countries," 31 *Journal of Sex Research* 125 (1994).
47. *Id.* at 127.
48. *Id.* (italics in original).
49. *Id.* at 129.
50. Charlene L. Muehlenhard & Stephen W. Cook: "Men's Self-Reports of Unwanted Sexual Activity," 24 *Journal of Sex Research* 58 (1988).
51. Shotland & Hunter: *Op.Cit.* Note 39.
52. See Lucia F. O'Sullivan & Elizabeth Rice Allgeier: "Feigning Sexual Desire: Consenting to Unwanted Sexual Activity in Heterosexual Dating Relationships," 35 *Journal of Sex Research* 234, 234 (1998) (describing but not endorsing this view).
53. *Id.*
54. Muehlenhard & Cook: *Op. Cit.* Note 50, at 69.

55. Shotland & Hunter: *Op. Cit.* Note 39.
56. O'Sullivan & Allgeier: *Op. Cit.* Note 52, p. 239.
57. Suppose that each adult engaged in one unwanted sex act every ten years—far fewer than the available studies indicate is likely. If so, more than one million acts of unwanted sex occur each month.
58. Perper & Weis, *Op. Cit.* Note 37.
59. Susan Haworth-Hoeppner: "What's Gender Got To Do With It: Perceptions of Sexual Coercion in a University Community," 38 *Sex Roles* 757 (1998).
60. *Id.* at 766, Table 1 (Situation 5).
61. *Id.* at 767 (Situation 15).
62. *Id.* at 774.
63. Judith S. Bridges: "Perceptions of Date and Stranger Rape: A Difference in Sex-Role Expectations and Rape-Supportive Beliefs," 24 *Sex Roles* 291 (1991); Mary E. Craig Shea: "The Effects of Selective Evaluation on the Perception of Female Cues in Sexually Coercive and Noncoercive Males," 22 *Archives of Sexual Behavior* 415 (1993).
64. O'Sullivan and Allgeier: *Op. Cit.* Note 52, at 242.
65. Some theorists warn against drawing inferences about reasonable mistakes involving sex from other examples on the ground that "rape is sui generis." Robin West: "Comment on Beyond Rape," 93 *Columbia Law Review* (1993), p. 1442, 1449. Such a view, however, fails to describe how allegations of reasonableness in sexual contexts *should* be assessed.
66. See *Supra* Part II.
67. We put to one side whether any of the various formulations of rape shield laws would preclude introduction of any of the evidence we describe here. The point of these laws is to protect the privacy of the victim, even when the evidence might be relevant to the issue of consent. See *State v. Colbath*, 540 A.2d 1212 (N.H. 1988) (holding that the defendant had a constitutional right to introduce evidence barred by the state's rape shield law).
68. *Regina v. Morgan*, [1976] A.C. 182 (House of Lords).
69. Two examples of this criticism should suffice. First, "Why aren't Husak and Thomas worried about all the women who are sexually violated when they said no?" Joan McGregor: "A Critical Reconstruction of Consent, Sex, and the Law," 2 *Legal Theory* 175, 205 (1996). Second, "The very idea that there is some way "women" behave (including verbal behavior) that licenses a man's belief about what some particular woman, in a particular setting, desires, degrades her. It treats her as an object (a variable) rather than as a person (a constant). A law that allows this as an excuse degrades all women." Keith Burgess-Jackson: *Rape: A Philosophical Investigation* (Dartmouth Pub. Co., 1996), p. 152.
70. McGregor: *Id.*, p. 205.
71. Some commentators are concerned that a few of the proposals that have been defended will undermine much of what is valuable about sexual relations, such as their spontaneity. Although some proposals may be vulnerable to this difficulty, we do not pursue this response here.
72. Schulhofer: *Op. Cit.* Note 10, p. 267.
73. In "Date Rape: A Feminist Analysis," 8 *Law and Philosophy* 217 (1989), Lois Pineau offers perhaps the only competitive theory about the conditions

under which mistakes about consent to sex are reasonable or unreasonable. Her argument involves two steps. The first is an empirical claim about the kind of sex that women like. Pineau alleges that "sexologists are unanimous ...in holding that mutual sexual enjoyment requires...communication, a minimum of pressure, and an ongoing checking up on one's partner's state." The second claim is not empirical. Pineau maintains that it is unreasonable for a man to believe that a woman would consent to a kind of sex she does not find to be enjoyable.

We are far less confident than Pineau that persons share a unanimous preference for the kind of sex she describes. Moreover, the phenomenon of unwanted sex indicates that consensual sex need not be enjoyable. Our main reservation, however, is with the means by which Pineau purports to reach her conclusion, viz., it is unreasonable for a man to believe that a woman would consent to noncommunicative sex. Belief in a false proposition is unreasonable only if a person should believe otherwise. Thus, Pineau must show that men **should** believe that a woman would not consent to noncommunicative sex. But why does the allegedly unanimous agreement that Pineau posits among sexologists entail that men should not have the beliefs that they in fact have? Does Pineau think that men should be under a duty to consult the writings of sexologists to correct their misapprehensions? That seems unlikely.

74. Someone might protest that the reasonableness of a belief about consent should not be assessed relative to empirical data at all, even if these conventions are "clear" and "easily manageable." After all, the determination that something is reasonable—a normative judgment—cannot be derived simply from a description of how persons actually behave. Our claim is not that all judgments of reasonableness should be assessed by empirical studies of how persons actually behave. Our claim is more narrow. We contend that the reasonableness of a belief about a mental state is to be assessed relative to descriptions of how persons who have that mental state typically behave.
75. Our theory, for example, would easily show the defendants to have behaved unreasonably in the celebrated case of *Regina v. Morgan*, *Op.Cit.* Note 68. The defendants in *Morgan* argued that they were not guilty of rape because the woman's husband had told them that she liked kinky sex and would enjoy being forced to have intercourse with them. Thus, they claimed, they proceeded on the mistaken view that her protests did not indicate nonconsent. But the belief that a screaming, protesting woman who has to be held down is giving consent would not be reasonable by the standards of the late twentieth century.
76. As Bryden puts it: "Granting that law can help to change folkways, but also that folkways can nullify law...." *Op.Cit.* Note 8, p. 409.
77. See, e.g., William J. Chambliss: "Types of Deviance and the Effectiveness of Legal Sanctions," *Wisconsin Law Review* (1967), p. 703.
78. Sherwin: *Op.Cit.* Note 20, p. 219.
79. McGregor: *Op.Cit.* Note 69, p. 205.
80. See Bryden: *Op.Cit.* Note 8, p. 409: "While many of us might criticize a man who fails to ask, or at least to wait for an affirmative signal, in the absence of at least verbal resistance by the woman few observers would say

that the man's conduct was so unusual and immoral that it warrants the extreme sanction of punishment."

81. Schulhofer: *Op.Cit.* Note 10, pp. 64–65 (italics in original).
82. *Id.*
83. *Id.* p. 264.
84. *Id.*, pp. 264–265.
85. *Id.*, p. 267.
86. This position, inter alia, would seem to violate the principle of legality. If nonconsent is an element of the crime of rape, and a woman consents to sex despite saying "no," the man who proceeds simply has not committed the offense of rape for which Schulhofer proposes to punish him.
87. Such information is most easily disseminated in a small, closely-knit community, such as a college campus. But there is no obvious mechanism for publicizing this information throughout all of society.
88. See some of the data presented in David Bryden and Sonja Lengnick: "Rape in the Criminal Justice System," 87 *Journal of Criminal Law & Criminology* 1194 (1997).
89. See, for example, Schulhofer: *Op.Cit* Note 10, Chapter Six.
90. For example, Dripps, in *Op.Cit.* Note 1, provides a narrow characterization of the concept of personal autonomy that is at stake in the area of sex. "By sexual autonomy," he writes, "I do not mean *positive* sexual autonomy—that is, the freedom to have sex with whomever one wishes." (p. 1785, emphasis in original). His reason for rejecting the positive account of autonomy is that "a right to sex would mean an obligation on another's part to participate." Instead, "What is meant by sexual autonomy is the freedom to refuse to have sex with any one for any reason." He continues (at p. 1786): "Sexual autonomy means freedom from illegitimate pressures to provide [sexual] service." But there is no good reason to suppose that sexual autonomy is involved only when persons **refuse** sex, or are unfairly pressured to engage in sex. Surely sexual autonomy should also encompass the freedom to **have** sex with any one for any reason. And why shouldn't sexual autonomy also encompass the freedom to **express** (or withhold) consent to sex in any manner the person chooses? Such freedoms or "rights" would be Hohfeldian liberties (or privileges), not claim-rights; thus they would not entail correlative obligations in other persons.

5

PHILOSOPHICAL ISSUES, 11
Social, Political, and Legal Philosophy, 2001

What We Can Reasonably Reject[1]

Thomas W. Pogge

I.

In his recent book, Tim Scanlon is "dealing with three concentric and successively narrower normative domains: reasons, values, and what we owe to each other" (13).[2] The third of these domains, the book's central subject, is understood as including only a subset of what is generally placed under the heading of 'morality'—namely that "narrower domain of morality having to do with our duties to other people" (6). I will refer to this domain as DDO (for 'domain of duties to others'). Scanlon asserts that "this part of morality comprises a distinct subject matter, unified by a single manner of reasoning and by a common motivational basis" (7). And he adds that these two unifiers of DDO—its *single* manner of reasoning and its *common* motivational basis—in turn share a deeper unity, which his contractualist account of DDO seeks to explicate (4, 10–11, 13, 189). Scanlon's contractualism thus tackles two distinct but related tasks: It tells us how to identify our duties within DDO; and it also characterizes and, as he says, explains what moves agents to attach importance to, and to honor, these moral duties.

Each of these two central achievements of Scanlon's contractualism can be condensed into a formula. With regard to the content of the moral demands arising within DDO, Scanlon offers what he calls a "general criterion of wrongness" (11), which he formulates as follows (4):

C *An act, A, is wrong [in the narrow sense of violating moral demands arising within DDO] if and only if any principle that permitted A could reasonably be rejected by people moved to find principles for the general regulation of behavior that others, similarly motivated, could not reasonably reject (or, equivalently, if and only if A would be disallowed by any principle that such people could not reasonably reject).*

For Scanlon, the task of explaining moral motivation is the task of understanding "the normative basis of...morality" (189)—of understanding, that is, the reasons people have for honoring their duties to others (147). Now if we took this to be an empirical task, we would have to conclude that the reasons people have for honoring duties to others are diverse: They may be moved by their religious faith, by some concern for the general happiness, by enlightened self-interest, by some contractualist aim, and/or by yet further reasons. Scanlon is interested in only one of these diverse normative bases of morality. He says that it "accurately describes moral motivation as many of us experience it" (158)—but then the same could be said of some others. What especially draws Scanlon's attention to the contractualist explanation of moral motivation is, first, that it is "phenomenologically accurate" with regard to himself[3] and, second, that it "seems to offer the right kind of response to Prichard's dilemma, by describing an ideal of relations with others which is clearly connected with the content of morality and, at the same time, has strong appeal when viewed apart from moral requirements" (155).[4]

Scanlon's contractualist account characterizes moral motivation as the ideal or aim of justifiability to others (157), as "the aim of finding principles that others, insofar as they too have this aim, could not reasonably reject" (191). We can restate this, somewhat more elaborately and in closer conformity with **C**, in the following second formula:

M *To have the contractualist moral motivation is to be moved by the aim of finding, and of being able to justify one's conduct by appeal to, principles for the general regulation of behavior that no one similarly motivated could reasonably reject.*

The two formulas, **C** and **M**, are related. They entail that a person who has the contractualist moral motivation (a CMM person, for short) is moved to avoid acts that are wrong in the sense of **C**.[5]

Scanlon's contractualist account of DDO has an air of triviality. This is due in part to his awkward suggestion that the domain of our duties to others is *defined* as the domain for which his proposed account works. Thus he writes of the values of friendship and sexual enjoyment that "these values go beyond what we owe to each other (as is shown by the fact that one cannot arrive at an understanding of them just by thinking about what principles others could not reasonably reject)" (176). But if the fact that something does not fit Scanlon's account suffices to show that it falls outside of DDO, then it becomes trivially true that everything within DDO fits his account. Moreover, by seeking a limited account for only one part of morality, Scanlon leaves out the important question how moral demands arising in different domains are to be balanced against one another. Though an act violates demands arising within DDO, its alternatives may be even more strongly disapproved by moral demands arising outside of DDO, and the act may then be morally right all things considered even though it is wrong according to **C**.[6] By not tackling this important question of balancing across domains of morality, Scanlon greatly limits the usefulness of his exercise.

The content of the proposed account may seem trivial as well: Why do we care to honor our duties to others? Because we care to avoid conduct we cannot justify to them. Scanlon's answer may seem to shed little light on the matter, especially when the idea of justifiability is then connected to the vague, moralized, and subjective notion of the reasonable.[7] But I will set this worry aside for now in order to examine the guidance that Scanlon's two formulas, as he interprets them, do give to agents in regard to how they should act and be motivated. This examination will show six distinct problems. The first four of these can be resolved through clarifications and refinements of Scanlon's account, I believe, while the last two seem more difficult.

II.

Let us begin with two problems specifically about Scanlon's first formula, **C**, which encapsulates his contractualist account of the content of our duties to others.

First problem: The word 'act,' left unanalyzed by Scanlon, poses various well-known problems of individuation and description. A given extended course of conduct may be describable as a single act or as a sequence of acts. And, even when the individuation of acts is held fixed, the same act description can be applied to very different physical events, and the same physical event can be brought under very different act descriptions. It would be tedious to rehearse here all of these issues, so let me just point to one difficulty as it arises within Scanlon's account. Suppose that Joe, exhausted and hungry after a hike, breaks into another's currently unoccupied country house, eats her food, and sleeps on her sofa. Are these acts wrong according to **C**? Joe might deny this by adducing a principle that permits such acts when the agent contacts the owner soon afterwards and gives her generous compensation that leaves her quite satisfied with the whole episode. If there is such a principle not reasonably rejectable from the standpoint of owners,[8] then, according to **C**, Joe's break-in is not wrong—even though Joe does not in fact compensate the owner. To be sure, **C** does allow us to classify as wrong Joe's more extended act of breaking-in-and-not-compensating-the owner; and **C** may also (assuming 'act' is to be understood as including omissions) allow us to classify as wrong the latter part of this extended act, Joe's subsequent failure to compensate. Still, it may be a disadvantage of **C** that it fails to support what seems the more natural view: Joe's break-in was wrong. The wrongness of this act could have been subsequently removed, but it was not. Preserving this more natural view would require significant further complications of Scanlon's formula.

Second problem: **C** sets a high threshold for wrongness. Scanlon believes that there are indefinitely many valid moral principles (201).[9] If A is permitted by just one single not-reasonably-rejectable principle, then A is not wrong. Now there are at least two ways of understanding what it means for an act to be *permitted* by a principle. Principles may permit in the weak sense, passively, merely by not disallowing A; and principles may, in addition, permit in the strong sense, actively, by expressly authorizing A. The clarification Scanlon adds in parentheses resolves this ambiguity in favor of the weak sense. Unfortunately, his clarification resolves the ambiguity in just the wrong way. If 'permitted' in **C** is understood in the weak sense, then there are, contrary to Scanlon's manifest intent, no wrong acts at all. This is so because, for any act, there will be at least one not-reasonably-rejectable principle that does not disallow this act. For example, most acts of telling malicious lies are not disallowed by the principle that forbids murder—and most acts of committing murder are not disallowed by the principle that forbids malicious lies.[10] To make sense of **C**, we must then resolve the ambiguity in favor of the strong sense of 'permitted': An act is wrong unless there is at least one not-reasonably-rejectable principle that expressly authorizes this act.[11] Correspondingly, we must either delete the bracketed paraphrase altogether, or else change the 'would be disallowed' in this paraphrase to 'would fail to be authorized.' Incorporating these revisions, we get:

> **C0** *An act, A, is wrong (in the narrow sense of violating moral demands arising within DDO) if and only if any principle that authorized A could reasonably be rejected by people moved to find principles for the general regulation of behavior that others, similarly motivated, could not reasonably reject (or, equivalently, if and only if A would fail to be authorized by any principle that such people could not reasonably reject).*

III.

Let me next raise two further, similarly straightforward questions about notions that occur in both **C** and **M**.

Third problem: Scanlon characterizes the contractualist moral motivation in terms of a certain class of people: A CMM person is one who is concerned that no one in this specific class of people should be able reasonably to reject the principles to which she appeals in justification of her conduct. So which class of people does Scanlon have in mind? The class of people who are "similarly motivated," that is, the class of CMM persons. So Scanlon's second formula is circular. Its flaw is analogous to, if somewhat less obvious than, that involved in defining a cooperator as someone disposed to be kind to other cooperators. This latter flaw can be brought out by imagining two persons who are unkind to each other, each coding herself as a cooperator and coding the other, in virtue of her unkindness to a cooperator, as a non-cooperator. The flaw in Scanlon's second formula can be displayed in a similar manner by imagining two persons, neither of whom cares about being exposed to reasonable rejections by the other because each sees herself as a CMM person and sees the other, in virtue of her lack of concern about being exposed to reasonable rejections by a

CMM person, as a non-CMM person. This flaw renders Scanlon's characterization of a CMM person indeterminate.

Fourth problem: Read literally, Scanlon's formulas are morally appalling. To avoid acting wrongly, and to be a CMM person, one must be concerned to avoid the possibility of reasonable rejection *by other CMM persons*. One need not be concerned to avoid reasonable rejectability by those whose compliance with their duties to others is motivated differently (e.g., in a religious or utilitarian manner)—no matter how strong grounds such others may have for rejecting the principle one invokes in justification of one's conduct. To take an extreme example: A CMM person might arrive at the principle, P, that Catholics may be killed whenever this can be done without collateral damage to CMM persons. To be sure, Catholics have very strong grounds for rejecting P. But then Catholics are not "similarly motivated," assuming that what motivates them is the aim to comply with the injunctions of God and the Church. There is nothing in the contractualist moral motivation that would incline a CMM agent to pay any heed to these Catholics and their grounds for rejecting P. On the contrary, the contractualist moral motivation *discourages* concern for Catholics insofar as such concern competes with concern for other CMM persons: A CMM person is motivated to render as weak as possible the grounds that *CMM persons* have for rejecting the principles she invokes in justification of her conduct.

These last two flaws in Scanlon's formulas can be repaired. The idea is to incorporate the thought Scanlon is after not by restricting the class of people whom a CMM person is concerned to render incapable of reasonable rejection (to those who are "similarly motivated"), but by restricting the class of possible rejections that a CMM person is sensitive to. Scanlon should characterize CMM persons as being concerned to avoid the possibility of reasonable rejection *by anyone* and then count a conceivable rejection as reasonable if and only if it is consistent with the aim of finding principles for the general regulation of behavior that no one could reasonably reject.

Now for Scanlon the rejection of a principle is consistent with that aim if this rejection is based on grounds that are stronger than the grounds on which some alternative to this principle could be rejected.[12] After the repair, Scanlon would hold, then, that any person can reasonably reject a principle if she can adduce grounds against this principle and there is some alternative principle that no one can reject except on weaker grounds. Or, equivalently, any person can reasonably reject a principle if she has a complaint against it and there is an alternative principle against which no one can lodge as strong or stronger a complaint (*cf.* 229). A particular person whose moral motivation is importantly different may not actually formulate, and may even actually reject, such a winning complaint available to her. Nonetheless, CMM persons should be conceived as acknowledging that the mere fact that *any* person *could* lodge such a winning complaint suffices to show that the principle against which it is lodged is reasonably rejectable.

This revision is, I believe, in line with some of what Scanlon says elsewhere[13] and, in any case, it is systematically necessary. (The revision also raises an interesting question, which I will come back to: Can the specifics of a person's moral motivation, her reasons for honoring her duties to others, affect the grounds on which she could reject a principle and the strength of these grounds?) Let us then update Scanlon's two formulas in accordance with the revision:

C1 *An act, A, is wrong (in the narrow sense of violating moral demands arising within DDO) if and only if any principle for the general regulation of behavior that authorized A could reasonably be rejected by someone (or, equivalently, if and only if A would fail to be authorized by any principle that no one could reasonably reject). The rejection of such a principle is reasonable if there is an alternative principle that no one could reject except on weaker grounds.*

M1 *To have the contractualist moral motivation is to be moved by the aim of finding, and of being able to justify one's conduct by appeal to, principles for the general regulation of behavior that no one could reasonably reject. The rejection of such a principle is reasonable if there is an alternative principle that no one could reject except on weaker grounds.*

IV.

As these reformulations bring out, Scanlon wants the reasonable rejectability of principles to turn on the strength of available grounds for rejecting them in comparison to the strength of the grounds available for rejecting their alternatives. This raises further questions, of which I will explore two that, I think, are new and especially interesting.

Fifth problem: A central function of morality is the peaceful settlement of conflicting claims. We should ask then how CMM persons are to cope with ties, that is, with situations in which the grounds available for rejecting various alternative principles are equally strong. I have posed this question to Scanlon (at a lecture he gave at Princeton University in January 1994) in terms of competitive survival situations involving shipwrecks, and he briefly discusses the issue by reference to such an example (195–97). How should persons act in such situations when the means of survival (life jackets, say) are scarce? A vast number of principles could be formulated for resolving such conflicts. Some principles might call for settlement by lot or combat, others might—instead or in addition—give greater or lesser weight to various other factors such as the persons' ages, their past sufferings, their past moral merits and non-moral accomplishments, the survival prospects each has with and without a vest, the expected moral merits and non-moral accomplishments of each if she survives, the number of friends and family members each has and the quality of her relations with these, and so on. Even if many of the conceivable principles in this multi-dimensional space may be reasonably rejectable by reference to alternatives that cannot be rejected except on weaker grounds, there will surely remain many principles that could not be eliminated in this way. We can thus easily imagine people reaching different conclusions about which of these mutually inconsistent least rejectable principles should be used to settle some particular conflict.

This plurality of mutually inconsistent least rejectable principles brings on a dilemma: On the one hand, one might say that, in such a case, each can reasonably reject the principle proposed by any other. Each can justify her rejection in this way: 'My rejecting the principle you propose on the ground I give would be unreasonable, if you could reject the alternative principle I propose on stronger grounds. However, you are not able to adduce stronger grounds against my principle than I can adduce against yours. Thus it is perfectly alright for me to reject your principle in favor of my own.' Here the word 'reject' is taken in the weak sense of 'disfavor,' with the result that *each* of the competing principles can reasonably be rejected by proposing an alternative against which no stronger grounds can be adduced. The upshot is that each person acts wrongly by acting on a principle that, because it is no less rejectable than some alternative, others can reasonably reject. This is the upshot, remarkably, even if all happen to favor the exact same principle because what matters, according to Scanlon's formulas, is whether a principle *could* reasonably be rejected, not whether a reasonable rejection is actually expressed.

On the other hand, one might say that, in such a case, no one can reasonably reject the principle proposed by another. Each can justify the non-rejectability of her principle as follows: 'You could reasonably reject my principle only if you could present an alternative principle such that the available grounds against my principle are stronger than the available grounds against your alternative. Since you are unable to offer such an alternative principle, you cannot reasonably reject the principle I propose.' Here the word 'reject' is taken in the strong sense of 'dismiss,' with the result that none of the competing principles can reasonably be rejected. The upshot is that, although the protagonists act on mutually inconsistent principles, none of them acts wrongly so long as each acts on one of the least rejectable principles.

To be clear: I am not here making the point that Scanlon's formulas are vague about the content of morality and moral motivation, thus giving us little guidance on how we ought to act. I am raising a different problem, brought on and intensified by such vagueness: Are the aims Scanlon stipulates for DDO—that we are to avoid wrong acts and are to become CMM persons—to be understood stringently, by reference to principles that no one can reasonably *disfavor*, or liberally, by reference to principles that no one can reasonably *dismiss*? Scanlon's response to this dilemma is somewhat obscure. As I understand it, he tries to avoid the issue by suggesting that there will be a way to break the apparent tie by coming up with some further, uniquely least rejectable principle.[14] This suggestion is very hard to believe and also in conflict with what Scanlon himself claims elsewhere in his book, as when he writes, for instance, that "there are many ways of...assigning responsibility to fathers, mothers, siblings, children, teachers, and professional caregivers that satisfy the 'negative' requirements...of morality in the narrow sense" (343) and introduces his Principle of Established Practices (to be discussed below) by appealing to cases where "there is a need for some principle to govern a particular kind of activity, but there are a number of principles that would do this in a way that no one could reasonably reject" (339). These statements favor reading 'reject' in the sense of 'dismiss'; and Scanlon has confirmed this reading in correspondence.

Scanlon's two formulas can then be further sharpened as follows:

C2 *An act, A, is wrong (in the narrow sense of violating moral demands arising within DDO) if and only if any principle* *for the general regulation of behavior that authorized A could reasonably be rejected by someone (or, equivalently, if and only if A would fail to be authorized by any principle that no one could reasonably reject). The rejection of such a principle is reasonable if and only if there is an alternative principle that no one could reject except on weaker grounds.*

M2 *To have the contractualist moral motivation is to be moved by the aim of finding, and of being able to justify one's conduct by appeal to, principles for the general regulation of behavior that no one could reasonably reject. The rejection of such a principle is reasonable if and only if there is an alternative principle that no one could reject except on weaker grounds.*

To understand better what these two formulas now mean, let us simplify them by collapsing the two equivalencies contained in each into one and by making use of my expression 'least rejectable principle' defined as a principle to which there exists no alternative such that the strongest grounds anyone could adduce against that principle are stronger than the strongest grounds anyone could adduce against this alternative. Thus, 'least rejectable' is the favored interpretation of 'not reasonably rejectable.'

C3 *An act, A, is wrong (in the narrow sense of violating moral demands arising within DDO) if and only if no least rejectable principle for the general regulation of behavior authorizes A.*[15]

M3 *To have the contractualist moral motivation is to be moved by the aim of finding, and of being able to justify one's conduct by appeal to, least rejectable principles for the general regulation of behavior.*

V.

I am tempted into a slight digression here, as these stripped-down formulations highlight an interesting and quite fundamental asymmetry that makes Scanlon's account yield many more negative than positive identifications. To identify an act as right, it suffices to find one least rejectable principle that authorizes this act. To identify an act as wrong, by contrast, one must run through the indefinite multitude of conceivable principles, showing of each that it either fails to authorize this act or else can reasonably be rejected. The judgment of an act as wrong will then generally have a tentative character, which detracts from the practical usefulness Scanlon's approach can have.[16]

One may think that this is not a problem because Scanlon is not interested in applicability. He seeks to help us understand what wrongness is, not to help us decide what acts are wrong. But I find this incredible: Scanlon calls **C** a criterion (from the Greek 'kriteîn' = to decide) rather than, say, a definition. He brings **C** to bear on many moral issues. And it is, in any case, unclear how we could be said to understand what wrongness is without being able to identify it.

If applicability is important, one might consider yet another reformulation:

> [**C4**] *An act, A, is wrong (in the narrow sense of violating moral demands arising within DDO) if and only if some least rejectable principle for the general regulation of behavior, P, forbids A and there exists no least rejectable alternative to P that authorizes A.*[17]

As a matter of logic alone, [**C4**] is neither stronger nor weaker than **C3**. It is formally possible for an act to be wrong under **C3** and yet not wrong under [**C4**]; this is the case for any act that is neither authorized nor forbidden by any least rejectable principle. It is likewise formally possible for an act to be wrong under [**C4**] and yet not wrong under **C3**; this is the case for any act, B, such that some least rejectable principle, Q, forbids B and there exists no least rejectable principle alternative to Q that authorizes B and there does exist some least rejectable principle that authorizes B.[18] One may doubt, certainly in the first of these two cases, whether there are conceivable acts that would illustrate these formal possibilities. Only if there actually turn out to be such acts would one need to examine which of the two criteria may be favored by their extensional discrepancy.

[**C4**] may mitigate the inconvenience of **C3** in two ways. First and most importantly, [**C4**] is meant to introduce a dialogical element into Scanlon's account. Consider a Principle of Preliminary Injunction (PPI) that, in the absence of special time pressures, forbids the performance of acts that are forbidden by some least rejectable principle unless one can point to a least rejectable alternative principle that authorizes the act. If PPI could be justified under [**C4**]—that is, could be shown to be least rejectable and to have no least rejectable alternative—PPI would create a preliminary injunction against any act that is forbidden by a least rejectable principle. This preliminary injunction can be removed only by pointing to a least rejectable alternative principle that authorizes the act. Performing the act while one is (still) unable to point to such a least rejectable alternative principle authorizing it is forbidden by PPI and hence wrong under [**C4**]. In this way, [**C4**] may enable us to identify many more acts as wrong (in the narrow sense of violating moral demands arising within DDO) in a non-tentative way.

[**C4**] mitigates the inconvenience associated with **C3** also by shrinking the set of conceivable principles relevant to establishing wrongness. Once a least rejectable principle forbidding the act has been presented, only principles alternative to it need be considered. If there is no least rejectable alternative principle authorizing the act, then this act is judged wrong (turning a preliminary into a definitive injunction).[19]

One may think that the advantage [**C4**] has in regard to judgments of wrongness is balanced by the advantage **C3** has in regard to judgments of rightness: To judge that an act is not wrong, [**C4**] requires one to run through the indefinite multitude of conceivable principles, showing of each that it either fails to forbid this act or else can reasonably be rejected. Have we merely then traded in one inconvenience for another? In response, let me appeal once more to the dialogical element. The intuitive idea of Scanlon's contractualism is that an act is wrong, if it is wrong, in virtue of the complaint someone could make against it. Scanlon conceives such complaints as taking the form of adducing grounds against principles. But, accepting [**C4**], we might envisage them as also taking the form of adducing principles against acts. An agent need not silence all imaginable doubts about the rightness of her contemplated conduct by running through all conceivable principles for the general regulation of behavior before proceeding to act. But she must address any real doubts she encounters in herself and in others. These doubts are to be expressed in the form of a principle forbidding her contemplated act and, once so expressed, can then be dispelled only by showing that this principle either can reasonably be rejected or has a least rejectable alternative that authorizes her act.

[**C4**] can then be understood as a kind of dialogical game with shifting burdens of proof: An agent is contemplating or initiating an act while being open to objections arising from within herself or from anyone else. Such objections are to be formulated in the form of a plausible principle for the general regulation of behavior that forbids the act in question. When such an objection has been formulated, the agent must forego her act or else show that the formulated principle either can reasonably be rejected or has a plausible alternative that authorizes the act. The formulation of such a plausible alternative principle puts the ball back into the court of the objector, who can sustain the initial objection by showing that the alternative principle can reasonably be rejected. Though the details remain to be worked out, the basic idea, I hope, is clear enough. This basic idea is worth exploring, because **[C4]** has the potential greatly to enhance the applicability of Scanlon's proposed criterion of wrongness, and also because the dialogical element introduced through my explication of **[C4]** is especially congenial to Scanlon's contractualism, which presents the aim of justifiability to others as central within DDO.

VI.

Once final wording of the two formulas is on hand, two major problems must still be solved in order to clarify their content. We must settle how to understand Scanlon's quest for "principles for the general regulation of behavior" and, correspondingly, how to conceive the various *standpoints* that may provide grounds for rejecting candidate principles. And, since it must be possible to identify *least rejectable* principles, we must also settle how to compare the strength of the grounds for rejecting alternative principles. I will discuss these two tasks in order.

Sixth problem: Scanlon holds that, when searching for grounds for rejecting a principle, we should not look at what complaints fully situated individuals could make by reference to their unique interests and circumstances. Instead, we should assess the comparative rejectability of principles by reference to more abstract, generic standpoints: "Acceptable principles could not require us, in deciding what to do, to consider how every actual individual would feel about it. And in deciding which systems of principles are 'acceptable,' we cannot envisage the reaction of every actual person. We can consider only representative cases" (171). A principle is not to be assessed then by reference to particular situations in which particular persons affected by its application may have particular grounds for rejecting it (or its application in this particular instance). Rather, Scanlon makes the assessment of any principle turn on the *generic* rejection grounds, or *generic* complaints, that can be adduced against it from various *standpoints*, which are abstractly described as occupied by persons in various *representative* roles and/or situations (202–206).

Scanlon's accounts of wrong conduct and of the contractualist moral motivation lead us then to the perspective of a moral legislator seeking principles for the general regulation of behavior. We are to assess any candidate principle by imagining the social world in which behavior in general is regulated by it. The sixth problem concerns the way in which these fictional social worlds are to be imagined.

Scanlon is clear that, as far as capacities are concerned, the proposed moral reasoning takes human beings as they are: "finer-grained principles will create more uncertainty and require those in other positions to gather more information in order to know what a principle gives to and requires of them. For example, the principle of fidelity to promises protects us against being bound in ways that we do not like by specifying that only voluntary undertakings are binding. But individuals differ in their ability to foresee possible difficulties and to resist subtle pressures to enter an agreement. The protection offered by the requirement of voluntariness is therefore of different value to different people" (205).

Before proceeding, let me flag one obvious difficulty. It is not clear why a particular person who finds herself in a particular conflict situation with particular others ought to be willing to settle the conflict by reference to a comprehensive legislative perspective. Suppose she is told that the principle she has proposed for settling the dispute is too fine-grained to be suitable as a principle for the general regulation of behavior. Being too complex, the principle would frequently be misapplied and thus can reasonably be rejected from some standpoint. Our protagonist might concede all this and still stick to her proposed principle: 'Yes, this principle would not reliably guide people in general. But why should this fact speak against our use of this principle here and now, given that the capacities of all persons involved in *this* situation clearly suffice for their conduct and judgment to be reliably guided by it?' Without an answer to this challenge, there is no support for Scanlon's demand that our conduct and motivation should be guided by the legislative quest for principles for the *general* regulation of behavior.

Let us return to the problem of specifying how, in Scanlonian moral reasoning, the fictional social worlds corresponding to candidate principles are to be imagined. Without a solution to this problem, we cannot gain a clear understanding of the generic standpoints and the associated generic rejection grounds to which such principles give rise. We can begin to appreciate the complexity hidden here by considering three straightforward questions that together, each posed in its simplest binary form, yield eight possible specifications of the proposed method of moral reasoning.

Question One is whether CMM agents are to look for *ideally best* or for *best feasible* principles for the general regulation of behavior. Are we to imagine the fictional social worlds as ones in which all fully comply with the candidate principles under consideration or as ones in which some fail to comply? The former, full-compliance stipulation would lead us into highly idealized thought experiments much like those Kant invites us to conduct in his *Groundwork*. Each Kantian agent is concerned that the maxims on which she acts should be universalizable. Universalization transforms maxims into principles and our actual social world into a fictional one in which these principles are universally observed. For Kant, the decisive question an agent is to ask about her maxim, or system of maxims, is whether she can will it together with the fictional social world constructed by reference to it. For Scanlon, on this full-compliance specification, CMM agents are to assess principles in an analogous way. We are to imagine social worlds in which a certain candidate principle is universally observed and we are then to look, in that hypothetical world, for standpoints affording generic grounds for rejecting this principle. Alternative principles are subjected to analogous thought experiments. And any candidate survives the test and is certified as least rejectable if and only if the generic grounds adducible against it (in the corresponding full-compliance world) are no stronger than those adducible against any of its alternatives (in the corresponding world in which this alternative principle is fully complied with).

Adopting the latter, partial-compliance stipulation, we might base our construction of fictional social worlds and of the relevant standpoints therein on realistic estimates—derived from our understanding of the actual nature and psychology of human beings—of how much compliance each principle would actually engender on some suitable assumption (such as, perhaps, the assumption that this principle is known by all to be widely affirmed as morally regulative).

To see what difference this first choice makes, consider a principle of mutual aid that requires affluent persons to contribute to the relief of acute distress by donating a fraction of their discretionary resources, which fraction is calculated in such a way that the aggregate of all required contributions suffices for the relief of all acute distress. Pursuant to the full-compliance stipulation, this candidate principle would relieve all acute distress and would thus generate no standpoint from which a complaint based on unrelieved acute distress could be lodged. Pursuant to the partial-compliance stipulation, by contrast, some people would fail to comply and none of the others would be required to step in to pick up the slack. Some persons would thus remain in acute distress and would have strong grounds for rejecting the candidate principle on this basis.[20]

My study of the text had led me to interpret Scanlon as favoring the full-compliance stipulation. I relied mainly on his lack of attention to problems of non-compliance[21] and on the brief instructions he gives us for applying his method.[22] But Scanlon has indicated, in correspondence, that he meant to stipulate partial compliance.[23]

Question Two is whether we are to imagine the fictional worlds as ones in which *all* or only *some* are CMM persons. Only on the latter stipulation must we deal with an important class of grounds that persons have—or at least think they have—for rejecting principles, namely grounds that derive from their non-contractualist moral motivation. Here is an example: Pursuant to Scanlon's contractualist account of DDO, "the idea that masturbation is morally forbidden is ridiculous" (175). In a world populated solely by CMM persons, the grounds for rejecting a principle that authorizes loud public conversations about masturbation may then be quite weak, and such a principle might thus qualify as least rejectable. Does this show that such conversations are not wrong in the actual world? Or are we to imagine the relevant fictional social world as also containing the standpoint of faithful Catholics, say, who regard masturbation as deeply wrong in a way that gives them much stronger grounds for rejecting the principle under examination? If Scanlon chooses the latter option, his moral reasoning might yield the conclusion that loud public conversations about masturbation—at least when Catholics might overhear them and take offense—are wrong (in the narrow sense of violating moral demands arising within DDO).

Another example: A least rejectable principle of mutual aid among CMM persons presumably adjusts the demands it makes to take account of any special obligations persons have. Other things equal, less such aid will be required from persons with dependent children, for instance. Now, in the actual world there are not only these special obligations persons really have, but also further special moral or religious obligations that non-CMM persons merely take themselves to have. Do such supposed obligations have no bearing on the duties of non-CMM persons? Is it wrong for such a person to be unresponsive to the needy on account of her supposed special obligation to build a monument to her god? The answers to these questions are affirmative if the fictional social worlds of Scanlonian moral reasoning are populated exclusively by CMM persons. The answers may well be negative otherwise, at least in certain cases. Scanlon does not address such issues, and so I will not speculate how he would answer Question Two.

Question Three is whether we are to compare alternative *sets* of principles (each regulating all the various aspects of human behavior) or alternative *individual* principles (regulating only one such aspect). Again, a simple example may illustrate the point. Consider a principle, Z, that authorizes men to strike up conversations with married women. In certain cultures, this principle would be rejected by the women's husbands whom such conversations would expose to nasty gossip. Does the loss such conversations impose on these husbands furnish a ground for rejecting Z? The answer is negative, if Scanlon's method of moral reasoning examines alternative *sets* of principles—assuming there is no least rejectable set of principles that authorizes people to spread nasty gossip about men whose wives have conversations with other men. The answer is affirmative, if Scanlon's method examines alternative principles while holding fixed the rest of morality in accordance with the going beliefs and practices.

Scanlon writes that "a sensible contractualism, like most other plausible views, will involve a holism about moral justification: in assessing one principle, we must hold many others fixed. This does not mean that these other principles are beyond question, but just that they are not being questioned at the moment" (214). It is not clear from this passage whether those other principles are to be held fixed in accordance with the moral reasoner's best estimate of what principles are part of a least rejectable set or in accordance with prevailing belief and practice in the relevant social environment. Thus Scanlon seems to leave Question Three, too, unresolved.[24]

There is much more to be said about these three questions. It seems important to explore mixed answers along the following lines: Our assessment of principles should take existing dispositions toward non-compliance into account, but we should also strive to improve these dispositions. We should take non-contractualist moral motivations into account, but should also strive to win people over to contractualism. We should take into account how a candidate principle fits into an ideal set of principles and also how it fits with existing belief and practice. Such mixed answers would make Scanlon's account of right and wrong and of moral motivation within DDO much more complex than it is already, and I cannot develop, let alone defend, such complications here. I mention these mixed answers only to underscore how enormously large and difficult a gap Scanlon leaves by not properly explaining how we are to conceive the standpoints from which generic complaints against candidate principles are to be made. Needed here are not merely answers to my three questions, but also reasons for such answers as well as much work toward developing the favored specification to the point where it can give us a clear sense of how we are to conceive the relevant standpoints we need for comparing the strength of various generic rejection grounds across fictional social worlds.

Let me close this section by suggesting that *all* specifications of Scanlonian moral reasoning may in the end prove unsatisfactory on account of the abstract standpoints they involve. This is so, first, because the requisite thought experiments are very difficult to conduct. A world in which people do not steal would be different from ours in many ways, and it is difficult enough to work out what relevant standpoints and generic rejection grounds would exist in it. These difficulties increase exponentially when, in the spirit of Kant's realm-of-ends formula, we believe that persons ought to act in accordance with some least rejectable *set* of principles for the general regulation of behavior and thus try to compare full sets of principles with one another. The fictional worlds corresponding to such candidate sets of principles would differ dramatically from our world, and it might then prove impossible to work out what burdens people in such worlds would face—let alone to compare across such fictional worlds the strength of rejection grounds that appeal to such burdens. These difficulties are most severe, of course, if we give the first (or a mixed) answer to each of the three questions. They are least severe, but still daunting, if we give the second answer in each case.

Another reason to be skeptical about abstracting moral reasoning of the sort Scanlon envisages is that there may be a more plausible, non-abstracting contractualist method. This *political* interpretation of contractualism would focus not on *hypothetical* standpoints affording *generic* rejection grounds in *fictional* social worlds, but on the *actual* standpoints and rejection grounds of *real* people in the world *here and now.* This interpretation directs us then not toward a theoretical task of figuring out what principles would be best, but toward an eminently practical, political task of establishing the *best reachable* principles in the world as it is through actual agreement with the people around us. Agents motivated toward this aim would be sensitive to the values and interests of other agents. They would tailor their arguments to those concrete others and would be willing to compromise in order to establish principles that are as good as the current attitudes of their contemporaries will allow.

To illustrate. Suppose I believe that abortion is morally wrong in Scanlon's sense: I believe that any principle authorizing abortion can reasonably be rejected from the standpoint of human beings whose killing this principle would authorize.[25] In the country where I live, abortion is now legal. So I am wondering whether I am morally required to give any time and money I can spare to the campaign to outlaw abortion. As I see it, this requirement can most plausibly be opposed by the alternative requirement to give any time and money I can spare to the campaign to eradicate world hunger. How do I decide between these two putative requirements? Scanlon's contractualism would lead me to make my decision by conceiving the two requirements as alternative principles for the general regulation of behavior. I am to imagine one social world in which behavior in general is regulated by the principle, X, that priority must be given to outlawing abortion and another social world in which behavior in general is regulated by the principle, Y, that priority must be given to eradicating world hunger. I am then to compare the grounds that could be given against X from the standpoint of people starving in the social world regulated by X with the grounds that could be given against Y from the standpoint of human beings suffering abortion in the social world regulated by Y. The principle against which stronger grounds can be given is disqualified as reasonably rejectable.

We have seen that Scanlon leaves quite unclear how we are to imagine these fictional social worlds and, in particular, how we are to conceive the group of those who, in each such world, would conform their behavior to the principle under examination. The political interpretation, in any case, differs from Scanlon by not imagining any fictional social worlds at all. This interpretation directs me to examine *not* what would happen if X or Y were used for the general regulation of behavior, but rather what would happen if I were to act in accordance with X or with Y. In this way, the political interpretation focuses attention on an important difference between the two competing principles: Achieving a broad agreement and mobilization toward eradicating world hunger is much more realistic than achieving a broad agreement and mobilization toward outlawing abortion. This seems to be an important reason for me to adopt X rather than Y. But Scanlonian moral reasoning is blind to this reason, because it focuses on the hypothetical consequences of the *general* adoption of a principle. It thus neglects the actual consequences of its adoption by the reasoning agent and, in particular, the task of *getting* a principle to be generally adopted.

The political interpretation seems to me to be a formidable competitor which deserves consideration and refinement. To be sure, it may be of relevance to inquire what principles human beings would honor in the best social world we can imagine. But this cannot be the only task of moral reasoning in an actual world in which the urgent needs of so many persons remain unfulfilled. In this actual world, agents motivated according to the political interpretation would be much more effective than CMM agents in promoting moral progress for the benefit of those actual people who have the strongest grounds for rejecting the practices currently imposed upon them. Thus we should hesitate to classify their conduct as wrong for the mere reason that it fails to be authorized by any principle for the general regulation of behavior that would be best under hypothetical conditions.

Scanlon suggests a way of blunting this criticism with his Principle of Established Practices (PEP), which he formulates as follows: "In situations of this kind [where there is a need for some principle to govern a particular kind of activity, but there are a number of principles that would do this in a way that no one could reasonably reject], if one of these (non-rejectable) principles is generally (it need not be unanimously) accepted in a given community, then it is wrong to violate it simply because this suits one's convenience" (339). Yet, PEP only *appears* to allow Scanlon to incorporate into his account an important advantage of the political interpretation he rejects: sensitivity to actual political realities.

There are two independent limitations. First, PEP merely asserts—plausibly enough—the reasonable rejectability of a principle that authorizes persons to violate widely accepted least rejectable principles *whenever doing so suits their convenience*. But there are indefinitely many other principles authorizing the violation of widely accepted least rejectable principles. According to Scanlon's own account of wrongness, he would need to show that all of these other principles, too, are reasonably rejectable. What makes conduct wrong is not that some least rejectable principle forbids it, but that no least rejectable principle authorizes it. It is unclear how Scanlon could possibly show this.[26] But, for the sake of the argument, let us grant that he can show the much stronger PEP*: 'It is wrong to violate widely accepted least rejectable principles.'

The second limitation shows that even PEP* is of little help. PEP* is a principle for breaking ties, in favor of the status quo, among competing *least-rejectable* principles. It requires CMM persons to comply with socially established practices if and only if they are principles no one can reasonably reject.[27] Yet most socially established practices the world has seen thus far are *not* least-rejectable. The requirement of PEP*, while plausible, is then also largely irrelevant. Sensitivity to actual political realities is still missing with regard to that vast majority of socially established practices that are reasonably rejectable and ought to be reformed. Here we need to know what means and methods CMM persons may employ in pressing for the reform of reasonably rejectable socially established practices. We also need to know under what conditions, if any, a CMM person may act wrongly by the lights of the ideally best principles when others' noncompliance with these principles would render compliance very costly: Can others reasonably reject my acts of dishonesty toward them even if dishonesty is my only way of protecting myself against the pervasive dishonesty of others? Or can I reasonably reject the demand of honesty in such circumstance by appeal to a 'sucker exemption'? With regard to such questions, PEP* contributes very little to the guidance we can get from Scanlon's criterion of wrongness on any of its specifications.

VII.

The preceding section has shown that Scanlon does not tell us nearly enough about how to conceive the standpoints on the basis of which judgments about the rejectability of "principles for the general regulation of behavior" are to be made. This problem introduces considerable unclarity (and perhaps implausibility) into his account of the wrongness of acts and of the desirable moral motivation. I will show in conclusion how this unclarity is compounded by another, more obvious source of indeterminacy, which has been remarked upon by several readers: Scanlon's contractualism tells us very little about how to compare the strength of the grounds for rejecting alternative principles for the general regulation of behavior. If we do not know how to make such comparisons, then we cannot identify least rejectable principles. And if we cannot identify least rejectable principles, then we cannot identify either right or wrong acts or the desired moral motivation.

The magnitude of the gap becomes apparent by considering that substantive moral theories Scanlon clearly rejects—utilitarianism and David Gauthier's contractarianism,[28] for example—can easily endorse Scanlon's formulas while inserting their own instructions for how to compare the strength of grounds for rejecting principles for the general regulation of behavior. Thus when Scanlon, in regard to various moral issues he discusses, reaches substantive moral views that diverge from utilitarianism and from Gauthier's contractarianism, he must do so by invoking additional general moral commitments that—though he repeatedly assures the reader that they are not *ad hoc*—have no discernible basis in his formulas.

The foremost of these additional general commitments is Scanlon's stipulation that "a central feature of contractualism [is] that the justifiability of a moral principle depends only on various *individuals'* reasons for objecting to that principle and alternatives to it" (229). This commitment limits moral reasoning to the *personal* rejection grounds that can be presented from the various relevant standpoints. And this commitment also rules out the kind of aggregation characteristic of utilitarian theorizing, which may require the imposition of greater losses on a few for the sake of smaller gains for many. In first approximation we can then say that Scanlon allows the contest between alternative principles to be settled by the individual(s) on whom this choice has the *greatest relative impact.*

But this idea is clearly inadequate. Consider two alternative principles that would result in pay-offs 9-4-0 and 0-9-4, respectively, among three relevant parties. A relative impact criterion would prefer the first principle, because the loss for the first party from the choice of the second principle exceeds the loss for either of the other parties from the choice of the first principle. But this preference is a violation of anonymity[29] and problematic also in light of the fact that it may be possible to formulate a third principle with pay-offs 4-0-9 which, by the same token, would have to be ranked above the first and below the second principle, resulting in a circular ordering.[30]

Scanlon helps himself with the stipulation that aggregation is ruled out only when it would allow the imposition of greater losses on a few for the sake of *much* smaller gains for many: "within contractualism, the number of persons affected does not become relevant until the harm the members of the larger group suffer reaches the same degree of moral seriousness as that suffered by those in the smaller group" (239). It is questionable whether this second stipulation is compatible with the first.[31] And it cannot, in any case, solve the problem, because harms may be commensurable even if they differ in degree of seriousness.[32]

Appeals to relative impact face further difficult questions: How is relative impact to be measured for purposes of comparison—are we to use an interpersonally invariant metric or are we to take account of the diverse needs, interests, preferences, religious values, and/or moral motivations of different persons?[33] What weight, if any, is one to give to how badly off the losers from the choice of some particular principle would be?[34] Scanlon bravely discusses some of these questions, and others. In doing so, he introduces yet further general moral commitments.[35] Yet, in the end, he leaves the exercise open-ended: "On the version [of contractualism] I am defending...we must sometimes exercise judgment as to whether certain considerations are or are not relevant to the reasonable rejectability of a principle, since these grounds are not completely specified in advance" (218, *cf.* 157–8, 206). For all the guidance Scanlon provides, it may be more accurate to say that we must *always* exercise judgment. At minimum, any decision about whether some principle is or is not least rejectable involves the judgment that there are no further, heretofore unspecified grounds that could affect the decision made.

As I mentioned at the outset, Scanlon stresses the unifying power of his account. Thus he writes that his "contractualism...can account for the significance of different moral notions within a single moral framework, without reducing all of them to a single idea" (216), that it reveals how our duties to others are "unified by a single manner of reasoning and by a common motivational basis" (7) and how "the idea of justifiability to others can be seen to play an important role in shaping our thinking about right and wrong" (170). In innumerable passages, exemplified in the four preceding paragraphs, Scanlon presents the additional general moral commitments he invokes when addressing specific moral issues as integral parts of his contractualism. Such constant references to contractualism may create the impression, but cannot support the conclusion, that Scanlon's moral views are shaped and unified by the idea of justifiability to others. I must say that I fail to see either the shaping power of the idea or the unity of what Scanlon has to say about our duties to others. As far as I can see, the two formulas can easily be used to reach the opposite of moral conclusions Scanlon endorses by adding different general moral commitments instead—for instance, the consequentialist commitment that the number of affected persons always counts.[36] And, as far as I can see, the only common element in Scanlon's moral views is their uncanny coincidence with the moral views prevalent in his time and culture. Such a defense of moral commonplaces would be fine, an advantage even, if it were genuinely based on (derived from) the contractualist idea of justifiability to others as sharpened in the two formulas. But, since this is not the case, the lesson from these exercises is that a commitment to Scanlon's contractualism is cost-free: You can endorse the two formulas and still hold pretty much any moral views you like.[37]

It may be fortunate, in a sense, that the additional general moral commitments Scanlon liberally introduces are extraneous to his contractualism, because their flaws cannot then taint the two formulas. But what then is the point or purpose of these formulas? If moral judgments in the end turn on weighing the morally significant reasons for and against particular ways of acting, then all the complexities introduced by the formulas may merely translate the old moral disagreements into a new jargon. I am in some sympathy here with those who have criticized Scanlon's contractualist apparatus as an unnecessary shuffle that does not really provide any guidance for our conduct or motivation. Still, this challenge has been posed effectively by others,[38] and I see no point in belaboring it further.

VIII.

"I can only describe my feeling by the metaphor, that, if a man could write a book on Ethics which really was a book on Ethics, this book would, with an explosion, destroy all the other books in the world."[39] Wittgenstein had a sense how very hard it is to write on ethics. Scanlon's book is not the book Wittgenstein was hoping for. But it is an ambitious, serious, and impressive work—perhaps the most important book in moral philosophy since Parfit's *Reasons and Persons*. I have not here dwelled on the strengths of Scanlon's book. I have not discussed its stronger first part at all, and I have stated rather strongly several criticisms of Scanlon's account of wrongness and moral motivation in terms of what principles for the general regulation of behavior one can reasonably reject. I hope that these criticisms are constructive and that my respect for Scanlon's work will be gauged by the effort I have made rather than by the sharpness of my criticisms. In the end, one must wonder of course whether Scanlon's contractualist account can itself be reasonably rejected. I do not feel confident to answer this question, but the answer does seem to me to turn on a thorough examination of the criticisms here presented.

NOTES

1. Work on this essay originated in a graduate seminar in the spring of 1998, for which Tim Scanlon had generously made available a typescript of his then forthcoming book. I am indebted to the discussions in that course as well as for the constructive criticisms I have received from lively audiences at the Di Tella Law School (Buenos Aires) and the University of Chicago, from Rüdiger Bittner, Andreas Føllesdal, Alexander George, Sidney Morgenbesser, Gerhard Øverland, and especially from Tim Scanlon and Leif Wenar. I am grateful also for a grant from the Research and Writing Initiative of the Program on Global Security and Sustainability of the John D. and Catherine T. MacArthur Foundation, which supported the final composition.
2. Parenthetical numbers refer to pages in Scanlon, T. M. (1998) *What We Owe to Each Other*, Cambridge MA, Harvard University Press.
3. "When I reflect on the reason that the wrongness of an action seems to supply not to do it, the best description of this reason I can come up with has to do with the relation to others that such an act would put me in: the sense that others could reasonably object to what I do" (155, *cf.* 163, 187, 352).
4. Prichard's dilemma concerns the question why one should give moral considerations a substantial role in guiding one's conduct. Offering a moral reason in response would beg the question, while non-moral reasons (referring to the advantages of being on good terms with others, for instance) would fail to explain the categorical nature of moral demands. *Cf.* 149–150.
5. Scanlon holds that the contractualist moral motivation he describes "provides a plausible interpretation of reasons for avoiding [wrong] actions and criticizing those who perform them" (13). The latter reasons for criticizing others are not strictly entailed by the contractualist moral motivation.
6. *Cf.* 220–23. Conversely, an act may be disapproved by moral demands arising outside of DDO, and therefore be morally wrong all things considered even though it is right according to **C**. Throughout, I am using the word 'right' in the sense of 'not wrong.'
7. This worry is eloquently and disarmingly articulated by Scanlon himself: "By basing itself on reasonableness, it may be charged, a theory builds in moral elements at the start. This makes it easy to produce a theory which *sounds* plausible, but such a theory will tell us very little, because everything we are to get out of it at the end we must put in at the beginning as part of the moral content of reasonableness" (194).
8. In correspondence, Scanlon has denied that there is such a principle that property owners could not reasonably reject. But it should be possible to find some principle that would exemplify my point and would be acceptable to Scanlon.

9. It is not clear what exactly he means by a *valid* moral principle, but we can safely assume that a principle is valid only if it could not reasonably be rejected by anyone moved to find principles for the general regulation of behavior that others, similarly motivated, could not reasonably reject. For Scanlon's explication of the word 'principle,' see 199–200.
10. One might think that Scanlon must be taking principles to be complete in the sense of assigning every possible act its unique deontic status (e.g., mandatory, forbidden, or discretionary). But this reading conflicts with how Scanlon formulates the various sample principles he discusses. Thus consider the Principles M, D, L, F, which Scanlon defends in Chapter 7. Each of them plainly fails to disallow many acts that he considers to be wrong.
11. On this interpretation, there may need to be lots and lots of not-reasonably-rejectable principles to authorize all the many trivial things we do. I don't find this problematic. People need not actually formulate a principle for every act. They should merely have a well-founded confidence that they could formulate an appropriate principle and should also be prepared perhaps to offer such a principle when a (proposed) act of theirs is challenged.
12. Scanlon's use, in this context, of the word 'alternative' papers over great complexities arising from the fact that two principles may not be either coincident or disjoint in scope (the set of acts to which they apply). Nonetheless, I will here follow Scanlon in pretending that it is clear with regard to any given principle which other principles are, and which are not, alternatives to it.
13. There is a paraphrase of **C** that lacks the offensive restriction of the class of people whom a CMM person is concerned to render incapable of reasonable rejection (153). See also Scanlon's discussion of reasonable balancing (195). In fact, it is not clear that he ever intended the literal reading of his formula. The target of my critique, in any case, is not the author but the philosophical position advanced in the text. My objective is to facilitate the appraisal of this position by stating it clearly in its most plausible form.
14. Remarkably, he offers *two* proposals in this direction, namely a principle requiring the actors to take turns with the life jacket and a principle requiring them to draw lots (196).
15. A is wrong, that is, if and only if, for any principle V that authorizes A, there exists an alternative principle W that does not authorize A and is such that the strongest ground anyone can adduce against W is weaker than the strongest ground anyone can adduce against V.
16. This problem occurs within DDO. It is thus distinct from the problem of taking account of moral considerations arising outside DDO in order to arrive at an all-things-considered moral assessment (*cf.* note 6 above and accompanying text).
17. I have used brackets in '**[C4]**' as a reminder that this formula is put forward not as a plausible interpretation (clarification or specification) of Scanlon's own criterion of wrongness, but as a competing modification of it. If this modification were accepted, the contractualist moral motivation might also have to be reformulated slightly.

18. Evidently, this last principle could not be Q (which forbids B), nor any of Q's alternatives (which, if least rejectable, do not authorize B).
19. I leave aside here that Scanlon gives no satisfactory account of what is to count as an *alternative* principle (see note 12 above). Such an account is needed quite apart from the reformulation here under examination.
20. It does not follow that the partial-compliance stipulation favors a more demanding principle of mutual aid. On the assumption that those whose acute distress remains unrelieved have the strongest rejection grounds here in play, the partial-compliance stipulation would favor whatever candidate principle of mutual aid would actually minimize unrelieved distress. Here a less demanding principle engendering greater compliance may be better (produce a higher yield) than a more demanding principle that would be widely disregarded. These matters are interestingly discussed in Murphy, Liam (2000) *Moral Demands in Nonideal Theory*, Oxford, Oxford University Press.
21. Scanlon never considers any complaint that, like the one just considered, depends on the expectable incidence of non-compliance.
22. Among the instructions I have in mind are the following: "when we are considering the acceptability or rejectability of a principle, we must take into account...the consequences of general performance or nonperformance of such actions and of the other implications (for both agents and others) of having agents be licensed and directed to think in the way that principle requires" (203). "At least in most cases, all we need to take into account in deciding whether a principle could reasonably be rejected are such things as the following: (a) the importance of being able to get aid *should one need it*; (b) the degree of inconvenience involved in giving it, *should one be called upon to do so*; (c) the generic cost of having a standing policy of giving aid in the way this principle requires; and (d) the generic benefits of having others have this policy" (207). Discussing cooperative schemes such as observing restrictions during a drought (212), Scanlon writes: "If, for example, compliance by only 80 percent of the participants is enough to keep a scheme going, then the rule might be that each person should roll a die before deciding whether to contribute, and would be excused if the die came up 'six'" (213). Under anything like realistic compliance assumptions, this roll-your-own-die rule would *obviously* fail to generate the requisite 80 percent contribution rate. The fiction involved in Scanlon's proposed method thus seems to be ideal-theoretic by presupposing universal full compliance—even if it is not, as we have seen, ideal-theoretic in regard to human capacities.
23. He refers to an earlier passage: "According to contractualism, moral argument concerns the possibility of agreement among persons who are all moved by this desire, and moved by it to the same degree. But this counter-factual assumption characterises only the agreement with which morality is concerned, not the world to which moral principles are to apply. Those who are concerned with morality look for principles for application to their imperfect world which they could not reasonably reject, and which others in this world, who are not now moved by the desire for agreement, could not reasonably reject should they come to be so moved." Scanlon, T. M. (1982) "Contrac-

tualism and Utilitarianism" in Amartya Sen and Bernard Williams, eds.: *Utilitarianism and Beyond*, Cambridge, Cambridge University Press, 111.

24. Scanlon's endorsement of Principles D and L (300–01) suggests that he understands his method as seeking least rejectable *sets* of principles. In many actual social environments, including the competitive world of business in the US, it would not seem to be wrong to mislead others. In any case, it is surely not impermissible (*pace* D) to lead a determined and well-armed cannibal to form false expectations about where one is headed, nor mandatory (*pace* L) to compensate her for the nice meal she lost on account of the reasonable but false expectation one had intentionally led her to form about one's whereabouts.
25. I do not know if Scanlon's contractualism includes unborn human beings and/or infants among those who can have grounds for rejecting principles. I do not know whether it settles this issue at all and, if so, on what basis. For purposes of the present example, I simply take for granted that counting infants and unborn human beings is at least compatible with contractualism. It is a disadvantage of my example that it depends on this assumption. But the example has two offsetting advantages. It highlights the vagueness of the word "others" in the expression "domain of our duties to others." And it can draw on the independent exploration of this issue in Pogge, Thomas (1999) "Dworkin, the Abortion Battle, and World Hunger" in Veronique Zanetti and Steffen Wesche, eds.: *Ronald Dworkin*, Brussels, Ousia.
26. The substitution of **[C4]**—especially when complemented by PPI—for Scanlon's own criterion of wrongness would go a long way toward overcoming this first limitation of the PEP strategy.
27. With respect to socially established practices that are *not* least-rejectable, Scanlon's criterion of wrongness permits complying acts that are also authorized by some least rejectable principle; and it forbids complying acts that are authorized by no least rejectable principle.
28. *Cf.* Gauthier, David (1986) *Morals By Agreement*, Oxford, Oxford University Press. In this conception, each party's relative bargaining position (threat advantage) is a crucial factor in the formulation and rejection of principles. It has become customary to call such accounts 'contractarian' in contrast to the more strongly moralized 'contractualist' accounts offered by Scanlon or Rawls.
29. The two outcomes differ merely in allocation, and a relative impact criterion may here be colliding with another general moral commitment Scanlon invokes, namely that principles can reasonably be rejected when they are arbitrary or unfair (212).
30. Another problem with a relative-impact criterion is that it can lead to Pareto inefficiency: Many innocent persons have been convicted to 5-year prison terms. You can either spare each of these innocents one year in jail or a specific one of them her entire 5 years. The relative impact criterion directs you toward the latter option. If you and four similarly situated others follow this direction, five innocents go free. If the five of you had 'let the numbers count,' *all* innocents would have been spared.

31. *Cf.* Otsuka, Michael (2000) "Scanlon and the Claims of the Many versus the One," *Analysis* 60, 288–93.
32. Suppose with respect to some particular harm that a ninefold increase counts as affecting the degree of seriousness. We can then reformulate the previous example as follows: Consider two alternative principles that would result in pay-offs 9-8-7-6-5-4-3-2-1-0 and 0-9-8-7-6-5-4-3-2-1, respectively, among ten relevant parties. Etc. The example of note 30, too, can easily be adjusted.
33. Some discussion of this question is provided in Scanlon, T. M. (1993) "Value, Desire, and Quality of Life" in Martha C. Nussbaum and Amartya Sen, eds.: *The Quality of Life*, Oxford, Clarendon Press. It is unclear to what extent the positions Scanlon takes in this and other, even earlier essays are meant to be incorporated into our reading of his book.
34. *Cf.* 223–9. It may be that, though men would lose more if principle S were chosen instead of T than women would lose if T were chosen instead of S, women would be worse off under T than men would be under S. How is one to decide in such cases whether or not the first fact counts more strongly in favor of T than the second counts in favor of S?
35. Thus he posits that "in order for differences in level to affect the relative strength of people's moral claims to help, these differences have to be in an aspect of welfare that the help in question will contribute to" (227). To illustrate the meaning of this latter general moral commitment, suppose that you can spare Amy a great pain or instead can spare Judy a slightly smaller pain. In making this choice, it is appropriate for you to take into account that, no matter how you decide, Judy faces more pain overall than Amy does; but it is not appropriate for you to take into account that Judy is worse off than Amy in other ways, *e.g.*, less affluent, pretty, popular, or intelligent. As with the other general moral commitments Scanlon introduces, my question is how he can say that this commitment is 'shaped' by his contractualism. How would you go against contractualism if you took account of Judy's poverty as a reason to spare her the slightly smaller pain?
36. Or the maximin commitment to take account of *all* the ways in which Judy is worse off than Amy (*cf.* note 35).
37. Scanlon could have made clear that this is not the lesson to be drawn by giving just one moral issue on which his contractualism does not endorse the view widely held among his readers. Thus he might have explored, for instance, perhaps in connection with his Rescue Principle (224–8), how his contractualist moral reasoning might address our relation to the 800 million human beings who do not have enough to eat. One might have thought that the aim of justifiability to others might well lead to a dramatic departure from ordinary moral thinking on this issue. In a late draft for his book, Scanlon at least gives a hint: "For example, we often exaggerate the sacrifice that would be involved in paying higher taxes, and fail to appreciate the benefits that others would derive from the increased aid, especially foreign aid, that higher taxes would make possible." (Had it not been deleted, this sentence would have concluded the last full paragraph on 358.)

38. See, for instance, Pettit, Philip (2000) "Two Construals of Scanlon's Contractualism," *Journal of Philosophy* 97, 148–64, esp. section III.
39. Wittgenstein, Ludwig (1993) "A Lecture on Ethics" in Ludwig Wittgenstein: *Philosophical Occasions 1912–1951*, edited by James Klagge and Alfred Nordmann, Indianapolis, Hackett, 40.

PHILOSOPHICAL ISSUES, 11
Social, Political, and Legal Philosophy, 2001

A Place for Cost-Benefit Analysis*

David Schmidtz

What next? We are forever making decisions. Typically, when unsure, we try to identify, then compare, our options. We weigh pros and cons. Occasionally, we make the weighing explicit, listing pros and cons and assigning numerical weights. What could be wrong with that? In fact, things sometimes go terribly wrong. This paper considers what cost-benefit analysis can do, and also what it cannot.

1. What Is CBA, and What Is It For?

Here is an example of how things go wrong. Ontario Hydro is a Canadian government-owned utility company (a Crown Corporation, on a par with Canada Post). Ten years ago, Ontario Hydro was expecting to become a hugely profitable provider of electricity to consumers all over the continent. At that time, Ontario circulated a report explaining how it planned to meet projected demand. Of interest to us is the report's admission that, "The analysis conducted in the development of the Demand/Supply Plans includes those costs which are borne directly by Hydro. It is these costs which can properly be included in Hydro's rates. Costs and benefits for the Ontario community, beyond these direct costs, are not factored into the cost comparisons." Why not? Because "even if desirable, these costs are difficult to estimate in monetary terms given the diffuse nature of the impacts and wide variety of effects." The costs that Ontario Hydro proposed to take into account "include the social and environmental costs incurred by Hydro but do not include social and environmental costs external to Hydro. This reflects normal business practice. In Hydro's judgment, including additional costs and benefits on an equitable basis would be impracticable." [1]

It is amazing that people would defend such a patently unethical stance by describing it as "normal business practice." Sadly, though, appealing to "normal business practice" is itself normal business practice, and Ontario Hydro is not especially guilty in that regard. Indeed, it is notable that Ontario Hydro was not duplicitous, since it did, after all, express its policy bluntly and publicly. Those who wrote the report evidently had no idea that what they were saying was wrong.

Environmentalists have their own "normal business practices," though, and it is too easy to condemn organizations like Ontario Hydro without thinking things through. Many critics of cost-benefit analysis (henceforth CBA) seem driven by a gut feeling that CBA is heartless. They think that, in denouncing CBA, they are taking a stand against heartlessness. This is unfortunate. The fact is, weighing a proposal's costs and benefits does not make you a bad person. What makes you a bad person is *ignoring* costs—the costs you impose on others.

The problem with Ontario Hydro arose, not when Ontario Hydro took costs and benefits into account, but rather when it decided *not* to do so. The problem in general terms is a problem of *external* costs. External costs are costs that decision makers ignore, leaving them to be paid by someone else. Ontario Hydro makes a decision that has certain costs. Some of the costs will fall not on Ontario Hydro but on innocent bystanders; following normal business practice, Ontario Hydro seems to say, "That's not our problem."

Decision makers naturally are tempted to ignore external costs. It is only human. Almost everyone does the same sort of thing in one context or another. Every time you leave an empty popcorn box in a theater rather than dispose of it properly, you are doing the same sort of thing as the person who dumps industrial waste in the river rather than dispose of it properly. Every time you drive a car, you are risking other people's lives, and you probably have never wasted a minute feeling guilty about it. (And just like you, industrial polluters defend themselves by saying, "But everybody does it!") It is not only bad people who ignore the costs they impose on others. Part of the problem is simple laziness, when we think no one is watching. Another part of the problem is the normal human desire to conform, even when "normal practice" is unconscionable.

2. Is CBA Anti-Environmentalist?

CBA comes in many variations, and there are many that no ethicist would defend. Needless to say, no ethicist would defend conventional CBA, that is, CBA in the narrowly focused way that Ontario Hydro used it at the end of the 1980s. All sides agree: there can be no general justification for foisting external costs on innocent bystanders. Any controversy concerns whether there exists some other form of CBA that can, in general, be justified.

Those with expertise in accounting are trained to draw fine-grained distinctions between different variations on the basic theme of conventional CBA. Full Cost Accounting, for example, refers to an attempt to carry out CBA in such a way as to take *all* known costs, external as well as internal, into account.[2] From here on, except where otherwise noted, when I speak of CBA, I will be referring to cost-benefit analysis with Full Cost Accounting. As E. J. Mishan's influential text defines it, "in cost-benefit analysis we are concerned with the economy as a whole, with the welfare of a defined society, and not any smaller part of it."[3]

Understood in this way, CBA is not merely an accounting method. It is a commitment to take responsibility for the consequences of one's actions. That is why, historically, environmentalists were among the most vocal *advocates* of CBA as a vehicle for making industries and governments answerable for the full cost of their decisions. It can work. Indeed, there has been an interesting further development in the case of Ontario Hydro. Perhaps having learned something about environmental ethics, Ontario Hydro changed its stance in 1993 and now trumpets its use of Full Cost Accounting methods.[4]

Under what general circumstances, then, should we want policy makers to employ CBA? Two answers come to mind: first, when one group pays the cost of a piece of legislation while another group gets the benefit; second, and more generally, whenever decision makers have an incentive not to take full costs into account. Where benefits of political decisions are concentrated while costs are dispersed, special interest groups can push through favorable policies even when costs to the population at large outweigh benefits.[5] To contain the proliferation of such unconscionable policies, we might require that policies be justified by the lights of a proper CBA. Requiring decision makers to provide a CBA, which is then made available for public scrutiny, is one way of trying to teach decision makers to take environmental costs into account. We do not want upstream people ignoring costs they foist on downstream people.[6] We want social and cultural and legal arrangements that encourage people to be aware of the full environmental cost, and also the full human cost, of what they do.

The most fundamental argument in favor of CBA has to do with CBA's role as a means of introducing accountability into decisions that affect whole communities. Think about it. If a business pollutes, would it be wrong to insist that the business should be paying the true full cost of its operation? As a mechanism for holding decision makers publicly accountable for external costs, CBA has the potential to constrain activities that are not worthwhile when external costs are taken into account. Accordingly, the National Policy Act of 1969 required CBA of all environment-related federal projects. To that extent, CBA is a friend of the environment. Or at least, it seemed that way at one time.

The tables seemingly have been turning, though. Throughout the 1970s, the Council on Wage and Price Stability and the Office of Management and Budget pressured the Environmental Protection Agency to pay more attention to the costs of complying with standards the EPA was trying to impose on industry. Finally, in 1981, President Reagan issued an Executive Order requiring government agencies to justify new regulations by submitting a formal CBA (of which an environmental impact statement would be only one part) to the Office of Management and Budget. Why? Why force agencies to perform CBA of their regulatory proposals? The point, very generally, was to force agencies to take into account costs they otherwise would have preferred to ignore. The Reagan administration reputedly felt some regulations were being pushed through by environmental zealots who did not care what their proposals cost in human terms. Accordingly, the Executive Order mandating CBA was perceived as having an anti-environmental thrust. Perhaps partly because of that bit of recent history, current environmentalist opinion remains, on the whole, anti-CBA. The following sections consider some of the main reasons (some cogent, some not) for distrusting CBA.

3. Is CBA Anthropocentric?

Is it only the interests of human persons that can be taken into account in a CBA? If so, then isn't CBA essentially anthropocentric? The answer is no. CBA as construed here is partly an accounting procedure, and partly a way of organizing public debate. In no way is it a substitute for philosophical debate. Animal liberationists who think full costs must (by definition?) include pain suffered by animals, for example, must argue for that point in philosophical debate with those who think otherwise. If CBA presupposed one or the other position, thereby preempting philosophical debate, that would be a flaw.

4. Does CBA Presuppose Utilitarian Moral Theory?

Utilitarian moral theory holds roughly that X is right if and only if X maximizes utility, where maximizing utility is a matter of producing the best possible balance of benefits over costs. It may seem obvious that CBA presupposes the truth of utilitarian moral theory. In fact, it does not. CBA is a way of organizing a public forum expressing respect for persons: persons present at the meeting and other persons as well, on whose behalf those present can speak (citizens of faraway countries, future generations, etc.). For that matter, those present at the forum will speak not only on behalf of other persons but on behalf of whatever they care about: animals, trees, canyons, historic sites, and so on.

The forum therefore is defensible on utilitarian grounds, but it does not depend on utilitarian moral theory, for this sort of CBA could and probably should be advocated by deontologists.[7] A conventional CBA that ignored external costs would be endorsed neither by deontologists nor utilitarians, but CBA with Full Cost Accounting, defended in a public forum, could be endorsed by either.[8]

5. Does CBA Tell Us to Sacrifice the One for the Sake of the Many?

We can imagine advocates of CBA jumping to the conclusion that policies are justified whenever benefits exceed costs. That would be a mistake. We need to be more circumspect than that. When benefits exceed costs, the conclusion should be that the policy has passed one crucial test and therefore further discussion is warranted. On the other hand, when a proposal *fails* the test of CBA, when costs exceed benefits, the implication is more decisive, namely that further discussion is not warranted. If enacting a certain proposal would help some people and hurt others, then showing that winners are gaining more than losers are losing counts for something, but it is not decisive. One must then argue that the gain is so great for some people that it justifies imposing a loss on other people. In contrast, to show that losers are losing more than winners are gaining should pretty much end the conversation. Failing CBA is a fairly reliable test of when something is wrong.[9] Passing CBA, however, is not a reliable test of when something is right.

Consider the following case.[10]

> HOSPITAL: Five patients lie on operating tables about to die for lack of suitable organ donors. A UPS delivery person just walked into the office. She is a suitable organ donor for all five patients. If you kidnap her and harvest her organs, you will be saving five and killing one.

Suppose we perform CBA in that case, and it yields the conclusion that, well, five is more than one. Would that imply that taking the delivery person's life is permissible? Required, even? No. Of course, we could quibble about how the calculation works out, but that would miss the fundamental point, which is that when we are talking about killing people, costs and benefits are not the only issue. CBA offers us guidance when our objective is to promote the best possible balance of costs and benefits, but not all situations call on us to maximize what is valuable. Promoting value is not always the best way of respecting it. There are times when morality calls on us not to maximize value but simply to respect it.

I argued that CBA does not presume the truth of utilitarian moral theory. Now it may seem that what I call CBA presumes that utilitarian moral theory is false! On the contrary, even from a broadly utilitarian perspective, we do not want ordinary citizens to have a license to kill whenever they think they can do a lot of good in the process. Some institutions have their utility precisely by *prohibiting* decisions based on utilitarian calculation. Hospitals, for example, cannot serve their purpose if they are a menace to innocent bystanders. Hospitals cannot serve their purpose unless people can trust hospitals to treat people as rights-bearers. Respecting people's rights is part of what helps make it safe to visit hospitals. And making it safe to visit the hospital is a prerequisite of hospitals functioning properly. Accordingly, we cannot justify cutting up one patient to save five simply by saying five is more than one. Sometimes, numbers do not count. It is good policy to forbid killing, requiring ordinary citizens to respect human rights, period.

Therefore, there are limits to the legitimate scope of CBA, and must be, even from a utilitarian perspective. Consider the case of *Peeveyhouse vs. Garland Coal.*[11] Having completed a strip-mining operation on the Peeveyhouse property, Garland Coal refused to honor its contractual promise to restore the land to its original condition. The restored land would have been worth only $300 and it would have cost $29,000 to restore it. Still, Peeveyhouse wanted the land restored and Garland Coal had promised to do it.

Incredibly, the Oklahoma court awarded Peeveyhouse only the $300, judging that Garland Coal could not be held financially liable for a restoration when such restoration would not be cost-effective. The Court's verdict generally is regarded as utterly mistaken, though, and one way of understanding the mistake is to see it as a case of failing to understand the limits of CBA's legitimate scope. We live in a society where hospitals cannot take organs without consent. We live in a society where Garland Coal normally would have to honor its contract with Peeveyhouse. Thus, we know where we stand. We need not be perpetually preparing to prove before a tribunal that strip-mining our land or harvesting our internal organs without consent is not cost-effective. Instead, we have a right simply to say no. In giving us moral space that we govern by right, our laws limit the energy we have to waste: trying to influence public regulators, fighting to keep what belongs to us, fighting to gain what belongs to others. In treating us as rights-bearers, our laws enable us simply to decline proposals that would benefit others at our expense.

Crucially, our being able to say no teaches people to search for ways of making progress that benefit everyone. CBA in its simplest form allows some to be sacrificed for the sake of the greater good of others, and therefore CBA in its simplest form is morally problematic. In contrast, CBA as a framework for public discussion, in a regime that treats people as rights-bearers, creates at least some pressure to craft proposals that promise benefits for all.[12]

Again, part of the message to take away from these discussions is that the proper purpose of CBA is not to show when a taking is permissible. If we see CBA as indicating when takings are permissible, we will have a problem, because breaking contracts, or taking things from people (including their lives) whenever the benefit is worth the cost is not a way of respecting people. But if we treat CBA as a *constraint* on takings, ruling out inefficient takings without licensing efficient takings, then it is not disrespectful.

Therefore, it would be a mistake to see CBA as an *alternative* to treating people as ends in themselves. On the contrary, when CBA is working properly, and in particular when treated not as a seal of approval for good proposals but rather as a means of filtering out bad proposals, CBA becomes a way of preventing people from treating each other as mere means. The point is to stop people from foisting the costs of their policies on innocent people without consent. In other words, requiring people to offer an accounting of the true costs and benefits of their operations is a way of holding them publicly accountable for failing to treat fellow citizens as ends in themselves. CBA will not filter out every proposal that ought to be filtered out, but it will help to filter out many of the most flagrantly disrespectful proposals, and that is its proper purpose.

6. Must CBA Treat All Values as Mere Commodities?

As Mark Sagoff nicely expresses the point, "There are some who believe on principle that worker safety and environmental quality ought to be protected only insofar as the benefits of protection balance the costs. On the other hand, people argue—also on principle—that neither worker safety nor environmental quality should be treated as a commodity to be traded at the margin for other commodities, but rather each should be valued for its own sake" (Sagoff 1981, pp. 1288–89). The second argument, though, presents a false dichotomy. CBA is perfectly compatible with the idea that worker safety and environmental quality ought to be valued for their own sake.

To see why, imagine a certain recycling process is risky to the workers involved. The process improves environmental quality, but inevitably workers risk getting their hands caught in the machines, and so on. Notice: although we treat both environmental quality and worker safety as ends in themselves, we still have to weigh the operation's costs and benefits. Is recycling's environmental benefit worth the risk? It is a good question, and we would be missing the point if we tried to answer it by saying environmental quality is valued for its own sake.

Nor must we imagine cases of different values (worker safety and environmental quality) coming into conflict. The need for CBA can arise even when environmental quality is the sole value at stake. For example, suppose the recycling process in question saves paper (and therefore trees), but saving trees comes at a cost of all the water and electricity used in the process; gasoline is used by trucks that collect the paper from recycling bins, and so on. Therefore, the very recycling process that reduces pollution and natural resource consumption in some respects also increases pollution and natural resource consumption in other respects. In this case, our reason to do CBA is precisely that we care about environmental quality. (If maintaining a politically correct environmentalist appearance were our only concern, we would not worry about it.)

Again, it would be beside the point to talk about environmental quality being valued for its own sake. In a nutshell, we sometimes find ourselves in situations of conflicting values, where the values at stake are really important. Critics of CBA sometimes seem to say, when values at stake are really important, that is when we should *not* think hard about the costs and benefits of resolving the conflict in one way rather than another. They seem to have things backwards.

Sagoff (1981, pp. 1290–91) asserts, "It is the characteristic of cost-benefit analysis that it treats all value judgments other than those made on its behalf as nothing but statements of preference, attitude, or emotion." There are several things going on in this passage. I will mention three. First, the words "other than those made on its behalf" are a jest at the pseudo-scientific posturing of radical subjectivists, and the jest is on target. Second, Sagoff is insinuating that it is a mistake simply to assume that all values are reducible to costs and benefits, and here too, Sagoff is on target. On the one hand, it is an economist's job to go as far as possible in treating values as preferences, and within economics narrowly construed, the reductionist bias serves a purpose. On the other hand, when we look at values in more philosophical terms, we cannot treat all values as mere preferences, as if attaching value to honesty were on a par with attaching value to chocolate. Accordingly, there is a problem with jumping from economic to philosophical discussions without stopping to remind ourselves that what is taken for granted in one kind of discussion cannot be taken for granted in the other.

The third thing Sagoff is saying is that CBA characteristically treats all values as mere preferences. Now, if Sagoff means to say CBA *typically* does so, he may be right. But if Sagoff were saying CBA *necessarily* does so, he would be mistaken. CBA is about weighing costs and benefits. It does not presume everything is either a cost or a benefit. We have to decide which values can be treated as mere preferences, costs, or benefits, and which have to be treated separately, as falling outside the scope of CBA. CBA itself does not make that decision for us. It is true by definition that to care about X is to have a preference regarding X, but we can care about X without thinking X is merely a preference. CBA assumes nothing about the nature of values, other than that they sometimes come into conflict and that no matter what we do, we will in effect be trading them off against each other.[13] It does not assume trading off values is unproblematic; it assumes only that we sometimes have no choice.

"Recycling" is a politically correct word, to be sure, but does that mean we should support any operation that uses the word in its title, even if the operation is environmentally catastrophic? Or should we instead stop to think about the operation's costs and benefits? Contra Sagoff, if we stop to think, that does not mean we are treating environmental quality as a mere "preference, attitude, or emotion." Stopping to think can be a way of showing respect.

7. Can CBA Handle Qualitative Values?

Steven Kelman (1981, p. 33) says CBA presupposes the desirability of being able to express all values as dollar values. However, as Kelman correctly notes, converting values to dollars can be a problem. It can distort the true nature of the values at stake. On the other hand, it would be a mistake to think CBA *requires* us to represent every value as a dollar value. For example, Kelman and Sagoff surely would agree that if we care about Atlantic Green Turtles and do a CBA of alternative ways of protecting them, nothing in that process even suggests we have reduced the value of turtles to dollars.

We can do CBA with respect to different values; we can accept conflicts of value that prevent definitive answers. Kelman is right that something is gained when we genuinely and fairly can reduce all values to dollar values, because if we can do that, then there will be a "bottom line." We can simply tally up values, and it will be clear what CBA recommends. Often, though, trying to force the process to yield an unambiguously numerical bottom line would be to chase a mirage. If the art museum is about to close and I have one last chance to see either my beloved Vermeer or my beloved Seurat, but there is no time to see both, then I must make a choice. The interesting point is, even when I know precisely what the costs and benefits will be of seeing the Vermeer versus seeing the Seurat, that does not entail that there will be an unambiguous bottom line. Normally, people do not attach numbers to their values. You never hear people saying, "Well, according to my calculations, the Vermeer experience is seven percent more valuable than the Seurat experience, so clearly Vermeer is the way to go." Nor do we hear, "Although I'm more in the mood for Seurat, the rational choice is the Vermeer, since appraisers say the Vermeer is worth more money." The latter thought would be irrelevant when the values at issue concern my own appreciation of the paintings' intrinsic merits as paintings rather than the paintings' value as instruments for raising cash. In cases like that, the bottom line will be qualitative rather than quantitative. No matter how accurately I appraise the intrinsic merits of the paintings, my appraisals will still be qualitative.

An object's *intrinsic* value is the value it has in and of itself, beyond any value it has as a means to further ends. Note that an object's having intrinsic value does not imply that the object is priceless. There is such a thing as limited intrinsic value. A painting can have an intrinsic value that is real without being infinite, or even particularly large. The value I would get from selling it is its instrumental value to me. The value it has to me in and of itself, simply because it is a beautiful painting, is its intrinsic value to me.[14] Both values are real, but one is instrumental and the other is intrinsic. Neither is necessarily large.

A related point: it would be better if Kelman (1981, p. 39) had not said, "selling a thing for money demonstrates that it was valued only instrumentally." [15] Suppose I sell a painting. The money I receive from the sale is the painting's instrumental value to me, but does my decision to sell imply that the painting had no intrinsic value? No. Suppose I love the painting, but I need to raise a large sum of money to save my life, so I sell the painting. What this implies is not that the painting has zero intrinsic value but rather that the instrumental value of selling it outweighs the intrinsic value of keeping it, in that circumstance.

More generally, we sometimes put dollar values on things even when their value to us is essentially different from the value of dollars. Incommensurability of different values is not generally an insurmountable obstacle to CBA. Still, there often is no point in trying to convert a qualitative balancing into something that *looks* like a precise quantitative calculation and thus *looks* scientific but in fact remains the same qualitative balancing, only now its qualitative nature is disguised by the attaching of made-up numbers.

Policy decisions can be like that. We can make up numbers when assessing the value of a public library we could build on land that otherwise will remain a public park. Maybe the numbers will mean something, maybe not. More often, even when we can accurately predict a policy's true costs and benefits, that does not entail that there will be any bottom line from which we simply read off what to do. When competing values cannot be reduced to a common measure without distortion, that makes it harder to know the bottom line. It may even mean there is no unitary bottom line to be known. Sometimes the bottom line is simply that one precious and irreplaceable thing is gained while another precious and irreplaceable thing is lost. Even so, that does not mean there is a problem with the very idea of taking costs and benefits into account. It just means we should not assume too much about what kind of bottom line we can expect to see.[16]

Ontario Hydro (since its reorganization), and the City of Vancouver Planning Department, to name two examples, say that in striving to provide a Full Cost Accounting, they try not to ignore vague nonmonetized costs, even though in practice such sensitivity means their bottom line will reflect not (or not only) numerical inputs so much as their version of informed common sense.[17] Consider an analogy. A computer program can play chess by algorithm. Human chess players cannot. Human chess players need creativity, experience, alertness to unintended consequences, and other skills and virtues that are not algorithmic. People who formulate policy need similar skills and virtues, and interpersonal skills as well. Employing CBA cannot change that.

8. Some Things Are Priceless. So What?

Critics of CBA think they capture the moral high ground when they say some things are beyond price. They miss the point. Even if Atlantic Green Turtles are a priceless world heritage, we still have to decide how to save them. We still need to look at costs and benefits of trying to protect them in one way rather than another, for two reasons. First, we need to know whether a certain approach will be effective, given available resources. Dollar for dollar, an effective way of protecting them is better than an ineffective way. Second, we need to know whether the cost of saving them involves sacrificing something else we consider equally priceless.

If baby Jessica has fallen into an abandoned well in Midland, Texas and it will cost nine million dollars to rescue her, is it worth the cost? It seems somehow wrong even to ask the question; after all, it is only money. But it is not wrong. If it would cost nine million dollars to save Jessica's life, what would the nine million dollars otherwise have purchased? Could it have been sent to Africa where it might have saved nine thousand lives? Consider an even more expensive case. If a public utility company in Pennsylvania (in the wake of a frivolous lawsuit blaming its high-voltage power lines for a child's leukemia) calculates that burying its power lines underground will cost two billion dollars, in the process maybe preventing one or two deaths from leukemia, is it only money? If the two billion dollars could have been sent to Africa where it might have saved two million lives, is it obvious we should *not* stop to think about it?

Critics like to say not all values are economic values. They are right, but no values whatsoever are purely economic values in that sense. Even money itself is never only money. In a small town in Texas in 1987, a lot of money was spent to save a baby's life—money that took several lifetimes to produce. It was not only money. It did after all save a baby's life. It also gave a community a chance to show the world what it stands for. These are not trivial things. Neither are many of the other things on which nine million dollars could have been spent.

There are things so valuable to us that we think of them as beyond price. Some economists might disagree, but it is, after all, a fact. What does this fact imply? When we have no choice but to make tradeoffs, should we ignore items we consider priceless, or should we take them into account?[18] The hard fact is, priceless values sometimes come into conflict. When that happens, and when we try rationally to weigh our options, we are in effect putting a price on that which is priceless. In that case, CBA is not the problem. It is a response to the problem. The world has handed us a painful choice, and trying rationally to weigh our options is our way of trying to cope with it.

Note in passing that although critics often speak of incommensurable values, incommensurability is not quite the issue, strictly speaking. Consider the central dilemma of the novel, *Sophie's*

Choice (Styron, 1979). Sophie's two children are about to be executed by a concentration camp commander. The commander says he will kill both children unless Sophie picks one to be killed, in which case the commander will spare the other one. Now, to Sophie, both children are beyond price. She does not value one more than the other. In some sense, she values each of them more than anything. Nevertheless, she does in the end pick one for execution, thereby saving the other one's life. The point is, although her values were incommensurate, she was still able to rank them in a situation where failing to rank them would have meant losing both. The values were incommensur*ate*, but not incommensur*able*. To Sophie, both children were beyond price, but when forced to put a price on them, she could.

Of course, the decision broke her heart. As the sadistic commander foresaw, the process of ranking her previously incommensurate values was psychologically devastating. At some level, commensuration is *always* possible, but there are times when something (our innocence, perhaps) is lost in the process of making values commensurate. Perhaps that explains why some critics want to reject CBA; they see it as a mechanism for ranking values that should not be ranked. Unfortunately, although we can hope people like Sophie will never need to rank their children and can instead go on thinking of each child as having infinite value, and although we can wish we never had to choose between worker safety and environmental quality, or between different aspects of environmental quality, the real world sometimes requires tradeoffs.

9. Does CBA Work?

When individuals engage in CBA, they typically are asking themselves how much they should be willing to pay. That is an obvious and legitimate question because they are, after all, constrained by their budget. In contrast, legislators ask themselves how much they are willing to make *other* people pay, and that is a problem. In that case, paying has become an external cost, and it is no surprise if legislators seem rather cavalier about how much they are making other people pay. I said earlier that if the analysis shows that losers are losing more than winners are gaining, that should pretty much end the conversation. Unfortunately, in the real world, the conversation does not always stop there. When a program's benefits are concentrated within influential constituencies, legislators conceal how costly the program is to taxpayers at large. Similarly, owners of dogs that bark all night ignore the costs they impose on neighbors. Again, it is not because people are evil. They are only human. Situations where we are not fully accountable—where we have the option of not paying the full cost of our decisions—tend not to bring out the best in us. CBA with Full Cost Accounting is one way of trying to introduce accountability.

In theory, then, CBA is a way of organizing agenda for public debates that respect all persons, and valuable nonpersons, too. How does it work in practice? An effective resolution to hold decision makers and policy makers accountable for all costs would, in theory, make for a cleaner, safer, more prosperous society. The prospect of a public accounting can make corporations and governments rethink what they owe to the environment, and in Ontario Hydro's case, it seems to have done exactly that. Still, there is much corruption in the world and nothing like CBA will ever put an end to it. As with any other accounting method, the quality of the output typically will be only as good as the quality of the inputs. The valuations we supply as inputs drive the results, so how to avoid biased valuations? Biased inputs generate biased outputs. CBA, then, has the potential to be a smokescreen for the real action that takes place before numbers get added.

Can anything guarantee that the process of CBA will not itself be subject to the same political piracy that CBA was supposed to limit? Probably not. As I said earlier, the verdict in *Peeveyhouse* generally is regarded as mistaken. What I did not mention is that, as Andrew Morriss (2000, p. 144) notes, "Shortly after the *Peeveyhouse* decision, a corruption investigation uncovered more than thirty years of routine bribery of several of the court's members." CBA per se does not correct for corrupted inputs. Neither does CBA stop people from applying CBA to cases in which CBA has no legitimate role. However, if the process is public, with affected parties having a chance to protest when their interests are ignored, public scrutiny will have some tendency to correct for biased inputs. It also will encourage planners to supply inputs that can survive scrutiny in the first place. If the process is public, people will step forward to scrutinize not only valuations, but also the list of options, suggesting possibilities that planners may have concealed or overlooked.

Even if we know the costs and benefits of any particular factor, that does not guarantee that we have considered everything. In the real world, we must acknowledge that for any actual calculation we perform, there could be some cost or benefit or risk we have overlooked. What can we do to avoid overlooking what in retrospect will become painfully obvious? Although it is no guarantee, the best thing I can think of is to open the process to public scrutiny.

Kelman (1981, p. 33) says CBA presumes we should spare no cost in enabling policy makers to make decisions in accordance with CBA. Kelman is right to be critical of such a presumption, for CBA is itself an activity with costs and benefits. The activity of analyzing costs and benefits is not always warranted on cost-benefit grounds. It can be a waste of time. Therefore, CBA on its own grounds ought to be able to recognize that there is a limit to CBA's legitimate scope. Decisions have to be made about what options are worth considering in cost-benefit terms. When we bring people together to scrutinize a proposal, we risk starting a fight over how to distribute costs and benefits. We take people who otherwise might peacefully mind their own business, and we teach them to think of each other as political adversaries. Not all problems can be solved by community policy. Often enough, neighbors are perfectly capable of quietly working things out among themselves, and often enough it is best simply to let them.

10. Must CBA Measure Valuations in Terms of Willingness to Pay?

Suppose we want to assess the costs and benefits of building a library on land that otherwise would remain a public park. How are we supposed to measure costs and benefits? Must we look into people's souls to see how much they really want the library? What alternative do we have? What if we asked people how much they are willing to pay to have the library, and compared that to what they say they are willing to pay to keep the park? Would that be a reasonable way of ascertaining how much they care?

CBA often is depicted as requiring us to measure a good's value by asking how much people would pay for it. Such a requirement is indeed problematic. One problem: willingness to pay is a function not only of perceived values but also of resources available for bidding on those values. Poorer people show up as less willing to pay even if, in some other sense, they value the good as much.

Is there anything we could do to make it legitimate to use willingness to pay as a surrogate for value in some other sense? Perhaps. Part of the problem, to judge from the literature, is that surveys designed to measure willingness to pay do not in fact take willingness to pay seriously. What they ask subjects to declare is not willingness to pay but *hypothetical* willingness to pay. The idea is, we justify building a waste treatment plant in a poorer neighborhood when we *judge* that poorer people would not pay as much as richer people would to have the plant built elsewhere. Critics call this environmental racism (because minorities tend to live in poorer neighborhoods). Whatever we call it, it looks preposterous.

Is there an alternative that would be more respectful of neighborhoods that provide the most likely building sites? Suppose we initially choose the site by random lottery, and suppose that by luck of the draw, Beverly Hills is selected as the site of the new waste treatment plant. Suppose we then ask Beverly Hills's rich residents what they are willing to pay to site the plant elsewhere. Suppose they say they jointly would pay ten million dollars to locate the plant elsewhere. Suppose we then announce that the people of Beverly Hills are actually, not just hypothetically, offering ten million to any neighborhood willing to make room for a waste treatment facility that otherwise will be built in Beverly Hills. Suppose one of the poorer neighborhoods votes to accept the bid. Would that be more respectful? Or instead, suppose no one accepts the Beverly Hills offer, and therefore the plant is built in Beverly Hills. Is there anything wrong with richer residents moving out, selling their houses to poorer people willing to live near the plant in order to live in better houses than they otherwise could afford? If siting a waste treatment plant drives down property values so that poorer people can afford to live in Beverly Hills, while rich people take their money elsewhere, is that a problem?

Note that even a random lottery will produce nonrandom results. No matter where the waste treatment facility is built, people who can afford to move away from waste treatment plants tend to be richer than the people who cannot. Home buyers who move in, accepting the nuisance in order to have a nicer house at a lower price, will tend to be poorer than buyers who opt to pay higher prices to live farther from the nuisance. One thing will never change: waste treatment facilities will tend to be found in poorer neighborhoods. Not even putting them all in Beverly Hills could ever change that.

Oddly, activists in effect are agitating for plants to be sited as far as possible from people who work in them, since siting waste treatment facilities within walking distance of the homes of people who might want the jobs they provide is classified as environmental racism. Perhaps the question of how far people have to commute is not important; normally, though, environmentalists urge us to pay more attention to such issues. In any case, if a waste treatment plant must be in a populated area, neighbors will be affected. Someone will have to pay, and no accounting tool is to blame for that.

Critics presume the process of siting waste treatment facilities will *not* be conducted in a respectful manner. They presume politicians will site waste treatment facilities not in response to actual negotiations with communities but rather in response to calculations about what will minimize adverse effects on campaign contributions and ultimately on reelection bids. The critics may be right.[19] If that is how it actually works, then politicians are asking the wrong question, morally speaking. In that case, no accounting method can yield the right answer. Under those circumstances, the point of subjecting the decision to public scrutiny is to lead (possibly racist) politicians not to recalculate answers so much as to start asking the right questions.

11. Must Future Generations Be Discounted?

In financial markets, a dollar acquired today is worth more than a dollar we will acquire in a year. The dollar acquired today can be put to work immediately. At worst, it can be put in the bank, and thus be worth perhaps $1.05 in a year. Therefore, if you ask me how much I would pay today to be given a dollar a year from now, I certainly would not pay as much as a dollar. I would pay something less, perhaps about ninety-five cents. Properly valued, then, the future dollar sells at a discount. Therefore, there is nothing irrational about borrowing against the future to get a profitable project off the ground, even though the cost of borrowing a thousand dollars now will be more than a thousand dollars later.

But here is the catch. There is nothing wrong with taking out a loan, so long as we *pay it back*. But there is something obviously wrong with taking out a loan we have no intention of repaying. In other words, discounting is one thing when the cost of raising capital is internalized; it is something else when we borrow against *someone else's* future rather than our own. We have no right to discount the price that *others* will have to pay for our projects. We have no right to discount externalities. *Redistributive* discounting is objectionable: morally, economically, and sometimes ecologically as well.

Some critics worry about the moral status of the discounting they think CBA presupposes. Thus, Peter Wenz (1989, p. 100) says, "Absurdities arise when the current worth of future human lives is discounted, as CBA requires of all values that will be realized only in the future." As an example of such an absurdity, Wenz (p. 100) goes on to calculate that at a five percent discount rate, "a human life today is worth four human lives that will not be realized for 28.8 years, eight lives that are 43.2 years in the future, and so on." Obviously, Wenz is right: that would be absurd.[20] So, why think CBA requires that life's value, or any other value, be discounted? Some economists say it does not, and few (none that I know) would discount the value of lives in the way Wenz says they must.[21] There are economists who go so far as to claim a proper analysis requires that values *not* be discounted.[22] In any case, if we undertake a CBA, we must decide whether to introduce a discount rate. CBA will not make the decision for us. We also must decide whether to discount all considerations or only some. For example, we must decide whether to discount a life in the same way we discount the financial cost of *saving* a life (say, by building safer highways). To philosophers, the decision appears clear-cut: human lives are not commodities, although things we use to save lives typically are.

The thing about affluent people, and the reason why environmentalists are correct (not merely politically correct) to worry about poverty, is that affluent people can afford to be more future-oriented, that is, to operate with lower discount rates. The task, then, is two-fold: first, to teach people to see their future as depending on resources they are in a position to preserve, conserve, or degrade, and, second, to put them in a position where they can afford to be future-oriented.

Conclusions

What can you do with a CBA? You can draw conclusions like this: "We conducted CBA, taking the following costs and benefits into account. The proposal before us appears to pass inspection by the lights of such analysis. We therefore recommend further discussion. Or where the proposal does not pass inspection, where the losers would lose more than the winners would gain, we recommend that the proposal be rejected. In either case, we could be wrong. First, there may be costs or benefits we have not anticipated. Second, even known costs and benefits are often impossible to quantify precisely; therefore, our numbers must be viewed with caution. Third, when used in support of a given proposal, CBA need not be decisive, for there are other grounds upon which policies can be prohibited, favorable CBA notwithstanding. Nevertheless, until someone either identifies additional costs or benefits for us to consider, or else informs us that the proposal violates a treaty (for example) that created rights and obligations that render costs and benefits moot, all we can do is go with our best understanding of the information before us. Barring new information, proceeding in accordance with the result of this CBA appears to be the best we can do."

I talked about doing CBA with Full Cost Accounting, but no mechanical procedure can be guaranteed to take all costs into account. For any mechanical procedure we devise, there will be situations where that procedure overlooks something important. This is not a reason to reject the very idea of CBA, though. Rather, it is a reason to be wary of the desire to make decisions in a mechanical way. We cannot wait for someone to devise the perfect procedure, guaranteed to give everything its proper weight. Whatever procedures we devise for making decisions as individuals or as a community, we need to exercise judgment. At some point we draw the line, make a decision, and get on with our lives, realizing that any real-world decision procedure inevitably will be of limited value. It will not be perfect. It never will be beyond question.

CBA with Full Cost Accounting is only one form of CBA. Many other forms of CBA are indefensible, and no ethicist would defend them. We do well not to conflate different forms of CBA, though, and we do well not to demonize the general idea of weighing costs and benefits. CBA is an important response to a real problem. However, it is not magic. There is a limit to what it can do. CBA is a way of organizing information. It can be a forum for eliciting further information. It can be a forum for correcting biased information. It can be a forum for giving affected parties a voice in community decision making, thereby leading to better understanding of, and greater acceptance of, the tradeoffs involved in running a community. CBA can be all of these good things, but it is not necessarily so. CBA can constrain a system's tendency to invite abuse, such as the environmental racism just discussed, but CBA is prone to the same abuse that infects the system as a whole. It is no panacea. It is an antidote to abuse that is itself subject to abuse.

CBA is not inherently biased, but if inputs are biased, then so will be the outputs, generally speaking. However, although the method does not inherently correct for biased inputs, if the process is conducted publicly, so that people can publicly challenge suppliers of biased inputs, there will be some tendency for the process to correct for biased inputs as well. We can hope there will be adequate opportunity for those with minority viewpoints to challenge mainstream biases, but we cannot guarantee it. The most we can say is that CBA done in public view helps to give democracies a fighting chance to operate as democracies are supposed to operate.

NOTES

*A version of this paper will appear in Schmidtz and Willott (2002).

I thank Maggie Julian and Michael McDonald for sharing their expertise regarding cost-benefit analysis in general, and regarding the case of Ontario Hydro in particular. Thanks also to Tyler Cowen and Elizabeth Willott. Errors, of course, are my own. For nurturing my research on this and other topics in 1999–2000, I am grateful to the University of Arizona, the Social Philosophy and Policy Center at Bowling Green State University, and the Centre for Applied Ethics at the University of British Columbia.

1. Demand/Supply Report of the Ontario Hydro Commission, as quoted in McDonald, Stevenson, and Craig, (1992) pp. 33–34.
2. In speaking to different people, I find that the terms are not quite standardized. What I have in mind when I speak of Full Cost Accounting is what some people call Multiple Accounts Analysis or Life Cycle Analysis. They might reserve the term 'Full Cost Accounting' to refer to a kind of CBA that considers all costs, but only in terms of their impact on current stakeholders. Whatever term we use, though, suffice it to say I have in mind a kind of CBA that does not deliberately ignore any cost whatever, including costs imposed on future generations.
3. Mishan, (1976) p. 11.
4. I do not know whether Ontario Hydro's change of heart was partly in response to the 1992 *Ethical Assessment* of McDonald, Stevenson, and Craig, cited above.
5. And if everyone belongs to one interest group or another, that does not mean we all break even in the final accounting. It is as if a hundred of us sat in a circle, and the government went round the circle collecting a penny from each, then favoring one of us with a fifty cent windfall. After repeating the process a hundred times, we are each a dollar poorer, fifty cents richer, and happy. So Friedman (1989) describes the game.
6. This is the illuminating central metaphor used by Scherer (1990).
7. In modern moral theory, deontology often is thought of as the main theoretical alternative to utilitarianism. Generally and roughly, deontology is the

theory that X is right if and only if X expresses respect for all persons as ends in themselves, and treats no one solely as a mere means.

8. Shrader-Frechette (1998) offers different arguments for a similar conclusion.
9. Kelman (1981, pp. 34–35) argues that there are cases in which an action is right even though its costs exceed its benefits. Kelman has in mind actions that involve keeping a promise or speaking out against injustice, cases in which there is something wrong with the very idea of asking about costs and benefits. In such cases, the balance of costs and benefits normally is not decisive because we should not have been asking about costs and benefits in the first place. All of that is compatible with my claim that, in cases where costs and benefits *should* be taken into account, determining that the losers are losing more than the winners are gaining should be considered a conversation stopper.
10. For a classic discussion of this case, see Thomson (1976).
11. 382 P.2d 109 Oklahoma, 1962. For a discussion of what the case shows about relative merits of statutory versus common law, see Morriss (2000, p. 144).
12. In the terminology of welfare economics, a move is a pareto-improvement when it makes no one worse off and makes at least some people better off. In the most sophisticated critique of CBA of which I am aware, David Copp attributes to E. J. Mishan (citing an earlier work than the one cited above) the view that CBA's justification is linked with the notion of pareto-improvement because when benefits exceed costs, the move is *potentially* pareto-improving. Copp (1985, p. 143) finds this puzzling, and so do I. As Mishan himself admits in his later work (1976, p. 15), "A Pareto improvement which positively requires that when some are made better off, no one is actually made worse off, is assured of fairly wide acceptance. ...A *potential* Pareto improvement, which is consistent with a great many people actually being made worse off, has much less appeal."
13. Hubin (1994, p. 172n) says cost-benefit moral theories (admittedly a slightly different topic) are "absolutely agnostic on the question of what things are of intrinsic value."
14. There is also a debate over whether there is a kind of intrinsic value that does not presuppose the existence of a valuer. We often speak of persons as having a value as ends in themselves, independently of any value attributed to them by other valuers. The questions is whether trees, for example, also can in this sense be ends in themselves. The purpose of the "Last Man Argument" in environmental ethics is to set the stage for discussion of this latter question.
15. Kelman has authorized us to delete this phrase from the version of the paper to be reprinted in Schmidtz and Willott (2002).
16. See also Lindblom (1994).
17. As gleaned from case studies "Full Cost Accounting For Decision Making At Ontario Hydro" prepared by ICF Incorporated for the Environmental Protection Agency, and "Environmentally Sustainable Development Guidelines For Southeast False Creek," prepared by Sheltair Inc. For the City of Vancouver, 1998.
18. Hargrove (1989, p. 211) notes that quantitative analysis may be inappropri-

ate when dealing with intrinsic values. Fair enough, but quantitative analysis often is inappropriate with purely instrumental values too. Not all instrumental values are reducible to monetary values. For example, seat belts are of purely instrumental value, yet when the car hits the ditch and begins to roll over, no amount of money would be a reasonable substitute for having our seat belts fastened.

19. Bullard (1990).
20. Actually, it looks economically problematic as well. If we suppose a zero inflation rate, then a dollar in the future is not worth less than a dollar today. It is worth exactly one dollar. That does not change when we introduce the possibility of earning interest. The possibility of interest means only that it is better to get the dollar earlier because we then can earn additional interest. If lives are like dollars in that respect, then the implication is not that a life later is worth less than a life now. Rather, the implication is very roughly that, just as it would be better to have an extra year's interest, it would be better to have an extra year of life. (That is, if I were going to be given a second life, and if I knew my second life would end in the year 2150, I would pay to have that life begin in 2110 rather than 2130. For analogous reasons, the dollar that began to collect interest in 2110 rather than 2130 would sell at a premium.)
21. For a typically circumspect discussion, see Stiglitz (1994).
22. See Cowen (1992); see also Cowen and Parfit (1992).

References

Bullard, Robert. (1990) *Dumping In Dixie: Race, Class, and Environmental Quality*, Boulder: Westview Press.

Copp, David. (1985) "Morality, Reason, and Management Science: the Rationale of Cost-Benefit Analysis," *Social Philosophy and Policy* 2 (pp. 128–51).

Cowen, Tyler. (1992) "Consequentialism Implies a Zero Rate of Discount," *Philosophy, Politics, and Society*, sixth series, edited by Peter Laslett and James Fishkin, New Haven: Yale University Press (pp. 162–68).

Cowen, Tyler, and Derek Parfit. (1992) "Against the Social Discount Rate," *Philosophy, Politics, and Society*, sixth series, edited by Peter Laslett and James Fishkin, New Haven: Yale University Press (pp. 144–61).

Friedman, David. (1989) *The Machinery of Freedom*, LaSalle: Open Court Publishing.

Hargrove, Eugene C. (1989) *Foundations of Environmental Ethics*, Denton: Environmental Ethics Books.

Hubin, Donald C. (1994) "The Moral Justification of Benefit/Cost Analysis," *Economics and Philosophy* 10 (pp. 169–94).

Kelman, Steven. (1981) "Cost-Benefit Analysis: An Ethical Critique," *Regulation* (Jan./Feb., pp. 33–40).

Lindblom, Charles. (1994) "The Science of Muddling Through," *Foundations of Administrative Law*, edited by Peter Schuck, New York: Oxford University Press (pp. 104–10).

McDonald, Michael, J.T. Stevenson, and Wesley Craig. (1992) *Finding a Balance of Values: An Ethical Assessment of Ontario Hydro's Demand/Supply Plan*, Report to Aboriginal Research Coalition of Ontario.

Mishan, E. J. (1976) *Elements of Cost-Benefit Analysis*, 2nd ed., London: George Allen & Unwin.

Morriss, Andrew. (2000) "Lessons for Environmental Law from the American Codification Debate," *The Common Law and the Environment*, edited by Roger Meiners and Andrew Morriss, Lanham: Rowman & Littlefield (pp. 130–57).

Sagoff, Mark. (1981) "At the Shrine of Our Lady of Fatima, or Why Political Questions Are Not All Economic," *Arizona Law Review* 23 (pp. 1283–98).

Scherer, Donald. (1990) *Upstream/Downstream: Issues in Environmental Ethics*, Philadelphia: Temple University Press.

Schmidtz, David and Elizabeth Willott. (2002) *Environmental Ethics: What Really Matters. What Really Works*, New York: Oxford University Press.

Shrader-Frechette, Kristin. (1998) "A Defense of Risk-Cost-Benefit Analysis," *Environmental Ethics: Readings In Theory and Application*, edited by Louis Pojman, 2nd ed., Belmont: Wadsworth (pp. 507–14).

Stiglitz, J. E. (1994) "The Rate of Discount for Benefit-Cost Analysis and the Theory of the Second Best," *Cost-Benefit Analysis*, edited by Richard Layard and Stephen Glaister, Cambridge: Cambridge University Press (pp. 116–59).

Styron, William. (1979) *Sophie's Choice*, New York: Random House.

Thomson, Judith Jarvis. (1976) "Killing, Letting Die, and the Trolley Problem," *Monist* 59 (pp. 204–17).

Wenz, Peter. (1989) "Democracy and Environmental Change," *Ethics and Environmental Responsibility*, edited by Nigel Dower, Aldershot: Avebury (pp. 91–109).

PHILOSOPHICAL ISSUES, 11
Social, Political, and Legal Philosophy, 2001

Against Rights

Richard J. Arneson

Claims to rights and negotiation about their shape are pervasive in our public and private culture. Rights consciousness is surely desirable and is part and parcel of the transition toward a more democratic world. In this essay I consider the proper placement of moral rights in moral theory. In a famous essay, "Taking Rights Seriously," Ronald Dworkin argues that if it is accepted that individuals have moral rights against their government, that implies serious constraints on the conduct of government and the freedom of a political majority to enforce its wishes through law.[1] I endorse the thesis that individuals have such moral rights and support taking rights seriously in Dworkin's sense. My focus is elsewhere. In this essay I shall argue that moral rights do not and should not figure in our fundamental moral principles; rights enter at the level of subordinate principles. In a very broad way, to take this stand is to side with utilitarians and consequentialists, who see rights as instruments for achieving other values, not moral goals in their own right.[2]

Is this more than a verbal issue? We can say that act utilitarianism assigns each person the moral right not to be harmed by anyone unless doing so maximizes utility and to be benefited by everyone whenever doing so maximizes utility. Someone who believes that morality just is Pareto efficiency can say that each person has a moral right, if the status quo can be altered by making her better off without making anyone else worse off, either that the status quo be altered to her benefit or that some entirely new situation be brought about, establishing a new status quo to which no one can make a similar complaint. Given these implications, are act utilitarianism and the Pareto norm rights principles? Following J. S. Mill, we might hold that the idea of a right involves a duty imposed on some person or persons along with a specifiable person or persons who are wronged if the duty is violated.[3] Rights utilitarianism and the Pareto rights view, advanced as fundamental moral principles, would qualify as including rights on this understanding of a right. To block this result, we might try stipulating that when a right exists, the performance of the associated duty would necessarily provide a benefit to the person who would be wronged if there is nonperformance.

We can do better. Following a suggestion first made by Joseph Raz, let us say that a person has a moral right to X just in case her interest in X (a) establishes a claim to X that should be honored, other things being equal, and (b) is a rationale for assigning other people duties to act or refrain from acting so as to secure X for her (or is a reason for holding that other people are bound by duties to act or refrain from acting so as to secure X for her).[4]

This analysis of what it is to have a right needs further elaboration. For the purposes of this essay, I note that on this analysis, the existence of a moral right implies a right-holder who benefits if the right is fulfilled. The right-holder's interest that the right protects may be generic—X is the sort of thing that is standardly advantageous. So one can have an interest in X, in the intended sense, even if in one's particular circumstances X will not be to one's advantage all things considered. I may have a right that you return the money you borrowed and promised to repay on this date, even though it is certain that if I get the money I will use it to purchase and consume a harmful recreational drug to my detriment.

In addition, for purposes of this analysis I accept a further definitional stipulation introduced by Ronald Dworkin.[5] According to Dworkin, one has a genuine moral right only if the right should be upheld even against the general welfare. That is to say, a valid claim of moral right trumps utility, takes precedence over the goal of bringing it about that utility is maximized. This trumping stipulation is consistent with the claim that if upholding a moral right in a particular case requires a sufficiently large loss of utility, the right should not be upheld in this case. The trumping priority need not be absolute. Rights trump utility to the extent that a valid claim of moral right should be upheld even if its nonfulfillment would bring about a marginal or modest increase in aggregate utility.

Since I want it to be an open question whether rights should be included as fundamental values in a consequentialist theory, at this point I do not insist that the essence of a right is to function in practical deliberation as a side constraint that removes some actions from the set of an agent's eligible options rather than as a goal to be promoted. I would suppose that the common-sense understanding of a moral right is the side constraint view, but consequentialism is subversive of common-sense moral views in several ways and its construal of rights might be another instance.[6]

Several types of moral views give no place to moral rights at the foundational level. Here we concentrate on views in the utilitarian and consequentialist family. The fundamental principles of such moral theories state what is morally valuable for its own sake and indicate what it is right to do, given what is morally valuable. With fundamental principles on hand, one knows how to proceed if one knows the facts of one's situation that these fundamental principles pick out as relevant for choice. Nonfundamental principles specify means to the moral goals affirmed by fundamental principles. If a consequentialist moral theory does not assign positive (or negative) weight to the fulfillment of moral rights in the evaluation of states of affairs and the determination of what should be done, moral rights are nonfundamental in that theory. My thesis is that moral rights should not be included at the level of fundamental moral principles.

Being nonfundamental is not the same as being unimportant. The story I tell about moral rights is not intended to be deflationary or debunking. Moral rights are important; my aim is to clarify how they are important, not deny their significance. The important means to what matters do themselves matter.

The position that moral rights are noninstrumentally valuable and belong in fundamental principle gains support from a variety of considerations. Many forces are mobilized under this banner. The overall strategy of this essay is to concede ground without losing the battle. I believe that the reasons that people offer for holding rights to be fundamental include important concerns and considerations which moral theory should accommodate, but this can be done without recognizing rights at the level of fundamental principle.

Reasons for Taking Rights to Be Fundamental

The case for recognizing rights as fundamental looks compelling if one supposes the exclusionary alternative is utilitarianism, the doctrine that one should always do whatever most promotes utility (human good).

John Rawls argues that utilitarianism fails to match our considered moral judgments on such topics as freedom of expression and the moral status of a feudal order in which caste privileges are assigned to an aristocratic elite on a basis of birth.[7] For utilitarian doctrine, the judgments that wholesale denial of freedom of expression is wrong and that feudalism should not be reinstituted depend on the answers to complex and uncertain empirical questions as to whether these policies would fail to maximize human happiness over the long run, compared to feasible alternative regimes. Since these matters are contingent and uncertain, our confidence that these policies of repression are morally wrong should also be contingent and uncertain, if the basis for deciding these issues is utilitarian calculation. But reasonable moral conviction diverges sharply from the utilitarian pattern of reasoning. Our confidence that tyrannical censorship and caste hierarchy are wrong is firm and unshakable and rests on the belief that these policies violate fundamental rights, and are morally beyond the pale whatever their consequences for long-run human happiness might or might not be.

In a similar spirit, Joseph Raz observes that according to hedonistic act utilitarianism, if we must choose between denying a large number of people the trivial pleasure of eating a lick of ice cream and killing an innocent individual, then provided that the number of potential ice cream eaters is sufficiently large, we should sacrifice the one for the many.[8]

Amartya Sen describes an example in which several thugs would enjoy severely beating a well-off shopkeeper to such an extent that principles that require equalizing utility among persons, equalizing utility among persons at the highest feasible level, maximizing the utility of the individual who has least utility, and maximizing average and aggregate utility would all favor enabling the beating to go forward rather than preventing it.[9] According to Sen, only a moral principle that includes fulfillment of human rights at the fundamental level among the goals to be maximized can plausibly endorse the common-sense conviction that the right-violating utility-promoting beating would be morally undesirable.

These considerations are weighty. My argument will be that these arguments for inclusion of rights at the level of fundamental moral principle combine several different strands of argument. Once the strands are separated and examined one by one, no one or combination looks compelling, and exclusion looks plausible.

Sen's Argument

Sen's counterexample merits close attention. A line of thought running through several of his writings argues that utilitarianism is defective not in virtue of its consequentialist structure but in virtue of its claim that nothing matters morally except utility.[10] The counterexample he presents in "Rights and Agency" is directed against any utility-based fundamental moral principle.[11] A utility-based principle is a consequentialist principle that identifies morally right action with action that maximizes some function of human utility. Maximize aggregate utility, maximize average utility, maximin utility, prioritize utility,[12] equalize utility, and equalize utility at the highest possible level would all qualify as utility-based fundamental moral principles. Sen construes utility as desire or preference satisfaction of life plan fulfillment or pleasure. He urges that an adequate morality (which might be consequentialist) must assign positive weight to the fulfillment of individual rights in the evaluation of states of affairs and the determination of what should be done.

In the example that Sen presents, Ali the shopkeeper is menaced by a gang of thugs, the Bashers, so-called because they intend to give him a bashing. If the threatened bashing occurs, it is stipulated that total utility, average utility, the utility of the worst off, and the degree to which utility is equalized across persons will all increase, compared to the alternative in which the bashing does not occur. Any of these utility-based principles would then have to recommend that the Bashers ought to inflict a bashing on Ali, even though his right not to be severely assaulted would be violated in this scenario. Sen hopes to elicit the reader's agreement that in this example bringing it about that Ali's important right is respected is morally more valuable than bringing about the net utility increase that would accompany the violation of Ali's right.

Sen elaborates the story to make two further points. Donna, Ali's friend, can prevent the violation of Ali's right not to be bashed, but only by inspecting the files of Ali's therapist Charles, thereby violating Charles's right to privacy. She correctly believes that Ali's right not to be bashed is morally more important than Charles's right to privacy in these circumstances, so if she adopts an act-consequentialist morality with rights as trumps, she will act to violate the little right in order to protect the bigger right, thereby bringing about a higher level of rights fulfillment on the whole. If on the other hand she adopts a morality in which rights are side constraints, so that any action that would violate a right is removed from the set of eligible acts from which one chooses, then her choice is to do nothing, violating no one's rights but allowing the Bashers to abolish Ali, or to violate Charles's right to privacy. (In this essay, given my purposes, I can sidestep the issue whether rights should be understood as goals to be promoted rather than as side constraints to be respected.)

In a further elaboration, Sen imagines that there are no Bashers, and Ali is menaced by some natural event such as a landslide that does not involve human agency. The landslide will inflict damages on Ali equivalent to the damage he would have suffered from being bashed. In this version of the example Donna can still save Ali by violating Charles's right to privacy in order to discover Ali's whereabouts just prior to the landslide. But if the threat of being hit by a landslide does not implicate any of Ali's rights, we no longer have a case in which Donna must choose either to bring about the fulfillment of Charles's less important right to privacy or to bring about the fulfillment of Ali's more important right not to be bashed. No bashing is in prospect.

Sen takes the lesson of this version of the example to be that we should see Donna as having equally good reason to violate Charles's right to prevent Ali from being mashed by a landslide as she would have to prevent Ali from being identically mashed by subjection to a violent beating. If we think of rights as relations between an individual and some significant capability, if rights in general are rights to capability, then we can account for the sense that Donna's two decision problems posed by the two versions of the example are morally equivalent. In each case Ali's right to the capability of moving freely about the city without injury is at risk, in one case menaced by the prospect of bashing and in the other case threatened by landslide. If I have a capability to achieve X then if I choose to achieve X, I do so, and if I choose not to achieve X, I do not do so. Capability is effective freedom. Sen's proposal then is that the fundamental human rights that can trump utility in the determination of what we morally ought to do are rights to important capabilities.

Several ideas are interwoven in Sen's ingenious story. Let us examine some of the separate strands, focussing first on the issue whether exclusion of rights from fundamental principle blocks one from formulating an adequate morality.

Construed Subjectively, Utility Is Not so Important

It is plausible to think that in the example the Bashers might draw a significant amount of subjective satisfaction, pleasure or preference satisfaction or the like, from inflicting a thrashing on an innocent victim. Such acts do prove enticing to people. But it is implausible to think that gaining pleasure or desire satisfaction or life plan fulfillment from inflicting a savage beating on someone makes one's life go better. If this is so, then what Sen's example suggests is that the attainment of utility construed as subjective satisfaction does not take precedence over rights fulfillment. This leaves it open that utility identified as what objectively makes a person's life go better does deserve pride of place in moral theory. Robert Adams proposes that "what is good for a person is a *life* characterized by *enjoyment of the excellent*."[13] My view is that a person's well-being can be augmented by excellent achievements that are not enjoyed, and also by some ordinary enjoyments such as the slaking of thirst that cannot be stretched to fit within the category of excellence enjoyment, but I agree that enjoying what is bad has less value than enjoying what is good and the taking pleasure in deliberate infliction of gratuitous pain on another person is valueless or virtually valueless.[14] If we identify utility or well-being with what is objectively worth seeking, what makes one's life go better, Sen's critique of the position that the amount and distribution of utility are all that fundamentally matters morally loses its force.

This response invites the reply that one can rewrite the Donna and the Bashers example so that the Bashers stand to gain significant objective utility. It turns out that they need to inflict a bashing on Ali (from which none derives any pleasure) so that they can secure the means to gain significant objective utility not otherwise obtainable. Subjection to violent assault significantly worsens the victim's life, so the gains the Bashers will secure must be large to offset Ali's loss.

But this version of the example is less compelling. Sen's case does not collapse, but is less powerful. I find it unobvious that the bashing as described is not justified by the significant objective utility gain it secures for persons with poor overall life prospects. Others may disagree. The point is that to test the resources of utility-based views, to give them a fair run for their money, we must develop the most convincing account of utility or well-being or what is good for people and then see how the utility-based views fare.

Moral Limits on Trade-offs

Another reason for rejecting utility-based views and including rights at the fundamental level is perhaps suggested in Sen's story and definitely pressed by Raz. The worry is that any moral principle that bids us to maximize the sum of benefits that accrue to an aggregate of persons when benefits range widely in quality will in some possible circumstances grind out the disturbing result that gaining very small, trivial benefits for a very large number of persons can yield a larger sum of benefits than achieving overwhelmingly urgent and important benefits for a very few persons. Against the morality of aggregation we might urge that morality must have greater internal structure, with lexical (strict) priority relations.[15] Rights might be thought to incorporate morally compelling priority relations and to express our commitment to rejecting promiscuous aggregation.

This issue may be a red herring in this context. For the same issue can arise when we reflect on intrapersonal comparisons and no conflict of interest among persons is in view. One might deny that any number of years of life that is barely worth living, muzak and potatoes in Derek Parfit's phrase, could render my life better than a normal life span filed with the best things.[16] Of course, asserting this discontinuity raises problems, given that the best things and the barely-good-at-all things in life lie on a continuum, and at any point on the continuum it would seem that some sufficiently large quantity of lower-quality life just below that point should outweigh any given quantity of higher quality life just above the point, so by transitivity the barely-good-at-all things should trade off against the best things. At any rate, one might either incorporate lexical priority relations into the understanding of utility or reject such thresholds in the interest of continuity. Either way, Raz's concern about many frivolities outweighing urgent needs need not force the rejection of utilitarian aggregation. Either we judge that continuity rules, which is the same as denying that

Raz's worry is compelling, or discontinuity rules, in which case utilitarian aggregation can accommodate Raz's concern.

Another reason to doubt that the problem of promiscuous aggregation supports the inclusion of moral rights in fundamental moral principles is that rights are susceptible to the same problem. Some moral rights are important, some less important, some trivial. I have a right that other people should not steal my extra shirt button. But then we can generate a version of Raz's puzzle involving moral rights. If a huge number of people are threatened with violation of their right that their shirt buttons not be stolen, the combined moral weight of this huge number of tiny rights can outweigh a single individual's important moral right not to be murdered. If so, then if one must choose between acting to prevent the huge number of shirt button thefts and acting to prevent the one murder, one should act to prevent the greater aggregate rights violation, the button thefts. Again, I take no stand on the issue whether this apparent problem is really a problem, whether we should formulate moral principles that avoid the implication that many small rights should take priority over one big right. My point is just that if there is a difficulty here, one can avoid it by assigning some rights lexical priority over others, so that no degree of fulfillment of the lexically prior rights should ever be sacrificed to secure any gain, no matter how great, in the degree to which lexically less favored rights are fulfilled. But the recourse to lexical priority is available for the pure welfarist (whose fundamental moral principles hold that nothing matters except utility and its distribution) as well as to the one who insists on taking rights seriously.

Driving Someone to the Wall

Suppose we are led to insistence on inclusion of moral rights at the level of fundamental principle by reflecting that utilitarian aggregation can yield the outcome that it is morally right to drive someone to the wall, to an intolerable and horrible condition, in order to secure benefits for persons who are already very well off. We have a moral aversion to pressing Smith into a hellish condition in order to gain benefits for those already in heavenly bliss.

Again, the consideration fails to support the proposed rights affirmation. If avoidance of intolerable and horrible conditions for a person is taken to be an urgent matter for moral theory, we could incorporate the concern directly into a principle that bids straight maximization of good consequences. For example, we might identify a threshold of decent existence and postulate that getting people up to this threshold level is a matter of utmost moral urgency. This yields a triage morality, which insists on using resources and setting policies and actions so that as many individuals as possible are raised to the threshold level. (Notice that this might require driving some, or even a great many individuals to the wall, when doing that is required to get as many people as possible up to the threshold of decent existence. One could avoid this result, if one wishes, by stipulating that moral priority is to be given to achieving gains in well-being for people below the threshold of decent existence. The farther one is from the threshold, the greater the priority that attaches to getting one benefits. Strict lexical priority is given to the aim of advancing the well-being of people below the threshold when their interests conflict with those of people above the threshold level.)

I am not endorsing triage morality (or the alternative threshold prioritarianism described in the previous sentence), merely noting that its assertion does not commit one to individual rights at the fundamental level. What we would have instead is a variant of a utility-based consequentialism in which one particular level of utility, the level deemed to mark the level of a decent existence, is given privileged status.[17] This would not be a consequentialism of rights. A principle that assigns each person the "right" that as many people as possible be boosted to the threshold of decency may not be beneficial to the "right"-holder (since the principle may require that the "right"-holder be driven to the wall).

Distribution across Persons Is Morally Significant

One might hold that there is no moral bar against aggregation of any sort within a single life, but that aggregation across persons, which may require violating the rights of some to secure small benefits to others (licks of ice cream) who may already be extremely well off, is morally dubious. Distribution across persons matters, and might be thought to generate a case for insistence on rights and for their inclusion.

To evaluate this point we need to consider the ways that distribution might be incorporated in moral principles without asserting rights. If we agree that the distribution of utility matters and that bringing about one outcome may be morally superior to bringing about another even if the utility sum is made highest in the second outcome, we are agreeing to reject utilitarianism but not yet to leave behind the utilitarian family of moral views. Let's say very roughly that a moral theory lies within the utilitarian family if it is consequentialist (acts, motives, rules, institutional arrangements, and practices are to be evaluated according to the moral value of the consequences they produce) and nothing affects the moral value of consequences except utility and how it is distributed across persons. So accepting this point that distribution across persons matters fundamentally, as I think we should, moves us beyond utilitarianism but not beyond the family of utility-based views. (Utility-based principles that are distribution-sensitive fall into the category of what Nozick called "end-state principles".[18])

I will give an example of such a distribution-sensitive view that I find plausible. *Weighted utilitarianism* or *prioritarianism* holds that we should act, and set policy, so that moral value is maximized. Moral value is utility weighted by the utility level of the person who gains or loses as a result of what we do. The value of achieving a benefit for a person is greater, the larger the utility she gets from the benefit, and greater, the lower the person's lifetime utility level would be absent this benefit.[19] (This formulation just identifies a class of principles; to specify a principle one would need a weighting of the mentioned factors.) Later I shall further amend prioritarianism; for now I want to trumpet its merits as stated.

If part of our response to Raz's example is revulsion at the idea of driving someone to the wall just to achieve a marginal gain in aggregate utility that takes the form of a trivial increase that goes to boost the well-being of many already advantaged persons, weighted utilitarianism allays this concern, at least to some extent. This distribution-sensitive principle counts at a discount making gains and avoiding losses for those who are already well off and gives extra weight to making gains and avoiding losses for those who are badly off. It is arguable that such a principle captures our intuitive judgments about how to decide on action and social policy when we must choose between grain for the peasants (the worse off) and cakes and ale for the lords (the better off).

If a unit of resource would give the same amount of utility to someone whose lifetime expectation of utility is now low or to someone whose lifetime expectation is high, the distribution-sensitive principle holds that it is morally more valuable to bring it about that the disadvantaged person gets the resource. But the right discount rate is not infinite. As we imagine a unit of resource producing less and less grain and eventually less and less well-being for me, whereas it could produce more and more cakes and ale and eventually more and more well-being for the lords, at some point as a reasonable person I will say, "All things considered, it is morally better that I sacrifice a bit to produce a big increase in well-being for the lords."

Return now to the contemplation of the distribution problem set by Raz. With limited resources and very severely limited flexibility in our deployment of resources, we face a stark choice: we can cut short a single human life in its prime and simultaneously gain the pleasure of a lick of ice cream for many, many people, or we can sustain the life in its prime at the cost of taking away a huge number of small ice cream pleasure experiences. Which to choose? For whatever it is worth, I find the distribution-sensitive principle yielding a close fit to my judgments. If we suppose that the masses of potential ice cream lick beneficiaries are extremely rich in utility to begin with, and the lone individual to be sacrificed is badly off at the outset, then a high discount rate kicks in and the numbers of persons who benefit at the expense of the sacrificed victim must be astronomically large. Galaxies teeming with individuals for tens of thousands of years must be anticipating their ice cream. On the other hand, if we picture initial well-being reversed, so that the lone individual has led an incredibly rich and fulfilling existence, and the many for whose sake he is to be sacrificed are living on hell on earth, so that the moment's respite of delicious ice cream provides huge numbers of people the single rewarding moment of their lives, I find myself inclined to stop resisting the sacrifice of the one for the many at a huge, but smaller number.

Given that our imaginative capacities that enable us to make moral comparisons involving large numbers are quite limited, our intuitive confidence in our judgments about cases involving very large numbers becomes quite weak. But this outcome is not fatal to the prospects for distribution-sensitive views in their rivalry with rights-based approaches. Consternation when faced with moral problems involving either (1) infinitesimal risks of enormous losses versus the certainty of small losses or (2) huge numbers of very, very small benefits versus very, very small numbers of huge benefits and the like will doubtless occur whether our fundamental moral principles are good-based, right-based, or based on whatever. On the rights-based approach, questions must be faced such as whether the violation without compensation of many people's right not to be lightly assaulted is morally worse than a single violation of an individual's right not to be killed. Recall the discussion above under the heading "Moral Limits on Trade-offs."

Absolutism and Deontology

If rights are absolute, and must never be violated whatever the consequences, then it is not true that the difficulties of aggregating moral values in calculations that involve tiny and huge numbers will arise within a rights-based approach. Another possible construal of the Raz and Rawls counterexamples would understand their lesson to be that our discomfort with utilitarian aggregation extends to any consequentialist aggregation and ultimately reflects our allegiance to a side constraint understanding of the place of rights in moral decision making.

According to the conception of rights as side constraints, each individual as she decides what to do will have available an array of disjoint actions any one of which she might choose. Some of these available actions would violate someone's individual rights. These are to be deleted from her options. She may choose any of the actions available to her that do not violate anyone's right and must not choose any that do. Rights constrain the set of permissible actions, and if rights are absolute, these constraints must always be respected. In order for it to be the case that it will always be possible for an individual to avoid violating any rights when she acts, whatever the circumstances in which she finds herself, the specification of the substance of rights must satisfy conditions that guarantee that the individual rights will always be co-possible—all may be satisfied together in any circumstances. Given that all rights, the lesser along with the greater, are all always absolutely to be respected, the issue of how best to aggregate the moral value of disparate rights so as to be able to decide which to prefer when they conflict does not arise. The conditions that serve to guarantee the co-possibility of rights may severely limit the kinds of moral considerations that can figure as rights, and may in this way diminish the plausibility of assigning respect for rights an absolute priority in the determination of right action. This issue I set aside.

I assume here without argument that if moral rights have a place at the level of fundamental moral principles, these will be consequentialist in structure. The proper doctrine that takes rights seriously would be a consequentialism of rights, not a deontology. Although absolutist construals of moral rights are widely rejected, the idea of a side constraint morality that gives weight to traditional deontological distinctions is popular. I note that its appeal might be accommodated to some extent in a hierarchical position, in which rights are not regarded as morally foundational but find a place in derivative, secondary principles. These are instruments to secure the foundational values. Against this demotion of moral rights to secondary status, it is said that the side constraint understanding of rights, implying that each person is inviolable up to a point, in effect confers a high status on everyone, the status of inviolability-up-to-a-point, which has great value. Leaving aside the worry that we seem to be justifying choice of nonconsequentialist principles by appeal to the good consequences of such choice, I note that the appeal to the value of status is question-begging in this context, as Shelly Kagan has noted.[20] For a consequentialist position assigns everyone the status of unignorability, meaning that when one is a potential beneficiary of an infringement of a right, one's interest may not be ignored in the moral calculation that determines what ought to be done all things considered. To inquire whether the status of inviolability up to a point is morally more desirable than the status of unignorability is just to raise in other words the initial question whether the side constraint or consequentialist construal of rights is correct.

Another reason to doubt whether deontology is as firmly rooted in common-sense intuition as is often supposed comes from recent theoretical work that attempts to articulate the fine structure of a morality of side constraints. Theorists who have done excellent work in this tradition recently include Frances Kamm and Judith Thomson.[21] But the structures elaborated in these analyses are increasingly baroque in their complexity and lack strong intuitive appeal. One possibility here is that we need to do more work to uncover the intuitively compelling deep structure of principles that rationally organizes the morality of side constraints. This may be. But the longer the project is continued without discernible progress toward this result, the more the alternative possibility that we have strong responses to some paradigm cases but that these do not cohere in any intuitive system becomes salient.

The Promotion of Goods other than Utility Matters Intrinsically

The issue of utility versus rights touches on questions about monism versus pluralism in value theory. If matters other than utility and how it is spread across persons are intrinsically morally significant, then these significant values should register directly in moral principles at the fundamental level. This issue, it would seem, can only be addressed piecemeal, by taking up each putative intrinsically morally significant non-utility value and testing its claim to nonderivative importance. Moreover, if the answers should turn out to be that non-utility values are significant and nonderivative, on the face of it, this result would yield pluralistic consequentialism not yet consequentialism of rights.

To bring this issue into focus, I shall propose a version of pluralistic consequentialism that strikes me as promising and plausible and that emphatically is not a consequentialism of rights. Suppose we held that if our moral principles are responsive in the right way to information (a) about how much utility the actions and policies we might choose would achieve and (b) about the way in which the utility that might be achieved from each possible course of action would be distributed across persons and finally (c) about the lifetime utility those who might be affected by our choices would have absent those choices, we are responding to all of the genuinely morally relevant features of situations. No other information should affect our choices. This is the position espoused by weighted utilitarianism or prioritarianism as characterized so far. It is arguable that more factors are relevant to proper moral choice than I have so far countenanced.

Consider matters of responsibility and deservingness. No doubt within the framework of weighted utilitarianism there will usually be good instrumental reason to steer utility toward deserving and responsible individuals and away from others. Doing so will reliably tend to promote the weighted utilitarian goal in the long run. But the extent to which this is so depends on contingencies. Suppose it turns out that the normal instrumental relations between rewarding the deserving and responsible and maximizing weighted utility are reversed, so that punishing the responsible and deserving surprisingly would maximize weighted utility. Suppose that we combine responsibility and deservingness considerations so that in principle we can assign a number to each individual that indicates the extent to which she is virtuous or nonvirtuous. But a world in which good fortune goes to the nonvirtuous and bad fortune to the virtuous is not morally on a par with a world where good fortune goes to the virtuous to a greater degree than to the nonvirtuous, given that the two worlds are equal in their weighted utility score. To some extent we should favor channeling utility to the virtuous, and we should do this for its own sake, quite apart from any calculation about how rewarding virtue would boost weighted utility in the long run.

Weighted utilitarianism with this modification then becomes a form of pluralistic consequentialism. Of the available actions that might be chosen, one ought always to do the act that maximizes moral value. Bringing about a benefit for an individual always per se augments moral value (and bringing about a loss for an individual per se decreases moral value). The greater the utility gain that a benefit provides an individual, the lower in lifetime utility the person would be apart from this benefit, and the more virtuous the individual, the greater the moral value the benefit provides.

Weighted utilitarianism modified in this way strikes me as plausible, but for purposes of this essay, there is no need to defend it. Either the pluralistic consequentialism just described is adequate as stated or it should be modified to incorporate the intrinsic significance of further moral values. Suppose that this pluralistic consequentialism is modified so that it is properly responsive to all further moral values (if any) except the putative moral significance of rights. The reader can develop in thought her ideal version of pluralistic consequentialism subject to the constraint that moral rights are not incorporated into this fundamental moral principle. The question then becomes, why add rights to the pluralistic mix?

Normally protecting rights protects many important moral values including physical security, relationships of respectful community, the self-worth of the persons whose rights are respected, and so on. For simplicity I shall focus on the moral values of increasing total utility, achieving utility gains for those whose utility level would otherwise be low, and channeling utility gains to the virtuous. The reader may keep in mind a more complex rights-excluding pluralistic consequentialism, whatever strikes her as best. To decide whether we should further transform this pluralistic consequentialism into a consequentialism of rights, the cases to consider are those in which rights are secured but without any gain to any of the other moral values deemed intrinsically worthwhile. If there were such gains, there would be to that extent for such cases instrumental reason to bring it about that rights are secured. But the instrumental value of rights protection is not what is at issue. If rights are intrinsically morally significant, then securing rights must have moral value even if no other moral value is advanced. Contemplating these situations in which bare rights gains unaccompanied by any other benefits are secured, I find the protection of rights in these situations to be a blankly formal and barren enterprise. I have no argument that this is so, but I suspect that rights tend to enter our thought as a freight locomotive bearing many cars laden with important moral goods. We care about whether or not the freight train arrives, but we should care about the arrival of the locomotive only if it pulls cargo.

Consider an example. Suppose that we can perfectly protect and secure people's rights to freedom of speech, at some cost to other values. However, it turns out that no one ever exercises her free speech rights, so that the values of informed public deliberation are not achieved to any greater extent than they would have been had free speech rights not been secured. Nor does the protection of free speech rights deliver any other values beyond itself. Since the maintenance of these rights ex hypothesi is not morally costless, in this imagined scenario the pluralist consequentialist holds, and holds reasonably, that we should forego protecting free speech rights. Being a liberal democrat, I believe that the imagined scenario is wildly counterfactual, and that protection of free speech rights tends directly and indirectly to promote the achievement of significant values. But to hold this position is to favor protection of such rights for instrumental reasons, not on the ground that they themselves are per se morally valuable.

Capabilities as Rights and as Consequentialist Goals

Posed abstractly, the issue whether rights as such are intrinsically valuable is hard to get a grip on, because possible individual moral rights are so heterogeneous. The best procedure might be to consider specific claimed values whose fundamental status would justify specific linked rights.

I propose to focus on Sen's suggestion on this issue.[22] Recall that he proposes that fundamental moral rights might be one and all rights to capabilities or to positive freedom. For Sen, if one has the capability to function in a certain way, then one can achieve this functioning if one chooses and sincerely tries to do so.

This suggestion resonates with the important view that protection of rights is above all protection of the individual rightholder's choice or discretion. Indeed, on one approach to the understanding of what it is to have a right, having a right is having a certain protected discretion or freedom, which amounts to a control on the freedom of others who have duties corresponding to the right.[23] Sen revives this idea by way of a claim about the substance or content of rights rather than a claim about the concept of a right.

Indeed, it may seem that in allowing an open-ended pluralistic consequentialism with plural values unspecified, which would allow that Senian capabilities are values of the first importance for an adequate consequentialist theory, I am merely splitting hairs rather than significantly differing from Sen's affirmation of a consequentialism of rights with rights to capabilities having pride of place in this system.[24]

I do not deny that for any system of moral goals that includes rights as fundamental goals, one could probably frame a system that is very similar in content, a close approximation to this rights inclusive system, by artful selection of values that will serve as goals, but that formally excludes rights. (One might deliberately select the values so that the practical effects of having rights are approximated as closely as possible.) Without trying to decide whether acceptance of capabilities to function in significant ways is tantamount to acceptance of rights in a consequentialist system, I shall resist the suggestion that capabilities or positive freedom should be included among an adequate consequentialism's list of fundamental moral goals.

This issue is delicate, because well-being does include aspects of freedom. Freely and willingly choosing to play the flute, for example, enhances one's well-being more than merely playing the flute (perhaps under coercion or duress). An important aspect of well-being is achieving agency goals, which we may define as goals that one advance a cause by one's own agency, the cause itself not being a part of one's well-being. I might have the goal to save the whales (not as an aspect of my well-being), but I might well have the desire that the whales be saved by my agency or that my choices and actions contribute significantly to the goal of saving the whales. The satisfaction of these latter agency desires, if reasonable, do contribute to my well-being. Having wide personal freedom is then in these and other ways important both as means and sometimes as partially constitutive of well-being.

But none of this goes so far as to admit that freedom itself or having capability is morally valuable except when it contributes to well-being or is partly constitutive of well-being. One should also notice cases in which one person's having freedom is morally valuable because its exercise contributes to the well-being not of the agent but of other people. If I exercise my freedom by smothering with my body a grenade about to explode in a crowded room, this does nothing for my well-being but a lot for the well-being of those who are saved from death by explosion.

The cases to consider to evaluate Sen's proposal that capability is morally valuable per se or that having one's right to capability protected is per se morally valuable are cases in which capability is not exercised in any way that enhances anyone's well-being or any other value beyond itself.

Think again of Sen's examples involving Ali and his capability to move about the city without bodily harm, which might be threatened either by violent assault or violent forces of nature. Suppose we know for certain that if the victim who is threatened with assault in Sen's example is not assaulted, he will immediately thereafter negligently choose a course of action that will result in damage to his capabilities identical to what the assault threatens, or will deliberately and wrong-headedly choose to impose damage to his capabilities identical to what the assault threatens. Or suppose we somehow know for certain that the capability sustained by having a healthy nonassaulted body will never be deployed by the person in any way that does him any good, advances his well-being in any way, and moreover will not be deployed to advance any other creature's well-being either. In these examples where the instrumental value of capabilities for well-being disappears, I lose the intuition that bringing it about that the right to capability is fulfilled is morally valuable.

Is it not disrespectful to a person to deny her a capability to which she has a right on the ground that others know for certain she will not exercise it to any useful purpose? This question may point to considerations that a view that regards capability and rights to capability as only instrumentally valuable can readily acknowledge. Perhaps Smith gains utility from being treated in a way she regards as suited to competent moral agents, or perhaps having one's rights respected when one will not exercise them well today may bring it about that one will buck up and be better capable of effective prudent and moral action in the future. These gains an instrumental view of rights will register. What is being denied is just that respecting and protecting rights is per se valuable even when it does no good.

Can Some Utility (or Other Value) Only Be Attained as a By-product of Protecting and Respecting Moral Rights?

The arguments advanced to this point do not rule out all possible arguments for inclusion of rights in fundamental moral principles.

Here is one argument. It might be the case that not being morally required to act so as to advance one's own or anyone else's utility to the maximal possible extent is itself a significant source of utility. Suppose rights to significant capabilities are understood as leaving one morally at liberty to exercise the capabilities or not, and that being morally at liberty in this way is itself a source of utility.

Here it is conjectured that establishing rights at the fundamental level is supposed to generate utility that would otherwise be unobtainable. The same point would apply if some other nonutility value could be secured only by establishing rights at the level of fundamental moral principle. Arguing that the consequentialist can recognize rights, Philip Pettit proposes that a person has dignity only if she has rights that ought morally to be upheld even if in particular cases bringing about nonfulfillment of the rights would produce better consequences overall than bringing about fulfillment.[25] If dignity itself has considerable moral value, then there is a moral gain that comes about not as a result of actions that people might or might not take but by virtue of the very existence of genuine, fundamental moral rights.

On this way of thinking, it is not that accepting moral rights as fundamental is itself an action that generates good consequences. Moral rights, we are supposed to think, do exist, and correct fundamental moral principles must incorporate moral rights. But we see that value that would not otherwise exist accompanies the existence of moral rights. Recognizing this value, we then see the point at which the constraints that moral rights establish should give way to the consideration that ideal consequences will be brought about in particular cases by bringing about or allowing their nonfulfillment. This is the point at which the dignity value that necessarily accompanies rights is outweighed by the better consequences that acting in disregard of rights could bring about. In principle, if dignity lexically outweighs all other values that might be arayed against it, this form of argument could establish absolute rights that may never legitimately be violated for any reason. If dignity has great but not overriding value, then we end up with a moral system in which fundamental moral rights exist but should be respected only up to a threshold of consequentialist value that disrespecting them could produce.

My response to this entire line of argument is that the possibilities envisaged are logical possibilities but we have no reason to think they actually obtain.[26] Supposing for the sake of the argument that there is a dignity value that the existence of fundamental moral rights brings into existence, one notes that if there are no fundamental moral rights and agents may always and should always act to bring about best consequences, one can just as well say that another sort of dignity accrues to the individuals who stand to benefit from the value-maximizing consequentialist acts (that is to say, all of us from an ex ante perspective). Pending further argument, the value that is thought to spring into being from the fact that one or another fundamental moral principle is correct can be invoked by the advocate of rights and the act consequentialist who denies such rights.[27] These ethereal dignity values offset each other so should not be thought to support one side or the other in argument about what does or does not belong in fundamental moral principles.

In the argument above I presented a bowdlerized version of Pettit's argument. I did so because I think this version of the argument is worth considering and needs to be cleanly distinguished from what I believe Pettit actually wants to assert. Pettit takes the view that with fundamental moral rights in place, people can and should take actions that will bring about a value that could not have been obtained if rights had not been in place. It is not that the very existence of rights somehow infuses the world with value, but that without fundamental rights, moral value cannot be maximized even if all agents always do what is best by act-consequentialist standards. One might say that moral rights facilitate the production of maximal consequentialist value.

By establishing and securing a system of fundamental moral rights, people thereby secure dignity for all. This dignity could not be secured for people if there were no fundamental moral rights. One has dignity only if one has the practical assurance that one's moral rights will actually be upheld and the theoretical assurance that one has rights, and no one legitimately may countenance nonfulfillment of one's rights even to bring about best consequences (up to a threshold at which the dignity value can be outweighed by consequentialist considerations).[28]

These claims about dignity and how it might be obtained strike me as having a gerrymandered, perhaps question-begging quality. Why think there is a special dignity that only recognition of rights at the fundamental level can provide? Recall that the act-consequentialist position I espouse happily concedes that moral rights may be efficient instruments for producing moral value and that at a derivative level, moral rights as instruments may well be established. These merely derivative and instrumental rights will not be genuine and hence will not be engines that promote dignity, it is claimed. The essential point is that if I have a merely derivative and instrumental right to X, my having this right is compatible with its being the case that I myself ought morally not act to secure X for myself and that other people who might act to fulfill my right to X ought morally not do so. This ever present possibility is thought to smother dignity.

Perhaps one acquires a special dignity by knowing that moral principles treat all people on a par and that whatever entitlements and duties and privileges are established for any humans by fundamental moral principles are established for all including oneself. But this formal notion of dignity can be secured no matter what the content of these universal principles that at the fundamental level treat all persons equally in some way. Why must the dignity-conferring fundamental principles entrench moral rights at the fundamental level? We are simply begging the question if we merely stipulate that the dignity one has in mind is the special dignity that only accrues to people if a system of fundamental rights is in place, recognized and established.

What holds true of dignity holds true of self-worth and other values that tend to be asserted in this context as essentially linked to fundamental moral rights. Understood straightforwardly, one has a sense of self-worth if one believes oneself to be a worthy being. Any of a wide range of universal moral principles including varieties of consequentialism imply that each human being has equal worth. Every one to count for one, nobody for more than one, as Bentham asserts. A caste principle that says that some people are essentially more worthy and have greater dignity than others might reasonably be thought likely to undermine the beliefs of the subordinate others in their dignity and worth, but we are not speaking here of such hierarchical fundamental principles. One can stipulate that real self-worth can be had only when one's self-worth is supported by society's recognition of fundamental moral rights, but such stipulation can be countered by counter-stipulation and one can see the argument on this path will lead to deadlock.

In this connection Pettit makes an interesting analogy to special ties between parents and children and among friends. A child gains an important sense of security by confidently believing that her parents will favor her and give special priority to her interests in their decisions about what to do. Loving their child, parents will favor their child and will not be motivated to behave in an impartial act-consequentialist fashion, which would mean favoring their child when and only when doing so produces best consequences overall. The acceptance of act-consequentialist morality by parents is incompatible with securing an important value, the children's confidence that parents will be especially solicitous of their welfare.

The claim then is that similar considerations hold true when it comes to moral rights. Those who are the intended beneficiaries of moral rights gain a confident sense of security and thereby a kind of assurance of worth and dignity that they could not obtain in a world in which moral rights were not morally fundamental and accepted as such.

But there is something peculiarly moralized about the assurance the child, the friend, and the right-holder are said not to be able to get if act consequentialism is the accepted morality and moral rights are not entrenched in fundamental moral principles and firmly established in practice. As a child, what I want to be assured of is that my parents love me and will be especially solicitous of my welfare. The world being as it is, this is an important good to the child, and those who lack it tend to be bereft. But it is no part of the assurance I need that my parents will favor me specially *and will be morally right in doing so.* The italicized phrase is neither here nor there. The same goes with friendship. Genuine friends give special extra consideration to the interests of their friends in their deliberations about what to do. Seeming friends who do not tailor their practical deliberation in this way are not genuine friends, and genuine friendship relations are a good. But for the existence of genuine friendship so characterized it is not plausibly required in addition that the friend give special weight to her friend in her deliberations *and be morally right to do so.*

Perhaps the argument is that if act consequentialism were accepted as the sole morally fundamental principle and if all perfectly conformed to it, best consequences would not be obtained, because the interests of those who gain from special ties and moral rights would not be fulfilled to as great an extent as would be possible in a world in which special ties and moral rights enter morality at the fundamental level and people conform their conduct to what fundamental moral principles require.

This might be so, but so far I do not see more than the invocation of logical possibility. If special ties and moral rights tend in practice to generate lots of moral value, then an adequate act consequentialism would provide free space for special ties and rights in derivative principles. Let us suppose that genuine parent-child relations, genuine friendship, and real moral rights would not exist in the perfect act-consequentialist world (this must be so if we have defined these special ties so that the genuine variety cannot exist if agents accept act consequentialist morality). But presumably ersatz parent-child relations, ersatz friendship, and a derivative facsimile of moral rights would have a significant place in human life in the perfect act-consequentialist society. These substitute versions of special ties and rights would be designed so as to achieve, so far as possible and desirable, the values generated by true special ties and moral rights but in ways that are consistent with act consequentialism. It is an empirical question whether act consequentialism if all were perfectly to conform to it would still be self-defeating in the way that the argument supposes, despite all mitigating and substituting of near-equivalents that a rational implementation of this moral doctrine would involve. Again, I do not see that the arguments do anything to advance the claim that the answer to this empirical question is negative beyond the bare invocation of logical possibilities. These should not faze the act-consequentialist advocate.

Can There Be Derivative Moral Rights?

Throughout this essay I have repeatedly allowed myself the assumption that moral rights, excluded from appearance in moral principles at the fundamental level, might yet appear in moral principles at a nonfundamental, derivative level. This assumption might well be subject to challenge. At any rate the assumption requires clarification and defense.

The fundamental moral principles as I see them state what is intrinsically morally valuable and what agents morally ought to do. That is, the fundamental principles include principles that determine the moral value of states of affairs that actions might produce. The principles include a statement of act consequentialism, that among the available alternatives on each occasion of choice, each person morally ought always to do an act the consequences of which would be no worse than those of any other act she could do. Finally, the principles state that institutions, social practices, rules, laws, constitutions, character traits and dispositions, and so on are to be assessed according to their tendency to produce consequences no worse than those of any alternatives.

Nonfundamental principles are instruments for bringing about the greater fulfillment of the fundamental moral principles, or in other words the greater achievement of the intrinsic moral values.

The considerations here are familiar from discussions of act utilitarianism. Humans tend to be not well informed, not very able at integrating such relevant information as they have into their deliberation about what they ought to do, and selfish rather than wholeheartedly dedicated to discovering and doing whatever they morally ought to do. Hence it may well better promote consequentialist values if people most of the time do not directly deliberate about what would produce best consequences but instead follow clear and relatively simple moral rules. Some of these rules should perhaps establish moral rights that leave specific forms of discretion to individuals and place others under duties to respect these rights or bring about their fulfillment. People are obligated to follow these rules and to conform to the duties implied by rights. If one is obligated to do X, one should be punished in some way, by law, public opinion or peer pressure, or pangs of conscience, if one fails to do what one is obligated to do. Socialization and social practices that sustain obligations through punishment maintain this network. In a decent society, the rules established are such that in the actual circumstances their maintenance efficiently promotes the moral values, and then the obligations people are trained to experience are morally genuine. When society's rules are not well directed toward the achievement of the moral values, people will feel obligated but are not genuinely obligated.

The objection is that if act consequentialism is asserted at the fundamental level, genuine moral rights cannot be established, because they would be incompatible with act consequentialism. David Lyons has pressed this objection.[29] If Mary has a moral right to go to the movies or stay home, then (a) she is morally at liberty to do either, and it is not the case that she morally must do one or the other, and (b) other agents are under a duty to let her do either, and it is not the case that anyone morally must bring it about that Mary does one or the other. But act consequentialism holds that if one of Mary's two choices would produce better consequences, then she morally must do that act, and if bringing it about that Mary's doing one of these two acts would produce best consequences, then the agent who can act in this way morally must do so. What must be true of Mary and other agents if Mary has a moral right cannot be true of Mary and other agents if act consequentialism is correct. The point generalizes, so acceptance of moral rights and acceptance of act consequentialism are incompatible.

The question then is whether the existence of moral rights, established as means to producing best consequences, is compatible with its being the case that each person always morally ought to do whatever in her circumstances would produce best consequences. My claim is that the existence of moral rights is linked to moral obligation, which can come apart from what one morally ought to do. If one has a moral right to X, there should be a social practice that secures one X, and people should be socialized and educated so that they are obligated to bring it about that one has X and experience punishment if they fail to carry out their obligation in this regard. What one morally ought to do according to act-consequentialism is not necessarily connected with sanctions and punishment for noncompliance. In the example, Mary is not obligated either to go to the movies or stay home and in this sense she is at liberty to do either, despite the fact that if one of these acts would produce better consequences she morally ought not to do the other. If you like, you can say that in a strong sense, one cannot have a moral right if others morally ought to deny one what one has a right to in order to secure small gains in good consequences, but in a weak sense, one can, as just explained. If weak rights are good enough instruments for promoting good consequences, the incompatibility of act consequentialism and strong rights is not problematic.

Applying this line of thought to Sen's counterexample, we get this result. If there is a derivative moral right not to be bashed, then Donna morally ought to act to bring about the bashing even though she is obligated not to do so and she therefore should not be blamed or feel guilty for not doing what she ought and perhaps should be punished for doing what she ought.

Weak, Instrumental Moral Rights as Side Constraints and as Moral Goals

For all that has been asserted to this point, it could turn out that the weak moral rights that would be the best instruments for the advancement of good consequences might be rights construed as side constraints on eligible choices of action rather than goals to be promoted. I do not wish to argue for this point, just note the possibility.

Notice that this possibility provides angle of insight into Sen's argument that moral rights should be included in fundamental moral principles as goals to be promoted rather than as side constraints to be respected. I have argued against Sen that moral rights should not be included in fundamental principles (and also that the fundamental moral principles, consequentialist in structure, should not make room for positive freedom or capabilities to function as fundamental value). It might also turn out to be the case that moral rights should be included in nonfundamental principles that state means to the fundamental goals and that at this nonfundamental level the rights that will be instrumentally best will have the character, to some extent, of side constraints to be respected rather than of goals to be promoted.

Conclusion

This essay has followed a path with many twists and turns. Its conclusion can be simply stated. I argue that moral rights should not be included at the level of fundamental moral principles. I concentrate on what can be said for and against the inclusion of rights in a consequentialist moral system. I reject the rights-inclusive positions defended by Sen and Pettit. I argue that capabilities to function in significant ways (positive freedom) as espoused by Sen should not be included among the fundamental goals of a consequentialist morality and I suggest—but only suggest—that a spare set of goals integrating weighted utility and the desirability of rewarding the virtuous and responsible individuals yields a morally adequate version of act consequentialism.

NOTES

1. See Dworkin (1977), the title essay.
2. Of course a consequentialist position might include protection of moral rights among the fundamental goals to be promoted. I argue against such a rights-inclusive consequentialism.
3. Mill (1957; originally published 1861), chapter 5.
4. Raz (1986), chapter 7. As Raz explicitly recognizes, this analysis must be qualified to allow for the evident fact that many rights such as the right of free speech serve the interests of people other than the right-holder and that the proper shape of such rights depends on a balancing of the interests of the right-holder and the interests of others who will tend to benefit if the right is upheld.
5. Dworkin (1977), p. 192.
6. Robert Nozick argues that rights are properly regarded as side constraints and hence that it is anomalous to suppose that rights can figure as "utilitarianism of rights" in Nozick (1974), chapter 3.
7. In Rawls (1971), chapter 1.

8. Raz (1986), chapter 6.
9. Sen (1982).
10. Sen (1979), (1982), and (1985).
11. Sen (1982).
12. On prioritarianism, see the text below.
13. Adams (1999), p. 93.
14. Arneson (1999a)
15. If value A has lexical priority over value B, one should not accept any loss in the maximal amount of A one can get, or the maximal extent to which A is fulfilled, no matter how tiny the loss, in exchange for any gain of any size, however huge, in the amount of B that one gets or the degree that B is fulfilled.
16. See Parfit (1986), p. 160.
17. For doubts about these sufficientarian moral views, see Arneson (1999b), (2000), and (2002).
18. Nozick (1974), p. 155.
19. Prioritarianism is formulated and discussed in Weirich (1983), McKerlie (1994), and Parfit (1995).
20. See Kagan (1991). An excellent further exploration of this issue is in Lippert-Rasmussen (1996).
21. See especially Kamm (1992) and the references she cites in this essay. For Thomson's views, see her (1990).
22. In Sen (1982).
23. See Hart (1962) and (1973), Sumner (1987), Wellman (1985), and Lyons (1994), Introduction.
24. In fact Sen does not commit himself as to whether he favors consequentialism of rights (a consequentialism in which rights are included among the fundamental goals) or a broader system that is not entirely consequentialist (that does not evaluate states of affairs impartially, for example). The point on which he wishes to insist is that rights must be included as fundamental in one's fundamental moral system, whatever its exact structure.
25. See Pettit (1988). It should be noted that my first presentation of "Pettit's view" does not describe the view I think he actually asserts.
26. A difficulty emerges here. If utilitarianism is defeated by the fact that it yields unacceptable implications for merely possible cases, why is not the exclusion of rights from fundamental moral status likewise defeated by the fact that it generates bad consequences in possible cases? My reply is that the logical possibility of bad consequences if rights are excluded is offset by the logical possibility of bad consequences if rights are included, so these possibilities cancel. In possible worlds "close" to the actual world, exclusion of rights fares well. Moreover, one would need to explore the issue whether the fact that rights exclusion generates bad consequences in a logically possible world is a morally unacceptable implication of the position (aside from the consideration that the logical possibilities are counterbalanced). If reason should favor principle A for a certain range of logical possibilities and Principle B for another range, one wants to know the underlying principle that generates this result.

27. This point is made in Lippert-Rasmussen (1996).
28. Feinberg (1980) asserts that having rights "makes claiming possible, but it is claiming that gives rights their special moral significance." Having rights enables an individual "to feel in some fundamental way the equal of anyone" (p. 155). Establishing and protecting equal rights induce a certain equality of self-respect among persons. From an act-consequentialist perspective, this might be read as recommending that acts of establishing and sustaining a system of rights produce better consequences than any alternative acts available even though they bring it about that many people will not act to produce best consequences in many circumstances (they will stand on their rights instead). So construed, rights are being viewed as complex instruments to other goals, not goals pursued for their own sakes. But Feinberg also suggests that respect for human dignity be understood as respect for rights and that self-respect be understood as respect for one's rights. This move renders rights fundamental goals.
29. See Lyons (1980) and (1994).

REFERENCES

Adams, Robert. (1999) *Finite and Infinite Goods.* (Oxford: Oxford University Press).

Arneson, Richard. (1999a) "Human Flourishing versus Desire Satisfaction," *Social Philosophy and Policy*, 13, 113–142.

______. (1999b) "Egalitarianism and Responsibility," *Journal of Ethics*, 3, 225–247.

______. (2000) "Perfectionism and Politics," *Ethics*, 111.

______. (2002) "Why Justice Requires Transfers to Offset Income and Wealth Inequalities," *Social Philosophy and Policy*, 15.

Dworkin, Ronald. (1977) *Taking Rights Seriously.* (Cambridge, Massachusetts: Harvard University Press).

Feinberg, Joel. (1980) "The Nature and Value of Rights," in Feinberg, *Rights, Justice, and the Bounds of Liberty: Essays in Social Philosophy.* (Princeton: Princeton University Press).

Hart, H. L. A. (1962) "Bentham: Lecture on a Master Mind," *British Academy Proceedings*, 48, 297–320.

______. (1973) "Bentham on Legal Rights," in *Oxford Essays on Jurisprudence: Second Series*, ed. A. W. B. Simpson (Oxford: Oxford University Press) pp. 171–201.

Kagan, Shelly. (1991) "Responses to My Critics," *Philosophy and Phenomenological Research*, 51, 919–928.

Kamm, Frances. (1992) "Non-consequentialism, the Person as an End-in-Itself, and the Significance of Status," *Philosophy and Public Affairs*, 21, 354–389.

Lippert-Rasmussen, Kasper. (1996) "Moral Status and the Impermissibility of Minimizing Violations," *Philosophy and Public Affairs*, 25, 333–351.

Lyons, David. (1980) "Utility as a Possible Ground of Rights," *Noûs*, 14, 17–28.

______. (1994) *Rights, Welfare, and Mill's Moral Theory.* (Oxford: Oxford University Press).

McKerlie, Dennis. (1994) "Equality and Priority," *Utilitas*, 6, 25–42.
Mill, J. S. (1969) *Utilitarianism*, in Mill, *Collected Works* 10, J. M. Robson, ed. (Toronto: University of Toronto Press (originally published 1861)).
Nozick, Robert. (1974) *Anarchy, State, and Utopia.* (New York: Basic Books).
Parfit, Derek. (1986) "Overpopulation and the Quality of Life," in Singer, Peter, ed., *Applied Ethics.* (Oxford: Oxford University Press). Pp. 145–164.
———. (1995) *Equality or Priority?* The Lindley Lecture. (Lawrence, Kansas: Department of Philosophy, University of Kansas).
Pettit, Philip. (1988) "The Consequentialist Can Recognise Rights," *Philosophical Quarterly*, 38, 42–55.
Rawls, John. (1971) *A Theory of Justice.* (Cambridge, Massachusetts: Harvard University Press).
Raz, Joseph. (1986) *The Morality of Freedom.* (Oxford: Oxford University Press).
Sen, Amartya. (1979) "Utilitarianism and Welfarism," *The Journal of Philosophy*, 76.
———. (1982) "Rights and Agency," *Philosophy and Public Affairs*, 11, 3–39.
———. (1982) "On Weights and Measures: Informational Constraints in Social Welfare Analysis," reprinted in Sen, *Choice, Welfare and Measurement.* (Cambridge, Massachusetts: MIT Press). Pp. 226–262.
———. (1985) "Well-being, Agency and Freedom," *The Journal of Philosophy*, 82, 169–221.
Sumner, L. W. (1987) *The Moral Foundations of Rights.* (Oxford: Oxford University Press).
Thomson, Judith. (1990) *The Realm of Rights.* (Cambridge, Massachusetts: Harvard University Press).
Weirich, Paul. (1983) "Utility Tempered with Equality," *Noûs*, 17, 423–439.
Wellman, Carl. (1985) *A Theory of Rights: Persons under Laws, Institutions and Morals.* (Totowa, New Jersey: Rowman and Allenheld).

PHILOSOPHICAL ISSUES, 11
Social, Political, and Legal Philosophy, 2001

Managing Scarcity: Toward a More Political Theory of Justice

Robert E. Goodin

Not just politics but all purposive human action involves the art of the possible. It is pragmatically pointless to pursue outcomes that are impossible—ones which will not occur, whatever we do. Pragmatically, it is equally pointless to expend efforts on outcomes that are inevitable—ones which will occur, whatever we do. Deliberation, intention and purposive action ought rationally focus on what lies in between. So sayeth Thomas Hobbes (1651, ch. 6).

The same is true at the collective level as well as the individual. Pragmatically, we ought concentrate our collective efforts on projects whose success is possible but not certain. That is one way, anyway, of understanding Hume's "circumstances of justice" (1739, bk. 3, pt. 2, sec. 2; 1777, sec. 3, pt. 1). Those can be read as delineating conditions under which the pursuit of justice would be neither superfluous, on the one hand, nor infeasible, on the other.

Consider the particular condition upon which I shall here be focusing, "moderate scarcity." In classing that among the "circumstances of justice," Hume reasons as follows. In a world of superabundance, everyone could have as much as they could possibly use without cost to anyone else: there, norms of justice would be unnecessary.[1] In a world of super-scarcity, abiding by the norms of justice would lead a person to starve: there, no one could reasonably be held to those rules.[2] The pursuit of justice makes pragmatic sense only in between those extremes, within the realm of "moderate scarcity." So sayeth David Hume, and many others (conspicuously among them Hart [1961, pp. 189–95] and Rawls [1971, § 22]) following him in this respect (cf. Barry 1989, pp. 152–63).

Most theories of justice strive for first-order principles and precepts of what, exactly, justice requires. Here I shall attempt to see how much by way of substantive conclusions we can get out of second-order enquiries alone—enquiries not into what justice requires, but what is required by way of background preconditions for any attempt to put social relations on a just footing at all.

I. Fixing the Meaning of "Moderate Scarcity"

There are different readings of what "moderate scarcity" might mean, with correspondingly many different implications for the appropriate social mechanisms for managing it. Here I canvas briefly three different interpretive options, and then (in the next section) discuss what that preferred interpretation implies for our choice among distributional mechanisms.

A. Individuals' Circumstances

On its face, Hume's condition of "moderate scarcity" refers simply to how much people have. But the reference cannot be to the holdings of people, taken individually. That would lead to obviously absurd results. Suppose, for example, that five percent of the population were in a situation of superabundance and the other ninety-five percent were starving. That would mean that no one among them, taken individually, would be in a condition of "moderate scarcity." But it would be absurd to say in such circumstances that the "circumstances of justice" do not obtain.[3] Among those people, discussions of the relative merits of alternative distributions are anything but pragmatically pointless.

B. Group Aggregates or Averages

Neither can "moderate scarcity" refer simply to aggregates or averages across society as a whole. There can be, and often are, pockets of poverty in societies that are rich overall. It is perfectly possible for goods to be superabundant, in the sense that if resources were averaged among everyone in society then everyone would have more than they could possibly use—and yet for those goods actually to be concentrated in the hands of a very few individuals. Think of all those real-world examples of Hume's "golden age," where resources were plentiful and needs simple, but rulers were more avaricious than nature was bountiful.

Conversely, there can be, and as often are, pockets of rich people in societies that are poor. It is perfectly possible that, averaged across everyone in society, resources would be below subsistence levels—and yet for those resources actually to be concentrated in the hands of a very few people. Again, there are plenty of countries where elites are very rich but people in general very poor, and would remain so even if all the elites' riches were redistributed (think, even today, of places like Duvalier's Haiti or Bokassa's Central African Republic).

C. Possible Distributions

Thus, "moderate scarcity" cannot plausibly refer either to the situation of individuals, taken one-by-one, or to the situation of societies, on aggregate or average. Instead, we ought understand the term to be referring to the *distributive possibilities* associated with any given stock of resources.

As a first approximation, we might suppose:

1) The circumstances of justice obtain if and only if:
   (a) it is possible to distribute a stock of resources in such a way that everyone's basic needs are met; and
   (b) it is not possible to distribute that society's stock of resources in such a way that all of everyone's desires are completely satiated.

That is not quite right, however. Reconsider clause (b). That suggests that we are beyond the bounds of justice wherever it is possible, somehow or another, to distribute social resources in such a way that all of everyone's desires are satiated. Were that distribution actually to be put into effect, then of course *at that point* considerations of justice would indeed be rendered irrelevant, for precisely the reasons Hume has given. But what is decisive in quietening Hume's "jealous virtue" of justice is the actuality, not the mere possibility, of resources being distributed in that way.

It may well be true that wherever that possibility exists it will be easily actualized. I shall say more about that below. For now, though, let us merely note that we are not outside the circumstances of justice until everyone is actually satiated.[4] Where everyone could be satiated, but is not, issues of justice can still arise.

In light of those reflections, it might seem better to rephrase the proposition along the following lines:

2) The circumstances of justice obtain if and only if:
  (a) it is possible to distribute a stock of resources in such a way that everyone's basic needs are met; and
  (b) the existing distribution of that society's stock of resources is not such that all of everyone's desires are completely satiated.

But that is still not quite right. If circumstances of justice, politically understood, obtain wherever distributions are pragmatically worth arguing about—and if we are supposed to understand this in counterfactual, possible-world terms—then even if the actual distribution is one in which everyone's desires are fully satiated, there might be alternative possible distributions in which they would not be. Blocking those possibilities from becoming actualities is then something that is, indeed, pragmatically worth arguing about, for anyone whose continuing satiation is potentially at risk.[5]

Again, in the circumstances here in view, that might (or might not) be an easy argument for those people to win. The reason to think it might be easy is this: where everyone is satiated under the present distribution, no one would have any motive to press for any other distribution. The reason to think it might not be easy is that the present situation might be unstable and unsustainable indefinitely; then there may well be some real scope for arguing over what distribution will replace it, wherever not everyone would be satiated under every alternative possible distribution. Be all that as it may, the larger point is simply that the litmus test for situations falling within the scope of the "circumstances of justice" is whether there would be any pragmatic point in arguing, not whether the argument would be hard or easy.

In light of those further reflections, our proposition ought finally be rephrased as follows:

3) The circumstances of justice obtain if and only if:
  (a) it is possible to distribute a stock of resources in such a way that everyone's basic needs are met; and

(b) it is not certain that society's stock of resources will be distributed in such a way that all of everyone's desires are completely satiated.

II. Possibilities and Mechanisms

The upshot of all that is that the "circumstances of justice" ought to be possibilistically understood. That simple fact has further consequences of a potentially surprising sort.

Focus particularly on the further fact, brought into sharp focus by that first finding, that what distributional outcomes are possible is in turn a joint function of two things. One is the size of the resource stock. The other is the capacities of the alternative available mechanisms for effecting those distributions.

Here I shall explore the possibilities contained within the two most standard distributional mechanisms—voluntary exchange in free economic markets, compared with socially-dictated allocations which are politically determined and imposed.

To foreshadow, my argument will be that the "natural processes" of the free market falter, confronted with the spectre of either superabundance or scarcity, in a way that the "natural processes" of politics do not. Evaluating those differential capacities, it turns out that the range of distributional possibilities under non-market processes is actually superior to the range of distributional possibilities under market ones.

A. Desiderata

First consider what ought be regarded as a "superior range of distributional possibilities," for these purposes. How ought we grade institution-based expansions and contractions of the set of alternative possible distributions, and expansions and contractions of the "circumstances of justice" that following from that?

We do not simply want to maximize our options, maximizing the set of distributions that are possible. It is tempting to think that, if justice is a virtue, then it is better that its writ run as widely as possible. Remember, though, that on the Humean account here in view its writ is bounded on two sides.

On the one side, it does indeed seem desirable to let the writ of justice reach as far as possible into the realm of scarcity.[6] The fewer exemptions there are from claims of justice the better, in that direction.

But the same is not true in the opposite direction. Surely it is better to expand the realm of superabundance as far as possible, even at the cost of rendering considerations of justice irrelevant.[7]

Our desiderata for distributional mechanisms, therefore, ought be twofold. First, we ought prefer mechanisms which expand the encroachment of justice into the realms of scarcity. That is to say, we ought prefer mechanisms which, by creating more possibilities for keeping everyone above subsistence, thereby prevent excuses of super-scarcity from cancelling considerations of justice altogether.

Second, we ought prefer distributional mechanisms which expand the scope of superabundance. That is to say, we ought prefer mechanisms that make it possible for all of everyone's desires to be satisfied to ones that do not. The fact that justice is thereby rendered irrelevant is, in those circumstances, something positively to be desired.[8]

In principle, those are two independent desiderata which might pull in different directions. In practice, as I shall go on to show, they line up nicely when comparing market versus political distributional mechanisms. Market procedures are prevented, by their own internal logic, from meeting either desideratum. Political procedures are permitted by their own logic to meet both. And what is possible in principle here will plausibly prove true in practice as well.

B. The Incapacities of Markets

The possibilistic construal of scarcity in Sec. I.C effectively echoes key features of the conventional economic account. For economists, to say that a good is "scarce" is invariably to say that it is "scarce *relative* to desires." By that they mean to say that there is no possible (re)distribution of goods such that that stock of goods can satisfy all desires for it.

The particular mechanism of (re)distribution that economists have in mind, here, is of course free market exchange. They construe the operational test of whether that condition is met accordingly. For economists, all desires for a good are deemed to have been satisfied—and hence that good deemed not to be scarce—whenever there is no (positive) price at which anyone would want to acquire any more of that good.

I shall elaborate the inadequacies of this market-based analysis shortly. But first let me put onto the table the equivalent economistic analysis of the second strand of Hume's "moderate scarcity." The standard analysis, sketched above, effectively captures what Hume means by calling goods "scarce" as opposed to "superabundant." Now, let us adapt that to capture what he means by goods being only "moderately scarce" rather than "super-scarce." For those purposes, we need to distinguish two different classes of desires: desires to have our basic needs satisfied; and all other desires.

Goods might then be said to be super-scarce when there is no possible redistribution of them such that everyone's basic needs would be met. To say that "goods are not super-scarce"—the second half of Hume's definition of "moderate scarcity"—is then equivalent to saying "goods are abundant relative to desires for basic-need satisfaction."

Once again, economists think of these matters primarily in connection with markets. Hence, they would operationalize this condition, broadly as before, by saying that "goods are not super-scarce" if and only if there is no (positive) price at which anyone would buy more goods for purposes of satisfying their basic needs.

That latter operationalization is problematic in various peculiar ways.[9] But let us set those peculiarities aside, concentrating instead on deeper problems which plague market-style approaches to superabundance and super-scarcity most generally.

Suppose some people are super-satiated (having enough goods to satiate all their desires, and then some) while other people are not satiated at all. How, exactly, is a free market supposed to work to effect the transfer of those superfluous goods from those who are super-satiated to those who are not satiated? What exactly are the non-satiated supposed to offer to the satiated, in order to induce them to part with some of their goods?

To be sure, the super-satiated have no particular interest in holding onto those goods. *Ex hypothesi*, the goods in question are superfluous, utterly of no use to them; they would not in the least mind losing them. But being already (super-)satiated, there is nothing else they want, either. So there is nothing that the non-satiated might offer them that could constitute a positive inducement of any sort for them to make the exchange. In short, there is no obvious way by which voluntary exchange in free markets can effect transfers from the super-satiated to the non-satiated.

(Economists like to model free markets in terms of equilibria. The most appropriate mathematical model for a society such as I have just been describing is not as an equilibriating system but, rather, a sink-hole or—if you prefer, a black hole. Goods pass into the hands of the super-satiated, never to reemerge onto the market.)

The converse occurs in the case of super-scarcity. Or at least it seems likely to do, on the standard assumptions of microeconomics. There, we are supposed to assume that the same resources which might be used to satisfy one person's basic needs could also be used to satisfy some of another person's non-basic desires. Hence, in ordinary economic markets, everyone who wants the good for whatever reason would be bidding against one another. Microeconomics also standardly asks us to assume that all resources are fungible for one another. Hence, anyone who is rich in some resources and poor in others can always trade away an excess in some dimensions to make up a shortfall in others. And anyone who is poor overall is in that state, on this analysis, because she has not enough of *anything* to trade.

But how, then, is someone with "too few" resources overall to meet her basic needs supposed to acquire "enough" resources, through ordinary market processes? Someone whose overall resources are inadequate to satisfy her basic needs cannot offer any of those resources in exchange for something to satisfy her need for X, without further compromising her capacity to satisfy her needs Y, Z and so on.[10]

In a bidding game on the open market, people in a situation of super-scarcity can never trade their way out of that situation. It is only too true (per the economistic operationalization of superscarcity) that there is no positive price they would pay for needed resources. But note well that the reason is simply this: any price they would pay would impoverish them in some other dimension.

Of course, they would pay more if they had more (money, or anything else with which to trade).[11] But that is just to say: they would not be impoverished if they were not impoverished. The point remains that they cannot trade their way out of poverty, because (by definition and the standard microeconomic assumptions set out above) poverty leaves them with no (discretionary, non-needed) resources with which to trade. Free markets offer no institutional mechanism by which poor people might escape their poverty.

In short, free markets fail both the desiderata set out above (Sec. II.A). Even where it looks as if overall social resources are objectively superabundant, free market exchange offers no mechanism by which people who are not yet satiated might induce people who are super-satiated to part with any of their superfluous goods. Free market exchange offers no way of expanding the range of superabundance. And even where it looks as if overall social resources are objectively adequate to overcome super-scarcity, free market exchange offers no mechanism by which people who have less than they need can acquire all they need from people who have more than they need. Free market exchange offers no way of reducing the range of super-scarcity.

C. The Potentialities of Politics

Requisitioning and rationing are standard political solutions to precisely those problems. Where some people have more than they can possibly use to meet all their hearts' desires, state officials can simply requisition some of the superfluous goods of the super-satiated and transfer them to people who are not yet satiated. Where some people have less than they need to meet their basic needs, once again state officials can simply ration resources in such a way as to ensure that no one has more than they need until everyone has all that they need (Pigou 1921, chs. 7 and 12).

Those policies are logically possible, anyway. (Indeed, they are more than mere logical possibilities: they have actually been implemented, from time to time, particularly in wartime.) It is another question, perhaps, whether or not they are politically likely to be common occurrences.[12]

I shall offer a few preliminary remarks designed to dispel such doubts shortly. But first let me say that, in one important respect, all that is merely by-the-way. Whether or not it is probable that political institutions will respond in these ways, it is at least possible that they will do so—in a way, note, that it is not possible that free market exchange will do so. It is not merely empirically unlikely but genuinely impossible, within the internal logic of systems of free market exchange, to see how these desired outcomes to come about. However probable or improbable these outcomes might be politically, that is still better than their being impossible altogether, economically.

That having been said, let me go on to show that the desired outcomes here in view are both possible and plausible, politically. Take first the case of extending the range of superabundance. Surely redistributing superfluous goods from people who are super-satiated to those who are not yet satiated should be politically straightforward. There is an obvious coalition in support of that act, consisting of everyone who is not yet satiated and who hence actually wants the goods. There is no obvious coalition against it.

The super-satiated are not going to go to any trouble to retain resources for which they have no use.[13] Thus, at least at the level of first-order political concerns, there should be no difficulty effecting the redistribution.[14]

(Note that Hume himself needs to assume some such dynamic, in leaping from the supposition that resources are superabundant in a society overall to the supposition that resources would be superabundant for each person in that society, who would therefore not argue over the justice of the distribution of those resources. That conclusion goes through only on the assumption that superabundant resources which are superabundant overall will be distributed equally, at least in the sense of equally "satiating everyone's desires." The argument of the previous paragraph would deliver him that result.)

Take next the case of reducing the range of super-scarcity. There I do not have nearly so compelling an argument. Regrettably, redistributing goods from people who "merely desire" them to people who "genuinely need" them is not at all politically straightforward. Quite the contrary: if people's political resources are a positive function of their other resources (recall the aphorism "money talks in politics"), then there is every reason to worry that that outcome might well not occur, politically either.

Still, let us suppose—as is officially the case virtually everywhere, and as is in practice the case to some greater or lesser extent most places—that people's votes cannot be literally bought and sold. To the extent that they cannot, political resources are therefore not fungible for other resources. Furthermore, political resources (votes) are generally distributed more equally than income or wealth (and hence than the various other resources exchangeable for income and wealth). A consequence of that is that poor people generally have *more* resources for meeting their basic needs politically—by voting for redistributive schemes transferring resources from the non-needy to the needy—than they do economically.

Whether their political resources will prove sufficient to carry the day is, perhaps, another issue. But at least it is possible politically, in a way it is not economically. The poor have votes to mobilize, even where they lack sufficient marketable resources to trade their way out of poverty. Thus, again at least at the level of first-order political dynamics, effecting the redistribution of resources from non-needy to needy should be easier politically than economically.[15]

III. Where the Action Is, Politically[16]

So far, I have argued that the "circumstances of justice" ought be understood politically. That follows from: (1) my initial argument that the "circumstances of justice" ought be understood pragmatically, as directing our intentional interventions to areas where they might be both necessary and the goals in view possible; combined with (2) the argument that "moderate scarcity" ought be construed possibilistically; combined with (3) the argument that the suite of distributional possibilities accessible through mechanisms of politics is superior to that accessible through free economic markets.

If all that is correct, then justice becomes a matter of what we can do, politically. That is not to say that anything we do, politically, will necessarily be just, of course. It is just to say that political possibilities help serve to fix the boundaries of the "circumstances of justice," on this preferred interpretation of that term. What can be done politically is what we ought properly regard as matters of justice.

We know a fair bit about what can and cannot be done, politically, to distribute and redistribute resources among people. Politics has long been understood as a study in distributional struggle: "who gets what, when, how."[17] That is not all there is to it, of course.[18] But whatever its other concerns, politics is centrally concerned with questions of distributions, every bit as much as are economics and markets.[19]

Politically, some redistributions will be easy and others hard. The politics of the situation differs importantly across the wide range that is described by the "moderate scarcity" component of Hume's "circumstances of justice."[20] Distributional politics will be relatively muted toward the top end of that continuum; they will be relatively heated in the middle ranges. Our real interest, both morally and politically, should however center on the bottom end of that spectrum—on circumstances of what I shall call "real but manageable scarcity."

It is easy to see why distributional struggles will be muted under circumstances of relative abundance, where each person has *almost* as much as she can possibly use. Note that I say "almost," not "fully" (that would make it a case of superabundance, thus rendering considerations of justice irrelevant even on Hume's own account). But even if people are not quite fully satiated, diminishing marginal utility being what it is, it really does not make very *much* difference at all to anyone whether she or someone else gets the last little bit.

Other things being equal, anyone who is not yet satiated would still prefer to have more than less, to be sure. Still, assuming that the political maneuvering required to effect any redistribution would be both costly and risky, and assuming agents are at least moderately cost-conscious and risk-averse, no one is going to be willing to bear the costs and risks of pressing the issue, politically.

Broadly the same would be true in circumstances of overall relative abundance, even where that abundance is distributed unequally. Thanks once again to diminishing marginal utility, those with relatively large shares of those goods have relatively little interest in retaining their last marginal unit of them; those with relatively small shares have relatively great interest in securing another marginal unit for themselves. Thinking of politics simply as the vector sum of forces, the forces in favor of redistribution will largely dominate the outcome.[21] More to the present point, they will do so largely without a fight, where what they take from the super-rich are things that the super-rich do not much care about losing, anyway.

Politically, the real fights will come over the distribution of resource stocks of middle size. Suppose resources are limited, and even dividing them equally would leave everyone seriously wanting more.[22] Then there will indeed be a genuine political struggle over how much each is to get. That, arguably, represents the real world of politics—or anyway the part of the real world that is dominated by politics.[23] That, politically, is where the action is.

IV. Politics at Its Best

Here, though, I want to focus on another special class of cases, right at the bottom end of Hume's range of "moderate scarcity." I do so not because they represent the most common case: quite the contrary. I focus on them, instead, because they represent one of the most interesting cases. They show politics at its best. They point to ways in which politics can, in the direst of circumstances, rise to the occasion and institute solutions which both morally empower and materially protect everyone within their reach.

A. Defining "Real but Manageable Scarcity

Let us define cases of "real but manageable scarcity" as being ones in which everyone can meet their basic needs if—but only if—everyone receives their due share of a just distribution of resources.[24]

The "if" portion of that biconditional serves to ensure that we remain within the realm of Hume's "moderate scarcity." Abiding by a just distribution will not cause anyone to starve. It will not entail an unrealistically heroic sacrifice from anyone, in that sense.[25] The "only if" portion of my biconditional serves to fix our focus on the lower end of the "moderate scarcity" scale, where it truly is a matter of very great consequence to people how goods are distributed.

B. The Politics of Real but Manageable Scarcity

Under conditions of "real but manageable scarcity," by definition, everyone's basic needs will be met *only if* everyone receives their due share under a just distribution of resources. That is to say, some people's basic needs will go unmet *unless* the requirements of the just distribution is implemented.

That, in turn, means that people will be vitally concerned with the distribution of resources in their society. Not only do people do have a strong reason to demand a fair share for themselves. They also have powerful reasons for insisting that others receive *no more* than their fair share—for in the circumstances here in view, if anyone receives more than her fair share then someone (perhaps you) will starve in consequence.

Exactly how much of a motive that latter consideration provides for our demanding distributive justice all around—not just for ourselves, but for all others in our society as well—is trebly contingent. It depends upon what *proportion* of us would fail to have our basic needs met, if the just distribution were not implemented. It also depends upon how *uncertain* it is who, among us, will have their needs go unmet. And it also depends upon how *averse* each of us is to bearing risks of that magnitude.

In the limiting case, suppose we know with absolute certainty that, unless the precepts of justice are respected, no one's needs will be met (thanks, perhaps, to the mutually destructive wrangling that would then ensue). In that case, each of us would indeed have a compelling motive for insisting upon a just distribution all around. Thus, paradoxically, the severest distributional problem actually proves politically the easiest to solve: everyone agrees.

But there are various limiting cases at the other end, as well. Here is one example. Suppose everyone can have substantially more than their just allocation, at the cost of a single identified individual's basic needs going unmet. Then no one except for that single identified individual would have any motive for insisting upon the just distribution. Or, for another example, suppose that each of N people can have substantially more than their just allocation, at the cost of a single randomly-chosen individual's basic needs not being met. Where N is very large (so the risk to each of us of being that unlucky individual is low), and the extra benefits that all the rest of them can expect (with high probability[26]) is large, everyone might well be prepared *ex ante* to take the risk. In those sorts of cases, we are politically back in the distributional wrangling that characterizes fights over stocks of middle size.

In the broad range of intermediate cases of real but manageable scarcity—cases where there is some real risk to all that their basic needs will not be met, unless a just distribution is implemented—most people would probably be inclined to demand that that be done. After all, having your basic needs go unmet is a seriously bad (yea, lethal) outcome. We may all be mildly risk-loving when it comes to small losses (betting on the horses, for example); but we are generally very averse to very large losses (that is why we buy insurance, after all [Arrow 1970]). People who are looking for assurance in such circumstances will particularly value "bright lines" and "Chinese walls." Even if the injustices being proposed at the moment work against someone else, once you step over the line and begin tolerating injustice at all a dangerous precedent will have been set; and everyone would rightly be nervous that they might be the next victim whose basic needs are thus sacrificed. In short, in most cases of real but manageable scarcity people would probably all agree more-or-less easily that the just distribution ought be implemented, without much of a political fight.[27]

These are all empirical speculations, to be sure. But, empirically, they seem to reflect what reasonably prudent agents ought themselves be thinking, when contemplating departures from the rule of justice in a world of "real but manageable scarcity." Such thoughts ought ordinarily lead them to insist upon scrupulous respect for principles of justice, in such circumstances.

C. Happy Consequence 1: Moral Empowerment

Imposing just distributions in circumstances of real but manageable scarcity give rise to happy consequences, both morally and politically. Begin with morality. The rich have long known that, as a matter of pure prudence, alleviating the poverty of others is a good way to forestall threats to their own holdings. Roman emperors' "bread and circuses," Bismarck's *Sozialstaat* and Roosevelt's New Deal were all devices for defusing more radical political demands, in just that way (Piven and Cloward 1971).

Note, however, that the prudence involved here is moral as much as it is political, however. A well-worn moral maxim tells us "ought implies can." Among other things, that maxim excuses people from any duty to respect others' property rights, whenever seizing that property is the only way to meet their own basic needs.[28] When the well-off discharge their duties of charity, thereby ensuring that the basic needs of the poor are met, they are therefore removing not only a motive but also a moral excuse for the poor seizing their property (Waldron 1986).[29]

There are good reasons for describing the logic underlying that scheme as a matter of "moral prudence." Clearly it is a matter of prudence, being as it is a calculated means by which the rich can effectively secure their riches. But it is a matter of "moral" prudence in two further respects. First, the threat that it removes is a moral one, viz., a moral excuse afforded to those in dire need. Second, the means whereby this maneuver removes that threat is itself a moral one, viz., discharging the standing imperfect duty of charity.

All that is true, and important. Still, stopping there strikes me as unduly cynical. Here let me sketch another approach. This is one which represents the "effective management of scarcity"—developing and enforcing principles of justice, such that everyone has their basic needs satisfied—as a means whereby each of us can effectively discharge both our rights and our duties.

This approach begins from the view that people want to discharge their duties as well as to demand their rights. Far from seeking out and reveling in excuses not to do their moral duties, suppose (as I do) that people genuinely regret the need to violate other people's rights and to default on their own moral duties.[30]

Seen in that light, a system of effective management of scarcity is a public good for both the poor and the rich alike. The rich get what we always imagined: more secure protection of their property from threats which are both political and moral as well. The poor get what they have long wanted in ways that cynics never imagined: the opportunity to meet their needs without defaulting on their moral duties, thereby branding themselves inferior members of the moral community. That their moral delicts would be excused, in the circumstances, does not make them any the less moral deficiencies. Recourse to such morally desperate measures is something that any morally conscientious agent would obviously strive assiduously to avoid.

Let me illustrate these themes by reference to an old moral chestnut, the famous case of "two sailors and a plank." [31] To set the scene: two survivors from a shipwreck find themselves clinging to the same plank of wood, which is buoyant enough to support only one of them; there is no other plank in sight and no prospect of prompt rescue. Morally speaking, what follows?

Hobbes, for one, would treat it as a "war of all against all" in which case "every man has a right to every thing, even to another's body" (Hobbes 1651, ch 14). Surprisingly many other legal philosophers—among them Bacon and Blackstone, Grotius and Pufendorf[32]—agree. The right of self-preservation, they say, logically (or, anyway psychologically[33]) trumps our duty not to kill. And that is true, they say, not only where it is literally a matter of killing or being killed, but also where it is merely a matter of killing or meeting our own certain death.[34]

Many others, of course, would strongly deny that proposition. But let us suppose for the sake of argument that it is true. Let us suppose that each of the shipwrecked sailors does indeed have a genuine moral right to push the other off the plank.

The point remains that to say that "X has a right to ϕ" is *not* to say that "it is right for X to ϕ." Built into the notion of a right is a choice, an option, to ϕ or not-ϕ. To assign X a right to ϕ is to empower X to choose, in that respect (Hart 1983, p. 35; 1955). But where one of the options is "morally right" and the other is "morally wrong" (as is often, if not always, the case), then assigning someone the right to choose between those options is to give the rightholder the "right to do wrong" (Waldron 1981). That is one of the choices open to him; indeed, it is one of the choices that is constitutive of the right itself. Yet one of the options he is entirely within his rights to choose is, by some standard, "morally wrong."

Apply this insight back to the case of two sailors and the plank. *Ex hypothesi*, each has a right of self-preservation. By virtue of that, each has a right to push the other off the plank, thereby causing the other's certain death. But to say that each "has a right" to do so is not to say that "it is right" for each to do so. The right that each of them has, stated in full, is "the right to push *or to refrain from pushing* the other off the plank." On the assumption that deliberately causing another's certain death is morally wrong, the "push the other off the plank" fork of that choice ought simply be seen as the "right to do wrong" that lurks within many rights.[35]

On this analysis, the two sailors on the plank have *both* a right *and* a duty. They each have the right to push (or to refrain from pushing) the other off the plank. But they each also have the *duty* not to push the other off the plank. Such is the teaching of moralists, both ancient (Cicero 44BC/1991, III.22) and modern (Kant 1797/1965, App. ii, 235–6); such is the finding of the British High Court, in the infamous case of shipwrecked seafarers convicted of slaughtering and eating one of their number to survive.[36]

Of course, were the two sailors on the plank each to exercise their right in a morally dutiful way, each plunks for the "not pushing" option and both would drown. That is what happens in the story as originally told.

But let us now vary the story slightly. Suppose that each is a sufficiently strong swimmer that, by taking it in turns to rest on the plank, both might be able to keep themselves afloat long enough for rescuers to reach them. Then the case of "two sailors and a plank" turns into one of my instances of "real but manageable scarcity." Then there is indeed a just distribution of resources—taking turns on the plank—by which the basic needs of each can be met. Indeed, the basic needs of both can be met only through the implementation of that just distribution.[37]

The great virtue of that just distribution from the point of view of the two sailors on the plank is that it enables each of them *both* to enjoy their moral rights *and* to discharge their moral duties. Morally conscientious agents should be glad of *both* facts. Morally conscientious agents would welcome that as a consequence of the effective social management of scarcity in all situations of "real but manageable scarcity," more generally.

D. Happy Consequence 2: Political Protection

Rationing, as I have said, is the social practice that corresponds to what I have been developing as the moral theory of the effective social management of real but manageable scarcity.

As a brute political fact, rationing is invariably resented—even in the face of objective wartime shortages[38] and generally unaffordable medical procedures (Aaron and Schwartz 1984). Rationing is resented all the more strongly where the shortages are seen as artificially engineered, or where unaffordability is seen as more a matter of unwillingness than genuine inability to pay.

Local authorities in Britain, for example, now regularly ration social services. They refuse, on grounds of affordability, to supply disabled people with home help that they have been officially assessed as needing; and they refuse, on grounds of affordability, to provide sick children home with schooling that the law requires they receive.[39] British courts refuse to intervene, saying that how much governments want to tax and spend on social services are political decisions into which they will not intervene. Welfare rights activists are up in arms (Harlow 1997; Palmer 2000). They regard it as a travesty to say, as the courts are thus implicitly saying, that rights do not ground claims to the resources required to give meaning to those rights. By any sensible standard, they say, people's welfare rights must be seen as being abrogated by government refusal to fund the welfare services to which they are rightfully entitled.[40] Either governments should pay the price or else they should legislate to withdraw the charade of rights.[41]

That is not only a claim *of* justice—a first-order political demand based on some particular, substantive theory of justice. Reflecting once again upon the "circumstances of justice," it can also be seen as *about* justice—a second-order precondition for ordering our society according to precepts of justice at all. The policies here in view, notice, amount to denying people resources they require to meet their basic needs, in circumstances in which there is some way it would be possible to let them have those resources (without similarly depriving anyone else).

That amounts to an instance of the state's being faced with circumstances of "real but manageable scarcity," and refusing to manage it. Although it would be possible for the state to manage the situation in such a way as to keep us within the bounds of justice, instead the state here deliberately pushes the situation over the border—putting us beyond the bounds of the "circumstances of justice," thereby excusing everyone thus deprived from any obligation of justice to the larger community.[42] The moral objection to needless rationing can, in this way, readily be assimilated to the present analysis of the "circumstances of justice."

Let us shift our focus, now, from cases of needless rationing to cases where rationing is genuinely needed, cases of "real but manageable scarcity" such that someone's basic needs will not be met unless the obligations of justice are respected all around. Rationing in such circumstances has the effect, which everyone notes well, of depriving everyone of the right to have more than they need (at least until everyone has as much as they need).[43] What is less noticed, but even more important, is the guarantee which this deprivation makes possible: everyone is guaranteed as much as they need, insofar as that is physically possible.

As one World War II ration book proudly proclaims on its back cover, "This book is your Government's assurance of your right to buy your fair share of certain goods made scarce by war" (US OPA 1943). Rationing is not just a matter of restriction. It also entails a concomitant: a "*right* to a ration." Guaranteeing people a fair share, as of right, in situations of scarcity in this way is an exemplary act of political authority to protect people when they are potentially most vulnerable. It is socially most necessary, yet politically most feasible, precisely where justice bumps up hardest against scarcity—where everyone's basic needs can be met if, but only if, there is a just distribution of resources.

V. Rationing Writ Large

Worlds of real but manageable scarcity, and the political responses which they evoke, thus have much to recommend them. Rationing in such circumstances can morally empower and politically protect the fundamental interests of everyone concerned. It is, in that way, a model response. Politically, no doubt it is a response that is most viable in precisely those dire (and happily rare) circumstances of "real but manageable scarcity." But the moral and political virtues of that response are such that we ought genuinely be tempted to see if there are ways to generalize it into a model for the social management of scarcity, more broadly.

Of course, we do not want to do that by artificially restricting supplies, so that some people unnecessarily end up with less than they need (as criticized above, in the cases of rationing of social services in the UK). Creating artificial scarcities for the sake of camaraderie takes us outside the "circumstances of justice" rather than helping us find a way to live within them.

Still, rationing of a sort might nonetheless make sense even in a world of considerable abundance. The general rule of rationing, stated above, is that "no one shall have more than she needs until everyone has all that she needs." That is perfectly consistent with circumstances of abundance, where a great many people have a great deal more than they actually need. All that that general rule of rationing imposes is a weak constraint, which is that everyone's basic needs first be met. Rationing writ large ought therefore be understood simply as a "basic needs strategy," one which prioritizes the meeting of basic needs over the satisfying of mere desires (Streeton 1981).

Defining basic needs and differentiating them from mere desires is, of course, a major challenge philosophically and practically as well. Notice however that it is not one peculiar to the generalized rationing model I am recommending. If the widely-accepted Humean analysis of the "circumstances of justice" is right, that is a task that implicitly figures on the "to do" list of any theory of justice. If Hume is right, then none of them can specify their range of application in the absence of some such analysis.

Neither is my rule that "basic needs must first be met" otiose, even in the richer corners of the world. There might be a few countries where resources are both abundant and broadly shared; where those conditions exist, distributional politics will be relatively muted and claims of justice rarely pressed hard. More commonly, even where resources are relatively abundant their distribution is badly skewed—so badly skewed as to leave non-negligible proportions of the population with their basic needs unmet. There, it is only to be expected that distributional struggles will be real, and claims of justice will be firmly lodged. In rich countries with pockets of poverty, like that, the rule that "basic needs must first be met" has very real application.

Understood as a rule "of" justice, that has a familiar ring about it. But on the present argument, that is less a rule of justice—less a first-order precept concerning what justice requires—and more a second-order precondition of justice. If we want to live in morally regularized relations with these people at all, Hume's analysis of the "circumstances of justice" tells us, we must first meet everyone's needs wherever we can.

NOTES

1. It had been long urged, as a substantive moral precept, that "if any assistance can be provided without detriment to oneself, it should be given" (Cicero 44BC/1991, I.51–2). Hume denies the need for moralizing at all, in such circumstances.
2. In contemporary parlance, such norms would be deemed "supererogatory," the stuff of saints and heroes (Urmson 1958).

3. Even if the needs of the starving can be satisfied by an utterly painless reallocation of the superfluity of the superrich, it would be absurd to deny that it could be a matter of justice that that should be done.
4. We would be all the more firmly outside the circumstances of justice where all of everyone's desires are necessarily (rather than just as it happens) satiated. But I take it that the simple actuality of their being satisfied is sufficient to take us outside circumstances of justice; that further step is not necessary.
5. That, arguably, is what environmental protection debates today are all about. Historically, air and water were regarded as paradigm instances of superabundant goods. Cicero (44BC/1991, I.51–2) takes them as unproblematically superabundant; Hume (1777, sec. 3, pt. 1, p. 145) had to dredge *Genesis* for a case in which they were not. The task of today's environmental planners is to prevent them from passing from the category of the "superabundant" into the category of "moderately scarce" commodities that have to be carefully husbanded.
6. More formally: Suppose each distributional mechanism has associated with it a set of distributional possibilities (d_1, d_2, ..., d_m, ..., d_{n-1}, d_n). For any two mechanisms, M_1 and M_2, that have the same upper limit, M_1 is superior to M_2 if and only if it has a lower lower limit, i.e., if the set of possibilities under M_1 is (d_1, d_2, ..., d_m, ..., d_n) and that under M_2 is (d_m, d_{m+1}, ..., d_n) where $1<m<n$.
7. In terms of the formalisms of the preceding note: For any two mechanisms, M_1 and M_2, that have the same lower limit then M_1 is superior to M_2 if and only if it has a lower upper limit, i.e., if the set of possibilities under M_1 is (d_1, d_2, ..., d_m) and that under M_2 is (d_1, d_2, ..,d_m, ..., d_n) where once again $1<m<n$.
8. Further to note 5, the "environmental justice" movement is indeed correct in seeing environmental quality as a matter of justice, when environmental quality has become a moderately scarce resource (Dobson 1999). But surely it would be better all around if environmental planners could restore environmental quality to the status it once enjoyed as a superabundant good over which issues of justice do not arise.
9. The main one is this. The purposes to which goods, once bought, will be put is not transparent in the act of exchange. In the case of superabundance that was not a problem: as long as any good would be bought for any purpose, that served as conclusive evidence that we were not in circumstances of superabundance. In the case of superscarcity, though, it is a problem: there, simply knowing that the good would be bought does not prove anything, one way or another; super-scarcity is proven only if it is bought *and* used to satisfy basic needs.
10. Supposing, anyway, that resources are universally fungible in the ways economists suppose—and need to suppose, to make market equilibriate in the ways they want.
11. As France and Italy did, when during World War I Britain and America provided them with loans which "made it possible for them to take up the 'rations' of imported wheat and other essential articles that were allotted to them by the various inter-allied commissions" (Pigou 1921, p. 143).

12. Even in the very special situations in view—of superscarcity or superabundance—which are themselves far from common occurrences, of course.
13. "[I]s it not possible that a king or an aristocracy may...be saturated with the objects of their desires, and may then protect the community in the enjoyment of the rest?" Macaulay (1829/1978, p. 104) asks—he supposes rhetorically.
14. There might of course be second-order concerns—people might want to protect property rights even in property regarded by its owners as superfluous, either out of high moral principle or extended prudence ("dangerous precedent," etc.).
15. Second-order issues might again intrude. Redistribution might compromise economic efficiency, reducing the overall level of resources in ways that (perhaps inevitably) leave the poor worse off after their smash-and-grab than they would have been without it. And so on.
16. With apologies to G.A. Cohen, whose concerns are rather different than my own in his own account of "Where the action is: on the site of distributive justice" (Cohen 1997).
17. The phrase is from Lasswell (1950). But the emphasis on distributional struggle among social classes is found even in Aristotle's *Politics*, of course.
18. David Easton (1965) characterizes politics generically as the "authoritative allocation of values"—not all of which are necessarily material in nature. See more generally Lowi (1969).
19. Indeed, markets themselves are underpinned by politics, in all the myriad ways seen in former communist economies making the transition to capitalism; see e.g. World Bank (1996).
20. As elaborated through more stylized game-theoretic representation in Goodin (1988).
21. Thinking of it in more complex terms of coalitional dynamics, broadly the same is likely to occur, at least wherever resources are very abundant and very unequally distributed.
22. I.e., diminishing marginal utility has not yet cut in, in any serious way.
23. There is of course a whole wide range of human affairs where this description is inapt; and arguments against the "political theory of scarcity" as being wrongly rooted in the "political theory of possessive individualism" insist that much more of politics ought be seen in those other lights. See, e.g.: Macpherson 1962; 1973; Cornford 1972.
24. "*A* just distribution": that is, "any of potentially many." Where the prescriptions of justice are indeterminate, in this way, there are then problems of coordinating on which one of them to implement. That would certainly complicate the story I shall be telling below, but it does not fundamentally alter it. In what follows, I shall therefore avoid those complications by assuming that the prescriptions of justice are determinate; and I shall subsequently talk, accordingly, in terms of "the just distribution."
25. As occurs in "triage" cases, where goods are so scarce that we have to concentrate resources on a few people in order to allow any of them to survive at all (Rescher 1966, pp. 95–8).
26. Where N is large, the probability $(N-1)/N$ approaches certainty, 1.0.

27. Assuming, as I said in footnote 24 above, that there is exactly one "just distribution," easily recognizable by all as the unique point upon which everyone should coordinate. Where there are multiple just distributions, or good grounds for honest disagreement over which distribution is truly just—as typically there are, over rationing schemes (Barry 1989, p. 156)—the politics gets messier. But even then, everyone can agree that we should coordinate on some one of these eligible, plausibly just options rather than not coordinating at all. Even where people have divergent interests in instituting alternative coordinated solutions, their overriding interest is in coordinating on one or another of those solutions rather than suffering some other which would be worse for all concerned (Luce and Raiffa 1957, pp. 90–4).
28. This was clear in the old natural lawyers: Grotius (1625/1964, bk 2, ch. 2, sec. 6) comments "that in case of necessity men have the right to use things which have become the property of another..."; and Pufendorf has a chapter "On the right and privilege of necessity" (1688/1934, bk 2, ch. 4). Locke (1690/1993, sec. 42) offers a garbled version conflating the duty (of charity) of the rich to give with the right (of necessity) of the poor to take.
29. As noticed in a rather different connection by Milton Friedman (1962, pp. 190–1) and David Miller (1988, pp. 163–88), undercutting such excuses constitutes a "public good" for all who are rich. The poor have an excuse to take property from any of the rich, so long as they are poor; depriving them of that excuse, by relieving their poverty, therefore benefits anyone who is rich, whether or not she actually contributed to the relief of the poor.
30. This might explain the appeal of notions of "mutual obligation" even among the poor, who like to feel they are doing something in return for their benefits. See Gutmann and Thompson (1996, ch. 12) and UK Secretary of State for Social Security (1998, ch. 11).
31. I am grateful to Claire Finkelstein for reminding me of this old example and for discussion of the issues it raises.
32. Under the heading "necessity carrieth a privilege in itself," Sir Francis Bacon writes, "So if divers be in danger of drowning, ... and one of them get to some plank, ... and another to save his life thrust him from it, whereby he is drowned; this is neither *se defendendo* nor by misadventure, but justifiable" (Bacon 1630, Regula. 5 at p. 29–30; spelling modernized). Sir William Blackstone writes, "He who thus preserves his own life at the expence of another man's, is excusable th[r]ough unavoidable necessity, and the principle of self-defence; since their both remaining on the same weak plank is a mutual, though innocent, attempt upon, and an endangering of, each other's life" (1765, bk 4, ch. 14, p. 186). Similar passages appear in Grotius (1625/1964, bk 2, ch. 2, sec. 8) and Pufendorf (1688/1934, bk 2, ch. 4, at p. 206).
33. Morally, what is beyond the psychological capacity of ordinary agents is deemed to be "supererogatory." Brian Barry (1989, p. 155) prefers this interpretation; so do I. Hume's position is ambiguous between these options, his talk of "motives of necessity" implying that the act is psychologically excused, his talk of "laws of justice" being "suspended" implying that it is morally excused (1777, sec. 3, pt. 1, p. 147).
34. This is subject to multiple caveats, of course. In ordinary cases of self-defense, one must first try to escape the threat, and only failing that may

one turn to fight: Blackstone says as much, in the paragraph immediately preceding the one just quoted. Or again, necessity excuses your taking from another only where you have not brought your plight upon yourself, and only where the person from whom you take is not in equal need; Grotius and Pufendorf emphasize that, in passages surrounding the ones just cited. It is unclear how all those caveats squares with their conclusions that the two sailors on a plank are morally at liberty to push each other off (the latter caveat, at least, certainly seems to apply).

35. Wherever there is a "right" and "wrong" thing to do, anyway.
36. In the words of Lord Coleridge, C.J., "the duty of dying for others has been laid down in glowing and emphatic language...from the principles of heathen ethics; it is enough in a Christian country to remind ourselves of the Great Example whom we profess to follow"; *R v Dudley and Stephens*, at 287. Lord Coleridge goes on to point out the obvious problems with a principle that "leaves to whom is to profit by it to determine the necessity which will justify him in deliberately taking another's life to save his own." For details, see Simpson (1984).
37. Indeed, the basic needs of each could only be met in that way, assuming each of them would drown if both of them exhausted themselves fighting over the plank.
38. The Minister responsible reported to the British Parliament in late 1916, "We have had two examples of rationing. We have rationed petrol, and we have had 200,000 letters in protest against it. Then we rationed sugar, and thousands and thousands of letters have come from the poor. God forbid that we should have to ration anything else" (alas for the poor Minister, wholesale food rationing was upon them within another month) (Runciman 1916, col. 509). Similarly, in World War II rationing officials were inevitably called "beasts," even from the floor of the House of Commons (Lipson 1941, col. 47). See more generally Goodin and Dryzek (1995).
39. Decisions which were upheld in court: see *R v Gloucester ex parte Barry* and *R v East Sussex County Council ex parte Tandy*. See more generally Foster (1983).
40. At least where government realistically could have done otherwise. In many of these cases it could.
41. As opponents of "social and economic rights," more generally, have always said coming from the opposite direction. See, e.g., Cranston (1962) and Raphael (1967).
42. In Hume's phrase, "Produce extreme abundance or extreme necessity...: [then] By rendering justice totally *useless*, you thereby totally destroy its essence, and suspend its obligation upon mankind" (1777, sec. 3, pt 1, p. 149).
43. During the world wars, much was made of the fact that "the king was on rations like all his subjects, and on exactly the same rations; his meat cards, duly registered with his butcher, were reproduced in all the [daily news-papers]" (Beveridge 1928, p. 232). Nor was it purely wartime propaganda. A similar story is told by Beveridge's successor moving into the Master's Lodge of University College, when Beveridge shifted to the Commons in 1945: "In those days there was very little in the shops for even the most basic things with which to set up a home. For instance, it took nearly a month to ac-

quire a washing-up bowl and equally long to buy a dustpan and brush. If one heard of a shop which had some of these precious objects in, one dropped everything and rushed to get there before they ran out. We only had plates and dishes because one of the College servants had a daughter who worked in a big local ironmonger and she procured them for the College Servants to give them to us as a magnificent wedding present" (Wild 1999, p. 93). When even the Head of an Oxbridge House is found experiencing such hardships, one can only suppose that the rigors of wartime rationing truly were broadly felt.

REFERENCES

Aaron, Henry J. and William B. Schwartz. (1984) *The Painful Prescription: Rationing Hospital Care.* Washington, D. C.: Brookings Institution.

Arrow, Kenneth J. (1970) *Essays in the Theory of Risk-bearing.* Amsterdam: North-Holland.

Bacon, Francis. (1630) "The maxims of the law," pp. 1–104 in Bacon, *The Elements of the Common Laws of England.* London: J. Moore.

Barry, Brian. (1989) *Theories of Justice.* Berkeley: University of California Press.

Beveridge, William H. (1928) *British Food Policy.* London: Oxford University Press.

Blackstone, William. (1765) *Commentaries on the Laws of England.* Oxford: Clarendon Press.

Cicero. (44BC/1991) *De Officiis*, ed. M. T. Griffin and E. M. Atkins. Cambridge: Cambridge University Press.

Cohen, G. A. (1997) "Where the action is: on the site of distributive justice," *Philosophy & Public Affairs*, vol. 26, pp. 3–30.

Cornford, James. (1972) "The political theory of scarcity," pp. 27–44. in *Philosophy, Politics & Society*, 4th series, ed. P. Laslett, W. G. Runciman and Q. Skinner. Oxford, Blackwell.

Cranston, Maurice. (1962) *Human Rights Today.* London: Ampersand.

Dobson, Andrew. (1999) *Justice and the Environment.* Oxford: Oxford University Press.

Easton, David. (1965) *A Systems Analysis of Political Life.* New York: Wiley.

Foster, Peggy. (1983) *Access to Welfare: An Introduction to Welfare Rationing.* London: Macmillan.

Friedman, Milton. (1962) *Capitalism and Freedom.* Chicago: University of Chicago Press.

Goodin, Robert E. (1988) "Some new sources of social conflict: transformations of mixed-motive games," *British Journal of Sociology*, vol. 39, pp. 441–51.

Goodin, Robert E. and John S. Dryzek. (1995) "Justice deferred: wartime rationing and postwar welfare policy," *Politics & Society*, vol. 23, pp. 49–73.

Grotius, Hugo. (1625/1964) *The Law of War and Peace*, trans. F. W. Kelsey, ed. J. B. Scott. New York: Oceana.

Gutmann, Amy and Dennis Thompson. (1996) *Democracy and Disagreement.* Cambridge, Mass.: Harvard University Press.

Harlow, Carole. (1997) "Back to basics: reinventing administrative law," *Public Law*, pp. 245–61.

Hart, H. L. A. (1955) "Are there any natural rights?" *Philosophical Review*, vol. 64, pp. 175–91.

Hart, H. L. A. (1961) *The Concept of Law*. Oxford: Clarendon Press.

Hart, H. L. A. (1983) "Definition and theory in jurisprudence," p. 21–48 in *Essays in Jurisprudence and Philosophy*. Oxford: Clarendon Press

Hofstadter, Richard. (1948) *The American Political Tradition*. New York: Knopf.

Hobbes, Thomas. (1651) *Leviathan*. London: Andrew Crooke.

Hume, David. (1739) *A Treatise of Human Nature*. London: John Noon.

Hume, David. (1777) *An Enquiry Concerning the Principles of Morals*. London: Cadell.

Kant, Immanuel. (1797/1965) *The Metaphysical Elements of Justice*, trans. John Ladd. Indianapolis, Ind.: Bobbs-Merrill.

Lasswell, Harold D. (1950) *Politics: Who Gets What, When, How?* New York: P. Smith.

Lipson, D. L. (1941) *Hansard's Parliamentary Debates* (Commons), 5th series, 371 (30 April), col. 479.

Locke, John (1690/1993) *First Treatise of Government*. Pp. 1–112 in *Two Treatises of Government*, ed. Mark Goldie. London: Everyman/Dent.

Lowi, Theodore J. (1969) *The End of Liberalism*. New York: Norton.

Luce, R. Duncan and Howard Raiffa. (1957) *Games and Decisions*. New York: Wiley.

Macaulay, T. B. (1829/1978) "Mill's essay on government: utilitarian logic and politics," pp. 99–129 in *Utilitarian Logic and Politics*, ed. Jack Lively and John Rees. Oxford: Clarendon Press.

Macpherson, C. B. (1962) *The Political Theory of Possessive Individualism*. Oxford: Clarendon Press.

Macpherson, C. B. (1973) *Democratic Theory*. Oxford: Clarendon Press.

Miller, David. (1988) "Altruism and the welfare state," pp. 163–88 in *Responsibility, Rights and Welfare*, ed. J. Donald Moon. Boulder, Colo.: Westview

Palmer, Ellie. (2000) "Resource allocation, welfare rights—mapping the boundaries of judicial control in public administrative law," *Oxford Journal of Legal Studies*, vol. 20, pp. 63–88.

Pigou, A. C. (1921) *The Political Economy of War*. London: Macmillan.

Piven, Frances Fox and Richard A. Cloward. (1971) *Regulating the Poor*. New York: Pantheon.

Pufendorf, Samuel. (1699/1934) *On the Law of Nature and Nations*, trans. C.H. and W. A. Oldfather. Oxford: Clarendon Press.

R v Dudley and Stephens [1884] 14 Q.B.D. 273.

R v East Sussex County Council ex parte Tandy [1998] AC 714, 2 All ER 770.

R v Gloucester ex parte Barry [1997] AC 584, [1977] 2 All ER 1.

Raphael, D. D. ed. (1967) *Political Theory and the Rights of Man*. Bloomington: Indiana University Press.

Rawls, John. (1971) *A Theory of Justice*. Cambridge, Mass.: Harvard University Press.

Rescher, Nicholas. (1966) *Distributive Justice*. Indianapolis: Bobbs-Merrill.

Runciman, Walter. (1916) *Hansard's Parliamentary Debates* (Commons), 5th series, 86 (17 Oct.), col. 509.
Simpson, A. W. B. (1984) *Cannibalism and the Common Law.* Chicago: University of Chicago Press.
Streeton, Paul et al. (1981) *First Things First: Meeting Basic Human Needs in the Developing Countries.* New York: Oxford University Press for the World Bank.
UK, Secretary of State for Social Security. (1998) *A New Contract for Welfare.* Cm 3805. London: HMSO.
United States, Office of Price Administration (US OPA). (1943) *War Ration Book No. 3.* OPA Form No. R-130. Washington, D.C.: Government Printing Office.
Urmson, J. O. (1958) "Saints and heroes." Pp. 198–216 in *Essays in Moral Philosophy,* ed. A.I. Melden. Seattle: University of Washington Press.
Waldron, Jeremy. (1981) "A right to do wrong," *Ethics,* vol. 92, pp. 21–39.
Waldron, Jeremy. (1986) "Welfare and the images of charity," *Philosophical Quarterly,* vol. 36, pp. 463–82.
Wild, Margaret. (1999) "The Lodgings 1945," *University College Record* (Oct.), pp. 92–6.
World Bank (1996) *World Development Report 1996: From Plan to Market.* Oxford: Oxford University Press for the World Bank.

Philosophical Issues, 11
Social, Political, and Legal Philosophy, 2001

A Critique of Philip Pettit's Republicanism

Charles Larmore

1. Three Concepts of Liberty

The contemporary renewal of republican theory has found in Philip Pettit its most ambitious architect. Pettit acknowledges his debt to a current of thought which goes back through Machiavelli to ancient Rome and which has been reconstructed in a series of important writings by Quentin Skinner.[1] But Pettit has given to the republican model of political life a systematic development it has never received before. His book, *Republicanism* (Pettit 1997), is a landmark work. All the same, I also believe that Pettit has not properly understood the true character of his achievement. I shall begin by laying out the basic principles of his republican theory, mostly in his own terms, though with some embroidering, which reflects my large measure of agreement. My ultimate aim, however, is to examine its problematic relation to the modern liberal tradition.

At the center of Pettit's enterprise is a conception of political liberty that he calls "non-domination". According to this conception, we are free to the extent that we do not find ourselves under the domination of others, subject to their will and exposed to the vicissitudes of their desires. Clearly, freedom thus conceived consists in the absence of conditions which are thought to diminish our possibilities of action. Freedom is not therefore identified with the exercise of a capacity, much less with some activity by which we supposedly realize our most significant possibilities or give expression to our true nature or "higher self". To invoke the taxonomy introduced by Isaiah Berlin in his classic essay of 1958, "Two Concepts of Liberty" (Berlin 1969, pp. 118–172), we may say that Pettit's idea of republican freedom counts as a "negative", not a "positive" conception. In particular, it does not denote the amount of control which an individual or a community exercises over its own existence. Freedom from domination by others is not equivalent to being one's own master, since in itself it is a condition which people may enjoy in a variety of ways, as much by letting themselves be carried away by passion as by bringing themselves under the rule of reason.

Thus, Pettit's conception differs from that prominent strand in the republican tradition which has sought to define freedom in a positive manner, as individual or collective autonomy and self-rule. In his eyes, and I agree, such definitions are too narrow. The freedom we prize includes other things too besides participating in democratic self-government or shaping our lives according to a plan of our own devising.

At the same time, however, Pettit does not endorse the particular notion of negative freedom that Berlin espoused. On the contrary, one of Pettit's most important contributions is to have broadened the range of theoretical options. Negative freedom as Berlin understood it is the domain of action where individuals can do as they may want without interference on the part of others. Like Hobbes and Bentham before him, he viewed individual freedom as the absence of obstacles.[2] To be sure, Berlin cautioned that a person's freedom should not be said to consist in the absence of obstacles *to the fulfillment of his desires*, for such a definition would allow the person to increase his freedom simply by extinguishing his unsatisfied desires. The obstacles relevant for judging the extent of a person's negative liberty are rather to be conceived as obstacles to his *possibilities*, as roadblocks standing in the way of the courses of action that he might choose to pursue.[3]

Nonetheless, Berlin did not waiver in defining our negative freedom by reference to actual interference, even when such interference works to limit our possibilities. As a result, people must count as free in this sense, even when another could encroach upon their projects (actual or possible) and yet decides in fact not to do so. Negative freedom, Berlin once remarked, is not compromised by a despotic regime, so long as the despot chooses to pursue an indulgent policy toward his subjects, reserving all political power to himself, while allowing them otherwise to act in large measure as they please.[4]

Yet surely it is wrong, Pettit objects, to hold that people are then free, inasmuch as they pursue their projects at the mercy of a prince who, well-disposed for the moment, can at any time change his mind and policy. Freedom really depends on an absence of both actual and possible interference at the hands of others. Or more exactly, Pettit adds, it consists in being exempt from all such *arbitrary* interference. For suppose that we inhabit a society governed in accord with just laws: we will consequently not possess an immunity from all interference in our affairs. Even then, the state must stand ready to discourage and to punish any infractions of the laws. But the point is that such conditions, where the threat of arbitrary interference has disappeared, mark a qualitative difference. The rule of law does not amount to one form of domination having been swapped for another, as though its utility consisted in offering us a greater net balance of freedom over constraint than we would otherwise have if living under despotic rule or under no rule at all (in a "state of nature"). Domination itself, so Pettit insists, has come to an end when the authority of just laws replaces the will of particular individuals.

Freedom as the absence of domination differs therefore in two respects from any view like Berlin's that equates negative freedom with the absence of obstacles (Pettit 1997, pp. 22ff.). On the one hand, domination can occur without any actual interference. Our freedom is abridged by the simple fact that we live at the mercy of others, since their power to meddle in our life can be so great that, even if they choose not to exercise it, we find ourselves obliged to anticipate their possible actions, modify our plans, and curry their favor. On the other hand, every act of interference need not be an instance of domination. If just laws have the function of making us free by checking the arbitrary will of others, their influence on our conduct and the prohibitions they impose do not amount to a reduction in our freedom.

It is on this latter score that the two "negative" conceptions of freedom differ most tellingly. For Hobbes and Bentham and those who follow in their footsteps, every law as such diminishes our freedom, even if its objective is to prevent the even greater loss of freedom which would ensue from the absence of law. Berlin himself made the point explicitly: "Every law seems to me to curtail *some* liberty, although it may be a means to increasing another"

(Berlin 1969, p. xlix). Civil freedom is deemed the silence of the law, since all law is in itself an intrusion and liberty begins where law ends.[5] According to the republican conception, by contrast, law and liberty are not intrinsically opposed. The exact nature of their relationship depends on the character of the law. To the extent that just laws rescue us from the relations of domination in which the natural course of things would otherwise place us, they constitute freedom's condition of possibility, not its antithesis (Pettit 1997, p. 35).

In the light of these initial observations, it becomes plain that Pettit's theory of freedom as non-domination, distinct though it is from the "positive" conception of freedom as autonomy, accords nonetheless an essential role to democratic self-rule (Pettit 1997, pp. 8, 183ff.). Only universal suffrage and the widespread participation of citizens in political life can ensure that the laws will be just, instead of serving particular interests and private concentrations of power. For those who see the essence of freedom as the absence of interference, there exists no such internal connection between liberty and democracy. Berlin, for example, declared that "freedom in [my] sense is not, at any rate logically, connected with democracy or self-government" (Berlin 1969, pp. 129–130).

Pettit's theory takes over therefore the venerable republican theme of active citizenship. But it does so without any tendentious equation of freedom itself with the exercise of self-government. Pettit distances himself emphatically from the republican strand that he calls "neo-Athenian", in other words, from the current of thought represented by Hannah Arendt, Michael Sandel, and other partisans of "the liberty of the ancients". They elevate political activity, the public discussion and implementation of a society's common purposes, to the rank of a supreme end in the constitution of the human good. Pettit, by contrast, urges that we take our bearings from a "neo-Roman" tradition that sees self-government as the essential means for the creation of a free society where each person, removed from the arbitrary will of others, can pursue his good as he understands it.[6]

Certainly, this version of republican theory accepts the need for civic virtue. But unlike the neo-Athenians, Pettit has no reason to exaggerate its importance as though it represented the very heart and soul of the moral life. He can rest content with delimiting the particular sorts of dispositions it must embody, if the distinctive feature of a republican regime, the substitution of the authority of law for personal dependence, is to be sustained.

Civic virtue, in Pettit's account, has three elements (Pettit 1997, pp. 246ff.).[7] First, the rule of law can be a reality only in a society where citizens respect the law for its own sake, instead of seeking to circumvent it or adhering to it solely out of a fear of sanctions. It is also necessary, if the law is not to turn into an instrument of particular interests, that citizens make a point of taking part in public life and thus making their own needs and concerns heard. Finally, they must practice a constant vigilance, staying on the lookout for excessive concentrations of power, which never cease to be a danger.

These traits of character are far from spontaneous. They require fostering, and may be considerably weakened today by countless pressures encouraging a consumerist approach to social life, where each person seeks to make the best bargain for himself instead of working with others to tame the powers, particularly economic, which set the terms for their calculations. But the key theoretical point is that civic virtue as Pettit defines it is a specifically political virtue, necessary for the securing of a society without domination. Its role is to make possible the pursuit of different visions of the good life and not to define the human good itself.

2. Republican vs. Liberal

Pettit's republican conception of freedom has many attractive features, some of which I have already indicated. It would be unwise, however, to conclude that non-domination constitutes the true meaning of political freedom. A number of distinct values, none of them negligible, have taken the name of "freedom", and our concern ought to be, not to determine which of them captures freedom's essence, but to recognize the differences between these ideals, chart their connections, and figure out whether one of them is of greater importance than the others. Berlin himself saw things this way. He had no intention of arguing that negative liberty (as he understood it) forms the whole of freedom. His aim was to point out the difference between non-interference and self-rule as well as to show that a single-minded devotion to the latter conception of freedom, pursued at the expense of the negative freedoms enshrined in individual rights, can have totalitarian consequences. In Berlin's eyes, the positive freedom involved in democratic self-government was also an important value, though one having chiefly an instrumental basis as the best means for protecting the rights of the individual.

I do not sense that the same spirit of value-pluralism informs Pettit's own examination of freedom. To be sure, freedom from domination represents an important value, and Pettit has shown how its contours differ significantly from those of non-interference and self-rule. He also has presented good reasons for attributing to this republican ideal a more fundamental role in our political thinking than the other two ideas of freedom. Pettit may well be right that democratic self-government draws its chief rationale from the need to abolish relations of domination, and that ceasing to live at the mercy of powerful individuals and interests is of far greater moment than simply living unobstructed by others. But freedom from interference is not nothing. Some laws, however just they may be (one need only think, for example, of tax codes), may require me to give up some of my freedom to do as I please which I may reasonably regret having to surrender, even if on balance I judge it to be for the best. Pettit seems often to suggest—to my mind, wrongly—that such freedom is not really a value at all.

There is another matter of greater theoretical consequence on which I do not agree with Pettit. It is the opposition he sets up between the republican conception of freedom and the modern liberal tradition. In his view, liberal thinkers have uniformly adhered to the idea that freedom means non-interference. "Liberalism", he writes, "has been associated over the two hundred years of its development, and in most of its influential varieties, with the negative conception of freedom as the absence of interference, and with the assumption that there is nothing inherently oppressive about some people having dominating power over others, provided they do not exercise that power and are not likely to exercise it" (Pettit 1997, pp. 8–9). As a result, when liberals have wanted to criticize relations of domination, such as poverty or job insecurity, in which no interference may actually take place, they have had, says Pettit, to fall back on other values such as satisfaction of basic needs or equality. Pettit believes that he has, by contrast, found in non-domination a principle which can serve all by itself as the basis of a cogent ideal of social justice. The republican conception of freedom represents, he claims, "the supreme political value" (Pettit 1997, pp. 80–81). Pettit's republicanism presents itself therefore as a rival to the liberal view of political life.

I find this line of argument mistaken for two important reasons. First of all, it is not right to suppose that the liberal tradition displays a monolithic allegiance to the notion of freedom as non-interference. The evidence which Pettit adduces to defend this interpretive thesis is unconvincing. But in addition, the exposition which he goes on to give of his republican theory does not really make of non-domination the supreme political value, and the character of this failure is quite significant. He finds himself, in fact, obliged to appeal to recognizably liberal principles in order to define the precise content of his republican conception of freedom. In the end, Pettit belongs to the very liberal tradition that he imagines he has transcended.

I shall begin with the first point, reserving a discussion of the second to the next section. Now indisputably Isaiah Berlin's thought fits the picture which Pettit draws of the liberal point of view. According to Berlin, there are two grand conceptions of freedom, the absence of interference and autonomy, and democratic self-government is a good only so far as it remains subordinate to a respect for individual rights. For this reason, liberalism tended to signify for him a political vision whose fundamental commitment is to the negative conception of freedom as non-interference. Nonetheless, the fact that this conception found its first detailed exposition in Hobbes' writings ought to give one pause. The Hobbesian theory of the state scarcely looks like a liberal philosophy.

Naturally, one might reply that Hobbes, while no liberal himself, furnished some tools—among them an idea of freedom—which later thinkers were able to exploit to construct a model of the open society that can properly be called "liberal". And indeed, freedom understood as the absence of obstacles and thus as the opposite of constraint was later taken up by Bentham, and it went on to inspire an important current of liberal thought. In the 19th century, its most eminent representative was John Stuart Mill, who argued that "the only freedom which deserves the name is that of pursuing our own good in our own way" and who conceived of law, which like "all restraint, *qua* restraint, is an evil", as a necessary limit on individual freedom so that "we do not attempt to deprive others of theirs".[8] Obviously, it has had its followers in the 20th century as well.

But the question is whether liberalism as a whole coincides with this line of thought. One signal difficulty is that John Locke, one of the founding fathers of the liberal tradition, clearly did not equate freedom with absence of constraint. Distinguishing sharply between "liberty" and "license",[9] he insisted on the role played by law in the very constitution of freedom—which is a corollary of the republican concern with non-domination. Consider what Locke wrote in §57 of the *Second Treatise of Government*:

> Law in its true notion is not so much the limitation as the direction of a free and intelligent agent to his proper interest....The end of law is not to abolish or restrain, but to preserve and enlarge freedom....Where there is no law, there is no freedom.

Pettit deals with this problem by placing Locke among the republicans (Pettit 1997, p. 40).[10] But that is a desperate remedy. Surely something is amiss in a definition of liberalism which accommodates Hobbes, but excludes Locke. The way out of this impasse is obvious, and it consists in admitting that the liberal tradition is not all of a piece. On the one hand, an identification of freedom with the absence of interference has often been at work, perhaps most explicitly in utilitarian thought. But on the other, a great many thinkers whom it would be hard to classify as anything other than "liberal" have rejected an essential opposition between freedom and law. We are entitled to suppose that in their eyes freedom meant, along the lines of Pettit's republican outlook, the absence of domination.

Let us take as another example Benjamin Constant and his famous evocation of "the liberty of the moderns". Pettit follows Berlin in regarding Constant as an illustrious advocate of the fundamental value of non-interference (Pettit 1997, pp. 18, 27, 50). But how did Constant himself portray modern liberty? Here is what he said:

> C'est le droit de *n'être soumis qu'aux lois*, de ne *pouvoir* ni être arrêté, ni détenu, ni mis à mort, ni maltraité d'aucune manière, par l'effet de la *volonté arbitraire* d'un ou de plusieurs individus.
> [It is the right to be subject only to the laws, such that one cannot be arrested, detained, executed, or mistreated in any way by virtue of the arbitrary will of one or more individuals.][11]

Freedom thus defined certainly differs from the collective exercise of sovereignty, that is, from the liberty of the Ancients in Constant's terminology. But does it therefore amount to the freedom of non-interference? I have underlined the phrases indicating that for Constant "modern liberty" consists in being subject to the *law*, not to the arbitrary will of another, and that its opposite is not merely actual interference in the harmful ways mentioned, but also the *possibility* of such mistreatment. The passage seems so clear an expression of the republican idea of freedom as the absence of domination that one might think it had been taken from the pages of Pettit's own book.

Naturally, one cannot be sure of Constant's intention, since he did not differentiate between the two negative conceptions of freedom—absence of interference, absence of domination—and therefore never formally rejected the one in favor of the other. But precisely in this respect Pettit's true achievement comes into view. He is the first to have analyzed in a systematic way the difference between these two conceptions. His work has put us in a position to appreciate some of the crucial obscurities and disagreements surrounding the notion of freedom in the liberal tradition. Having grasped the distinctive concerns that underlie the republican ideal of not living at the mercy of another's will, we can now devote ourselves to a more careful articulation of liberal principles. Pettit would have done better to present his own theory of government in that spirit.

Instead, he chose to set up a grand opposition between liberal and republican thought. Understanding is not thereby advanced. Consider as a final example Pettit's attempt to draw John Rawls too within the maw of his critique of liberalism. Rawls' idea of the "priority of liberty", the principle that "liberty can be restricted only for the sake of liberty" (Rawls 1971, pp. 244, 302), serves as Pettit's chief evidence for placing him among those who hold that we are free to the extent that we escape interference from others (Pettit 1997, p. 50). On Pettit's telling, that principle expresses the characteristic view of Hobbes and Bentham, for whom law, even when just, constitutes a restriction of freedom to be accepted only because its absence would entail an even greater loss of freedom. This interpretation misses, however, the real meaning of Rawls' principle. Its import is to require that liberty (or more exactly, the scheme of equal basic liberties) never be compromised in order to promote some other value such as a fairer organization of the economic conditions in society. Rawls invoked the "priority of liberty" precisely with the aim of underscoring the subordinate importance to be assigned to his second main principle of justice, the difference principle, whose domain includes the distribution of income and wealth. Consequently, this position does not differ very much from that of Pettit himself, when he declares that freedom is the supreme political value and that existing relations of domination should be tolerated only if they happen to constitute the best means for promoting nondomination overall (Pettit 1997, p. 102).

Pettit's argument for aligning Rawls with the Hobbesian theory of freedom is unpersuasive. That does not mean, of course, that we should abandon the idea of figuring out whether Rawls conceived of liberty as the absence of interference or as the absence of domination. Nonetheless, I believe that not only does there emerge no clear-cut answer to this question, but also that we should not be surprised to come up with none. Only as a result of Pettit's own work are we in a position to formulate precisely the distinction between these two conceptions and to grasp their different implications. One might well expect that Rawls sometimes leaned toward the one, and sometimes toward the other.

In fact, just this fluctuation is what we find when looking at Rawls' writings in the light of our preceding remarks. His general definition of liberty undeniably speaks the language of non-interference:

> This or that person (or persons) is free (or not free) from this or that constraint (or set of constraints) to do (or not to do) so and so....Persons are at liberty to do something when they are free from certain constraints either to do it or not to do it and when their doing it or not doing it is protected from interference by other persons (Rawls 1971, p. 202).

Yet many of the things that Rawls went on to say about political liberty show an affinity with the republican conviction that freedom consists in the absence of domination. The freedom which he made the object of his first principle of justice counts as a value only to the extent that it embodies an equal freedom for all, a scheme of basic liberties which each person enjoys compatibly with a similar scheme for everyone else. Why regard equality as essential to freedom? Were non-interference the only concern, then citizens ought not to worry about some people having a more extensive set of basic liberties than theirs, provided that they themselves are able to pursue unobstructed their individual purposes. If equal liberty forms the paramount principle, the point must be that people should be free, not only from undue interference by others, but also from the unfair influence or domination of others, when such fundamental matters as religious conscience, association, and political voice are at stake.[12]

Another reason for thinking that Rawls did not really equate freedom with the absence of obstacles is his evident reluctance to regard law as in itself an abridgement of liberty. "Whether men are free," he wrote, "is determined by the rights and duties established by the major institutions of society. Liberty is a certain pattern of social forms" (Rawls 1971, p. 63).[13] Note that in this statement the fundamental laws of society are described as determining whether citizens are free at all. Law is very far from appearing as a constraint on freedom designed to prevent a still greater loss of liberty. No devotee of the Hobbesian conception of freedom could have penned those words.

But again, my aim is not to suggest that in his heart of hearts Rawls adhered to the republican conception. A well-defined distinction between the two views of freedom was not available, when he wrote *A Theory of Justice* or *Political Liberalism.* Nothing impelled him to take a stand one way or the other. Here lies the great merit of Pettit's work. Casting light on these points of obscurity, it forces us to be more explicit about what we mean when we say that freedom is "freedom from".

What we should not do, however, is to seek in the republican ideal of freedom the makings of a non-liberal theory of political association. Pettit himself imagines that he stands outside the liberal framework. In reality he does not, and this will become clear as we examine more closely the way he proposes to understand freedom as the absence of domination.

3. Domination and Respect

So far little has been said about the nature of domination itself. Pettit holds, as I have indicated, that we are free from domination to the extent that we do not find ourselves subject to the arbitrary will of others. What, however, does this proposition mean exactly?

Pettit's analysis involves three components (Pettit 1971, p. 52). An individual A is dominated by another (individual or group of individuals) B to the extent that

(i) B has the capacity to interfere,
(ii) on an arbitrary basis, and
(iii) in certain choices that A is in a position to make.

Clearly, it is condition (ii) that raises the most delicate questions. The state has the capacity to interfere in the affairs of its citizens, but provided that the basis of its interference is not arbitrary, it does not count—so the republican believes—as exercising a power of domination. How then ought the key term "arbitrary" to be defined?

Pettit's answer is that the basis for possible interference is not arbitrary if it leads to interference aimed at "tracking" or pursuing the interests, or at least the relevant interests, of the individual who is its object (Pettit 1997, p. 55). For instance (this is Pettit's example), it is in my interest that each citizen pays his taxes, so that even if I do not want to pay my own, the coercion that the government may then employ to force my payment does not constitute an arbitrary interference. Yet how should the interests of the individual be ascertained? Is it a matter of the interests which the individual herself avows? And if so, what is the nature of the circumstances in which her own declarations count as authoritative? Or is it a matter instead of her "real" interests, of which she may or may not have any grasp?

Pettit contends that determining the interests which state power can pursue on a non-arbitrary basis is a question which only the political deliberation of the citizens themselves can ultimately decide (Pettit 1997, pp. 56, 63). This position is no doubt attractive. But it gives rise in turn to a further question, namely, that of the principles which ought to govern this collective deliberation. In the absence of both institutional and normative structures that are already in place, debate will lead to no result, or the outcome will have no claim to being fair and just.

The point is not lost on Pettit himself, who proceeds to lay down two conditions which political deliberation, as it determines the interests deserving legal protection, ought to satisfy (Pettit 1997, pp. 131f.). First of all, citizens should rely solely on conceptual distinctions and forms of inference which no one in the community has a serious reason to reject. And second, the fundamental notions on which they do rely must nonetheless be substantial enough to permit an adequate articulation of their various grievances and goals. Pettit argues that the value of non-domination fulfills these conditions far better than does the understanding of freedom as the absence of interference, which expresses the concerns of entrepreneurs and professionals seeking to curtail government intervention, but which does not resonate so well with workers, for example, whose lives are marked by economic insecurity and who stand to gain by state regulations. Pettit may well be right. But several crucial aspects of his argument demand comment.

As Pettit admits, the two conditions he places upon political deliberation have a normative content. Yet what is the underlying value they express? The requirement that citizens and legislators make their legally-binding decisions without appeal to convictions which their fellow citizens have good reason to reject embodies in fact a basic sort of respect for the individual. If, as Pettit claims (Pettit 1997, pp. 187ff.), just laws are based, not upon the bargaining power of various interests, but upon arguments that in principle can meet with the assent of each citizen's reason, then persons are being viewed as something more than simply means to an ulterior end. The good involved in their obedience to the law has to amount to more than whatever may be the benefits which their compliance affords everyone else. They are being seen as ends in themselves, in the sense that the exercise of their reason counts as having an intrinsic value, which the terms of political life ought to acknowledge.

This fundamental principle of respect for persons turns out therefore to constitute the deepest stratum in Pettit's republican theory. It guides the determination of the interests which non-arbitrary, that is, just laws ought to promote. And if such interests form part of the definition of what is to count as the absence of domination, then Pettit is hardly right to assert that the republican notion of freedom can serve as the supreme political value. We are not in a position to figure out whether domination is at hand or not, either in society at large or in the operations of the state, unless we rely upon the notion of respect for persons.

But there is more. For what does this norm of respect represent if not the cardinal principle of liberalism, at least as one important strand of the liberal tradition has conceived it? Respect requires, as we have seen, that the fundamental terms of political life be such as to meet with the reasonable agreement of all who are bound by them. Now Rawls' "liberal principle of political legitimacy", for example, says precisely that. It maintains that the exercise of political power is justified only if it accords with a constitution whose essentials citizens can endorse in the light of principles and ideals which they can regard as reasonable (Rawls 1996, p. 137).[14] From this principle derives the sort of neutrality which Rawls, in company with many other liberal thinkers, has held the state must practice with regard to those comprehensive conceptions of the good life which remain an object of reasonable disagreement. Yet Pettit, too, implicitly accords this conception of respect a fundamental importance, relying on it as he does to define what he wants to understand by non-domination. His republican model is therefore not really in conflict with the essentials of liberalism, even though it does stand opposed, that is clear, to the Benthamite current which conceives of freedom as the absence of interference.

No doubt there exist other ways to define non-domination than the one adopted by Pettit himself. Some ways of conceiving the idea of not being subject to the arbitrary will of another might very well deny that an individual's reason has any real bearing on the issue. We are truly free—so some may suppose—and no longer live at another's leave, when we place ourselves under the authority of God or the Nation, whatever our own reason may say. One might therefore be "republican" without being liberal. But that is manifestly not the sort of republicanism which Pettit espouses.

Again and again in his book, Pettit declares that contestability counts for more than consent in his ideal republic (Pettit 1997, pp. ix, 63, 184f.). Only if citizens stand ready to challenge the government's decisions, can they make sure that it will not slip into the arbitrary exercise of its powers, advancing its own particular interests and catering to the concerns of the powerful, as it can easily do. There is good sense in this observation, and certainly actual consent, shaped as it generally is by a motley of pressures, ought to be an object of suspicion. But Pettit goes too far when he asserts that "once a contestatory democracy is in place, then of course everything is up for grabs" (Pettit 1997, p. 201). Not everything can be subject to revision, if contestation is to mean anything like what Pettit himself has in mind. Not the principle of respect for persons which defines the very idea of arbitrary power, and which makes Pettit's ideal republic a liberal polity.[15]

Notes

1. See, most recently, Skinner (1998).
2. See Hobbes, *Leviathan*, chapter XIV, paragraph 2 ("By LIBERTY is understood, according to the proper signification of the word, the absence of external impediments") and chapter XXI, paragraph 2 ("A FREE-MAN is he that in those things, which by his strength and wit he is able to do, is not hindered to do what he has a will to do"). In a letter quoted in Pettit (1997, p. 44), Bentham wrote of his discovery that "the idea of liberty imported nothing in it that was positive: that it was merely a negative one: and that accordingly I defined it 'the absence of restraint'".
3. See Berlin, "Two Concepts" (Berlin 1969), p. 139 and also the "Introduction" in the same volume, pp. xxxviii–xxxix.
4. Berlin, "Two Concepts" (Berlin 1969, p. 129): "It is perfectly conceivable that a liberal-minded despot would allow his subjects a large measure of personal freedom".
5. Such of course was Hobbes' view. See Pettit 1997, pp. 37f.
6. Pettit introduced this distinction between neo-Athenian and neo-Roman versions of the republican tradition in his review (Pettit 1998) of Sandel (1996).
7. See also Pettit 1998, pp. 81, 87–89.
8. J. S. Mill, *On Liberty*, chapter I, paragraph 13, and chapter V, paragraph 4.
9. Locke, *Second Treatise of Government*, §6.
10. See also Pettit 1998, pp. 84–85.
11. Constant, "De la liberté des Anciens comparée à celle des Modernes", in Constant 1980, pp. 494–495 (emphasis added). I have amended the transla-

tion to be found in Constant 1988, p. 310, because it fails unfortunately to preserve the key terms which I have underscored.

12. Pettit himself notes that the value of equal liberty makes most sense when freedom is understood as absence of domination. See Pettit 1997, p. 111.
13. See also Rawls 1971, p. 202.
14. See also Larmore 1996, chapter VI, as well as Larmore 1999, in which I bring out more clearly, I believe, than Rawls himself the notion of respect at the basis of liberal theory.
15. For further reflections along these general lines, see Larmore 2000a. The present essay develops ideas first introduced in Larmore 2000b.

REFERENCES

Berlin, Isaiah. (1969) *Four Essays on Liberty*, Oxford: Oxford University Press.

Constant, Benjamin. (1980) *De la liberté chez les Modernes*, Paris: Pluriel.

Constant, Benjamin. (1988) *Political Writings*, edited by Biancamaria Fontana, Cambridge: Cambridge University Press.

Larmore, Charles. (1996) *The Morals of Modernity*, Cambridge: Cambridge University Press.

Larmore, Charles. (1999) "The Moral Basis of Political Liberalism", *The Journal of Philosophy* 96 (12), December 1999, pp. 599–625.

Larmore, Charles. (2000a) "Le 'nous' moral que nous sommes", *Comprendre: Les identités culturelles*, vol. 1, Paris: Presses Universitaires de France, pp. 219–234.

Larmore, Charles. (2000b) "Républicanisme et libéralisme chez Philip Pettit", *Cahiers de Philosophie de l'Université de Caen*, vol. 34, Caen: Presses Universitaires de Caen, pp. 115–125.

Pettit, Philip. (1997) *Republicanism. A Theory of Freedom and Government*, Oxford: Clarendon Press.

Pettit, Philip. (1998) "Review of Michael Sandel, *Democracy's Discontent*", *The Journal of Philosophy* 95 (2), February 1998, pp. 73–96.

Rawls, John. (1971) *A Theory of Justice*, Cambridge, Mass.: Harvard University Press.

Rawls, John. (1996) *Political Liberalism*, 2nd edition, New York: Columbia University Press.

Sandel, Michael. (1996) *Democracy's Discontent*, Cambridge, Mass.: Harvard University Press.

Skinner, Quentin. (1998) *Liberty Before Liberalism*, Cambridge: Cambridge University Press.

10

PHILOSOPHICAL ISSUES, 11
Social, Political, and Legal Philosophy, 2001

Classical Realism*

Brian Leiter

This essay offers a systematic reconstruction of a neglected perspective on questions of moral, political, and legal theory that I will call "Classical Realism." [1] The perspective is actually part of a long tradition of theorizing about morals, law, politics, and society that includes, to greater and lesser degrees, writers like Thucydides, Machiavelli, Freud, Marx, Nietzsche, and Holmes, among others. This tradition, however, has almost vanished from the modern academy. It is the most general aim of this paper to begin a revival of Classical Realism as a serious—albeit debunking—position in normative theory. It is the more specific aim to delineate the position, assign it a pedigree, and locate it in conceptual space. Subsequent papers will tackle specific thinkers and arguments that will be sketched more lightly in the historical survey that follows here.

I. Classical Realism

By using the label "Classical Realism" I wish to reclaim for the term "realism" a meaning both older than and different from that current in academic debates, especially in philosophy, where it names certain doctrines in semantics and metaphysics.[2] Classical Realism, by contrast, is a very different kind of position; indeed, it entails no particular semantic and metaphysical doctrines at all. Classical Realism denotes a certain hard-headed, unromantic, uncompromising attitude towards the world, which manifests itself in a brutal honesty and candor in the assessment of human motives and the portrayal of human affairs.[3] More precisely, Classical Realists accept the following three doctrines:

> **Naturalism**: there exist certain (largely) incorrigible and generally unattractive facts about human beings and human nature.
> **Pragmatism:** only theories which make a difference to practice are worth the effort: the effect or "practical pay-off" is the relevant measure of value in theoretical matters.
> **Quietism**: any normative theorizing which fails to respect the limits imposed by these facts about human nature is idle and pointless; it is better to "keep quiet" about normative matters, than to theorize in ways that make no difference to practice.

Many philosophers could, of course, agree in principle with the Naturalism and the Quietism, even if Classical Realists do distinguish themselves by the extent to which they view the unattractive facts about human nature as incorrigible. What is proprietary to Classical Realism is the insertion of Pragmatism in to the mix. For now the conjunction of the three doctrines means that the aim of theory-construction must be descriptive and explanatory adequacy to the incorrigible facts, rather than normative edification or rationalization: only the former kind of theorizing will pass the pragmatic test, given the Naturalism. Indeed, what is most striking about the pantheon of Classical Realists is that they do *not* pursue the sort of justificatory or normative projects that characterize contemporary moral and political theory (in writers like Rawls, Habermas, Dworkin and many others). Realists want to understand and explain *the way things really are*, rather than engage in idle talk about how they "ought" to be. To the extent they take theory-construction to have an important normative dimension, Realists view this normative advice as circumscribed by their Naturalism. Machiavelli provides a useful illustration of the Classical Realist attitude towards normative theory.

Complaining about earlier writers who offered advice to princes, Machiavelli says, "[I]t seems to me better to concentrate on what really happens rather than on theories or speculations" (Machiavelli 1988, XV).[4] Accordingly, Machiavelli proposes to "set aside fantasies about rulers...and consider what happens in fact" (XV). He proceeds with a point-by-point refutation of the utterly unrealistic "wisdom" of antiquity, especially in the person of Cicero (cf. Skinner 1988, xvii-xx). Thus, Machiavelli denies that generosity is a virtue (XVI); he says that "because men are excessively self-interested," it is better to be feared than loved, since fear appeals more directly to the self-interest of the subjects (XVII); he argues that a ruler should only feel bound by his promises "if all men were upright; but because they are treacherous and would not keep their promises to you, you should not consider yourself bound to keep your promises to them" (XVIII). Much of Machiavelli's advice is predicated on the supposition that "men are so naive, and so much dominated by immediate needs" that deception is both quite possible and profitable. "The common people," he says, "are impressed by appearances and results" (XVIII).

The Prince, in sum, "is passionately driven forward by a sense of what must realistically be said and done if political success is to be achieved" (Skinner 1988, xxiv). Machiavelli thinks this normative advice is constrained by the permanent facts about human nature. In his view, men are self-interested: "the end which everyone aims at...[is] glory and riches" (XXV). These facts make the normative advice of a Cicero or Seneca—the spokesmen for "classical humanism"—irrelevant at best and pernicious at worst. Cicero and Seneca, in short, fail to understand human nature, with the result that their theoretical advice fails the pragmatic test.

Classical Realism, then, stands in opposition to the dominant tradition in the modern academy, which maintains an optimistic view about the ability for normative theory to "make a difference."[5] The Realist view is deeply skeptical, in much the way the eminent political scientist Charles Lindblom has recently expressed:

> [T]here is no clear, unmistakable, demonstrated connection between...the distinguished contributions of a whole history of political philosophy and any of society's major ventures....We have to face, at one extreme, the *possibility* that the world of the 1940s and 1950s—and today's world, too—would look pretty much as it does had there never been a Plato or Aristotle or their equivalents; never a Hobbes, a Locke, a Weber, or their equivalents. (Lindblom 1997, 241–242)[6]

Judge Richard Posner of the U.S. Court of Appeals for the Seventh Circuit, who is perhaps the most influential living legal scholar, has recently articulated the same basic view (to a chorus of condemnation, unsurprisingly, from those with a professional stake in normative theory[7]). Attacking what he calls "academic moralism" (Posner 1999, 5)—"the kind of moral theorizing nowadays considered rigorous in university circles" (*id.*)—Posner claims that such theory,

> has no prospect of improving human behavior. Knowing the moral thing to do furnishes no motive, and creates no motivation.[[8]] Motive and motivation have to come from outside morality. Even if this is wrong, the analytical tools employed in academic moralism—whether moral casuistry, or reasoning from the canonical texts of moral philosophy, or careful analysis, or reflective equilibrium, or some combination of these tools—are too feeble to override either narrow self-interest or [pre-existing] moral intuitions. And academic moralists have neither the rhetorical skills nor the factual knowledge that might enable them to persuade without having good methods of inquiry and analysis. As a result of its analytical, rhetorical, and factual deficiencies, academic moralism is helpless when intuitions clash or self-interest opposes, and otiose when they line up. (Posner 1999, 7)[9]

This is a bracing and polemical statement of a kind of Classical Realist skepticism about normative theory, but perhaps we can try to say more systematically and precisely what considerations would underwrite such a view.

We must recognize at the start that Classical Realist skepticism need *not* depend on any general skepticism about whether ideas (or reasons) make a causal difference to the course of events.[10] Hardcore physicalists (like Quine) may embrace this kind of radical skepticism, but more relaxed materialists (like Posner and Marx) need not.[11] People *may* act *for reasons*, and ideas *may* be hugely influential, and all of that is compatible with Classical Realism. Realist skepticism is directed, rather, at one or both of the following claims: (1) that *moral* ideas and reasons make a causal difference to the course of events; or, (2) that certain normative ideas *in the form of a theory* make a causal difference to the course of events. The former claim would, of course, subsume the latter: if moral ideas make no causal difference, then of course moral theories will make no causal difference. The converse does not hold, however: (2) is a weaker claim than (1), which might explain why even some contemporary moral philosophers have embraced versions of (2) (e.g., Baier 1985).

This latter, more modest skepticism does require that we specify the distinctive *form* of normative *theory*, such that normative ideas so expressed are causally inert. A "theory" in the problematic sense, I take it, aims for a systematic and explicit justification of its normative claims. Moreover, this justification aims for a level of abstractness and comprehensiveness remote from the particularized decision-making of ordinary life. Of course, ordinary people have normative views, and these views may influence their actions. But ordinary decisions are not generally (if ever) informed by a normative *theory* in the sense at issue.

This characterization of normative theory certainly fits Posner's examples of "academic moralists" (like Dworkin and Rawls), and it also jibes with his criticism of academic moralism. For it is precisely the characteristics of academic moral theory—the drawing of fine distinctions, the mustering of careful arguments and counter-arguments, the parsing of concepts—that are supposed to explain its inefficacy for Posner: such stuff simply numbs the mind, bores the reader, and is ineffectual with respect to altering people's antecedent, basic motivations and desires.

But is Posner right? A bit of armchair sociology suggests he may well be. We do know, for example, that academic moral theory is little read, even within the academy.[12] We know that it bores many people, including students. We know that most people and most politicians are not especially smart or acute, and have trouble following a complex argument. We know that people are strongly moved by self-interest in many (perhaps most) circumstances. Given all that—who could seriously deny any of it?—it would, indeed, be surprising if academic moral theory made any difference at all to the course of events. The burden is properly placed on the proponents of the thesis that academic moral theory *matters* to make the case.

The first and less modest kind of skepticism—the one which questions whether *moral* ideas, theoretically expressed or otherwise, exert much force in the course of human affairs—is, in contrast to Posner's anti-moral theory stance, the predominant theme in the historical Classical Realists. This skepticism does share with the first, however, dependence upon Naturalism, i.e., upon the thought that there are incorrigible and unattractive facts about human nature. For both kinds of skepticism rest on the thought that *given what human beings are really like*, one should not expect moral claims or normative theory to have much impact upon them: either people are such that they won't answer to moral demands, or they are such that moral theory will not affect them. Naturalism conjoined with Pragmatism then forms the crux of Classical Realism in all its forms, since it underpins normative quietism and the conception of theory-construction as essentially descriptive and explanatory, rather than normative. It is crucial, then, to be clear about how Classical Realists conceive of human nature and the "incorrigible facts" about human beings. Two themes run through their writings.

First, Classical Realists view human beings as essentially selfish (or self-interested), and their actions as essentially immoral or amoral. (This means, of course, that normative theories *not* in tension with self-interest may turn out to be causally efficacious.) Human beings are "selfish" in the precise sense that in acting their *primary* (though perhaps not their exclusive) motivation is that they expect an action to: (a) constitute their well-being; or (b) contribute (as a means) to their well-being. Many Classical Realists have substantive views about what agents typically take to constitute their well-being: for example, power, fame, wealth, and sexual gratification.[13] But we can also speak generally about the Classical Realist idea that in acting an agent's primary motivation is his own well-being, however exactly well-being is construed.

Of course, this egocentric view of human nature can be strengthened or weakened by placing constraints upon the notion of an agent's "well-being." For example, to what extent can an agent's well-being depend on the satisfaction of other people's desires? To the extent it can, the egocentric view of human motivation risks triviality. The Realist, then, must claim that agents are characterized by a certain "self-regardingness" (Pettit 1995, 310–312). An agent's motivations *may* take into account other people's well-being ("other-regarding desires"), but the more others' well-being is to the agent's own advantage, then the stronger the agent's motivation will be. "[P]eople's self-regarding desires," in a nutshell, "are generally stronger than their other-regarding desires" (Pettit 1995, 312).

Secondly, Classical Realists, though thinking human beings are basically selfish, also have a fairly dim view of human intelligence and capacities.[14] Most people, on the Classical Realist view, are frequently susceptible to the force of irrational wishes and desires; they are essentially gullible, naive, and perhaps even foolish; and they are easily manipulated. Humankind constitutes, in large part, what Nietzsche called the "herd," with all the bovine (or sheepish) connotations of that label. This makes for a rather unhappy combination of traits. People are largely self-serving in their behavior, yet are prone to irrational behavior and are simple-minded, easily fooled, and susceptible to being controlled and used. As a result, while people are generally motivated by selfish concerns, they can not be expected to do particularly well in satisfying even their perceived self-interest, let alone what is *really* in their interest (should that be different).

It bears emphasizing that Classical Realism does not simply amount to a blanket anti-intellectualism. Classical Realists can think "theories" are worth having, even if they think normative theories are a waste of time (or at least normative theories unconstrained by Naturalism). The aim of theory-construction for most Classical Realists is to make perspicuous the causal forces at work in the natural world, including that part of the natural world populated by human beings and their institutions. Intellectual pursuits are not the problem for Realists; idle, normative speculation is.

In the rest of this paper, I want to illustrate Classical Realism in moral, political and legal theory with three historical examples: Nietzsche's Thucydides, Marx, and the American Legal Realists.

II. The Pedigree of Classical Realism

A. Thucydides (as understood by Nietzsche)

For Nietzsche, the story of ancient philosophy is the unhappy story of how Plato and Socratic rationalism triumphed over the Presocratics and, especially, the culture of the Sophists of the 5th century B.C.[15] For Nietzsche, Thucydides represents the high point of this period in Greek culture. In Thucydides, he says,

> that *culture of the most impartial knowledge of the world* finds its last glorious flower: that culture which had in Sophocles its poet, in Pericles its statesman, in Hippocrates its physician, in Democritus its natural philosopher; which deserves to be baptised with the name of its teachers, the Sophists.... (D 168)[16]

In Thucydides, in other words, "the culture of the Sophists, by which I mean the culture of the realists [*die Realisten-Cultur*], reaches its perfect expression" (TI X:2). The essence of Sophistic culture, for Nietzsche, is precisely its Classical Realism: "The Sophists are no more than realists....they possess the courage of all strong spirits to *know* their own immorality" (WP 429). It is, in turn, Thucydides, in his great *History of the Peloponnesian War*, who displays this courage more completely than anyone else. Thus, Nietzsche calls Thucydides,

...the great sum, the last revelation of that strong, severe, hard factuality which was instinctive with the older Hellenes. In the end, it is *courage* in the face of reality that distinguishes a man like Thucydides from Plato: Plato is a coward before reality, consequently he flees into the ideal; Thucydides has control of *himself*, consequently he also maintains control of things. (TI X:2)

In what, precisely, does the "courage" or "realism" of Thucydides consist? The most useful illustration is the dialogue between the Athenians and the vanquished Melians recounted in Thucydides' *History*—a dialogue that one distinguished commentator has called "the most famous example of amoral realism" (Guthrie 1971, 85). Negotiating over the terms of surrender, the Athenians address the Melians, in relevant part, as follows:

For our part, we will not make a long speech no one would believe, full of fine moral arguments–that our empire is justified because we defeated the Persians, or that we are coming against you for an injustice you have done to us....Instead, let's work out what we can do on the basis of what both sides truly accept: we both know that decisions about justice are made in human discussions only when both sides are under equal compulsion [i.e., only among equals does right prevail over might]; but when one side is stronger, it gets as much as it can, and the weak must accept that....Nature always compels gods (we believe) and men (we are certain) to rule over anyone they can control. We did not make this law, and we were not the first to follow it; but we will take it as we found it and leave it to posterity forever, because we know that you would do the same if you had our power, and so would anyone else. (Woodruff 1993, 103, 106 (¶¶89, 105)).

Nietzsche's own commentary on this particular dialogue highlights some of the key themes of Classical Realism:

Do you suppose perchance that these little Greek free cities, which from rage and envy would have liked to devour each other, were guided by philanthropic and righteous principles? Does one reproach Thucydides for the words he puts into the mouths of the Athenian ambassadors when they negotiated with the Melians on the question of destruction or submission? Only complete Tartuffes [i.e., Socrates and Plato] could possibly have talked of virtue in the midst of this terrible tension—or men living apart, hermits, refugees, and emigrants from reality—people who negated in order to be able to live themselves—The Sophists were Greeks: when Socrates and Plato took up the cause of virtue and justice, they were *Jews* [i.e., promulgators of Judeo-Christian, or slave, morality] or I know not what—Grote's tactics in defense of the Sophists are false: he wants to raise them to the rank of men of honor and ensigns of morality—but it was precisely their honor not to indulge in any swindle with big words and virtues. (WP 429)

Thucydides "the Realist" recognizes quite clearly that the Athenians are not moved by "philanthropic and righteous principles," that they are driven, instead, by selfish and self-aggrandizing concerns, restrained only by the limits of their own power. Socrates and Plato, by contrast, chatter irrelevantly about "virtue and justice," when, as Thucydides makes plain, virtue and justice play no role in human affairs.

Of course, the speeches Thucydides recorded are his own creations; in many cases (as with the Melian dialogue), he could not even have been present to hear them. Yet this is precisely why Thucydides is a Realist in Nietzsche's view: how he chooses to reconstruct events marks Thucydides as a Realist. As Paul Woodruff aptly observes:

> a frequent purpose of the speeches [in Thucydides' *History*] is to reveal the [true] motives of the speakers....Thucydides wants to bring the darker side of human nature to light by revealing motives such as fear that speakers would want to conceal in real life....Thucydides' speakers are made to say what Thucydides thinks they actually believe, whether they would have said those things in public or not....He shows us their speeches refracted through a lens of honesty. (Woodruff 1993, xxiii)

Thucydides, in other words, puts into the speakers' mouths their true, amoral motives, reflecting Thucydides' realistic view of human nature and human affairs, in contrast with the idealistic fantasies of a Socrates or Plato.[17] Thus, Nietzsche declares:

> my *cure* from all Platonism has always been *Thucydides*. Thucydides and, perhaps Machiavelli's *Principe* are most closely related to myself by the unconditional will not to gull oneself and to see reason in *reality*—not in "reason," still less in "morality." (TI X:2)

Thucydides the Classical Realist views humans as essentially motivated by selfish concerns—power, fear, wealth—and as creatures for whom moral considerations are at best rhetorical window-dressing, rather than a reason for action.[18] The *History of the Peloponnesian War* is a microcosm for what happens when the perennial dark facts about human nature encounter the recurring circumstances of human social existence. Nietzsche the Classical Realist, in turn, views Socrates and Plato as foolishly non-quietistic, since they promulgate theories about justice and virtue when, as Thucydides so vividly demonstrates, norms of justice and virtue play little or no role in human affairs.

Of course, as Nietzsche's earlier comments would suggest, Thucydides is not alone as a spokesman for Classical Realism in antiquity. The Sophist Gorgias, as well as Glaucon and Thrasymachus in Plato's *Republic*, are also Realists in large measure. As Guthrie puts it, they share "an attitude of hard-headed realism or fact-facing which without passing judgment declares that the more powerful will always take advantage of the weaker, and will give the name of law and justice to whatever they lay down in their own interests" (1971, 60). The Realists, according to Guthrie, all agree with Glaucon in the *Republic* that "[s]elf-interest...is what every nature (*physis*) naturally pursues as good" (1971, 99).

B. MARX

Marx may, at first, seem an unlikely candidate for membership in the pantheon of Classical Realists, since he is often thought to deny that there is any such thing as "human nature." For example, in the *Theses on Feuerbach* he sounds a familiar theme when he asserts that "men are products of circumstances and upbringing" (Tucker 1978, 144), while in *The Communist Manifesto* he derides the German socialists for claiming to speak for "the interests of Human Nature, of Man in general, who belongs to no class, has no reality, who exists only in the misty realm of philosophical fantasy" (Tucker 1978, 494).

Remarks like these, however, are misleading. Marx does want to argue, to be sure, that many features of human behavior that are chalked up to an invariant human nature by the forces of reaction are, in truth, the artifacts of socio-economic circumstances, and thus are malleable. Yet one can think conservatives are wrong about human nature, while still thinking, as Marx does, that there is an essential, unchanging human nature that conservatives have simply overlooked.[19]

Yet this may not help in the present context. For Marx held, famously, that the putatively "selfish" nature of human beings is a socio-economic artifact, not an enduring feature of the human condition. Thus, in a typical passage from *The Communist Manifesto*, Marx writes that:

> The bourgeoisie, wherever it has got the upper hand, has put an end to all feudal, patriarchal, idyllic relations. It has pitilessly torn asunder the motley feudal ties that bound man to his "natural superiors," and has left remaining no other nexus between man and man than naked self-interest, than callous "cash payment." It has drowned the most heavenly ecstasies of religious fervour, of chivalrous enthusiasm, of philistine sentimentalism, in the icy water of egotistical calculation. (Tucker 1978, 475)

One might, of course, simply repudiate this Marxist skepticism that "self-interest" and other "ugly" human character traits are deep facts about human nature. Perhaps Freud is right, and Marx wrong, about what is "natural" and what is mere "social construct" when it comes to the familiar, unattractive features of human social existence?[20] A more modest rejoinder, however, will suffice here: even if selfishness is not a permanent feature of human nature, it remains a permanent feature of human beings in capitalist society. Since capitalism remains dominant—indeed, will, by Marx's own theory, remain dominant for the foreseeable future[21]—Marx can agree with the Classical Realist appraisal of human beings in every respect except one: human beings must necessarily and always be this way.

Indeed, beyond this one issue, the points of affinity between Marx and Classical Realism are manifold. The standard Marxist refrains that, "The ideas of the ruling class are in every epoch the ruling ideas" (*The German Ideology*; Tucker 1978, 172) and that, "Law, morality, religion are to [the proletariat] so many bourgeois prejudices, behind which lurk in ambush just as many bourgeois interests" (*The Communist Manifesto*; Tucker 1978, 482) are simply modern translations of the Sophistic view "that the more powerful will always take advantage of the weaker, and will give the name of law and justice to whatever they lay down in their own interests" (Guthrie 1971, 60). Like Thucydides, Marx is also skeptical of self-serving explanations that agents proffer for their behavior. In fact, he endlessly derides non-realistic historians for taking actors and events at face value:

> Whilst in ordinary life every shopkeeper is very well able to distinguish between what somebody professes to be and what he really is, our historians have not yet won even this trivial insight. They take every epoch at its word and believe that everything it says and imagines about itself is true. (*German Ideology*, Tucker 1978, 175)

But in fact what people profess is a mere ideology, behind which lurks the real selfish interests of a particular class:

> For each new class which puts itself in the place of one ruling before it, is compelled, merely in order to carry through its aim, to represent its interest as the common interest of all the members of society, that is, expressed in ideal form: it has to give its ideas the form of universality, and represent them as the only rational, universally valid ones. (Tucker 1978, 174)

This is the essence of "ideology" on Marx's view—to present the (selfish) interests of a particular class as really being in the general interest.[22] Like Thucydides the Classical Realist historian, Marx would pull back the veils to expose the real motives of the ruling class and their ideological spokesmen.[23]

Perhaps the most striking affinity between Marx and Classical Realism concerns the Pragmatism and Quietism they share. For Marx's theoretical efforts are not spent in *justifying* communism (as, e.g., morally desirable or just): there is no analogue in the Marxian corpus to the Rawlsian defense of a liberal theory of justice. Rather, Marx tries to construct an adequate descriptive and explanatory account of human society and history that will have practical pay-offs in political organizing and revolutionary activity. (In this sense, Marx is the quintessential pragmatist: the value of any theory is measured by the difference it makes to practice.[24]) Making arguments about the "injustice" or "immorality" of capitalism has no practical value for Marx.[25] The ruling classes will not give up their privileges because philosophers show them that they are violating some putatively timeless moral precept, whether it be the Difference Principle, the Categorical Imperative or the principle of utility.[26] On normative matters, then, Marx keeps quiet—not in the sense that he has no normative beliefs, but rather in the sense that, *qua* theorist, he thinks there is no point in developing a philosophical account and defense of those beliefs. Thus, in *The German Ideology*, Marx says that "real, positive science begins" with,

> the representation of the practical activity, of the practical process of development of men....When reality is depicted, philosophy as an independent branch of knowledge loses its medium of existence. (Tucker 1978, 155)

For Marx, like the modern Quinean naturalist,[27] philosophy collapses into a certain sort of descriptive/explanatory theory of the kind typical in the empirical sciences. Theoretical accounts of justice play no role in theory-construction so understood.[28]

Marx's Classical Realism is most vivid when contrasted with the views of the currently most influential member of the quasi-Marxist Frankfurt School, Jürgen Habermas. I say "quasi-Marxist" not only because of the familiar fact that the early Frankfurt School breaks with Marx over a variety of issues (e.g., the revolutionary potential of the working classes).[29] Habermas represents, in a profound way, a complete betrayal of Marx's conception of philosophy. For at the center of Habermas's writings, there has been precisely a set of *normative* and "purely *scholastic*"[30] questions, indistinguishable in kind from the questions that have occupied all the great bourgeois moral philosophers from Kant to Rawls.[31]

Through "the ideal speech situation" (in his early work) and "communicative ethics" (in his later work), Habermas tries to *justify* a particular normative perspective on questions of right action and just social ordering.[32] One can well imagine what Marx, the Classical Realist, would have thought of such efforts. Recall, for example, Marx's complaint about the German socialists who present themselves as advancing "the requirements of truth; not the interests of the proletariat, but the interests of Human Nature, of Man in general, who belongs to no class, has no reality, who exists only in the misty realm of philosophical fantasy" (*The Communist Manifesto*; Tucker 1978, 494). Marx might just as well have been referring to the Habermas who thinks that "truth" in moral and social matters would be fixed by consensus in a situation of open and rational argument among free and equal persons. The revival of *normative* theory within critical theory marks a decisive turn away from the whole (realistic) spirit of Marx's own work.

C. American Legal Realism

The American Legal Realists of the 1920s and 1930s chose their name precisely for the reasons that Classical Realists earn theirs: the Legal Realists wanted to tell it like it *really* is, especially with respect to judicial decision-making. These themes are sounded in Oliver Wendell Holmes, Jr.'s seminal paper on "The Path of the Law" (Holmes 1897)[33] which introduces ideas that would become, thirty years later, central to the legal theory characteristic of American Legal Realism.[34] Holmes, the proto-Realist, wastes no time telling his audience that the object of legal study is neither moral truth or justice, nor abstract principles or logical systems, but rather "the prediction of the incidence of the public force through the instrumentality of the courts" (Holmes 1897, 457). The student of the law must know "what the courts will do in fact" (461) which requires that one "look straight through all the dramatic incidents [in order] to discern the true basis for prophecy" (475). This "true basis" demands neither an understanding of morality—for law is one thing, and morality another—nor even much of legal logic ("You can give any conclusion a logical form" (466)). Instead, it requires recognizing that every decision represents a "half conscious battle on the question of legislative policy" (467). For Holmes, "the man of the future," will be "the master of economics" (469) in part because economics will anchor prediction in the way Holmes's realistic perspective demands. Economics, in

Posner's words, provides "the key to an accurate description of what the judges are up to" (Posner 1990, 360). Of course, "such a mode of looking at the matter [may] stink[] in the nostrils of those who think it advantageous to get as much ethics into the law as they can" (Holmes 1897, 462). But this is of no concern to Holmes the hard-headed realist. We can imagine Holmes agreeing with Nietzsche in ridiculing those who "indulge in any swindle with big [moral] words and virtues" (WP 429), when all that is required is a willingness to confront the facts squarely. For Holmes, that meant the facts about what the courts really do.[35]

Holmes similarly anticipates the Legal Realists in his approach to normative theorizing about courts.[36] Although he speaks of the judge's "duty of weighing considerations of social advantage" (Holmes 1897, 467), he quickly makes clear that as normative advice it does not amount to much, for this is what courts do anyway! "The duty is inevitable," says Holmes, so telling judges that they "ought" to weigh social advantage only amounts to the modest suggestion that they do openly what they do anyway, albeit "inarticulate[ly], and often unconscious[ly]" (Holmes 1897, 467). Normative theory, at least in "The Path of the Law," takes a back seat to the practical task of making a systematic, empirical study of the real grounds of decision. We need to explain and describe judicial decision-making, rather than tell judges what they "ought" to do.

This type of normative quietism is prominent in the later Legal Realists. Jerome Frank, for example, commenting on what he called "Cadi justice" (essentially, justice by personal predilection), remarked that, "[t]he true question...is not whether we should 'revert' to [it], but whether (a) we have ever abandoned it and (b) we can ever pass beyond it" (Frank 1931, 31). Advocating a "'reversion to Cadi justice'...is as meaningless as [advocating] a 'reversion to mortality' or a 'return to breathing'" (31), because, according to Frank, "the personal element is unavoidable in judicial decisions" (25).

A more interesting example of normative quietism in Legal Realism is Karl Llewellyn's work on Article 2 of the Uniform Commercial Code. For drafting a Code is, of course, an explicitly normative enterprise, one a Realist, on my construal, shouldn't be able to undertake. In fact, though, Llewellyn uses Article 2 to tell judges that what they *ought* to do in commercial disputes is precisely what his *descriptive* theory claims they largely do already, namely enforce the norms of the prevailing commercial culture (or mercantile practice) in which the dispute arose.[37] Thus, for example, the Code imposes an obligation of "good faith" in all contractual dealings (§1-203) which means "the observance of reasonable commercial standards of fair dealing in the trade" (§2-103). But for a court, then, to enforce the rule requiring "good faith" is just for that court to enforce the relevant norms of commercial culture! The reliance of Article 2 throughout on norms of "good faith" and "reasonableness" is a constant invitation to the judge to do what he would, on the Realist theory, do anyway.

The Quietism of Holmes and the Legal Realists contrasts markedly with the *normative* ambitions of contemporary jurisprudents like Ronald Dworkin. Dworkin, of course, claims descriptive adequacy for his theory, at least with respect to the underlying logic of what it is judges are doing.[38] But it is not always clear that lawyers or judges find Dworkin's "description" of what they are doing recognizable.[39] And when Dworkin himself comes to actually discuss substantive legal issues—e.g., abortion, affirmative action, and the like—he seems to be doing something quite different from what lawyers do.[40] Certainly, Dworkin's most famous claim, that even "hard cases" have right answers, has won little acceptance among either academics or judges.[41] Rather than merely advising judges to do explicitly what they already do—as Holmes does—Dworkin wants to reform their practice in line with a philosophically superior theory of adjudication and political legitimacy. But such an undertaking, according to Realism, is an irrelevant undertaking.

Indeed, Quietist complaints about Dworkin are not merely speculative. There are empirical reasons for thinking his normative theory of how judges should decide cases really has been an idle exercise. Although Dworkin has been the most famous figure in Anglo-American jurisprudence for more than a quarter-century, he has been cited only *seven* times in U.S. Supreme Court opinions during this time–and only *once*, remarkably, in the majority (and even then, on a quite minor point).[42] This is surely striking, if defeasible, evidence that thirty years of telling courts how they *ought* to decide cases has made little difference to the practice of the courts.

It is possible, of course, that even without citing Dworkin, the Court might have adopted his distinctive way of thinking about legal problems. But even this seems, manifestly, not to have been the case. Over the quarter-century that Dworkin has been one of the leading defenders of "noninterpretivist" approaches to the Constitution—those approaches which defend the propriety of finding Constitutional rights beyond the history, structure, and text of the document itself[43]—the Court has gradually repudiated this entire approach to reading the Constitution, culminating with its 1986 decision in *Bowers v. Hardwick*.[44] Dworkin's rise to academic prominence, in short, has coincided exactly with the decline of his favored approach to Constitutional interpretation. Surely this fact supports the Quietist suspicion that certain types of normative theorizing are idle exercises, that "styles" of Constitutional interpretation (and the political consequences that flow from them) rise and fall for reasons that have *nothing* to do with the arguments of philosophers.

III: Concluding Thoughts

One might worry, to be sure, that the Classical Realist critique of normative theory presupposes an unrealistic time frame in which to register influence or impact.[45] Perhaps it is not thirty years, but a century that we must look at; perhaps it is not particular citations, but the gradual shaping of an *enabling ethos* which becomes the historical consciousness of a later period and, in turn, affects decisions and actions. Understood this way, of course, the claim of normative theorizing to have "made a difference" gets much harder to assess.[46] The fact that we speak of an "idea whose time has come" does not mean that its time has come because of the labor of moral philosophers. How are we, over the course of a century or two, to disentangle the causal mechanisms at work? If Marx or Braudel is right, can we expect anything more from normative theory than that it should make a difference *only in virtue of favorable material circumstances making the time ripe*? Do Lockean *arguments* influence the American framing, or is it that historical circumstances create a receptivity to some general ideas, for which Locke and his arguments provide "authority"? There are difficult questions here of social and historical causation, but the power of broadly materialistic explanations of phenomena across almost all domains might suggest that the Classical Realist is right to be skeptical about the claimed causal efficacy of moral norms or normative theory.[47]

Of course, it remains open to normative theorists to repudiate the pragmatic criterion of the Classical Realists, and certainly no argument has been given for thinking that practical cash-value should be a constraint on philosophical reflection. What bears emphasizing, however, is that there is an important tradition of normative thought which takes it for granted that Pragmatism, in the sense defined earlier, *is* a constraint on theory, and which thus approaches the phenomena of human moral and social life not with the goal of finding post-hoc rationalizations for our normative commitments, but rather with the aim of laying bare the actual causal structure of the world, including the normative commitments we find in it.

NOTES

*Thanks to Richard Posner for comments on the penultimate draft, to Paul Woodruff for useful discussion about Thucydides and Nietzsche, and to the audience members at the University of Toronto Legal Theory Workshop for their helpful comments and questions regarding an earlier version of some of this material. I am especially grateful to Arthur Ripstein for saving me from several errors.

1. I took a briefer, and less satisfactory, stab at the same enterprise in Leiter (2000), but the characterization of Classical Realism there now strikes me as problematic in respects I try to rectify here.
2. For a representative treatment of "realism" in current philosophy, see Railton (1996); for a somewhat different (though related) approach, see Pettit (2001).
3. One area in which the "realist" label has retained this kind of meaning is international affairs. See, e.g., Morgenthau (1967, 4–8); Forde (1995).
4. I take no position in this essay on the difficult interpretive question of whether the later Machiavelli of *The Discourses* is also a Classical Realist in my sense.
5. If the rationale for normative theory is only to achieve a certain reflective, albeit impotent, understanding of our normative talk, then the Classical Realist has no particular quarrel with normative theory (though he might not think it a kind of understanding worth having). Of course, it would be surprising if those who commit their lives to developing theories about what *ought* to be done, in fact entertained no hope of determining what *is* done.
6. I am grateful to Calvin Johnson for calling this article to my attention.
7. See, e.g., Dworkin (1998) and Nussbaum (1998). Dworkin's criticisms of Posner's uses of evolutionary theory, however, do strike me as correct. Posner sometimes comes close to running afoul of his own Classical Realist scruples.
8. Although Posner does not discuss the issue, he is, in fact, taking a position here on a controversial thesis in moral theory, namely externalism, which denies that there is any intrinsic connection between knowledge of the moral rightness of an action and an agent's motivation to perform it. Kantians deny externalism, while Humeans affirm it. I am inclined to think that the Humeans (and, *a fortiori*, Posner) are rather *clearly* right (certainly empirically, but also conceptually), but such an affirmation will merely strike Kantians as dogmatic.
9. Posner is well-aware that professional moral philosophers frequently claim influence for academic moral theory, but, as he notes, no empirical evidence

is ever adduced on behalf of these sanctimonious platitudes. See Posner (1999, 25 and n. 27) (discussing such claims by the moral philosophers Samuel Scheffler and J.B. Schneewind).

10. Dworkin simply caricatures Posner's view when he objects, "no doubt many people are never moved by the logic of a moral argument, even once in their lives, but it is absurd to suppose that no one ever is" (Dworkin 2000, 51). But nothing in Posner's view, or that of Classical Realism, requires maintaining that the argument of moral philosophers has never influenced *anyone*; the claim is that moral arguments make no difference to *the course of events*, which is, of course, compatible with their influencing persons on occasion. Indeed, it seems bizarre for Dworkin to lambaste Posner for his "a priori psychological dogma" (*id.*) regarding the influence of moral philosophy, given that Posner's claim, like Marx's related claim (see below), is manifestly *a posteriori*: where, one wonders, is the evidence for the great influence of the arguments of moral philosophers?
11. Materialists need only hold that ideas are causally efficacious *only in virtue of* opportune material circumstances. Thus, preaching communism in the fourteenth-century would be inefficacious because the level of material development is inadequate to support communism. By contrast, Marx believed (falsely as it turns out) that the level of material development was sufficiently high in the nineteenth century as to make the *idea* of communism, suitably promulgated, causally efficacious (but not causally sufficient) in bringing about the demise of capitalism.
12. The lone exception might be Rawls (1971), though it is unclear whether that distinguished work is widely *read* or just widely *referred to* for a few simple ideas. Indeed, one suspects the power of Rawls may be more a function of his pithy, memorable, metaphoric ideas—the difference principle, the veil of ignorance, the original position, overlapping consensus, and so forth—than his elaborate argumentative apparatus which purportedly generates these ideas. (I am grateful to Richard Posner on these points.)
13. President Clinton's recent address to the U.N. General Assembly (September 21, 1999) begins on a relevant Realist note: "the 20th century has been deeply scarred by enduring human failures, by greed and lust for power." The Classical Realist might add: not *only* the 20th century!
14. It is in this regard that economic theories, predicated as they are on rational actor models, depart from Classical Realism. Behavioral law and economics, in turn, may be understood as an attempt to bring Classical Realist concerns to bear on economic analysis. See generally, Jolls, Sunstein & Thaler (1998). Unfortunately, it seems more likely that the behavioral turn will simply accelerate the fading credibility of economics. On the latter, see Leiter (2000, 303–310).
15. E.g., "The real philosophers of Greece are those before Socrates" (WP 437); "for the whole phenomenon Plato I would sooner use the harsh phrase 'higher swindle'" (TI X:2). A note on citation format to Nietzsche: I cite to Nietzsche's texts by their standard English-language acronyms: *Dawn* (D), *The Gay Science* (GS), *Thus Spoke Zarathustra* (Z), *Beyond Good and Evil* (BGE), *On the Genealogy of Morality* (GM), *Twilight of the Idols* (TI), *The Antichrist*

(A), *Ecce Homo* (EH), *The Will to Power* (WP). Translations, with minor emendations, are by Walter Kaufmann and/or R.J. Hollingdale; for purposes of emendations, I rely on the Colli/Montinari edition of the *Sämtliche Werke*. Roman numerals refer to major chapters or divisions in Nietzsche's works; Arabic numerals refer to sections, not pages.

16. Cf. WP 428 (a note of 1888): "The Greek culture of the Sophists had developed out of all the Greek instincts; it belongs to the culture of the Periclean age as necessarily as Plato does *not*; it has its predecessors in Heraclitus, Democritus, in the scientific types of the old philosophy; it finds its expression in, e.g., the high culture of Thucydides...."
17. Of course, on one prevalent understanding of Plato, he too accepts that humans are self-interested, and tries to show them simply that "justice" and "virtue" are in their self-interest. The Realist might object that this identification of morality with self-interest is so implausible as to be no different from preaching "justice" and "virtue" quite apart from any appeal to self-interest.
18. Cf. Guthrie (1971, 85): "It is remarkable how seldom even [Thucydides'] orators, aiming at persuasion, see any point in appealing to considerations of right, justice or other normally accepted moral standards: it is taken for granted that only an appeal to self-interest is likely to succeed."
19. See the discussion in Cohen (1978, 151) and Wood (1980, 17–24).
20. The classic expression of this view is Freud (1961). Freud's embrace of the Classical Realist's Quietistic Thesis is strikingly explicit in the concluding pages of this seminal work:

    > [I]t is very far from my intention to express an opinion upon the value of human civilization....One thing only do I know for certain and that is that man's judgments of value follow directly his wishes for happiness—that, accordingly, they are an attempt to support his illusions with arguments....I have not the courage to rise up before my fellow-men as a prophet, and I bow to their reproach that I can offer them no consolation: for at bottom that is what they are all demanding—the wildest revolutionaries no less passionately than the most virtuous believers. (Freud 1961, 103, 104)

21. The party line of the capitalist media in recent years, at least in the U.S., has been that the collapse of the Soviet Union constitutes a "refutation" of Marx, assigning him to the "dustbin of history". But this is obviously silly. It is quite clear that the conditions for communist revolution that Marx explicitly sets out—that capitalism have produced the maximal development of the forces of production, reduced the great mass of humanity to a condition of poverty, destroyed all the hitherto-existing national, ethnic, and religious identities, and exhausted all the potential markets for goods (see *The Communist Manifesto*, in Tucker (1978, 475–483, 488))—were not satisfied in 1917, nor have they been satisfied even today. Nonetheless, it seems equally clear that current global economic tendencies and trends point precisely towards the conditions that Marx wrongly thought were around the corner in

the mid-19th-century. (Even the seemingly resilient national, ethnic and religious chauvinisms that have captured the headlines from the former Yugoslavia, Iran, and Rwanda (among other places) must be set against a backdrop of the gradual triumph of American pop culture over much of the globe, and the resulting homogenization of attitudes and values; no doubt the market will have similar effects in the aforementioned retrograde countries in due course.) In this regard, Marx was quite prescient in his understanding of the logic of capitalism, though his timing was badly off. It remains, in turn, an open empirical question whether the realization of these conditions will bring about the triumph of communism and an open empirical question whether selfishness will turn out to be a permanent feature of human nature or a mere socio-economic artifact of a particular era.

22. On the different possible senses of "ideology," see Geuss (1981, 13–14). Marx's usage is what Geuss calls an ideology in the "epistemic" sense.
23. One might also argue that Marx shares the Classical Realists' view that human beings are naive, gullible, and easily misled insofar as he thinks that the vast majority of people who embrace bourgeois morals, law, and religion have been badly duped about their own interests. But this aspect of Classical Realism is probably more vivid in the early writers of the Frankfurt School—like Theodor Adorno and Herbert Marcuse—who no longer share Marx's optimism about the revolutionary potential of the working classes, and have a far more contemptuous view of the intelligence and revolutionary capacities of ordinary persons.
24. This, in a nutshell, is one of the central themes of the *Theses on Feuerbach*, esp. Theses II, VIII, and XI. For a related understanding of pragmatism, in a more contemporary idiom, see Johnston (1993).
25. As one commentator aptly puts Marx's view: "The moralist turns out to be little help to a revolution and to be positively pernicious if many people take up her useless activity" (Brudney 1998, 324). Oddly, Brudney later claims that "if...any radical theory is to help change social conditions it needs a relatively explicit account of the good society" (*id.* at 353). No defense of this utterly unMarxian claim is given.
26. Thus, Marx derides the Young Hegelians and Feuerbach for wanting "merely to produce a correct [philosophical] consciousness about an *existing* fact; whereas for the real communist it is a question of overthrowing the existing state of things" (*German Ideology*, in Tucker (1978, 167–168)). This Marxist criticism is, ironically, apt with respect to parts of the Critical Legal Studies literature. See the discussion in Leiter (1997, 383–384).

The irrelevance of the arguments of moral and political philosophers to social change has sometimes been noted by such philosophers. See, e.g., Nagel (1979, xii) ("Moral judgment and moral theory certainly apply to public questions, but they are notably ineffective"). The Classical Realist explanation for this is straightforward: the great "herd" of humanity is too driven by selfish concerns and too uninterested (or unable) to understand moral argument for the labor of moral philosophers to make any difference.

Indeed, the often breathtaking moral illiteracy and self-serving pettiness of people is made vivid in the newspapers every day. Thus, a randomly chosen issue of *The New York Times* (January 8, 1997) reports that wealthy whites in a suburb of Johannesburg, South Africa, are refusing to pay their new, higher property taxes. The *Times* explains:

> [M]any of the whites here feel blameless for apartheid. They say that they never voted for the National Party, which devised and carried out South Africa's repressive racial policies when it headed a white minority government, and that they were active in various charities. For instance, [one wealthy white woman] says that she used to make peanut butter cookies for poor black children in Pretoria and that her husband's firm sponsors an adult literacy course for domestic servants. (p. A4)

Everything in my own experience suggests that these (no doubt) "educated" South Africans are the norm, not the exception, in the quality of their moral calculus.

27. On Quinean naturalism, see Leiter (1997a, 288–294; 1997b, 1746–1748; 1998). For a useful characterization of Quine for my purposes here, see especially, Kim (1994).
28. Notice that this interpretation is compatible with the possibility that Marx is a tacit (sophisticated) utilitarian, a view favored by contemporary analytical Marxists like Richard Boyd and Peter Railton. My point is not that Marx did not have what might fairly be called *moral* views, but rather that he did not view the construction of a moral *theory* as a worthwhile or necessary undertaking.
29. For a useful, but somewhat polemical account of the differences, see Kolakowski (1978, 341–343).
30. *Theses on Feuerbach*, in Tucker (1978, 144).
31. So, e.g., Roemer (1986, 99) betrays his lack of understanding of Marx's Classical Realism—or at least analytical Marxism's betrayal of that Realism—when he says "it is not at all clear how analytical Marxists will differ from non-Marxist philosophers like Ronald Dworkin, John Rawls, and Amartya Sen." To be sure, analytical Marxists correctly repudiate Marx's lunatic commitment to "dialectical" methodology, but it is not only that that sets Marx's whole approach apart from that of non-Realist normative theorists like Dworkin, Rawls, and Sen.
32. For description and criticism of the earlier versions of the normative argument, see Geuss (1981, 55–75) and Lukes (1982). Contrary to some defenders of Habermas, it does not seem to me that these critiques are deflected by the shifts in thinking of the later Habermas.
33. I make no claim here about the extent to which the rest of the Holmesian corpus is consistent with the Classical Realist themes sounded in this essay, or in his correspondence.
34. For a brief overview of the main themes of the Realist movement, see Leiter (1999).
35. I confess it is not clear to me how this aspect of Holmes's Classical Realism is to be squared with the concluding pages of Holmes (1897). Holmes may simply have shared another feature with the later Legal Realists: a tendency to say inconsistent things. Interestingly, though, Holmes explicitly admired *exactly* the same features in Thucydides as did Nietzsche: "I am struck [in

the dialogues of Thucydides]...by the absence of our notion of manners. They say what they think with no polite veils....I like the absence of the hypocritic Christian unction. They say outright that of course the crowd that has the force means to have the top–and everybody understands it" (Posner 1992, 60).

36. On this issue, see in particular Leiter (1996a, 276–278).
37. For the descriptive theory of the "Sociological Wing" of Realism, see Leiter (1996a, 272–275). For a more detailed discussion—one that supports the quietism I emphasize here—see White (1994).
38. See Dworkin (1986, 265); cf. the discussion in Leiter (1996b, 255–258).
39. See, e.g., Noonan (1986); see also Ely (1980, 56–60).
40. All of this is, admittedly, *defeasible* evidence as to the descriptive adequacy of Dworkin's theory.
41. See, e.g., Posner (1990, 233).
42. The majority cite comes in *Board of Pardons v. Allen*, 482 U.S. 369, 375 (1987). One citation, in a concurring opinion, is on a bioethical issue addressed in Dworkin (1996), one unrelated to his general jurisprudential views. See *Washington v. Glucksberg*, 521 U.S. 702, 747 (1997). The other citations, all in dissent, appear in: *Hewitt v. Helms*, 459 U.S. 460, 485 (1983); *Delaware v. Van Arsdall*, 475 U.S. 673, 698 (1986); *Young v. Community Nutrition Institute*, 476 U.S. 974, 988 (1986); *Webster v. Reproductive Health Services*, 492 U.S. 490, 541 (1989); *Planned Parenthood v. Casey*, 505 U.S. 833, 914 (1992). The citations to Dworkin in the dissents in *Casey*, *Webster*, and *Van Arsdall* are all a bit more substantive than in *Allen*. But in none of these cases could the Court, by any stretch of the imagination, be described as embracing Dworkin's theory of adjudication.
43. Dworkin has, rightly it seems to me, criticized the "noninterpretivist" label as question-begging (Dworkin 1985). This does not alter the fact that Dworkin's interpretive methodology is quite different from that of John Hart Ely or Antonin Scalia or Henry Monaghan.
44. 478 U.S. 186 (1986).
45. I am grateful to Maurice Leiter for a forceful articulation of this point, from which I borrow in the text.
46. Understood this way, the point is also of no help to Dworkin, who clearly expresses but one aspect of an enabling ethos created by others—e.g., Kant and Locke and Rousseau. And perhaps even these latter writers are mere expressions of an "ethos" whose sources are not at all philosophical—as, for example, Nietzsche argues in the *Genealogy*.
47. The moral explanations literature by moral realists suggests that normative claims do figure in the best explanations of phenomena. But the examples adduced by moral realists do not bear much scrutiny; see the discussion and critique in Leiter (2001b.)

References

Baier, Annette. (1985) "Doing without Moral Theory?" in *Postures of the Mind: Essays on Mind & Morals* (London: Metheun).

Brudney, Daniel. (1998) *Marx's Attempt to Leave Philosophy* (Cambridge, Mass.: Harvard University Press).
Cohen, G.A. (1978) *Karl Marx's Theory of History: A Defence* (Princeton: Princeton University Press).
Dworkin, Ronald. (1985) "The Forum of Principle," in *A Matter of Principle* (Cambridge, Mass.: Harvard University Press).
______. (1986) *Law's Empire* (Cambridge, Mass.: Harvard University Press).
______. (1996) *Life's Dominion* (Cambridge, Mass.: Harvard University Press).
______. (1998) "Darwin's New Bulldog," *Harvard Law Review* 111: 1718–1738.
______. (2000) "Philosophy & Monica Lewinsky," *New York Review of Books* XLVII/4 (March 9): 48–52.
Ely, John Hart (1980) *Democracy and Distrust* (Cambridge, Mass.: Harvard University Press).
Forde, Steven. (1995) "International Realism and the Science of Politics: Thucydides, Machiavelli, and Neorealism," *International Studies Quarterly* 39: 141–160.
Frank, Jerome. (1931) "Are Judges Human? Part I," *University of Pennsylvania Law Review* 80: 17–53.
Freud, Sigmund. (1961) *Civilization and Its Discontents*, ed. & trans. J. Strachey (New York: W.W. Norton & Co.).
Geuss, Raymond. (1981) *The Idea of a Critical Theory* (Cambridge: Cambridge University Press).
Guthrie, W.K.C. (1971) *The Sophists* (Cambridge: Cambridge University Press).
Holmes, O.W. (1897) "The Path of the Law," *Harvard Law Review* 10: 457–478.
Johnston, Mark. (1993) "Objectivity Refigured: Pragmatism Without Verificationism," in J. Haldane & C. Wright (eds.), *Reality, Representation, and Projection* (Oxford: Oxford University Press).
Jolls, Christine, Cass R. Sunstein, & Richard Thaler. (1998) "A Behavioral Approach to Law and Economics," *Stanford Law Review* 50: 1471–1550.
Kim, Jaegwon. (1994) "What is Naturalized Epistemology?" in H. Kornblith (ed.), *Naturalizing Epistemology*, 2nd ed. (Cambridge, Mass.: MIT Press).
Kolakowski, Leszek. (1978) *Main Currents of Marxism, Volume 3: The Breakdown* (Oxford: Oxford University Press).
Leiter, Brian. (1996a). "Legal Realism," in D. Patterson (ed.), *A Companion to the Philosophy of Law and Legal Theory* (Oxford: Blackwell).
______. (1996b). "Heidegger and the Theory of Adjudication," *Yale Law Journal* 106: 253–282.
______. (1997a). "Is There an 'American' Jurisprudence?" *Oxford Journal of Legal Studies* 17: 367–387.
______. (1997b). "Rethinking Legal Realism: Toward a Naturalized Jurisprudence," *Texas Law Review* 76: 267–315.
______. (1997c). "Why Quine is Not a Postmodernist," *Southern Methodist University Law Review* 50: 1739–1754.
______. (1998) "Naturalism and Naturalized Jurisprudence," in B. Bix (ed.), *Analyzing Law: New Essays in Legal Theory* (Oxford: Clarendon Press).
______. (1999) "Legal Realism," in C.B. Gray (ed.), *The Philosophy of Law: An Encyclopedia* (New York: Garland).

———. (2000) "Holmes, Economics, and Classical Realism," in S.J. Burton (ed.), *The Path of the Law and Its Influence: The Legacy of Oliver Wendell Holmes, Jr.* (New York: Cambridge University Press).

———. (ed.) (2001a) *Objectivity in Law and Morals* (New York: Cambridge University Press).

———. (2001b) "Moral Facts and Best Explanations," *Social Philosophy & Policy* (forthcoming).

Lindblom, Charles. (1997) "Political Science in the 1940s and 1950s," *Daedalus* 126: 225–252.

Lukes, Steven. (1982) "Of Gods and Demons: Habermas and Practical Reason," in J. Thompson & D. Held (eds.), *Habermas: Critical Debates* (Cambridge, Mass.: MIT Press).

Machiavelli. (1988) *The Prince*, ed. Q. Skinner & R. Price (Cambridge: Cambridge University Press).

Morgenthau, Hans. (1967) *Politics Among Nations*, 4th ed. (New York: Knopf).

Nagel, Thomas. (1979) *Mortal Questions* (New York: Oxford University Press).

Noonan, John. (1986) "Hercules and the Snail Darter," *New York Times Book Review* (May 25): 12.

Nussbaum, Martha. (1998) "Still Worthy of Praise," *Harvard Law Review* 111: 1776–1795.

Pettit, Philip. (1995) "The Virtual Reality of *Homo Economicus*," *The Monist* 78: 308–329.

———. (2001) "Embracing Objectivity in Ethics," in Leiter (2001a).

Posner, Richard A. (1990) *The Problems of Jurisprudence* (Cambridge, Mass.: Harvard University Press).

———. (ed.) (1992) *The Essential Holmes* (Chicago: University of Chicago Press).

———. (1999) *The Problematics of Moral and Legal Theory* (Cambridge, Mass.: Harvard University Press).

Railton, Peter. (1996) "Moral Realism: Prospects and Problems," in W. Sinnott-Armstrong & M. Timmons (eds.), *Moral Knowledge? New Readings in Moral Epistemology* (New York: Oxford University Press).

Rawls, John. (1971) *A Theory of Justice* (Cambridge, Mass.: Harvard University Press).

Roemer, John (1986) "'Rational-Choice' Marxism: Some Issues of Method and Substance," in J. Roemer (ed.), *Analytical Marxism* (Cambridge: Cambridge University Press).

Skinner, Quentin. (1988) "Introduction," in Machiavelli (1988).

Tucker, Robert C. (ed.) (1978) *The Marx-Engels Reader*, 2nd ed. (New York: W.W. Norton & Co.).

White, James J. (1994) "The Influence of American Legal Realism on Article 2 of the Uniform Commercial Code," in W. Krawietz et al. (eds.), *Prescriptive Formality and Normative Rationality in Modern Legal Systems* (Berlin: Duncker & Humboldt).

Wood, Allen. (1980) *Karl Marx* (London: Routledge & Kegan Paul).

Woodruff, Paul. (ed. & trans.). (1993) *Thucydides on Justice, Power, and Human Nature* (Indianapolis: Hackett).

11

PHILOSOPHICAL ISSUES, 11
Social, Political, and Legal Philosophy, 2001

Deliberative Democracy and the Discursive Dilemma

Philip Pettit

Taken as a model for how groups should make collective judgments and decisions, the ideal of deliberative democracy is inherently ambiguous. Consider the idealised case where it is agreed on all sides that a certain conclusion should be endorsed if and only if certain premises are admitted. Does deliberative democracy recommend that members of the group debate the premises and then individually vote, in the light of that debate, on whether or not to support the conclusion? Or does it recommend that members individually vote on the premises, and then let their commitment to the conclusion be settled by whether or not the group endorses the required premises? Is deliberative democracy to enforce the discipline of reason at the individual level, as in the first possibility, or at the collective level, as in the second?

Deliberative-democratic theory has not addressed this issue, perhaps because of an implicit assumption that it does not matter whether the discipline of reason is imposed at the individual or at the collective level. But that assumption is false and there is no excuse for neglecting the issue raised. The discursive dilemma of my title—a generalisation of the doctrinal paradox that has recently received attention in analytical jurisprudence—shows that the procedures distinguished can come apart. Thus deliberative democrats must make up their minds on where they stand in relation to the issue; they cannot sit on the fence.

This paper is an attempt to address the issue and look at the grounds on which it may be resolved. In the first section, I give a brief account of the ideal of deliberative democracy, as I understand it. In the second, I introduce the discursive dilemma with the help of some stylised examples and then in the third section I show why the issue that it raises is of relevance, theoretically and practically, to the deliberative-democratic ideal. How should deliberative democrats resolve that issue? I argue in the fourth section that the role in which republican theory casts deliberative democracy argues for preferring the imposition of reason, where possible, at the collective level. And then in the final section I argue for the consistency of that position with the main sorts of argument put forward by others in defence of the ideal.

1. The ideal of deliberative democracy

There are three issues on which deliberative democrats divide among themselves. First, the question of how many contexts—electoral, parliamentary, industrial, educational, and so on—ought to be democratised. Second, the question of how many issues in any democratised context ought to be under democratic control: just the choice of office-holders, or also the choice of policy-programs, or perhaps the choice of some detailed policies. And third, the question of how far a democratic character serves to justify or legitimate a regime and pattern of decision-making, or at least to give them a presumptive authority: to place the onus of argument on the shoulders of those who would not comply.

But there, or thereabouts, disagreement runs out. For no matter what their differences on such matters, deliberative democrats do show a remarkable degree of consensus on how democracy should be organised. Wherever democracy is instituted, however deeply democratic control runs, and whatever standing it is taken to give to decision-making, they agree that it ought to be inclusive, judgmental and dialogical (see the representative readings in Bohman and Rehg 1997; Elster 1998). These constraints spell out what I shall describe here as the deliberative-democratic ideal.

- *The inclusive constraint:* all members are equally entitled to vote on how to resolve relevant collective issues, or bundles of issues, with something less than a unanimous vote being sufficient to determine the outcome.
- *The judgmental constraint:* before voting, members should deliberate on the basis of presumptively common concerns about which resolution is to be preferred.
- *The dialogical constraint:* they should conduct this deliberation in open and unforced dialogue with one another, whether in a centralised forum or in various decentralised contexts.

The inclusive constraint means that deliberative democracy is to be contrasted with elitist or authoritarian schemes, even ones in which deliberation and dialogue have an important place. It will be satisfied in any context by having a representative democracy, if democratic control only runs to the choice of office-holders, but the general assumption is that where direct participation by all members is feasible—and is consistent with the general case for deliberative democracy—it will be preferred to indirect representation. The constraint includes the stipulation that unanimity is not required for the determination of an outcome by voting, since a combination of inclusiveness and unanimity would lead to a group's being unable to reach a common view on most significant issues; unanimity is probably achievable, at best, only on very abstract constitutional matters (Buchanan and Tullock 1962).

The judgmental constraint has got two sides to it. First, it requires voters to deliberate or reason about how they should vote, not just vote in an unreflective or spontaneous or reflex manner. And second, it requires voters to deliberate about how they should vote on the basis of considerations as to what is best for the society as a whole: what is likely to advance those common interests that people are capable of recognising as common interests. This constraint need not itself specify any particular conception of such common, perceived interests: that may itself be matter for the sort of deliberation recommended. What it counsels against is any pattern of voting in which each individual voter takes account only of what is good for his or her particular coterie or corner or circle. The model of voting recommended under this constraint can be described as judgment-voting rather than preference-voting (Cohen 1986; Coleman and Ferejohn 1986; Brennan and Pettit 1990). The idea is that each voter should make up his or her own mind as to what is for the good of the group in question and should vote on the basis of that judgment, not on the basis of brute preference (Sunstein 1993) or bargained compromise (Elster 1998, 5–8; cf. Pettit 1993, Ch. 5).

The third, dialogical constraint in the ideal of deliberative democracy marks a further, important level of differentiation. It rules out the sort of plebiscitarian dispensation in which each participant privately forms his or her judgment about common perceived interests, rather than doing so in dialogue with others, and then votes on the basis of that judgment. It is sometimes thought, on the basis of his remarks about the danger of faction, that Rousseau embraced this plebiscitarian ideal. According to Rousseau, so it is said, 'each voter is polled about his independently reached choice, without any group deliberation' (Grofman and Feld 1988, 570). But this interpretation is almost certainly mistaken, if only because it makes no sense of Rousseau's requiring that the people come together in an assembly. What he was anxious to guard against was not dialogue and debate, with the formation of individual judgment that this fosters, but rather the threat of some individuals' being so intimidated or impressed by others—so deferential towards them—that they vote according to the judgments of those others, not according to their own (Estlund and Waldron 1989).

The third constraint requires that the dialogue envisaged be open and unforced, while allowing that it may be centralised or decentralised. It must be open in the sense that each can get a hearing and it must be unforced in the sense that no one need fear to speak their mind; it must approximate the conditions for ideal speech that Juergen Habermas (1984, 1989) emphasises. Some will insist that dialogue must be centralised in a single forum, if talk of deliberative democracy is to be justified (Goodin 1999). But I think that it is better to leave that question open and to take the centralised or collective picture of deliberative democracy as a more specific version of a broader ideal.

2. The discursive dilemma

So much for the different elements in the ideal of deliberative democracy. In this and the next section I want to show that the ideal is seriously underspecified and, in particular, that there are two quite different ways in which it may be understood in any context.

My argument in this section derives from the recent discussion in jurisprudential circles of what its analysts have sometimes called the doctrinal paradox (Kornhauser and Sager 1986; Kornhauser 1992; Kornhauser 1992; Kornhauser and Sager 1993. See too Chapman 1998a; Chapman 1998b; Brennan 2001). This is a paradox that arises when a multi-member court has to make a decision on the basis of received doctrine as to the considerations that ought to be taken into account: on the basis of a conceptual sequencing of the issues to be decided (Chapman 1998a) . I describe the problem, in its general form, as a discursive dilemma. I prefer the word 'discursive', because the problem in question is not tied to the acceptance of common doctrine, only to the enterprise of making group judgments on the basis of reasons. I prefer the word 'dilemma', because while the problem generates a choice in which each option has its difficulties, it does not constitute a paradox in any strict sense. My analysis of the discursive dilemma derives directly from that jurisprudential literature, though many of the points I want to make do not appear there; where they do appear, I explicitly acknowledge them.

The discursive dilemma: the conjunction case

In order to introduce the discursive dilemma, consider an issue that might arise in a workplace, among the employees of a company: for simplicity, as we may assume, a company owned by the employees. The issue is whether to forego a pay-rise in order to spend the money thereby saved on introducing a set of workplace safety measures: say, measures to guard against electrocution. Let us suppose for convenience that the employees are to make the decision—perhaps because of prior resolution—on the basis of considering two separable issues: first, whether the danger is serious: say, whether the risk of electrocution is above some tolerable threshold; and second, whether the pay-sacrifice would make it possible to buy a safety measure that would be effective in reducing the risk below that threshold, in the event of its having been above it. If an employee thinks that the danger is sufficiently serious, and the safety measure sufficiently effective, he or she will vote for the pay-sacrifice; otherwise they will vote against. And so each will have to consider the seriousness issue and the effectiveness issue and then look to what should be concluded about the pay-sacrifice.

Imagine now that after appropriate dialogue and deliberation the employees are disposed to vote on the relevant premises and conclusion in the pattern illustrated by the following matrix for a group of three workers. The letters A, B, and C represent the three employees and the 'Yes' or 'No' on any row represents the disposition of the relevant employee to admit or reject the corresponding premise or conclusion.

	Serious danger?	Effective measure?	Pay-sacrifice?
A.	Yes	No	No
B.	No	Yes	No
C.	Yes	Yes	Yes

Matrix 1

If this is the pattern in which the employees are inclined to vote, then what decision or judgment will be made by the group under deliberatively democratic procedures? It turns out that a different decision will be made, depending on whether the group judgment is driven by how members judge on the premises or by how they judge on the conclusion. Looking at the matrix, we can see that though a majority rejects the pay-sacrifice, a majority supports each of the premises. If we think that the views of the employees on the conclusion should determine the group-decision, then we will say that the group-conclusion should be to reject the pay-sacrifice: there are more 'No's' than 'Yes's' in the final column. But if we think that the views of the employees on the premises should determine the group-decision, then we will say that the group-conclusion should be to accept the pay-sacrifice: there are more 'Yes's' than 'No's' in each of the premise columns. The fact that socially aggregating the conclusion-judgments gives us a different result from socially aggregating the premise-judgments illustrates the discursive dilemma.

It should be clear that the discursive dilemma will generalise from the three-person case to a group of any size. All that is required for the paradox to arise is that a majority in the group supports the first of the premises, a different majority supports the second—B and C rather than A and C—and the intersection or overlap of those majorities—C in our example—represents only a minority in the group as a whole. The fact that the intersection represents only a minority explains why there is a majority against the conclusion. But not only will the paradox generalise to groups of any size. It should equally be clear that it will generalise in other ways too: for example, to a case where there are any number of premises, not just two; and to cases that arise in quite different domains.

The structure required for the sort of paradox illustrated to be capable of generalising can be summed up in these points:

a. there is a conclusion to be decided among a group of people by reference to a conjunction of independent or separable premises—the conclusion will be endorsed if relevant premises are endorsed, and otherwise it will be rejected;
b. each member of the group forms a judgment on each of the premises and a corresponding judgment on the conclusion;
c. each of the premises is supported by a majority of members but those majorities do not coincide with one another;
d. the intersection of those majorities will support the conclusion, and the others reject it, in view of a; and
e. the intersection of the majorities is only a minority in the group as a whole.

The discursive dilemma, as illustrated in our workplace example, stems from the fact that the group can make its judgments in the conclusion-driven way or in the premise-driven way and that in many cases those procedures yield different results. It constitutes a dilemma, so far as each option has its problems. As the example shows, going the conclusion-driven way means adopting a course that is inconsistent with the premises endorsed by the group and going the premise-driven way means adopting a course that a majority individually reject. Going the first way means sacrificing collective rationality for the sake of responsiveness to individuals, going the second means sacrificing responsiveness to individuals for the sake of collective rationality.

There are familiar practices of group deliberation and decision-making corresponding to those different approaches. Thus the group would go the conclusion-driven way if members entered into deliberation and dialogue and then each cast their personal vote on whether to endorse the pay-sacrifice or not; in that case the decision would be against the pay-sacrifice. The group would go the premise-driven way, on the other hand, if there was a chairperson who took a vote on each of the premises—say, a show of hands—and then let logic decide the outcome; in this case the decision would be in favour of the pay-sacrifice.

THE DISCURSIVE DILEMMA: THE DISJUNCTION CASE

But the sort of discursive dilemma illustrated is not the only sort there is. Another version of the dilemma arises when the issue facing a group has to be decided, not by reference to a conjunction of premises, but rather by reference to a disjunction. In this case the conclusion will be endorsed if any one of the premises is endorsed—any, not all—and otherwise it will be rejected. (It might also be required, of course, that any two of three or more premises would have to be endorsed—or any three of four or more premises, and so on—but I shall ignore that possibility here.)

The second variety of the discursive dilemma can be illustrated with another sort of decision that our workplace group might face. Suppose that the group has to decide on whether to introduce a clocking-in and clocking-out system and that by their shared lights the decision should be made on the grounds, and only on the grounds, either that such a time-check would increase productivity or that it would serve to reassure everybody that others are pulling their weight in the joint enterprise. Let someone decide the productivity question in the affirmative, or let them decide the reassurance question in the affirmative, and their conclusion will be that the time-check should be introduced; otherwise they will conclude that it ought not to be introduced. The conclusion will be judged by reference to a disjunction of those independent premises: endorsing either premise on its own will be enough to support the endorsement of the conclusion; rejecting both of the premises will be enough to support the rejection of the conclusion.

Imagine now, as in the conjunction case, that after appropriate dialogue and deliberation the employees are disposed to vote on the relevant premises and conclusion in the pattern illustrated by the following matrix for a group of three workers. The letters A, B, and C represent the three employees, as before, and the 'Yes' or 'No' on any row represents the disposition of each to admit or reject the corresponding premise or conclusion.

	Productivity issue?	Reassurance issue?	Time-check?
A.	Yes	No	Yes
B.	No	Yes	Yes
C.	No	No	No

Matrix 2

Where votes follow this pattern, then the premise-driven approach will yield one group-judgment, as in the previous sort of case, the conclusion-driven approach another. Each of the premises is rejected by a majority, as we can see by considering the premise columns, so that if we go by the premises, then we will take the group-decision to be against the time-check proposal. But the conclusion, on the other hand, is endorsed by a majority so that if we go by the conclusions the employees individually reach, then we will take the group-decision to be in favour of the time-check.

This sort of dilemma allows of generalisation in just the same way as the first. The salient points to preserve in this case mirror the points mentioned with the other:

a. there is a conclusion to be decided among a group of people by reference to a disjunction of independent or separable premises—the conclusion will be endorsed if any of the premises is endorsed, and otherwise it will be rejected;
b. each member of the group forms a judgment on each of the premises and a corresponding judgment on the conclusion;
c. each of the premises is supported by a minority of members but those minorities do not coincide with one another;
d. the union of those minorities will support the conclusion, and the others reject it, in view of a; and
e. the union of the minorities is a majority in the group as a whole.

In this case, as in the last, there are familiar decision-making practices that differ in implementing either a conclusion-driven mode of group-judgment or a premise-driven mode. The workplace ballot in which each casts his or her vote privately would implement the conclusion-driven mode, whereas the workplace meeting in which the chair takes a vote on each of the relevant considerations and then announces the significance for the conclusion would implement the premise-driven mode.

3. The relevance of the dilemma for deliberative democracy

The relevance in principle

Under the regime of deliberative democracy, it is required that with any logically connected propositions in the domain of discussion—the premises and conclusion of our examples—people make up their minds about the propositions in such a way that reason is satisfied. They do not endorse inconsistent or otherwise incoherent sets of propositions; they do not fail to derive conclusions that are supported, even saliently supported, by what they already endorse; and they do not follow a procedure—say, one of unanimitarian voting—that gives them nothing to say on most issues (List and Pettit 2002).

The question raised by the discursive dilemma is whether this discipline of reason is meant to apply to each individual, taken singly, or to the group taken as a whole. Under the conclusion-driven, majoritarian way of voting the discipline is applied to each individual, under the premise-driven, majoritarian way of voting it is applied to the group taken as a whole. The question is a pressing one, where it arises, because it represents a hard choice or dilemma. Let a group individualise reason, and it will ensure responsiveness to individuals in its collective view on each issue but it will run the risk that the views will be irrational. Let a group collectivise reason, and it will ensure the rationality of the collective views maintained but run the risk of adopting a view on one or another issue that is unresponsive to the views of individuals on that issue.

The choice with which groups are faced is not necessarily a choice between following a conclusion-driven, majoritarian procedure and following a premise-driven, majoritarian one. Individualising reason and ensuring responsiveness to individual views will always involve having members vote, whether on a majoritarian or some other basis, about each of the issues involved, and then letting that vote determine the collective view; this, in effect, is a generalisation of the conclusion-driven procedure. But collectivising reason and ensuring collective rationality will not always involve privileging certain issues in the manner of premises and letting the collective views on those issues logically determine the collective view on the conclusion. Consistently with behaving in a deliberative democratic manner, the group might let the presumptive set of collective views be determined by having members vote on each issue and only consider moderating those views—amending one or other of them—in the event of the collective views proving to be irrational in some way. The amendment chosen might involve letting the views with the presumptive status of premises—if that can be agreed—determine the view on the conclusion. But it might also involve holding onto that conclusion and revising the collectively endorsed view on one of the premises. In short, it might involve practising *modus ponens*—letting the premises dictate the conclusion—or *modus tollens*—keeping the conclusion and revising one or more of the premises.

To sum up, then, the discursive dilemma is relevant in principle to deliberative democracy so far as it raises the question as to whether deliberative democrats require people to be disciplined by reason at the individual or, where this is feasible, at the collective level. There is a dilemma involved, because each of the options available has its problems. Let people be disciplined by reason at the individual level and they may collectively endorse an irrational set of propositions. Let them be disciplined by reason at the collective level and they may collectively endorse a conclusion that a majority of them individually reject.

THE RELEVANCE OF THE DILEMMA IN PRACTICE

But is the discursive dilemma relevant in practice to the way the ideal of deliberative democracy is specified? Some might say that it is not, on the grounds that it is rarely going to be a feasible option for people to discipline themselves by reason at the collective level and that all deliberative democracy can require is that individuals do this in the formation of their opinions at the individual level. The problem raised will be that if people are to discipline themselves collectively by reason, then they must agree on what are the relevant considerations by reference to which various issues are to be decided. But that agreement, so it will be said, is rarely going to be available. Thus sceptics will maintain that the assumption that the parties in my workplace examples agree on the premises by reference to which the pay-sacrifice and time-check issues are to be decided is an idealisation rarely satisfied in practice.

This point is well taken for large scale collectivities such as an electorate and it may well be the case that all deliberative democrats can seek in such contexts is a discipline of reason imposed at the individual level.[1] But the point does not hold more generally. There are two sorts of groups that routinely confront the possibility of collective self-discipline, and that must therefore decide on whether to follow reason at the individual or at the collective level. And there is a further, more general consideration why any groups that seek to advance a common purpose, and not just the two sorts mentioned, are going to confront that possibility in the course of their development.

The first sort of case is that of a group that is charged by an external authority with making certain decisions on the basis of designated considerations, and on that basis only. Examples of such groups are appointment and promotions committees; committees charged with deciding who is to win a certain prize or contract; trusts that have to make judgments on the basis of a trustee's instructions; associations or the executives of associations that have to justify their actions by reference to the group's charter; corporations that have to comply with policies endorsed by their shareholders; public bodies, be they bureaucratic committees or appointed boards, that have to discharge specific briefs; and governments that are more or less bound to party programs and principles. In all of these cases deliberative democrats will want their ideal to apply and in each case there will clearly be an issue as to whether the discipline of reason should be imposed at the individual or at the collective level.

In the second sort of case, it will be a matter of internal aspiration in a group that members find common grounds by which to justify whatever line they collectively take. Think of the political movement that has to work out a policy program; or the association that has to decide on the terms of its constitution; or the church that has to give an account of itself in the public forum; or the learned academy that seeks a voice in the larger world of politics and journalism. In such cases members of the group may not have access to an antecedently agreed set of considerations on the basis of which to justify particular judgments. But their identification with one another will support a wish to reach agreement on such a set of reasons. To the extent that that wish gets to be satisfied, the discursive dilemma will generate the issue as to whether the group should make its decisions in a premise-driven or conclusion-driven way.

These two cases are special in a certain way. They contrast with the case of a group that has to advance a purpose, as those groups have to do, but that may be quite happy to have its members reach a judgment on any issue without their agreeing on the reasons that support that judgment; a majority may vote for the judgment but, theorising it only incompletely (Sunstein 1999), different people within that majority may support it for different reasons. Will a group of this laid-back kind ever confront the possibility of imposing reason at a collective level and ever have to face the discursive dilemma? I believe that it will (Pettit 2001).

Like the other groups envisaged, this sort of group is bound to generate a history of judgments that it is on record as making, when it seeks to pursue its purposes. But those past judgments will invariably constrain the future judgments that it can rationally maintain at the collective level: this, in the way that a political party's past commitments on reducing taxes but increasing expenditure in certain areas will constrain the other decisions it has to make about expenditure. And so there will be a serious question for the group as to whether or not it should impose reason at the collective level, letting later judgments be dictated in a premise-driven way by earlier ones or disowning some of the earlier judgments; after all, the lesson of the discursive dilemma is that though every individual holds a rational set of views on the issues involved, voting independently on each issue could lead to a collectively irrational result. That question will arise to the extent that effective, joint action requires collectively rational judgments. And it will assume a particularly sharp form so far as members or outsiders are ready to charge the group, perhaps even mock it, for any failure of collective reason.

The upshot, then, is this. Take those groups where the ideal of deliberative democracy apparently applies and where the collectivisation of reason is not made infeasible by numbers or disorganisation. Are such groups likely to face the hard choice between individualising and collectivising deliberation? Yes, they are. They will certainly face that choice if they are commissioned to make their decisions on the basis of certain criteria or if they succeed in establishing criteria by which to make those decisions. But even if they do not have such criteria imposed on them, or cannot agree on any criteria by which to operate, they will still face the hard choice represented by the discursive dilemma; they will not be able to rest content with their members each voting according to their own particular reasons on the different issues that come before the group. The reason is that any such group will build up a history of judgments over time and those judgments are bound to provide reason, now here, now there, for taking a certain line on some new issue. Thus the group will have to choose either to let their line on this new issue be governed by majority vote, at a risk of proving inconsistent over time, or to enforce collective reason in the event of such inconsistency, whether by letting the previous judgments dictate that line or by allowing the new vote to stand and by revising one or more of those judgments. The discursive dilemma is, quite simply, unavoidable.

4. The resolution in republican theory

The republican argument for deliberative democracy

Republican theory, as I have argued elsewhere, puts a premium on people's enjoying freedom as non-domination: that is, on people's having a status such that ideally no one else is able to interfere arbitrarily in their lives. If any other person or agency is able to interfere in their lives, then they must be forced to track people's perceived interests in the interference they practise; they must not have a power of arbitrary interference.

That ideal raises the question of how the state can be blocked from enjoying a power of arbitrary interference in the lives of citizens. The state is a necessary institution and it necessarily has a power of interfering with people: it cannot operate without being able to tax, legislate and penalise the governed. So how is its power of interference to be made non-arbitrary? Republican constitutional theory is built around that question and has consistently sought to describe various devices whereby non-arbitrariness may be furthered. These include familiar mechanisms such as democratic election, rule of law, separation of powers, limitation of tenure, rotation of office, and so on.

In this republican tradition of constitutional discussion, one important strand has been the idea that if the state's power of interference is to be rendered non-arbitrary then whatever other devices are in place, people must be able to contest the decisions made by various arms of government. They must have access to the reasons supporting those decisions and they must be able to contest the soundness of those reasons or the degree of support they offer to the decisions made. Moreover they must be in a position, ideally, to expect that such contestations will be heard, will be impartially adjudicated and, if necessary, will be implemented against those in government. The general message is that so far as a government is effectively contestable, to that extent it is less likely to enjoy arbitrary power.

The effective promotion of contestability in the political sphere requires a variety of institutions, especially if it is to guard against unwieldy levels of complaint, and I have tried elsewhere to review some of them (Pettit 2000). From our point of view, however, only two observations are relevant. The first is that putting in place a regime of participatory or representative democracy is essential in guarding against certain possibilities of non-contestability and domination: the colonial, the authoritarian, and so on. And the second is that any such regime still leaves striking possibilities of non-contestability and domination in place: possibilities associated with the tyranny of the democratic majority, in particular, and the tyranny of what we might describe as the democratic elite: those in the corridors of power—for example, in the bureaucracy, the cabinet, the courts, the prisons, or the police force—

who can impose their own will in how they interpret and implement democratic policy.

How are people to be empowered in relation to democratic majorities and democratic elites? How are they to be given a power of contestation against them? Whatever else is necessary, it seems clear that they must be able to ask after the reasons that support the decisions, they must be able to question the relevance of the reasons and they must be in a position to expect a fair hearing. And all of that is going to be possible, of course, only so far as the democratic bodies in question operate in a deliberative mode. There must be a dispensation of deliberation in place in the community as a whole, and in the microcosm of parliament, which establishes a currency of considerations that are admitted on all sides to be relevant to the doings of government. There must be a commitment in the different arms of government to justifying whatever decisions are taken by reference to the considerations that are relevant, by common consent, in their case. And it must be possible for private individuals, or perhaps for designated representatives, to challenge such decisions on the grounds that the reasons quoted are not sound or do not offer the requisite support for the decisions taken. It is only in the event of democracy having this deliberative cast that contestability, and ultimately non-arbitrariness, can be furthered.

This republican argument for deliberative democracy applies also, of course, to forums beyond those of government. Take the workplace community or the community organisation or indeed the family. Even if decisions are taken democratically in such a body, there will be little protection against arbitrariness—short of exit—unless the democracy in question operates in deliberative mode, giving individuals a chance to contest the decisions made. If decisions are made on the basis of interest-group politics, or bargaining from different levels of power, then there will be no grounds on which any contestation can be made. Brute force or naked preference will rule.

Cass Sunstein (1993) probably has this republican case for deliberative-democratic procedure in mind when he describes deliberative democracy as a 'republic of reasons'. Just as people are in a position to know where they stand in relation to a court judgment, only so far as the judges have to provide statements of their reasons, so more generally people can know where they stand in relation to public decisions only if they know what the grounds adduced in support of those decisions are. They will not be able to take a stand in relation to public decisions, if those decisions are the outcome of interest-group bargaining or of voting on the basis of naked, unargued preference. Such non-deliberatively generated decisions would have the profile of dictates or fiats from on high, where the products of deliberative-democratic procedure would present themselves as reasoned—well-reasoned or badly-reasoned—judgments that people are in a position to examine, assess and if necessary, challenge.

APPLYING THE REPUBLICAN ARGUMENT

The contestability argument for deliberative democracy ought to have persuasive force, quite apart from its connection with republican theory (see Pettit 2000). It is of particular interest here because—unusually among such arguments, as we shall see in the next section—it provides a firm ground for wanting, where that is feasible, to impose the discipline of reason at the collective, not at the individual, level.

If I am to be able to judge the actions of another individual or agency in relation to alleged reasons—and, ultimately, if I am to be able to contest those actions in the relevant sense—then the individual or agency must prove answerable to those reasons. The individual or agency must be disposed to act as the reasons require or, at the least, to adjust in response to the criticism that the reasons adduced in support of something they did are not appropriate or that what they did was not supported by those reasons. In a word, the individual or agency must prove to be conversable: that is, must prove to be an interlocutor whose words can be taken at face value and, where appropriate, invoked in effective criticism of the things they later do.

A group that records its assent to certain considerations on the basis of majority vote and which then proceeds to make its judgments and decisions according to the premise-driven strategy will prove conversable in this sense. Its judgments, decisions and actions will track those reasons in the ordinary case. And where they do not, or where the reasons adduced are shown to be in some way inappropriate, then it can be called effectively to book. The group will acknowledge a role for the consideration of reasons or premises in relation to any case; it will decide the group commitments in regard to those reasons or premises on the basis of majority vote, or some such measure of social aggregation; and it will then accept that how it judges or decides on the case in hand should be answerable to those commitments. You can deal with such a group as you might deal with an individual person;

indeed the group will deserve to be regarded as a legal or at least cultural person: a unified, corporate entity.

A group that makes its judgments and decisions on the basis of individualising reason, however, will have a very different profile. What the discursive dilemma reveals is that such a group may reach theoretical and practical conclusions that are completely out of kilter with the majority disposition of its members in relation to related propositions. There will be little or no point in interrogating the group for its view, under majority rule, of the different premises that might be thought to be relevant, for example, and might be acknowledged as relevant by members of the group. For it will be a permanent possibility that the conclusion it reaches is not the conclusion that those majority views would deliberatively support.

Consider the workforce in our earlier example. We might discover that the majority view among its members is that electrocution is a serious danger, and that a pay-sacrifice would solve the problem—and that those premises imply that a pay-sacrifice would be desirable; and yet it should be no surprise to find that the group comes down against a pay-sacrifice. There is no talking to a group that operates like this. It is inherently unconversable. Where the group that runs by premise-driven judgment and decision is a unified, corporate entity, the group envisaged here would be a disparate, aggregate sort of thing. It would not be one, but many.

Consider an analogy. Imagine that I am composed of many different personalities, as in some sense I undoubtedly am. There is the ecologically minded self, the economically minded self, and the socially minded self that likes to keep up with the neighbours. And now suppose that I face a decision about whether to buy a Volvo. That decision, let us say, will be determined by the views I take on two issues: one, whether to get a car; and two, whether the best car for someone like me to buy, assuming they do buy a car, is a Volvo. It is quite possible, that faced with a decision like this, my different selves will go quite different ways. My economic self, A, may say that a car is desirable, but not a Volvo: it's too expensive. My ecological self may say that a car is undesirable but agree that a Volvo is the best sort of car to buy: it is environmentally the friendliest kind available. And my social self may hold that it would be good both to buy a car, in order to keep up with the neighbours, and that from this point of view a Volvo is the best sort there is. This, then, is the pattern of voting among my selves.

	Car desirable?	Volvo a desirable car?	Get a Volvo?
Self A.	Yes	No	No
Self B.	No	Yes	No
Self C.	Yes	Yes	Yes

Matrix 3

Constituted though I am in such a multiplex mode, I would pass as a unified, conversable agent were I to make my judgments and decisions in this and similar cases on a premise-driven basis. I would decide to buy a Volvo in the case on hand, reporting as I presumably would do that I think a car desirable and that I view a Volvo as the most desirable car there is; after all, those are the views defended by a majority of my selves. But imagine that I made my judgments and took my decisions in a way that individualised reason in my different selves, rather than collectivising it in my person as a whole. I would decide in a case like this not to buy a Volvo. And yet, interrogated about the relevant reasons—reasons that I myself might declare to be relevant—I would be found to defend considerations supporting the purchase of a Volvo. It should be clear that did I operate in this way, then I could not prove to be a conversable subject. I would be taken at best as a multitude of disorganised voices, at worst as someone without anything recognisable as a mind.

Might the demands of contestability be satisfied to the extent that the individuals in a group, though not the group itself, are conversable and contestable agents? Might they be satisfied in the way in which they are satisfied by the multi-judge court? In this case, the group is relatively small and the differing individuals or subgroups give their differing reasons for taking their different lines, or indeed their differing reasons for taking the same line. It is not clear how satisfactory a model the judicial bench offers, given evidence that members switch votes in order to avoid problems and given recent critiques of the system (Kornhauser and Sager 1993; Stearns 1999). But those issues aside, I think that there are good reasons why contestability should be secured at the level of the group, not at the level of the different individuals who comprise it.

The group is the entity that continues over time despite changes in its membership, and that fact alone makes it the salient agency that we should want to be contestable and conversable. And not only does the group continue in time across changes in membership. It will often have so many members that no one could hope to secure contestability at the individual level. It will often be, not just the salient agency to make contestable, but the only feasible one available for that role.

These considerations of salience and feasibility are supported by a thought that would apply, even in their absence. It is only under a regime of group-level contestability that the relevant judgments will be made in a way that answers to reasons alone and that can be challenged on the basis of reasons alone. Where a group makes its judgments in the conclusion-driven way, there are two distinct factors that determine what judgment it makes in a given case: one, the reasons that receive majority support among members of the group; and two, the degree of overlap between the supporting majorities. But the second factor is not relevant from the point of view of contestability and so it is better for the group to give authority to the first factor only, as it does under the premise-driven procedure and, more generally, under any procedure that collectivises deliberation.

Finally, a word in defence of sticking with this collectivising procedure, even in cases where its results may be counter-intuitive. Imagine that a court has to make a decision on whether or not someone should be given a retrial; that a retrial is required either in the event of inadmissible evidence having been used previously or in the event of the appellants's having been forced to confess; and that the voting goes as follows among three judges (Kornhauser and Sager 1993, 40).

	Inadmissible evidence?	Forced confession?	Retrial?
A.	Yes	No	Yes
B.	No	Yes	Yes
C.	No	No	No

Matrix 4

It is plausible in such a case that the person ought to be given a retrial, despite the fact that a majority rejects each of the relevant grounds. Does this suggest that there is a general problem of plausibility attached to the procedure that collectivises reason? I think not.

While it is certainly implausible in such a case that the defendant should be denied a retrial, that implausibility can easily be registered in the approach of a group that seeks to collectivise deliberation. The implausibility can be taken by the group to indicate that the majority vote in favour of a retrial is more compelling than either premise-vote and that one or more of the premise-votes should be revised. Or the group may think that there is only one proposition which they each have to make a judgment on: viz., the disjunctive claim that there was inadmissible evidence or a forced confession. Or the implausibility may prompt members of the group to argue that while the representation in Matrix 4 is fine, what collective deliberation should be designed to secure in such a case is primarily the avoidance of a false negative—denying a retrial to a deserving appellant—and that only a unanimously rejected ground of appeal should be dismissed by the group. Under any of these interpretations, the collectivising procedure would enable the group to grant a retrial.[2]

5. This resolution and other arguments for the ideal

There are many different arguments in support of deliberative democracy to be found in the recent literature. The question that we must consider, then, is whether the position taken in favour of the premise-driven version of the ideal—and, more generally, in favour of the version that collectivises deliberation—runs seriously counter to any of those other arguments. I devote the final section to that issue.

ARGUMENTS FOR MAKING DEMOCRACY DELIBERATIVE

Most of the arguments in the literature focus on the virtue of making democracy deliberative: that is, on the benefit to a democratic process or society of having deliberation of an inclusive, dialogical kind (see Cohen 1989; Dryzek 1990; Sunstein 1993; Benhabib 1994; Gutmann and Thompson 1996; Bohman and Rehg 1997; Elster 1998). Some assert that making democracy deliberative should help to ensure that people's preferences are reflective and informed, not just the brute product of their adaptation to circumstance (Sunstein 1993); or that it should enable people to do better in reaching beyond the chasms of difference that separate the members of certain groups, even if it does not bring them into consensus (Young 1990); or that it should stretch people's imagination and empathy as they are forced to take a general point of view (Goodin 1999). Without alleging any such psychological transformation, other arguments maintain that making democracy deliberative should at least have the effect of screening out self-regarding concerns in favour of more public-spirited considerations, thereby approximating or advancing an ideal of public reasoning among free and equal participants (Habermas 1984, 1989; Elster 1986; Cohen 1989; Elster 1998). And yet a further range of arguments urge that making democracy deliberative would promote such effects as legitimising whatever decisions are reached, making them more likely to take account of the relatively powerless, increasing transparency among members of the group, or promoting just outcomes (see Elster 1998, 11, for a summary).

There is no likelihood that any arguments of this kind could be invoked against the view that deliberative democracy ought to impose reason at the collective rather than the individual level. We do not eliminate deliberation by making deliberative democracy premise-driven, for example, and thereby imposing reason at the collective level, and benefits of the kind invoked in these arguments all look to be consistent with such a procedure. Consider the case of the workforce deliberating on whether to introduce a safety measure or to establish a time-check. Even if they agree to reach a decision in a premise-driven way, they will first be required under the deliberative-democratic ideal to discuss the matter in public. And the benefits that come of making democracy deliberative, according to the arguments under consideration, would all seem to be available under the premise-driven way of doing things; in particular, they would seem to be available as readily and as richly as under the alternative. The premise-driven procedure makes ample room for achieving the psychological and other transformative effects mentioned in the arguments in question. And so of course would any other procedure that collectivised reason in a democratic way: say, as mentioned earlier, a procedure that allowed *modus tollens* as well as *modus ponens*.

Not only that. Among such benefits there are some that look much more likely to be realised under a reason-collectivising procedure. With many democratic bodies, it is important by our general lights that members not be prejudiced in the conclusion they draw, for example, and not be lazy about the consideration they give to relevant premises. But if they are allowed to vote their individual judgments on the conclusion to be decided, then there is more room for prejudice and laziness than would be available under a collectivising procedure. Not having to give their judgment on the relevant premises, members of the body may find it easier to hide the influence of prejudice on their views. And not having to give their judgment on each premise, members may be tempted, once they have made a premise-judgment that determines their conclusion-vote, not to bother giving consideration to the other premises relevant.

ARGUMENTS FOR MAKING DELIBERATION DEMOCRATIC

But there is another sort of argument for the ideal of deliberative democracy that raises a sharper challenge to the republican position. This is the type of argument that makes a case, not for having deliberation present in democratic process, but rather for having democracy present in deliberative process; it argues for making deliberation democratic, not for making democracy deliberative. The claim is that if there are matters of truth involved in political deliberation—as in the question, most abstractly, of whether this or that is in the common interest—then the chance of reaching the truth, or of reaching the truth according to received views of reliability, is increased by having in place a regime of democratic decision-making. The argument may be recast for goals other than that of maximising the chance of reaching the truth or minimising the chance of falsehood. It applies just as readily to a more specific goal like that of minimising the chance of a false negative, for example: say, minimising the chance of finding an innocent defendant guilty. But I shall restrict myself here to the original truth-centred case.

This type of argument has been forcefully defended by David Estlund (1993a;1993b; 1997) but the most famous version, and the one I shall consider here, derives from the Marquis de Condorcet's work in defence of his so-called jury theorem (Black 1958; Condorcet 1976, 33–70; Estlund 1994). The theorem presupposes that the voters are independent of one another: while they may certainly form their opinions on the basis of dialogue, none of them votes in a way that is blindly deferential to others (Estlund and Waldron 1989; Estlund 1994). It shows that if voters each have the same, greater than evens chance of being right on some yes-no issue then, first, their collective resolution of the issue, under majority rule, will have a yet greater chance of being right and, second, it will have a progressively greater chance of being right as the size of the group increases. Indeed the latter element is assured, even if some voters have a less than evens chance of being right; it will hold so long as the average chance of voters being individually right is greater than evens (Owen, Grofman and Feld 1989).

Let competence in a person be identified with the probability that on being forced to choose between the answers, they will choose the right one. Suppose that the person has to choose, then, between judging that p and judging that not p. Their competence will be given by the probability associated with its being the case: either that p, and they judge that p; or that not p, and they judge that not p. The message of the jury theorem is that if the the competence of individual voters is greater than 1/2, then the competence of the group operating under majority rule will be greater still and will approach 1.0 as the number of members increases.

We cannot go through the proof of the jury theorem here—for an excellent presentation, see Estlund (1994)—but the idea is reasonably intuitive. Suppose that each of us in a certain group has a two thirds chance of being right on some sort of issue. If I provide an answer on my own as that sort of issue comes up instance after instance, then in the long run I may expect to be right two thirds of the time. But if three of us, A, B and C, decide what to say instance by instance, on the basis of a majority vote, then under the standard probability calculus (Skyrms 1966, 111–37), our performance ought to be better than mine on my own.

Here, in brief, is why. On any occasion the group will be right so long as at least two of us—so long as three of us or any two of us—are right. If the chance of any one of us being right on a given occasion is two thirds, then the chance of at least two of us being right is the chance that A and B but not C are right, or that A and C but not B are right, or that B and C but not A are right, or that A and B and C are right. The chance that A and B but not C are right—assuming independence—is the chance of A being right times the chance of B being right times the chance of C not being right: i.e. $2/3 \times 2/3 \times 1/3$, or 4/27; and similarly for the other pairs. The chance that A and B and C are all right is $2/3 \times 2/3 \times 2/3$, i.e. 8/27. And so, the chance that at least two of us are right is the sum of these four figures: 4/27 plus 4/27 plus 4/27 plus 8/27; with disjuncts that are mutually incompatible the probability of the disjunction is the sum of the disjunct-probabilities. Thus the chance that at least two of us are right on any occasion is 20/27; and this is higher than the two thirds chance—18/27—of any one of us being right. The reasoning continues in the same way for each increase in the size of the group, supporting the Condorcetian conclusion that group competence approaches 1.0 as the size of the group increases.

The question now is whether the jury theorem provides any reason for resisting a mode of democratic judgment-making that imposes reason at the collective level. Is there a general argument for thinking that it is better, in Condorcetian terms, to collectivise reason rather than individualising it? In particular, to make the issue more specific, is there a general argument for going the premise-driven rather than the conclusion-driven way? As the answer goes in this case, so it should go more generally.

I raise the question under the assumption that a conclusion in the conjunctive case will be supported if the premises are supported and will be rejected otherwise. This is the assumption, in effect, that if the premises are 'p' and 'q', then the conclusion is just the conjunction of those premises. We need only consider the conjunctive case, since under our interpretation the chance of an individual or group being right about a disjunction, p or q, is just the chance of their being right about the conjunction, not(not p and not q).

The calculation of the relevant probabilities is a complex matter that Wlodek Rabinowicz and I address in an appendix, but the overall picture suggested by those calculations—suggested, not definitively established—is relatively clear. The premise-driven approach does better, according to that picture, provided we focus on the case where the individual or group is right about the conclusion through being right about the premises: provided they are right about the conclusion for the right reasons. But it is possible for an individual or group to be right about whether a conjunctive conclusion obtains, while being wrong about some or all of the conjunct-premises: it is possible to be right about the conclusion for the wrong reasons. Suppose that it is not the case that p and q. I may be right in thinking that it is not the case that p and q through thinking that not p and q, or not p and not q, when it is rather the case that p and not q; or I may be right through thinking that p and not q, or not p and not q, when it is rather that case that not p and q; or, finally, I may be right through thinking that p and not q, or not p and q, when it is rather the case that not p and not q. It turns out, surprisingly, that if it does not matter what the reasons are for which an individual or group is right about a conclusion, then the conclusion-driven approach does better in Condorcetian terms: it offers a better chance of the group's making the correct judgment on the conjunctive conclusion.

How should we respond to this finding? It is not the most welcome result possible from the point of view of the argument in the last section; the most welcome result would have been that the premise-driven approach is better either way. But it is much more welcome than would have been the result that the conclusion-driven approach is better either way. And it is a result that, on reflection, proves to be quite congenial.

When a person or community makes a correct judgment that p for the wrong deliberative reasons, then we deny that they understand why it is the case that p, or that they know that p. But the ideal of deliberative democracy, as that has been articulated on all sides, is closely bound to the alleged prospect of an increase of understanding and perhaps knowledge on the part of individuals in the community, and the group as a whole; there is no suggestion that it merely increases the likelihood of serendipitous error. The ideal supposes that in relying on deliberation to guide them towards a collective judgment, people will be guided by right reasons: that is, by reasons that are sound as well as supportive.

This line of thought suggests that when we try to determine how satisfactory the premise-driven approach is in Condorcetian terms, the question we should ask is whether it does better than the conclusion-driven approach in promoting the chance of the group's getting the right result, assuming that the result is to be reached on the basis of right reasons. And the answer to that question, happily, does go the way of the premise-driven approach. Not only does the approach make contestability possible and so answer to republican concerns. Under the assumption that judgments are to be reached via right reasons, which is common to all theorists of deliberative democracy, it also holds out the best prospect of enabling the group to get at the truth.

I said that the picture defended in the appendix, on which we have been relying, is not definitively established there. What is worth noting, however, is that the less secure element in that picture is the suggestion that the conclusion-driven approach will do better when it does not matter whether the moving considerations are the right reasons or not. The claim that the premise-driven procedure will do better than the conclusion-driven when only right reasons are in play—that is, the claim on which the validity of the comments just made depends—looks to be much more firmly supported.

I conclude, to return to the general line, that the various arguments in the literature for deliberative democracy are consistent with the republican way of resolving the question that the discursive dilemma raises. The republican concern with contestability gives powerful reason for wanting democratic procedure to be deliberative, where possible, in a way that imposes the discipline of reason at the collective level. And the other considerations that are more generally invoked to support deliberative democracy do not represent countervailing forces.[3]

NOTES

1. This means that there would be nothing to be gained by having electoral democracy impose the discipline of reason at the collective level. But it does not mean that we should abandon the ambition, common to most deliberative democrats, to make electoral democracy and politics as deliberative as possible. There may be reasons of a non-republican kind for seeking a deliberative dispensation, as we shall see in the fourth section. But in any event the republican rationale introduced in the third section itself suggests an argument in support of electoral discussion and deliberation. This is that such debate is likely to be important for a political democracy in helping it to establish a currency of considerations that can be invoked to support or challenge decisions of government. It can serve as a filter such that those considerations that go unchallenged in the electoral forum have a good claim to express common perceived concerns.
2. Kornhauser and Sager (1993) suggest that while the straightforward premise-driven procedure is generally more satisfactory—more satisfactory from the point of view, roughly, of contestability—the court should resort to a higher-level procedure in any case, like the one illustrated, where there is any doubt about this. It should take a majority meta-vote on which procedure to employ at the lower level, undertaking 'to justify its decision' (31; cf 33–36): that is, undertaking to find agreed premises such that the meta-vote can be represented as itself driven by majority endorsement of those considerations in a premise-driven way. Thus the higher-level considerations might be, first, that going along with the lower-level premise-driven decision in this instance would generate a certain result and, second, that the court ought to avoid such a result. Such considerations, if endorsed by a majority, might provide a higher-level, premise-driven case for going along with a different result from that which was supported by a lower-level, premise-driven procedure.
3. I am indebted to Geoff Brennan, who first made me aware of the dilemma. I was helped by comments received when versions were presented at Lund University, Nov 99; at a conference on 'Deliberating about Deliberative Democracy', University of Texas, Austin, Feb 00; at the annual Analytic Legal Philosophers' Conference in New York, April 00; and at seminar presentations in Johns Hopkins University, New York University, and Princeton University. I owe a particular debt to Wlodek Rabinowitz for his helpful comments and I was also greatly aided by discussions with a number of other people: David Estlund, Christian List, Victoria McGeer and Fred Schick. Bruce Chapman and Lewis Kornhauser sent me useful written comments on the paper.

REFERENCES

Benhabib, S. (1994). "Deliberative rationality and models of democratic legitimacy." *Constellations* 1: 26–52.

Black, D. (1958). *The Theory of Committees and Elections.* Cambridge, Cambridge University Press.

Brennan, G. (2001). "Collective Coherence?" *International Review of Law and Economics* 21.

Brennan, G. and P. Pettit (1990). "Unveiling the Vote." *British Journal of Political Science* 20: 311–33.

Buchanan, J. and G. Tullock (1962). *The Calculus of Consent.* Ann Arbor, University of Michigan Press.

Chapman, B. (1998). "Law, Incommensurability, and Conceptually Sequenced Argument." *University of Pennsylvania Law Review* 146: 1487–1582.

Chapman, B. (1998). "More Easily Done than Said: Rules, Reason and Rational Social Choice." *Oxford Journal of Legal Studies* 18: 293–329.

Cohen, J. (1986). "An Epistemic Conception of Democracy." *Ethics* 97: 26–38.

Cohen, J. (1989). Deliberation and Democratic Legitimacy. *The Good Polity.* A. Hamlin and P. Pettit: 17–34.

Coleman, J. and J. Ferejohn (1986). "Democracy and Social Choice." *Ethics* 97: 6–25.

Condorcet, M. D. (1976). *Condorcet: Selected Writings.* Indianapolis, Bobbs-Merrill.

Dryzek, J. S. (1990). *Discursive Democracy.* Cambridge, Cambridge University Press.

Estlund, D. (1993). Making Truth Safe for Democracy. *The Idea of Democracy.* D. Copp, J. Hampton and J. E.Roemer. Cambridge, Cambridge University Press: 71–100.

Estlund, D. (1993). "Who's Afraid of Deliberative Democracy?" *Texas Law Review* 71: 1437–77.

Estlund, D. (1994). "Opinion Leaders, Independence, and Condorcet's Jury Theorem." *Theory and Decision* 36: 131–62.

Estlund, D. (1997). Beyond Fairness and Deliberation: The Epistemic Dimension of Democratic Authority. *Deliberative Democracy: Essays on Reason and Politics.* J. Bohman and W. Rehg. Cambridge, Mass., MIT Press.

Estlund, D. and J. Waldron (1989). "Democratic Theory and the Public Interest: Condorcet and Rousseau Revisited." *American Political Science Review* 83: 1317–1328.

Goodin, R. E. (1999). Democratic Deliberation Within. Canberra, Research School of Social Sciences, Australian National University.

Grofman, B. N. and S. Feld (1988). "Rousseau's General Will: A Condorcetian Perspective." *American Political Science Review* 82: 567–76.

Gutmann, A. and D. Thompson (1996). *Democracy and Disagreement.* Cambridge, Mass, Harvard University Press.

Habermas, J. (1984, 1989). *A Theory of Communicative Action, Vols1 and 2.* Cambridge, Polity Press.

Kornhauser, L. A. (1992). "Modelling Collegial Courts. I. Path-Dependence." *International Review of Law and Economics* 12: 169–85.

Kornhauser, L. A. (1992). "Modelling Collegial Courts. II. Legal Doctrine." *Journal of Law, Economics and Organization* 8: 441–70.
Kornhauser, L. A. and L. G. Sager (1986). "Unpacking the Court." *Yale Law Journal* 82.
Kornhauser, L. A. and L. G. Sager (1993). "The One and the Many: Adjudication in Collegial Courts." *California Law Review* 81: 1–59.
List, C. and P. Pettit (2002). "Aggregating Sets of Judgments: An Impossibility Result." *Economics and Philosophy.*
Owen, G., B. Grofman, et al. (1989). "Proving a distribution-free generalization of the Condorcet jury theorem." *Mathematical Social Sciences* 17: 1–16.
Pettit, P. (1997). *Republicanism: A Theory of Freedom and Government.* Oxford, Oxford University Press.
Pettit, P. (2000). "Democracy, Electoral and Contestatory." *Nomos* 42: 105–44..
Pettit, P. (2001). *A Theory of Freedom: From the Psychology to the Politics of Agency.* New York: Oxford University Press.
Skyrms, B. (1966). *Choice and Chance: An Introduction to Inductive Logic.* Belmont, Cal., Dickenson.
Stearns, M. L. (1999). "Should Justices Ever Switch Votes? Miller v. Albright in Social Choice Perspective." *Supreme Court Economic Review* 7: 87–156.
Sunstein, C. (1999). *One Case At A Time.* Cambridge, Mass., Harvard University Press.
Sunstein, C. R. (1993a). *The Partial Constitution.* Cambridge, Mass., Harvard University Press.
Young, I. M. (1990). *Justice and the Politics of Difference.* Princeton, Princeton University Press.

Appendix. The jury theorem and the discursive dilemma

Philip Pettit and Wlodek Rabinowicz

Background

Let us assume that in a society, S, everyone has a greater than evens chance, k, of being right in respect of each of two unrelated propositions, φ and ψ. This, to take the case of φ in illustration, means that for any member, x, the probability *that x judges that φ, and φ, or that x judges that not φ, and not φ,* is greater than 1/2. If we use R_φ for 'is right in respect of φ', i.e., as short for the italicized proposition in the preceding sentence, then we can express the assumption by saying that for every x and y in S, $P(R_\varphi x) = P(R_\varphi y) = k > 1/2$; and similarly for ψ.

Let us assume, in addition, that the chance of any individual's being right about one of the propositions is independent of the chance of any other individual's being right about it. Thus for all x and y in S, $P(R_\varphi x \ \& \ R_\varphi y) = P(R_\varphi x).P(R_\varphi y)$, and similarly for ψ.

Under these assumptions, the Condorcet jury theorem gives rise to an interesting question. We know from the theorem that given the two assumptions, the probability of a majority's being right about either proposition is greater than k and that it approaches 1 as the size of the group increases. But what is the probability of a majority's being right about the conjunction φ & ψ? That question divides into two, in the light of the discursive dilemma. First, what is the probability of a majority's being right, if the group follows the premise-driven procedure? And second, what is the probability of a majority's being right, if the group follows a conclusion-driven procedure?

We explore the answers to these questions in this appendix, entering specific values for the size of the group and for the chance of an individual's being right about a proposition. In pursuing this exploration we add some further assumptions, in order to make the questions tractable. We take it, not only that φ and ψ are unrelated propositions in respect of content, but also that the competence of each individual in respect of those propositions is unrelated. Thus, the probability that the individual correctly judges one proposition to be true or false is independent both of the truth value of the other proposition and of his judgment of that proposition (*Independence*). We assume that each individual is opinionated with respect to both φ and ψ, i.e., the probability that he judges φ (ψ) to be true or to be false—the probability that he judges that it holds or judges that it does not hold—equals 1 (*Opinionation*). We assume also that, for each of these propositions, its being true is equiprobable with its being false (*Equiprobability of Propositions*). And we assume that the competence of each individual is evenhanded as far as each proposition and its negation are concerned: that he judges it to be true and it is true is just as probable as that he judges it to be false and it is false (*Evenhandedness*).

A complexity: being right for the wrong reasons

These questions involve a complexity that is not at first obvious. If we ask about someone's—or indeed some group's—chance of being right about a conjunction like φ & ψ then we have to consider the chance of their being right in each of four (as we assume, equiprobable) scenarios:

1. φ & ψ 2. not φ & not ψ. 3. φ & not ψ 4. not φ & ψ.

In each of those scenarios we have to determine the chance of the person's being right for the right reasons, i.e. through being right about each of the conjuncts; or being right for the wrong reasons, i.e. through being wrong about one or even both of the conjuncts. A person can be right in scenario 1 only through being right about both conjuncts; in 2 through being right about both or wrong about one and right about the other; in 3 through being right about both, through being wrong about both, or through being wrong about the first and right about the second; and in 4 through being right about both, through being wrong about both, or through being right about the first and wrong about the second.

First question, re premise-driven procedure

Let us now consider the first question. Specifically let us consider it under the assumption that we have a group, S, of just three members and that the chance, k, of an individual's being right is 2/3. Under the premise-driven procedure we first have to determine the chance of the group's being right about each of the propositions, φ and ψ. The Condorcet jury theorem, applied as illustrated in the text, tells us that this chance is 20/27. So what, then, is the chance of the group's being right about the conjunction φ & ψ?

The elements required for making this calculation are presented in this table, where 'J' indicates that the proposition following is judged to be true by the relevant subject: in this case, the majority and so the group.

Scenarios	Ways of being right	Chance of being right
1. φ and ψ	Jφ and Jψ	20/27 × 20/27
		Total: 400/729
2. not φ and not ψ	Jnot φ and Jnot ψ	20/27 × 20/27
	Jnot φ and Jψ	20/27 × 7/27
	Jφ and Jnot ψ	7/27 × 20/27
		Total: 680/729
3. φ and not ψ	Jφ and Jnot ψ	20/27 × 20/27
	Jnot φ and Jnot ψ	7/27 × 20/27
	Jnot φ and Jψ	7/27 × 7/27
		Total: 589/729
4. not φ and ψ	Jnot φ and Jψ	20/27 × 20/27
	Jnot φ and Jnot ψ	20/27 × 7/27
	Jφ and Jnot ψ	7/27 × 7/27
		Total: 589/729

The table displays the fact that it is harder for the group to be right in scenario 1 about the conjunction than in other cases; in those cases the group can be right about the conjunction while being wrong about one or both of the conjuncts. The overall probability of the group's being right about the conjunction will equal the sum of the four totals, divided by 4, since the scenarios are equiprobable. And that figure comes out as 1129/1458. This is the chance of the group's being right about the conclusion, for right or wrong reasons, under the premise-driven procedure.

But what is the chance of the group's being right for the right reasons? The answer is given by the sum of the first row totals for the four scenarios, divided by 4. And the figure in this case is 400/729: i.e. 800/1458 as against 1129/1458.

Second question, re conclusion-driven procedure

Now for the second question, which bears on the group's chance of being right in the event of following a conclusion-driven procedure. Here the first calculation involves the random individual's chance of being right about the conjunction, given an independent 2/3rds chance of being right about any conjunct. The elements required in this calculation are given in the following table:

Scenarios	Ways of being right	Chance of being right
1. φ and ψ	Jφ and Jψ	2/3 × 2/3
		Total: 4/9
2. not φ and not ψ	Jnot φ and Jnot ψ	2/3 × 2/3
	Jnot φ and Jψ	2/3 × 1/3
	Jφ and Jnot ψ	1/3 × 2/3
		Total: 8/9
3. φ and not ψ	Jφ and Jnot ψ	2/3 × 2/3
	Jnot φ and Jnot ψ	1/3 × 2/3
	Jnot φ and Jψ	1/3 × 1/3
		Total: 7/9
4. not φ and ψ	Jnot φ and Jψ	2/3 × 2/3
	Jnot φ and Jnot ψ	2/3 × 1/3
	Jφ and Jnot ψ	1/3 × 1/3
		Total: 7/9

What is the chance of a random individual's being right about the conjunction for any reasons, right or wrong? This is given by the sum of the four totals, divided by 4, which is 13/18. And what in that case, using Condorcet's theorem, will be the chance of a majority being correct? This will be the sum of the chances attaching to the possibilities that all three members are correct, that the first two are correct and the third wrong, that the first and third are correct and the second wrong, and that the second and third are correct and the first wrong. And that works out at 1183/1458. This is somewhat greater than the chance of the group's being right, no matter for what reasons, under the premise-driven approach: 1183/1458 as against 1129/1458.

What is the chance of the group's being right when the individuals are right for the right reasons? In order to get an individual's chance of being right for the right reasons about the conjunction, we need to go back to the calculation for the random individual, add up the first row totals for each scenario, and divide by 4. This gives us a figure of 4/9. Using the now familiar Condorcetian calculation, we then find that the chance of a majority being right about the conclusion is 648/1458. This is considerably smaller than the chance of the group's being right for the right reasons under the premise-driven approach: 648/1458 as against 800/1458.

Does this last result depend crucially on the fact that the random individual's chance of being right about the conjunction for the right reasons is less than a half, i.e. 4/9? We do not think so. If we do the corresponding calculations where the individual's chance of being right about either proposition is taken to be, say, 8/9—and so with his or her chance of being right about the conjunction for the right reasons being 64/81 and greater than evens—we still find that the group's chance of being right for the right reasons is higher under the premise-driven approach. It is 495,616/531,441 as against 471,040/531,441.

Conclusion

These calculations give us solid if not absolutely certain grounds for the claims made in the text. These are, first, that the premise-driven procedure looks likely to do considerably better than the conclusion-driven in securing the chance of a majority being right for the right reasons about a conjunction; and second, that the conclusion-driven procedure appears to do better than the premise-driven one, though not by the same sort of margin, in securing the chance of a majority being right for no matter what reasons, right or wrong, about a conjunction. This conclusion applies to disjunctions as well. Any disjunction 'p or q' can be expressed as a negated conjunction: not(not p and not q); and being right about a conjunction is equivalent, under our assumptions, to being right about its negation.

PHILOSOPHICAL ISSUES, 11
Social, Political, and Legal Philosophy, 2001

On the Territorial Rights of States[1]

A. John Simmons

I. When officials of some political society portray their state as legitimate—and when do they not!—they intend to be laying claim to a large body of rights, the rights in which their state's legitimacy allegedly consists. The rights claimed are minimally those that states must exercise if they are to retain effective control over their territories and populations in a world composed of numerous autonomous states. Often the rights states are trying to claim in asserting their legitimacy go far beyond this minimum. But whether a state's claims are modest or extravagant, the rights claimed invariably fall into three categories.[2] The first category is a set of rights held over or against those persons who fall within the state's claimed legal jurisdiction—what I will call *rights over subjects*. The second is a set of rights claimed against those persons *without* the state's jurisdiction—what we can call *rights against aliens*. And the third category is a set of rights held over a particular geographical territory (whose extent largely determines the scope of the state's jurisdiction)—call these *rights over territory*. The rights states claim in these three categories jointly define their conception of the *sovereignty*[3] that they (or their governments or institutions) enjoy, sovereignty that is more extensive (strong, absolute) as the rights asserted in these categories are more numerous and wide-ranging.[4]

It is principally on the third of these categories—on the nature and possible moral bases for the claims states make over geographical territories—that I will focus in this essay. The modern state is a *territorial* entity, and it claims to be legitimately so. Sidgwick was surely correct when he wrote that "it seems essential to the modern conception of a State that its government should exercise supreme dominion over a particular portion of the earth's surface...Indeed, in modern political thought the connection between a political society and its territory is so close that the two notions almost blend."[5] Common sense seems to view the territoriality of the modern state as natural and unquestionable. That, perhaps, explains why so little has been written, either by contemporary theorists or by the authors of the classics of modern political philosophy, on the *moral* bases of the modern state's claimed rights over territory.[6] States typically claim not only *legal* authority over their territories (i.e., that their rights over those territories should be affirmed by international law), but *moral* authority as well—at the very least insofar as the relevant principles of international law are thought themselves to have moral weight. My concern here, then, will be with the possible moral bases for the kinds of claims made over geographical territories by typical modern states.[7]

Much has been written (particularly during the last three decades) discussing the first category of rights claimed by states: the state's rights over subjects. The large contemporary literature on political obligation and civil disobedience is centrally concerned with the nature and extent of the state's rights over subjects, and most contemporary discussions of state (or governmental) legitimacy likewise concentrate (correctly, I will suggest) on this first category of rights. Similarly, there is a significant body of contemporary writing that deals with the second category of claimed rights, the state's rights against aliens. Concerns about the extent of states' rights over those within their claimed jurisdictions have led naturally to discussion of the rights of groups (principally, minority groups) to secede or to otherwise limit their subjection; and concerns about the rights of groups to secede have naturally focussed attention on groups' rights of self-determination, leading inevitably to discussion of *states'* rights of independence and self-government, held against alien persons, groups, and states. Arguments for states' rights in the first category thus have clear implications for a state's rights in the second category.

It seems just as clear, of course, that arguments concerning the rights in these first two categories must tell us something important about the legitimacy of states' claims over territory. Yet the problem of justifying the state's territorial claims—its claimed rights in my third category—still seems "intimidating" or "intractable" (to quote the authors of two of the very few recent discussions),[8] perhaps in part because it has been so little addressed. Of the great classical political philosophers, only one—John Locke—seems to have devoted any serious thought to this issue.[9] And contemporary political philosophers, like their historical predecessors, have almost always *begun* with the idea of states as units with legitimate territorial dimensions, proceeding more or less immediately to questions about how such territorial states can be justly governed.

For instance, John Rawls, by far the most influential of these philosophers, barely mentions the territorial dimension of political societies. Rawls begins with the idea that "political society is closed: we come to be within it and we do not, and indeed cannot, enter or leave it voluntarily...The government's authority cannot be evaded except by leaving the territory over which it governs, and not always then" (Rawls [1993], 136, 222). For Rawls, the fundamental question of political philosophy is: how can political power ("which is always coercive power" [Rawls (1993), 136]) be justifiably wielded over such a "captive audience"? But there is a logically prior question to be asked: what is the nature and basis of states' claims over those territories within which each of us comes nonvoluntarily to be? An answer to this prior question seems necessary before Rawls' question can be persuasively answered; and a sufficiently skeptical answer to this prior question can make Rawls' question seem otiose. For surely most would agree that even the most reasonable sort of political authority cannot be justifiably wielded by a state over territory (and the persons on it) to which that state has no legitimate claim. No matter how just its Constitution and its policies might be made, the United States could still not justifiably extend its political power to include, say, Pakistan or Antarctica within its jurisdiction. The question of *territorial* sovereignty, then, needs answering first.

Where this question has been addressed at all by contemporary theorists, the tendency has been[10] to focus on the ways in which injustice, cultural needs, or status as a "nation" might ground *new* territorial claims for groups, especially seceding groups—claims which might override the territorial claims made by the states from which they wish to separate themselves. My prior question, however, concerns the bases for the "old" territorial claims made by longstanding political societies, for secession is a far less serious moral problem if the states from which groups wish to secede have no rights to begin with over the territories at issue.

We mostly think of states' territories, of course, either purely or largely "positivistically". Thus, a state's territory is that portion of the earth's surface acknowledged to "belong" [11] to the state by the "world community" or by an appropriate international agency; or, following Weber, we think of a state's territory as the area within which it possesses a monopoly on the legitimate use of physical force. But such accounts either ignore altogether or merely push one step back questions about the *moral* bases for states' claims to those areas within which they do in fact exercise largely unchallenged control.[12] And we know that the actual means by which existing states have established their territorial claims have seldom been morally exemplary. Boundaries expand and contract by simple seizures or annexations, by military conquest and intimidation, and by negotiation under duress. The international community generally accepts these changes after a suitable mourning period.[13] States tend to lay claim to (and try to defend their claims to) all territory extending to salient or defensible geographical features (like coastlines, rivers, or mountains), regardless of whether they extend services to those areas or whether those areas are used or inhabited by their subjects. Even where new territories have been acquired by settlement or by uncoerced agreement between states, these processes have frequently involved displacement of (or other severe impact on) native peoples.

Now it might, I suppose, seem to some that political philosophers *should* leave to one side questions about the legitimacy of states' territorial claims. For political philosophy does, after all, have to accommodate itself to the real world if it is to avoid reasonable charges of utopianism.[14] We cannot, for instance, do political philosophy while ignoring basic and (virtually) unchangeable facts about human nature, human motivation, and the human condition. Why, then, should we not also simply accept as a datum for political philosophy the basic and (virtually) unchangeable fact that the world is made up of states that have territories? The answer, of course, is that nobody denies the *fact* that all modern states claim territorial rights; but these territorial claims are often controversial, contested, or plainly unjust. And further, at an even more fundamental level, a world of territorial states is not an unalterable feature of the human condition, nor is such territoriality even a necessary feature of organized, law-governed human associations (as humanity's past shows quite clearly[15]).

It is thus perfectly appropriate for political philosophers to question the claims states make to geographical territories. And we can begin by distinguishing between two kinds of claims to territory that merit examination: the particular claims made by particular states to particular territories, and the general claims made by states together to the entire world (indeed, to the entire usable universe). First, what is it that justifies states' enforcement of their particular territorial claims? Indeed, why should states be thought entitled to control territories at all, rather than, say, to just control persons? Second, how did states collectively acquire the right to divide among themselves all usable territory, thus producing the many "captive audiences" with which Rawls' (with so many others') political philosophy begins? We seem, of course, mostly to accept these claims made by states without question. But it is surely on reflection a quite striking and remarkable feature of our political lives that the usable earth is entirely claimed by states—and that of the territory remaining in the usable universe that is claimed by no particular state (e.g., the high seas, Antarctica, the earth's moon, outer space), nearly all is regarded in international law as *res communis* (i.e., as held in common by *all* states and unavailable for acquisition). Virtually nothing usable is treated as *res nullius* (i.e., as what I will here call "unsubjected" territory) and thus as available for appropriation or settlement.[16]

But however little we may actually question such arrangements, it is unquestionable that they have profound effects on individual and group liberty, effects to which Locke's political philosophy is appropriately sensitive. Locke famously wrote that "any number of men may" join together in political society, but only because their doing so "injures not the freedom of the rest".[17] Where the territorial claims made by political societies (on behalf of their willing members) *do* injure the freedom of other (less willing) individuals, are those territorial claims indefensible? Further, of course, Locke famously argued that *individuals* may only legitimately appropriate unowned land where there is "enough and as good left in common for others" (II, 27; see also II,33). We may not by our appropriations deny others similar opportunities to appropriate. But are *states* immune from this Lockean proviso, free to take all usable territory as their own, without regard for actual or potential rival claimants? If we take at all seriously the Lockean concern with the state's impact on individual freedom, how must we view the legitimacy of states' general and particular territorial claims?

II. To this point, I have referred to the three categories of rights claimed by states, but only in reasonably vague terms. I want now to pause momentarily to be more specific about the contents of these categories, so that I can be more specific as well about the *relations* that might be thought to hold between the rights in these categories. Since different states may claim different sorts of rights, I propose to emphasize here only those claims that I think are made by all states that we would consider decent and tolerably just. In evaluating the claims, then, we will be evaluating the best case that states can make for themselves.

In the first category—that which I've called "rights over subjects"—reasonable states claim: (a) the right to be the exclusive imposer of law[18] on those within their jurisdictions (i.e., on their "subjects", in one natural sense of that term); (b) the right to be obeyed by their subjects (i.e., the right to have those within their jurisdictions perform their imposed legal duties); and (c) the right to threaten all subjects with the legal use of coercion and to use such coercion against noncompliers. The first of these rights—the legislative power—is generally taken to be limited to making only tolerably just (or, at the very least, procedurally legitimate) law. The relevant jurisdiction states claim is always defined principally in terms of the territory over which they claim rights of control, so that "jurisdiction" has come to have as a secondary meaning that particular territory itself: states claim a right to make law for and enforce that law on those within a territory. But the class of a state's subjects (those within its jurisdiction) is seldom thought to be identical to the class of persons within its claimed territory. States normally claim some, typically partial, jurisdiction over persons outside of their territories (e.g., their citizens abroad or those who have committed crimes against their citizens).[19] And they claim only limited jurisdiction over some persons within their territories (e.g., diplomats or visiting aliens who, while generally held to the observance of the laws establishing "peace and good order", may not be subject to other laws—such as parking or traffic, tax, or military service laws).

These rights in the first category—rights to make and enforce law (broadly, within a territory) and to be obeyed by those subject to the law—are normally taken to correlate with the *obligations* of other persons, groups, or states. Some of the correlative obligations are the obligations of subjects: obligations not to attempt rival legislation or enforcement, to fulfill lawfully imposed requirements, and not to resist the state's lawfully employed coercive powers. Other of these correlative obligations, however, are the obligations of *non*-subjects, of those *without* the state's claimed jurisdiction.

Here the first category of rights makes contact with the second, with the "rights against aliens" claimed by states. States claim the right not to be interfered with or usurped by alien persons, groups, or states in the exercise of those rights claimed in the first category. States claim rights to non-interference, self-determination, self-government, or external sovereignty. This is generally intended to include not only obligatory alien respect for the state's exercise of its first-category legislative and executive powers, but also for the state's exercise of what is sometimes called its *federative* power—what Locke describes as "the power of war and peace, leagues and alliances, and all the transactions with all persons and communities without the commonwealth" (II, 146). States claim the right to "do business" in the world as a legal person, as an autonomous, equal corporate entity—including the "business" of conducting just war—without alien interference. This business may even be taken to include the enforcement against aliens of "natural law", God-made law, or "human rights", which will, of course, inevitably bring the rights claimed by some states in category two ("rights against aliens") into conflict with those claimed by other states in category one ("rights over subjects").

Finally, the rights claimed by states in category three—the "rights over territory" which are here my principal concern—normally encompass the following: (a) rights to exercise jurisdiction (either full or partial) over those within the territory, and so to control and coerce in substantial ways even non-citizens within it; (b) rights to reasonably full control over land and resources within the territory that are not privately owned; (c) rights to tax and regulate uses of that which is privately owned within the state's claimed territory; (d) rights to control or prohibit movement across the borders of the territory (which, of course, involves as well certain quite direct "rights against aliens" from our second category); and (e) rights to limit or prohibit "dismemberment" of the state's territories, by prohibiting unencumbered transfer of land to aliens, alienation of land to "the common", or private or group secession.

These, then, are the principal rights claimed by reasonably just states in each of the three categories. How might these categories of claimed rights be taken to be *justified* relative to one another (hence, how might the state's "rights over territory" be taken to be justified at all)? Given the clear connections we have seen between the categories of rights, one natural approach to justifying the rights in the three categories is to defend what we might call a "hierarchical" account. On hierarchical accounts, one of the three categories of right is regarded as primary or basic, with the others being derivative. For instance, we might regard the state's claims to territory as its most basic rights and attempt to justify those claims independently. We could then derive the state's rights over subjects and the state's rights against aliens by arguing that these are rights that are necessary to the state's free exercise of its more fundamental (and already justified) rights over territory.

A more plausible hierarchical account, I think, begins with a different category of right as primary. This model, familiar to us from Locke's political philosophy—and on the discussion of which I will spend some time in this paper—begins with the state's authority over its subjects as its fundamental or primary right. On Locke's own version of this model, of course, the state's rights over subjects are independently justified in terms of the subjects' free consent. The state's rights against aliens are then derivatively justified as what is necessary to properly exercise authority over subjects, with the state's rights to non-interference, self-determination, and free interaction with other agents being understood on the model of individuals' natural rights to self-government. Indeed, on Locke's version of the model, the state's rights against aliens just *are* (a subset of) individual rights against aliens, transferred to and exercised collectively by the state. Finally, on this model the state's *territorial* rights are derived as well from its rights over subjects. For a state's rightful territory is to be understood as that geographical area exclusively and legitimately owned, occupied, or used by the state's subjects. In order to effectively control and protect its subjects (in the exercise of its first- and second-category rights), the state requires as well control of various sorts over the territory in which those subjects lead their lives. Thus, the derivative third-category rights of states over territories.

As I suggested above, I regard this Lockean hierarchical account as more plausible than a hierarchical account that takes the state's rights over territory to be primary. For the Lockean account is not forced, as is this latter account, to regard the state as an independent agent, prior in moral standing to the citizens it serves, with claims to the earth that are more basic than those of individuals. It is difficult (for me, at least) to see how the state's claim to territory could be justified *except* through the claims or needs of the persons it rules, making it essential to begin any derivation with the state's right to act on behalf of those subjects (as on the Lockean derivation). But even if the Lockean account is admitted to be superior to alternative hierarchical accounts, our account of the relations between the three categories of states' rights need not be hierarchical in this way. For instance, a utilitarian might try to justify the state's rights over territory by direct or indirect appeal to the effects of such state control on human (or animal) happiness[20]. But she could justify the state's rights over subjects and against aliens by precisely the same kind of appeal to utility, with none of the categories of right defended as primary and none derived from others regarded as more basic. Before returning to the Lockean hierarchical account, what can be said about such non-hierarchical accounts of states' rights over territory?

III. Let us start by noting that any acceptable account of states' rights over territory must do more than simply explain why states should have territories; it must explain how a state can be morally justified in claiming rights over a *particular* territory. The first sort of explanation is (relatively) easy: without various kinds of control over a reasonably fixed territory (within which its subjects mostly remain), it is difficult for a state to effectively protect and advance the interests of its subjects (or itself)[21]; and state responsibility for, e.g., environmental protection and other shared ends with territorial dimensions might be the best means of advancing such ends. It is, however, the second, harder explanation we seek here, for the first sort of explanation never tells us why *this* state has a right to *this* land, a right that might triumph in an actual controversy over territorial title. By analogy, we can also (relatively) easily explain why *individuals* ought to have personal *property*: without enduring control over external goods it is far more difficult for persons to secure essential interests and exercise self-government. But it has proved far more difficult for theorists to explain how individuals can be justified in claiming *particular* external goods as their property.

The only non-hierarchical accounts of states' territorial rights that appear to stand any real chance of explaining particular states' particular territorial entitlements are either consequentialist, conventionalist, or some combination of the two (as in a non-ideal, conventional-rule consequentialism, like Hume's). I find none of the moral theories at issue in such accounts at all compelling. But here I want only to try to briefly argue that these non-hierarchical accounts are unconvincing in the ways they approach territorial rights, regardless of what we might think of the moral theories that drive them. Such accounts are, I will suggest, distinctly less persuasive than the rival Lockean hierarchical account that I will go on to discuss.

To begin, let us focus on those justifications offered by the most defensible of the consequentialist moral theories, utilitarianism. It is difficult to see how *act*-utilitarian reasoning could succeed in justifying much of anything in the way of enduring territorial rights for states. If a state's particular territorial rights are to be determined at any moment by the extent to which those rights facilitate the promotion of ends like pleasure, happiness, or desire-satisfaction (or, say, by the extent to which drawing the boundaries of the state in that particular place effectively internalizes externalities [Barry (1999a), 254]), there may of course be some tendency to determine legitimate territories to be those in fact currently effectively ruled by existing states—since utility tends to favor present settled possession (due to transfer costs). But even taking such tendencies into account, it seems likely that act-utilitarians will have to allow that state territories should change quite frequently, following the dramatic shifts in national or group needs produced by natural disasters, crop failures, droughts, exhaustion of natural resources, increases or decreases in population, and so on (see, e.g., Moore [1998], 149). And such an account will be unlikely to capture many people's intuitive sense of the particular territorial rights of states. In any event, I will focus my attention here on the non-hierarchical accounts of states' rights over territories that feature instead *rule*-utilitarian or conventionalist reasoning (despite the familiar and, in my view, compelling objections to such approaches to moral reasoning).

Rule-centered moral reasoning will account for states' legitimate territorial rights in terms of the extent to which states' particular claims conform to the ideal or conventional rules governing such claims. Rule-centered reasoning of this sort seems likely to yield conclusions far more amenable to a state's possession of relatively stable (hence intuitively satisfying) territorial rights over a particular area, due not only to high transfer costs, but as well to the need for viable rules to both eliminate the necessity of complex calculation (so that the rules are relatively simple and memorable) and to look beyond utilities in the particular case to the general felicific tendencies of competing *policies*. There are, however, some obvious problems with appeals to such ideal or conventional rules that are special to this context. The actual international conventions governing the titles to and boundaries of state territories are sufficiently vague and controversial as to be virtually useless in any attempts at justification.[22] And appeals to ideal rules seem likely to face difficulties just as severe, in light of the difficulty of the calculations required to generate clear rules for the legitimacy of states' particular territorial claims.

The difficulty with rule-utilitarian and conventionalist accounts of states' territorial rights that I want to stress here, however, is even more general than this concern about the clarity of the rules those accounts can justify. It is rather the built-in and, I think, unjustified *conservatism* of such accounts that makes them most questionable. The actual conventions that govern territorial claims (insofar as these are clear enough to discuss) are heavily, and not surprisingly, biased in favor of settled possession and the power to defend a territorial claim, both of which strongly support the claims of the winners in the land game, regardless of the apparent moral merits of their claims.[23] One needn't be an ardent Marxist or an embittered Thrasymachean to acknowledge this simple truth. Appeals to *ideal* rules might seem to promise less conservative conclusions. But while utilitarianism is by no means conservative in all of its practical implications, on the question of states' territorial rights it seems bound to be so. For once anything like a particular territorial order is solidly entrenched, the levels of inconvenience, frustrated expectations, and other utilitarian "mischief" that would attend changes is likely to be so high that the ideal rules assigning territorial rights in such contexts will almost certainly be just as conservative as our actual conventions.

Admittedly, the conservative conclusions of ideal rule utilitarianism are better motivated by underlying theory than are those of simple conventionalism. But one of the fundamental problems with all varieties of consequentialism is the way in which they permit their conclusions to be strongly influenced by the weight of frustrated expectations and desires, however unjustified these might be, and by considerations of simple convenience, thus biasing the theory against those who have "lost out" in the relevant context and against claims on behalf of alternative forms of social organization that are not instantiated. In particular, I want to emphasize three kinds of claims that seem intuitively forceful but that are unlikely to be recognized within any utilitarian system of rules. The first kind is the historical claims of small groups of persons to territories currently controlled by states, claims often stemming from acts or events in the distant past. The second kind is the claims of (actual or potential) groups of people desiring to found new states in unsubjected territories. And the third kind of claim is that of those who desire (or a claim on behalf of those who might desire) independence from the state-system altogether, and who thus count as another class of rival claimants to the territories carved up by states.

Claims of the first sort are unlikely, if honored, to yield utilities sufficient to outweigh the disutilities involved in the disruption of settled state mechanisms and the frustrated expectations of states' willing subjects. When the number of rival claimants is small and when the state's territorial claims are enforced in practice, utilitarian rules are bound to favor state claims. Yet, intuitively, the claims to land and to substantial territorial sovereignty made by tribes and other small groups, based on past use or possession and on unwilling subjection, seem forceful and morally considerable in ways utilitarians seem bound to deny. Similarly, states' claimed right to simply divide up the entire surface of the earth, leaving no possible unsubjected holdings for new groups or independents (our second and third classes of claimants)—and basing territorial claims on little more than the willingness to defend claims with force—seems simply unjustifiable. The rival claims of new groups and independents, along with simple considerations of the value of human liberty, ought to make us deeply skeptical of such general territorial claims by states,[21] hence deeply skeptical as well of many of the particular territorial claims made by particular states. Utilitarian theory seems ill equipped to challenge this aspect of the state-system, unlike the Lockean hierarchical account to which I will turn momentarily.

Theorists who defend conservative rules of territorial integrity, whether or not they are consequentialists, regularly disregard these issues. Allen Buchanan, for instance, favors a "progressive" understanding of such rules, according to which "the territorial integrity of existing states is not to be violated", provided they are legitimate states (Buchanan [1997], 50). But the idea of legitimacy at work in Buchanan's account is apparently to be characterized *independently of* any justification for the state's claim to particular territories (or of states' claims to all available territory) (Buchanan [1999], 52–62), which threatens to simply beg the questions I raise here. For these questions are not questions about the justification of secession—that is, questions about the possibility of groups having special claims to land of their own based on the oppression or abuse they suffer within some state, or based on threats to their culture or their "national self-determination" (Miller [1995], 112). Mine are the *prior* questions about the general and particular state claims to territory which form the background against which such special group claims are made (and which are presupposed as legitimate by the terms in which such special claims are made) (see Moore [1998], 135).

The claims of states to territories can be challenged *without* alleging that states are abusing their subjects and *without* alleging that cultural or national needs ground special (possibly rival) rights to land. I do not intend to deny, of course, that states have an interest, even a "morally legitimate interest in maintaining their territorial integrity" (Buchanan [1997], 46). But such an interest does not necessarily rise to the level of a *right* for states to the territories they claim. By analogy, for instance, individual persons have an interest, even a morally legitimate interest, in maintaining the integrity of their current holdings in external goods—an interest made legitimate, we can suppose, by their own reasonable desires for subsistence, moderate comfort, security, and self-government, along with the needs of those who depend on them, their descendants, and so on. But these interests are not sufficient to ground for individuals a *right* to whatever holdings they happen at any particular time to possess. To deny this, either in the case of individual holdings or in the case of the territories claimed by states, is simply to favor the status quo without warrant (Moore [1998], 140). I want to explore the possibilities for an account of states' territorial rights that does not, as do most non-hierarchical (and, indeed, most other) accounts, simply build in a conservative bias without sufficient justification. For that purpose, I return now to the Lockean hierarchical account, an account that *can* have (and was thought by Locke himself to have) conservative *implications*, but that by no means *presupposes* such results.[25]

IV. Locke, remember, begins by imagining groups of loosely associated persons, many of whom possess property in land, and attempts to describe how such persons might create a territorial state. All legitimate political societies originate for Locke in consent (or contract). But such consent, be it tacit or express, is typically vague or inexplicit, amounting to little more than an agreement to join together into one society. And this leaves us with the question of what subjects' consent is actually consent *to*. Locke argues that we should interpret inexplicit political consent as follows:[26]

> Whosoever therefore out of a state of nature unite into a community must be understood to give up all the power necessary to the ends for which they unite into society ... And this is done by barely agreeing to unite into one political society, which is all the compact that is, or needs be, between the individuals that enter into or make up a commonwealth (II,99).

The principle of interpretation suggested here (and elsewhere) by Locke is this: consent should always be understood to be consent *to* all and only that which is necessary to the purpose for which the consent is given, unless otherwise explicitly stated.

When people consent to make or join a political society, then, their consent should normally be understood as consent to whatever arrangements are necessary for a peaceful, stable society. This, Locke thinks, means consent to majority rule, to obedience to and support for law (within the limits set by natural law), to mutual defense, and so on. Most important for our purposes here, political consent is normally consent to incorporate one's rightful landholdings into that territory over which the society will have jurisdiction. It would, Locke thinks, be "a direct contradiction" for us to suppose that a person's "land...should be exempt from the jurisdiction of that government to which he himself, the proprietor of the land, is a subject" (II, 120). More generally, we might say, the state cannot effectively protect its subjects from domestic or alien aggression if it cannot exercise certain kinds of control over (including enforcement of the law on) the territory where its subjects mostly reside and work.

Further, stability in this preservation of peace requires that the society's territories not be dismembered or perforated by the individual decisions of subjects, allowing alien presences within established defenses, and so on. So a subject's consent should also be understood to be consent to the following arrangement: subjects will not bequeath, sell, or otherwise alienate land incorporated into the state's territories except on the condition that subsequent holders of that land will also be bound by the obligations of membership, including subjection of the land to state jurisdiction (II, 116–17, 120). Thus, Locke argues, the consent that legitimates political society will normally legitimate as well that society's claims to jurisdiction and control over a particular, (more or less) fixed and stable area of the earth's surface.[27]

Territory can be legitimately *added* to the state, of course, as new subjects or subject-settlers join new land to it, or as the state otherwise makes legitimate acquisitions (through purchase, say, or through seizures justified by prior alien aggression). The process that creates a state's territories needn't be an "all at once" contract, as Locke's remarks perhaps suggest. But for Locke's account to end up justifying anything remotely like the territorial claims of actual modern states, he needs to explain why they should end up with legitimate *continuous* boundaries, not just how they can end up with legitimate jurisdiction over various chunks of land. Locke tries to do this, I think, by making two assumptions. The first is that there will be no "interior dissenters"—i.e., landowning persons who decline membership but whose holdings are surrounded by those of consenting members.[28] The second is that *unowned* interior land (i.e., unowned land surrounded by the holdings of subjects) will, by international understanding, be accepted as the common property of all members of that political society within whose exterior boundaries it lies.[29]

Neither supposition, perhaps, seems very plausible on its face; but both can be made to seem more reasonable with further elaboration. Interior dissenters are not very likely for a variety of reasons (at least where states do not attempt, as modern states in fact routinely do, to subject all adjacent land to their jurisdictions). States' territories can be expected to initially form by expanding outward from cores of already associated persons with common goals. Dissenters who find themselves surrounded by consenters, or consenters who find themselves separated by dissenters' lands from the core of members, both have strong self-interested reasons to exchange land (or seek new holdings) in ways that will tend to create continuous boundaries for political societies. While being a dissenter surrounded by consenters might provide some attractive opportunities for riding free on the society's provision of public goods, the amounts of control over the lives of interior dissenters that Lockean states could still legitimately exercise (e.g., by controlling their movement and opportunities for productive interaction with others, by enforcing natural law against them, etc.) would in fact provide much stronger motivations for dissenters to either consent to membership or relocate to exterior spaces (supposing such spaces exist, as Locke does suppose).

The international "common consent" that Locke thinks creates "the commons" within states is, perhaps, an even more questionable Lockean assumption, for such consent would seem to bind neither independent persons (i.e., those who are subjects of no state) nor new states formed subsequent to such common consent, leaving both free to establish property in the allegedly common land. But the spirit of Locke's theory of property is, I think, consistent with allowing that *modest* common holdings of land can be legitimated by the exclusive use of the commons by society's members for gathering, recreation, or shared activities, *independent of* any "common consent" to this that other societies may have given. What the spirit of Locke's account *condemns*—rightly, I think—is the familiar practice of states' declaring as the common property of their members (perhaps on the grounds of their "manifest destiny") vast and unused spaces, simply to facilitate defense or future settlement and expansion.

We've now seen the essentials of Locke's account of the territorial rights of states. Legitimate territorial claims are established through the subjection, by free consent, of persons and their land to state authority. A natural first complaint about such an account, of course, is that *no* states' claimed territories are actually legitimated in this fashion, so Locke's account condemns all territorial states to illegitimacy. Since I believe that Locke's consent theory of the state's "rights over subjects", by itself, condemns all existing states to some measure of illegitimacy (Simmons [1993], esp. Part 4), I find this implication of his theory of territorial rights unsurprising. Nor do I find these anarchistic consequences of Lockean political philosophy particularly unsettling, regardless of how unsettling Locke himself would have found them.[30] Standards of legitimacy may surely be correct, even if no actual states fully satisfy them. An account of territorial rights of the sort we seek should perhaps be required to show how states *could* acquire such rights; but it needn't imply that any actual states' territorial claims are fully, or even partially, legitimate, any more than an adequate theory of justice must imply that some actual states are just to a satisfactory extent. Theories of legitimacy and justice should, in my view, have as their contents genuine moral ideals, uncompromised by allowing moral justification to be held hostage to a rationalization of our own familiar or preferred political arrangements.

For the many who, with Locke, would find such conclusions about territorial rights difficult to countenance, however, it should be emphasized that states can be morally evaluated in many different ways other than by their legitimacy or illegitimacy. Possession of the rights in which a state's legitimacy consists is not the only positive moral quality a state can possess. States can be more or less well justified in terms of their justice, their efficiency, the extent to which they help to meet their subjects' needs and those of others in the world, etc.[31] And even if all actual states fail to live up to Lockean standards of legitimacy, they do not all fail in equal measure. Just as states can more or less closely approximate Locke's ideal of the voluntary political association, so can states more or less closely approximate the Lockean ideal of territorial rights that we've just examined.

So Lockean theory need not deny that some states' claims are *nearer* to being legitimate than are others', and this includes states' claims to territorial sovereignty. Further, we can surely identify *portions* of existing states' claimed territories that more or less closely satisfy Lockean standards. Importantly, I think that we do intuitively take closeness to satisfying Lockean standards for territorial rights as indicating closeness to the legitimacy of states' territorial claims. Where states' territories have histories that approximate Locke's conjectural history—where persons have (relatively) innocently acquired or (relatively) exclusively used land that has been (relatively) freely subjected to state jurisdiction—we tend to be *least* skeptical about states' claims to territorial sovereignty and *most* skeptical about rival claims to that territory. Where territories have been forcibly subjected, where "unimproved" lands have been claimed without use, or where claimed territories have been the subject of rival use or ownership claims, for instance, we tend to be most skeptical about states' claims.

This suggests to me that the Lockean account of legitimate territorial rights is at the heart of our common sense notion of rightful territorial sovereignty, with much of the remainder being mere accommodation to the (grim) realities of international political life. This should prove unsurprising when we remember that the few early modern political philosophers who wrote anything at all about the state's territorial dimension—these being the serious philosophers who had the best historical perspective on the *rise* of the territorial state—seem to have agreed with Locke in taking legitimate state territory to be derived from the rightful property of the state's subjects.[32] The great strength of the Lockean hierarchical account, then, is that it captures deeply entrenched and rationally supportable intuitions about what counts as a rightful territorial claim. And, importantly, it captures as well the force of many of the world's most persuasive actual claims raised *against* internationally condoned assertions of state territory. When native peoples press their claims to lands central to their history, we can easily understand the force of their claims, for their central force is really based, I think, on intuitively plausible claims of Lockean rights from use or ownership. When oppressed subjects or displaced groups deny state sovereignty over the lands they worked or owned, or when they decry the absence of unsubjected land in which to relocate and freely associate in their own ways, their denials speak to us in a Lockean voice.

On the other hand, the Lockean account also accords in a special way with much that we think states *are* entitled to when they make *legitimate* claims to territory. First, Lockean rights of jurisdiction, as we've seen, derive from individual rights of use or property; and even those who emphasize the differences between jurisdiction and property have to allow (as Sidgwick does) that state territorial jurisdiction (what Sidgwick misleadingly called "dominion") is strongly "analogous to private ownership from an international point of view" (Sidgwick [1908], 252). Second, thinking of state jurisdiction as a kind of (limited) property, as the Lockean claims we should, helps to explain why we think states have rights over windfalls (e.g., of natural resources) that happen to lie within their legitimate territories; for on the Lockean model, individual property holders have rights over all that flows from their labors, including both intended products and windfalls (provided that these holdings leave "enough and as good for others"). Likewise, where we think states are obliged to share with or donate to others their wealth or land, the Lockean account accords well with our sense of how this should be done. For if the state's rights over territory constitute a weak form of property, then the state, like a property-holding individual, has certain rights of discretion and administration over charitable distributions to other states or groups (just as we normally suppose states do). Even states' *legitimate* claims to territory may sometimes have to give way to more pressing claims based on need.[33]

V. The Lockean account of the state's valid rights over territory, then, has a great deal to recommend it. It also, of course, has been widely criticized. To be perfectly honest, I have been unable to find a single other philosopher who supports it. So I will try in closing to respond here to a few of what I take to be the most serious of the criticisms of the Lockean account. I will not even attempt to deal now with one complaint even more basic than those I will address: namely, that the Lockean account presupposes the possession by individuals of natural, pre-political (hence pre-legal) property (or, at least, use-rights) in land, which many critics regard as impossible or even incoherent. I have tried elsewhere to defend the Lockean position on this issue (Simmons [1992], ch. 5), and I can do no more here than refer the reader to those arguments.[34]

The first of the serious criticisms that I *will* address here is this: Locke understands state jurisdiction or territorial sovereignty as a kind of property or ownership; but there are enormous differences between jurisdiction and property,[35] which fact alone discredits the Lockean account. One simply cannot explain the territorial sovereignty of the modern state in terms of Lockean property. In my view, however, the Lockean account has ample resources to convincingly deal with this objection. State jurisdiction is not, according to Locke, supposed to be *identical* to private property, since individuals can privately own land over which a state has legitimate jurisdiction.[36] State jurisdiction is composed of some of the "incidents" (Honore [1961]) (or component rights) of the fuller ownership of land that individuals can enjoy in the state of nature, along with some of the rights that individuals there possess over themselves. When persons subject themselves and their land to the state, they transfer to the state some of their rights over each. They then enjoy a less full property in their land (e.g., they can no longer accomplish unencumbered transfer of their land to others) and a less full freedom in their persons (e.g., they are now obligated to comply with valid law). State jurisdiction differs from individual property by including only some of the rights of natural property in land (e.g., the rights to control borders and regulate uses) and by including some rights over persons which are *not* components of natural property in land (e.g., the right to make and coercively enforce law within the area). There is, as far as I can see, nothing particularly mysterious about our ordinary conception of states' rights over territory that cannot in this way be accounted for "by subtraction" from individual natural rights over land and over their persons (i.e., from individuals' natural "property" in the broad, Lockean sense of that term).

The second criticism of the Lockean account that I will address here is that when such an account is applied in practice, it cannot hope to yield any clear *resolutions* of states' (or others') territorial claims. Given the long human history of injustice with respect to land, both by individuals and by states, along with the controversial nature of even many respectable claims to property, we simply cannot expect to be able to untangle the various strands of entitlement to lands in a way that can illuminate any actual territorial controversies. This problem appears to be part of what makes Brian Barry call the Lockean account "absurd" (Barry (1999a), 252).[37] It is also, of course, a charge that has been frequently levelled (*mutatis mutandis*) against Robert Nozick's related "entitlement theory" of "justice in holdings".

Aside from the fact that alternative accounts of states' rights over territory seem to me to fare even *worse* in related respects than the Lockean account does in this—since they either cannot recognize at all the kinds of forceful historical claims at issue or must without adequate justification strongly privilege the status quo, whatever the history leading to it—the problems for the Lockean account are not as dire as it may seem. While I do not pretend that a Lockean account can without difficulty neatly determine the proper distribution of rights over, say, Kosovo or Palestine, at least some of the most serious problems are *evidentiary* (which is not a problem with the *theory*), while other of the questions central in actual political debates over such territories are of either marginal or no relevance on a Lockean accounting. Appeals to "national homelands" or to the cultural significance of a territory are relevant to a Lockean determination of territorial rights only to the extent that these correspond to claims of past productive use of the land or clear entitlement as just reparation for injuries, and even then only to the extent that the states or groups in question enjoyed (something like) a freely chosen subjection by the relevant persons or nations.

There are thus far fewer *legitimate* claims (to either property in land or jurisdiction over land) to be assessed on the Lockean account than there are claims passionately advanced and defended in actual political debates over territories. Further, I have argued elsewhere (Simmons [1995]) that many compelling and perfectly valid Lockean claims to land have only vague or "limiting" contents, rather than precisely delineable contents. Even, then, on a perfectly articulated and well justified Lockean theory, we should *expect* many property claims (hence jurisdictional claims) to be controversial and to require the use of judgment, not merely calculation, for their satisfactory resolution. For instance, the compelling historical claims to control over territory made by the descendants of some aboriginal peoples, though perfectly legitimate in Lockean terms, may not be precisely delineable due to the requirement that claims to large amounts of land (such as those necessary to a hunter/gatherer economy) may have to be "downsized" in the face of the needs of other potential users (in order to leave "enough and as good for others"). So a Lockean accounting of the valid territorial rights of states is likely both to be clearer and less tangled than its critics suggest and to be less vulnerable to the force of apparently outrageous claims that Lockeans might appear to be committed to accepting.

The Lockean hierarchical account of states' rights over territory, then, is less obviously vulnerable to serious objections than it might at first seem. There is no doubt that on this account the state territory legitimated by Lockean argument may not "coincide with the territory that is intuitively associated with a state" (Copp [1999], 15), at least if our intuitions simply follow international convention. But this does not seem to me to be a defect of the Lockean account; indeed, it seems vastly preferable to a built-in and ill-justified conservatism about states' territorial claims.

But even if the potential "revisionism" of the Lockean model seems an undesirable consequence, this cost may be one we should be prepared to bear in light of the clear shortcomings of alternative philosophical approaches to state territoriality.

NOTES

1. For their helpful comments on an earlier draft of this paper, I would like to thank audiences at Bowling Green State University and the University of Virginia Law School. Some of the work on this paper was done during a brief stay as a Visiting Scholar at the Social Philosophy and Policy Center at Bowling Green.
2. These categories correspond roughly to the three sorts of rights noted in Copp (1999), 18. I characterize the categories slightly differently and suggest a different set of constituent rights for them than does Copp.
3. Sovereignty is thus often characterized in international law as consisting of that set of rights normally exercised by modern states. Jurisdiction is then defined as that particular set of rights that entitles a state to govern persons and property by the state's municipal law. See, e.g., Brownlie (1998), 106 and Wallace (1997), 111. "International law is based on the concept of the state. The state in its turn lies upon the foundation of sovereignty, which expresses internally the supremacy of the governmental institutions and externally the supremacy of the state as a legal person" (Shaw, [1997], 331). For a good recent philosophical discussion of the concept of sovereignty, see Morris (1998), ch. 7.
4. In my view, both state legitimacy and state sovereignty consist in the state's possession of complex and internally related sets of these three kinds of right. A state is sovereign if it possesses reasonably extensive and exclusive (but not necessarily absolute) claim rights over a citizenry and territory, rights that entitle it to both internal control and external independence. A state (like any other institutional arrangement) is legitimate if it actually possesses the rights to do what it does (or what it attempts to do). Since the rights modern states claim and try to exercise add up to various kinds of sovereignty, discussions of legitimacy and sovereignty will naturally tend to converge. But the differences in the concepts allow the possibility of legitimate but non-sovereign political institutions (which might or might not qualify as "states"). The old (16th- and 17th-century) debates about sovereignty concerned principally questions of internal sovereignty (e.g., who has *de jure* authority over whom within a political society, the limits on political authority, etc.). More recent debates have concerned primarily external sovereignty (e.g., when and why nations have a right to self-determination, when international intervention is justified, etc.). My topic in this paper touches on both aspects of state sovereignty.
5. Sidgwick (1908), 221, 222. In international law (e.g., under the 1933 Montevideo Convention on the Rights and Duties of States [Article I]) states are *defined* as entities with fixed territories (and permanent populations) under

government control (and with the capacity to enter into relations with other states). The territorial state is thus the principal type of "legal person" recognized in international law.

6. Two recent works which strongly emphasize the territorial nature of modern states and the need to justify this dimension of states are Copp (1999) and Morris (1998).
7. I will not try to discuss here the question of whether the law (i.e., international law) ought to recognize all or only distinctively *moral* grounds for claims to territory, though I think it clear that no such position can be convincingly defended.
8. Buchanan (1991), 107; Morris (1998), 228. Morris writes at the conclusion of his discussion: "it is not evident that there are any general solutions for the question of determining the boundaries of states." (265) Courts have similarly been reluctant to address this question directly. As Malcolm Shaw argues, "the problem of how a state actually acquires its own territory in international law is a difficult one... With long-established states one may dismiss the question on the basis of recognition and acceptance." With respect to new states, "there has been relatively little discussion of the method by which the new entity itself acquires the legal rights to its lands. The stress has instead been on compliance with factual requirements as to statehood coupled with the acceptance of this by other states" (Shaw [1997], 335).
9. And the neglect of this issue is even more strikingly demonstrated by the fact that almost none of the numerous commentaries produced by Locke scholars over the years pays any careful attention to Locke's views on state territoriality. Two exceptions are Beitz (1980) and Grant (1987), ch. 3.
10. As in Buchanan (1991) and, to a lesser extent, in Morris (1998).
11. The sense in which a state's territories "belong" to it, of course, can only be clarified by clarifying the extent of a state's sovereignty. Centuries ago, feudal law conferred title to the state's territories on the ruler, as a virtual private owner. Contemporary law views a state's powers of government, administration, and disposition of territory as a kind of *imperium*, not as a form of *dominium*.
12. Thomas Baldwin claims that there is no real alternative to relying on the international community's judgment as a "justification" for "the territorial rights that states claim for themselves" (Baldwin [1992], 225). This seems to me false, as my arguments below indicate.
13. While many such acquisitions are prohibited under widely accepted principles of law, the legal force of subsequent international recognition in effect undermines those principles. The rules of international law have often "had the effect of legitimising the results of the exercise of power... Law must come to terms with power and force... The international community has accepted the results of illegal aggression in many cases by virtue of recognition" (Shaw (1997), 332, 340). See also Wallace (1997), 98–99.
14. On the problem of avoiding utopianism, see Nagel (1991), ch. 3.
15. See, for instance, Hendrik Spruyt's extensive discussion of the differences between the modern territorial state and its immediate, non-territorial pre-

decessor forms of association in Spruyt (1994). See also Morris (1998), esp. ch. 2.

16. More precisely, international law recognizes four types of territory: that which is subject to the sovereignty of some state (or states); that which is not so subject, but which has its own legal status (e.g., trust territories); the *res communis*; and the *res nullius* (Brownlie [1998], 105).
17. Locke, *Second Treatise of Government*, para. 95. Future references to this text will be noted as "II", followed by paragraph number.
18. For these purposes, we can think of law as a set of nonvoluntary binding duties and enabling mechanisms, ultimately backed by the legal powers of coercion and official recognition.
19. States claim jurisdiction not only under the "territorial principle", but also under the "nationality principle" (which determines jurisdiction by an *offender's* nationality) and the "passive personality principle" (which can determine jurisdiction by a *victim's* nationality). Other non-territorial principles of jurisdiction include the "protective principle" (according to which those who threaten or injure state security are held liable) and the "universality principle" (which makes, e.g., pirates, war criminals, and perpetrators of genocide subject to every state's jurisdiction). See, e.g., Wallace (1997), 111–19.
20. As when Sidgwick vaguely gestures in this direction: "the main justification for the appropriation of territory to governments is that the prevention of mutual mischief among the human beings using it cannot otherwise be adequately secured" (Sidgwick [1908], 252).
21. This is true both for the obvious reasons and for some that are subtler—e.g., that territorial states constitute a less immediate threat to other states or groups (and so are more likely to be able to peacefully coexist with them), since they recognize a territorial *limitation* to their jurisdiction (see Spruyt [1994], 169–70).
22. These conventions, of course, are largely given force in the relevant rules of international law. And many of the traditionally recognized bases for legitimate territorial acquisition (e.g., accretion, cession, occupation [of *terra nullius*], prescription) are still widely acknowledged. But in many cases the proper mode of application of these rules to contemporary circumstances is obscure, while in others the rules are either largely irrelevant (as in rules governing occupation) or clearly morally suspect (as in the rules of acquisitive prescription). Further, of course, actual rulings by international courts are muddied by their appeal to a huge variety of additional historical, cultural, economic, and geographical factors (e.g., contiguity, continuity, and geographical unity). And, as Martti Koskenniemi observes, "late modern practice of solving sovereignty disputes pays hardly more than lip-service to the traditional bases of territorial entitlement. Deciding such questions is now thought of in terms of trying to establish the most equitable solution" (Koskenniemi [1999], 505). Finally, as previously noted, international acceptance and recognition confers eventual effective title on all manner of acquisitions, despite the law's contemporary condemnation of (e.g.) conquest as a source of territorial title.

23. "It is a settled principle of the law of nations that a state of things which actually exists and has existed for a long time should be changed as little as possible" (Scott [1916], 121, 130).
24. Harry Beran has argued that political societies need to set aside ungoverned "dissenters' territories" in order to create the genuine options that would make free consent fully possible for persons living within political societies (Beran [1987], 59, 67, 104, 125). The maintenance of unsubjected territory of this sort seems to me unlikely by itself to solve any real problems for the consent theorist, since the high costs of relocation to such territory simply mirror the high costs of emigration generally, generating similar (and familiar) worries about the voluntariness of remaining (and consenting). But the rather different problem of *territorial* legitimacy that I am addressing in the text seems to me to push us by a different argumentative route toward practical recommendations similar to those made by Beran. The requirement that states leave enough and as good land for rival (i.e., non-state) claimants may oblige states to downsize and create unsubjected territories, available for appropriation by individuals or groups.
25. It may seem, I know, that my argument displays a bias toward a "natural law" approach to international issues, paying inadequate attention to more positivistic accounts of territorial title—for instance, to the traditional reliance in positivist theories of international law on general consent, treaty, and custom. I pay little attention to this tradition of thought because I think it is relatively easy to dispatch. Custom and tradition have in themselves no moral authority at all, since they can have pernicious contents and be maintained by morally despicable means. Customary rules may, of course, acquire moral sanction if, say, they are freely agreed to by all concerned or if they are utility-maximizing. But to say no more than that is to give up on custom as in itself morally authoritative (notice that even theorists like Burke end by defending custom as the content of an implicit social contract). As for general consent and treaty, there are two additional problems. First, appeals to the general consent of humankind (e.g., consent to certain customary rules for territorial title) tend to confuse mere acquiescence (which may be a product of ignorance, inability, or fear) with genuine, binding consent. Second, appeals to the consent of *nations* (e.g., on the basis of treaties concerning or common practice with respect to territorial claims) fail to establish *first* what must be established for such consent to justify binding rules: namely, the moral authority of states to *decide* the relevant questions (that is, states' priority over individuals or non-state groups). It is to this *prior* question—of the authority of states to by themselves resolve questions of territorial title—that this paper addresses itself.
26. The discussion immediately below draws on my more detailed defense of this reading of Locke in Simmons (1998), esp. 168–70.
27. Beitz summarizes Locke's argument as follows: "The founders restricted both the uses to which they (and their heirs and assigns) could put their land and created a limited power in the government to regulate its use. Since the territory of the commonwealth is like a quilt patched together from individ-

ual holdings in land, the system of covenants envisaged results in a uniform diminution of the ownership rights of the original owners and in the creation of a uniform set of rights in the government in respect of all the land in the commonwealth" (Beitz [1980], 493).

28. Jean Hampton objected to Locke's account precisely because the possibility (likelihood?) of such interior dissenters leaves as the only legitimate state "a patchwork state, which is so impractical as to be impossible" (Hampton [1997], 62). But Hampton did not consider the points noted below in the text concerning the unlikelihood of interior dissent. She also mistakenly supposed that *tacit* consenters in Locke would not count as having joined their land to the state, making discontinuous boundaries for the state seem virtually inevitable. This supposition is perhaps not unreasonable in light of the fact that Locke's principal example of tacit consent is that of enjoying land *already* under a state's jurisdiction (II,119). But Locke plainly allows that tacit consent can be given in other ways; and tacit consent to join a political society given by those holding *unsubjected* land is clearly intended by Locke to involve incorporation of that land into the society's territories. See my defense of this reading of Locke in Simmons (1998), esp. 164–66, 168–70, 176.
29. "And though it be common in respect of some men, it is not so to all mankind, but is the joint property of this country or this parish" (II,35). The "several states and kingdoms" have "by common consent given up their pretenses to their natural common right, which originally they had to those countries" (II,45). "By consent they came in time to set out the bounds of their distinct territories, and agree on limits between them and their neighbors" (II,38).
30. Locke's avowed purpose in the *Treatises* was "to make good [King William's] title, in the consent of the people" (*Two Treatises of Government*, Preface).
31. See my discussion of the relevant distinctions at issue here in Simmons (1999).
32. As Baldwin (Baldwin [1992], 213) correctly notes. Grotius and Pufendorf, for instance, while saying very little on the subject, plainly take the state's territory to be established in some way by adding together the original members' legitimate holdings. See, for example, Samuel Pufendorf, *De jure naturae et gentium, libri octo*, VII, 2, 20.
33. Just as Locke allows that the legitimate claims to land (and other property) of a just conqueror may have to "give way to the pressing and preferable title of those who are in danger to perish without it" (II,183). See also Locke's *First Treatise of Government*, paras. 42–43.
34. Baldwin believes that even should we accept Locke's theory of property, his account of the state's territorial rights cannot succeed. But even were Baldwin correct that for Locke the holdings of individuals and groups are "called into question" when land becomes scarce (Baldwin [1992], 215), it surely does not follow that these holdings are simply "invalidated" (as opposed to, say, "adjusted") in a way that undermines Locke's account of the state's territorial rights. Nor, of course, is it necessary for a Lockean to follow Locke in accepting either the premise or its (alleged) implication.

35. See, e.g., Buchanan (1991), 108–9; Morris (1998), 262–65; Brilmayer, (1989), 15–16.
36. It is common for those writing about Locke's views to simply confuse jurisdiction with ownership, as Locke plainly does not. For just one of many such examples, see Gale (1973).
37. Exactly what makes Locke's account "absurd" is unclear from this article. But elsewhere Barry writes that, because of their enormous complexity and controversial nature, adjudicating historical claims to territory is "like asking philosophers and lawyers to rule on the question of whether the number seven is orange" (Barry [1999b], 41). This also, of course, leaves the precise nature of the alleged problem unclear. But it can certainly fairly be said that Barry's language in both articles is far stronger than any arguments he actually advances.

REFERENCES

Baldwin, Thomas. (1992) "The Territorial State", in H. Gross and R. Harrison (eds.), *Jurisprudence: Cambridge Essays.* Oxford: Oxford University Press.

Barry, Brian. (1999a) "Self-Government Revisited", in R. Beiner (ed.), *Theorizing Nationalism.* Albany: S.U.N.Y. Press.

Barry, Brian. (1999b) "Statism and Nationalism: A Cosmopolitan Critique", in I. Shapiro and L. Brilmayer (eds.), *Nomos XLI: Global Justice.* New York: New York University Press.

Beitz, Charles. (1980) "Tacit Consent and Property Rights", *Political Theory* 8:4 (November 1980).

Beran, Harry. (1987) *The Consent Theory of Political Obligation.* London: Croom Helm.

Brilmayer, Lea. (1989) "Consent, Contract, and Territory", *Minnesota Law Review* 74:1 (October 1989).

Brownlie, Ian. (1998) *Principles of Public International Law,* Fifth Edition. Oxford: Clarendon Press.

Buchanan, Allen. (1991) *Secession.* Boulder: Westview.

Buchanan, Allen. (1997) "Theories of Secession", *Philosophy and Public Affairs* 26:1 (Winter 1997).

Buchanan, Allen. (1999) "Recognitional Legitimacy and the State System", *Philosophy and Public Affairs* 28:1 (Winter 1999).

Copp, David. (1999) "The Idea of a Legitimate State", *Philosophy and Public Affairs* 28:1 (Winter 1999).

Gale, George. (1973) "John Locke on Territoriality: An Unnoticed Aspect of the *Second Treatise*", *Political Theory* 1:4 (November 1973).

Grant, Ruth. (1987) *John Locke's Liberalism.* Chicago: University of Chicago Press.

Hampton, Jean. (1997) *Political Philosophy.* Boulder: Westview.

Honore, A. M. (1961) "Ownership", in A. Guest (ed.), *Oxford Essays in Jurisprudence.* Oxford: Oxford University Press.

Koskenniemi, Martti. (1999) "The Politics of International Law", in K. Culver (ed.), *Readings in the Philosophy of Law.* Peterborough, Canada: Broadview Press.

Miller, David. (1995) *On Nationality.* Oxford: Oxford University Press.

Moore, Margaret. (1998) "The Territorial Dimension of Self-Determination", in M. Moore (ed.), *National Self-Determination and Secession.* Oxford: Oxford University Press.

Morris, Christopher. (1998) *An Essay on the Modern State.* Cambridge: Cambridge University Press.

Nagel, Thomas. (1991) *Equality and Partiality.* New York: Oxford University Press.

Rawls, John. (1993) *Political Liberalism.* New York: Columbia University Press.

Scott, J. B. (1916) *Hague Court Reports*, Vol. I.

Shaw, Malcolm. (1997) *International Law*, Fourth Edition. Cambridge: Cambridge University Press.

Sidgwick, Henry. (1908) *The Elements of Politics.* London: MacMillan.

Simmons, A. John. (1992) *The Lockean Theory of Rights.* Princeton: Princeton University Press.

Simmons, A. John. (1993) *On the Edge of Anarchy: Locke, Consent, and the Limits of Society.* Princeton: Princeton University Press.

Simmons, A. John. (1995) "Historical Rights and Fair Shares", *Law and Philosophy* 14 (May 1995).

Simmons, A. John. (1998) "'Denisons' and 'Aliens': Locke's Problem of Political Consent", *Social Theory and Practice* 24:2 (Summer 1998)

Simmons, A. John. (1999) "Justification and Legitimacy", *Ethics* 109:4 (July 1999)

Spruyt, Hendrik. (1994) *The Sovereign State and Its Competitors.* Princeton: Princeton University Press.

Wallace, Rebecca. (1997) *International Law*, Third Edition. London: Sweet and Maxwell.

PHILOSOPHICAL ISSUES, 11
Social, Political, and Legal Philosophy, 2001

Inequality: A Complex, Individualistic, and Comparative Notion[1]

Larry S. Temkin

Introduction

Equality has long been among the most potent of human ideals, and it continues to play a prominent role in political argument. Views about equality inform much of the debates about such wide-ranging issues as racism, sexism, obligations to the poor or handicapped, relations between developed and developing countries, and the justification of competing political, economic, and ideological systems. Unfortunately, these debates have been shrouded in error and confusion, for few ideals have been more widely discussed, yet less well understood, than the ideal of equality.

This essay is divided into two main parts. In part I, I distinguish between different kinds of egalitarian positions. I show that numerous so-called egalitarian positions are compatible with the central tenet of non-egalitarianism, and suggest a core notion that would distinguish egalitarians from non-egalitarians. In addition, I claim that there is an intimate connection between equality and fairness, and suggest that egalitarians should be pluralists both in terms of other ideals and in terms of the kinds of equality that matter. In part II, I gather together, for the first time in an essay, some of the central results of my book, *Inequality.*[2] I introduce my approach to understanding equality as a complex, individualistic, and comparative notion. In addition, I briefly address several questions about which many have been confused or mistaken. These include whether inequality matters more at high levels or low levels, whether variation in population size affects inequality, and whether one should focus on whole lives in comparing individuals with respect to inequality. Finally, I briefly consider a possible implication of my work that would be surprising and dismaying.

The aim of my essay is modest, but important. It is to contribute to a better understanding of the ideal of equality. I do not argue that one *should* care about equality. Nor do I address the question of how much one should care about equality, assuming one should. It seems to me that until one *understands* the notion such questions are premature.

One preliminary comment. The set of issues that most philosophers and political scientists cast in the terminology of *equality*, most economists cast in the terminology of *inequality.* The issues are the same, but there are two ways of talking about them. Thus, the egalitarian's concern to promote equality, just is the concern to reduce inequality. In general, I shall follow the economists' usage, which I find more perspicuous. However, in contexts where it would be misleading or awkward to do so, I shall follow the philosophers' usage. I trust, in each case, context will make my meaning plain.

Part I

Egalitarians come in many stripes. Too many, I'm afraid. There is no consensus as to what egalitarianism is, hence no single position being defended or attacked. Worse, both advocates and opponents conflate equality with a host of other positions. This is unfortunate. We cannot make progress in this difficult area until we are clear what we are arguing about. The main aim of this part is to help rectify this situation. I want to carefully distinguish between different possible egalitarian positions, so that future debates can be more focused and effective. Unfortunately, to do this properly involves some boring taxonomy. Nevertheless, years of reading and lecturing about equality have convinced me that although some of these distinctions have long been recognized, too often they are overlooked or ignored. Moreover, much needless confusion could be avoided if they were kept in mind. In the interests of space, I shall largely restrict myself to bald—but not, I think, unwarranted—assertions.

A. Philosophers have long distinguished between purely *formal* principles of equality and *substantive* principles of equality, where, roughly, a formal principle is one that demands *universality* in its application, while a substantive principle is one that demands that people be treated equally in certain respects. Unfortunately, this distinction is neither as clean, nor as helpful as one might hope. Many positions meet the criteria of both formal and substantive principles of equality, and among positions that meet the stated criterion of a substantive principle of equality, some are associated with a deep and thoroughgoing commitment to equality, while others are not. Consequently, it may be useful to distinguish between *equality as universality* principles, *equality as impartiality* principles, and *equality as comparability* principles.

Roughly, equality as universality reflects the view that all reasons and principles must be universal in their application. The view that all blue-eyed people should be made kings, and all brown-eyed people paupers meets the equality as universality criterion! So too would the more restricted view that all blue-eyed people named Temkin should be made kings, and all brown-eyed people not named Temkin paupers. Thus, no matter how inegalitarian a view may be in its motivation and implications, all that matters for a view to be egalitarian in *this* sense is that it apply universally. Equality as universality corresponds to the notion of pure formal equality noted above. It is widely regarded as a basic principle of rationality.

Equality as impartiality reflects the view that all people must be treated impartially. Of course, positions can vary dramatically in their understanding of what treating people impartially requires. Kantians believe we treat people impartially by treating them all as ends, and never merely as means. Utilitarians believe we treat all impartially when we count each person's interests as of equal weight in deciding what maximizes the good. Certain Marxists believe we treat all impartially by following the dictum "from each according to his ability, to each according to his need." Though each of these views has its own conception of impartiality, each is committed to treating people equally in the sense of being impartial between them. Note, those committed to equality as impartiality will also (tend to) be committed to equality as universality, but the reverse need not hold.

Equality as comparability reflects a different kind of commitment to equality. Equality as comparability reflects a fundamental concern with how people fare *relative to others*. More particularly, I believe the fundamental view underlying equality as comparability is that it is bad for some to be worse off than others through no fault or choice of their own. Importantly, those committed to equality as comparability will also be committed to both equality as impartiality and equality as universality, but their substantive views extend significantly beyond a concern for universality or impartiality. Correspondingly, many committed to equality as universality or equality as impartiality lack the concern for equality as comparability. Thus, one might say that equality as comparability reflects a deeper and more thoroughgoing commitment to equality than either equality as universality or equality as impartiality. Such a view reflects a significant and distinctive commitment to equality as an independent substantive ideal.

To see the value of these distinctions, let us consider some claims of Amartya Sen, one of the most thoughtful and influential writers on equality.

Most philosophical discussions of equality have focused on two questions: Is equality really desirable? And what kind of equality should we seek—that is, insofar as we are egalitarians, should we want equality of opportunity, primary goods, need satisfaction, welfare, or what? Sen has suggested that only the second question is really in doubt. According to Sen, virtually all moral theories "want equality of *something*," what they differ about is "equality of *what*?" Thus, "income-egalitarians...demand equal incomes,...welfare-egalitarians...equal welfare levels,...classical utilitarians...equal weights on the utilities of all, and...libertarians... equality with respect to...rights and liberties." [3]

Sen's view is interesting and important. Yet many will find it hard to believe that utilitarianism and libertarianism—two views most widely associated with non-egalitarianism—are in fact egalitarian positions. Indeed, it seems clear that there is something distinctive about positions like income-egalitarianism, primary goods-egalitarianism, or welfare-egalitarianism, and that such positions share a spirit or focus that is *fundamentally* different from that of utilitarianism or libertarianism.

So what are we to make of Sen's claims? I think Sen is right that there are important senses in which virtually all contemporary moral views incorporate commitments to equality. But what they are committed to are equality as universality and equality as impartiality. They are *not* all committed to equality as comparability. Indeed, notoriously, both permit gross inequalities between better- and worse-off. The utilitarian's fundamental concern is to maximize utility; the libertarian's fundamental concern is for people to act freely, without interference, as long as they respect the rights and liberties of others. Neither has a fundamental concern for how people fare *relative to others.*

Aristotle's famous principle of equality, that likes should be treated alike, and unalikes should be treated unalike, has long been regarded as a merely formal principle of equality. It corresponds to what I have called equality as universality. By itself, such a principle tells us nothing about how "likes" or "unalikes" should actually be treated, it is not committed to treating all people impartially, and it neither approves, nor condemns, some being worse off than others through no fault or choice of their own.

The widely-held view that all person's should be treated with equal consideration and respect[4] expresses a commitment to equality as universality, but it is not just a formal principle like Aristotle's. It is also a substantive principle of equality, in that it expresses a commitment to impartiality that Aristotle's principle lacks. Still, by itself, the view is sufficiently broad as to be compatible with any moral principle that insists on impartiality, and so might be endorsed by such diverse positions as Kantianism, utilitarianism, Marxism, or libertarianism. Correspondingly, while such a position is compatible with equality as comparability, it does not entail it. Thus, it need not reflect the distinctive thoroughgoing commitment to equality expressed by equality as comparability.

Virtually all agree that equality as universality is necessary as a condition of rationality. And virtually all contemporary theorists agree that equality as impartiality is a requirement of any plausible moral principle. But whether a further, deeper, commitment to a distinctive principle of equality as comparability is desirable remains highly disputed.

B. Let us next distinguish between *instrumental egalitarianism* and *non-instrumental egalitarianism.* On instrumental egalitarianism, equality is extrinsically valuable—that is, valuable because it promotes some other valuable ideal. On non-instrumental egalitarianism equality is intrinsically valuable—that is, valuable in itself, over and above the extent to which it promotes other ideals. On instrumental egalitarianism, the value of equality is derivative from the value of the ideal it promotes. Thus, the ideal of equality does not play a fundamental role in one's account of the moral realm. On non-instrumental egalitarianism, equality is a distinct moral ideal with independent normative significance. Thus, a complete account of the moral realm must allow for equality's value.

Non-egalitarians can readily admit that equality sometimes promotes other desirable ideals. Their central tenet is that equality is not a *fundamental* ideal. Those who would refute the non-egalitarian must endorse non-instrumental egalitarianism.

Unfortunately, failure to recognize the distinction between instrumental and non-instrumental egalitarianism is responsible for much confusion regarding the nature and value of equality. Many who think of themselves as egalitarians are in fact only instrumental egalitarians, though they may not realize this. Moreover, they believe, wrongly, that a defense of instrumental egalitarianism is sufficient to refute non-egalitarians. Similarly, many non-egalitarians are in fact instrumental egalitarians, but they think, wrongly, that they must reject the arguments of instrumental egalitarians if they want to remain non-egalitarians.

Defending an instrumental egalitarian position requires two moves: a defense of the ideal that equality is purportedly promoting, and a defense of the claim that in certain circumstances equality promotes that ideal. Neither move has *any* bearing on whether equality is a fundamental ideal. The first involves a normative claim about the value of an ideal *other* than equality; the second strictly involves an empirical fact. Thus, one hoping to respond to the non-egalitarian's central tenet in fact gains nothing by supporting instrumental egalitarianism.

Let me illustrate some of these claims. Many people argue *for* equality—and in so doing think of themselves as opposing non-egalitarianism—because they favor significant redistribution from the better- to worse-off. But the *reasons* they have for favoring such redistribution vary markedly, and may have nothing to do with a concern for *equality itself*. For example, some favor such transfers for *humanitarian* reasons—they favor equality *solely* as a means of reducing suffering, and given the choice between redistribution from the better- to worse-off, and identical gains for the worse-off with equal, or even greater, gains for the better-off, they would see *no* reason to favor the former over the latter. Such people are instrumental egalitarians, rather than non-instrumental egalitarians. Their position offers no more support of equality as an independent ideal than utilitarianism, which, of course, also favors transfers from better- to worse-off on all and only those occasions that maximize utility. Similarly, some would favor transfers from better- to worse-off as a way of promoting *freedom*—they believe that genuine freedom involves the autonomous formulation and effective implementation of a meaningful life plan, and this requires satisfaction of one's basic needs, acceptable levels of resources or primary goods, and freedom from social, economic, and political coercion of a sort incompatible with great inequality. And the list goes on. Socialists, capitalists, communitarians, and others all might favor redistribution from better- to worse-off purely for instrumental reasons.

Instrumental reasons for promoting equality may have tremendous moral significance—but, as noted, they do not support the value of equality *per se*. Unfortunately, many have not recognized this, and thus concern for equality is often conflated with other concerns that equality may, under certain circumstances, promote. One striking example of this is Rawls's maximin principle, which requires that we maximize the expectations of the representative member of the worst-off group.[5] Maximin is widely regarded as an egalitarian principle, and many who accept maximin think of themselves as egalitarians. Yet maximin is concerned with how well off the worst-off fare, it is *not* concerned with how the worst-off fare *relative to others*. Thus, maximin licenses vast *increases* in inequality, if necessary for improving—however slightly—the worst-off. Of course, in most cases promoting equality *will* improve a situation according to maximin. Hence maximin *is* plausible as an instrumental egalitarian position. Moreover, like most plausible moral principles—maximin is acceptable both as a principle of equality as universality, and also as a principle of equality as impartiality. But maximin is no different from utilitarianism in these respects. It is *not* plausible as a non-instrumental egalitarian position in the sense I am concerned with in this essay. It does not express a distinctive thoroughgoing commitment to equality as comparability.

We have distinguished many different kinds of egalitarian positions: equality as universality, equality as impartiality, equality as comparability, instrumental egalitarianism, and non-instrumental egalitarianism. Having done this, in the remainder of this essay, I shall use the term *egalitarian* and its correlates to refer to those who share the deep thoroughgoing commitment to equality as comparability, and in particular to those who believe in the non-instrumental value equality. So, for my purposes, egalitarians believe that how people fare relative to others has independent moral significance, and in particular, they believe that it is bad for some to be worse off than others through no fault or choice of their own. Naturally, those who wish to continue to use the term *egalitarian* to refer to other positions may legitimately do so, but it is important not to conflate distinct positions.

C. I have claimed that a principle of equality as comparability is one whose principal concern is with how people fare *relative to others* and which regards it as bad for some to be worse off than others through no fault or choice of their own. I have also claimed that only non-instrumental egalitarianism conflicts with the central tenet of non-egalitarianism. Many have wondered how there *could* be anything bad about inequality *itself*, over and above the extent to which it affects other ideals. Notoriously, egalitarians are accused of engaging in the "politics of envy," as if only envy could account for a concern with how people fare *relative to others*, rather than a concern with how people fare. In addition, many wonder about the relevance of the "no fault or choice of their own" clause. After all, if inequality really is bad "in itself," what difference does it make how it comes about?

These worries raise a host of important questions. Unfortunately, I can only say a few words about each. Let me begin by carefully interpreting, or qualifying, my claim that inequality is bad "in itself." If I give one piece of candy to Andrea, and two to Rebecca, Andrea will immediately assert "unfair!" This natural reaction suggests that equality is intimately connected with notions of fairness. I say "intimately connected with" advisedly. On my view, equality is a subtopic of the more general—and even more complex—topic of fairness. Specifically, concern about inequality is that portion of our concern about fairness that focuses on how people fare relative to others. So, our concern for equality is not separable from our concern for a certain aspect of fairness; they are part and parcel of a single concern. We say that certain inequalities are objectionable because they are unfair; but by the same token, we say that there is a certain kind of unfairness in being worse off than another through no fault or choice of one's own.

This explains the importance of the "no fault or choice" clause. Egalitarians are not committed to the view that deserved inequalities—if there are any—are as bad as undeserved ones. In fact, I think deserved inequalities are not bad *at all*. Rather, what is objectionable is some being worse off than others *through no fault or choice of their own.* The reason for this is simple. *Undeserved* inequality is unfair, but *deserved* inequality is not.

The egalitarian is *not* committed to the implausible view that it is bad for parents or citizens to freely and rationally sacrifice for their descendants so that their descendants will be better off than they. Nor is the egalitarian committed to the implausible view that it is bad for imprisoned criminals to be worse off than regular citizens, *if* the egalitarian believes that the criminal could have been as well off as others, but freely and rationally chose a life of crime. In such cases, the unequal outcomes are not unfair, and hence not objectionable, because the worse-off are so by their own free choice. These cases presumably differ from those where the worse-off are so because they were unlucky enough to born into poverty, or with severe handicaps, or with the "wrong" color skin in a racist society.

The preceding reminds us that egalitarians are not simply concern with *how much* inequality obtains, they are concerned with how *bad* the inequality is. Thus, while there may be *more* inequality in one situation than another, that needn't be *worse* if the greater inequality is deserved, but the lesser is not.

In thinking about this it helps to remember a simple point. Inequality is rampant in the universe. There are more electrons than protons, more roaches than whales, more numbers than mountains. These inequalities are real. But they are merely factual, descriptive, or arithmetical inequalities. Of the innumerable descriptive inequalities, only a few have normative significance. Egalitarians may argue as to which inequalities have normative significance, or whether some inequalities are more significant than others. But they can agree, I think, that only undeserved inequalities matter.

It is, of course, *extremely* difficult to decide when people *are* worse off than others through no fault or choice of their own. Egalitarians tend to think this is often, or nearly always, the case. Non-egalitarians tend to think this is rarely, if ever, the case. This raises enormous practical and theoretical issues for egalitarians. But it is important to distinguish the difficulty of determining when inequalities are undeserved from the crucial normative question of whether only undeserved inequalities are objectionable. It is an interesting question to what extent debates between people who think of themselves as egalitarians or non-egalitarians actually turn on whether prevalent inequalities, such as those produced under capitalism, are undeserved.

Are egalitarians necessarily envious? Are they "maliciously covetous or resentful of the possessions or good fortune of another" (as *Webster's Third New International Dictionary* defines the term "envious")? Surely not. When an egalitarian condemns past inequalities between clan leaders and their followers, or servants, she is not "maliciously covetous" or "resentful" of the clan leader's possessions or good fortune. Indeed, she may well believe, rightly, that she is *much* better off than the clan leader ever was. Nevertheless, she believes it is bad—because unfair—for some to be much worse off than others through no fault or choice of their own. Thus, the egalitarian's judgment is not motivated by *envy*, but by a sense of *fairness*. At least, I believe that is what an egalitarian's judgment should be motivated by, whether considering other societies or one's own.

D. Milton Friedman reputedly claimed that people can serve only one master, and that master is freedom. Those sharing Friedman's view that the true, or correct, moral theory must be *monistic*—that there can be one and only one "true" moral ideal—often argue against equality by appealing to examples like the following.

Imagine two alternative outcomes, A and B. A and B are each perfectly equal outcomes, that is, within each outcome each person would be as well off as every other. However, those in A would all be *much* better off than those in B in terms of resources, welfare, freedom, opportunity, etc.

Surely, A is a better outcome than B, since everyone in A is equally well off, and much better off than those in B. However, A is *not* better than B regarding equality; they are equivalent, since, by hypothesis, both are perfect regarding equality.

Monistic egalitarians—those who believed that equality was the *only* moral value—would have no reason to prefer A to B. But this, we agree, is implausible. A *is* better than B. But what does this show? All it shows is that if we are egalitarians we should be *pluralists*. We should admit that equality is not our only ideal, that it is but one, among others, that we value. Correspondingly, we should distinguish between our "purely" egalitarian judgments—our judgments about how situations compare regarding equality, and hence the judgments we would make *if* equality *were* our only concern—and our *all things considered* judgments—our judgments about how situations compare after giving each ideal its due weight.

If we were committed to moral monism, arguments such as the preceding would successfully undermine egalitarianism. (Though the stubborn monistic egalitarian could, of course, implausibly insist that there *is* nothing to choose between A and B, since inequality *is* all that matters.) But there is little reason to believe moral monism is true, and good reason to believe it is false.

Equality is not the only ideal that would, if exclusively pursued, have implausible or even terrible implications. The same is true of justice, utility, freedom, and probably every other ideal. Recall Kant's view that "justice be done though the heavens should fall." Do we really think, with Kant, that it would be wrong to falsely imprison an innocent man for even five minutes, if that were necessary to save 1,000,000 innocent lives? Or consider the principle of utility, which would require us to torture an innocent person if only *enough* people had their lives improved by the tiniest of amounts because of our action. Or finally, consider the implications of unfettered freedom to act as one wants without government interference, as long as one doesn't interfere with the rights or liberties of others. Such a principle could allow *complete* neglect of the least fortunate, even regarding basic necessities such as food, clothing, shelter, and healthcare. Considerations such as these do not show that each of these moral ideals should be rejected, only that morality is complex.

As noted, one of the most widely debated issues among egalitarians concerns what *kind* of equality is desirable. This issue is extremely important, both practically and theoretically. Clearly, different outcomes or choices will seem better or worse regarding equality, depending on what kind of inequality one is concerned with. Moreover, one must be particularly careful in determining what kind of inequality matters, since, as has long been recognized, equality of one kind will often require inequality of another. For example, equality of income may correlate with inequality of need satisfaction between the handicapped and the healthy, and vice versa. Similarly, in many circumstances equality of opportunity may correlate with inequality of welfare, and vice versa.

Many assume that concern for one kind of equality rules out concern for others. Correspondingly, philosophers favoring different conceptions of what kind of equality matters have gone to great lengths illustrating cases where rival conceptions have implausible implications. Unfortunately, on a pluralistic view of morality the assumption in question is dubious. Perhaps different kinds of equality matter in different contexts. Or perhaps even in the same context there are strong reasons for promoting different kinds of equality. Thus, the question "equality of what?" may have several plausible answers.

As we have just seen, the fact that ideals like equality, utility, or freedom sometimes have implausible, or even terrible, implications, does *not* show that those ideals do not matter. It merely shows that each ideal, alone, is not *all* that matters. Likewise, the fact that different conceptions of what kind of equality matters sometimes have implausible implications does not necessarily show that those conceptions do not matter. Equality, like morality itself, is complex. And more than one conception may be relevant to our "all things considered" egalitarian judgments.

My own view is that a large component of the egalitarian's concern should be with equality of *welfare*; but as I use it "welfare" is a technical term that needs to be interpreted broadly, and with great care. It must appropriately include, among other things, most of the elements that Amartya Sen carefully distinguishes in his sophisticated account of functionings, capability sets, freedom, agency, and well-being.[6] However, I also think the egalitarian should give weight to equality of opportunity.

Suppose, for example, that we lived in a world not too unlike the actual one, in which a relatively small percentage of people were very well off, while the vast majority were much worse off. Concern for equality of welfare would impel us to raise everyone to the level of the best-off. But suppose, for empirical reasons of limited resources, this were not possible. Concern for equality of welfare might then impel us to redistribute from the better-off to the worse-off. But if the percentage of better-off were small, this might do little to actually improve the lot of the worse-off, its main effect might be to reduce the better-off to the level of the worse-off. Even if we think this *would* be an improvement regarding equality of welfare, we might agree it would *not* be an improvement all things considered. Thus, we might conclude that in such a case we must accept, even if not happily, a *significantly* unequal situation regarding welfare.

Still, we might distinguish two versions of this scenario. In one version, the better-off group are members of a hereditary aristocracy. They, and their descendants, have been guaranteed a place in the better-off group. Likewise, the members of the worse-off group, and their descendants, are destined to remain in the worse-off group regardless of their abilities or efforts. In the second version there is genuine equality of opportunity. At birth, each person, and her descendants, has an equal chance of ending up in the better-off group.

By hypothesis, the two versions of the scenario are equivalent regarding equality of welfare. Yet, I think many would agree the second is better than the first all things considered, and better largely, if not wholly, because it is better regarding equality of opportunity. I think, then, that qua egalitarian, one should care about equality of opportunity. But this concern should be *in addition to*, rather than *in place of*, a concern for equality of welfare. The second situation may be *perfect* regarding equality of opportunity—but it still involves many people who are worse off than others through no choice of their own. The egalitarian, *qua* egalitarian, will regard this as objectionable. It would be better, regarding equality, if, in addition to everyone having equal *opportunities*, they actually fared equally well.

Does the egalitarian have to make room in her spectrum of concerns for other kinds of equality? Perhaps, but I am inclined to think that, *theoretically* at least, the plausible elements of most other kinds of equality will be captured by a sufficiently sophisticated interpretation of welfare. Still, in the real world it may be extremely difficult or undesirable to pursue equality of welfare, for a host of political, practical, and moral reasons. Given this, it may well be better to pursue equality of other kinds, such as income, resources, primary goods, or need satisfaction. However, we must be careful to distinguish our ultimate reasons for advocating one kind of equality over another. There may well be a difference between the option that is most desirable, from an egalitarian perspective, and the option that is most desirable or feasible all things considered, and we must not fool ourselves that the latter is necessarily the same as the former.

Part II

The considerations in this part are addressed to those who accept non-instrumental egalitarianism. I claimed that according to this position it is bad—because unfair—for some to be worse off than others through no fault or choice of their own. Unfortunately, as we shall see next, it is one thing to note such a position, quite another to accurately interpret it, or unpack what it involves.

As noted, most philosophical discussions of equality have focused on two questions: Is equality really desirable? And what kind of equality should we seek? These are important questions. But egalitarians must address a slew of other questions as well, including, but by no means are limited to, the following: When is one situation worse than another regarding inequality? Does inequality matter between groups, or between individuals? Does inequality matter differently at high levels than low levels? Is inequality affected by variations in population size? If one compares individuals with respect to inequality, should one focus on their lives taken as complete wholes, on contemporaneous portions of their lives—say, the elderly of today with the youth of today—or on corresponding segments of their lives—say, the elderly of today with the elderly of tomorrow?

Those who believe that inequality matters must ultimately address each of these questions, and others as well. After all, it does no good to claim that inequality matters, if one cannot determine what factors affect inequality and whether one situation is worse than another regarding inequality. I believe the answers to the preceding questions are not only interesting and important, in many cases they are perplexing, disturbing, and controversial. They have significant implications not only for our understanding of equality, but for our understanding of morality itself, including the structure and relation of our moral ideals. Unfortunately, I cannot defend these claims here. Instead, I wish to present a brief overview of a few conclusions I have arrived at in thinking about these questions, and convey some sense for the kinds of considerations underlying my thinking.

Most of this part will discuss the general question, "when is one situation worse than another regarding inequality?" This is my book's central question, and it is one that led me both to develop a new approach to understanding inequality, and to consider the other, more specific, questions. After discussing the general question, I shall briefly comment on the other questions noted above. For the interested reader, extensive arguments are available in *Inequality*.[7]

A. When is one situation worse than another regarding inequality? In some cases the answer to this question can be easily given. We know, for instance, that among equally deserving people a situation where some are worse off than others is worse than one where everyone is equal, in terms of inequality. We also know that among equally deserving people the inequality in a situation would be worse if the gaps between the better- and worse-off were large, than if they were small. Consider, however, a situation where many are better-off, and a few are worse-off. How would the inequality in such a situation compare to the inequality in a situation where a few are better-off and many are worse-off? How would both of these compare to a situation where the better- and worse-off groups were similar in size? It turns out that these are complicated questions, and ones to which several plausible but conflicting answers might be given.

For example, one way we may judge inequality is in terms of how "gratuitous" the inequality seems. Consider a situation where many are better-off, and only a few are worse-off. Call this *the first situation*. In such a situation the inequality may seem "pointless and unnecessary." If direct redistribution were possible to bring about equality, the better-off would hardly lose anything and the worse-off would gain tremendously. Hence, the inequality in the first situation may seem particularly offensive as there seems to be virtually nothing gained by it.

Next consider the situation where half of the people are better-off, and half are worse-off. Call this *the middle situation*. It seems that in the middle situation redistribution would "cost" a lot. A large number would have to sacrifice a great deal to achieve equality. In such a situation, we could understand the reluctance of the better-off to redistribute, and while we might think it would be good if they were to voluntarily do this, we might not think they were morally *required* to do this. In that situation, then, the inequality might strike us as more excusable, and hence less disturbing, than the inequality in the first situation.

Finally, consider a situation where only a few are better-off, and the vast majority are worse-off. Call this *the last situation*. In the last situation direct redistribution from better- to worse-off would involve tremendous loss for some, with virtually no gain for those thus "benefited." Therefore, the inequality might seem least offensive in the last situation, where the "cost" of the inequality might seem smallest, and the "gain" highest.

This position might be summed up as follows. Egalitarians will think it unfair if, through no fault or choice of their own, some are badly-off (e.g., struggling to survive) while others are well-off (e.g., living lives of ease and comfort). But from one perspective, at least, egalitarians may be most offended if just a few are badly-off while the vast majority are well-off, since the inequality then seems particularly gratuitous. Thus, in accordance with this way of thinking, it will seem that the three situations are getting *better and better* regarding inequality.

Another reason egalitarians may think the three situations are getting better and better is that it appears to be less and less the case that those who are worse-off are being especially victimized by the situation. In the first situation, for instance, it is as if the entire burden of the inequality is borne by those few who are unfortunate enough to be among the worse-off. Given that those few people are much worse off than *every other* member of their world, it may seem that they have a very large complaint regarding inequality, and correspondingly, that the inequality is especially offensive. By contrast, the last situation's inequality may seem relatively inoffensive. In that situation each member of the worse-off group is as well off as *all* but a *few* of the other members of her world. Hence, in that world it may seem as if nobody has much to complain about regarding inequality.

This view is plausible, and it expresses itself in the way we react to the actions of bullies or tyrants. If a bully or tyrant decides to humiliate certain people, from a utilitarian standpoint we may well hope that it is a small portion of the population that is so mistreated. Nevertheless, from an egalitarian standpoint we may well find the mistreatment most offensive if it applies to only a small segment of the population. Thus, it may seem particularly unfair for a few people to bear the brunt of their world's unfairness; and it may seem especially galling that the vast majority should be leading normal happy lives, while one small segment of it gets "crushed beneath the heel of oppression."

One way of putting this point is that certain egalitarian intuitions are especially attuned to instances of invidious or capricious discrimination where a particular person or small number of people is *singled* out for discriminatory treatment. In fact, I think it is the *singling out* in this way of an individual or small number that is the paradigmatic case of where we judge a (harmful) discrimination to be grossly unfair.

I suspect this element of our thinking may be one of the reasons it has taken many people so long to recognize pervasive discrimination against women. Even though women were (and still are) being treated very differently than men, half of the population was being treated in the same way. Because of this, and because of the fact that certain of our egalitarian intuitions are especially attuned to discrimination against individuals and small numbers, it was easy for both men and women to realize that women were being treated differently, and yet fail to recognize that women were actually being *discriminated* against.

There are, then, several ways of thinking that might lead one to think the three situations are getting better and better regarding inequality. But there are also ways of thinking that might lead one to judge that the situations first get worse, then better. It is easy to be drawn to such an ordering by reasoning as follows. In the first situation, everyone is perfectly equal except, regrettably, for a few isolated individuals. In that situation, then, the worse-off represent an ever-so-slight perturbation in an otherwise perfectly homogeneous system. Therefore, since in the first situation there is just a slight deviation from absolute equality that situation may seem nearly perfect regarding inequality. In the middle situation, the deviation from absolute equality is much larger. *Half* the population is much better off than the other half. In the last situation, there is once again just an ever-so-slight deviation from absolute equality. Everyone is perfectly equal except, regrettably, for a few isolated individuals. Like the first situation, therefore, that world may appear almost perfect regarding inequality. In sum, it seems there is a natural and plausible way of looking at the three situations such that we would judge they first get worse, then better.

Another line of thought also supports the "worse, then better" ordering. In the first situation, only a *few* people have a complaint regarding inequality, so as large as their complaint may be that situation's inequality may not seem too bad. However, in the middle situation, it may seem *both* that a large number have a complaint (half of the population), *and* that the magnitude of their complaints will be large (they are, after all, worse off than half the population through no fault or choice of their own). In the last world, on the other hand, the situation may seem analogous to, though the reverse of, the one obtaining in the first. Although almost everyone has *something* to complain about, it may seem that the size of their complaints will be virtually negligible, as they are as well off as almost every other person in the situation. Hence, as with the first situation, the inequality may not seem too bad.

It seems, then, there are egalitarian reasons to rank the three situations as getting worse, then better, as well as reasons to rank them as just getting better. Still other reasons seem to support ranking them as getting worse and worse. In the first situation, only a few people are worse off than the better-off. In the middle situation, half the population are worse off than the better-off. In the last situation, virtually everybody is worse off than the better-off. Since the size of the gap between better- and worse-off is the same in each situation, we may conclude that the first situation is the best regarding inequality, and the last situation is worst.

Before going on, let me note two examples where such reasoning seems to be in involved. First, if one asks audiences to think of the worst periods of inequality in human history—as I have many times over the years—one of the most common responses is that of medieval Europe. But the common conception of medieval

Europe involves a few—kings, queens, and noblemen—living in the lap of luxury while the vast majority—peasants and serfs—struggle to survive. Such a situation resembles the last situation, rather than the first or middle one. And while here, as elsewhere, I think people's intuitive responses may be partly influenced by non-egalitarian factors as well as various different egalitarian factors, I think *one* reason so many think of medieval Europe as among the worst periods of inequality is that the number of worse-off is so large relative to the fortunate few who are well off. This way of thinking is compatible with the judgment that the three situations are getting worse and worse, but not with the ways of thinking discussed previously.

Another example where such thinking seems operative is illustrated by a Marxian analysis of the advance of capitalism. On a Marxian view, as capitalism advances more and more people are squeezed out of the ranks of the bourgeoisie into the ranks of the proletariat; hence, fewer and fewer people come to reap the benefits of capitalism.

Now whatever one thinks of its ultimate accuracy, it must be admitted that as stories go a Marxian analysis of capitalism exerts a strong pull on one's egalitarian intuitions. Specifically, egalitarians would find advancing capitalism increasingly objectionable for (at least) two reasons: first, because the rich become richer and the poor (at least relatively) poorer; and second, because the ranks of the worse-off swell and the ranks of the better-off shrink. It is the latter point that concerns us here. It suggests that certain egalitarian intuitions will be increasingly offended as more and more people are worse-off relative to the better-off. These intuitions support the judgment that the three situations are getting worse and worse.

This discussion has been vastly oversimplified. But I hope to have conveyed some sense for why I claim inequality is complex. There are many different positions, or aspects, capable of underlying and influencing our egalitarian judgments. In fact, in my book I argue there are at least twelve such aspects. I do not claim each of these aspects is equally appealing. But I do believe each represents elements of the egalitarian's thinking that are not easily dismissed.

Given that equality's different aspects often diverge in the judgments they yield, and that, on examination, many apparently rest on contrary views, one may come to conclude that the notion of equality is largely inconsistent and severely limited. Alternatively, one may try to maintain that it is complex, multi-faceted, and partially incomplete. Either way, once one understands what the notion of equality involves, many of one's common-sense judgments about equality will need to be revised.

Reflecting on considerations like the preceding, led me to develop a new way of thinking about inequality. The common view is that the notion of inequality is simple, holistic, and essentially distributive. This view is thoroughly misleading—the notion of inequality is complex, individualistic, and essentially comparative. Let me briefly explain.

Simple versus *complex*. People have long recognized that there are complicated issues *connected* with inequality, such as whether inequality is truly undesirable, and if so, with respect to what. Still, most have thought the notion of inequality *itself* is simple. We *all* know what equality is, it has been thought, that's where everybody has the same amount of x (for whatever x we are interested in). Similarly, we *all* know what inequality is, that's where some have more x than others. What could be simpler? Thus, it has been assumed that once we determine with respect to what, if anything, we should care about inequality, it will be easy to rank situations regarding inequality.

As we have seen, there is reason to reject this. Inequality is very complex, as many aspects with different implications underlie and influence our egalitarian judgments.

Holistic versus *individualistic*. Most who learn that I work on inequality immediately ask something like the following: "inequality between whom: blacks and whites, women and men, Americans and Ethiopians, or homosexuals and heterosexuals?" The assumption is that the egalitarian should be concerned about (in)-equality between *groups* or *societies*.

Again, there are powerful reasons to question this assumption. The notion of inequality has a strong *individualistic* component. Looking at situations we are capable of making judgments as to which individuals fare better or worse regarding inequality. Thus, for any situation where some are better off than others through no fault or choice of their own, we can say that the best-off have nothing to complain about regarding inequality—since they are already as well off as every other member of their situation—while the worst-off have the most to complain about regarding inequality—since, by hypothesis, they are worse off than every other member of their situation. Moreover, on reflection, not only can we make judgments about how different individuals fare with respect to inequality, but our overall judgments regarding inequality are generally based on how individuals fare regarding inequality.

In addition, it seems clear that *groups* or *societies* aren't the proper objects of moral concern, *individuals* are. Thus, although different individuals or social institutions often discriminate against groups, and though, for political and practical reasons we may need to focus on groups in responding to such discrimination, our *ultimate* concern is for the individual members of the affected groups.

While on average whites may be much better off than blacks, some blacks will be much better off than others, and some whites will be much worse off than some blacks. Correspondingly, insofar as one is concerned about inequality, one will favor transfers from better-off whites to worse-off blacks, but should oppose transfers (except, perhaps, for indirect long term reasons) from worse-off whites to better-off blacks. Likewise, one should favor transfers from better-off blacks to worse-off blacks, or for that matter, from better-off blacks to worse-off whites. Similarly, for the case of men and women, or other cases of general inequality between groups or societies.

Essentially distributive versus *essentially comparative.* I agree that the egalitarian is not merely concerned with *how much* good obtains, but with how the good is distributed. But, fundamentally, the concern for equality is not so much *essentially* distributive, as it is *essentially comparative.* Equality is a *relation* between individuals and, as previously suggested, the egalitarian's fundamental concern is with how individuals fare *relative to each other.*

B. Does inequality matter more at high levels or low levels? This is a question about which there has been much confusion. Some argue that inequality matters more at high levels than low levels because they think that only at high levels can one "afford the luxury" of equality. So, for example, they point out that in a situation of *extreme* scarcity, inequality might allow some to live, while perfect equality might result in everyone dying. Others argue that inequality matters the same at high and low levels. They claim that whether one is at level 1,000 or level 1,000,000 makes no difference to how bad it would be to be worse off than another by 1,000 units, since in each case it would take an increase of the same amount—namely 1,000—to make you equal with the other. In addition, many economists' measures of inequality are indifferent between proportional increases in people's levels. So, on those measures, the inequality between someone at level 1 and someone at level 10 would be just as bad as the inequality between someone at level 100 and someone at level 1000. Economists have assumed these so-called "mean-independent" measures of inequality are *neutral* with respect to whether inequality matters more at high or low levels, and debated the desirability of this feature.

All these views are mistaken. The first conflates an all things considered judgment with an egalitarian one. All things considered, a perfectly equal situation where everybody *dies* will be much worse than an unequal situation where some live and others die, but surely this doesn't show that the inequality in the latter situation doesn't *matter*! The inequality in the latter situation involves a difference measured in terms of life's necessities, it involves a difference, quite literally, between who lives and who dies. The person who responds to such a situation with the truism "whoever said that life is *fair*?" acknowledges, even in his cynicism, the egalitarian's basic view of the situation. For the egalitarian, if the people are equally deserving such inequality is *very* bad, and it matters a great deal. Still, as bad as the inequality is, if the cost of removing it is that everyone die, even the egalitarian can admit—as a pluralist—that the cost is too high.

The second view conflates a *descriptive* question, how *much* inequality obtains, with a *normative* question, how bad is the inequality. In a sense, of course, there is the same *amount* of inequality in the two described cases. In each someone is 1000 units worse off than another. But a person at level 1,000 fares much worse *relative to* someone at level 2,000, than does someone at level 1,000,000 *relative to* someone at level 1,001,000. The first person has only 33 per cent of what there is to be shared, and is only 50 per cent as well off as the better-off person. The second person has 49.98 per cent of what there is to be shared, and is 99.9 per cent as well off as the better-off person. Clearly, insofar as one is concerned with how people fare *relative to others*, the first person fares worse than the second.

Such considerations suggest that inequality matters *more* at low levels than high levels, in the sense that regarding inequality, it is worse for someone to be worse off than another by a certain amount if that person is poorly off than if that person is well off.

As for the third view, economists were mistaken in thinking that mean-independent measures were *neutral* regarding the question of whether inequality matters more at high or low levels. On a mean-independent measure, to be 9 units worse off than another if one is at level 1 is as bad as being *900* units worse off than another if one is as level 100. So, on a mean-independent measure inequality matters much more at low levels than high levels. The problem is that it matters *too* much more. To be worse than another by 9 units matters more if one is at level 1 than if one is at level 100, but it doesn't matter 100 times more!

C. Does variation in population size affect inequality? Most economists and others assume that mere proportional increases in a population's size would not affect inequality. On this view, if the *pattern* of inequality is the same in two situations, it doesn't matter how many people are actually in the better- and worse-off groups. This position has great plausibility, and it is supported by numerous important aspects of inequality. Ultimately, however, this position needs revision. If it is genuinely bad for some to be worse off than others through no fault or choice of their own, then the more people there are who are in such a position the worse the situation should be.

One way of putting this point is as follows. In general, numbers count. This is true in most spheres of life, and morality is no exception to it. Moreover, it is not only true for utilitarians, it is true for most who employ moral ideals in the assessment of outcomes. Other things equal, more pains are worse than fewer pains, more infringements of liberty are worse than fewer infringements of liberty, more injustices or inequalities are worse than fewer injustices or inequalities. Even deontologists can accept such claims (though they deny that what we ought, morally, to *do*, is always to maximize the good or minimize wrong doing).

Not everyone accepts the view that numbers count in the moral realm.[8] But most do. And I think they are right in doing so.

Some will insist that while numbers count for certain moral ideals, such as utility, they do not count for equality. They will insist that equality and utility are different *kinds* of moral ideals and that the two ideals can, and should, be treated differently. On this view, the fact that numbers count regarding ideals like utility is completely irrelevant to—i.e. suggests *nothing* about—whether numbers count regarding equality.

This contention has some plausibility, but ultimately I think it should be rejected. As I argue in my book, it turns out that different moral ideals cannot be fully and adequately characterized in isolation from each other. Specifically, a plausible and coherent account of the role moral ideals play in relation to each other and our all things considered judgments may require at least some ideals to share certain formal or structural features. In particular, if we want to hold on to the view that numbers count regarding utility, we may also have to hold that numbers count regarding equality, if we want to avoid inconsistency in our all things considered judgments. The argument for this is interesting, and ultimately has implications that extend far beyond the topic of equality. Unfortunately, I cannot pursue it here.

D. In comparing individuals with respect to inequality should one focus on their lives taken as complete wholes? Most discussions of equality, as well as other ideals such as Rawls's maximin principle, have implicitly assumed that the proper unit of moral concern should be individual lives taken as complete wholes. Following a fascinating article by Dennis McKerlie,[9] I reject this position.

Consider the following example. Suppose that God has two faithful servants, Job_1 and Job_2. Suppose each is equally deserving in all respects, yet for 40 years Job_1's life has been filled with all the blessings that life can bestow, while Job_2's life has been one of continuous wretched misery. If we questioned God about treating two equally deserving people so *grossly* unequally, would an adequate response be that during the second 40 years of their lives their situations would be reversed, so that in fact the overall quality of their lives, taken as a whole, would be *completely equal*?

Analogously, do we think there would be no egalitarian objection to a caste system involving substantial differential treatment of caste members, as long as the demographic composition of the castes changed periodically so that each person was a member of each caste and the *overall* quality of each life was equivalent?

I believe the answer to both these questions should be "No." I reject the implication of whole lives egalitarianism that there can be no objection to a situation involving vast inequalities between equally deserving people—no matter how significant, sustained, widespread, systematic, and even perverse those inequalities were—as long as the roles of the equally deserving individuals were interchanged so that each receives an equivalent share of the different experiences.

Does this mean that we should reject whole lives egalitarianism and replace it entirely with some alternative? No. Once again, equality is a complex ideal. Besides focusing on complete lives, inequality might be measured by comparing *simultaneous*, or overlapping, segments of people's lives—for example, by directly comparing the current lives of aged A and youthful B, or by comparing *corresponding* segments of people's lives—for example, aged A's youth, with B's youth. In fact, I believe that each of these views is plausible in some cases, and implausible in others.

These different views have practical significance. For example, many would urge transfers from the young to the elderly partly on egalitarian grounds—since the elderly are often much worse off than the young due to losses of health and loved ones. But while many of today's elderly are currently worse off than many of today's youth in terms of the simultaneous segments of their lives, it is much less clear that they are worse off in terms of the corresponding segments of their lives, or taking their lives as complete wholes. Thus, it may make a substantial difference to the nature and extent of our obligations to the elderly, which views we accept, or how we weight them relative to each other.

E. Let me conclude this part by discussing a possible implication of my work that is both surprising and somewhat dismaying.

Unfortunately, the real world resembles the third kind of situation discussed earlier. A relatively small percentage are well off, while the vast majority fare poorly. In addition, a combination of moral, political, and practical considerations make it extremely unlikely that we will raise most of the worse-off to the level of the better-off, or that the better-off will substantially sacrifice their well-being so as to benefit the worse-off. This raises the worry that practically, perhaps the most we can hope for in the foreseeable future is that the better-off will make some small sacrifices enabling some of the worse-off to raise themselves to the level of the better-off. That is, one might worry that for the foreseeable future, perhaps the most we might reasonably hope for would be to transform our world from one resembling the last situation I discussed, to one resembling the middle situation, where a fairly large percentage of people are better off, though a fairly large percentage remain worse-off.

Unfortunately, it is unclear that this would be an improvement regarding *equality*. To the contrary, it is almost certain that when one fully takes into account each of equality's plausible aspects a situation like the middle one will be *worse* regarding *equality* than one like the last one. After all, in the middle situation *half* the population is much worse off than the other half through no fault or choice of their own, while in the last one *most* of the people are equal, but a fortunate few are better-off.

If the foregoing were the implication of my view, would it mean that we should oppose programs aimed at improving the lot of the worse-off? Certainly not. But it suggests that we would have to rethink the grounds of such programs, and the extent of our commitment to non-instrumental egalitarianism in the face of other competing ideals. Most programs benefiting the worse-off have been defended largely in the name of equality. Yet, if the situation were as described, the effect of some such programs would be, at least for the foreseeable future, to *worsen* inequality, not improve it.

I mention the foregoing, because it is important in assessing the relative strength of our commitment to moral ideals to squarely face their unpalatable implications. However, it is unclear whether egalitarianism would actually have the implications noted. Thus, it has been claimed that a mere half of one percent of the income of the top 20% of income earners, would be more than sufficient to double the income of *everyone* in the bottom 20% of income earners. Even more strikingly, perhaps, it has been claimed that "The additional cost of achieving and maintaining universal access to basic education for all, basic health care for all, reproductive health care for all women, adequate food for all and safe water and sanitation for all is ... less than 4% of the combined wealth of the 225 richest people in the world."[10] Together, these considerations suggest that the egalitarian could clearly and unequivocally favor relatively small losses to the better off so as to achieve substantial gains for all of the worse off. The worry that for the foreseeable future we may only be able to benefit a relatively few while per force leaving most behind, may be moot.

In sum, arguments for effective transfers from the very best off to the world's worse off may, indeed, be justified on egalitarian grounds, as has long been supposed. Still, we must be alert to the possibility that in some cases effective efforts to improve some of the world's worse off might actually worsen inequality not improve it. This might be so if most of the worse off are left behind, so in essence we would be transforming our world from one resembling the last situation I discussed into one more resembling the middle situation.

Conclusion

In my book, I discussed at some length a position I then called *extended humanitarianism*, and which I now call *prioritarianism*.[11] On this view, one wants each person to fare as well as possible, but is especially concerned with—and hence gives extra weight or priority to—the worse-off. I argued that many people mistake prioritarianism for egalitarianism, and that while prioritarianism is a plausible position in its own right, it is a non-starter as a non-instrumental egalitarian position.

Roger Crisp accepted my claims, alas, with a bit too much enthusiasm. At the end of a generous review of my book in the *Times Literary Supplement*, Crisp wrote "The clarity of Temkin's distinction between genuine [non-instrumental] egalitarianism and extended humanitarianism [prioritarianism] marks the end of egalitarianism as a coherent political doctrine."

I hope Crisp is mistaken, since I believe there is an important place for equality in our pantheon of moral ideals. But even if, as I believe, egalitarianism remains as a coherent practical doctrine, I think it is extremely important for people to accurately recognize its nature, scope, and implications. The common tendency to argue about virtually every major social and political issue largely in egalitarian terms, especially in the absence of a clear understanding of the full complexity of the notion and its implications, does a disservice to both many pressing issues *and* the ideal of equality.

NOTES

1. This essay was originally written as an invited paper, delivered at the American Political Science Association Meeting in San Francisco in the summer of 1996.
2. Oxford University Press, 1993.
3. *Inequality Reexamined*, Harvard University Press, 1992, p. ix.
4. The substance of this view has been held by many philosophers over the years. But in this formulation it has been powerfully championed, and come to be associated with, Ronald Dworkin (see, for example, *Taking Rights Seriously*, Harvard University Press, 1978).
5. John Rawls, *A Theory of Justice*, Harvard University Press, 1971.
6. See *Inequality Reexamined*, and also Sen's "Well-being, Agency, and Freedom: The Dewey Lectures 1984." *Journal of Philosophy* 82 (1985): 169–220.
7. Oxford University Press, 1993.
8. John Taurek explicitly denies that numbers should count in his rich and widely discussed article "Should the Numbers Count?" *Philosophy and Public Affairs* 6 (1977): 293–316.
9. "Equality and Time." *Ethics* 99 (1989): 475–91.
10. I am most grateful to Thomas Pogge for sending me this quotation as well as defending the claim made in the previous sentence (personal correspondence). Pogge cites the United Nations' *Human Development Report*, 1998, p. 30, as the source of the quote, and based his calculation about incomes on other information contained in the Report. Pogge's observations considerably weaken the force of the worries expressed in the preceding paragraphs.
11. See my "Equality, Priority, and the Levelling Down Objection," in *The Ideal of Equality*, eds. Clayton, Matthew and Williams, Andrew, Macmillan Press

Ltd and St. Martin's Press, 2000, pp. 126–161. Derek Parfit has called the position in question the *Priority View* (first in his unpublished manuscript, "On Giving Priority to the Worse-off," 1989, and later in his Lindley Lecture "Equality or Priority?" The University of Kansas, 1991.) Since Parfit's terminology has some advantages and has largely taken hold, I have amended my terminology accordingly. However, I might note that while Parfit is widely credited with launching the equality versus priority debate, my initial discussion of extended humanitarianism—which makes many points Parfit is credited with—first appeared in chapter six of my 1983 Princeton University PhD thesis, *Inequality*. This chapter was completed seven years earlier than Parfit's widely circulated and cited 1989 draft, "On Giving Priority to the Worse-off."

PHILOSOPHICAL ISSUES, 11
Social, Political, and Legal Philosophy, 2001

The Conventionality Thesis[1]

Jules L. Coleman

The law purports to govern our conduct, and to do so in virtue of its status as law. The first, and perhaps the most philosophically difficult question of jurisprudence is: how is that possible? What accounts for the fact that a particular rule can make demands on our conduct in virtue of its bearing the mark of law? In some cases, a rule's claim to govern conduct as law can be explained by appeal to a more basic authorizing rule. For example, the laws a legislature promulgates may be authorized by the law that authorizes the legislature as a source of law. It should be apparent, however, that we cannot keep up this form of explanation indefinitely; for instead of explaining the possibility of law's claim to govern our behavior, we would simply be assuming that possibility by an infinite regress of "legal" authorizations. Nor can we accept a vicious circle in which some finite set of rules putatively authorize one another. The problem, in a nutshell, is how to explain the possibility of legal authority without appealing to legal authority itself. The recognition of this problem marks the beginning of jurisprudence.

Historically, jurisprudential theorists have adopted one of two alternative solutions: Each explains the possibility of legal authority in terms of something other than legal authority. In the case of the Natural Law tradition, the possibility of legal authority is explained in terms of *moral* authority. There are numerous variations on this theme, and I mention only a few to provide a feel for the strategy of argument: On one view, legal authority is the institutional embodiment of the Natural Law, and thus is to be explained as being made possible by Natural Law; a related view is that legal authority is made possible insofar as it is an expression of God's will; alternatively, legal authority is sometimes said to be derived from (and in that sense made possible by) the correct political morality, and in that case legal authority is an institutional expression or realization of political morality. The key to all such arguments is that the concept of legal authority is explicated in terms of, broadly speaking, moral authority. This is one sense in which the concepts of law and morality are thought to be conceptually connected.[2]

The prevailing view is that what distinguishes legal positivism from natural law theory is that the former denies what the latter asserts—namely, that there is a conceptual connection between the concepts of law and morality. In the context of current discussions of the possibility conditions of legal authority, this denial amounts to the claim that the possibility of legal authority is not to be explained as being an instance of moral authority.

Positivism claims that the possibility of legal authority is to be explained not in terms of substantive morality, but rather, in terms of certain *social facts*. Call this the Social Fact Thesis; no claim is more central to legal positivism.[3] John Austin's legal philosophy provides an important 19th Century example of the approach. For Austin, law is "the command of a sovereign-properly-so-called." The sovereign is conceived as an actual person: that individual who has secured the habit of obedience to his commands and who, himself, is not in the habit of obeying anyone.

There is no infinite regress or vicious circle in this account—the chain of authority is firmly anchored in the person of the sovereign, who is in turn defined without a circular appeal to law (the sovereign is not, for example, defined as the legally authorized source of law). Yet Austin's solution does not rely on introducing a new set of normative terms. Legal authority is a matter of "hard facts" about habits of obedience and patterns of sanctioning.

Austin's explanation of law's existence conditions in terms of habits of obedience came under devastating attack by positivism's greatest contemporary proponent, H.L.A. Hart. In the first place, the sovereign in many cases is no single individual but a collective body, such as a legislative assembly. Even if everyone else is in the habit of obeying the assembly, there is no explanation on Austin's account for the procedural rules (among others) that bind the assembly's members. Moreover, even when a single individual is the sovereign, as in the case of an absolute monarch, Austin can provide no explanation of the rules of succession, which authorize the transfer of sovereignty from a monarch to his heir. A deeper and on Hart's view more important objection is that in effectively reducing authority to habits, Austin throws out the baby with the bath water: for the idea of legal authority is the idea that the law claims to provide *reasons* for acting, and not simply that it exploits a habit of obedience.

Hart's own formulation of positivism retains the Social Fact Thesis, while avoiding the difficulties of Austin's account. Hart's position—widely misunderstood and mistakenly criticized—is that law is made possible by an interdependent convergence of behavior and attitude: a kind of *convention* or social practice that we might characterize as an "agreement" among officials on the criteria for membership in the category "law".[4] The relevant social practice is comprised of two elements: convergent behavior and a critical reflective attitude toward that behavior—an acceptance of it. In other words, officials behave in a manner that is consistent with their following the same rule for validating laws; and this reflects a set of normative commitments which endorse the convergent behavior as justified, and which would condemn deviations from it. This reflective, critical attitude is the so-called "internal point of view." It is expressed in and manifested by, but is not reducible to, the behavior of offering justification and condemning noncompliance.

For Hart, this practice of officials creates and sustains criteria for membership in the category "law." Law is made possible by the existence among officials of a practice of adhering to criteria of legality or validity. The rule that captures this practice is what Hart calls "the Rule of Recognition": it is the signature of a legal system. The Rule of Recognition is a necessary, but not a sufficient condition for law. In addition, Hart identifies various efficacy conditions: e.g. that the bulk of the populace comply with the rules recognized under the Rule of Recognition.

Law exists (is actual) when there is a Rule of Recognition and rules valid under it that are generally followed by the majority of the population. Acceptance of the Rule of Recognition from the internal point of view by officials is a conceptual requirement of the possibility of law; acceptance from the internal point of view by the bulk of the populace is neither a conceptual nor an efficacy requirement. Even if they characteristically do, the majority of persons need not *as a conceptual matter* adopt the internal point of view toward the behavior by which officials validate law, nor toward the subordinate rules that are validated under the legal system. (Of course, it may be desirable on efficiency grounds that a population treat law as legitimate or obligation imposing, since fewer public resources might then be required to insure compliance.)[5]

An additional feature of Hart's account that differentiates it in a fundamental way both from Austin and from some more recent positivists, such as the Scandinavian Realists, is that Hart explicitly rejects a certain reductive approach to the analysis of law. As we saw above, Austin reduces legal authority to power and habits of obedience; the Scandinavian Realists reduce law to predictions of untoward consequences in the event of noncompliance and thus—by Hart's lights as well as my own—define the internal point of view out of existence.[6] The failure here is not, as some have mistakenly thought, limited to the reductionist's inability to account for the obvious *empirical* fact that individuals sometimes comply with law because the law requires it. Rather, the failing is also, and more significantly, *conceptual.* Law is not *possible* unless officials accept the Rule of Recognition from the internal point of view; that is, law is possible only if the relevant officials treat the rule as their reason for compliance with it. By defining the internal point of view out of existence, the reductionist is left with no way of explaining the very possibility of law.

Like every legal positivist, I maintain that the possibility of law is to be explained in terms of social facts. Like Hart, I further maintain that the possibility of legal authority is to be explained in terms of a *conventional* social practice, namely the adherence by officials to a Rule of Recognition that imposes a duty on them to apply all and only those rules valid under it. Call that the Conventionality Thesis. In explaining the possibility of legal authority in terms of a Rule of Recognition, the Conventionality Thesis gives content to the idea that law is a normative *social* practice, which while satisfying the Social Fact Thesis, nevertheless avoids *reducing* legal authority to social facts. The Conventionality Thesis provides an answer to what is perhaps the most fundamental question of jurisprudence: what are the possibility conditions of legal authority?

The Conventionality Thesis is central to the form of legal positivism I defend. In this essay, I wish to clarify a number of important philosophical issues surrounding that thesis (some of which we have briefly alluded to already) and in doing so, to articulate my particular version of it. I begin (1) by considering the widely misunderstood relationship between the Rule of Recognition and the social practice of officials. I go on to argue (2) that, contrary to the views of many positivists, the Rule of Recognition purports to be, and can be a duty-imposing rule. This leads to the general question of how the Rule of Recognition can impose duties on those whose conduct it purports to govern, and to the particular question of what role, if any, the internal point of view plays in the explanation of the normativity of social rules. I close (3) by considering the objection that to explain the existence conditions of legal authority in terms of a Rule of Recognition whose existence depends on the behavior of "officials" is, in the end, to explain law in terms of law. According to this objection, rather than counting as a solution to the problem it addresses, the Rule of Recognition merely reformulates or restates the problem. We begin with the relationship between the Rule of Recognition and the relevant social practice.

(1) Though many writers—Hart himself occasionally—identify the Rule of Recognition with a social practice, the two cannot possibly be the same thing. The Rule of Recognition is a rule, and thus an abstract, propositional entity.[7] The practice is constituted in part by behavior, and is thus not a propositional entity. The Rule has conditions of satisfaction; the practice does not. If the Rule is not identical with the practice, what is the relationship between them?

The most important point about the relationship between rule and practice is that the Rule of Recognition comes into existence as a rule that regulates behavior only if it is *practiced.* The practice, we can say, is an existence condition of the Rule of Recognition. This feature falls out of the fact that the Rule of Recognition is a social or conventional rule: like the convention of driving on the right hand side of the road, its claim to govern conduct depends on its being generally observed.[8] By contrast, the legal rules that are validated by a Rule of Recognition purport to regulate behavior regardless of whether or not those rules reflect actual practice. For example, a valid law setting the legal drinking age at twenty-one years purports to regulate conduct despite its being flouted.[9] Thus, while the Rule of Recognition can impose an obligation on officials (to evaluate conduct by applying all those rules that satisfy the criteria of legality set forth in it) only insofar as it is actually practiced, this conventional rule in turn grounds the claims of the rules validated under it to regulate conduct regardless of whether or not those subordinate rules are adhered to. Put precisely, while the claim to legal authority requires that all laws be capable of regulating conduct, the claim of legal norms generally to regulate conduct depends on the existence of a rule whose own claim to do so depends on its being practiced.[10]

Scott Shapiro has expressed very much the same point in a slightly different, and helpful way. Shapiro claims that the distinctive innovation of Hart's positivism is the claim that (legal) *norm-governed* behavior is made possible by (legal) *norm-guided* behavior. Norm-guided behavior is behavior in which the norm is the reason on which the agent acts; norm governed behavior is behavior that is subject to a norm. The vast majority of legal rules purport to *govern* behavior whether or not they are practiced, that is, whether or not they actually *guide* behavior. But the possibility of a legal rule's governing depends on the analytically or conceptually prior existence of a convention among officials, a convention whose ability to govern their behavior depends on their being guided by it.

This brings us to a related point about the relationship between Rule and practice. It is often said, mistakenly, that because the Rule of Recognition is a social or conventional rule, its *content* is constituted by the behavior of officials; and that because its capacity to impose duties depends on its being practiced, the scope of the obligations it imposes on officials is coextensive with their actual behavior. The issues of semantic content and scope of obligation are of course closely related, but let us set that aside for the moment and focus on the claim about content. The standard view, implicit in almost all writing on the subject, is that because the Rule depends on convergent behavior for its existence as a regulative rule, its content is determined fully by that behavior. Those who object to characterizing the Rule of Recognition as a conventional rule have exploited this standard view in order to undermine the Conventionality Thesis.

Here is the worry. If the content of the rule is determined by the convergent behavior, it seems to follow that whatever description captures the range of that convergence just is the Rule of Recognition. This would be at best a cramped and unilluminating form of explanation—in effect, we would be saying, "whatever it is that officials do, they are following a rule whose content tells them to do that." Moreover, some have thought that if the behavior determines the content of the rule, then the scope of obligation imposed by the rule must be coextensive with the actual convergence of behavior of officials. But in that case, the rule could impose no duties beyond the scope of convergent behavior, and thus no behavior could fail to satisfy the rule. All and only convergent behavior would be subject to the rule, and there would be no sense in which it could govern behavior that failed to converge. Here it is difficult to see in what sense we would be talking about a rule at all.[11]

While the objection seems quite powerful, it is able to get off the ground only by presupposing a mistaken picture of the relationship between the content of the rule and the convergent behavior (a picture that, regrettably, is owed in part to positivist supporters of the Conventionality Thesis). The mistake is to suppose that the semantic content of the Rule of Recognition is determined by the range of the convergent behavior. To make this mistake is not to take seriously the claim that the practice of officials is a practice of *following a rule*. For there must always be a gap between the mere description of rule-guided behavior and the content of the rule that guides it.

The point is familiar from a variety of sources, most famously perhaps from Wittgenstein's *Philosophical Investigations*. A pattern of behavior can never fully determine the content of a rule, because any pattern of behavior is consistent with an indefinite number of different rules, each of which "covers" past behavior, yet each of which would result in different future behavior.[12] If the behavior alone determined the rule, then the rule would be so indeterminate that any future course of behavior would be consistent with it—which is to say that there would be no rule at all.

The crucial point is that in saying that there is a *practice* of officials of adhering and conforming to certain criteria as constitutive of the class "law", we mean to be asserting more than that their behavior converges on applying these criteria. In order for their behavior to constitute a *practice* in the relevant sense, it must reflect a shared grasp of the rule they are applying. The practice requires not only that officials' past behavior has accorded with the rule, but also that they share a grasp of how to "go on" or to "project" the rule to cover future behaviors. They must tend to agree, in other words, on which future behavior will accord with the rule and which will not. This commitment to going on in a particular way is part of what distinguishes merely convergent behavior from rule-following behavior.[13] Here we are merely emphasizing that officials really do *follow* the Rule of Recognition, in the everyday sense of "following" that we always mean when we say someone follows a rule. It is only in this sense that the Rule of Recognition is capable of having explanatory power with regard to officials' behavior.

A related point, articulated first by Wittgenstein in his discussion of rule following, is that the grasp of a rule—the ability to "go on"—cannot be exhaustively articulated in propositional form. Saul Kripke has explicated this point forcefully, showing that even the apparently hard-and-fast rule for our practice of addition cannot be stated in such a way that it uniquely determines what we all know to be the criteria of correctness for that practice.[14] There is always the possibility of interpreting a propositional expression of the rule of addition in an indefinite number of non-standard ways. Since in fact we all converge in interpreting it in the same way, our understanding of the practice must go beyond propositional knowledge.

It should be unsurprising, therefore, if participants in a convergent or conventional practice—such as that explained by the Rule of Recognition—were to provide somewhat different formulations of the rule they were following; especially if they were asked to specify it in all its details, or to project it to cover a range of difficult hypothetical cases (here the analogy with addition breaks down: not all rules have a standard interpretation which admits of no variations). We should not want to overstate the degree of allowable disagreement or difference in formulations, however; if the same rule is being followed, then participants must share a grasp or understanding of the rule that is reflected both in convergent behavior and in broadly shared understandings of the rule's application to a range of paradigms and hypotheticals.[15] At a minimum, they must share a framework of interaction.

Instead of saying that the content of the rule is determined by the convergent behavior, we might say that the behavior *fixes* the rule.[16] By this I mean, first, that the behavior can help us to identify which rule is being practiced; certainly it can eliminate the vast majority of potential candidates. Moreover, given the background of a common culture and language (in which the capacities needed to grasp the standard interpretation of a rule are embodied) the convergence of behavior can suffice to enable succeeding generations of officials to gain the requisite grasp of how to "go on," thus enabling legal systems to persist over time.

We come finally to the relationship of the Rule of Recognition to the internal point of view. Hart's introduction of the internal point of view into jurisprudence is one of his great contributions. Unfortunately, his occasionally equivocal use of this term has led to at least as much confusion as insight. As we characterized it above, the internal point of view is an attitude of the participants toward a pattern of convergent behavior. Hart suggests in some contexts, however, that the internal point of view is an attitude not toward patterns of behavior, but toward *rules*. This has led to a variety of misunderstandings about the role of the internal point of view.

Hart often refers to social rules as having an "internal aspect." Many writers in the field take this to mean that the Rule of Recognition is a social rule that is itself accepted from the internal point of view, or in other words that the internal point of view is simply an attitude (acceptance) taken toward the Rule. While not strictly incorrect, this characterization obscures the key element of the relationship between the internal point of view and the Rule of Recognition, namely the fact that the internal point of view is an *existence condition* of the Rule. There is no Rule of Recognition independent of convergent behavior toward which participants take the internal point of view. It is the shared attitude toward the pattern of behavior that constitutes the fact that the behavior is governed by a rule.[17]

A social rule exists when convergent behavior is conjoined with a critical reflective attitude toward that behavior. The critical reflective attitude is the internal point of view. Its object, in the first instance, is the pattern of behavior, not the rule. The existence of the internal point of view is what marks the difference between regularized behavior—or behavior that people engage in "as a rule"—and rule-governed behavior—behavior *that is regulated by a rule*. If the majority of those whose behavior has converged in some way (for example, habitually) do not share the view that their behavior in the convergent area is governed by a rule, then it is not governed by a social rule. A social rule's ability to govern behavior depends on the fact that individuals take the convergent behavior of themselves and others to be guided by the rule.

In contrast, compliance with most ordinary rules does not imply taking the internal point of view toward them. One might comply with a moral rule for fear of an afterlife in hell, for example; or one might comply with the tax law for fear of imprisonment. This would not be to take the internal point of view toward the rule. To take the internal point of view toward rule-governed behavior is to take the rule—and not an external sanction—as the reason for one's compliance. This is the difference between merely *complying* with a rule that governs one's behavior, and being *guided* by that rule. In the latter case, but not the former, the rule is the reason for compliance.

Of course one could take the internal point of view toward moral rules or tax laws; some people do. But the relationship of the internal point of view to such non-social rules would still be different from its relationship to the Rule of Recognition, and to social rules more generally. For one could in principle take a non-social rule as the reason for one's compliance even if no one else did. By contrast, if there is no general practice of compliance with the Rule of Recognition, there is no Rule of Recognition, and *a fortiori* one cannot take it as a reason for action. This is the key to the special relationship of the internal point of view to the Rule of Recognition. The widespread adoption of the internal point of view by officials toward their convergent behavior—as evidenced in consistent appeals to the Rule as a basis of justification or condemnation—is *an existence condition of the rule, and thus a possibility condition for the rule's providing reason for action.*

As we have seen, the claim of rules subordinate to the Rule of Recognition to regulate conduct does not depend on their being practiced, but depends instead on another rule—the Rule of Recognition—whose claim to regulate conduct does depend on *its* being practiced. The point currently under discussion is analogous. The claim of subordinate rules to regulate behavior does not depend on anyone's adopting the internal point of view towards them, though it does depend on the existence of a rule whose own existence depends on the bulk of those whose conduct it purports to regulate (i.e., officials) adopting the internal point of view towards *it.*

Let me summarize this discussion of the relationship between the Rule of Recognition and the practice of officials. Being practiced is an *existence condition* of the Rule of Recognition. The practice consists in a convergence of behavior and an internal point of view. The convergent behavior fixes the Rule, but does not determine its content; nor does the range of convergent behavior determine the scope of obligations the Rule purports to impose. As with any rule, the content of the Rule of Recognition extends beyond any finite pattern of behavior; and as with any obligation-imposing rule, the obligations the Rule imposes are determined by its *content*, and are not limited to the convergence of behavior of those subject to the rule. Finally, the internal point of view is a necessary element of the practice of a Rule of Recognition, and is therefore itself an existence condition of the Rule. However, the claim of subordinate rules to regulate behavior does not depend on anyone's adopting the internal point of view towards them.[18]

(2) I turn now to the second main topic of this essay, the question of whether the Rule of Recognition can be a duty-imposing

rule. Hart famously distinguishes primary from secondary rules: primary rules are those that purport to impose obligations, whereas secondary rules confer powers. The Rule of Recognition is on Hart's view the most important of the secondary rules, and thus is typically conceived as a power-conferring rather than a duty-imposing rule.[19] Some commentators have noted that because the Rule of Recognition simply states what the criteria of legality are, it should be thought of as neither power conferring nor duty imposing. This has prompted some theorists sympathetic to Hart's overall project to re-draw the distinction between primary and secondary rules. They prefer to say that primary rules claim to impose obligations, while secondary rules are rules about primary rules; secondary rules are in this sense second-order or meta-rules. They include rules of legislation, which enable individuals to make, amend and alter primary rules; rules of adjudication, which establish the power to adjudicate disputes and the conditions under which that power can be legitimately exercised; and finally, the Rule of Recognition, which sets out the criteria of legality.[20] The Rule of Recognition is a rule about other rules, but on this view it is neither power conferring nor duty imposing. Rather, it merely states when norms that purport to be power conferring or duty imposing are valid law; or, to put it slightly differently, it states the test which norms must satisfy in order to be law.

Joseph Raz, for example, adopts what we might call a "semantic" conception of the Rule of Recognition. He acknowledges that the criteria of legality are conventional in the sense that their existence depends on the practice of officials, and not on the quality of argument that can be mustered on their behalf. He is committed, as well, to the view that these criteria constitute *a* "test" of legality—criteria of membership in the category "law." He does not, however, treat the statement of these criteria as a *regulative rule* that purports to govern anyone's behavior. In that sense, he treats the Rule of Recognition as having a *semantic* character only. Put another way: the Razian view is that wherever there is law there are criteria that constitute a test of the legality of any norm. These criteria may in principle be articulated in propositional form, and that proposition may be called "the Rule of Recognition." Understood thus, however, the "rule" is not part of the community's law; it simply states what the criteria of legality in a given community are. In doing so, it guides no one's conduct and imposes no duties. It is just a conceptual tool that helps those of us who think about law to organize our thinking about it.

Thus, in claiming that the criteria of legality are conventional, one is not thereby committed to the existence of a Rule of Recognition as a potentially duty-imposing or regulative rule; it remains a matter of dispute among legal positivists whether or not it is necessary or helpful to invoke the concept of a Rule of Recognition in any sense that goes beyond the semantic conception. Raz thinks not, while a number of positivists—Hart and I among them—have characterized the Rule of Recognition in a stronger sense, as a rule that purports to impose a duty on officials: specifically, the duty to evaluate conduct by appealing to all those norms that are valid under the rule.[21] Often, the reluctance of those positivists who have shied away from characterizing the Rule of recognition as a duty-imposing rule stems from doubts they have about the possibility of conventional rules to create or impose duties. Thus, one burden that falls to those who view the Rule of Recognition as purporting to impose a duty on officials is to explain how conventional rules can be duty imposing. This is a serious challenge to the Conventionality Thesis, and I respond to this challenge below.

To be perfectly fair, there may be no theoretically compelling reason to say that the duty judges have to evaluate conduct by appealing to all and only those norms that are valid under the rule is a duty that originates in, or is explained by the Rule. One might wish to reserve the expression "Rule of Recognition" to mean a merely semantic entity that captures the content of the criteria of legality without imposing any duty. Nonetheless if one does not treat the Rule of Recognition as a duty-imposing rule, one still needs to explain why, and under what conditions, judges are obligated (or have reason) to apply the criteria of legality, as well as how the fact that other judges apply the criteria can be a reason for each judge to do so. Even if it is not strictly speaking necessary to explain these things in terms of a Rule of Recognition, it is both natural and perhaps helpful to do so. It reflects the ordinary way in which we characterize or talk about conventional practices and authority—that is, as rule-governed concepts. At the same time, speaking in terms of freestanding criteria of legality does not eliminate any of the philosophical puzzles that a positivist must confront. On balance, it seems preferable to follow Hart by understanding the criteria of legality as being expressed in a Rule of Recognition that purports to be a regulative or duty-imposing rule.[22] In the end, however, it may be of little importance whether or not the term "Rule of Recognition" is attached to the explanation of the purported duty; what is important is to explain—in a way consistent with the positivist commitment to the conventionality of law—the nature and possibility conditions of the duty of officials to apply the criteria of legality.

One of Hart's most familiar and important objections to Austin is that his analysis of law in terms of commands and habits of obedience is incapable of explaining law's normativity—that is, law's claim to provide reasons for action. Because habits are not reasons, an analysis that reduces law to habits lacks the resources necessary to explain the role law plays in our deliberative and normative lives. This is why Hart places at the center of his analysis of law the concept of a rule. Rules can be reasons for action in a way in which mere habits cannot be.

It is a further and important philosophical question how, or in virtue of what feature, a rule purports to be reason giving. In the case of the rules of critical morality, the claim to provide reasons for action derives from the claim to truth; or, put slightly differently, from the fact that such rules can express bona fide moral reasons independently of whether or not anyone heeds them. The existence of such rules as normative entities does not require that they be practiced or accepted. The opposite is true of social rules, however, whose existence as regulative rules always depends on their being accepted and practiced. This is important in the present context because the rule of Recognition is, according to positivists, a social rule and not a rule of critical morality.

The Rule of Recognition can be a reason for action only if social rules can be reasons for action. What we need is an account of how social rules, which purport to be reasons for action independently of their content, can nevertheless be bona fide reasons. Providing such an account is especially important to the theory being developed here, because the existence of a Rule of Recognition is being put forward as part of the explanation of the very possibility of legal authority. Since the claim of rules subordinate to the rule of Recognition to provide reasons for action depends on their being authorized by the Rule, it is crucial that we be able to explain *its* normativity.

It is reasonable to suppose that such an explanation will follow from a more general account of the normativity of social rules. Like any social rule, the Rule of Recognition exists only if there is a convergence of behavior conjoined with the reflective, critical attitude that Hart calls the internal point of view. The internal point of view thus marks the difference—on Hart's account—between mere convergent or regular behavior (habits of obedience, for example) and social-rule-guided behavior. It is natural to read this account as entailing the claim that the internal point of view *explains the Rule of Recognition's normativity.* The Rule of Recognition is capable of regulating the behavior of officials—capable, in other words, of imposing a duty on them to evaluate conduct by applying the standards that satisfy the criteria set out in it—*just because* the Rule is accepted from the internal point of view.

Having read Hart this way, many commentators have gone on to assail the claim that the internal point of view could transform a behavioral fact (a regularity of behavior) into a normative fact (the existence of a regulative rule). How, these critics ask, can a rule give reasons or impose an obligation just because people treat it as doing so? A rule cannot be said to impose an obligation simply because those individuals who are its intended subjects *believe* they are obligated by it. To hold otherwise is to engage in a form of objectionable "bootstrapping," in which that which purports to explain the normativity of the Rule of Recognition—the internal point of view—is partly constitutive of what is to be explained.[23] On the other hand, if Hart does not claim that the internal point of view explains the Rule of Recognition's normativity, he appears to have no explanation of it.

Though nearly universally accepted as devastating to Hart's project, the objection is not, in the end, persuasive. Social rules can be reasons for action, and properly understood, the internal point of view is pivotal to the explanation of how they can be. Moreover, though a conventional rule, the Rule of Recognition can nevertheless be a duty-imposing rule. The internal point of view, however, plays no role in the explanation of how conventional rules can be duty imposing. The arguments for each of these claims—that social rules can be reasons, and that they can impose duties—draw on important, but largely overlooked distinctions, and require a more philosophically sophisticated understanding of the internal point of view.

Let us begin with the important distinction between the claim that the Rule of Recognition can be a *reason* for acting, and the very different claim that the kind of reason it provides is a *duty* specifically a duty to evaluate conduct in the light of those norms that satisfy certain criteria of legality. The Conventionality Thesis entails both of these claims, but they are importantly different. First, if legal governance or legal authority is made possible by rule-guidance in the form of adherence to a social practice that guides the behavior of officials, then we need an account of how certain social practices can be *reasons*—how social facts can be norms. Not every reason is a duty; however, both Hart and I treat the Rule of Recognition as purporting to be the source of judicial duty or obligation, that is, as the explanation of the duty judges have to apply certain criteria of legality. Thus, we need an account of the possibility of social rules being reasons, as well as an account of the distinctive kind of reason the rule of Recognition purports to be—namely, a duty to apply certain criteria of legality.

The criticism of Hart just outlined treats him as attempting to show that the internal point of view can explain how a social rule of recognition could be a *duty-imposing* rule. I do not believe, however, that Hart meant for the internal point of view to explain how the Rule of Recognition could be a source or explanation of judicial *duties*. In any case, I certainly hold no such view. The internal point of view figures in the explanation of how social rules can be reasons for action: how certain practices can be norms. It is not an explanation of the character of the reason that a social rule can provide. Thus, while Hart's critics may be right to insist that the internal point of view cannot explain the Rule's capacity to impose a duty, their criticism is probably misplaced.

In order to understand how social rules can be reasons, and to demonstrate the role of the internal point of view in that explanation, it is important that we begin with a proper understanding of the internal point of view.[24] Hart's critics mischaracterize the internal point of view in a way that makes it seem impossible that it could even *enter into* an explanation of the Rule's normativity. If we regard the internal point of view as simply the *belief* among officials that their behavior is governed by a rule—then it is indeed difficult to see how this belief could give rise to a regulative rule or a reason for acting. If convergent behavior alone cannot create reasons for action, then how can convergent behavior conjoined with the belief that the behavior is rule governed create such reasons?

Put this way, the objection is compelling; but as I said, this mischaracterizes the internal point of view. The internal point of view should not be understood as a belief of any sort, but rather, as the exercise of a basic and important psychological capacity of human beings to adopt a practice or pattern of behavior as a norm. This capacity can be given a philosophical analysis in terms of behavioral and psychological dispositions—among them, the disposition to conform to the norm or rule, to evaluate oneself and others on its basis, and to form certain beliefs and other intentional states associated with such a commitment. However, there may be no further *philosophical* explanation of the grounds or source of this capacity. Its existence is to be explained in some other way—causally, sociologically, biologically or, more broadly, by invoking an evolutionary argument that identifies the adaptive value of such a capacity (for example, its usefulness to individuals in enabling them to undertake projects and to secure the gains of coordinative activity). Understood in this more sophisticated sense—not as a belief, but as the exercise of a basic capacity to adopt a pattern of behavior as a norm—the internal point of view is essential to the explanation of the Rule of Recognition's normativity.

We can illustrate the role the internal point of view plays in this story by considering the case of a self-imposed or "personal" rule—say the rule I might adopt to do a hundred sit-ups every day. If I should happen to be in the habit of doing that many sit-ups every day, my habit of doing so gives me no reason to do sit-ups. Of course I already have plenty of good reasons—having to do with health and fitness—for doing such exercises; but my *habit* of doing them does not add any further reason. Now suppose that I take a certain stance towards my doing sit-ups each day, a stance we can characterize as "adopting the behavior as a norm." This stance can be explicated in terms of a set of normative dispositions: the disposition to conform to a certain standard of behavior, and to engage in reflective evaluation of my conduct on the basis of that standard. By thus adopting my behavior as a norm (and provided I regularly conform to it) I have made the behavior a rule or norm for me. In doing so, I have created a reason that is additional to and different from the reasons of fitness and health that I already had.[25] The internal point of view creates an analogous reason for those who adopt it. In this sense, the internal point of view actually *does* "turn behavior into a rule"; it turns a social fact into a normative one. Hart's emphasis on the explanatory value of the internal point of view is thus vindicated.[26] Social rules can be reasons for action, and the internal point of view figures prominently in the explanation of that fact.[27]

However, while the internal point of view explains how the Rule of Recognition can create reasons for acting, this does not yet explain how those reasons can be *duties.* If I can create a reason by adopting a pattern of behavior as a norm, then it would seem that I can subsequently *extinguish* the reason that norm provides simply by withdrawing my commitment to it. Yet it is the nature of duties that those bound by them cannot voluntarily extinguished them as reasons. It would be odd if not incomprehensible to say that the reason my self-imposed rule creates for me to do sit-ups is a *duty*; for if I withdraw my commitment to follow that rule, then I extinguish the reason it creates. The many other reasons I have for doing daily sit-ups remain, but the reason I create by adopting the rule disappears.[28]

The situation is no different if the same behavior is adopted as a personal rule by others besides me. If each of a thousand people decides to do daily sit-ups, then there are a thousand new personal rules, each providing a new reason for acting for the individual who adopts the rule, and each extinguishable as a reason by that individual. Such reasons cannot be characterized as duties, for it is in the nature of duties that one cannot—at least not in the usual case—autonomously extinguish a duty.

By analogy, if each of a thousand individuals separately and as it were, "personally" commits to evaluating conduct by all and only those norms that satisfy certain criteria of legality, those separate acts of commitment do not impose any duties. There may be independent reasons—even duties—for each to evaluate conduct according to the norms that the criteria specify (for example, the content of those norms might express requirements of morality. However, the additional reason created for each by her separate, personal commitment to the criteria is a reason that can be extinguished at will by her withdrawal of that commitment. In short, not every reason is a duty, and the explanation we have offered of the capacity of the Rule of Recognition to be a reason falls short of explaining how the Rule can impose a duty.

The solution to this problem requires that we turn our attention from the psychological capacity to adopt a practice or a pattern of behavior as a norm, and focus instead on the normative structure of the pattern of behavior to which we commit. In other words, if we wish to explain the character of the reason that the Rule of Recognition creates, we must look beyond the internal point of view that officials adopt toward their practice, and consider instead the structure of the practice that the Rule governs.

Margaret Gilbert provides the helpful example of two people going for a walk together. Part of what distinguishes this activity from the activity of two people who are simply walking alongside one another is that the former activity has a normative structure that the latter lacks. If you and I are taking a walk together, your actions and intentions create reasons for me, and mine create reasons for you. For example, the fact that you turn to the left—or even that you intend or prefer to do so—can give me a reason to turn left. Similarly, when Judges adopt the practice of applying the Rule of Recognition, the actions and intentions of the other judges are reasons for each; it is as though they are going for a walk together, rather than simply walking alongside one another. It is this feature of the normativity of the Rule of Recognition that is left unexplained by the internal point of view. For it is not just that different judges decide individually and separately to evaluate conduct in the light of standards that satisfy certain criteria, thereby creating reasons for themselves that they can unilaterally extinguish; rather, they are engaged in a practice that has a certain normative structure—where, among other things, the fact that some judges apply criteria of legality is a reason for others to do so. It is this fact about legal practice, and not the internal point of view that judges take towards it, that is the key to understanding how the conventional practice of applying criteria of legality can be a source of a duty to do so.

I cannot say whether Hart fully appreciated the difference between these two aspects of the Rule's normativity—that is, its ability to be a reason for action, and the fact that the kind of practice the Rule governs is one in which the behavior, intentions and preferences of some participants are (or can be) reasons for action for others. I am inclined to believe that Hart was, at least implicitly, aware of both aspects—since he did in fact offer two different kinds of arguments regarding these different normative dimensions of the Rule of Recognition: one emphasizing the internal point of view, the other emphasizing the coordinative features of the Rule of Recognition. While his critics certainly conflated these two elements, I do not believe that Hart himself did.

Arguably, Hart conceived the Rule of Recognition as what we would nowadays refer to as a 'coordination convention', in the formal or game-theoretic sense. Coordination conventions solve recurrent problems that arise as a result of structural features of human action. For example, when a telephone conversation is cut off, it is useful for each party to know who will call back; a convention establishing that it is the original caller who resumes the call solves the problem by coordinating the parties' actions.

Suppose it has been agreed that for some reason a legal system is a desirable thing. If there is to be law, then some group of individuals must commit themselves to applying a rule that specifies the membership conditions for the category "law." Surely there will be a broad range of possible sets of membership conditions, and each person may, *ex ante*, prefer a different set. Although each person's first preference is that all apply his favored set, each prefers (second) that all apply the *same* set—regardless of which one it is—over the (third-ranked) alternative of applying his own first-choice set while others apply their own (which is to say, the alternative of having no legal system at all). This situation reflects what in game theory is called a "Battle of the Sexes," or a game of partial conflict. Typically, solutions to these games are coordinating conventions, and this is how Hart seems to believe the Rule of Recognition is best understood. It solves a partial conflict game whose resolution is necessary if law is to be possible.

In the present context, the importance of coordinative conventions is that the actions of some whose behavior is governed by them can be reasons for others. Thus, the fact that the other motorists drive on the right side of the road typically gives me a reason for doing so as well. The fact that everyone else in our group is going to the opera gives me a reason for doing so as well, and so on. Coordinative conventions create normative relationships of just the sort officials—especially judges—appear to have towards one another.

In imputing to Hart the view that the Rule of Recognition solves a coordination problem, I certainly do not mean to impute to him the view that *law* solves a coordination problem; rather, the Rule of Recognition solves a coordination problem that must be solved if law is to be *possible*.[29] To illustrate: If Hobbes is right, then the state of nature is a situation that may best be modeled game theoretically as a Prisoner's Dilemma. Law provides a potential solution to the Prisoners' Dilemma. But law can solve this problem only if legal authority is possible; and legal authority is possible, on Hart's view, only if there is a Rule of Recognition that sets out criteria of legality and imposes a duty on officials to apply the norms that satisfy those criteria. *The Rule of Recognition does not solve the Prisoner's Dilemma. Law solves that problem.* Instead, the Rule of Recognition solves a coordination problem that must be solved if law is to be possible.

Though I use the Hobbesian example of the Prisoner's Dilemma to distinguish the problem law solves from the one the Rule of Recognition solves, we need not regard law as a solution to any sort of problem at all—let alone one that can be modeled game-theoretically. Law may exist in order to make more determinate the requirements of a shared political morality, or to organize society in a way that enables individuals to be responsible for the lives they lead. Or law can create an efficient scheme of production and distribution. Law can have any number of legitimate purposes, not all of which can be usefully modeled game theoretically. The point is just this: in order for there to be a legal system that can serve any end through rules that govern behavior, there must be a Rule of Recognition. That rule is not the solution to the structural problem (if any) that makes law *desirable*. It is the solution to the problem of coordinating officials on a set of criteria of legality necessary to make law *possible*.

Understanding the Rule of Recognition as a coordination convention has the advantage of capturing the fact that the behavior of some participants can create reasons for others. The internal point of view, moreover, has a subsidiary role to play in this explanation. To see this, recall that since each individual prefers (on the explanation we are considering) that all adopt the *same* criteria for membership in the category "law," no member has any reason to defect unilaterally—which is to say that no official has reason to apply his own first-choice set of criteria of legality. This is just another way of expressing the well-known fact that coordinating conventions are 'Nash equilibria'. As long as others comply, no individual has sufficient reason to defect unilaterally.

Though it is irrational for any official to apply her own criteria of legality unilaterally, it need not be irrational to defect if others do so. Thus, parties to the coordinating convention need periodic assurance that the observable behavior of others is correctly interpreted as compliance with the "agreed upon" or conventionally accepted criteria. The requisite assurance can be provided by the causal role the internal point of view plays in affecting the expectations of officials. The internal point of view—understood as an exercise of the capacity to enter into normative commitments, and expressed in officials' public appeals to the Rule of Recognition as justification for their behavior, or as grounds of condemnation—gives each a reason to believe that a convention is well established and that others will continue to uphold it. It also communicates when the criteria of legality are being revised. The point here is that the *reason* an official has for believing that others will continue to comply with the Rule of Recognition—and thus, the reason for complying herself—rests on a *causal* story about the psychological capacity of humans to form reliable expectations about future human behavior on the basis of stable and consistent behavior and declarations about that behavior's significance.

Both the internal point of view and the fact that the Rule of Recognition is a coordination convention contribute to an explanation of the fact that the Rule of Recognition is a social rule in which the behavior of participants is authoritative with respect to the action of others. Like coordination conventions generally, the Rule of Recognition creates a system of interdependent and reciprocal expectations.

While I believe that the coordination convention account represents a genuine advance in interpreting Hart's position, and in our understanding of the Rule of Recognition, I fear that it is ultimately not an adequate solution to the problem under discussion, which is to provide an account of the Rule of Recognition that explains why the behavior of some judges is or can be a reason for other judges.[30] The difficulty with the coordination convention account is that coordination conventions are solutions to games in which the participants' *ex ante* preferences have a specific structure, or are ordered in certain specific ways—ways that constitute what we call "partial conflict" or "Battle of the Sexes" games. These are only a small subset of our social or conventional practices, however; the large majority cannot be modeled as solutions to partial conflict games. It would place an arbitrary and baseless constraint on our concept of law to stipulate that the social practice among officials necessary for the existence of a Rule of Recognition must always be representable as a game of partial conflict: to claim, in effect, that it is a conceptual truth about law that it can exist only if officials have *ex ante* preferences over possible criteria of law that are structured in a certain way—one that is amenable to a certain kind of game-theoretic representation of them. In this sense, the coordination convention account is too strong or demanding.

In another sense, the coordination convention account is too weak, since such conventions do not seem to capture well the kinds of reasons officials have for acting as other officials do. While it is true that the fact that judges apply certain criteria of legality can be a reason for any particular judge to do so, it is not simply the fact that others do so that explains the character of the reason that any particular judge has. A full explanation of the character of the reason any judge has to apply the relevant criteria will accommodate the fact that these criteria have been adopted as part of a plan or project (a legal system) that can serve valuable ends—though individual judges may be committed to that project for any number of different personal reasons.

In short, it is simply not plausible to suppose that all rules of recognition must be coordination conventions—even if, as positivists rightly believe, such rules are conventional. If such rules are conventional, but not necessarily coordination conventions in the game-theoretic sense, what can be said about the kind of conventional rules they are?

Let us take a moment to frame this question in terms of the broader argument. The positivist project demands an account of the normativity of the Rule of Recognition. This is because the capacity of almost all legal rules to *govern* conduct depends on their bearing a certain relationship to another rule—the Rule of Recognition—whose capacity to govern the behavior of those to whom it is addressed (namely, officials) depends on its *guiding* their behavior. A rule guides an individual's behavior only if it is his reason for acting in compliance with it. A philosophical account of the very possibility of governance by law, then, rests on the possibility of a philosophical account of how the Rule of Recognition can be a reason for action. I have suggested that, contrary to prevailing wisdom, the internal point of view is perfectly well suited to an explanation of how convergent practices can be norms of conduct. Providing this sort of account of the normativity of the Rule of Recognition meets a burden incumbent on those who maintain that the Conventionality Thesis can explain the possibility of legal authority. However, the Conventionality Thesis—which I am defending, and which Hart also endorsed—entails the further claim that the Rule of Recognition can be a duty-imposing rule. While the argument just summarized may explain how practices can become norms—how social rules can be reasons—it falls considerably short of explaining how a social rule can impose duties.

Two aspects of the claim that the Rule of Recognition is a duty-imposing rule cannot be explained by the internal point of view. First, a duty-imposing rule cannot normally be extinguished unilaterally, whereas rules that are reasons solely in virtue of one's commitment to them can, in the typical case, be unilaterally extinguished. Second, the particular kind of duty one has under a Rule of Recognition is to act in a coordinative way with others to achieve certain ends, and in doing so to be responsive to the interests, intentions, preferences and actions of others. Nothing in the internal point of view addresses either of these features of the duty imposed by the Rule of Recognition. Many forms of social life, not just the legal practices of officials, have these features. The general problem is to offer a philosophical explanation of such practices. This is a problem in social theory, not in jurisprudence as such; nonetheless a general philosophical explanation of the structure of such practices might help us understand the nature of the practice of legal officials.

A general philosophical analysis of exactly this sort has been proposed by Michael Bratman, who identifies a class of practices that he calls "Shared Cooperative Activity" (SCA).[31] SCA is something we do together—taking a walk together, building a house together and singing a duet together are all examples of SCA. I would like to suggest that the practice of officials of evaluating conduct in the light of rules that satisfy certain criteria of legality is an instance of SCA.[32]

Bratman identifies three characteristic features of SCA:

> (i) *Mutual responsiveness*: In SCA each participating agent attempts to be responsive to the intentions and actions of the other...Each seeks to guide his behavior with an eye to the behavior of the other, knowing that the other seeks to do likewise.
> (ii) *Commitment to the joint activity*: In SCA the participants each have an appropriate commitment (though perhaps for different reasons) to the joint activity, and their mutual responsiveness is in pursuit of this commitment.
> (iii) *Commitment to mutual support*: In SCA each agent is committed to supporting the efforts of the other to play her role in the joint activity...These commitments to support each other put us in a position to perform the joint activity successfully even if we each need help in certain ways.[33]

The practice of officials of being committed to a set of criteria of legality exhibits these features. Judges coordinate their behavior with one another through, for example, practices of precedent, which are ways in which they are responsive to the intentions of one another. The intention of an appellate court is that its decisions be binding on lower courts. Lower court judges typically respond to these intentions by treating higher court judges' decisions as constraints on their own behavior. The best explanation of judges' responsiveness to one another is their commitment to the goal of making possible the existence of a durable legal practice (though judges may have different reasons for thinking that a durable, sustained legal practice is desirable). Abiding by a practice of precedent is one way in which each judge helps the other do his part in fulfilling the aims of a legal practice.

While Hart was right to identify the normative structure of the practice of officials, he was wrong (as was I and Gerald Postema as well) to conclude that the Rule of Recognition represents, in effect, a Nash-equilibrium solution to a game of partial conflict.[34] The practice of officials necessary to create and sustain law is a more general form of social coordination, a form that is otherwise familiar to us. Bratman has a plausible and attractive account of such practices and of their possibility conditions.

Among the possibility conditions of SCA are what Bratman refers to as "shared intentions."[35] Despite the name, a shared intention is not actually a kind of intention at all. Intention (as Bratman notes at the beginning of his essay) is an *attitude*; by contrast, he writes,

> [S]hared intention, as I understand it, is not an attitude in any mind. It is not an attitude in the mind of some fused agent, for there is no such mind; and it is not an attitude in the mind or minds of either or both participants. Rather, it is a state of affairs that consists primarily in attitudes (none of which are themselves shared intentions) of the participants and interrelations between those attitudes.[36]

The particular form of interrelated responsiveness constitutive of shared intentions is not important for my purposes.

It is important, however, that shared intentions function in our practical lives by helping to "coordinate our intentional actions,"[37] to "coordinate our planning,"[38] and to "structure relevant bargaining."[39] In the latter case, our shared intentions "will tend to provide a background framework that structures relevant bargaining"[40] between us about how the joint activity is to proceed. In other words, when we participate jointly in SCA, we must share an intention that converges on a common goal—even if our reasons or motives for doing so are importantly different. The content of our shared intention is not fully specified, and indeed is specified more fully by the course our activity takes.

Moreover, carrying on together may require a continuous process of "give and take," as increasingly specific actions are required of us. Thus, we negotiate or bargain with one another in a particular way—that is, within a particular framework. The framework itself creates the parameters of reason that are recognized as appropriate or good ones, and so on.

The distinctive, though by no means unique normative structure of SCA can be seen as conceptually necessary elements of the practice of constituting a rule of recognition, a point that Ken Himma explicates in discussing my view of the Rule of Recognition,

> What is conceptually essential to the social practice constituting a conventional rule of recognition...is that it has the normative structure of an SCA. It is a conceptual truth about law that officials must coordinate their behavior with one another in various ways that are responsive to the intentions and actions of the others; what a judge, for example, does in a particular case depends on what other judges have done in similar cases. Similarly, it is a conceptual truth that officials be committed to the joint activity and to sup-

porting one another; officials responsible for promulgating law require an assurance of continuing support from officials responsible for enforcing and executing those law...[41]

Bratman's notion of an SCA also makes intelligible the claim that the Rule of Recognition can be a duty imposing rule. To quote Himma again—

> While the point of Coleman's analysis of the rule of recognition as an SCA is to make explicit the normative structure of the supporting social practice-...the notion of an SCA might contribute to an explanation of how a social practice can give rise to obligations. The notion of an SCA involves more than just a convergence of unilateral acceptances of the rule of recognition. It involves a joint *commitment* on the part of the participants to the activity governed by the rule of recognition...And there is no mystery (at least not one that a legal theorist is obliged to solve) about how joint commitments can give rise to obligations; insofar as such commitments induce reliance and a justified set of expectations (whether explicitly or not), they can give rise to obligations.

Bratman's account of SCA thus helps to make intelligible the Rule of Recognition as a duty-imposing rule, as well as providing philosophical insight into the normative structure of judicial practice. In doing so, his account helps to discharge the remaining burden Positivists face concerning the normativity of the Rule of Recognition.[42]

In addition to making explicit the way in which the conventional Rule of Recognition can be duty imposing, Bratman's analysis provides a unified philosophical framework from which I can defend several controversial claims I have made about the conventionality of the Rule of Recognition. Many of these claims have been controversial among my positivist allies as well as among my critics. Until now I have defended them in a more or less ad hoc fashion. Bratman's account of SCA enables me to defend these claims in a more unified and systematic way. Let me explain.

Beginning with "Negative and Positive Positivism," I have argued that while the conduct of participants is an existence condition of a conventional rule of recognition, the content of the rule is not determined by their behavior. Second, and relatedly, I have argued that conventional practices or conventional rules can—indeed almost certainly must—admit of the possibility of disagreement. Moreover, I have argued that such disagreements may take either of two forms: disagreements about how to apply the rule, or disagreements about its content. Whereas others have claimed that the latter kind of disagreement is not compatible with conceiving of the rule as conventional, I have argued not only that disagreement about content is possible in a conventional rule, but also that there is no reason to believe that such disagreement must be reserved for the "penumbra" case.[43] Finally, whereas no one else, to my knowledge, has allowed that appeal to substantive moral argument to resolve disputes in the Rule of Recognition can be compatible with conceiving of the rule as a convention, I have steadfastly asserted that compatibility.[44] There can be general and widespread appeal to moral principle to resolve controversies about the rule of recognition, I claimed—if the rule itself specifies that controversies about its content are to be resolved that way.[45]

I have defended these positions, until now, simply by responding to particular objections to them. As I said, there has been something philosophically unsatisfying about this strategy of response. Though I am satisfied that I have adequately met individual challenges to my claims as those challenges have arisen, I have not done so in a way that expresses or yields a unifying account of the conventionality of the Rule of Recognition. Conceiving of shared intentions and the SCAs they make possible as frameworks for bargaining provides such an account, and reinforces each of the positions I have taken about the conventionality of the Rule of Recognition. The framework is created and sustained by the behavior of participants, but the content of the rules that constitute the practice is not. The rules are the result of ongoing negotiations. Thus there may well be disagreement about their content—disagreement, moreover, that is substantive and important, and which, given the framework, might well be settled by an appeal to substantive moral argument about how one ought to proceed, and that may invite discussion about the point of the practice.

Dworkin has rightly argued that in a mature legal practice, disagreement about the content of the criteria of legality will exist, and that such disagreement is likely to invite discussion about the best interpretation of the practice. The best interpretation, in turn, will invoke discussion of the proper point or purpose of the activity. Where Dworkin goes wrong—as I have argued here and elsewhere—is in inferring that such disagreement and the means available to its resolution are incompatible with the criteria of legality being conventional in the way positivists claim they are and must be. Positivism—as I have argued—is compatible with everything Dworkin says about the possibility and character of disagreement in legal argument. More importantly, in characterizing judicial practice as SCA, positivists have an explanation of the sense in which law is a social or conventional practice—an explanation that is unavailable to Dworkin, given the structure of his theory.

My views about the conventionality of the Rule of Recognition have also been criticized, at least implicitly, by other positivists. For example, Andrei Marmor appears to believe that we must appeal to a novel kind of convention—what he calls a constitutive convention—in order to accommodate the facts of disagreement and the relevance of appeals to evaluative argument.[46] The implicit objection is that a view like mine cannot have it both ways: it cannot claim that the Rule of Recognition is a convention *and* that disputes about its content are subject to resolution by moral argument. I have responded that there is no contradiction in holding such a position, since it could be part of the conventional practice surrounding the Rule of Recognition that individuals resolve disputes about its content by appealing to certain kinds of moral arguments. Though obviously coherent, this response, I admit, has always struck me as somewhat ad hoc. We are now in a position to provide a far more satisfying response. Since the Rule of Recognition is itself a framework for bargaining about how to go on, there is nothing at all ad hoc in supposing that such bargaining might involve moral or political arguments about the point of the practice. In short, positivism never needed a new kind of convention—for example, constitutive conventions. It only needed a better philosophical account of conventional practices.

(3) Before concluding, I would like to consider an objection that will allow us to revisit the question with which this essay began, the question of how to explain law without appealing to law. The objection is along the following lines.

The Rule of Recognition, we are told, exists only when officials act in a certain way; but whether or not individuals are *officials* in the relevant sense seems to depend on the existence of a Rule of Recognition. After all, persons are officials in virtue of the laws that create officials. But those laws, we are told, are valid only if they are validated by the Rule of Recognition, which leads us back to where we started. So it appears that the Conventionality Thesis has not solved the original problem. It explains law in terms of law after all.

This is indeed a clever objection, but there is a clear and decisive response. We must differentiate between two distinct roles that the same group of individuals plays in the conventionalist story. First, some group of individuals—we do not call them officials and we need not identify them by reference to laws—choose to have their behavior guided by a certain rule. In other words, they take the rule as giving them good reasons for action. If that rule takes hold in the sense of establishing membership criteria in a system of rules; and if those rules are complied with generally; and if institutions of certain types are then created, and so on, it is fair to say that a legal system exists. If a legal system exists, then that rule which guides the behavior of our initial group of individuals is correctly described as the Rule of Recognition for that legal system. And those individuals who guide their behavior by that rule are thus appropriately conceived of as "officials". They are, in a sense, officials in virtue of that rule, but they are not officials prior to it (in either the factual or the logical sense). Their behavior makes the rule possible; but it is the rule that makes them officials.

In this essay I have offered a distinctive account of the positivist claim that legality is conventional—what I have called "the Conventionality Thesis." In this account, the Rule of Recognition expresses a conventional practice among officials, in virtue of which (though only together with certain other necessary conditions) a legal system can be said to exist. The possibility of legal rules purporting to govern conduct depends on the existence of a rule whose claim to govern conduct depends on its being practiced from an internal point of view. As Shapiro puts it, legal rule governance is made possible by rule guidance.

In explaining how legal governance is possible we have not explained *how* law governs; nor have we determined the conditions, if any, under which legal governance is or can be morally legitimate. The legitimacy of legal authority will no doubt depend on the value of the ends law serves. These ends may be heterogeneous—they may include personal security, an efficient cooperative system of production and exchange, or the creation of conditions under which individuals can be responsible for the lives they lead. Any or all of these are possible functions of law, but none is necessary to the concept of law.

NOTES

1. This essay is drawn from Chapter 7 of my Clarendon Lectures, *The Practice of Principle: In Defense of a Pragmatist Approach to Legal Theory* (Oxford: Oxford University Press, 2001).

2. Being conceptually connected in this way does not immunize law from moral criticism, nor does it preclude the natural lawyer from explicating in some other way the distinctive way in which law purports to govern human action.
3. For a fuller discussion of the Social Fact Thesis and an explanation of why it is more central to legal positivism than is the Separability Thesis, see *The Practice of Principle*, (Oxford University Press: 2001) Chapter 11.
4. The idea of agreement is slightly misleading in this context since a formal act of agreement is not necessary to Hart's or to my account. Below, I reformulate this idea in terms of participation in a social practice having a certain normative structure.
5. To say that it is desirable that individuals find the law legitimate and obligation imposing is not to say it is invariably desirable that, when individuals comply with the law, they act on the reason the law provides. That they should act on law's reason may normally be preferable to their acting because of sanction; but in many cases, for example the case of a law prohibiting murder, it is of course preferable that individuals act not on law's reason but on the independent moral conviction that innocent human life is valuable and not to be destroyed.
6. The Work of Alf Ross exemplifies this approach. See *On Law and Justice* [translated by Margaret Dutton] (Berkeley: University of California Press, 1959).
7. I am extremely grateful to Scott Shapiro for discussions that have shaped my thinking about the issues that I take up in the section on the relationship between rule and practice.
8. For the purpose of this example, I treat the practice of driving on the right as merely a convention, not as a practice required by law.
9. In this sense, a *law* requiring driving on the right hand side of the road could regulate conduct independently of its being practiced. Its claim to provide a reason for driving on the right would stem not from its being a conventional practice, but from its being a legally prescribed practice.
10. Another example: If I "adopt the rule" of running for one hour three times a week, I have not yet brought that rule into existence *as a regulative rule*, that is, as something that can give me reasons for acting (I may, of course, have reasons for running that are not created by any rule—for example, running may be good for my health). Even if, having decided to run three times a week, I am henceforth disposed to criticize myself for failing to adhere to that decision, I have still not given myself a regulative rule until I have practiced it to some degree (think how odd it would be to say, "I make it a rule to run one mile three times a week, but never actually do so"). This is one feature that social rules have in common with self-imposed rules.
11. It is this unhappy formulation of the relationship between behavior and Rule that Dworkin's arguments implicitly target. The mistake here lies at the other extreme from the mistake noted earlier—namely, the failure to recognize that being practiced is an existence condition of a social rule (as it is for self-imposed rules). Those who fail to recognize that practice is an existence condition of social rules will not be tempted to question the possibil-

ity of disagreement about the content of the obligations imposed by social rules, or to wonder how a social rule can give rise to a particular obligation in a case in which there is no established convergent practice. By contrast, while Dworkin rightly notes that being practiced is an existence condition of a social rule, he takes this to mean that the convergence of behavior *fully determines the content* of the rule and, thus, delimits the scope of the obligations it imposes. It is this mistaken interpretation of the relationship between rule and practice that Dworkin's objection seeks to exploit.

A view about social rules may fail either by holding that the mere adoption of a rule is sufficient for its existence as a social rule; or by holding that the practice of a social rule determines its content. In what follows, I offer a view that steers a middle course between both of these mistaken extremes. The appropriate account is one that explains what is distinctive about social rules—namely, that their existence as regulative rules depends on their being practiced—while also explaining how they are similar to other (non-social) regulative rules, insofar as their capacity to regulate is compatible with disagreement about the nature and scope of the duties they purport to impose.

12. Nelson Goodman has shown that an analogous problem arises in the area of confirmation theory: Suppose "grue" is a predicate that applies to any object that is seen to be green when first observed before a given time t, or that is seen to be blue when first observed after t. The same evidentiary base at any time, t seems to provide equally good confirmation for "all emeralds are green" and "all emeralds are grue." See Nelson Goodman, *Fact, Fiction and Forecast* (Boston: Harvard University Press, 1979) 74 ff.
13. This idea is further developed below and in *The Practice of Principle* (Op. Cit.) Chapter 11. I argue there that social practices are constituted by social rules that are best characterized as "frameworks of interaction." Their existence depends on "shared intentions," The full content of which is filled out as the participants go along. In that sense, social rules are parameters within which the terms of ongoing interaction are negotiated or evolve.
14. See Saul Kripke, *Wittgenstein on Rules and Private Language: An Elementary Exposition* (Cambridge, MA.: Harvard University Press, 1982).
15. Each case is revisible at any given time, but they are not all revisible at once. See Chapter 11 of *The Practice of Principle* for a discussion of the impact of this claim on Dworkin's "Semantic Sting" argument.
16. I am grateful to Scott Shapiro for suggesting this way of putting the point.
17. This is a conceptual point about what it is for something to be a social rule—not an explanation of how social rules create or give rise to reasons for acting. See below for a discussion of the way in which this shared reflective attitude contributes to an explanation of the normativity of the Rule of Recognition.
18. This is why "sanction" or "command" theories—views that, as Hart puts it, "leave no room" for the internal point of view—fail as a *conceptual* matter. It is not just that they ignore the obvious fact that some people comply with the law for the reason that the law requires it; rather, as I emphasize

below, failure to countenance the internal point of view makes it impossible to explain the very possibility of legal authority. Similarly, Hart's argument is *not* that it is preferable for the law to secure compliance through individuals' adopting the internal point of view. Rather, Hart claims that the internal point of view is a conceptual necessity of legality. There is nothing in Hart that even suggests the preference that ordinary citizens' compliance be motivated by the internal point of view. I take this issue up in greater detail in *The Practice of Principle* Chapter 12.

19. In fact, despite classing it among the secondary, power-conferring rules, Hart treats the Rule of Recognition primarily as a duty imposing rule: that is, a rule that purports to impose a duty on officials to evaluate conduct in the light of norms that satisfy the criteria of legality set out in it.
20. To say that the Rule sets out the criteria of legality is ambiguous. It could mean that the rule simply marks some norms as valid law, and thus renders the law *determinate*. But it could mean that in addition to that, the Rule also plays the role of enabling individuals to identify which of a community's norms are its laws, and thus makes the law *determinable*. Making the law determinate in this sense would be an *ontological* function of the Rule of Recognition, while making the law determinable would be an *epistemic* function. The key point here is that on either interpretation, the Rule of Recognition may appear to be neither power conferring nor duty imposing.
21. In saying that the Rule of Recognition purports to impose a duty on officials to evaluate conduct in the light of those norms that satisfy the conditions set forth in a Rule of Recognition, I mean to include norms immediately valid under the rule as well as norms that are not immediately valid under the rule, but to which officials are directed by the immediately valid norms.
22. The idea of legal authority is, for a positivist, tied up with the concept of a rule. Understanding the possibility of legal authority in terms of an authorizing rule and not just free-standing criteria of legality enables us to explain the concept of legal authority in terms of rules; and to do so in a way that creates no additional conceptual problems.
23. Though the objection is sometimes formulated this way, it is not clear that, as a formal matter, A's being partly constitutive of B makes it objectionable to explain some feature of B by appealing to A. There need be nothing objectionable about an explanation of that form—though of course not every explanation like that will be a good one. The present objection is most charitably understood as asserting that Hart offers a bad explanation of this form—not that this is a bad form of explanation.
24. Hart's introduction of the internal point of view is one of the great contributions *The Concept of Law* makes to legal philosophy. But this notion has also been a tremendous source of confusion. I try to sort through some of this confusion in "The Internal Point of View" [essay on file with the author].
25. The existence of the additional reason is apparent if we consider how it can affect my motivations (that is, adopting the rule might strengthen my will to do what I already have good reasons to do).

26. I am grateful to Christopher Kutz for suggesting this interpretation of the internal point of view along Gibbardian lines.
27. In saying that law is normative, one is saying that the language of the law is the language of obligation, right, duty, privilege and so on. An account of the law's normativity must at a minimum make this fact about law intelligible. In claming that the language of law is the language of "ought," one is not thereby committed to a certain view of the *nature* of the legal "ought"; nothing about whether it is a moral "ought," a prudential "ought," or some other kind altogether. One illuminating way to read Hart's objection to Austin is to see him as claiming that Austin's theory—which reduces law to power, habit, and command—lacks the resources to make intelligible the appropriateness of the normative vocabulary of the law; that it lacks the resources to make out distinctions that are central to legal practice, for example, between being obligated and being obliged. In contrast, Hart claims, an analysis in terms of rules and an internal point of view has the resources adequate to make the deployment of the normative language of law intelligible. The concepts of obligation, authority, right and duty make sense in the language of rules; and the internal point of view signals acceptance or commitment to rules as legitimate. That is why I am inclined to view the primary function of the internal point of view in Hart's theory as *epistemic.* It is a reliable indicator that individuals treat the law as reason giving. For Hart, it indicates the existence of norm-governed behavior, and thus renders the use of the normative language of law intelligible.

Hart's commentators have demanded more, however, of the internal point of view. They have read Hart as claiming not just that the internal point of view is a mark of law's normativity that helps us explain the appropriateness of the distinctions drawn in law between, for example, being obliged and being obligated; but that the internal point of view is the *source* of that distinction. Social rules obligate because they are accepted from the internal point of view. If this is Hart's argument, they claim, it is a bad one. Believing one is obligated does not make one obligated. It should be clear that I, for one, doubt that Hart ever claimed or meant to claim that the internal point of view turns a habit into an obligation.

Those who wish to saddle Hart with this obviously bad argument make either of two moves in response. Either they just reject his account outright, or if they are more sympathetic, they reinterpret him. Instead of explaining how social rules of Recognition can obligate, they take Hart to be providing a social scientific account of the existence conditions for a legal system. On this reading, Hart is claiming that a legal system exists when a group of individuals—officials—believe that they are under an obligation to apply certain criteria of legality. Hart's answer to this question, his friends suggest, may be wrong, incomplete or less than fully satisfying—but at least it is not fatuous.

It may well be that among Hart's projects is to provide a social scientific account of the existence conditions of a legal system; but I doubt that Hart should be read as claiming that among those conditions is that officials must believe they are obligated to apply certain criteria for assessing conduct. Even if Hart did not think the internal point of view explained how social rules can obligate, he did believe, I have argued, that the internal point of view could figure in an explanation of how social rules could be reasons for acting. Whether the account I defend is also Hart's view is neither here nor there. It is consistent with, and of a piece with Hart's jurisprudence.

In my view, the internal point of view plays several roles. It helps make intelligible the normative discourse of law and is thus a reliable indicator of an "ought," and thereby help make intelligible the aptness of the normative language of law. It is an existence condition of social rules and, a fortiori, of the Rule of Recognition. Finally, and most importantly, as I argue above, it is part of the explanation of how social rules can be reasons.

28. I am extremely grateful to Ken Himma for impressing this point on me. Much of the discussion that follows has benefited greatly from his insightful thoughts on the relationship between duties and the internal point of view.
29. Thus, the familiar objection that by conceiving of the rule of Recognition as a coordination convention one is committed thereby to viewing law as a solution to a coordination problem is shown to rest on a confusion.
30. As many readers will know, I have previously defended the view that the Rule of Recognition is plausibly analyzed as a coordination convention. I was convinced of the inadequacy of such an account by Scott Shapiro, who also suggested the alternative account of the Rule of Recognition sketched in this essay.
31. Michael E. Bratman, "Shared Cooperative Activity," *The Philosophical Review*, Vol. 101, No. 2 (April 1992) and "Shared Intention," *Ethics* 104 (October 1993): 97–113
32. The argument that follows was heavily influenced by Scott Shapiro, who suggested that it might be illuminating to think of the Rule of Recognition as a Shared Cooperative Activity in Bratman's sense. Shapiro develops this idea far beyond my limited purposes here. I introduce the idea to make intelligible the normative structure of the practice of officials and to provide a philosophical grounding for several of the claims I have made elsewhere concerning the conventionality of the Rule of Recognition—in particular, that the rule can be conventional yet controversial, and that controversy regarding either its content or application can be resolvable by substantive moral argument.
33. Bratman, "Shared Cooperative Activity" 328.
34. Gerald Postema and I have also made this error.
35. Michael Bratman, "Shared Intention."
36. Bratman, "Shared Intentions" 107.
37. Bratman, "Shared Intentions" 99.
38. *Ibid.*
39. *Ibid.*
40. *Ibid.*

41. Kenneth Einar Himma, "Inclusive Legal Positivism" in Jules Coleman and Scott Shapiro eds, *The Oxford Handbook on Jurisprudence and Legal Philosophy* (Oxford University Press, forthcoming 2002).
42. I am grateful to Michael Bratman for his comments on a previous draft of this section of the essay, and to Scott Shapiro for formulating many of the ideas pertaining to the Rule of Recognition that have been outlined in skeletal form here.
43. I take this issue up again in more detail in The Practice of Principle Chapter 11.
44. The objection is that if the proper interpretation of the Rule's content depends on moral argument, the Rule itself has to be a moral rule, not a conventional one.
45. See "Negative and Positive Positivism" Journal of Legal Studies Vol. 11, no. 1 (Jan. 1982) 139–164.
46. See Andrei Marmor, "Legal Conventionalism" in Legal Theory, Vol. 4, no. 4, (Dec. 1998) 509–31.

15

PHILOSOPHICAL ISSUES, 11
Social, Political, and Legal Philosophy, 2001

Egalitarianism and the Problem of Tort Liability*

Michael L. Corrado

1. Introduction.

Where should the egalitarian stand on the question of tort liability? Should she prefer strict liability to negligence? Or should she abandon both and support a system of social insurance that ignores questions of responsibility? The egalitarian I am thinking of here is one who qualifies her preference for equality with a principle of responsibility. She believes that the community has an obligation to compensate an individual for his losses, but only for those losses he is not responsible for, losses that cannot be attributed to his voluntary and knowing risk-taking. In other words, he must be compensated only for those losses that are *brute luck*.[1] We may call this responsibility-egalitarianism.[2]

Tort law is, on the face of it at least, a problem for the egalitarian. There is a relatively strong case to be made that American tort law, in its current form, promotes the aim of economic efficiency, in particular that brand of efficiency known as *wealth maximization* (Posner 1972, 29), and the aim of maximizing wealth is inconsistent with the principles of egalitarianism. An action or institution is said to be wealth maximizing when it leads to a greater satisfaction of preferences than any alternative action or institution—the intensity of a preference being measured by the actor's willingness and ability to pay for the satisfaction. Efficiency in this version raises the same problems for the egalitarian that utilitarianism raises, and more. Indeed, as I will try to show, tort law in its present form has a tendency to redistribute wealth from the less well-off to those better-off, to force people to invest their resources in commercial enterprises without compensation or return, and to permit actors to treat potential victims with differing levels of respect.

Of course, the egalitarian might want to ignore those flaws in the existing system. If she is concerned about productivity, if she is concerned about inefficiencies that will reduce the surplus to be distributed, then she might recognize discrete areas of the law as properly taking the reduction of inefficiency as their sole or primary goal. She might do so in spite of the fact that she considers that some form of egalitarianism ought to be the *overall* aim of the law. Amartya Sen says:

> The need for incentives may be rightly seen as including an element of blackmail. It would typically include the claims to higher reward for the better endowed and the more productive, who can decide to do less of those of their activities that benefit others, unless they receive more 'compensation'. If this connection does actually work this way, then an uncompromising pursuit of equality may be self-defeating. Blackmail or not, the incentive connections must be taken into account by someone trying to promote equality. (Sen 1996, 9, 15).

So the egalitarian might actually prefer the existing system.

Still, that is something we cannot know until we have examined the possible alternatives. As I will try to show, if there is an alternative more attractive to the egalitarian than the current system, then it must, like the current system, be a system of negligence liability. Neither strict liability nor social insurance can claim to be more compatible than negligence with egalitarian principles—at least not the principles of responsibility-egalitarianism. It is precisely the egalitarian's strong focus on responsibility that rules out these two alternatives. For an egalitarianism concerned with responsibility, tort law would have an actor compensating his victim for all and only those losses he was responsible for—that is, for all and only those losses that he could reasonably have avoided. But if this principle of negligence is not going to collapse into the efficiency understanding of negligence, it must be because the notion of reasonableness involved is different from the current, efficiency-promoting notion of reasonableness. The aim, then, is to explore the idea of reasonableness, to see whether it can be made to support a principle of liability which, while friendly toward egalitarian principles, is nevertheless suitable for negligence liability.

2. Tort Law.

Tort law, or at least that part of it that has to do with accidents, is about shifting losses. The rule of liability, generally, is negligence. That means that you will be responsible for the loss someone else suffers only if it is due to your negligence. If you exercise the proper level of care but your activity nevertheless results in an injury to another, then the victim must bear her own loss. There are some exceptions, isolated areas in which the rule is strict liability. If you are engaged in blasting a roadway, for example, and as a result of your blasting someone is injured, you will be liable whether or not you took an appropriate level of care. But for the most part you can injure others and avoid compensating them as long as you have taken that level of care that the law requires of you. If you are driving carefully and injure someone, you do not have to pay: you are innocent and it is unfair, according to the law, to make an innocent person pay for an injury that could not be avoided with ordinary care.

Of course the victim may also be innocent; but the law requires the innocent victim to bear losses caused by an equally innocent—that is, nonnegligent—injurer. Negligence is a rule which, by comparison with strict liability, protects the injurer. The saying is that as between an innocent injurer and an innocent victim, the loss should lie where it fell. But why is that so? Why should the loss not go to the one who caused it? In continental European countries, for example, the rule in traffic accidents is strict liability. Indeed, when the legislature in France failed to respond to the heavy damage imposed by industry in the nineteenth century and the automobile at the beginning of the twentieth century, the French courts took it upon themselves to reconstruct the rule of liability under the Civil Code.[3] Or why not say that as between two innocent parties neither should bear the loss, and that somehow the community is responsible for faultless losses?

Some writers argue that the rule of negligence is the kind of accommodation required to make life in a complex society possible. It permits greater freedom of action and greater productivity by permitting a greater reciprocal imposition of reasonable risks. Someone who, through her carelessness, imposes an unreasonable risk and as a result injures another must pay compensation; but if her behavior creates only reasonable risks, she will be insulated from liability. In this way we can move about in a crowded world knowing that we are safe from liability so long as we take the appropriate amount of care in our activities, and do not expose others to risks that we are not willing to undergo ourselves. If we had to bear the consequences of every risk we created, no matter how small or reasonable, no one could afford to take any action at all.

However romantic this explanation of the function of tort law, it simply is not supportable. Recent work makes clear that, on the same assumption of rationality that the current negligence formulation depends upon, actors would take more or less the same level of care if they were subjected to strict liability for all their actions.[4] (Landes and Posner 1987, 64–73). For if they were forced to pay for the consequences of all their actions, they would perform only those actions that imposed reasonable risks—that is, risks to which they were willing to subject their own property. What makes those risks reasonable is that they would be worth it in the end; the actor would benefit in spite of having to pay for the accident costs created by the activity.

So although the rule in accident law is negligence, it does not have to be. Moreover, the existing rule of negligence carries with it a particular understanding of just what negligence is, an understanding refined in recent decades by a particular economic approach to accident law. And so the further question is whether that understanding is an unavoidable part of the rule of negligence. That means that there are two sorts of questions the egalitarian might raise about tort law: First, should there be a rule of negligence at all? And second, if there should be a rule of negligence, should negligence be understood in the particular way in which it is in fact currently understood in the courts? Let's begin by looking at the current formulation of negligence.

A. Learned Hand and the Economic Interpretation. Negligence law has always been a matter of balancing. The Romans considered the injurer to be faultless if he was engaged in an activity that was normal in its time and place (throwing javelins on a military practice field), but not if the activity was unusual and thus would create risks that were harder for the victim to avoid than for the actor to prevent. Germanic law, of which our common law is a descendant, attached liability to the *act*, and was not concerned about fault. The common law, thus, was a little slower to protect injurers with a rule of negligence. Negligence liability came fully into its own in this country and in Britain only in the nineteenth century (while strict liability was coming into its own in France) largely due, it is said, to the sympathy of common law judges for the vulnerability of newly created industries. The rationale developed by legal commentators was explicitly a cost-benefit sort of thing. Terry, for example, proposed such an understanding of what negligence meant in 1915. For behavior to constitute negligence, he said, it must raise an unreasonable risk:

> The reasonableness of a given risk may depend upon the following five factors:
>
> 1. The magnitude of the risk. A risk is more likely to be unreasonable the greater it is.
>
> 2. The value or importance of that which is exposed to the risk, which is the object that the law desires to protect, ...
>
> 3. [The value or importance of the risk-taker's own object (the collateral object) in engaging in the risky conduct.]
>
> 4. The probability that the collateral object will be attained by the conduct which involves risk to the principal...[and]...the probability that the collateral object would not have been attained without taking the risk. (Terry 1915, 42–43).

Thus Learned Hand's introduction of his famous formula for assessing negligence in the *Carroll Towing Case* was simply a formal recognition of the direction in which tort law was headed. What Hand did in that case was to make the judgment of negligence depend upon a comparison of the cost of preventing the accident with the cost of the accident itself, discounted by the beforehand likelihood the accident would occur given the injurer's activity. In other words, if I do something that creates a ten percent chance that someone will suffer a hundred dollar loss, and if I can do something to prevent that loss for less than ten dollars, then it will be negligent of me not to have prevented it. If the loss occurs, I must pay the hundred dollars to compensate the victim. But if I can prevent it only by doing something that will cost more than ten dollars, then I may proceed without paying the cost of prevention, and I will not be negligent; and if an accident occurs because of my activity, I will not have to compensate the victim. According to Hand, if the cost of care is less than the cost of the harm that might be caused discounted by the probability of the harm occurring, and I do not pay the cost of care, then I am negligent.[5]

So suppose, for example, that I own a railroad that runs through a series of cornfields, and every time I run a steam engine through those cornfields I create a ten percent chance of setting one cornfield on fire and causing $500 worth of destruction. And suppose that I can prevent such destruction entirely by purchasing a device that costs me $20 each time I run an engine through those fields. Then if I fail to purchase the device and end up causing a fire, I am responsible and must compensate the farmer the full $500 for his loss: it would have cost less to prevent the accident than the discounted cost of the accident itself, which was $50 (10% of $500). But if it would cost me $60 on each such trip to purchase such a preventive device, then the device would not be cost-effective, and I would not be negligent if I did not purchase it. If I ended up causing a fire, I would not have to compensate the farmer whose field I destroyed. In a seminal study Richard Posner argued that in fact the negligence cases of the nineteenth century could be explained on the assumption that judges were in fact acting upon this principle. (Posner 1972, 29).[6]

Though in Hand's formulation that was all there was to it, the calculation turns out to be a little more complex in its implementation. For one thing, it is marginal costs and losses that are at issue. Since there are usually varying levels of accident prevention that an actor can purchase, with corresponding levels of reduction in accident losses, the real comparison is between the cost of the next increment of care and the corresponding reduction in losses. For another thing, the victim might also purchase accident prevention, and might purchase it for less than it costs the injurer, so that there is a question about who, in a particular situation, is the appropriate party to pay for prevention. This translates into the tort law issue of contributory or comparative negligence.

The idea is that in the long run if people pay for accident prevention only when it costs less than the accidents it is supposed to prevent, the cost of accidents will be minimized.[7] Negligence interpreted in this way promotes efficiency, or is supposed to. There are a number of propositions that have to be accepted on the way to this conclusion: that the way to promote efficiency through tort law is by minimizing accident costs; that getting people to compare costs and benefits, and to take only cost-effective measures of prevention, will minimize accident costs; and that the way to get people to act in that way is by imposing the negligence rule in its Hand-formulation. This last is the assumption of rationality, which is often criticized and is probably false, but which need not concern us here.[8] The first two propositions have to do with a particular definition of efficiency; more about that in a moment. Beyond all this there is the implicit claim that the law, including the common law, *ought* to be efficient. The assumption here is that judges work not to do the right thing between the parties before them, but to find rules under which they can operate to benefit society as a whole; that it is not only legislators but also judges who must be concerned about questions of policy.

For judges and lawyers schooled in the Hand approach, efficiency means wealth-maximization. That, in its turn, means maximizing the total satisfaction of preferences, measured by the willingness and ability of individuals to have those preferences satisfied. If there is some commodity for which I am willing to pay $5 and you are willing to pay $10, then your preference for the thing is twice as intense as mine, and more value—more wealth—is created and society as a whole is better-off if the commodity goes to you rather than to me. When all commodities go to those who value them most, wealth is maximized. This version of efficiency would be attractive to a utilitarian, provided she believed that utility consisted in the satisfaction of preferences, that the quantity of the preference satisfied could be measured by willingness and ability to pay, and that the value or wealth measured by a dollar was the same for all, regardless of the size of an individual's holdings.

B. Egalitarianism and the Hand Rule. But the existing system of negligence law, thus understood, has certain redistributive tendencies that should bother the egalitarian: it tends to redistribute resources from the less well-off to the more well-off. This tendency has three different aspects: it shows a *lack of equal concern in compensating losses*; it shows a *lack of equal concern in imposing losses*; and it incorporates an element of *forced investment* in surplus-generating activities, with no return to the investor. To illustrate these points, let's begin with an example involving the sort of redistribution in question.

Suppose that Jones has a choice between two activities that may cause harm. The two activities are very much alike, and aside from the liability question Jones is otherwise indifferent between them. But the first, let's call it A, may cause harm to Poorman's property, and the second, call it B, may cause harm instead to Richman's property. The same *probability* of the harm occurring exists in the two cases: the probability that A will harm Poorman is identical to the probability that B will harm Richman. Altogether Jones has three choices: She may take appropriate care to avoid causing harm to either property; she may fail to take care and engage in activity A, putting Poorman's property at risk; or she may fail to take care and engage in activity B, putting Richman's property at risk. Taking the appropriate level of care would cost her $20; the projected damage to Richman's property, discounted by the probability of the damage occurring, is $30; and the projected damage to Poorman's property, discounted in the same way, would be $10. The benefits to her are the same, before accident costs or the cost of prevention is taken into account. What does the law say that Jones ought to do?

The harm that Jones could inflict on Poorman is very similar to the harm that she could inflict on Richman. What accounts for the difference in the projected loss is the difference in the value of the property damaged. Richman is relatively well-off, and his property is worth more; Poorman is less well-off, and his property is worth less. It may be, for example, that Poorman owns a Ford and Richman owns a Lexus, and Jones' choice is between endangering Poorman's automobile and endangering Richman's automobile. The Hand interpretation of the negligence standard gives Jones clear directions: She should subject Poorman to the risk of harm rather than either taking care to prevent the harm or imposing the risk on Richman. If she imposes the risk on Richman without taking care, then she is negligent and will have to pay if harm occurs. That would of course be foolish; over time she will pay more in damages ($30) than she would have paid for prevention ($20). And she could of course pay to prevent the harm, but that course will seem foolish as well. For if she imposes the risk on Poorman (that is, without paying for prevention) she will not be liable under the Hand rule if harm occurs: Care costs more ($20) than the expected accident cost ($10). Thus if she goes ahead and imposes the risk on Poorman, she will neither have to pay the cost of prevention nor compensate for the loss to Poorman if it occurs. And so that is what the law will tell her to do, if efficiency is the rule.[9]

We may call this the problem of environmental elitism.[10] Where the value of property enters into the negligence calculation, the negligence rule systematically favors the wealthy, and it tends to shift wealth in a regressive way from poor to rich. It is true that if Jones is engaged in commercial activity Poorman may benefit from it, but then so will Richman—and probably to a greater extent. Poorman is financing part of Jones' activity and is getting nothing in return. If there is a cost to permitting mutual imposition of risk, then in this case Poorman bears that cost. I am not arguing that this is the result in every case; much of tort law is neutral in terms of redistribution. But there are a number of sorts of cases in which there is this sort of tendency to redistribute from poor to rich, and there are no compensating sorts of cases in which redistribution goes in the opposite direction. There are several classes of cases in which tort law obviously realizes the redistributive tendency, including nuisance cases,[11] but the threat is there whenever an actor can choose between courses of action that affect groups of people in different economic classes. The effect was especially clear in the compensation of workers for injuries suffered on the job, before the introduction of workers' compensation rules. When risking harm to workers was an industry's cheapest alternative, workers were subjected to risk.[12] Had the risk been imposed on members of another economic class, where the threatened economic loss was greater, the outcome in many cases would have been different.

The egalitarian has got to want a different outcome in cases of this sort. It ought not to be the case that the market value of Poorman's property can determine whether Jones ought to take care. The problem here is the result, at least in part, of treating losses of the same monetary amount as equal in value. For then it turns out that since Poorman's resources are worth less, society is better-off in terms of *the total expenditure on resources* if Jones takes Poorman's resources rather than Richman's.[13]

1. Lack of Equal Concern in Compensating Losses. The example illustrates all three of the problems mentioned. Take the discrepancy in compensating losses. If Jones chooses activity B, threatening the better-off class of victims, she will have to either take care or risk paying damages. But if she chooses activity A, threatening the worse-off, she will have to do neither. If the wealthier are harmed, in this scenario, they will be compensated; if the poorer are harmed, they will not be. The rule demonstrates a lack of equal concern in compensation. Compensation for some victims has to be taken into account; compensation for others does not; and the difference lies in the different value of the victims' property.

2. Lack of Equal Concern in Imposing Losses. From that lack of concern follows another. Because compensating poorer victims does not have to be taken into account, Jones is not indifferent between activity A and activity B. She will systematically choose the activity that imposes losses on Poorman and on the less well-off generally. There is therefore a lack of equal concern in imposing losses.

Notice that these are not the same issue. The first problem, but not the second, can be solved by changing the liability rule to universal strict liability. If the victim is always compensated, then there is no lack of equality in compensation: all are compensated the full amount of their losses. (The results of accidents would then always be Pareto superior—on the usual assumptions of rationality and information.) But the same victims would be subjected to the threat of harm and the disruption that goes with it.

3. Forced Investment. Suppose that the activities that Jones is considering, A and B, are commercial activities. The cheapest alternative for Jones is to risk injury to Poorman, and so that is what he does. If Poorman was *not* to be compensated for his loss, then he would be helping to finance Jones' activity. If Jones' activity resulted in a product to be purchased by both Poorman and Richman, for example, Poorman would have borne part of the cost of the production of that item. But things are not that different in the scenario in which Poorman is compensated. Jones has used Poorman's resources without Poorman's consent, and if injury results he need only pay the market value of those resources in compensation.[14] Thus Poorman has been forced to invest in Jones' project by being subjected to the risk of harm, and for his trouble receives only his investment back, and no part of the surplus created by Jones' activity. (That is not quite true: If he and Richman both purchase the resulting product, they will find the price reduced in proportion to Poorman's contribution. But that is the extent of the return on his investment.) So in that sense he is still helping to fund Jones' activity.

This arrangement denies Poorman a say in how his resources are to be used, and it gives him no part of the surplus that he has helped to create. If the risk is to an automobile that Poorman owns, then Jones may take the automobile in an accident, and compensate only at the market rate for automobiles. On the other hand, if Jones had been forced to negotiate beforehand for the car, he would have been prepared to offer something over market value for the right to acquire just that car. The inequity is starkest when it is Poorman's physical integrity that is involved. Suppose the injury in question is to Poorman's body. As a result of the injury, he will be unable to work. If there is appropriate compensation under the present system, Poorman will be compensated for his lost wages and for other associated losses. Compare compensation for lost wages with what Poorman might have demanded if Jones had approached him beforehand and asked him to give up his right to work for a living. If Jones' enterprise had required that, Poorman would consider himself entitled to some part of the profit if he agreed to the deal, and surely he would be entitled to ask for more than lost wages. Indeed, if Jones had approached him beforehand looking for that sort of investment, Jones herself would have been prepared to share the profits. The question is why it is not so if the investment is made without Poorman's consent.

Under the rule of negligence, then, the potential victim loses out on the benefits his resources are capable of producing, and the egalitarian cannot be happy with that. In one way or another it is precisely the surplus created by cooperative activity that the egalitarian claims must be used to promote equality. Everyone has a certain basic entitlement—which may vary with the individual's ability to convert resources into welfare—but beyond that what is created is considered common property. It may be divided up to create equal opportunities for welfare, or a certain inequality may be necessary to increase production to everyone's advantage. The community may confer on Jones the right to keep some of the surplus he has created: without that right he may have no incentive to undertake either A or B, and everyone in society may be worse-off because of it. But there is no reason that Poorman must do his part unrewarded, and no reason why he may not insist on a share for his investment. We may see that share as inducement to support productivity by permitting Jones to subject him to the risk. To treat him otherwise is to deny him the equal respect to which the egalitarian insists he is entitled.

C. Egalitarianism and Strict Liability. Is the solution a rule of strict liability? Even with strict liability it is cheaper for Jones to risk harm to Poorman than to either take care or impose the risk on Richman. If she engages in A, threatening harm to Poorman, then one time in ten she will damage Poorman's property, which will cost her $100. Taking care ten times would cost her $200; ten repetitions of B, threatening harm to Richman, would in the end cost her $300. Poorman is the preferred victim, even though he must be paid if injured. A society that permits its rule of negligence to discriminate in that way does not show equal concern in imposing losses. Strict liability offers a solution for inequality in compensation, but no solution for this second sort of inequality.

There are two other reasons why a rule of universal strict liability is not the egalitarian answer. The first is that the egalitarian cannot support strict liability in general. One of the basic principles of the sort of egalitarianism we are considering is that someone must bear a loss if and only if that person is responsible for the loss. But causation is not enough for responsibility; if it were, then any catastrophe that resulted from any choice an individual made would be considered her responsibility, and the egalitarian would saddle her with the cost of it. Suppose, for example, that someone is struck by lightning in the park and disabled. Had he not been in the park he would not have been struck by lightning, and so his being there contributed causally to his injury. Yet the egalitarian believes (or should believe) it wrong to say that he was responsible for his injury, and to make him bear the cost. Mere causation is not enough; whatever responsibility means, it means more than that. Under strict liability, the injurer pays for injuries she causes, whether or not she is responsible for them. Where both parties are innocent, where neither is responsible for the injury, neither must pay. That seems to be the appropriate outcome under an egalitarian scheme. What then? Who will bear the loss? The answer must be that in cases of this sort the community will bear the cost; compensation for the injured party must come out of the general fund.

D. Egalitarianism and Social Insurance. The question, then, is whether the egalitarian ought to dismiss tort law altogether as an instrument for allocating losses and allow all tort injuries to be compensated out of the general fund, or whether there is some way of modifying the principles of tort law to meet the concerns of the egalitarian. There is plenty of reason to think that the tort system ought to be done away with in favor of a system of social insurance; but that is not a move that follows from the principles of egalitarianism.[15] The egalitarian wants to hold people accountable for the losses they are responsible for, while compensating them for the losses for which they are not responsible. When someone is responsible for someone else's loss, he must be held accountable for that loss; he and not society must pay for it. There must be a mechanism for deciding on responsibility, then, even if liability is covered by insurance, and in the end the principles that govern that mechanism will be principles of tort law. On the assumption that what we are looking for is an egalitarian institution rather than one that merely serves egalitarian purposes (Arneson 2000, 13–14), the egalitarian cannot reject tort law, and cannot accept the general application of a principle of strict liability. But the existing negligence principle, embodying as it does the development of an efficiency standard, raises significant problems for the egalitarian. Where does she go from here?

3. An Egalitarian Rule for Tort Law?

The fact of the matter, then, is that at least in the case of tort law the law is not neutral with respect to egalitarian principles.

Of course, tort law is not an instrument for *creating* equality. Instead the egalitarian must look for a rule of liability that will prevent tort law from undermining equality, just as the economist looks for a rule that will prevent inefficiencies. Here are the features an egalitarian principle must have: The rule must not be a rule of universal strict liability; in addition to compensating victims for losses they are not responsible for, it must acknowledge the responsibility of individuals for the losses for which they are in fact responsible. It should also reflect the fact that the same losses may involve the loss of different levels of utility, or different levels of opportunity, for different individuals. It should not be regressive—that is, it should not tend to redistribute wealth from poor to rich—and it should not force individuals to invest in commercial activity with no promise of a share in the surplus. And finally the rule must not unnecessarily destroy incentives, either the incentive to take appropriate levels of care, or incentives for reasonable increases in production.

A. Self-inflicted harms. Let's begin by considering how we might decide on an individual's responsibility for her own losses, when she smashes up her car, for example, or suffers a gambling loss.[16] Something very much like the Hand rule sometimes makes sense in this context. If we are egalitarians, we will want to compensate the actor for losses due to "reasonable" risks without destroying the incentive for the actor to avoid foolish (unreasonable) risks; and at the same time the rule should not deprive the actor of the freedom to make foolish choices so long as she pays for them with her own resources. Suppose she took a foolish risk with her money and lost it. We would not want to compensate her. But on the other hand she takes a risk every time she leaves the house; suppose she leaves the house and is struck by lightning, for example. She could have avoided the risk by staying in the house; there was some infinitesimal probability that she would be hit by lightning, and she would probably have acknowledged it if we had raised the issue. But we would not want to consider the risk unreasonable or the loss foolish. In some sense or other the risk would have been reasonable, and the egalitarian would want to compensate her for her loss.

One plausible interpretation of "reasonable" in this individual context, perhaps the only plausible interpretation, is the Hand interpretation: the risk is reasonable if the probable (discounted) harm is less expensive than any form of prevention of the harm, including forgoing the activity.[17] To say that our actor's risk was reasonable is to say that the risk of harm when leaving the house is so small that the probable loss is much smaller than the cost either of remaining at home or purchasing the extensive protection that would be necessary. And if the risk was reasonable we will not hold her responsible for the consequences. To say that the cost of preventing the harm is greater than the cost of the harm itself is to say that the cost of the harm is inevitable, and there is nothing the actor can do to avoid it. She either suffers that lesser amount, or expends that amount and more to prevent the harm. Holding her responsible for the harm in cases in which the risk is reasonable, therefore, is holding her responsible for harm she cannot avoid, or at least for costs she cannot avoid. We might think of this as a kind of Hand rule of personal responsibility.[18]

But there are other considerations; the question of responsibility is not merely a question about costs and benefits. Suppose our actor was given the opportunity to make a bet: She could invest $10 with a chance of winning $100. If her chance of winning were one in twenty, we might consider the bet unreasonable, and the resulting loss, if she lost, foolish. If her chance of winning were one in three, on the other hand, she ought not to pass up the bet. It is a reasonable risk and, if she loses, the loss will be not be foolish. But I cannot imagine that anyone would suppose that she ought to be compensated in either case. We would not want to compensate people for gambling losses, even when the wagers they make are very good ones. And yet the structure of the wager might appear to be precisely the same as the structure of a risk that will be compensated. What precisely is the difference?

The answer, I suspect, lies in the object that is put at risk. Roughly speaking, and as a first approximation, a loss due to the individual's free choice should be considered for compensation only if the loss takes the individual's holdings below some level bearing some appropriate relationship to the level of resources the egalitarian feels everyone is entitled to—whether it is an equal share of the surplus, or merely some level of sufficient resources, depending upon the egalitarian. The idea is this: In those gambles that we feel ought not to be compensated it would seem to be the case that the individual's risk is limited to something he can "afford to lose," in a sense to be explained in terms of the individual's basic entitlement. The gambler does not put his estate or his life at risk, typically. He bets $10 on a lottery, or $100 on a ball game, or $1000 in the stock market.[19] His risk is limited to his bet, the sum of money he puts up. So perhaps we can say this: Compensation is due for a loss that follows from a reasonable risk *only where* what was risked was something that the bettor could not afford to lose. For example, what I put at risk (however slight the risk) when I step into the elements is my bodily integrity or my life. If I lose the risk, if I am struck by lightning, and the risk was reasonable, then I ought to be compensated. But if I risk a fixed sum betting on sports or investing in the stock market, then (pathological cases aside) however reasonable the risk my loss should not be compensated.

There is, I think, some intuitive force behind this distinction. The question is whether we can get any clearer about what it means to be able to afford to lose some sum of resources. Does it mean that having lost that sum the individual will not be absolutely destitute? Does it mean instead that the individual might still maintain a moderately full and satisfying life, even without the sum he has lost? Or does it mean that the loss of that sum will affect the individual's lifestyle hardly at all? Without attempting to be too precise at this point, I would suggest that the notion of affordability might be a function of whatever notion of equality, or sufficiency, or priority the egalitarian might have, independent of questions of responsibility. Either the individual can afford to lose whatever, by the egalitarian standard, he is not entitled to as what we might call his basic allotment; or what he can afford to lose is some function of that basic allotment. Beyond his allotment, questions of reasonableness (or responsibility) do not enter the picture. Whatever he puts at risk, he stands to lose. It is only when he puts part of that allotment at risk that reasonableness comes into play: he will be compensated only if the risk was reasonable.

On one side of this line fall (or are meant to fall) risks reasonably taken to maintain a living wage and to otherwise take advantage of the opportunities available for a decent life. On the other side fall (or are meant to fall) not only traditional forms of gambling, where fixed sums of money are at risk, but also equity investment, and perhaps commercial activity in general (however reasonable) where risk is limited to a fixed amount (as in a limited liability corporation), an amount the investor can afford to lose. I acknowledge that the distinction based upon affordability is a crude one, and at best will have to be refined. But I think that the cases it is meant to divide really are different and that some distinction of this sort will have to be found in the end. The division between the cases is significant, in ways that will become apparent.

I will use the phrase "aggressive resource investment" to designate those cases in which the individual puts up sums of money or other resources he can afford to lose in the hope of making a profit. Making use of the distinction between aggressive investment and other sorts of risk taking, however we denominate it, we might formulate the following rule governing responsibility for losses in the one-party case as a rule the egalitarian might want to accept:

> A party is responsible for a loss she has suffered, and will not be compensated, if:
> (1) the loss was due to the party taking an unreasonable risk; or
> (2) the loss was due to an aggressive resource investment.

Thus, any time a party engages in an unreasonable risk, where no risk to anyone else is involved in the calculation, that party must take the consequences; she could have avoided the risk by taking the proper care. And here, in the one-party case, we give reasonableness its cost-benefit meaning; whatever we may think of the Hand definition of reasonableness in two-party cases, it seems perfectly adequate for assessing reasonableness in the one-party case. On the other hand, where the loss is due to a risk that constitutes aggressive resource investment, it will not be compensated. The person who suffers losses due to the risks associated with the ordinary activities of life, in which the resources involved are not employed in a profit-making venture, will have some of those losses compensated—those that are the consequence of reasonable risks. The person who gambles and loses, on the other hand, will not be compensated for the loss no matter how attractive the odds were; and the person who invests in a commercial enterprise for a share of the surplus will not have the costs that arise from risks associated with that enterprise compensated, however reasonable the risk may have been, provided that her investment is something that is not part of her basic allotment.

I am more confident about the first of these two points. Ignoring for the time being epistemic questions and questions about the difference between subjective and objective probabilities, there is nothing inegalitarian about compensating only reasonable choices.[20] Losses from reasonable choices are unavoidable, and by compensating only reasonable choices we tend to discourage avoidable losses without depriving an individual of the right to make those choices if she is willing to suffer the consequences. The second point, on the other hand, is much less clear, but it opens up areas that are worth exploring, and I will follow out its implications in what follows. I'm sure there is much more to be said about self-inflicted losses, but what I would like to do now is to explore the implications of these insights for accident law and the two-party case.

B. Harm to Others. The question for accident law is when a person should be held responsible for the losses they inflict upon others. Following the line set out in connection with self-inflicted harm, we should begin by exploring the possibility that commercial activity, or aggressive resource investment in general, should be treated differently from other sorts of activity.

1. Aggressive Resource Investment. Suppose, then, that Harris enters into a business that requires her to engage in a certain activity, and suppose further that the investment is one that she can afford to lose, by whatever egalitarian standard is in play. By engaging in that activity, Harris causes harm to Smith. Is Harris liable to Smith for the harm? Starting up her business is like entering a lottery for Harris; she undertakes certain risks in the hope of making a profit, of gathering in some of the surplus that exists. We have already seen that Harris would be held responsible for the losses she suffered if she entered into a lottery; it is hard to imagine an alternative outcome in that situation. And I have suggested that if she went into business she would have to be responsible for the costs she experienced in the course of running the business—but in that case we were thinking of the ordinary costs such as labor and materials, not of liability for harm or injury to another person. What about the injury to Smith?

Assuming that Smith, the victim, is not himself responsible for his injury, there are (for the egalitarian) only two possible answers to the question of compensation: Either Harris is responsible and must compensate Smith, or Harris is not responsible and the community must compensate. Smith must, in any event, be compensated for a loss that was not his responsibility. Under the Hand rule responsibility would be a question of reasonableness, and reasonableness would be decided by balancing the benefit to Harris against the harm to Smith. In the one-party case we saw that reasonableness was not appropriate for deciding responsibility where aggressive surplus-seeking activity was in question. The egalitarian might reach the same result here in the two-party case by reasoning in the following way: No individual is entitled to any part of the surplus generated by cooperation or trade. At best an individual might be granted some part of the surplus as an incentive for an activity that might increase the surplus. Any such grant would be a subsidy. But any such subsidy should be calculated after all other calculations have been made, including the costs of running the business, so that the question of the profitability of the enterprise and the desirability of incentives and subsidies can be kept relatively clear.

To hold Harris responsible, from this point of view, is just to chalk Smith's injury up to the enterprise Harris is running; to deny that Harris is responsible is to chalk Smith's injury up to Smith's bad luck. Although there is no essential difference from Smith's point of view, there may a considerable difference from Harris' point of view. If Harris is held responsible for the injury, then Harris will suffer financially and might be forced to go out of business. It doesn't matter whether Harris must pay damages from her own pocket and decide on her own to close down, or society pays Smith directly and closes Harris down; either way Harris has been held responsible. If Harris is not held responsible then Harris will be insulated from Smith's loss and from similar losses, and will continue to operate, even though the losses are losses to the surplus and are caused by Harris' activity, and even though Harris' activity may be a net loss for the community. The injuries caused by the enterprise ought, therefore, to be treated as costs, and Harris held responsible for Smith's injury.

Remember that in the environmental elitism case Jones chose harming Poorman over either taking care or harming Richman, and was not held responsible for the harm under the negligence standard. Holding commercial actors responsible would solve one problem, the problem of inequality in compensating losses: Jones, if a commercial actor, would be responsible for the harm to Poorman and would have to pay damages. But as we have seen it would not solve the other problem, the problem of inequality in imposing losses. Jones would still choose harming Poorman over harming Richman. (The only solution to this problem seems to lie in the calculation of damages, to which we will turn later.)

2. Nonaggressive Activity and Proportional Responsibility. Harms caused in the course of nonaggressive activity, on the other hand, ought to be treated differently. All human activity creates a certain amount of risk of harm. Some of the risk is risk of harm to the actor herself, but a substantial proportion of what we do creates a risk of harm to others. On the assumption that there is a certain basic entitlement to possess and use resources, including our own innate abilities, an entitlement that nevertheless does not confer on us the right to any surplus created by the trading of those resources, the question is whether society ever has the right to take some of that entitlement away from an individual on the ground that he is responsible for some loss to another person. The answer here, I think, must be that under some but not all conditions he may be charged with the losses that his behavior causes. If he was charged with none of them, that would mean that he was not responsible for any of the harm he caused, a possibility that simply does not square with our notion of responsibility. Surely we are responsible for the intentional harm we cause; surely we are responsible for the harm we cause through recklessness, to use the more extreme examples. On the other hand, it would not square with our notion of responsibility to hold him responsible for all harms he causes, either. Some things are due to bad luck.

It seems therefore that the answer for nonaggressive, noncommercial harms will have to be a variation on the negligence rule: responsibility and an obligation to compensate for some harms caused; no responsibility and no duty to compensate for the others. The question then is where to draw the line, whether to draw it in the same place the Hand rule draws it or somewhere else entirely. The point is both to find a reasonable dividing line for a person's responsibility for himself, and to encourage nonfoolish behavior. In the case of one-party harms the Hand rule for responsibility seemed perfectly adequate for egalitarian purposes: A person must bear those losses that it would have paid him to try to prevent, what we called foolish losses. The Hand rule's function in that setting would be to encourage rationality in our activity: injuries that befall us in spite of a wise management of our resources must be attributed to bad luck. In a sense they are unavoidable costs: to have prevented them would have cost more than the loss did, in the long run, and a cost that is unavoidable by human action is bad luck. The question now is whether that same reasoning should apply to two-party cases. If it should, then the prevailing economic version of tort liability would be perfectly adequate for noncommercial cases.

Notice first that as long as tort law damages are limited to actual harm[21] there is not much the civil law can do to get equality in the imposition of risk. Even with strict liability Jones will not take as much care to prevent harm to Poorman's property as she would take to prevent harm to her own. If prevention costs more than the expected harm, she will cause the harm and pay for that instead. No matter how responsibility is allocated, Jones will prefer Poorman as a victim. The possible solution to this problem will have to be deferred until we talk about damages.

But things are different with the issue of equal regard in compensating harms. The problem here is that the care that would be sufficient to protect Jones against having to compensate Poorman is not sufficient to protect her against having to compensate Richman. Under similar circumstances—say where Jones failed to invest the $20 in purchasing care—harm to Richman would have to be compensated, while harm to Poorman would not. If we want Jones to pay compensation to both under the same circumstances, if we want to make her liable to Poorman when and only when she would be liable to Richman, then the Hand formulation of the negligence standard will not do.

Even if Jones continues to prefer Poorman as a victim, requiring her to pay for the harm expresses a minimal sort of regard on the part of the community; and if Poorman is in fact fully compensated he is no worse-off financially than he was before the accident. The least the community can do is to require Jones to pay in this case: she ought to be liable if she did not take the sort of care of Poorman's car that she would take of her own. If the law cannot make her indifferent between Poorman and Richman, it can at least require this acknowledgment that she did not show Poorman's property the same concern she showed for her own and for Richman's property. And the way to do that would be to hold her responsible for the harm to Poorman's property unless she took the amount of care to prevent it that would be sufficient to prevent a harm to herself which was proportional, given their respective estates, to the harm she risks causing to Poorman's property. The following rule is intended to capture the idea of proportional responsibility:

> An individual is responsible for the harm his nonaggressive, noncommercial activities cause to another provided that the cost of preventing the harm would have been less than the loss of a part of his estate proportional to the part of the victim's estate threatened with destruction, discounted by the probability of the harm occurring.

In other words, if it was Jones' own car she was putting at risk, and if it would have paid her to spend a certain amount to purchase preventive measures to protect it, then she would be responsible for the harm to Poorman's car unless she paid at least up to that same amount to purchase preventive measures to protect his car. Suppose, for example, Jones' car was a new Lexus worth $50,000, and Poorman's car was a used Ford worth

$2,500. There is a one percent chance that Jones will demolish it, doing what she is doing. It would pay her to spend up to $500 to prevent a one percent chance of harm to her own car. Therefore under this rule she would be liable to Poorman unless she pays whatever it takes up to $500 to eliminate this risk of harm to Poorman.[22]

One effect of such a rule would be to segment the field of accident-causing behavior into three parts. There would be that behavior for which the injurer will not be held responsible. (This is the case where care costs more than the expected harm to either Richman (who is in the same economic situation she is) or Poorman.) The actor will go ahead and risk the accident, and will not compensate if the accident does occur. It is here that the proportional responsibility rule differs from a rule of strict liability. There is that behavior for which the actor will be held responsible, where the expected damages are greater than the cost of prevention. (Jones' activity threatens Richman's property, and cost of care is less than the expected harm to Richman.) In those cases the actor will either take the preventive measures or will forgo the activity. In this respect the rule has the same consequences as both the Hand rule and a rule of strict liability. Finally there is that behavior for which the injurer would be held responsible, where the expected damages do not exceed the cost of prevention. (Jones activity threatens Poorman's property, and the cost of care is more than the expected harm to Poorman but less than an equivalent expected harm to herself or to Richman would amount.) In those cases, the actor will go ahead and risk the accident, and will pay compensation if an accident does occur. It is here that the rule can be distinguished from the Hand rule.

Here then are three rules the egalitarian can choose from: the Hand rule; the proportional responsibility rule; and strict liability. Imagine a population that consists of two groups, owners of old Fords worth $2,500 each and owners of new Lexuses worth $50,000 each. The three charts below show the consequences of adopting each of the rules in two different auto accident settings in that population, first where a rational Lexus owner has a choice between an action that endangers Fords and one that endangers Lexuses, and second where a rational Ford owner has the same choice. Whichever action is chosen, the benefits to the actor (aside from the damage calculation) will be the same. The harm in each case, if it occurs, will be the total destruction of the automobile. The probability in each case is one in one hundred that an accident will occur; thus the expected harm where Fords are threatened is $25, and where Lexuses are threatened it is $500. "Care" refers to preventive measures other than choosing the cheaper of the two risks; there is no liability under the Hand rule when the actor either takes independent preventive measures to prevent the threatened harm, or independent measures are more expensive than any alternative facing the actor and the actor chooses the cheaper of the alternatives. In this example the cheaper alternative will be putting Fords at risk rather than Lexuses.

I. UNDER THE HAND RULE

COST OF CARE	ACTION TAKEN BY LEXUS OWNER	ACTION TAKEN BY FORD OWNER
Less than $25	Takes care; is indifferent between victims; no liability and no accident	Same
Between $25 and $500	Does not take care; chooses action that endangers Fords; no liability for resulting accident	Same
More than $500	Does not take care; chooses action that endangers Fords; no liability for resulting accident	Same

II. PROPORTIONAL RESPONSIBILITY

COST OF CARE	ACTION TAKEN BY LEXUS OWNER	ACTION TAKEN BY FORD OWNER
Less than $25	Takes care; is indifferent between victims; no liability and no accident	Same
More than $25 but less than $500	Does not take care; chooses to endanger Fords and pay damages	Does not take care; indifferent between victims; no liability

More than $500	Does not take care; is indifferent between victims; no liability for resulting accident	Same

III. STRICT LIABILITY

COST OF CARE	ACTION TAKEN BY LEXUS OWNER	ACTION TAKEN BY FORD OWNER
Less than $25	Takes care; is indifferent between victims; no accident so no liability	Same
More than $25 but less than $500	Does not take care; chooses to endanger Fords and pay damages	Same
More than $500	Does not take care; chooses to endanger Fords and pay damages	Same

The three rules give identical results where care costs less than $25: both the Lexus owner and the Ford owner will take care, will be indifferent, and no accident will result. And where care costs more than $500 the only rule that gives a different result is strict liability which, if I am correct, is not available to the egalitarian. The other two render both owners indifferent between courses of action; neither will take care, and neither will be responsible for the resulting accident. It is where care costs more than $25 but less than $500 that the differences between negligence and proportional responsibility show up. Under the Hand rule both owners take the same course of action: both choose to put the Ford owners at risk and thereby avoid responsibility though an accident may occur. With proportional responsibility neither owner will take care, but the Ford owner will avoid liability that way, and be indifferent between the courses of action, whereas the Lexus owner will put Ford owners at risk.

One objection to both the Hand rule and the rule of proportional responsibility, therefore, is that both encourage discrimination between victims in favor of those who are better-off; the Hand rule is the worse of the two, since it encourages every actor to behave in that way, while the other encourages only those who are better-off to behave in that way; and while proportional responsibility does nothing about equality in imposition, it does require equal concern for compensation. But there is another objection to proportional responsibility from the point of view of efficiency understood as wealth maximization. If Ford owners who do not take care are genuinely indifferent between courses of action that threaten Fords and courses of action that threaten Lexuses, there will be as many Lexuses lost as there are Fords lost, and there is a loss to the community of wealth equivalent to the difference between the cost of a Ford and the cost of a Lexus, for every Lexus lost.

Which rule the egalitarian favors would seem to depend upon the role she grants to tort law as an instrument of productivity, and whether she is willing to discriminate between injurers on the basis of economic condition. Some acknowledgment of the significance of the relative economic condition of the parties in determining liability has appeared here and there in the common law.[23] German tort law explicitly recognizes this point. According to Markesinis:

> If...the tortfeasor is incapable of all fault (and therefore not personally liable) the innocent victim might run the risk of being left without any compensation....The German legislator, however, foresaw this eventuality and included a provision in the Code—s. 829 BGB—which enables the judge to take into account the financial situation of the parties (including the insurance situation) and to oblige the innocent tortfeasor to pay...as equity demands. (Markesinis 1990, 662).

In making this choice between negligence and proportional responsibility, it is important to remember that wealth maximization is not the same as utilitarianism. If an old Ford represents, for its owner, roughly the same utility that a new Lexus represents for its owner, then there is no difference in the utility effect between the loss of one and the loss of the other. And if that is so then the fact that the Ford owner, as injurer, is indifferent between victims does not pose any threat to utility.

C. Damages. A rule of proportional responsibility addresses the issue of equality in connection with compensation. But it does nothing about the issues of equality in imposition of risk, or about forced investment. Both of these, I think, require discussion of damage rules. In the end there may be nothing to do about our preference for making the less well-off our victims. The sort of damage rule that would be required to make injurers indifferent between victims who are better-off and victims who are less well-off simply cannot be justified. On the other hand, there is something that can be done about forced investment.

1. Proportional Damages in Commercial and Noncommercial Cases. The proportional responsibility rule does not resolve the problem of inequality in imposing losses but merely requires an acknowledgment of the harm done. It forces the injurer to acknowledge that he has preserved his own property at the expense of the property of another, that he has not taken the care that he would have taken to preserve his own property or the property of someone in his own economic circumstances. Still, it permits the activity to proceed, and that may be a desirable consequence. Compare this with a rule that required the measure of damages to be determined in a similar proportional way. Under that rule, for example, when Jones destroyed Poorman's car she would have to pay not \$2,500 but \$50,000—the value of a resource that meant the same thing to her—in compensation. That would prevent Jones from engaging in activity that did not demonstrate her equal concern for all; she would no more undertake an activity that threatened cars like Poorman's than she would undertake an activity that threatened cars like her own or Richman's. Either she would not be responsible in either case for harm that occurred, or she would be responsible in both and would either take care or forgo the activity.

There is a certain appeal to such a rule.[24] The very wealthy would not endanger the property of others by their activity unless there would be a net benefit from their activity regardless of whether it endangered the property of the wealthy or the property of the very poor, and there seems to be a certain fairness in that. But such a rule would be neither fair nor efficient. Activity that would increase the surplus available for all would be prevented in order to protect property worth much less than the proposed gain, and activity would effectively grind to a halt. And the rule is not symmetrical. It is true that it would make all potential injurers, regardless of their economic status, indifferent between victims. But the indifference would show itself in different ways. The wealthy would engage in too little risky activity, but the very poor would engage in too much; there is a much larger area of activity in which the cost of prevention would be greater than the proportional expected harm to the poor than to the well-off.

2. Forced Investment in Commercial Cases. The final issue has to do with forced investment in commercial activity. Let's return to our example in which Jones, the entrepreneur, has a choice between courses of surplus-seeking activity which threaten the property of Poorman and the property of Richman. Imposing the loss on Poorman without compensation was an objectionable feature of the Hand rule; but even if we choose a rule under which actual damages are paid, there is a problem that remains. If Jones is free to choose to injure Poorman provided that he is willing to pay damages, Poorman is in effect helping to finance Jones' enterprise. Since consuming Poorman's resources is the cheapest way for Jones to proceed, Poorman is involuntarily contributing his good in the service of Jones' project. If he does it without compensation, he is robbed; but even if there is compensation, he is being wronged; or so at least it may seem to the egalitarian. We may, therefore, want to supplement actual damages with damages representing the victim's share of the commercial enterprise.

It would be wrong, for example, to allow an enterprise to seize an individual's home to use as a place of business; and if the enterprise paid the market price it would still be wrong. If the goods are to be used in furtherance of a commercial enterprise, they should not be taken without consent and without a share in the profits. And if it is essential under some circumstances to allow an enterprise to take resources—if certain injuries are an inevitable consequence of a desirable and surplus-creating activity, I mean—that is no reason why those who are forced to contribute ought not to share in the surplus. Suppose that Jones is allowed to injure Poorman's property, paying only actual damages under our strict liability rule. Had Jones been required to bargain with Poorman beforehand, he would have had to offer to share the proposed surplus in order to persuade Poorman to give up his property. If Jones provides a product that both Poorman and Richman will purchase, the price of that product will perhaps be lower if Poorman does not share in the surplus; but Poorman gets no more of the benefit than Frederick does, who has not contributed anything.

So it does not seem unreasonable to expect Jones to give Poorman some share of the profits of the enterprise. The question is how that share should be calculated. If Poorman is treated as a debt-holder for the enterprise, then his share of the surplus should be based in some fixed way upon the size of his contribution. That would mean that he would be assured something over his actual damages whatever the fate of the enterprise, short of bankruptcy. On the other hand, he might be treated as someone who holds equity in the enterprise, in which case he would share proportionately in the good fortunes of the enterprise, but also in the bad. There is also the question whether Poorman is entitled to something for having his resources used without his consent. How we choose to calculate the additional damages is not as important at this point as merely acknowledging some additional payment is due as a fair return on the investment.

D. An Egalitarian Rule. An egalitarian rule governing the adjudication of accidents might look something like the following:

> An individual is responsible:
> a. for the harm his noncommercial activities cause to another provided that the cost of preventing the harm would have been less than the loss of a part of his estate proportional to the part of the victim's estate threatened with destruction, discounted by the probability of the harm occurring; and
> b. for the harm his commercial activities cause [with damages supplemented to represent the victim's share in the commercial enterprise].

For injuries caused in the course of noncommercial, nonsurplus seeking, activities the rule is negligence, with responsibility assessed by comparing the assets of the injurer with the assets of the victim or the class of victims threatened by the injurer's activity. This rule might be extended with a damage rule of a similarly proportional nature. Where the activity is a commercial enterprise, however, the rule would be strict liability, with a possible extension to take account of the investment the victim is forced to make in the enterprise.

4. Conclusion.

The negligence standard, as it is currently understood in tort law, is based upon a notion of reasonableness that the egalitarian should find perfectly suitable for the one-party case, in which the question is whether a person should bear the cost of harms he has caused himself. Once we see that that notion of reasonableness cannot be extended to the two-party case, the search begins for an interpretation of reasonableness and a rule of negligence that might offend less against the principles of egalitarianism.

The rule we ended up with certainly has an alien feel to it. But is it really so far from the existing principles of tort law? Notice that much commercial activity is already governed by a kind of strict liability. Extrahazardous activities like blasting and those we see in the Rylands/Fletcher progeny are governed by strict liability; so is the keeping of wild animals. The manufacture and sale of products has drifted quite a way toward strict liability, even if a persistent emphasis by industry on the cost-benefit consequences of that policy has succeeded in reversing the drift. Of course the rise of negligence law in the country was largely the outcome of railroad litigation in the nineteenth century, when judges purported to feel the need to protect industry. But what those judges did was to grant a subsidy to industry; there is no basis for the rule in fairness, and it is questionable whether the rule was required by efficiency. In France and Germany an entirely different rule arose, a rule of strict liability for such injuries.

That part of the rule that addresses noncommercial activity is of course a form of negligence rule, reflecting the fact that in some cases injurers are to be held responsible for what they have done and in other cases they are not. To that extent the rule resembles the rule actually in effect. The difference, of course, is that the rule of proportional responsibility makes those who are well-off responsible in more cases that those who are poorly off would be. It sacrifices something in terms of efficiency (add the rule of proportional damages and you sacrifice a *great deal* of efficiency), in order to secure more equal treatment of victims. But side by side with rules designed to subsidize industry the common law is full of instances of judicial action designed to protect those who are less well-off, from the rescinding of the fellow servant rule and the contributory negligence rule in torts to the rules governing contracts of adhesion. And at least in cases in which the abuses of the Hand formula are obvious, as in nuisance cases involving elements of environmental elitism, it would not be surprising to find the courts carving out rules more to the liking of egalitarians.

You might argue, as Arthur Ripstein does, that tort law should treat everyone the same, and that that is what treating everyone as equals consists of. I agree that in a world in which there was in fact equality a single standard of negligence would be appropriate, and I think that is consistent with what I have argued here. But in a world of striking inequalities the principle of equality is served by treating differently people who are differently situated. This need for different treatment, I suggest, can be implemented in part through the definition of reasonableness in tort law.

NOTES

*My thanks to Peter Vallentyne and Marc Fleurbaey for their comments and criticisms.

1. "Option luck is a matter of how deliberate and calculated gambles turn out....Brute luck is a matter of how risks fall out that are not...deliberate gambles." (Dworkin 2000, 73.)
2. I will try to avoid taking a position on one of the more controversial questions in the egalitarianism debate, the question of the nature of the value to be equalized. (Dworkin 2000, chapter 7; Arneson 1989; Cohen 1989.)
3. All the more surprising, of course, since French courts, like the courts of most civil law countries, technically lack the power to make law. Even so, the courts can have a profound effect on the law simply by maintaining consistent positions, and that is what happened here. The cases through which this was accomplished in France can be found reprinted in von Mehren and Gordley 1977, 575–632. In 1985 the French legislature finally passed legislation acknowledging the change for traffic accidents.
4. This does not hold where the victim can take care more efficiently; contributory negligence would have to be added to strict liability to cover that case.
5. United States v. Carroll Towing, 159 F.2d 169 (2d Cir. 1947). (The issue in that case was contributory negligence, though the principle he developed was intended by Hand to apply to all questions of negligence.)
6. As the quote from Terry makes clear, the considerations that the courts relied on from, say, 1850 to 1950, though not explicitly economic, took costs and benefits into account in precisely the way that the economic approach proposes. And whether or not judges in the past were after efficiency in accident law, enough judges are currently persuaded that efficiency both has been and should be the aim of the law that for all practical purposes we may consider the economic interpretation to be the leading interpretation of negligence.
7. That is, the total of losses and costs of prevention will be minimized. Incidental costs like the costs of litigation must also be taken account of; see Calabresi 1970, 225.
8. The fact that this assumption is false is not, by itself, any reason for abandoning the economic approach. If the economic approach is right about how people should act, then the question is: what rule will cause that sort of behavior? Triple damages in antitrust law, for example, is a recognition of the sort of difficulty that is at issue here. Although the assumption of rationality raises problems about the proper rule to implement, and raises those problems not only for the economic approach but for any approach, including some that might appeal to egalitarians, I will not spend much time on it in this paper. The very fact of its universality makes it a topic for a discussion all of its own.
9. Ripstein suggests this point as a criticism of the Hand formula: "If those who might be injured have smaller incomes to replace, ... , correspondingly less by way of precautions are justified by their costs." (Ripstein 1999, 59.)

What he sees as an objection to the Hand formula seems to me to be an objection to tort law generally. The Hand formula did not appear in a vacuum; it was seized upon by the courts because it fit pretty well with the way in which tort law had developed.

10. Notice the similarity to the so-called environmental racism problem, in which the locating of waste facilities seems too often to end up in minority neighborhoods.
11. In some jurisdictions nuisance law is governed by a negligence standard. See Copart Industries v. Consolidated Edison, 362 N.E.2d 968 (NY 1977), for example, where a plaintiff forced out of business by pollution from a neighboring generating plant lost because the value of the defendant's business (and consequently the cost of closing it down) was greater than the loss from closing down the plaintiff's business.
12. There are astonishing examples of the indifference of some courts to the plight of workers. In one Massachusetts case a worker had notified his employer of the risk caused by a certain way of hanging axes in the workplace. The court took this as evidence that the worker was aware of and had "assumed" the risk; he did not recover. Workers' compensation rules permit recovery, but at rates that will not cover all of the worker's damages.
13. There are other consequences of this assumption of equal value that will bother the egalitarian. Consider, for example, the question of cost-spreading. Assuming there is no negligence, who should pay for the harm caused by commercial products? The choice is to allow the injured party to pay for the injury she suffers, or to require the manufacturer or seller to pay. If the loss stays with the victim, she must either pay for it out of her own pocket; or she will be covered by insurance which she will have paid for out of her own pocket. If the loss belongs to the manufacturer whose product caused it or the seller of that product, either the cost of the loss or the cost of insurance to cover it will be spread over the consumers of the product. Which of these two outcomes is preferable? This is a point at which utilitarianism and law and economics part ways. Suppose the choice is between imposing a $10,000 loss on a single person, on one hand, and imposing a one dollar loss on 10,000 people, on the other. The utilitarian must compare the difference in utility that results from these two different allocations, and on the assumption that the first dollar a person loses means less, in terms of happiness or utility, than the second, and the second less than the third, and so on, it follows that it is a very bad idea to impose the loss on a single person when it could be spread out over a great number of people. The assumption mentioned—a rather reasonable assumption—is the assumption of the declining marginal value of money, and it appears to be an assumption that early utilitarians made. The implication appears to be that, other things being equal, the way to minimize accident costs is to spread the losses caused by a commercial product over the consumers of that product. On this issue the egalitarian and the classical utilitarian are on the same side (reflecting, some say, the egalitarian bent of the early utilitarians). To ignore the fact that a dollar must necessarily mean less to the well-off than to someone who is badly off, or that the loss of a dollar will mean less to a person who has

his entire estate than it will to the same person after he has already lost half his estate, is to ignore what is self-evident. On top of that the rate of conversion of money into utility or opportunities for welfare will vary from individual to individual.

14. "If [damages] were the only remedy in this case, though, the defendant would have effectively forced the plaintiff to sell the logs at their market price. In so doing, the defendant would have deprived the plaintiff of one of the central rights of ownership, namely, the right to refuse to sell something at its market value." (Ripstein 1999, 150) Ripstein is talking only about intentional cases; his solution is punitive damages.
15. Such remarks always carry with them the same proviso: Though no-fault insurance is not an egalitarian institution, the egalitarian may have good reason to prefer certain nonegalitarian institutions. See the quote from Sen, above, page 389.
16. The project here is to distinguish between option luck and brute luck as described above in footnote two. See the recent work by Marc Fleurbaey, Fleurbaey 2000.
17. Richard Arneson does not find the Hand rule so plausible even for the one-party case. He points out (citing Fleurbaey's example) that the result would be to saddle an individual for the full extent of his loss, whether it was the result of his repeatedly running unreasonable risks, or the result of what was simply a one-time mistake. Such a conception of justice, he says, is too unforgiving. (Arneson 2000; Fleurbaey 1995.)
18. It is an important feature of the one-person case, a feature that we will return to later on, that in this situation every dollar is worth the same to injurer and injured, since injurer and injured are the same person.
19. Where he does risk his estate, or his life, or his family's well-being on such matters, other considerations arise, and the egalitarian must consider whether compensation is due. A *reasonable* gamble that puts such things at risk for the sake of a sports bet or an investment raises questions the egalitarian cannot ignore.
20. But see the questions raised by Arneson and Fleurbaey, above.
21. Punitive damages are another matter entirely; nothing I say here has anything to do with that question.
22. A proportional rule may be subject to the same objections that would be raised against a rule that made someone liable only according to his talents. If it is wrong to subject the more clever person to a higher standard of liability than the less clever person (Ripstein 1999, 84–85), then perhaps it is wrong to subject the person with greater financial resources to a higher standard as well. But it is not self evident that the existing objective standard of liability is a proper one. (See Arneson 2000, 10–12.) Should such things as cleverness be taken into account in working out the implications of proportional liability? That would take us into a part of the egalitarian debate that I would prefer to avoid right now.
23. For example, in the law of contracts.

24. Ripstein proposes punitive damages for the case in which the actor has knowingly subjected the victim to the risk. (Ripstein 1999, 60.) There are a number of problems with this proposal. One is that punitive damages have no rational boundaries, and thus may or may not deter the objectionable activity. The lack of boundaries in fact makes punitive damages one of the great problems of American tort law, if only because the abuse of punitive damages lends some credibility to those who seek limits to tort recovery. Another is that this reasoning might justify punitive damages in every case of negligence; all that would seem to be necessary is that the actor was aware of the risk of harm.

REFERENCES

Arneson, Richard. (1989) "Equality and Equal Opportunity for Welfare," 56 *Philosophical Studies* 77.

Arneson, Richard. (2000) "Egalitarianism and Tort Law," (manuscript).

Calabresi, Guido. (1970) *The Costs of Accidents* (New Haven: Yale University Press).

Cohen, G.A. (1989) "On the Currency of Egalitarian Justice," 99 *Ethics* 906.

Dworkin, Ronald. (2000) *Sovereign Virtue* (Cambridge, Mass.: Harvard University Press).

Fleurbaey, Marc. (2000) "Egalitarian Opportunities," (manuscript).

Fleurbaey, Marc. (1995) "Equal Opportunity or Equal Social Outcome," 11 *Economics and Philosophy* 25.

Landes, William, and Richard Posner. (1987) *Economic Structure of Tort Law* (Cambridge, Mass.: Harvard University Press).

Markesinis, B.S. (1990) *The German Law of Torts* (New York: Oxford University Press).

Posner, Richard. (1972) "A Theory of Negligence," 1 *Journal of Legal Studies* 29.

Ripstein, Arthur. (1999) *Equality, Responsibility, and the Law* (New York: Cambridge University Press).

Sen, Amartya. (1996) "Social Commitment and Democracy: The Demands of Equity and Financial Conservatism," *Living as Equals* (Paul Barker, ed.) (New York: Oxford University Press).

Terry, Henry. (1915) "Negligence," 29 *Harvard Law Review* 40.

von Mehren, Arthur, and James R. Gordley. (1977) *The Civil Law Tradition.* (2nd ed.) (Boston: Little, Brown and Company).

PHILOSOPHICAL ISSUES, 11
Social, Political, and Legal Philosophy, 2001

Reconciling Autonomy and Efficiency in Contract Law: The Vertical Integration Strategy*

Jody S. Kraus

The economic analysis of law dominates contemporary contract theory. Economic contract theories seek to explain and justify contract law by analyzing the extent to which contract doctrines promote efficiency. Philosophical contract theories seek to explain and justify contract law by analyzing the extent to which contract doctrines accord with an ideal of autonomy. As normative theories, economic contract theories would seem to be logically incompatible with autonomy contract theories for the same reason that consequentialist moral theories are logically incompatible with deontological moral theories: The former claim that moral justification is solely a function of consequences, while the latter claim that moral justification is logically independent of consequences.

There are three strategies for reconciling these apparently incompatible approaches to contract theory. The first strategy is *the convergence strategy*. It attempts to demonstrate that efficiency and autonomy contract theories happily converge in their normative assessment of most contract doctrines, even though they do so on logically incompatible grounds. On this view, although efficiency and autonomy theories make logically incompatible claims, it is not necessary to adjudicate between them in order to evaluate contract law.[1] The convergence strategy has long been thought a promising avenue for reconciling autonomy and efficiency theories of contract law and has been the subject of extended analysis.[2] The second strategy is *the horizontal independence strategy.* It reconciles efficiency and autonomy contract theories by construing them as making either different kinds of claims or claims about different kinds of things. For example, by distinguishing between the explanatory and normative enterprises of contract theory, the horizontal independence strategy might reconcile efficiency and autonomy theories by insisting that the former make only explanatory claims and the latter make only normative claims in contract theory. Or the horizontal independence strategy might instead argue that efficiency theories seek to explain and justify case outcomes, while autonomy theories seek to explain and justify the plain meaning of doctrinal statements. In either case, the theories are rendered logically compatible because they are either making different kinds of claims, or making the same kind of claims about different kinds of things. The third strategy is called *the vertical integration strategy.* It reconciles efficiency and autonomy contract theories by construing them as comprising logically distinct elements within one unified theory.

The convergence strategy is not a genuine reconciliation strategy because it purports merely to demonstrate the mere compatibility of efficiency and autonomy contract theories in practice, while conceding their logical incompatibility in principle. The horizontal independence strategy offers genuine reconciliation, but it requires each theory to concede its irrelevance to either the explanatory or normative project of contract theory, or for example, to concede it explains either case outcomes or plain-meaning doctrinal statements, but not both. I explore both of these possibilities at length in other writings.[3]

In this Article, I focus exclusively on the vertical integration strategy. It provides the only principled reconciliation of efficiency and autonomy approaches within a unified normative contract theory. The vertical integration strategy combines both approaches by preserving the most defensible claims, and subordinating or abandoning the weakest claims, of each kind of theory. I argue that efficiency and autonomy theories of contract can be vertically integrated either by according the former lexical priority over the latter, or by treating the former as normatively foundational and the latter as normatively derivative. I suggest that the most theoretically plausible vertical integration strategy requires autonomy theories to abandon fine-grained, institutional prescriptions, and efficiency theories to subordinate their normative claims. The resulting unified theory these concessions make possible promises to combine the comparatively superior normative credentials of autonomy theories with the comparatively superior operational virtues of efficiency theories.

I. Two Vertical Integration Strategies

Vertical integration strategies reject the view that efficiency and autonomy contract theories are either competitors or logically independent because devoted to entirely different enterprises. They contemplate instead that both approaches may be combined as logically distinct components of a unified theory. There are two different vertical integration strategies for understanding how two apparently incompatible theories can be combined into one coherent theory. Both strategies rely on a "division of labor" approach to theory construction: They assign each theory a different role within one overall theory.[4]

A. Lexical Ordering of Competing Theories

The first vertical integration strategy conceives of the overall normative justification of an area of law as a two-part enterprise. One version of this strategy begins by defending a general moral theory. This theory then provides a constraint on the specific institutions permissible in any society: Any specific institution that permits violation of the theory's requirements is unjust. Thomas Scanlon's moral theory provides one example.[5] Scanlon argues that an act is wrong if and only if it could not be justified to others on grounds that they could not reasonably reject. Scanlon then assesses the moral permissibility not only of contract law generally (the legal enforcement of promises), but of specific remedy rules within contract, such as the rule providing for expectancy damages in the event of breach.[6] Scanlon's moral principle sets out a standard against which any legal institution can be measured. But it must be understood as providing merely a side-constraint. Although Scanlon's principle might require certain legal institutions to be created,[7] in assessing the law of contracts it purports only to establish the moral permissibility of having a law of contracts in general, and one with expectancy damages in particular. Thus, it does not purport to constrain, let alone supply, the kinds of reasons that might justify the decision to create a *particular* law of contracts, and to include within contract a *particular* rule, such as expectancy damages. It simply grants jurisdiction, so to speak, to other kinds of reasons[8] to decide the question of whether to have a particular institution, or a particular rule within it. Scanlon's theory therefore has no bearing on the choice among institutions and rules that are not subject to reasonable rejection.[9] Thus, his theory provides a necessary but not sufficient condition for justifying particular legal institutions and their constituent rules.

The form of Scanlon's theory suggests that otherwise opposing theories of contract might be reconciled by assigning one the role of providing a *lexically prior* moral justification of contract law (e.g., setting out the grounds for its moral permissibility), and the other the role of providing a *lexically subordinate* justification of the choice to have a law of contracts, as well as the choice of specific contract rules. For example, one might justify the law of contracts on the ground that it is permitted by an autonomy-based moral theory,[10] and yet hold that this justification leaves the selection among the many possible variants of contract law it would permit to be justified on the basis of other reasons. One would therefore be free to argue that, for example, the justification of the particular body of contract law that we have can be based on the value of efficiency, rather than autonomy. The point, of course, is neither that the form or content of Scanlon's view is correct, nor even that if the form of Scanlon's theory is possible, then some non-economic theory in fact explains and justifies the moral legitimacy of contract law, and economic analysis in fact explains and justifies the law of contract in all its detail. Rather, the form of Scanlon's theory demonstrates that, at least according to one quite respectable view of the nature of institutional justification, it might be possible to combine two otherwise apparently incompatible theories by interpreting them as playing different roles in the overall justification of contract law.

Rawls's approach to political philosophy provides another example of how the device of lexical ordering can accommodate otherwise incompatible theories within a unified theory. Rawls states that the subject of (his) political philosophy is the basic structure of society, rather than particular transactions, distributions, or individual decisions.[11] Thus, Rawls often writes that the two principles of justice apply to the basic structure, and not to particular transactions, distributions, or individual decisions. Although Rawls puts the point this way, the claim that the principles of justice apply to the basic structure is elliptical and therefore potentially misleading. It should be understood as shorthand for the claim that the basic structure is the only mechanism for insuring the justness of a society as measured by the principles of justice. In Rawls's view, justice is a property of a society as a whole, rather than a constituent part of it. Neither the basic nor the non-basic structure of society can be in itself just or unjust. A society is just if and only if it insures that the conditions set out by the two principles of justice will be satisfied. Rawls argues that the only feasible means for insuring a society's conformance with the requirements of the principles of justice is to design its basic structure to achieve that end. Thus, the basic structure of a society is justified by demonstrating that it will insure that the society it regulates will satisfy the principles of justice. Once such a basic structure is in place, the particular non-basic institutional forms that it permits can be characterized as just only in the sense that they are components of a society that is just. Hence, Rawls claims that transactions, distributions, and individual decisions that occur in society are neither fair nor unfair in their own right, but instead are fair only if the basic structure of the society in which they are permitted is justified.[12] Thus, a justified basic structure insures a fair background of social conditions.[13] Against this background, there are a wide range of permissible non-basic institutions that provide for relatively free and unfettered individual and associational conduct. So long as individuals conform to the requirements of these non-basic institutions, they need not take considerations of justice into account in choosing how to behave.[14] The basic structure guarantees that conduct permitted under non-basic structures will not compromise the justness of the society. Any necessary adjustments to the results of conduct in accordance with the terms of non-basic institutions will be made by the basic structure.[15]

Thus, Rawls's strategy is to "start with the basic structure and try to see how this structure itself should make the adjustments necessary to preserve background justice. What we look for, in effect, is an institutional division of labor between the basic structure and the rules applying directly to individuals and associations and to be followed by them in particular transactions."[16] Rawls therefore distinguishes between the basic structure of society and non-basic institutions such as the law of contracts.[17] In Rawls's theory, once a justified set of basic institutions is in place, there is a wide range of permissible non-basic institutions among which a just society can choose.[18] Rawls's theory of justice, then, has no bearing on the choice among these non-basic institutions, such as the choice among the many varieties of contract law permitted under a justified basic structure.[19]

Thus, quite apart from its substantive content, the form of Rawlsian institutional justification, which calls for a division of labor between the basic and non-basic structure of society, implies that the justification of these two kinds of analytically distinct but related structures within society must be provided by an overall theory composed of analytically distinct, but therein unified, justificatory principles. Rawlsian justification of non-basic institutions, such as contract law, consists in two analytically distinct components: a lexically prior theory justifying the basic structure of society, and a lexically subordinate theory justifying the choice of non-basic structures that are compatible with the just basic structure of their society.[20] This lexically structured, dual component approach to institutional justification, like Scanlon's side-constraint approach, readily accommodates otherwise incompatible principles within a unified justificatory theory. For example, an autonomy-based political theory might provide the justification for the basic structure of a society, even though an efficiency-based theory might provide the justification for some non-basic institutions, such as contract law.

The first half of this illustration is hardly implausible: Rawls's own theory constitutes a paradigm instance of an autonomy-based political theory that purports to justify the basic structure of a society.[21] The second half might plausibly be advanced by any number of theorists subscribing to an economic analysis of contract law. But again, the point here is not that Rawls's political theory and some efficiency theory in fact combine to provide a successful justification of contract law at any level. Instead, the claim is that autonomy and efficiency theories can be combined *in principle* (without pain of logical inconsistency) as lexically ordered components in an overall institutional justification with a Rawlsian form.

On both Scanlon's and Rawls's views, the unified theory is most naturally interpreted as providing an external justification of contract law. Scanlon's moral theory and Rawls's political theory can be viewed as establishing the legitimacy of the law of contracts, and economic theory can be understood as providing the reasons for selecting a particular form of contract law. In both cases, the economic theory might allege that the reasons it supplies are justificatory because they are moral reasons in their own right or because they fall within the domain of reasons allowable under the lexically prior moral or political theory. The resulting theory would constitute an external justification because it purports to justify a particular practice on the basis of reasons independent of the practice itself (here, reasons based on moral, political, and economic theory).

Thus, both Scanlon's and Rawls's theories can accommodate two otherwise incompatible normative principles by treating one as lexically prior to the other. Scanlon's moral principle is lexically prior to any other normative principles because it sets out a necessary condition for the legitimacy of any social institution and any rule within it. Rawls's principles of justice are lexically prior to any other normative principles because they determine the set of basic institutions that will determine the range of particular institutional variations permissible within a society. Both accounts allow other normative principles to determine the kind and detail of the social institutions consistent with lexically prior normative principles.

B. Foundational v. Derivative Normative Theories

The second vertical integration strategy unifies two otherwise incompatible justificatory theories into one coherent justificatory theory by assigning one theory to a normatively foundational role and the other to a normatively derivative role. The clearest example is again provided by a structural feature of Rawls's theory, but not the lexical priority of the principles of justice over other supplementary principles that guide institutional design and decision-making. Rather, it is the original position as a procedural device for expressing the requirements of autonomy. As Rawls now understands his theory, the original position embeds certain autonomy values (the Kantian ideals of the reasonable and the rational). Rawls argues that whatever principles would be chosen in the original position are, by virtue of that fact, the principles of justice justified by the autonomy ideal the original position embeds. In other words, Rawls's theory provides an autonomy-based justification of the principles of justice chosen in the original position.

Rawls's theory therefore makes two independent claims. The first is that the principles chosen in the original position are justified by the (autonomy) ideals it embeds. The second is that the principles of justice he describes in fact would be chosen in the original position. The former claim is structural, the latter is substantive. One could accept the view that Rawls has appropriately constructed the original position so that it guarantees that the principles chosen in it will be justified by the ideals it embeds, and yet reject the claim that the principles of justice he describes would be chosen in the original position. This is precisely what John Harsanyi did when he argued that the parties in the original position would chose a principle of average utility maximization rather than Rawls's two principles of justice.[22] If Harsanyi is right, then Rawls's (structural) theory provides a deontological, autonomy-based justification[23] of a consequentialist, utilitarian principle of justice. However, Harsanyi's argument, even if sound, does not provide an illustration of how an efficiency justification for the law of contracts can be derived from an autonomy theory. As we have just seen, the principles derived from the original position apply directly to the basic structure of society, and not institutions like contract law. The point here is simply one of logical possibility and theoretical plausibility: Rawls's structural theory for deriving the logical consequences of a deontological justification—the methodological commitment to a "pure procedural justice" approach to deriving the principles of justice themselves—demonstrates that it is at least logically possible that a consequentialist principle could be derived from a deontological normative foundation; Harsanyi's argument demonstrates that this position is not merely logically possible, but at least theoretically plausible as well.

II. The Plausibility of Vertical Integration in Contract Theory

I have so far characterized the vertical integration as an interpretive strategy for reconciling autonomy-based and efficiency-based legal theories. Although vertical integration may be a viable strategy for reconciling explanatory theories, its most obvious application is to normative theories. Hence, the illustrations that I have provided demonstrate how normative legal theories might be reconciled. It should be clear, however, that such reconciliation comes at a price. The vertical integration of normative legal theories requires one theory to concede that it is either lexically subordinate to or normatively derivative of a competitor theory. At the same time, the lexically prior, or normatively foundational, theory must concede that it normatively under-determines the choice of legal institutions. Hence, the illustrations reinterpret the normative claims of economic theories of contract as lexically subordinate to, or normatively derivative of, autonomy theories of contract, but reinterpret the normative claims of autonomy theories so that they under-determine the content of contract law. The conflict between many, perhaps most, normative theories of contract is, at its core, probably based on each theory's refusal to make the concession required by the vertical integration strategy. It is appropriate, therefore, to suggest why, at least as between legal theories based on autonomy and efficiency, the strengths and weakness of each theory lend themselves to a vertical integration reconciliation.

Each of the illustrations I provided interpreted an autonomy theory as lexically prior to or normatively foundational of an efficiency theory of contract law. As a logical matter, of course, the reverse is possible as well. But the illustrations took this form for two reasons: (1) The normative credentials of the economic analysis of law, including the economic analysis of contract law, have not been, and are not likely to be, established, and (2) The normative implications of autonomy theories for fine-grained institutional analysis have not been, and are not likely to be, established.

A. The Normative Foundations of Economic Analysis: A Review

The classic debate over the normative foundations of the economic analysis of law reveals that wealth maximization, the most plausible efficiency criterion for economic analysis, must be grounded in some independent moral theory. A brief review of Posner's initial normative defense of wealth maximization, and his subsequent fallback positions, provides good evidence for this claim. Efficiency analyses of contract law are therefore poor candidates for the role of the lexically prior or normatively foundational theory in a vertical integration of competing autonomy and efficiency theories.

The assessment of the normative foundations of economic analysis has not changed since it was first explored two decades ago. When the foundations of the economic analysis of law were initially debated, Richard Posner first advanced the view that economic analysis constituted a moral theory in its own right. The economic analysis of law, in Posner's view, provided not only a compelling description but also a moral justification of various legal institutions. After conceding that other notions of efficiency, like Pareto efficiency, were too stringent for the economic analysis of law, Posner argued that economic analysis relied on the principle of wealth maximization. He defended wealth maximization on the grounds that it avoided the traditional objections to utilitarianism and Kantianism, and yet produced "an ethically attractive combination of happiness, of rights (to liberty and property), and of sharing with the less fortunate members of society."[24] Posner claimed that the principle of wealth maximization constituted an ethical system superior to both utilitarian and Kantian ethics.[25] But the instrumental nature of Posner's defense of wealth maximization actually undermined the claim that it should be viewed as a moral principle. An instrumental defense of wealth maximization presupposes the value of the ends it promotes. Thus, on his initial view, despite his claim that wealth maximization constituted a moral principle itself, the normative value of wealth maximization is derivative of some unspecified moral theory.[26]

Posner's second defense held that many wealth-maximizing social decisions are normatively defensible because they would receive the implied consent of the people they affect.[27] But virtually no wealth maximizing institution would receive the consent of all of the affected parties at the time of the decision whether to adopt it. Some of those individuals would expect to be net losers under the institution and they would not give their consent. Posner presented two responses to this problem. The first redefined hypothetical consent to avoid the possibility that, at the time they are supposed to consent to wealth maximizing institutions, any individuals will know they will suffer uncompensated losses. For example, Posner revised his definition of implied consent so that an individual impliedly consents if he would have agreed to the institution behind a modified version of the Rawlsian veil of ignorance.[28] But as Dworkin argued convincingly,[29] Posner offered no defense of the normative significance of the hypothetical choice he imagined. Some argument from political morality, deep equality, or fairness, akin to Rawls's justification of the original position, would be required to support Posner's hypothetical consent argument. As Posner presented it, it is no more than an ad hoc justification of wealth maximization.

Posner's second response rejected the claim that an autonomy-based justification requires unanimous consent, actual or implied. Posner argued that the Pareto criterion justifies a strong majoritarian rule, but does not require unanimity.[30] But a social decision receiving anything short of unanimous consent cannot be justified on Pareto grounds.[31]

Finally, Posner claimed that the principle of wealth maximization provides moral justification because it yields a moral system that combines the insights of deontological, autonomy-based theories with those of consequentialist, utility-based theories.[32] Posner's final defense of wealth maximization returned to his original claim that wealth maximization constituted a moral principle in its own right. He presented wealth maximization as a hybrid moral principle itself, allegedly incorporating the insights but avoiding the pitfalls of both utility and autonomy principles. This defense of wealth maximization implicitly denied that deontological and consequentialist moral theories are mutually exclusive and jointly exhaustive categories of moral theory.

If this defense were successful, Posner would have provided not only a normative foundation for the economic analysis of law, but a break-through in the foundation of morality, and perhaps logic, as well. Unfortunately, there is good reason to doubt the coherence, let alone success, of this defense of wealth maximization.[33] Indeed, it is doubtful that any objective reader of the initial debates between Posner and others over the normative foundations of wealth maximization could believe that wealth has any inherent moral value, or that the exclusive pursuit of wealth in all common law adjudication, let alone in all social decisions, is morally defensible.

The lesson that emerges from this debate over the normative foundations of economic analysis is not that wealth maximization cannot be given an adequate foundation in some moral theory. Although he rightly rejects Posner's "modified" Rawlsian defense of wealth maximization, Dworkin himself leaves open the possibility that a genuine Rawlsian original position (one that, for example, maintains Rawls's thick veil of ignorance) might justify a principle like wealth maximization (again, recall Harsanyi's argument roughly to that effect). More modestly, a moral case might be made for seeking to increase wealth within certain constraints and in addition to the pursuit of other ends, or even for seeking to maximize wealth exclusively in some institutions.[34] Nonetheless, there is a justified presumption against treating wealth maximization as a free standing moral principle. If the principle of wealth maximization has normative force, it must be *derived* from some independently established moral theory.

Thus, when adjudicating between an efficiency-based and an autonomy-based normative analysis of contract law, there is a justified presumption against according the efficiency theory a normatively foundational role. To the extent that it has normative power, that power must be presumed to derive from some independent moral (or normative political) theory. Of course, this does not mean that the competitor autonomy theory constitutes such a theory, is correct, or is necessarily compatible with the efficiency theory. It merely means that when considering a vertical integration reconciliation between a normative efficiency theory and a normative autonomy theory, there is a strong presumption against interpreting the former as lexically prior to, or normatively foundational to, the latter.

B. AUTONOMY AND FINE-GRAINED INSTITUTIONAL ANALYSIS

Despite the almost undeniable relevance of considerations of autonomy to institutional analysis, theories of autonomy are notoriously difficult to apply to actual questions of institutional design. The difficulty has two causes. The first can be called "the problem of incompleteness." Some questions cannot be answered by autonomy theories, *even in principle.* Autonomy theories, like all theories, can answer only certain questions. Taken on their own terms, this is not a problem. But if they are offered as a theory of an independently specified domain, such as the law of contracts, incompleteness constitutes a disabling defect. The best example is provided by Richard Craswell's critique of promise-based theories of contract.[35] His claim is that these theories have no implications, even in principle, for how contract default rules should be designed, a central and unavoidable question of contract law. I have argued elsewhere that Craswell's criticism of Charles Fried's and Randy Barnett's theories is not convincing.[36] Craswell's case against other particular autonomy theories, however, appears to demonstrate that they have no bearing on how contract default rules should be selected.[37] I suggested above that this fact constitutes grounds for criticism only if the criteria of adequacy for these promise-based theories of contract is that they provide a "complete" theory of institutional design that is, that at least in principle they generate answers to all questions of how to design, and perhaps how to decide cases in, contract law. If they can instead be interpreted as offering a theory only of, for example, the normative implications for contract law of the moral obligation to keep a promise, then the fact that they do not speak to some questions of contractual design is of no moment. But the point here is that such theories nonetheless do not qualify as competitors against contract theories that purport to constitute complete theories of design, including a theory of default rules. Again, the reason is that they simply have no bearing on these questions.

The other difficulty in applying autonomy theories to institutional design is that they are "indeterminate." Although this problem is hardly unique to autonomy theories, it is most extensive in, and corrosive of, them (as compared to economic theories). The problem of indeterminacy comes in two forms: epistemic and metaphysical. Epistemic indeterminacy holds that although a theory may have a precise answer to the question raised, we currently lack the ability to determine what that answer is.[38] Metaphysical indeterminacy holds that a theory's answer to the question is in fact indeterminate. As a conceptual matter, this position is distinct from the prior difficulty of incompleteness, in which a theory simply does not by its own terms apply. Here, the theory applies, but indeterminately only. For example, the question raised might clearly implicate the concept of autonomy, but perhaps because the implications fall within a vague area in the extension of the concept, the concept fails to provide a determinate answer. For purposes of practical, institutional analysis, both kinds of indeterminacy are defects. But while epistemic indeterminacy is only potentially disabling (there is the hope of overcoming it), metaphysical indeterminacy, like incompleteness, is permanently disabling for a theory that takes an independently specified domain (e.g., an area of law) as its object of inquiry.

As the previous example suggests, one source of indeterminacy in autonomy theories is the fundamentally vague, and perhaps essentially contestable,[39] concept of autonomy. Its paradigm instances and counter-instances may well be uncontroversial, and as a general matter, its justificatory credentials are as well-established as any (in Kant, for example). The problem is that institutional design inevitably raises questions that fall within the grey area of the concept itself. The problem is not that the concept, or the theory that relies on that concept, simply has no application to the question raised (the problem of incompleteness). Rather, the question falls squarely within the domain of the concept and theory, but in practice the theory lacks the resources to translate the value of autonomy into any concrete analysis that is not a purely speculative, rather than logically supported, extension of the concept and theory. Depending on how this shortcoming is described, it renders the theory epistemically or metaphysically indeterminate.

Trebilcock's discussion of the so-called "rights-based" theories of Nozick, Fried, Feinberg, and Wertheimer, and of Margaret Radin's "theory of personhood," provides good examples of indeterminacy. To distinguish between an (impermissible) threat and a (permissible) offer from A to B, each of these theories requires specification of B's "base-line." On Wertheimer's view, for example, the base-line refers to the statistical, phenomenological, and moral expectations of the party receiving the proposal. The most critical of these base-lines is the "moral base-line:" "what B is morally entitled to expect in her future."[40] As Trebilcock argues,

> while it is possible to determine whether A's proposal is coercive once B's moral base-line has been set, once B's moral base-line has been set all the interesting theoretical work has been done....Presumably, any general normative theory of rights is likely to be highly contestable, at least any theory that goes beyond proposals by A that entail committing torts or crimes, as currently defined, against B, as the extensive philosophical debates over the base-line in the threat-offer distinction (and intermediate categories of "throffers") clearly attest.[41]

Radin's theory of personhood consists in her theory of human flourishing, which in turn relies on the notions of freedom, identity, and contextuality. Freedom is defined as the power to choose for one's self. "The identity aspect of personhood focuses on the integrity and continuity of the self required for individuation. To have a unique individual identity, we must have selves that are integrated and continuous over time. The contextuality aspect of personhood focuses on the necessity of self-constitution in relation to the environment of things and other people."[42] Radin argues that "universal commodification undermines personal identity by conceiving of personal attributes, relationships, and philosophical and moral commitments as monetizable and alienable from the self. A better view of personhood should understand many kinds of particulars, including one's politics, work, religion, family, love, sexuality, friendships, altruism, experiences, wisdom, moral commitments, character, and personal attributes, as integral to the self."[43] Radin concedes that "there is no algorithm or abstract formula to tell us which items are (justifiably) personal. A moral judgment is required in each case."[44] Radin counsels that we rely "on our best moral judgment in light of the best conception of personhood as we now understand it."[45] As Trebilcock notes, "[t]his seems inevitably to lead to...arbitrary and conclusory judgements on a case-by-case basis."[46]

The problem with both the rights-based and personhood theories Trebilcock outlines is that they lack an operational component. Quite apart from the normative underpinnings of the foundational concepts they embrace (abstract moral rights and a moral ideal of personhood, respectively), their failing, *as complete, practical institutional theories*, is that their policy prescriptions lack an argument based on their concepts of autonomy or individual rights. That is, the policy conclusions reached by proponents of these theories cannot be demonstrated to follow, even "loosely," from any premise their theories provide. When a practical, institutional question is posed, both theories require a substantive moral judgment that is presupposed by, rather than derived from, the theory. In the end, the theorist's own subjective intuitions fill the gap between the theory and its application. The theory itself is a fifth wheel.

There are three reasons such theories might lack an operational component. First, they might simply be uncompleted theories. In principle, they could be operationalized, but their proponents have failed to operationalize them so far. Second, they might be epistemically indeterminate. Although they in principle determine an answer for the question raised, it is currently impossible to know what that answer is. Third, the theories might be metaphysically indeterminate. They simply cannot answer the question raised, even though the question clearly falls within their domain. Much more analysis would be required to determine which of these is in fact the case for these theories. But it is possible, even plausible, that the very ideas of a "moral base-line" or "moral personhood" on which these theories rely are vague and essentially contestable concepts. If that is so, then no theory will be able to draw out an operational principle—one that provides clear purchase on every practical question raised within its domain—that logically follows from its core normative conception. If this is the case, such theories are metaphysically indeterminate, and thus seriously defective as complete, practical theories of an institution, such as contract law.

Nonetheless, the insights of such theories might be incorporated into a vertically integrated normative theory as part of a lexically prior normative theory. For example, Radin might be able to construct an original position based on her theory of personhood. That in turn might produce an operational, but lexically subordinate, normative principle useful for providing practical answers for questions raised in actual institutions. Or either the rights-based theories or Radin's theory might restrict their domain of application to those clear, or paradigm, cases in the core of their fundamental, normative concepts. Their theories would then disavow any claim to completeness within their domain, and instead follow the structure of Scanlon's theory by purporting to provide only a side-constraint on institutional design. Decisions governing controversial cases that fall outside of the core of their fundamental concepts would be left to other theories.

Of course, efficiency theories are not perfectly operational either. But by and large they are far more suitable for practical application than autonomy theories. In one sense, efficiency theories of contract are incomplete because they fail to answer precisely the question Radin's theory attempts to answer: What rights are inalienable? Efficiency theories do not even purport to answer that question directly. Clearly, some moral theory, whether Radin's or another, is required. But efficiency analysis does recommend the elimination of sources of market failure that might be responsible for creating the problems that give rise to questions of inalienability. For example, instead of addressing the moral question of how to allocate rights to scarce human organs, body tissues, or fluids, Trebilcock presents efficiency-based arguments for eliminating the scarcity of those "commodities," which creates the need for allocative mechanisms in the first instance. On the question of coercion, efficiency analysis is to some extent disabled because its central methodological tenet requires it to base its determination of whether a transaction is wealth maximizing on its voluntariness.[47] But the problem of coercion requires a method for determining voluntariness. Nonetheless, economic theories offer various efficiency-based analyses of coercion, each with fairly determinate results.[48]

Incompleteness, then, is a problem facing both autonomy and efficiency approaches to contract. For example, although autonomy approaches lack a theory of default rules, efficiency approaches lack a genuine theory of "commodification" or inalienable rights. But the significant difference between these approaches to contract law is their comparative determinacy and ease of application. When efficiency theories apply to their domain, they typically do so in a clear and straightforward manner. Their application difficulties concern complex modeling questions and difficult empirical questions. In contrast, even when autonomy theories apply to their domain, their implications in difficult cases are rarely clear even in principle. Their lack of clarity stems not from modeling complexities or empirical uncertainties, both of which are relatively tractable using the methods of rigorous disciplines, such as mathematics and empirical research. Instead, the unclarity is typically a function, as we have seen, of one form or another of indeterminacy. Often, the indeterminacy is metaphysical because the central concepts of the theory are themselves indeterminate.

However, none of this provides any reason for supposing that efficiency theories are correct, or even likely to be correct. It merely suggests that as between autonomy and efficiency theories of contract, the latter are more suited to the role of the lexically subordinate, rather than lexically prior, normative theory. It may well turn out that efficiency theories cannot be successfully married to autonomy theories, or any other credible normative theories. Virtues in applicability are no virtue at all for a normative theory that lacks any normative force. The only point I have tried to make is that the efficiency theories have a comparative advantage over autonomy theories as practical, applied theories, and autonomy theories have a comparative advantage over efficiency theories as foundational normative theories. Thus, I presume that reconciliation of these theories through vertical integration is more likely to succeed if the efficiency theory is given lexical priority over the autonomy theory.

III. Conclusion

Autonomy and efficiency approaches to contract theory have long been thought to be incompatible in principle. Recent scholarship casts serious doubt on the convergence claim that they are nonetheless compatible in practice. I have argued that autonomy and efficiency theories might be reconciled in principle by either the horizontal independence or the vertical integration strategies. Whereas the former restricts each kind of theory to mutually exclusive domains, such as explanation and justification, the latter combines both approaches in a unified theory. In this Article, I have focused exclusively on the vertical integration strategy. The vertical integration strategy permits the combination of efficiency and autonomy approaches in a unified contract theory by according one theory lexical priority over the other, or by treating one as normatively foundational and the other as normatively derivative. As a logical matter, reconciliation could be achieved by according either theory lexical priority over the other, or treating either theory as normatively derivative of the other. But as a methodological matter, the superior normative credentials of autonomy theories, and the superior operational virtues of efficiency theories, argue in favor of treating autonomy theories as lexical prior, or normative foundational, to efficiency theories. Autonomy theories are unlikely to succeed as practical, applied theories unless they are integrated with principles, whether economic or otherwise, that operationalize their basic insights. And efficiency theories are unlikely to justify contract law unless they are integrated with autonomy principles. Given its precedents in political theory, vertical integration is the most promising approach to constructing a comprehensive theory that justifies the law of contract.

NOTES

*I thank Jules Coleman, Roberto Gargarella, Ken Kress, Brian Leiter, Stephen Perry, Robert Scott, Scott Shapiro, Alan Schwartz, Steven Walt, Ben Zipursky, and participants at The Ohio State University Law School Legal Theory Workshop, the University of Virginia Legal Theory Workshop, and the Sociedad Filosofica Ibero Americana (SOFIA)/Instituto de Investigaciones Juridicas de la UNAM XII Conference on Philosophy of Law and Politics, Mazatlan, Sinaloa State, Mexico, December 11–14, 1999.

1. In the parlance of philosophers of language, the theories would be intentionally incompatible but extensionally equivalent.
2. *See* Michael J. Trebilcock, THE LIMITS OF FREEDOM OF CONTRACT 247 (1993).
3. In Part II of Jody S. Kraus, *Legal Theory and Contract Law*, in THE JOURNAL OF SOCIAL, POLITICAL, AND LEGAL PHILOSOPHY (forthcoming 2001), I provide a general analysis of the horizontal independence strategy. In *The Methodological Commitments of Contemporary Contract Theory*, in (Jules L. Coleman and Scott Shapiro, eds.) THE OXFORD HANDBOOK ON JURISPRUDENCE AND LEGAL THEORY (Oxford: Oxford University Press, forthcoming, 2002). I argue that apparently first-order disagreements between efficiency and autonomy contract theories are, upon analysis, second-order disagreements over incompatible methodological assumptions. I argue that four methodological issues often divide efficiency and autonomy contract theories, including the commitment of efficiency theories to explaining case outcomes (and dismissing plain-meaning doctrinal statements) and the commitment of autonomy theories to explaining plain-meaning doctrinal statements (and ignoring or dismissing case outcomes).
4. Although the precedents for the vertical integration strategies I discuss in this section are provided by normative theories, I believe the vertical integration could be applied to explanatory theories as well.
5. Thomas Scanlon, WHAT WE OWE TO EACH OTHER (1998).
6. Thomas Scanlon, *Promises and Contracts*, in THE THEORY OF CONTRACT LAW: NEW ESSAYS (PETER BENSON ED., 2001).
7. Presumably on the ground that all grounds for failing to legally prescribe or proscribe some behavior are reasonably rejectable.
8. Scanlon's moral principle applies "to the domain of morality having to do with our duties to other people." Scanlon, *supra* note 5, at 9. Thus, the

other reasons for or against institutions of particular sorts may be other kinds of *moral* reasons, as well as non-moral reasons. *Id.* at note 41.

9. On Scanlon's view, the claim that legal institutions or rules are subject to reasonable rejection must be understood elliptically. They are reasonably rejectable only if they permit or require action that cannot be justified to others on grounds that are not reasonably rejectable.
10. In fact, it would seem that Scanlon's own theory could be construed as based on the value of autonomy, suitably construed.
11. John Rawls, POLITICAL LIBERALISM 283 (1993).
12. Or as Rawls puts the point, transactions, distributions, and individual decisions are just only as a matter of "pure procedural justice"—that is, by virtue of their resulting from a fair process that is guaranteed by a justified basic structure:

    > A fair distribution can be arrived at only by the actual working of a fair social process over time in the course of which, in accordance with publicly announced rules, entitlements are earned and honored. These features define pure procedural justice. Therefore if it is asked in the abstract whether one distribution of a given stock of things to definite individuals with known desires and preferences is more just than another, then there is simply no answer to the question.

    Id. at 282.
13. Note that in my view, a basic structure, strictly speaking, can be *justified*, but cannot itself be *just*. Its justification consists in demonstrating that it insures the justness (according to the principles of justice) of the society whose basic structure it provides.
14. Indeed, Rawls argues that individuals *cannot* take considerations of justice into account adequately in their private conduct. *See id.* at 267–68, 284–85.
15. According to Rawls, "[t]he basic structure comprises first the institutions that define the social background and includes as well those operations that continually adjust and compensate for the inevitable tendencies away from background fairness, for example, such operations as income and inheritance taxation designed to even out the ownership of property." *Id.* at 268.
16. *Id.* at 281–82.
17. Rawls specifically singles out the law of contracts as an example of a non-basic institution:

    > [W]e arrive at the idea of a division of labor between two kinds of social rules, and the different institutional forms in which these rules are realized. The basic structure comprises...the institutions that define the social background....This structure also enforces through the legal system *another* set of rules that govern the transactions and agreements between individuals and associations (*the law of contract* and so on). The rules relating to fraud and duress, and the like, belong to these rules....

    Id. at 268 (emphasis added).
18. Put somewhat more precisely, though less elegantly, Rawls's view permits any non-basic institutions within a society that do not create any conditions of injustice not corrected by the background set of basic institutions in that society.

19. However, Rawls's theory quite plausibly could be read *to require* that there *be* a law of contract, of some variety or other. This much might be "read off" the principle of justice as a basic right, and from the efficiency motivation underlying the choice of the difference principle behind the veil of ignorance. To explain the parties' choice of the difference principle in the original position, Rawls argues that the parties "must take organizational requirements and efficiency into account. Thus, it is unreasonable to stop at equal division." *Id.* at 281–82.
20. Note that Rawls himself invokes the idea of lexical priority (and indeed is largely responsible for introducing the term, if not the concept, to political philosophy) in explaining the logical relationship between the first and second principles of justice. The idea is employed in the text, however, to describe the relationship between "justice as fairness" (which consists in the two principles of justice, themselves lexically ordered), which serves to justify the basic institutions, and other theories, principles, or reasons that might justify non-basic institutions.
21. Note that although the *form* of Rawls's institutional justification requires one theory to justify the basic structure, and another to justify choices among non-basic institutions, Rawls's substantive theory provides only the former. The latter is left largely unspecified by Rawls.
22. *See* John Harsanyi, *Can the Maximin Principle Serve as a Basis for Morality? A Critique of John Rawls's Theory*, 59 AMERICAN POLITICAL SCIENCE REVIEW 594, 596–7 (1975).
23. Arguably, in A THEORY OF JUSTICE, Rawls would say "morally justified," but in POLITICAL LIBERALISM, Rawls clearly now says "politically (and not necessarily morally) justified."
24. Richard Posner, *The Ethical and Political Basis of the Efficiency Norm in Common Law Adjudication*, 8 HOFSTRA L. REV. 487, 487 (1980).
25. Richard Posner, *Utilitarianism, Economics, and Legal Theory*, 8 J. LEGAL STUD. 191 (1980).
26. At best, this defense of wealth maximization was incomplete. At worst, wealth maximization did not even lead to the outcomes Posner claimed for it. And in any event, even if wealth maximization did lead to an ethically attractive combination of outcomes, it was persuasively argued that such values could and should be pursued directly (for example, in adjudication and legislation) on the basis of the moral theory that accounts for their moral attractiveness.
27. Posner argued that, "[i]f there is no reliable mechanism for eliciting express consent, it follows, not that we must abandon the principle of consent, but rather that we should look for implied consent, as by trying to answer the hypothetical question whether, if transaction costs were zero, the affected parties would have agreed to the institution." Posner, *supra* note 24, at 487.
28. Posner defines his veil of ignorance to allow individuals to know their productive capabilities—their skill, energy, and character—but claims it will prevent them from knowing whether the wealth-maximizing institution they are considering will impose losses on them, even though they know it will impose aggregate wealth losses on some individuals that are smaller than the aggregate wealth gains to others. Posner, *supra* note 24, at 499.

29. Dworkin, *Why Efficiency?*, 8 HOFSTRA L. REV. 563 (1980), AT 578–79.
30. "No institution, of course, will command the implicit consent of everyone. But only a fanatic would insist that absolute unanimity is required to legitimize a social institution....While Kaldor-Hicks is not a Pareto criterion as such, it will sometimes function as a tolerable and, more to the point, administrable approximation of the Pareto-superiority criterion." Posner, *supra* note 24, at 495.
31. Dworkin, *Why Efficiency?*, *supra* note 29, at 582–83.
32. Posner claimed that a system of wealth maximization "could be viewed as one of constrained utilitarianism. The constraint, which is not ad hoc but is supplied by the principle of consent, is that people may seek to promise their utility only through the market or institutions modeled on the market." Posner, *supra* note 24, at 497.
33. *See* A. Kronman, *Wealth Maximization as a Normative Principle*, 9 J. LEGAL STUD. 227, 228 (1980); Dworkin, *Why Efficiency?*, *supra* note 29, at 206–7; Jules L. Coleman, *Efficiency, Utility, and Wealth Maximization*, 8 HOFSTRA L. REV. 509 (1980).
34. For a recent attempt to use a modified Rawlsian original position to derive a limited principle of efficiency for the domain of corporate and commercial law, see Daniel Farber, *The Shift to the Ex Ante Perspective*, in THE JURISPRUDENTIAL FOUNDATIONS OF CORPORATE AND COMMERCIAL LAW (Jody S. Kraus & Steven D. Walt eds., 2000).
35. Richard Craswell, *Contract Law, Default Rules, and the Philosophy of Promising*, 88 MICH. L. REV. 395 (1989).
36. I defend Fried against Craswell's criticism in *The Methodological Commitments of Contemporary Contract Theory*, Part IIC, *supra* note 3. Barnett provides his own reply to Craswell in Randy Barnett, *The Sounds of Silence: Default Rules and Contractual Consent*, 78 VA. L. REV. 821 (1992). I provide a detailed discussion of Barnett's response to Craswell in *Theories of Contract*, to appear in E. Zalta (ed.), THE STANFORD ENCYCLOPEDIA OF PHILOSOPHY (on-line), (L. Murphy & J. Raz (eds.), sections on philosophy of law).
37. In *Methodological Commitments*, I argue that Craswell's claim tells against purely deontological theories such as Peter Benson's. *See supra* note 3, part III.
38. Ordinarily, "epistemic indeterminacy" is not understood to have a temporal dimension. If something is epistemically indeterminate, it is necessarily the case that we cannot know it. My usage departs from this convention. For our purposes, a necessarily epistemically indeterminate implication of a theory is, for purposes of theory application, functionally equivalent to metaphysical indeterminacy. Hence, I use epistemic indeterminacy to refer to a current state of affairs that might be overcome in time. The contrast between this sense of epistemic indeterminacy and metaphysical indeterminacy is then relevant to assessing the prospects of a theory's success.
39. The seminal work on essentially contested concepts is W.B. Gallie, *Essentially Contested Concepts*, in PHILOSOPHY AND THE HISTORICAL UNDER-

STANDING (1964). Gallie's article has spawned a cottage industry. *See, e.g.*, John Gray, *On the Contestability of Social and Political Concepts*, 5 POLITICAL THEORY 331 (1977); John Gray, *Political Power, Social Theory, and Essential Contestability*, in THE NATURE OF POLITICAL THEORY (David Miller & Larry Siedentop eds., 1983); Alasdair MacIntyre, *The Essential Contestability of Some Social Concepts*, 84 ETHICS 1 (1973–4); W.N.R. Lucy, *Rights, Values, and Controversy*, 5 CANADIAN JOURNAL OF LAW AND JURISPRUDENCE 195 (1992); David Miller, *Linguistic Philosophy and Political Theory*, in THE NATURE OF POLITICAL THEORY 35–51 (David Miller & Larry Siedentop eds., 1983); Quentin Skinner, *The Idea of a Cultural Lexicon*, 29 ESSAYS IN CRITICISM 205, 207–13 (1979); Christine Swanton, *On the 'Essential Contestedness' of Political Concepts*, 95 ETHICS 811 (1985).

40. Trebilcock, *supra* note 2, at 80.
41. *Id.*
42. Margaret Jane Radin, *Market Inalienability*, 100 HARV. L. REV. 1849, 1904 (1989).
43. *Id.* at 1905–6.
44. *Id.* at 1908.
45. *Id.* at 1909.
46. Trebilcock, *supra* note 2, at 26.
47. *Id.* at 84.
48. *See, e.g.*, Anthony Kronman, *Contract Law and Distributive Justice*, 89 YALE L. J. 472 (1980); Frank Buckley, *Three Theories of Substantive Fairness*, 19 HOFSTRA L. REV. 33 (1990).

PHILOSOPHICAL ISSUES, 11
Social, Political, and Legal Philosophy, 2001

The Judicial Community*

Christopher Kutz

1. The root of positivism is the idea that a legal system's criteria of legal validity have authoritative status just in virtue of social facts, where "social facts" consist of the behavior, beliefs, dispositions, and attitudes of certain persons in the community whose legal system it is.

So put, the claim of positivism is simple—deceptively simple, for it masks controversies about, for example, how facts can determine normative criteria, whether the criteria can incorporate moral claims, the way those criteria may brought to bear on the legal propositions to which they potentially apply, the degree of indeterminacy they permit, and so forth. But this simplistic formulation nonetheless captures a thought: what counts as law is wholly a function of what (some) people do, and moreover of what they do together. To put the point more strongly, the positivist thesis locates the possibility of law with the possibility of community.

Relating positivism to community may be surprising, since positivism, at least in its contemporary form, was born amid metaphysical (and normative) doubts about collectives and communities as the source of law. But, I shall argue, the truth of positivism does indeed invoke claims about community, and in two ways.

Neither of these ways, however, contradicts ontological individualism. The first invocation is the community to which the legal system applies and in which it operates—to those governed by it. And second is the community from whose practice emerges the criteria of legality, a community rarely coincident with the first. This paper addresses the second community, of law-determiners, whom I will call "judges" for simplicity's sake. It asks, what must be true of the members of that community such that they can make law possible? How does what they do together create law?

2. I will first refine the positivist thesis that what counts as law is a matter of social fact. Positivist theories are traditionally understood by opposition to natural law theories, according to which legality turns on moral facts, not social facts. But this opposition is too crude, for some reasons that, though evident, it will be useful to detail.

Let us say generally that a proposition P correctly states the law of a given community if and only if P meets the criteria of legal validity applying in that community. (This is simply a definition of legality.) Where natural and positivist theories of law differ is on the source of authority for the criteria of legality, as well—on some versions of positivism—as on the possible content of those criteria.

The social world is deeply implicated in even a natural law view. What is now taken as definitive of natural law theory is the claim that legal validity turns, in part, on normative criteria. But that "in part" masks a complex of social dependencies. Imagine a legal system for a given society in which the question is raised whether a judge's decision that the state is immune from tort damages really is valid law. On a natural law view, the criteria of legality necessarily include so-called "pedigree" criteria for those forms of law emanating from social institutions, such as legislatures, court chambers, and custom, as well as substantive moral and political criteria. In the example above, the pedigree criteria will refer to the authority of the judge whose decision is at question: on the basis of what set of rules or institutional norms is she authorized to make legal judgments? The moral and political criteria, by contrast, will make the legality of the decision turn either directly on its substantive merits as a matter of political morality, or indirectly, on the moral merits of the lawmaker. But, and this is the key point, those moral and political criteria can only be deployed through propositions of law whose truth depends on social facts.

Let me explain. Even if a natural law view validates as law some propositions that satisfy *only* moral and political criteria—for example, background principles of justice such as "no one should be judge in his own cause" [1]—such principles can only be effective as law in virtue of what I will call their "social instantiation." This is true in at least three ways. First, the very terms of such background principles—what is a "cause," a "judge"?—only have determinate semantic content in relation to the particular social institutions to which they refer.[2] Whatever one's preferred ontology for generic moral properties like "just" or "wrong," the propositions making use of those properties must relate them to entities and institutions in our social world. Otherwise, such principles are not propositions of law, but simply expressions of value.

Second, even on a natural law view, the criteria of legality are necessarily instantiated in the community's adjudicative institutions. This point is explicit in Ronald Dworkin's version of natural law, in which normative criteria are derived from a constructive interpretation of political institutions.[3] But even on a traditional view, the tests for law are deployed (or deployable) by the institutions charged with its determination. This is not meant to be a controversial claim, but simply flows from the observation that "legal system" is a success-term: to describe something as "a legal system" is to presuppose some set of institutions capable of determining what the elements of that system are. The institutions may be highly imperfect, generating both false negatives and positives, for any proposition tested. But there must be some sense in which the legality criteria, normative and pedigree alike, are deployed by those institutions, else we are not talking about a legal system at all, but only a fantasy of one.

Third, and relatedly, there is a necessarily social dimension to the application of any legal system's criteria of legality, for they are mediated through processes of reason essentially embodied in social agents. It is, I take it, a widely accepted lesson of Legal Realism that legal argument is not simply a matter of deductive reasoning. And it is (or should be) a widely accepted lesson of post-Realist jurisprudence that legal reason is not exhausted by deductive reasoning, so that Legal Realism does not entail skepticism.[4] To put the point positively, the determination of what counts as law, as much as determinations of what the substantive law on a given point is, draws on analogical and other projective forms of reasoning, forms whose normative boundaries are at least in part matters of what the community of reasoners counts as legitimate non-deductive inference.[5]

3. So even on a natural law view, legality must turn on matters of social fact: institutions and practices give content to background principles of justice, and mediate their application to the putative legal norms they assess. On a natural law view, social instantiation is a necessary condition of the authoritative status of legality criteria, just because social instantiation is a necessary condition of the functional existence of those criteria. But those criteria are only adequate to the task of determining law if they (or some subset) incorporate moral criteria as well. The moral constraint on the criteria of legality is not a product of their social instantiation; it follows, rather, from the concept of law. The source of those criteria's authority is independent of their social instantiation.

Natural law theories insist that the judges only have reason to apply the criteria they do because those criteria test for moral merit in the underlying law. Positivist views are distinguished by the claim that social instantiation, understood at least partly in terms of behavioral regularities, is both necessary and sufficient for the authority of the community's legal criteria—to their claim to be *the* criteria of what counts as law. To the question, "why are these the marks of legality?" it is a sufficient answer that "that's how we do things around here." A principal challenge for positivism, as Jules Coleman has laid out in his new book, *The Practice of Principle*, is to show how that can be a sufficient answer.[6] How can what we in fact happen to do around here be a *reason* for us to keep doing it? An imitative disposition may be reasonable, or it may be pathological—a compulsion to repeat. If law is in some sense a rational activity, then the dispositions in which it is grounded had better lie in the former camp. Positivism needs to show why.

Now, this challenge for positivism, explaining the authority of criteria of legality, may seem like one that can just as readily be skipped. If one understands the project of jurisprudence purely descriptively, then the relevant question simply is why the relevant social agents *believe* they have reason to do what they do. And one might then posit, as one answer, that social agents are simply disposed to follow each other's lead, to continuc longstanding traditions, and so forth. The judges of the community could simply regard the criteria as authoritative in virtue of their social source, for example because that's what they learned in law school. Or it could turn out as a matter of social fact that judges abide by the legality criteria they do because they accept the force of certain moral arguments. Indeed, as I will suggest, an adequate positivist theory needs to save a range of phenomena, accounting for very different explanations of judicial practice, both individual and collective—that is, individual judicial decision as well as judicial debate and disagreement. (The challenge of accounting for systematic and profound disagreement within the institution is one posed most acutely by Dworkin, and I therefore will refer to it as "Dworkin's challenge."[7])

But saving the phenomena, in the sense of offering a description adequate to the range of reasons believed by participants, is not enough for a philosophical theory of law. Such a descriptive project would be the jurisprudential analog of Mannheim's sociology of knowledge, eliminating the epistemological dimension of the inquiry. In fact, the classical positivism of John Austin is, arguably, more sociological than philosophical.[8] Philosophy's role might then seem to be a sort of conceptual housekeeping, albeit the keeping of a large and rococo house. Given the role law claims as a source of reasons, and the role it demonstrably has in people's practical reasoning, stopping the inquiry at the sociological level is either to accept without argument a skepticism about reason that must surely be argued for; or it is to leave uninterpreted the central terms of the social practice at issue. Positivism must be not only hermeneutic, in the sense of accounting for judicial motivation and deliberation as well as action, it must also be normative in testing and rendering an account of the reasons structuring judicial practice. The alternative is to concede the normative notion of legal validity to the natural lawyer. This was, I think, also H.L.A. Hart's conception of positivism, implicit in his assertion *contra* the Holmesian predictive theory of law, that a judge's "statement that the rule satisfies the tests for identifying what is to count as law in his court [] constitutes not a prophecy of but part of the *reason* for his decision."[9] What we need, then, is a positivist account that does two things: one that both reflects the structure of actual social institutions, including the structure of participants' deliberations, while explaining how those institutions can provide their participants with genuine reasons for action.

4. Because I have laid great stress on the descriptive aspect of positivism, it is worth getting clear, albeit in compressed form, about the relevant object of study.[10] The study of judicial behavior, and in particular the study of judicial *collective* behavior, is a well-mined vein in contemporary political science. Most of the studies have concerned the U.S. Supreme Court, but despite (and in part because of) the narrow focus, the work has been revealing

and is of considerable importance for philosophers. The dominant strands of work have been behavioralist, attempting to correlate judicial votes (whether at conference or in the final decision) with some set of causal factors. So-called "attitudinalist" models of judicial behavior correlate votes with judges' ideological positions, as measured by pre-judicial statements or editorial comment. The findings of this model have been stark: in the words of the leading attitudinalists, Jeffrey Segal and Howard Spaeth, "Simply put, Rehnquist votes the way he does because he is extremely conservative; Marshall voted the way he did because he is [*sic*] extremely liberal."[11] A corollary of this view is that citation to precedent appears purely epiphenomenal, as dressing for decisions more parsimoniously explained by ideological commitment.[12] Law withers to a husk.

Despite the robustness of the correlations between votes and political positions, attitudinalists have been criticized for failing to attend to the difference that legal institutions make to judicial decisionmaking. A particularly striking factor in the history of the Supreme Court is the rise in the proportion of dissenting opinions and concurrences accompanying judgments, a proportion that hovered around 15–20% from the early 19th century until 1935, then suddenly shot up to the 50–80% range where it hangs today.[13] Although the passage of the Judiciary Act of 1925, which gave the Court discretion over its docket, made a clear difference, the ten year lag in the rate of unanimity can only be explained by pro-consensus norms among the justices, norms which eroded over that period. Furthermore, as Robert Post has shown, research into justices' private papers and into court docket books (which record conference votes) reveals the very deliberate attempts by Chief Justices—Taft, successfully, and Stone, unsuccessfully—to forge consensus amid disagreement, as evidenced by justices' switching their votes (or not) between the conference and the final draft.[14] Cross-temporal comparisons of the opinions themselves reveal large differences in the kinds of authorities cited, with a sharp increase (particularly among dissents) in the citations to academic literature.

This evidence has given rise to two different kinds of theories that both complement and complicate the attitudinal model. On the one hand, rational choice approaches model well the extent to which judicial behavior must be seen as essentially strategic, with justices staking out legal positions that fall short of their individual policy preferences, in order to maximize the degree to which the collective decision approaches their individual preferences.[15]

On the other hand, "historical institutionalist" approaches emphasize the endogeneity of judicial preferences, particularly the degree to which judicial behavior can only be explained by institutional norms and legal traditions, traditions that shift in their meaning over time, and whose futures are functions of their pasts.[16]

Of course, it is dangerous to generalize from the behavior of the U.S. Supreme court, not just to make a point about legal systems as such, independent of time and place, but even to make a point about U.S. legal practice. The U.S. Supreme Court has highly distinctive internal norms, methods of recruitment, and public visibility, and only self-imposed precedential requirements—factors all of which may explain the law-determining practices of its justices.[17] The bulk of law-determining goes on in the trial courts and courts of appeals, state and federal, where it is more plausible to assume that judicial determinations are made largely by reference to legal criteria whose force stems from their conventional acceptance.[18]

On the other hand, two factors make the Supreme Court studies worth taking into account. The first is empirical. While trial courts and collegial appellate courts have not been studied nearly as much, the studies that do exist point in a similar direction. The decisions of trial court judges appear to line up more strongly with a set of individually varied, exogenous goals, including policy preferences, reversal-avoidance, re-election seeking, and time-saving. As with the Supreme Court justices, "following the law" does not seem to name an explanatory factor.[19] And studies of appellate courts have shown the same kind of strategic behavior and masked dissensus that characterizes the Supreme Court, as well as significant cross-temporal change in published dissent rates.[20]

The second reason is conceptual: the top of the legal hierarchy is a particularly salient point for positivist theory. It may be true that the legal system as a whole is sustained through reliance on criteria of legality by lower-tier courts—on the everyday practice of recurring to statute books, case reporters and the like to determine what counts as law. But those criteria do not function as what Hart called "the rule of recognition," a canonical statement of the supreme and authoritative norms of legality for a given legal system.[21] Lower-courts' use of those norms can be invalidated by norms established by the higher-court, while the highest-courts' norms can only be invalidated by a change in the practice of the high court (putting aside the possibility of constitutional change). The superiority within the system of high-court established norms means that those norms, as understood by the high court members, must be considered the actual criteria of legality.[22] And so we have to confront the question whether acceptance, simply put, constitutes the basis of their authority.

What of philosophical use emerges from the studies of judicial politics? One point that should be resisted, I think, is the purely skeptical reading of the legal process, even though that is a clear lesson of the more reductionist literature. We must recognize that legal deliberation is thoroughly political, and that ideological conviction and strategic calculation play a great part in explaining behavior. But we can recognize this without eliminating law as a mediating set of reasons, a grammar through which this particular dialect of politics is spoken, as well as a framework which makes available certain choices and not others.

The lesson to take away is more modest: the norms governing judicial behavior, especially judicial collegiality, are not conceptually fixed, but are rather historically-specific products of interpersonal relations, particular leaders, and relations to other political actors and institutions, notably the legislature. Judicial behavior ranges from the extremely collegial to the strategic to the autarkic. To put the point as charitably as possible, as an actual social process, judicial behavior seems better explained as an attempt to further individual substantive views of the good in a complex strategic environment, than as an attempt to reflect some prior agreement. A secondary task may follow, of effectuating the right decision within the institutional framework, by persuading or bargaining with other judges. But that is secondary, consequent upon the project of considering the matter aright.

So an account of law grounded in judicial behavior had better not place too many demands on how judges conceive their relations to their colleagues, or, more generally, how they understand their relation to the institution of the law. It is, of course, a direct implication of positivism that judicial norms are matters of social practice—the fact of their contingency is recognized. But positivism has been markedly reluctant to take seriously the import of that contingency, instead deriving virtually *a priori* the content of its account of the social foundations of law. What we need in its place is a less restrictive philosophical account of the judicial community, one ranging over very different degrees of interdependency and independence.

5. The philosophical tradition of positivism has not followed what we could call the positivist tradition of positivism. Philosophical accounts, by contrast, have portrayed judicial practice

not in terms of a mix of politics, individual goals, and strategy, but rather in univocal terms of rule-following. The challenge philosophical positivists have tried to meet is not actual descriptive adequacy, but rather the conceptual problem of showing how any social practice can give rise to reasons. And while positivism has succeeded in the second challenge, it has largely failed in the first. Surveying the reasons will be instructive.

H.L.A. Hart's solution to the problem of showing how social practice could give rise to reasons was, famously, the claim that the criteria of legality were elements of a social convention among the judges of that system. By "social convention" Hart meant a "convergence of behavior" by a group of individuals, towards which the individuals take a distinctive "critical attitude," an attitude Hart also refers to as an "internal point of view."[23] In taking this point of view, the members of the group see themselves as having reason to conform their own behavior to the convergent regularity, as well as to criticize others' deviations from that convergence. A positivist account of law emerges from Hart's further claim that the authority of the community's legality criteria derives from the acceptance of those criteria as conventional. That is, the tests for law deployed by the community of judges are the proper tests just because those tests are matters of convergent behavior towards which the members of the community adopt a distinctive critical attitude. Social facts, therefore, are sufficient for the existence and authority of the criteria of law.

There are, equally famously, many obscurities and difficulties about this account of social conventions, let alone its application to law. A central obscurity lies in the question how taking an attitude toward a practice can provide a reason to engage in that practice. And one difficulty lies in the extension of the account of convention from the kinds of easily identifiable convergence of social mores—e.g., hat-tipping, not slurping, conversational distance—to behavior whose convergence seems to exist only at the most abstract level, namely in a practice of arguing what proper behavior is in the first place. A second, closely related difficulty follows: how to extract propositional content (the content of the rule) from a range of behavior. There is always a problem of characterizing behavior in terms of a rule, even behavior of a heretofore thoroughly consistent sort; this is the problem of rule-underdetermination made prominent by Wittgenstein, especially as interpreted by Saul Kripke.[24] But the problem with divergent behavior is not simply that indefinitely many rules are consistent with prior practice but diverge in future prescription. The problem is, rather, that divergent behavior can only be seen as exemplifying a rule through an exercise of what Dworkin has aptly called "interpretation," in which core instances are identified and deviations rejected.[25] But interpretation is necessarily a subjective process, in the weak sense that one's interpretation of something (an inscription or utterance, an object, a set of historical facts) is a matter of trying to make sense of that thing relative to a set of expectations and beliefs whose source is in the interpreter. Such subjectivity, or individual variance, is consistent with plenty of objectivity, in the form of constraints on what sort of expectations it is reasonable to have about the thing. But these constraints make room for plenty of indeterminacy in what counts as a plausible interpretation.[26] (It would, for example, be unreasonable to try to interpret a bird song as an instance of a disquisition on physics, but perhaps not as a poem.) Where the data to be interpreted are complex, as is often the case in a complex legal system, disagreement is likely. If it is contested what the content of the rule of recognition is, then the rule cannot function as a rule, as an objective point around which participants can converge their behavior. Each, rather, is likely to be attempting to converge around different interpretations of the rule. Hart's response to disagreement is to say that where there is disagreement, there is no rule; but this response only works so long as the disagreement is closely cabined, for if there is generally no rule of recognition, there is also no legal system. So if disagreement is in fact pervasive, the problem for Hart's account is real.

I will deal with the obscurity first, deferring discussion of the difficulties till later in the paper, when we will be able to avoid them instead of having to solve them. Participation in a social convention *is*, on Hart's view, sufficient for its own warrant. But how can engaging in a practice be a reason to engage in that practice?[27] The central point for understanding Hart is to see that the "internal point of view" names not a belief about what one should do, but a complex motivational state, a state consisting in part in beliefs about the desirability of the practice, but also pro-attitudes towards the practice, and dispositions to act on those attitudes and beliefs, both positively (conformity) and negatively (critically).[28] "Accepting" a practice, in this sense, is closely analogous to forming an intention, a state whose reason-generating powers are evident.[29] Take the case of intention: casting about for a way to spend the evening, I decide, and so form the intention, to go to the movies. It being a weekend night, I now have reason to check the schedule, make sure there's gas in the car, buy tickets ahead, and so forth. None of these are reasons I had prior to or independently of forming the intention. Nor do any of these reasons count in support of my forming the intention in the first place. My reasons for that rest with my interest in amusement, the fact that I have no competing obligations, etc. Indeed, it may be that I have overall reason not to decide to go to the movies. What matters here is simply the observation that forming the intention structures my deliberation and motivation such that I now have reason to perform those acts constitutive of fulfilling my aim.

Similarly in the case of conventions: we must distinguish someone's reason for accepting the rule from the reasons that accepting the convention provides one with. In many cases accepting a rule is not a matter of decision. It may be, as with social norms, a matter of inculcation—discipline, in the Foucauldian sense. Alternatively, accepting a rule may be a deliberative or non-deliberative consequence of forming an intention or taking on a goal, as when one accepts the conventions of a genre in trying to produce an art work of a certain sort, or when one selects a set of rules to govern one's conduct in a game for which alternative rule-sets exist. Whatever the etiology of the rule's acceptance, its acceptance makes true claims about the reasons the agent has.

Nor should there be a problem in understanding conventional practices as generating not just reasons but duties. The crucial point is that the relevant sense of duty here is not that of an overriding moral obligation, but rather a category of reason that, within its domain, is mandatory rather than permissive, such that an agent may be subject to criticism for not acting on its basis. Certain sorts of conventions are defined by mandatory practices; to accept the convention is to accept that the practice is something one may be criticized for not doing. Games are the standard examples: to play chess is to make true claims that one must not move rooks diagonally, that one can only move pawns one square at a time, etc. The "musts" and "oughts" of the game masquerade as categorical imperatives, but that is only because the antecedent "if one is to play the game" is presupposed.[30] The situation is more complicated, as is well known, for social norms, where it may be hard to identify an antecedent "if" that an agent might voluntarily accept or withdraw from. But that complication arises chiefly in the second- and third-person deployment of the language of "ought" and "duty," as in: "Young man, I don't care what you want—you ought not chew with your mouth open!" As Bernard Williams and Phillippa Foot have written, these deployments can best be made sense of as devices for recruiting agents into a normative system, not as representations of the reasons they actually have.[31]

Indeed, it seems a strength in a positivist account that there should be an ambivalence about the status of duty claims, including duties of applying certain criteria of legality. On the one hand, the account needs to show in what sense the reasons to apply the criteria do present themselves as mandatory if it is to make sense of the normative vocabulary of law. On the other, a positivist account should make plenty of room for the renunciation of that vocabulary, for example to make room for the claim that an anti-slavery judge ought, morally, to have rejected the conventional criteria of legality and refused enforcement of the Fugitive Slave Acts. Understanding the normativity of legality as a consequence of acceptance precisely makes room for that ambivalence.

6. So the difficulty with Hart's convention account is not that acceptance of a convention is inadequate to explain that convention's authority. Such an account *could* provide an adequate analysis of a system of rules under deliberate institutional control. The problem, rather, lies in the account of the reasons provided by the criteria of legality, a problem whose symptom is divergence and disagreement over the content of those criteria. And here I think the conventionalist account must be rejected.

The problem is that the conventionalist account seems to deeply mischaracterize the way in which judges decide what the criteria of legality are. Hart's account of convention makes the reason-generating capacity of conventions a brute fact, proceeding directly from acceptance of the rule, where "rule" is understood as a summary of collective behavior. One who accepts a convention of hat-tipping sees himself as having reason to tip his hat just in virtue of accepting the convention. As I argued above, there is nothing in principle wrong with this account—indeed it better captures the role of social conventions in practical reasoning than does Dworkin's proffered alternative of an independent "consensus of conviction," according to which the reason to tip one's hat is that one really does have an independent moral duty to hat-tip.[32] Clearly there must be room for reasonable but unreflective conformity to account for some social norms.[33] The trouble is that judicial conformity is not like that, at least in core instances. To take a central case, U.S. judges do not accept the status of the Constitution simply because it is *comme il faut.* Rather, they accept the Constitution in virtue of seeing reason to do so. Its authority is not brute, but is rather the product of deliberative reflection. Hart's theory is unacceptable because it appears to make no room for that reflection.[34]

Alternative models of convention improve on Hart by accommodating the possibility of reflection, but they too fail to give judicial deliberation its due. According to David Lewis' influential account (adumbrated in the legal context by Coleman and Gerald Postema), conventions are best understood as solutions to coordination problems—that is, the problem facing individuals who most prefer acting together to any particular way of acting.[35] One who is a party to a convention in this sense takes current practice as a reason to conform, not unreflectively, but because conformity delivers the good of coordination. (Why participants believe they have a coordination problem is an independent question.) As with Hart's brute convention model, Lewis conventions are reason-providing to their participants, and moreover, unlike brute conventions, they are stable under reflection. To mangle Holmes, participants do have a better reason to follow the rule than simply that it was laid down by Henry IV: following the rule achieves coordination.[36]

There are three serious problems with this model. The first, laid out by Scott Shapiro and Coleman, is that Lewis conventions exist only in a restricted domain, when all participants prefer conformity in a rule to any particular rule.[37] But it is antecedently unlikely that this distribution of preferences actually characterizes the judicial community, many of whom may well prefer that a particular rule obtain to general conformity.[38] More importantly, the possibility of law should not turn on such a distribution of preferences as a conceptual matter; the condition is far too strong. Second, the form of justification available to participants in Lewis conventions covers only a small range of the types of justification characteristic of adjudication. At most it would seem to cover the behavior of inferior court judges, who justify their behavior by reference to norms issued by superior court judges. Now, it is true that the preference-structure underlying Lewis conventions should be understood counterfactually, so that a participant need not be motivated by the desire to coordinate so long as she would not have chosen otherwise if her choice did not, in fact, coordinate. Thus, a judge could opt for an individually preferred legal rule because that rule seems right, but only so long as she would reject the rule if it weren't generally followed. But that is a very meager form of deliberative autonomy, for it still requires that, ultimately, the judge must prefer getting along to getting it right. And this does not seem to mesh with either actual studies of judicial politics, nor with the imaginative phenomenology that forms the basis of Dworkin's critique.

Third, Lewis conventions are incompatible with the kind of systematic disagreement among participants that characterizes adjudication, and so cannot meet Dworkin's challenge. While it is possible, as a formal matter, to identify "rule-governed disagreement over the relevant criteria" as the solution to a coordination problem, such a "solution" would be an evident practical failure. Since the very point of a Lewis convention is to eliminate disagreement over the proper rule, building disagreement into the convention would defeat the point. Hence positivism cannot explain the practice of pervasive disagreement by reference to conventions. Any theory of law that aims at descriptive adequacy, as positivism does, had better be able to capture the non-conventional aspect of practice. While Lewis conventions may well have a significant role to play in explaining law, it would seem a mistake to build them into the center of legal theory.

Coleman, in *The Practice of Principle*, has sought to remedy the deficiencies of the Lewis convention model by looking instead to the model of cooperation put forward by Michael Bratman in an important series of papers in the philosophy of action.[39] Bratman's goal is to characterize a significant set of highly interactive activities—the examples he gives include singing a duet, painting a house together, or running a basketball play.[40] Abstracting from these instances, Bratman tries to provide a model that captures their distinctive features: (i) mutual responsiveness, in the sense of participants' dispositions to adjust their behavior in light of what others do; (ii) commitment to a joint goal, with (i) in service of (ii); and (iii) commitment to mutual support, in that each will try to make sure the others are able to perform their parts of the joint goal. Bratman's resulting analysis is complex, but the general idea is that such instances of cooperative action can be broken down into interlocking sets of individual intentions to bring about the joint goal, where each intends that the goal be realized in part through the agency of the others. The commitment to the joint goal, however, need not presuppose that the way to achieve the goal is settled; to use his example, you and I could both be committing to singing a duet together without having decided what song to sing. Thus, commitment to the joint goal is consistent with discussion and bargaining over how to achieve it.

Coleman suggests understanding the social practice constitutive of the rule of recognition as a Bratman-type shared cooperative activity (SCA). This conception, he thinks, helps us account for the way in which judicial practice is genuinely collective without presupposing an absolute preference for coordination, as with Lewis, as well as accommodating the kind of disagreement and bargaining that presents a problem for both Hart and Lewis. Moreover, conceiving the rule of recognition as an SCA can explain the rule's normativity, for the reciprocal expectations and reliance proceeding from the commitment to mutual support generate duties owed towards the other participants.[41]

The problem with invoking this model of shared cooperative activity is that it precisely repeats the problem with Lewis conventions: it makes a much too strong assumption about the nature of judicial interaction. The central feature of SCA's is that participants unite in a shared project, shared in the strong sense that each aims at its realization through the agency of each. This is a very high degree of interdependence; indeed, one of the routine motives for engaging in SCA's is the intimacy of the association. But—as Bratman recognizes—there are many forms of genuinely collective action which do not meet the criteria of SCA's, particularly the very demanding criterion of mutual support.[42] You and I might, for example, have an understanding that we will walk together, but with no commitment to stay the course; we each might peel off at any time without apology. So long as each of us pursues the walk together, each will try to match the other's stride, turning as the other turns. If we do so, we will genuinely be walking together. But neither need be committed to slowing down for the other's sake, so that we can finish the walk together. Neither of us, in other words, need treat the other as a source of reason nor ground of obligation; we can treat the other instrumentally, as a means of temporary entertainment. This would, of course, be a highly unusual way to walk together, but the point is that the presence of the relevant mutual commitments is a contingent matter, not a conceptual one, at least insofar as an account of collective action goes.[43]

It may be that some collegial courts function as cooperative teams, each trying to support the efforts of the other to arrive at the correct determination of law. It is even more likely that coalitions of judges on collegial courts see their projects as cooperative, and not merely strategic. But it surely goes too far to characterize the judiciary as a whole in cooperative terms. To repeat the point above, it is a salient feature of adjudication that getting it right is often more important than getting together, and the SCA model doesn't make room for that degree of independence within the collective institution. To put the point another way, the SCA account is over-moralized as a description of institutionally-structured collective behavior.[44] It is a further point that the normativity generated by SCA's does not well account for the normativity possessed by the criteria of legality. For the duties generated by the SCA model are duties owed to the other participants; they are the correlates of rights of performance. But that doesn't seem to characterize the normativity of institutionally-defined criteria. If, in fact, judges do have genuine moral duties to apply some and not other criteria, those duties are owed to the beneficiaries of the institution, not to their fellow participants.[45] In any event, as I argued above, there is no reason for the positivist to search for genuine moral duties; institutionally-defined duties suffice, and those can be generated by reference to institutional roles. Cooperation need not enter the picture.

7. So what we need is an account of collective behavior capacious enough to encompass the Scalias and the Brennans, the lone rangers and the coalition builders, an account that makes the constitutive institutional norms matters of contingent emergence, not conceptual necessity. I am going to present such an account. But first, to put it in context, let's imagine a collegial setting with which most of us have more experience than the judicial conference room: the faculty meeting. Say that the faculty is trying to decide which of two candidates to hire, each of whom does clearly strong but not perfect work, in the sense that the work is of obvious interest but has identifiable errors; and each of whom would complement the department's strengths in different ways. We can imagine at least the following deliberative scenarios taking place:

(1) Each member of the faculty speaks his or her views, doesn't listen to anyone else, considers the matter individually, then votes. **(Pure Autarky)**
(2) Each member of the faculty considers the matter individually, listens to others' views in order to detect colleagues' preferences, then advances arguments aimed at bringing those colleagues to his or her individual preference, or otherwise bargains for the preferred candidate. **(Pure Strategy)**
(3) Each member is mainly concerned to agree with each other member of the department, so as not to have a split vote. So each searches for some point of salience around which to coordinate, for example, the candidate who satisfies the same criteria as the last hire. **(Pure Convention)**

(4) Each member believes that the majority of the faculty is likely to have considered the matter aright, and so each is concerned to vote with the majority. **(Pure Authoritative Deference)**
(5) Each member advances arguments and listens to the arguments of the others, comparing point against point, and attempting to work out a consensus position that accommodates all valid claims. **(Pure Cooperation)**

Following the deliberative (or not) process, the faculty members vote, a winner is selected, and dissenters (if any) nurse their wounds and grouse in private.

Pretty obviously, no faculty meeting matches any of these pure types, in part because individual members vary in their attitudes towards others' views, taken as a whole; and in part because individuals vary in their attitudes towards particular others, treating the comments of some as signal and others as noise. Moreover, people's interests in real or feigned unity vary in response to both the likely effects of disagreement on interpersonal relations, as well as pressures from the broader institutional environment. But whatever the general interactive profile of the department, and whatever the mix of individual attitudes, what happens at the end is the same: the department chooses a candidate.[46]

Pay attention to that last sentence: "the department chooses." We ought to be more puzzled than we are, for choosing is something people do, and departments are not people (though they are made of people). And yet, unless this is the choice of the department, not just of a person or group of persons, it has no institutional significance—no authority, in a word. So how can a department choose? More abstractly, when can we attribute an act to a collective?

Two elements of the example are key: a set of rules structuring the institution, and collective action by the institutions' members. The rules of the department prescribe roles for the members to play, as interviewers, deliberators, voters, and employers; and those rules are embedded within the rules governing the larger institution of the university. And those rules define a space of collective action, in which the department members can engage in the joint project of making the hire, for example by talking (in turn, more or less), voting, and finally acquiescing in the institutionally recognized collective decision. Indeed, the second element, collective action, would seem to have explanatory priority, since the rules structure the institution only insofar as they are instantiated in the practice of the institution's members.

What we need, I believe, is what I have called in other work a "minimalist conception" of collective action.[47] As with Bratman's account of SCA's, but without the strong conditions of interdependence, individuals' intentions and the relations among them are what turns a group of people acting into a collective, turns what they do into collective action. According to the minimalist conception, a group of people acts collectively when, and only when, each acts with what I have called a "participatory intention"—an individual intention to contribute to some collective end—and there is sufficient overlap among individual conceptions of that end. More stringent conditions of mutual support, responsiveness, and the like may be implicated by particular types of collective action—tangos come to mind. But the crucial idea for collective action as such is the idea of overlapping participatory intentions, or, more broadly, of individual action oriented around a collective goal.

When individuals act together in this manner, they justify claims of *inclusive* authorship, claims that "we did so-and-so," when spoken by a member of the group. Such claims are inclusive because they can only be made by someone included in the group that together did something. (Contrast these with claims of *exclusive* authorship, claims that something is what "I have done.") Assertions of inclusive authorship are, of course, a deep and familiar part of our social life. We teachers together, in our universities, educate our students, though each of us teaches only a few students and a few courses. We together, in our departments, deliberate, vote and hire, though only some read the files, others skip the meeting, only the chair writes the offer letter. And we judges together, in our courts and chambers, distinguish the licit from the illicit, law from policy, and render judgments, though some hear trials, others reverse us, and others recuse themselves for fear of conflict. These are all things we do together, acts and events for which each can say, for better or for ill, "we did this." We do these things cooperatively, fractiously, and in various forms of hierarchical discipline and divided labor. But what makes it true that we do these things together is that each does his or her part of a collective project.

The move from "we did it" to "the department did it" should now be obvious. Third-personal claims that a collective acts are parasitic on the first-personal inclusive claim—deeply parasitic in the sense that they are rooted in what Gerald Postema has nicely called "deliberation in the first person plural."[48] The department does what we do, when we are the members of the department and act with that identity in mind. Of course, our acting as members of the department—orienting our action within that institutional space—is necessary but not sufficient for the department's acting, for we might be posers. But assuming we meet the relevant criteria for being members of the department, when we vote the department chooses, and our collective choice will be authoritative, in the sense that each must recognize it as a product of our institutional voice. Here we see the importance of interdependence of institutional rules and collective action: only because we satisfy the criteria of the institution does what we do count as institutional action. These criteria, moreover, are criteria both of pedigree and substantive performance. Just as someone not properly appointed could not be considered a member of the department in the formal sense, so also someone whose behavior was so out of line with institutional norms would also be excluded from the inclusive "we." ("He's not really a member of the department," we say of the madman in the attic.)

Now there is one last point to clarify before returning to the case of law. I have said that participants' conceptions of the collective goal must overlap, but that leaves matters too vague, for there is inevitably difference in individual conceptions of the collective goal, indeed debate about how to understand that goal. One member might, for example, think that our actual goal is to promote social justice by looking for a member of an underrepresented group, another that our goal is to show the dean that we are truly self-governing through exercising contentious choice, a third that we need to improve our curricular offerings in political theory. Our individual goals differ, but they overlap with respect to engaging in the hiring process, and that is sufficient to make hiring something we do together, even if fighting for social justice, etc., is not. So overlap is essentially a pragmatic concept and always a matter of degree, given inevitable differences in each agent's expectations and conceptions of the group act. Agents will have more or less determinate conceptions of the group act, they may be more or less willing to compromise after bargaining on the character of that act, and they may have very different ideas about the scope of the group act, its duration and membership. As a result, a group act can be collective under one description and not collective intentional under another.

8. Let us return to law, and the problem for positivism of accommodating disagreement while retaining authority. This can be

brief, since most of the work has already been done. Conceiving judging as collective action shows how law can be the product of social instantiation, while making room for the kinds of disagreement, normative argument, judicial politics, and Herculean deliberative jurisprudence that Dworkin rightly insists is part of the culture of mature legal systems.

Here is the model: a legal system consists of a set of individuals each intentionally doing his or her part in a collective project of establishing a set of criteria for distinguishing those norms that have a privileged status in social ordering from other social norms, and determining the proper application of the privileged norms, plus institutions for generating and revising the privileged norms, plus some extensive set of social practices in a population governed effectively by those norms. We can, without vicious circularity, refer to the privileged norms as "legal" norms, understanding "legal" in terms of the uncontroversial social marks of governing potentially harmful behavior, channeling disputes, empowering contractors susceptible to political change, claiming supreme authority, and so on; and we also can refer to the individuals as judges, though the defense against circularity is slightly more complicated, and I will address it below. So, even more simplified, the model is this: A legal system consists of a set of judges, each intentionally contributing to the systematic distinction of legal from non-legal norms and regulating their application, plus other institutions capable of generating and enforcing those norms.

This model modifies the traditional positivist account by replacing the idea of a regulative convention with respect to the criteria of legality, with the idea of collective action. Alternatively put, it replaces the idea of a regulative convention with the social conditions of its possibility—but these are conditions as well of the possibility of institutionalized disagreement, considered consensus, and strategic bargaining. Regulative conventions still play an indirect role, in structuring the general institution, but they do not directly determine what counts as law within the system. So the institutional unity through content—a conventional set of criteria—becomes institutional unity through agents' orientation towards a collective goal. This orientation consists in part of agents' acceptance of the norms constitutive of the institution—what we could call acceptance of the job description and personal appearance rules (be disinterested, supply reasons for your decision, wear black robes...). It consists in a shared argumentative sensibility, concerning what sort of claim counts as a reason, what the limits of precedential assimilation and distinction are, what level of confidence in a decision is required. And it consists in an acceptance of the project of determining law under some description, be it using legal power to fight social power, or ensuring a social environment predictable enough for citizens to plan their lives, or acting as the agent of the legislature. But it need not consist wholly in acquiescence in a set of shared legal criteria, though such acquiescence may be a consequence of the unified orientation. Consider the analogy of conversation, as developed by Paul Grice.[49] To engage in conversation is to accept certain linguistic conventions, as well as conventions of turn-taking, tone, and the like. And it is to accept a set of pragmatic norms, of relevance, economy, sincerity, and clarity. Sharing these norms (at least some of them) makes conversation possible; but the resulting conversation can be anything from flirtatious banter to consensus-building to a shouting match. Acceptance of the structural norms entails almost nothing about the nature of the conversational content.[50]

Before addressing the problem of normativity, let me defuse the worry of circularity in presupposing an institutional space—the courts, more or less—that serves to orient judicial behavior. The worry is that the rules constitutive of the institution and its offices are legal rules, and so must be validated by the criteria established by the "judges." But the judges are, by hypothesis, only able to establish legality criteria within the context of the constitution, and so circularity seems to be built in. There are two responses. First, as Coleman has argued, the circularity is only apparent, for the *legal* status of the institutional rules is not prior to the acts of the individuals who collectively establish the legality criteria.[51] In establishing the criteria of legality, they make true the claim that they hold legal offices, and that (some of) the norms governing judicial behavior are legal. But the behavior precedes the ascription of legal status, not vice versa. Second, what is necessary is that there be *social* institutions that provide the environment in which what becomes legal practice can take place. Whether such social institutions exist is a contingent matter, a fluke of historical process.[52] But if they do exist, then law is possible. The worry about circularity is analogous to a worry about Hobbesian political theory, namely that a solution to the collective action problem of the state of nature (the prisoner's dilemma) can itself only be established by a collective attempt to solve the problem. But of course a political solution to the prisoner's dilemma—a monopoly on violence, for Hobbes—can be the product of a non-collective process. What *sustains* the monopoly is that it does solve the collective action problem, but the explanation of its emergence can look quite different.

9. When judges do share an institutional orientation, no matter how they disagree in their decisions, their decisions count as conclusions of law, not of men. By acting collectively, judges warrant the attribution of their decisions to the institution as a whole: their decisions are decisions of law; their decisions therefore claim the authority the institution claims, and have the authority the institution deserves. The legitimating effects of the institutional attribution resonate both externally and internally to the institution. Externally to the institution—from the perspective of a legal subject—some judge's determination that proposition P is law marks P as authoritative, as coming from a particular instantiation of authority, and so gives the subject reason to comply. And internally to the institution, the judge's decision is—from the perspective of another judge—something we have done, and therefore a move in the collective project that demands response. The response may be acquiescence, or it may be rejection, but a response is demanded nonetheless. Compare liability: if I am a member of a group that together causes some disaster, I owe a response to that harm, and its victims, that I would not if I were not a member. Its being our act makes a difference, even if the act was not mine.[53] Similarly, some judge's decision that P is law is now an element in how other judges must understand what they together have done; it partly defines, by modifying, how the collective project is realized.

Here is the truth in Dworkin's claim that precedents have "gravitational force" even when the rule they stand for does not apply in the instant case. As a matter of phenomenology, the explanation lies in judges' realization that the decision is one for which, and to which, they are responsible, since it is, in the inclusive sense, their decision. And as a matter of jurisprudence, the decision now exists as a kind of disequilibriation of the collective project of discovering the law, a shift in collective direction that may call for correction or endorsement. What does not seem true is that it should have even defeasible binding force as a precedent—that *stare decisis* should, as a conceptual matter, be a norm of the institution. Again, the comparison with liability is instructive. The proper response from me to a harm caused by a fellow actor may be sympathy, if my fellowship gives me insight into a basis for excuse; or it may warrant special condemnation, if my insight makes me see how stupid what he did was. Errors by others, in pursuit of the collective project I share, attract my attention, to be sure, but not necessarily my loyalty.

One consequence of this revision to positivism is that the criteria of law are no longer usefully represented in terms of a rule of recognition. Some rule-like generalizations, of course can be made—e.g., the Constitution is law, custom is law, legislative history is not law. And some of these generalizations may be supported by argumentative consensus, or by conventional acceptance. But the source of their support is a contingent feature, and the only general thing that can be said of the community's criteria of law is that, ultimately, they consist in what the judges offer as contributions to the collective project of law-determination. Any statement of a "rule" represents merely a temporary equilibrium in an ongoing collective project. Fortunately, we do not need rules to account for normativity at the foundations of law. The duties of the judges to find law come from a shared conception of the institution in which they find themselves: to accept the job is to accept the norms, mandatory and permissive both, that structure the institution, and so make one liable for deviations therefrom. And the normativity of the decisions themselves, as I have argued, consists in their being products of the collective project, and so constituting grounds for deliberative response. The criteria are not, therefore, duty-generating, but they are response-demanding, and this seems normativity enough—moreover it is normativity whose ground is purely social. The distinction between positivism and natural law is thus preserved. Last, because inconsistent decisions need not be reconciled into a rule, this version of positivism escapes the problem of extracting a univocal, propositional rule from divergent behavior.

It also follows from this account that the criteria of legality cannot serve the function of guiding conduct as exhaustively as some positivists, notably Shapiro, have claimed, since that function can only be performed by rules.[54] And since I have left open the possibility that the criteria of legality deployed by some or all judges may include, as a contingent matter, moral and political criteria, the account is open to Joseph Raz's related argument that moral and political criteria cannot perform the validating function that law must perform if it is to be law.[55] This is a complex debate, into which I do not wish to wander far. The response I can offer is this: insofar as the objection to non-rule-based criteria derives from the function of law, it would seem that it could be satisfied as a matter of degree.[56] This account does permit the coalescence of legality criteria into rules, as a contingent matter. So, even if as a conceptual matter a legal system is characterized in terms of a certain, very high degree of rule-guidance with respect to the criteria of legality, it may be a contingent matter whether collective attempts at legal organization actually satisfy the success criteria. This seems intuitively correct, for a social institution characterized by nothing but disagreement over the criteria of legality could not, as a matter of practice let alone principle, perform the social ordering that is an existence condition of a legal system. On my account, law is grounded in an adjudicative community, and while that community may be fractious, that fractiousness must be understood against a background of common purpose. The mistake, however, is to build agreement into the account of normativity at the root of law, or to think that normativity can only be provided by either rules or morality. Rather, what we do together can be a source of reasons.

Notes

*I am very grateful to Jules Coleman and Scott Shapiro for early conversations about the topic of this essay—indeed, it was Scott who argued for the need for understanding positivism in terms of judicial collective action, and who made clear the form such a theory could take. Joseph Raz has provided wonderfully helpful comments as have members of the Bay Area Forum for Law and Ethics (BAFFLE), and the Analytic Legal Philosophy (ALP) conference. And I am also grateful to Mark Antaki for his very helpful research assistance, and to the Townsend Humanities Center for fellowship support during this essay's writing.

1. "[A]liquis non debet esse judex in propria causa." Sir Edward Coke, *The First Part of the Institutes of England* (London: J. & W.T. Clarke, 18th ed. 1823), §141a.
2. I don't mean to imply that their content is exhausted by actually existing institutional structures, for there can be questions whether, for example, a matter for a court counts as a "case"—questions that cannot simply be answered ostensively. But actual institutions will supply something like a focal meaning for the term. I return to these semantic issues below.
3. Ronald Dworkin, *Law's Empire* (Cambridge: Harvard University Press, 1986), ch. 2.
4. I argue for the consistency of indeterminacy and rational justification in "Just Disagreement: Indeterminacy and Rationality in the Rule of Law," *Yale Law Journal* 103 (1994): 997–1030.
5. Compare Stanley Cavell, *The Claim of Reason* (New York: Oxford University Press, 1979), ch. 5, on the grounding of reason in "form of life." Wittgenstein may be read to suggest that the rules of deductive inference, too,

are grounded in forms of life, but this claim is highly controversial, to the extent it is not tautological. See Ludwig Wittgenstein, *Remarks on the Foundations of Mathematics* (Cambridge: MIT Press, 1967), esp. §§I, 149–155. I do want to distance myself from any claim, rightly or wrongly associated with Wittgenstein, that community approval is *sufficient* warrant for rules of inference. There may well be objective limits on how any particular community of reasoners can construct their rules of inference, just as there are natural limits on how a community can construct rules of eating. For discussion, see David Cerbone, "Don't look but think: imaginary scenarios in Wittgenstein's later philosophy." *Inquiry* 37 (1994):159–184.

6. Jules Coleman, *The Practice of Principle* (New York: Oxford University Press, 2001), ch. 7.
7. See Dworkin, *Law's Empire*, esp. ch. 1.
8. John Austin, *The Province of Jurisprudence Determined* (New York: Prometheus Press, 2000).
9. H.L.A. Hart, *The Concept of Law* (New York: Oxford University Press, 2nd ed., 1961), 105 (emphasis in original). Joseph Raz, in "Kelsen on the nature of normativity," claims that Hart was merely trying to account for what Raz calls the "social" as opposed to "justified" normativity of law. Raz, *The Authority of Law* (New York: Oxford University Press, 1979), 134. But Hart's distinction in his account of conventional rules between genuine obligation and the belief that one is obligated, clearly presupposes a distinction between subjective and objective reasons. Hart, *Concept of Law*, 88.
10. This survey is indebted to the review article by Keith Whittington, "Once More Unto the Breach: PostBehavioralist Approaches to Judicial Politics," *Law and Social Inquiry* 25: 601–633 (2000). See also Lawrence Baum, *The Puzzle of Judicial Behavior* (Ann Arbor: University of Michigan Press, 1997), for a useful overview. The argument of this section is indebted to Robert Post, "The Supreme Court as Institutional Practice: Dissent, Legal Scholarship, and Decisionmaking in the Taft Court" *Minnesota Law Review* 85 (2001: 1267–1384).
11. Jeffrey Segal and Howard Spaeth, *The Supreme Court and the Attitudinal Model* (New York: Cambridge University Press, 1993), 65. There would be an obvious problem of circularity, if evidence of the justices' politics were taken from their decisions. Spaeth and Segal confront the objection squarely, however, and I am convinced they separate the two data sets adequately.
12. One measure of the force of precedent is that in only 10% of the studied cases does a dissenting Justice in the original precedent later shift toward that precedent. Spaeth and Segal, *Majority Will or Minority Rule: Adherence to Precedent on the U.S. Supreme Court* (New York: Cambridge University Press, 1999), 287–288.
13. See Lee Epstein and Jack Knight, *The Choices Justices Make* (Washington, D.C.: CQ Press, 1998), Figure 2-1.
14. See Epstein and Knight; and Post, "Supreme Court as Institutional Practice."
15. Epstein and Knight, *supra*, is the canonical work in this vein.
16. See, e.g., Rogers Smith, *Liberalism and American Constitutional Law* (Cambridge: Harvard University Press, 1988).

17. For example, it is suggested that Supreme Court justices clearly play to a public, seeking to enhance public reputations, through their practices of dissent. See Baum, *Puzzle of Judicial Behavior*, 47–55.
18. Alternatively, one might see lower courts as applying norms validated by higher legal norms, and doing so not because they accept the conventional authority of those norms, but because of other, external pressures to do so (for example the embarrassment of being overturned). This view would put lower courts in the role of ordinary citizens, whose practice of obedience is not necessarily constitutive of the system's rule of recognition, but may be simply a function of the exercise of power.
19. Baum, *Puzzle*, 24–25.
20. See, e.g., Justin J. Green, "Parameters of Dissensus on Shifting Small Groups," in *Judicial Conflict and Consensus*, ed. Sheldon Goldman and Charles M. Lamb (Lexington, Kentucky: University Press of Kentucky, 1986), 139–153; and Henry R. Glick and George W. Pruet, Jr., "Dissent in State Supreme Courts: Patterns and Correlates of Conflict," also in Goldman and Lamb, 199–214.
21. Hart, *CL*, 94–95.
22. This is to neglect Kent Greenawalt's point that, strictly construed, the rule of recognition for the federal system therefore consists of the amending clause of the Constitution, since the rule of recognition is also, according to Hart, the supreme criterion of law. But this point depends on Hart's particular formulation of the criteria of legality. See Kent Greenawalt, "The Rule of Recognition and the Constitution," Michigan Law Review 85 (1987): 621–671. I am indebted to Greenawalt's article.
23. Hart, *CL*, 86ff.
24. Wittgenstein, *Philosophical Investigations*, trans. G.E.M. Anscombe (New York: MacMillan, 1953), esp. §§177–202; Saul Kripke, *Wittgenstein on Rules and Private Language* (Cambridge: Harvard University Press, 1982).
25. See Dworkin, *Law's Empire*.
26. I mean here to allude to Donald Davidson's account of interpreting an idiolect, a condition of whose possibility is objective constraints on the belief attributable by the interpreter to the speaker, but which leaves room for a range of plausible interpretations. See, e.g., Davidson, "The Inscrutability of Reference," in *Inquiries into Truth and Interpretation* (New York: Oxford University Press, 1984).
27. For this statement of the problem, and a discussion of the solution, see Coleman, *Practice of Principle*, ch. 7.
28. In the jargon of philosophy of mind, the "internal point of view" has in part a world-to-mind direction of fit, unlike belief which has a mind-to-world direction of fit.
29. For discussion, see Michael Bratman, *Intentions, Plans & Practical Reasoning*, ch. 5; T.M. Scanlon, *What We Owe to Each Other*, 45–47.
30. Thus I agree with Andrei Marmor that worries about the duty-generating capacity of conventionalist accounts are spurious. See his "Legal Conventionalism," *Legal Theory* 4 (1998): 509–531, 530, an article with which I have considerable sympathy in its emphasis on historical contingency. But cf. Cole-

man, *Practice of Principle*, 90–91. Coleman's and Kenneth Himma's reference to reliance-based obligations can only be understood as a way to show that judicial conventions impose *prima facie* moral obligations, a task beyond that called for by the positivist program. Coleman, *Practice of Principle*, 98; quoting Kenneth Himma, "Inclusive Legal Positivism," in Coleman and Scott Shapiro (eds.), *The Oxford Handbook of Jurisprudence and Legal Philosophy* (Oxford: Oxford University Press, forthcoming 2001).

31. See Philippa Foot, "Does Morality Consist of Hypothetical Imperatives?" *Virtues and Vices and Other Essays* (Berkeley: University of California Press, 1978); Williams, "Internal and External Reasons," *Moral Luck* (New York: Cambridge University Press, 1981); "Internal Reasons and the Obscurity of Blame," *Making Sense of Humanity* (New York: Cambridge University Press, 1995). I mean only to invoke the language of "recruitment" for the uncontroversial case of etiquette norms. No one, I think, thinks that chewing with one's mouth closed is a categorical imperative.
32. Ronald Dworkin, "The Model of Rules II," in *Taking Rights Seriously* (Cambridge, Mass.: Harvard University Press, 1978), 51. Dworkin's argument is effectively criticized by Hart in his Postscript, *CL*, 256–257.
33. Indeed, most rules of etiquette could not survive rational reflection if they needed to be supported by Dworkin's "normative state of affairs."
34. I do not mean to claim that Hart thought judging purely unreflective, only that the theory of convention he provides makes no room for that reflection. The problem, as Marmor notes, may be that his paradigms of convention, social norms, are too arbitrary to serve as an appropriate model for law. And indeed, it is a notable feature of social norms that they erode under reflective scrutiny.
35. David Lewis, *Convention: A Philosophical Study* (Cambridge: Harvard University Press, 1969); Jules Coleman, "Incorporationism, Conventionality, and the Practical Difference Thesis," *Legal Theory* 4 (1998): 381–425; Gerald Postema, "Coordination and Convention at the Foundations of Law," *Journal of Legal Studies* (1982): 165.
36. Oliver Wendell Holmes, "The Path of the Law," *Harvard Law Review* 10 (1897): 457, 469.
37. See Coleman, *Practice of Principle*, 94–95 (citing Shapiro), for an explanation of this point.
38. It would, for example, be difficult to explain the behavior of the U.S. Ninth Circuit Court of Appeals on any other basis; the frequency with which they are reversed suggests a counter-conformity strategy.
39. Coleman, *Practice of Principle*, 96ff. See generally Michael Bratman, *Faces of Intention* (New York: Cambridge University Press, 1999), Part II, especially "Shared Cooperative Activity," 93–108.
40. Bratman, "Shared Cooperative Activity," 93.
41. Coleman, *Practice of Principle*, 98–99.
42. Bratman, "Shared Cooperative Activity," 103–104.
43. Bratman makes a similar point, criticizing Margaret Gilbert's claim that mutual obligation is partly constitutive of collective action. See his "Shared Intention and Mutual Obligation," 130–141.

44. Surely the explanation of, say, Justice Scalia's angry dissents is not that they are his means of meeting his commitment to ensuring that his colleagues interpret the law aright. Rather, they are his means of stating what the right view is, period.
45. They may have other duties towards fellow participants, such as courtesy, but that is a separate matter.
46. This example is developed, although very differently, in J. David Velleman, "How to Share an Intention," reprinted in *The Possibility of Practical Reason* (Oxford: Oxford University Press, 2000), 200–221.
47. See my "Acting Together," *Philosophy and Phenomenological Research* 61 (2000): 1–31. That article provides a criticism of more elaborate conditions of collective action claimed to be constitutive of it.
48. Gerald Postema, "Morality in the First Person Plural," *Law and Philosophy* 14 (1995): 35–64.
49. Paul Grice, "Logic and Conversation," in *Studies in the Way of Words* (Cambridge: Harvard University Press, 1989), 22–40.
50. Hence Grice is wrong, I think, to say that conversation is intrinsically cooperative, at least if "cooperative" is understood in Bratman's sense. Sharing the project of talking together is necessary, but the commitment to mutual support need not be present.
51. Coleman, *Practice of Principles*, 101.
52. See Marmor, "Legal Conventionalism," 528, for a similar point.
53. The importance of collective action for ascriptions of liability is the subject of my book, *Complicity: Ethics and Law for a Collective Age* (New York: Cambridge University Press, 2000).
54. Scott Shapiro, "On Hart's Way Out," *Legal Theory* 4 (1998): 469–508.
55. See, e.g., Joseph Raz, "Legal Positivism and the Sources of Law," in *The Authority of Law* (New York: Oxford University Press, 1979).
56. See Coleman, *Practice of Principle*, Lecture Nine, for a better defense of this claim.

PHILOSOPHICAL ISSUES, 11
Social, Political, and Legal Philosophy, 2001

Law as Command: The Model of Command in Modern Jurisprudence

Gerald J. Postema

> Statutes are not Philosophy as is the Common-Law, and other disputable Arts, but are Commands or Prohibitions...
>
> Thomas Hobbes, *Dialogue*

I. Command as a jurisprudential commonplace

The command theory of law is widely associated with classical positivist jurisprudence. In an early manuscript, Bentham boldly and simply announced, "A law is a command....Thus much we must conceive of it on all occasions, to conceive clearly. Everything that is not a command therefore is not a law." [1] His most important jurisprudential work, *Of Laws in General*, opens with a *definition* of law that elaborates this simple thesis into a sophisticated, "imperatival" version of the command theory.[2] The definition was not theoretically innocent, of course, since Bentham used it to condemn English common law as "a thing merely imaginary." [3] John Austin, while much more willing to grant residency to common law in the province of jurisprudence, nevertheless also opened his treatise with the sentence, "Laws proper, or properly so called, are commands..." and he never repented of his use of this model.[4]

What is remarkable to early 21st century readers of Bentham and Austin, perhaps, is not the fact that they used the concept of command to model core ideas of law, but rather that they felt no need to *defend* this use. This is especially surprising in view of the fact that both seemed aware of at least some of the important limits of the model.[5]

If we travel back into the history of modern jurisprudential theory we may find an explanation of this remarkable feature of classical positivist writing. In fact, the definition of law as the general command of a superior addressed to an inferior was a jurisprudential commonplace already in the 17th century. Hobbes's familiar definition of law comes to mind immediately. "Law in generall, is not Counsell," he wrote, "but Command...addressed to one formerly obliged to obey him."[6] The "philosopher" of Hobbes's *Dialogue* elaborates: "A Law is the Command of him, or them that have the Soveraign Power, given to those that be his or their Subjects, declaring Publickly, and plainly what every of them may do, and what they must forbear to do."[7] It is especially noteworthy that Hobbes made a special point of conceding that the Laws of Nature he defended (for example in *Leviathan*, chs. 14 and 15) are not *proper laws*, but "only Conclusions, or Theoremes concerning what conduceth to the conservation and defence of [men]". They can be regarded properly as *laws*, he argued, only "if we consider the same Theoremes, as delivered in the word of God, that by right commandeth all things".[8]

Of course, Hobbes was not the only writer known to Bentham and Austin who defined law in terms of sovereign commands. Even standard-bearers of the common law tradition, who had every reason to give no jurisprudential quarter to the concept of command, can be found to utter the commonplace. Blackstone, in his general introduction to *Commentaries* (entitled "Of the Nature of Laws in General"), wrote "Law in its most general and comprehensive sense signifies a rule of action...prescribed by some superior, and which the inferior is bound to obey....[Law] is a rule of action dictated by some supreme being..."[9] Blackstone, of course, was a common law jurist, not a legal philosopher, and may simply have been mouthing platitudes without appreciating fully their implications for his own understanding of the nature of common law. But we find that even Sir Matthew Hale, perhaps the most powerful common law intellect of the 17th century, who penned a vigorous defense of common law against Hobbes's attack in the *Dialogue*,[10] nevertheless could write the following in an essay entitled "On the nature of laws".

> [A] law I take to be a rule of moral actions, given to a being endued with understanding and will, by him that hath power and authority to give the same and exact obedience thereunto per modum imperii commanding or forbidding such actions under some penalty expressed or implicitly contained in such law.[11]

Laws differ in this respect from other "prescript rules" like the prescription of a physician, Hale insisted, for the latter "is a rule indeed, but not juncta cum imperio." And he concluded, echoing Hobbes, "if atheistical persons could, as they would, exterminate the great God of heaven from having to do in this world, that, which they call reason and the law of reason, would be indeed a rule, but not truly and formally a law." [12] It is relevant that Hale is focusing here on *moral* laws and, as a devout Christian, he was convinced that the moral order depended on a legislating God. Yet, the key concept he used to express this conviction was *law*, and the application to the juridical phenomena with which he dealt on a daily basis could not have escaped his view. This same common law jurist argued vigorously against Hobbes for the view that the common law of England was rooted ultimately not in the expressions of the sovereign will, but in common custom of the land and especially the "artificial reason" of those trained in its common law.

There is a deep antipathy between the way law is conceived by classical common law jurists and the model of law as sovereign commands. In view of this incompatibility—which Bentham, of course, trumpeted without mercy—it is more than surprising that staunch defenders of common law could embrace such general definitions of law. An explanation may be possible, but it must wait for another occasion. I mention it here only to emphasize that the power of this model of law was great enough to insinuate itself even into the vocabulary and frame of mind of common lawyers of the 17th and 18th centuries.

It was also pervasive in the work of writers in the medieval and early modern natural law tradition, both its Scholastic and Protestant wings. Indeed, the command model of law had a recognized albeit contested place in the natural law tradition at least since the Ockham in the 14th century, and it was revived during the Reformation in the strongly voluntarist moral and political theories of Luther, Calvin, and their followers.

However, it is reasonable to assume that the headwaters of this intellectual stream were classical. We might find a clue in Heraclitus, who is reported to have said, "To obey the will of one man is also *nomos*."[13] This suggests that we could trace the command model of law to ancient Greece, but to do so would misunderstand both Heraclitus and the command model. For "*nomos*" is probably best translated here as "statute" rather than (more generally) as "law".[14] Moreover, *nomos* is only one of several overlapping terms used in classical Greece for the legal or juridical, and *nomos* itself had a wider meaning than that suggested in the Heraclitean fragment. As Martin Ostwald writes,

> *nomos* denotes an order of living, a way of life...[It] describes an order of some kind, which differs from the order expressed in the early archaic age by *themis* in that it sees its sanction in its acceptance by those who live under it and who acknowledge it as valid and binding for themselves. It is, therefore, not part of a universal order but of a limited social order, nor is it like *thesmos* something imposed by an external agent; even when it is attributed to a god or a lawgiver, the source of its validity always remains its general acceptance as a norm by those who constitute a given milieu (Ostwald, p. 682).

In this sense, Aristotle wrote of *nomoi* when he had a conventional, but not necessarily legislated, order in mind.[15]

More likely, the source can be found in the 6th century *Corpus Juris Civilis*, and the much debated doctrine announced at the opening of the *Digest*: *quod principi placuit, legis habet vigorem*—what pleases the prince has the force of law.[16] This doctrine attracted vigorous debate throughout medieval Europe over the foundations and scope of imperial authority, and over the relationship between imperial legislation (*lex*) and custom, both local and general (*mos, consuetude, ius gentium*).[17]

The influence of Justinian's definition also greatly influenced the debates between intellectualists and voluntarists concerning the foundations of morality from the 14th to the 17th centuries.[18] The issues were, of course, principally theological, yet implicit assumptions about the nature of law powerfully shaped the debate. In 1612, Suarez effected a brilliant reconciliation of these embattled wings of the Scholastic natural law party, at the core of which was a concept of law modeled on that of command.[19] Although they differed with the Scholastics on philosophical fundamentals, especially over the soundness of Aristotelian metaphysics, leaders of the Protestant natural law tradition, especially Pufendorf, reached a reconciliation that was in several respects similar. Indeed, the 17th century produced a distinctive and powerful conceptual framework for understanding law that provided a kind of common language in which competing theories of law and morality were articulated and debated.

What characterized the command tradition of thinking about law, if I may refer to it in this way, was that it took the command of a superior to an inferior to be a defining feature of law, not of a certain kind of law—statutes, for example—but of law in general. On this view, this feature distinguishes law from other requirements, rules, norms, conventions, and forms of order. We see this idea at work in the point made by Hobbes and Hale, and uttered regularly by writers on law and morality at least since the 1600s, that requirements on human behavior may be wise, good, or even rationally necessary, but they are not *laws* unless commanded by a superior (e.g., God). That which is reasonable, prudent, right, or just is one thing, but law is another. For the *legal* is not (or not merely) the right (*ius*), it is law (*lex*), and its distinguishing mark is that it is obligating, binding (from *ligare*, as they often point out). The conduct to which we are *bound* is not merely good, proper, reasonable, wise, advisable, right, recommended, or even something one ought or is required to do, it is *commanded*; and that which we are obligated to forbear is not merely inadvisable, imprudent, unreasonable, improper, or even evil or wrong, it is *forbidden*. Law, or rather *laws*, alone articulate and underwrite these obligations. To use language now fashionable, law is not merely normative; it is a distinct species of the normative.

Contemporary jurisprudence has abandoned the language of command. However, it is an interesting question whether, or to what extent, it has abandoned the conceptual model to which that language pointed. In this essay, I wish to identify and articulate some of the assumptions of this model. I will focus on key figures in 17th century jurisprudence because they seem to have developed the model most richly. (I will also consult Austin from time to time to bridge the centuries to our era.) I will then look at Bentham's 18th century empiricist version of the model because there is reason to think that he, not Austin, began to break with this tradition, but in ways that some contemporary jurisprudence—for example, that of Hart[20]—is unwilling to follow.

I should say at the outset that the ideas and assumptions I will highlight are not in every case shared by all those we might want to locate in the "command tradition," as I have called it. Yet, they tend to hang together philosophically, and departures are remarkably few and relatively minor. Moreover, although I will take the 17th century, and especially Suarez and Pufendorf, as my primary sources, what I hope will be clear is that the general conceptual contours of the assumptions of the command model remain even when we vary substantially the metaphysical and epistemological framework in which they are located. In that respect, the model is remarkably resilient.

II. Background assumptions of the command model

The concept of command has attracted a wide variety of legal theorists from medieval to modern times as an apt model of the nature of law. These theorists share a number of background assumptions—sometimes explicitly articulated and defended, sometimes functioning only vaguely in the background—which give a distinctive shape to the inquiries into the nature of law these theorists pursue. I will mention three structuring assumptions that seem to me to be of some importance.

First, typically jurisprudential inquiry was regarded as part of a larger project of philosophical inquiry. The domain of the *juridical*—typically called "human law" or "positive law"—was seen as a species of a genus that also includes morality, religious duties, and politics.[21] Unlike much contemporary jurisprudence, the initial theoretical aim of this tradition is not to find a way to *distinguish* law from morality, but rather to *relate* them; or rather, to locate important differences against a background of common features.

Second, writers in the command tradition typically assumed that common to laws of all kinds was the fact that they "pertain to" intelligent, rational, free beings, and order their behavior;[22] correlatively, law properly so called orders behavior in a way appropriate to such beings. The proximate aim of such directives is the ordering of their behavior in this distinctive way. Thus, laws properly speaking have a distinctive *modus operandi*, and an anticipated outcome of this operation is that the behavior of free intelligent beings will manifest a certain order. Thus, it was widely assumed that the juridical was a department of the practical, that inquiry into the nature of law was part of a more general inquiry into the domain of practical life. Three aspects or implications of this structuring assumption call for further comment: (1) the idea of law's having a distinctive proximate aim, (2) the relation of the juridical domain to the rest of practical inquiry, and, most importantly, (3) the conception of the subjects of law common to the command tradition.

(1) The fact that it was commonly assumed that the law had as its proximate aim to guide the behavior of free intelligent beings does not imply that laws were thought necessarily (at least, at this level of abstraction) to have a single or dominant function. This is a common thought in this tradition and in jurisprudence generally, of course, but it is not entailed by this structural assumption. It was simply assumed that laws operate (and, so, to achieve whatever ends to which they were ultimately directed) in a distinctive way because they were addressed to beings of a certain kind. We can perhaps speak of the "proximate aim" of laws, on this view, but to say that the *function* of law is to "guide behavior" or "to seek compliance" would be at best misleading and at worst would just be an empty claim. To say that normative guidance (of a special kind) is law's distinctive business does not specify anything like a "function" or "task". Compliance with rules cannot intelligibly be put forward as an end in itself. Even in the limiting case of the absolute autocrat, the autocrat's aim is not simply to produce compliance with his dictates; rather, he seeks compliance as a public expression of their subjection to his will. This is an intelligible, if highly objectionable, further aim. Thus, to say the law's business is normative guidance only identifies a *distinctive way* in which law seeks to achieve whatever ends or aims it has (whether these be aims it has by nature or contingently by assignment). The philosophical task, then, according to this tradition, is to explain this distinctive kind of ordering. The juridical is seen as part of the general philosophical enterprise of understanding the practical domain; jurisprudence is a key part of practical philosophy.

Thus, the motivation for the inquiry was usually not narrowly metaphysical. Some legal philosophers, especially those with strongly empiricist leanings, might have been drawn to the command model in some part because it enabled them to offer a minimalist ontology of norms—for example, in terms of norms reduced to wishes, their public expressions, and likely sanctions. This was not typically what attracted theorists to the model throughout the history of this broad and motley tradition. Most of the theorists who use the command model were already committed to a rich ontology in virtue of their theology. They had no reason to be especially scrupulous about the ontology of norms.

(2) These writers were keenly aware that law, and the kind of normative guidance it claims to provide, does not exhaust the field.

There are norms, rules, and guides of several different kinds. Law is a special case, and, in their view, an especially important one. They regarded law as a species of the normative, and the juridical (human law) in turn as a species of the law-normative. They took the first task of jurisprudential inquiry, then, to be to explain the law-normative. For this purpose, *command* offered a ready metaphor and delivered to the theorist a handy set of conceptual tools.

Thus, the idea of command typically was not used in this tradition to mark the broad meta-ethical distinction between fact and value, or to explain the motivational power of evaluative, moral, or legal judgments. In this tradition, law was distinguished from evaluative judgments, standards of instrumental rationality, and even judgments of moral right and wrong by the fact that law alone imposes *binding obligations*. A law, says Suarez, is not merely a rule or measure of action; it is a binding precept (OL I.1.5–7). Thus, "the will of God", for example, "assumes in the actions themselves [that it commands or forbids] some necessary rightness or wrongness, and *joins to them* a special obligation of law" (OL II.6.11, emphasis added).[23] Hobbes, too, as we noted above, recognized the practical force of "dictates of reason" (his "laws" of nature), but distinguished them from laws proper, which were thought to have a special binding force that is best modeled by a command. The concept of law qua command was not introduced to help answer a meta-ethical question; rather, it gave shape to that question. What this tradition sought to explain with the model of command is not normativity *in general*, but a specific kind of normativity.

Austin's use of the command model is instructive in this respect. His famous positivist dictum—"the existence of law is one thing, its merit or demerit is another"—and his attack on the alleged natural law slogan, "an unjust law is no law at all", both implicitly rely on the command model (*Province*, pp. 184–5). Yet, his account of the sole "measure or test" of law "as it ought [morally] to be" *itself* relies on the command model: morality properly speaking is God's command (*Province*, pp. 6, 12, and Lecture II *passim.*) Thus, Austin holds that the nature of the demands of both morality and positive law—of law-like normativity in both domains—is captured by the idea of sovereign commands. The *positivity* of positive law, for Austin, is a *further* matter, which is to be spelled out against the background of this feature shared with (non-positive) morality.

(3) The command tradition rests on a strong assumption about the nature of beings subject to law. Laws properly so called do

not (merely) characterize or describe an ordering, either real or idea, it was assumed. Neither do they merely create or sustain (or, as we would say, "cause") that ordering. Although it was important to explain how law could be *productive* of behavior, the manner in which law sought to be productive, on this view, was determined by the nature of the beings whose behavior it governed. Thus, the characteristic response sought by law of a law-subject is not that of the snake to its charmer.[24] To be sure, laws and sanctions sometimes do influence behavior of rational agents in this way—they may merely succumb to the policeman's voice or bearing, as Falk points out—but when law has this effect it does not influence them *qua* free beings. And a defining fact about law, in this tradition, is that it pertains to—it is directed to—free, intelligent beings.[25]

This freedom was understood to involve, at the most fundamental level, a degree of understanding of oneself, one's actions, and the world in which one acts, and a capacity based on this understanding to direct one's actions according to a rule or norm, or according to the reasons available to one (Pufendorf, OLN I.1.7). Joseph Raz captured this assumption concerning the nature of law-subjects in his recent exploration of normativity. Persons have a "capacity to perceive and understand how things are, and what response is appropriate to them" and an "ability to respond appropriately", he wrote. They are able to direct their lives "in accordance with their appreciation of themselves and their environment, and of the reasons with which, given how they are, the world presents them."[26] Some command theorists insist, further, that freedom involves what is now called freedom of alternative possibilities, that is, an ability to do or not do an act as one wills.[27]

Law, then, was said to "pertain to" its subjects regarded as free, self-directing beings. They pertain to such beings not merely in the sense of being *concerned with* them or their behavior, as, for example, rules for the care of pet turtles pertain to turtles, but in the stronger sense of being *addressed to* them in their capacity as free, self-directing beings. To them law addresses rules, norms, and requirements. In doing so, it assumes that they are capable of grasping them and acting in accord with them based on this understanding, and expects them to behave in certain ways because they exercise these capacities effectively. On this view, it is an essential feature of laws that they seek to play a special role in the practical reasoning of those to whom they are addressed.

This structuring assumption is reflected in the fact that writers in this broad tradition naturally and almost exclusively speak of *lex* rather then *ius*.[28] Both terms can be translated "law," of course, but they give very different shape to the idea thus conveyed. Three differences are especially important at this point in our discussion. First, *lex* is easily thought of in the plural, *leges*, without any risk of a substantial change of meaning. In contrast, *ius* typically undergoes a change in meaning when made plural. This is not merely a linguistic oddity; it reflects the fact that *lex* encouraged theorists to think of individual laws, subjected, perhaps, to some systematizing, but the system would seem to be imposed as it were from the outside, not entailed by the very concept. The distinction is not, strictly speaking, the distinction Austin identified, namely the distinction between law and justice.[29] It is, rather, a distinction between law regarded as an order or structure (of behavior of rational beings, for example) and law regarded as individual rules or norms. Aquinas captured the implicit difference. *Ius*, he claimed in the *Summa Theologiae*, is an objective, rational ordering of social behavior and relations amongst members of a community (ST 2a2ae 57.1). Human beings participate in this ordering as rational beings, discovering the principles of this ordering and self-consciously directing their actions in accord with it (ST 1a2ae 90.1; 93.5). *Ius* refers to the order conceived as a whole and in respect of its ordering; *lex* refers to precepts or ordinances (*rationes ordinatio*) defined with respect to it. Hence, "*lex non est ipsum ius proprie loquendo, sed aliqualis ratio iuris*" (ST 2a2ae 57.1 ad 2, see also ST 1a2ae 90.4). Thus, the preference of writers in the command tradition for *lex* over *ius* reveals not a bias against the marriage of law and justice usually associated with natural law jurisprudence, but rather a strong tendency to think of law (whether linked to justice or not) in terms of *laws*, the systematic relations amongst which are not presupposed by the notion of law itself, as might have been suggested by the term *ius*.

Second, common to this tradition is the idea that law (*lex*) arises from and takes shape in the relations between or among rational beings, that legal norms (moral as well as juridical) are expressions of certain social relations (taking "social" in a sense sufficiently wide to include that between Creator and creature). For the command tradition, this social relation, we shall see, is that between a superior being or person and those inferior to that being. Finally, the third way in which the choice of *lex* over *ius* shaped jurisprudential thinking follows on the previous two. It is natural (albeit not logically necessary) to regard these individual legal norms as the product of some (and so someone's) making or at least of more or less explicit adoption, hence as the product of legislation.

Thus, to summarize, the command tradition started from the assumption that laws typically do, or must claim to, provide distinctive practical guidance to free, self-directing beings. In view of its background assumptions, the concept of command offered a model, a particular interpretation, of this special kind of normativity, distinctive of *law's* rational guidance, whether it be law of God, moral law, or law of the state.

III. Normativity according to the command tradition

I propose to take a closer look at the model of command as it was developed especially in 17th century legal philosophers. This model was built out of three basic concepts: will, unequal social relations, and generality. These concepts provide the terms in which the special conception of normative guidance attributed to law was expressed.

Will. The concept of will bears the largest part of the explanatory burden. Writers in this tradition sought to model several important features of law's normativity with the help of this notion. First, will was typically understood to be the faculty that is most nearly proximate to rational action. Will, says Suarez, is "the principle that moves and brings one to the performance of an action..." (OL I.5.15). Hobbes famously defined will as "the last Appetite, or Aversion, immediately adhaering to the action, or to the omission thereof" (*Leviathan*, ch. 6, p. 127). Pufendorf calls will "a determinative principle" (EJU, p. 49). According to this tradition, will is a rational faculty in the sense that it is responsive to reasons and judgment, but its job is strictly *executive.* It is, in Pufendorf's word, the "internal directress of [one's] action" (OLN I.4.1); Suarez calls it "the executory power" (OL I.4.11). Will is "the starting point of voluntary actions", wrote Hobbes, "hence it is not capable of deliberation and agreements" (DC, ch. 5.8).

The nature of self-directed action (that is, *imperium*—command) was a contested issue in Scholastic philosophy.[30] Aquinas, for example, insisted that *imperium* was an act of intelligence, setting the decided-upon course of action, the product of deliberation and decision, before one as one proceeds (ST 1a2ae 17.1). Suarez accepted that in order for the command of the lawmaker to direct the action of the subject that subject must bring the command "before and into direct contact with" his will, which is an act of judgment or the intellect (OL I.4.5). However, with respect to self-chosen, freely-willed action, Suarez thought that Aquinas's *imperium* was a fiction. In his view, Aquinas had introduced an unnecessary step in his account of the process of intelligent movement from deliberation to action; indeed, he declared that such an act of the intellect was impossible (OL I.4.11). Will or command, as Suarez saw it, was just that which "moves" the subject to action (OL I.4.10–12, I.5.6). However, it is clear that in this debate all parties assumed that will (and hence command) appears only at the stage of *executing* deliberative resolution.[31] As Suarez put it, "To the will pertains the subsequent application of the other power in actual use"—including judgment or the intellect (OL I.4.11). With the concept of will the command tradition captured the *executive* nature of commands (and hence of law).

Second, not only is will the faculty by which one moves *oneself* to action; it is equally the faculty by which one "moves" another to act.[32] Will, we might say, is *transitive*; it somehow communicates its "motion". A decree does not remain in the mind and will of the person who makes it, says Pufendorf; rather, "it is instilled into a subject's mind in such a way as to make him understand the necessity of conforming himself to it" (OLN I.6.4). Suarez even maintains at one point that no act of will by the law-subject to accept the prince's command is necessary for it to do its action-guiding work, "unless it be on account of some defect of power in the lawmaker" (OL I.4.5). This "transitive" aspect of the will and commands was used to capture what theorists in this tradition took to be a salient feature of law: law was *active* and *productive*, in the sense that its commands are oriented to producing behavior of some sort.

However, third, the tradition's understanding of the "power" and "moving" involved in commanding the behavior of another person was subtle. The way commands, and hence laws, direct action, according to this tradition, respects the fact that the beings that the commander seeks to move are free, self-directing beings. As we have seen, a straightforward, mechanically causal account of this directing was ruled out from the start. Writers in this tradition would have agreed with Peter Railton's characterization of normative guidance as involving a "peculiar mix of force and freedom".[33] The force of one's will on another is not "physical", but "moral", as Suarez puts it.[34] Obligation, he says, "is a certain kind of moral moving [of someone] to act".[35] The commander addresses the will of the other person; he does not manipulate the body, or even the motivations, of his subject. The moral force ("moral moving") necessitates in a way consistent with freedom; the mode of address is obligation. Suarez goes so far as to maintain that the commander wills not the action of his subject, but rather wills *to bind* his subject (OL I.4.8).[36] The will's power is not causal, but normative. It "moves" by addressing the moral capacities of agents.

Pufendorf was even clearer on this score. In *On the Duties of Man and Citizen* he wrote, law is a "decree by which a superior obliges anyone who is subject to him"; the command creates an obligation, "a bond of right by which we are constrained by the necessity of making some performance" (DMC I.2.2–3). Yet, the necessity of conforming one's action to obligation rooted in command never compromises the subject's freedom to act or refrain from acting.[37] Obligation, he maintains, "contains sufficient force to bend the will", but it does so "morally". Unlike coercion, which "shakes the will in an external fashion only and impels it to select an unwelcome thing solely through the awareness of an impending evil," obligation "farther engage[s] the Person".[38] One both "understands the necessity of conforming himself to it" (OLN I.6.4) and one is disposed to judge his own behavior in light of the obligation-imposing norm. The will is imbued "with a special internal sense that compels it to censure its own actions and deem itself blameworthy if it has not conformed itself to the prescribed norm" (OLN I.6.5; see also DMC I.2.3).

Fourth, will expressed in commands is thought by writers in this tradition to be, in a certain respect, normatively *creative*. Through the exercise of will obligations are imposed on others, new "moral entities" (as Pufendorf would put it) are *created*.[39] The commander addresses the will, not the intellect, of the subject. Recognizing the risk of distorting the views of some contributors to this tradition, we can make their point most clearly using the language of reasons for action. As we have seen, the will is conceived, in this tradition, as a rational—in the sense of reason-responsive—faculty, and the reasons supplied to it by the command of another are not merely the reasons already available, or that already apply, to the agent addressed. This is one important respect in which law is repeatedly said to differ from advice or counsel.[40] One who offers advice or counsel seeks to influence another person's behavior by rehearsing "considerations drawn from the thing itself", as Pufendorf puts it (OLN I.6.1). The advisor may issue imperatives, Hobbes wrote, but he only "deduceth his reasons from the benefit that arriveth by it to him to whom he saith it" (*Leviathan*, ch. 25, p. 303). In contrast, the reasons addressed to the will by command, and hence by law, are in some sense *new*, supplied by the commander, not merely adduced or proffered by him.

Moreover, that new reason has a very definite content, namely the (expression of the) will of the commander, and it alone. The "moving force" in law, according to Suarez, lies in the prince's will (OL I.5.21). Hobbes's formulation of this point in the *Leviathan* is perhaps the most familiar: "Command is, where a man saith, *Doe this*, or *Doe not this*, without expecting other reason than the Will of him that sayes it" (p. 303). Elsewhere Hobbes wrote even more pointedly: "Commanding...is that speech by which we signify to another our appetite or desire to have anything done, or left undone, for reasons contained in the will itself: for it is not properly said *Sic volo, sic jubeo*, without the other clause, *Stet pro ratione voluntas*".[41] Pufendorf adds, commenting on a parallel passage in *De Cive* (ch. 14.1), "And so laws are obeyed principally because of their prescriber's will and not because of their content" (OLN I.6.1; see also EJU, p. 58). These reasons are regarded, as we now say, as "content-independent." It is the fact of the commander's having issued the command—the commander's "will," they would say—and not anything about the action commanded that is supposed to give sole and sufficient reason to do the commanded action.

It would seem that this fits nicely into positivist jurisprudence, but not its natural law counterpart. Yet, we find Pufendorf explicitly arguing that although a law "should also have its reasons, to be sure," nevertheless, "these are not properly the ground of obedience to it. This lies rather in the authority of the one prescribing the law who, in announcing a decree of his will, obligates a subject to act in complete accord with his prescription..." (OLN I.6.1). Suarez, similarly, concedes that, while law directs us to that which is good and necessary, nevertheless, the moving force of law regarded as imposing obligations rests solely in the will of the prince (OL I.5.21). His explanation of the Augustinian conundrum, "an unjust law is not a law," underscores his commitment to this aspect of the command model (see OL I.9.4). A prince may prescribe unjust things, he concedes, but his precepts lack validity as law, and hence fail to impose binding obligations on their subjects. But this is not due merely to the fact that they are inconsistent with precepts of natural law understood as principles of justice. It is due rather to the fact that natural law is commanded by God, the proper (and only) superior of the prince, and no inferior can create or impose an obligation contrary to the will of his superior. The unjust precept is strictly void, formally invalid, we might say, because "it is not possible that men should be bound, at one and the same time, to do and to abstain from doing a given thing" and "no law made by an inferior can annul the obligation imposed by the superior" (OL I.9.4).

Finally, these newly supplied reasons are of a special kind. They are not merely recommendatory, but rather are categorical. They make the action prescribed *non-optional* in a special way. They "induce" action "by imposing a moral necessity" (Suarez, OL I.1.8–9). They make action "necessary" while at the same time respecting the agent's freedom (Pufendorf, OLN I.6.5, also EJU, 50). Legal obligations "bridle" the will of the parties obliged. The subject is free to act as he wills, but in a key sense he is not free to will. He is deprived of rational choice. He has no choice, not in the physical sense, but rather in the sense that no other rationally appropriate option is open to him. Moreover, he is precluded from considering those options or reasons for them.[42] The commands are peremptory.

This peremptory, deliberation-precluding aspect of commands reinforces the *executory* aspect of commands that we noticed earlier. It leads Pufendorf, for example, to deny that it is possible for one to bind oneself (OLN I.6.6–7), or for the sovereign to make "perfect," that is, binding promises to his subjects (OLN I.1.19 and III.5.6). To take on the nature of commands, these devices must preclude all deliberation, but they are unable to do so. "Even after he has made a final determination and firmly committed himself to something, the force of his decision (insofar as it stems from his will) is not so strong as to prevent him from changing or abrogating it at his own pleasure...unless, that is, external considerations prohibit him from altering his will once it has been determined and declared" (OLN I.6.6). Perhaps it was a similar thought that actually led Hobbes to his famous definition of will as the last appetite before action. For until the action takes place, there was, in his view, still room for further deliberation.

Social relations. According to the command tradition, commands presuppose the existence of a certain kind of relationship between the commander and the subject addressed. The key difference between *counsel* and *law* is consistently characterized by the difference in the relationships between the parties. While counsel is guidance addressed by one rational agent to *an equal*, petition and command presuppose inequalities between the parties. Petitions are addressed to a superior, Suarez observes, while commands are addressed to an inferior (OL I.12.4). To this standard Scholastic point, Hobbes and Pufendorf add that law must also be distinguished from covenant or pact, again on the ground that the latter involve exchange of promises among equals, while command presupposes superiority.[43] The exchange of promises yields *obligations*, they maintain, but not obligations *of law*, unless sovereignty is involved.[44]

Commands create new, peremptory constraints, as we have seen, but judgments of counsel or advice are not able to create such constraints. This is because the reasons are not new, and because the reason they offer are not peremptory. To explain this distinctive feature of commands the tradition appeals to the inequality of the relationship between the parties. Command entails the subordination of the will of one person to that of another.

I hasten to add that, for writers in this tradition, this unequal social relationship is never portrayed as simply a matter of inequality of sheer physical power, the subjection of one person to the physical power of another. Rather, law's distinctive normative force arises from, and is an expression of an unequal social relationship that is normatively charged. This is clearly the case for the religious tradition on which the command theory draws. For God's authority to command was always seen to be rooted in, and an expression of, the covenant relationship between God and His people. (This covenantal context was especially important in the 16th century to voluntarists in the Calvinist camp.) Some writers in the command tradition, Suarez, for example, explained our subjection to God in terms of our status as *creatures* of the creator (OL I.3.3). But this relationship is itself characterized in moral terms, not merely factual ones. The Creator is, in virtue of being creator, the trustee and guardian of His creation, and we acknowledge His superior authority out of gratitude for His continued superintendence.[45] In this tradition, Hobbes comes closest to treating the relationship as one of sheer power. Commands, by definition, are addressed to those who are "formerly obliged to obey him", he maintained (*Leviathan*, ch. 26, p. 312), but God's commands rest ultimately on God's "irresistible power" (DC, ch. 15.5). It is not clear whether that power alone gives God sovereignty, or whether it still requires as well (possibly coerced, but, for Hobbes, no less voluntary) acceptance of His creatures. Pufendorf (OLN I.6.10) argues at length against Hobbes's "irresistible power" thesis, taking it to mean nothing more than God's power to physically compel action and hence obedience. Against Hobbes, he insists that this logically cannot ground our obligation to obey because "compulsion and obligation are different" (OLN I.6.10). And he argues at length that the *potestas* to command rests neither on superior strength or sheer ability to compel, nor on any other measure of "natural eminence" (OLN I.6.9–12). Still, for all that, the relation between commander and subject, for all theorists in this tradition, is, necessarily, a matter of *subordination*, the subordination of one will to another will. The inequality, whatever its ground, consists in, or entails, the subordination of one will to another.

This allows us to put sharply into perspective the role of coercive sanctions in law according to the command tradition. Sanctions are logically, not just pragmatically, necessary to the command relationship, yet they are thought to provide neither the primary motivation for compliance nor the ground of the superiority of the commander over the subject. Sanctions supply useful, indeed indispensable, auxiliary motives, but the primary impelling reason from the point of view of law, is acknowledgement of the will of the superior (Pufendorf, OLN I.6.12). Coercion is always "external" and supplementary to the law's norm; obligation is the "internal" reflection of the law's normativity, it "engages the person" (OLN I.6.5). Because the fear of coercive sanction is always external to the norm, and contingent upon the particular circumstances in which agents find themselves, it cannot explain the normative force of law, which claims to persist despite these contingencies. "It is true", Pufendorf writes, "that strength alone can set me against my own inclination, so that I prefer temporarily to obey another's will instead of experiencing his power. But once my fear is gone, there is nothing to prevent me from acting more according to my discretion than according to his" (OLN I.6.9).

In a similar vein, Hobbes argues in *Leviathan* that counsel and command are distinguished precisely in that counsel points to benefits and harms that are likely to attend one's compliance with the counselor's imperative, while command relies *solely* on the expression of will of the commander: "a man may be obliged to do what he is Commanded;...But he cannot be obliged to do as he is Counselled, because the hurt of not following it, is his own" (*Leviathan*, ch. 25, p. 303, see also 305–6). Sanctions always concern the benefit, or rather, the "hurt," of the subject. To motivate only by such incentives is not to command, he argues.

Yet, the ability to back up commands with credible sanctions is (logically) necessary to command authority. For, as Pufendorf puts it, "it is vain to prescribe something that can be neglected with impunity" (EJU, p. 59) and "one who can be disregarded with impunity rules only by the indulgence of others" (OLN I.6.12). That is, while power to coerce is not the *ground* of the commander's authority (as we saw above), it is a *necessary mark and com-*

ponent of that authority.[46] To lack the power, and the title to exercise that power, to coerce is to lack the requisite superiority. To rule "only by the indulgence of others" is not to command.

Hence, on this view, the relation between commands and sanctions is logical, not merely empirical or instrumental.[47] That is, the relationship between command and punishment, on this view, is not like that of a threat of retaliation between rival political powers. The logic of law, on this view, is very different from the logic of threats. This may be what lies at the root of retributivist intuitions about punishment, but we must keep in mind that this notion has nothing to do with justice. On this way of thinking, punishment is normatively required for the simple logical reason that it is part of what is involved in subordination of the will of another. To fail to punish disobedience is like refusing to draw the conclusion *q*, although one believed *p* and *p logically implies q*. In the latter case, one is forced on pain of inconsistency to abandon either the belief that *p* or the belief that *p logically implies q*. So, too, upon pain of inconsistency, one is forced to abandon one's claim to dominion over the will of the other. It is consistency (consistency of willing, we might say), and not justice, on this view, that demands punishment.

Thus, according to this tradition, law is an expression of *dominion*, the power of one will over another will. Suarez wrote, "lawmaking is an act of jurisdiction and of superior power... Consequently, it is...the use of a form of dominion" (OL, I.5.15). Similarly, Pufendorf argued, "the faculty of enjoining something in the manner of a law or precept implies superiority, just as the obligation to obey proves that we are inferior to one who is able to prescribe to us" (EJU, p. 59). Subordination of the will is the mode in which intelligent, free beings are *necessitated*. Subjects retain the *ability* to will, and so do, otherwise—therein lies their "freedom." Yet they are not *free to will* to do otherwise. Law (that is, the law-giver) imposes constraints on an inferior's willing. Disobedience is possible, of course, but in that case dominion is expressed in punishment, the imposition of suffering designed to humble the disobedient will. Hence, punishment upon disobedience is not something *added to* the command to motivate behavior in accord with it; rather, punishment is simply another form in which the subordination of the will of the inferior to the superior is expressed. Moreover, dominion is a defining feature of law—of any kind of law, of anything that purports to be law. According to this tradition, dominion expresses the special kind of normativity of law.

Generality. Implicit in the discussion thus far, according to our writers, is the fact that the commands that lawmakers give are necessarily characterized by generality (or at least most laws will take this form).[48] This is thought to follow from the nature of *law*, not from the nature of command, and so it is, strictly speaking, an addition to the concept of command. Law is a *species* of commands. The necessary generality is of broadly two kinds: the law's commands are addressed to classes of persons, not to specific individuals, and direct them to types of actions. These conditions put a strain on the command model.[49] The fact that law's commands are addressed not merely to a plurality of persons but to *classes* of persons introduces a degree of impersonalism into a relationship that is otherwise portrayed as personal in nature. The personal nature is suggested by the characterization of the social relation between superior and inferior, and the idea, especially strong in Suarez, that it is an act of mind of the sovereign lawgiver that communicates its motion to the minds of his subjects. Suarez, however, admits the tension and actually identifies a further one. He argues for the necessary generality of law in part on the ground that it is a direct consequence of the necessary "perpetual" nature (Hart would call it "persistence") of the law. But this requires, he recognizes, that "it is inherent in the nature of law that it shall not depend on the life of the lawmaker.[50]

It might be argued that the fact that law commands (often broad) *types* of actions also qualifies its strictly *executive* and deliberation-precluding properties. This is partly correct. Since legal norms direct subjects to types of action, those subjects must exercise their judgment at least insofar as it is necessary to identify a concrete action open to them as a token (or rather, a more specific sub-type, since such judgment always works with representations of actions considered *ex ante*) of the prescribed time. Yet, on this view, deliberation is still strongly channeled. For subjects are required only to ask whether the action falls under the norm, not to determine whether the action is in some broader view good, right, or wise, or whether the norm meets certain standards of rationality (or justice). Thus, command model does not preclude any practical reasoning on the part law-subjects, but it does strongly tend to represent this practical reasoning, and so to characterize the reasoning proper to law, as deductive in form, or at least as a matter of applying pre-established general norms to concrete facts. In this respect, the command model remains faithful to its basic intuition that law represents to those who fall under its authority the *result* of deliberation carried on elsewhere, expecting them to *execute* the deliberative decision of the law-giver. The normativity of law, we might say, is still distinctively executory. So, subjects addressed by law are expected to hold the pattern of action defined by the norm before their mind's practical eye and act in accord with it.[51] Thus, some deliberation, or at least interpretation, is typically required, but it is still ratiocination at the executive stage of practical deliberation.

In sum, the command model assumes that law, *qua law*, creates new, categorical reasons for acting that are intended to operate at the executive stage of practical deliberation. They are imposed by directives to rational agents and they have their moral or practical force in virtue of the special relationship that exists between law-giver and subject. It is possible to see now why this model might be attractive to both natural law and positivist legal philosophers. Because it focuses exclusively on the executive stage of deliberate action, it can be silent about whether, and what kind, of reasons must lie behind it. It is possible to debate whether, *in addition* law's directives must meet conditions of justice or reasonableness in order to be valid. But that dispute is about how best to characterize law as depicted by this model. That is, this dispute does not challenge the model, and both sides can in fact presuppose it as common ground. The model structures that dispute. The dispute turns in part on whether the model alone adequately captures certain fairly abstract beliefs we have about law and its mode of operation in practical reasoning and on possibly conflicting ideas about the tasks or functions of law.

IV. Bentham's revisionist command model

Most of the key features of the command model of law outlined above can be found in Austin's definition of law in the middle of the 19th century. In contrast, Bentham reworked the model offered by the 17th century jurists in some important respects. I wish to sketch only briefly some features of Bentham's revisionist command model.

Bentham began in his early work (mid- to late-1770's) with an orthodox understanding of the command model. The idea of "[l]aw was invented to denote a General Command of Public Government" (UC 69.142), he wrote. In his essay "What a Law Is,"[52] he developed this thought. A command, he wrote, is the verbal expression of the wish of a superior addressed to an inferior that he act in a certain way. In expressing this wish, the superior seeks to produce this conduct in the inferior, and for this to occur two ideas must be communicated: an idea of the type of action he has in mind and an idea of his wish or volition. This volition of the commander, Bentham says, is meant to furnish the requisite motive to perform the action (Parekh, p. 148). Petitions, requests, and commands are all expressions of volition aimed at producing conduct in others; they differ only with respect to the social relations between the parties: requests are made of equals, petitions of superiors, commands to inferiors.

The inequality Bentham seemed to have in mind in these early manuscripts was primarily, but not exclusively inequality of physical power—that is, differential ability to inflict suffering on a person. But he was keenly aware, especially in *Of Laws in General*, that such physical power was not of the right kind to explain what we have called the special normativity of law. He distinguished sharply between "the power of contrectation"—the power of physically affecting bodies—and "the power of imperation"—power of command (OLG, pp. 81, 137–9 n. h). The power of imperation depends often (but not exclusively) on the power of contrectation, but it is fundamentally different from it. The power of imperation is a power over the "active faculties" of persons whereas the power of contrectation is power over their "passive faculties". Like the earlier command tradition, Bentham seemed to recognize that law depends on a normative relation. It is a mistake, I believe, to think that Bentham sought to reduce law to strictly factual relations, like those of sheer physical power.

Finally, in his early work Bentham insisted that law is a species of commands. In virtue of being general, their effects can be seen in certain regularities of behavior. This, he argued, has led many to confuse law properly so-called with other phenomena or fictions (UC 69.142–3). Law must not be confused with an order or regularity of behavior of inanimate or animate beings, whether actual or in some sense ideal. Law, he wrote, "came to be considered as a cause of uniformity among such acts...Looking forward from the Law [i.e., juridical law], men observed an uniformity produced by it: and looking backwards from an assemblage of uniform actions, saw them resulting by a law" (UC 69.142). Law, however, is not just any regularity, nor just any cause of such regularity. Law is a matter of command, and legal order is that produced by such commands. Hence, he argued that the claims that natural law and custom are types of *law*, in virtue of some ideal or real order or regularity of behavior, rest on an elementary confusion. Similarly, law is not utility or a dictate of utility, he argued. For utility is a fact that operates as a reason for action (or law), but it is not law; neither is a "dictate of utility", which is just an opinion about utility (Parekh, pp. 151–53). On the contrary, law is a command, an *act of will*, not an act of the understanding. Law is the expression of the will of one person communicated to the will of another. Furthermore, laws are *general* commands. Hence, common law decisions, while they may actually produce some degree of uniformity of behavior, appear to have "somewhat of the effect of general laws" only "in virtue of the more extensive interpretation which people are disposed to put upon" those particular commands (OLG, p. 152). Common law is not law, it is only "a thing merely imaginary" (*Comment*, p. 119), because insofar as it involves commands they are particular, and insofar as it pretends to be general (as represented in propositions inferred or "abstracted" from particular decisions) it fails to take the form of commands.[53]

Thus far, Bentham seems to be walking a familiar jurisprudential path (albeit begging many important questions along the way). But even in these very early manuscripts he departs from the orthodox command model in one respect. He held that sanctions may be needed for the law to be "effectual", but he was willing to concede that they are not logically required by the concept of command, or even the concept of law (UC 70a.5). Sanctions play an important role in law, but they are only instrumentally and contingently necessary. He argued from the beginning that laws typically have a complex command structure: a "primary" law addresses individual law subjects and commands a certain action (or refraining), while a "secondary" law commands a third party (official, for example) to punish disobedience of the primary law (Parekh, pp. 155–56). Sometimes the secondary law is not needed, or is replaced by promise of reward, or ambient reasons are sufficient to provide addressees with reasons to comply.

In *Of Laws in General*, written in the early 1780's, he makes a more substantial break from the received command model. First of all, he realized the idea of command was too narrow, for laws necessarily involve not only commands (and prohibitions), but also permissions and countermands. Perhaps his most impressive work in OLG is his attempt to work out a "logic of imperations"—what we would now call a deontic logic (OLG, ch. X). In OLG he also makes much clearer that sanctions in the form of evils threatened by the sovereign for disobedience are not logically necessary, and may not even be practically necessary in all contexts. He regards it as an open, practical question just what auxiliary motives it is appropriate to attach to sovereign general commands (OLG, ch. XI). And, unlike Austin (*Province*, p. 16) and Pufendorf (OLN I.6.14), he is willing to consider rewards as well as punishments as useful motivational aids. This departure allowed him to provide an account of *legal* limits on sovereign power. He treated them as *leges in principem*, undertakings by the sovereign addressed to future sovereigns supported not by any formal legal sanction, but rather by informal, moral sanction of public opinion (OLG, ch. VI.15–19).

A second major task of OLG stretched the command model near to breaking. The driving force behind the researches that resulted in OLG was Bentham's puzzlement and desire to articulate the logic and structure of "*a* law...meaning one entire but single law" (IPML, ch. XVII.29), and on that basis to work out the formal, structuring principles of a complete code of laws, his *pannomion*. While he opened OLG with a definition of law on the model (albeit extended) of command (OLG, p. 1), he focused increasingly in later chapters, and in subsequent work, on "expository", "exceptive", and "adjective" portions of the law—that is, on legal material defining not only action types (for offenses) but also relationships among persons (legal status), conditions by which property or offices or legal recognized relationships were vested, defining various conditions and constraints on offenses (e.g., excuses) and the vesting of status, and, finally, setting up and maintaining of adjudicative procedures and legal processes of all kinds. As he dug deeper into the law and its mode of operation, this expository or definitional material took on increasing importance. The "ideal object" he began to describe, looked less and less like the direct command of a superior and more and more like an impersonal, logical construct. His comment at the end of the "Concluding Note" of IPML, which is in fact a comment on the results of his extended researches reported and articulated in OLG, indicates his own sense of the complexity of a single, complete law: "Leaning on his elbow, in an attitude of profound and solemn meditation," the dancing master Marcel asked, " 'What a multitude of things there are...in a minuet—May we now add?—and in a law" (IPML, p. 310).

These are, perhaps, interesting departures from the orthodox command model, but it may seem that they represent only differences of emphasis. However, I think they mark a further, more substantial, departure.[54] First, while Bentham sustained throughout his vast writings the view that the proper model of the logical structure of a single law was that of command—with two major parts, a punitory and an expository part[55]—he gave the expository/definitional elements far greater emphasis. He even toyed with the idea, from time to time, of trying to capture the entirety of the law in (or from the point of view of) the civil code.[56] Law is not, or not merely, a means of "inducing" behavior. It is also, and more importantly, a means of making known to citizens what each person's property is, what relationships each bears to others, and the like (Bowring, v. 9. p. 12). Law plays at least as large an epistemic role in society as a directive role, and it does so by defining and for legal and public purposes constituting, social and political relationships. Bentham came to the realization that in large part law does its practical, directing, action-guiding work indirectly, through this "expository" or constituting work.

Second, Bentham seems to have rejected one key feature of the orthodox concept of command. Hart argued Hobbes rightly recognized that commands take the commander's will to be the exclusive reason for the subject's acting as commanded.[57] Bentham failed to see this, he complained. Unlike Hobbes, Bentham did not seem to regard the expression of volition in the command to constitute in itself a reason, let alone a peremptory reason, for the subject to act. Thus, again in contrast with the orthodox command model, Bentham thought that all commands needed to be supplemented with some sort of motive or sanction. But, I believe Hart was wrong to think that this was an oversight or failure of analysis on Bentham's part. On the contrary, it highlights the fact that Bentham came to hold a very different (albeit inadequately developed) conception of the authority and normative force of law. Bentham followed, but in a profound yet subtle way challenged, the command tradition. In Bentham's view, the command was designed ultimately not to directly address the will of law-subjects; rather, it addressed their "understanding," he maintained. Law's "commands" were to perform, first of all, an epistemic function. Law's fundamental task was to facilitate the coordination of social interaction,[58] and for this purpose law sought clearly and publicly to mark out social and political relationships and corresponding patterns of interaction. Clarity, publicity, and manifest authenticity of the rules of law focus expectations, he argued; and when mutual expectations are focused on the rules, each law-subject has reason to comply. Sanctions still play an important role, of course, but only as auxiliaries, complementing the primary epistemic function of identifying potentially successful coordination patterns. Unlike Hobbes, Bentham did not fear individual rational decision-making, once a manifest pattern of expectations was established. So Bentham did not believe, as Hobbes did, that displacing individual judgment entirely onto the judgment of the sovereign was essential for social order.

This seems to put Bentham's disagreement with Hobbes on a merely pragmatic basis, but there are reasons to think that the difference had far deeper roots in Bentham's understanding of law. Bentham's view, emerging first in his critique of Blackstone's defense of English common law, and elaborated frequently later as he worked out his scheme for a complete code of laws, was that law's proper role, and its only possible claim to legitimacy, was to address the wills of citizens and thus to guide their actions *through* their "understanding". In his *Comment on the Commentaries*, he argued that law's objective was peace and social order through "submission of conduct", *not* through "submission of judgment" (*Comment*, pp. 346–47). Common law, he argued repeatedly, failed *as law*. It was "fit only for Beasts" (UC 69.151), because in countless ways it "torpedo[ed]" individual judgment and fostered submission to authority in both conduct and judgment, based on ignorance and blind fear (*Comment*, p. 346). It issued particular coercive commands and then expected citizens to anticipate the next strike of the hidden judicial sword. The prevalent mode of governance was by way of "influence of the will on the will" rather than by way of "influence of understanding on the understanding" (UC 126.1).[59] He insisted that obedience to law must spring "not from a passive principle of blind fear alone, but with the concurrence of the will also" and insisted that law seek compliance "from conciliating the approbation of all minds, by satisfying the public judgment" (Bowring, v. 1, p. 161). "Those who are able to convince men, will treat them like men;" he argued, while "those who only command, avow their inability to convince" and lose their right to command (Bowring, v. 1, p. 160). Concurrence of the will was to be achieved through addressing reasons to the understanding. Thus, consistent with this understanding of the only possible ground of the legitimacy and authority of law, Bentham could not adopt the orthodox command model of law, for it located law entirely in the will, the *executor* of deliberative judgments that are made elsewhere. Law at its best, on Bentham's view, addresses and engages the deliberative reason ("understanding") of law subjects. He could not, then, adopt a view of the essential nature of law that necessarily precludes this possibility.

These developments of Bentham's jurisprudence stretched the orthodox command model, challenged it, and exposed some of its weaknesses. Indeed, the challenge is so fundamental that it seems to cry out for a very different model. But the attractions of the command model were too powerful for Bentham and he never clearly abandoned it. Austin, lacking an appreciation of the subtlety of Bentham's thought, and much influenced by his early study of Roman law, restored the orthodox model and made it the centerpiece of classical positivism.

V. Concluding reflections

Command theories of law and legal obligation have passed from sophisticated jurisprudence. Yet the criticisms of the tradition have often been superficial and fail to address the hard core of its conception of the nature of law and it characteristic *modus operandi.* For example, from our survey of the tradition in its heyday it is clear that any attempt to dismiss the command model as reductionist, that is, as attempting to reduce law to normatively inert social facts, or attempting to explain law's normativity solely in terms of such facts, fails to understand the tradition.

At its core was a conception of the authority and distinctive normativity of law, its distinctive mode of guiding action. This conception, shorn of its outmoded vocabulary, to be sure, is still very much in play in contemporary jurisprudence. Commands remain as a model, but they are commands without a commander. So, unequal social relations are no longer assumed, also eliminated is any sense of a "communication" from one party to another. Law is still thought to guide (or at least purport to guide) action, but the idea of *transitivity* is lost. Law guides in its distinctive way to the extent that officials, or citizens, or both, *take* them so to guide. Law's normativity is understood entirely on the model of an individual's guiding herself by rules. On the account preferred by Hart and Raz, this is understood in terms of the content-independent and peremptory reasons one adopts.[60] On a recent account proposed by Scott Shapiro, it is understood in terms of certain psychologically constraining dispositions one develops.[61] On these representative views, law guides when officials or citizens guide *themselves by* law in the way they describe. But the mode of guidance they propose closely resembles that portrayed vividly by the orthodox command tradition. Law is still identified with the *execution* of deliberation carried on elsewhere. Law claims to guide citizen/official action, to make a difference to their practical reasoning by displacing individual deliberative judgment from them onto a surrogate. Hobbes's words still fit this conception: law is a matter of commands, not philosophy.

This is a compelling conception of law's authority, but it is not without internal tensions, or external challengers. Bentham appears to have felt one of these tensions and he struggled to carve out a place for deliberative judgment within the normal operation of law conceived on the command model. It is doubtful that the view he suggested can succeed, but it raises an important question. Does the conception of law's authority assumed by orthodox command theory and latter-day revisions of it adequately capture law's distinctive mode of guiding the action of free, self-directing agents? To what exactly in the daily practice of law and its impact on the agents it seeks to govern does this conception respond? Does it obscure from view other general features of law that might be equally important? Is there a viable alternative that does justice also to these features? These questions and many others remain. This review of a broad and diverse jurisprudential tradition, it is hoped, sheds some light on them.

NOTES

1. J. Bentham, "What a Law is" (Bentham Manuscripts, University College London, box 69, folios 69–76), UC 69.71. This essay is reproduced in B. Parekh, ed., *Bentham's Political Thought* (London: Croom Helm, 1973), pp. 146–56. The passage quoted is at p. 149. All subsequent references to this essay will be to its appearance in Parekh's volume.
2. J. Bentham, *Of Laws in General* [OLG], H.L.A. Hart, ed. (London: Athlone Press, 1970), p. 1.
3. J. Bentham, *Comment on the Commentaries* [*Comment*], J.H. Burns and H.L.A. Hart, eds. (London: Athlone Press, 1977), p. 119.
4. J. Austin, *Province of Jurisprudence Determined* [*Province*] (London: Weidenfeld and Nicolson, 1971), p. 1.
5. Austin takes great pains to distinguish between "proper" and "improper" uses of the term "law". *Province*, Lecture I, esp. pp. 26–33, and throughout Lecture V. He tries to explain, or explain away, a host of potential embarrassments like declaratory laws, repealing laws, laws that seem merely to create rights (*Province*, pp. 26–29). Unlike Bentham, he found it especially important to account for custom, and most notably the judicial custom of common law, within this conceptual framework. See *Province*, pp. 31–32, 191 and *Lectures on Jurisprudence*, R. Campbell, ed., 3rd edition (London, 1869), pp. 621–30. Bentham delayed the publication of his *Introduction to the Principles of Morals and Legislation* nine years because he ran into a "metaphysical maze" trying to find a place for the civil law within the framework of the command model. (See *Introduction to the Principles of Morals*

and Legislation [IPML], J.H. Burns and H.L.A. Hart, eds. (London: Athlone Press, 1970), editors's introduction, p. xxxvii.) He presents his brilliant, if controversial solution in OLG. Hart's classic demonstration of some of these deficiencies can be found in *The Concept of Law* [*Concept*] (Oxford: Clarendon Press, 1961), chs. 2–3.

6. T. Hobbes, *Leviathan* [*Leviathan*] (1651), C.B. Macpherson, ed. (Baltimore: Penguin Books, 1968), ch. 26, p. 312. See also *On the Citizen* (*De Cive*) [DC] (1642), R. Tuck and M. Silverthorne, eds. and trans. (Cambridge: Cambridge University Press, 1998), ch.14, para. 1: "LAW is a command of that person...whose instruction is the reason for obedience....law comes from one who has power over those whom he instructs...."
7. T. Hobbes, *A Dialogue between a Philosopher and a Student of the Common Laws of England* [*Dialogue*], J. Cropsey, ed. (Chicago: University of Chicago Press, 1971), p. 71. Hobbes wrote the *Dialogue* sometime between 1664 and 1673; it was first published in 1681.
8. *Leviathan*, ch. 15, p. 217. See also *Leviathan*, ch. 26, p. 314; DC, ch. 3.33, and *The English Works of Thomas Hobbes* (ed. W. Molesworth), 11 vols., London, 1839–45, vol. 4, pp. 284–85: "After I had ended the discourse he mentions of the laws of nature, I thought it fittest in the last place, once for all, to say they were the laws of God, then when they were delivered in the word of God; but before, being not known by men for any thing but their own natural reason, they were but theorems, tending to peace and those being uncertain, as being but the conclusions of particular men, and therefore not properly laws."
9. W. Blackstone, *Commentaries on the Laws of England* (1765–69), 4 vols. (Chicago: University of Chicago Press, 1979), vol. 1, pp. 38, 39.
10. "Reflections by the Lrd. Cheife Justice Hale on Mr. Hobbes His Dialogue of the Lawe" (probably 1673) published in W. Holdsworth, *A History of English Law*, 7th ed. (London, 1956), vol. 1, pp. 499–513.
11. British Library, Hargrave MS 485, fo. 3; quoted in A. Cromartie, *Sir Matthew Hale 1609–1676* (Cambridge: Cambridge University Press, 1995), p. 90.
12. British Library, Hargrave MS 485, fo. 4; quoted in Cromartie, p. 91.
13. Heraclitus, Fragment 32, in K. Freeman, *Pre-Socratic Philosophers* (Oxford, 1946), p. 27; quoted in D.R. Kelley, *The Human Measure* (Cambridge, MA: Harvard University Press, 1990), p. 19.
14. See M. Ostwald, "Ancient Greek Ideas of Law," *Dictionary of the History of Ideas*, P. Weiner, ed., (New York: Charles Scribner's Sons, 1968), p. 681.
15. Aristotle, *Nichomachean Ethics*, 1094b15–16, 1134b18–1135b6.
16. *Digest* I, 4, 1; see also *Institutes* I, 2, 6.
17. See, for example, N. Cantor, *Imagining Law* (New York: Harper Collins, 1997), ch. 3; Kelly, *The Human Measure*, ch. 4. *Quod principi* was not merely a Continental or Civilian doctrine. All the major medieval treatises of English common law addressed it as well, often on their first few pages. See the "Prologue" of "Glanvill's" 12th century treatise, *The Treatise on the Laws and Customs of the Realm of England Commonly Called Glanvill*, G.D.C. Hall (with M. T. Clanchy), ed. (Oxford: Clarendon Press, 1993), p. 2; Bracton, in the 13th century, *On the Laws and Customs of England*, S. Thorne, trans.

(Cambridge, MA: Belnap Press, 1968), vol. 2, pp. 19, 21–22, 33, 305–6; Sir John Fortescue, in the 15th century, *In Praise of the Laws of England* in Fortescue, *On the Laws and Governance of England*, S. Lockwood, ed. (Cambridge: Cambridge University Press, 1997), pp. 17, 27. Generally, see J.W. Tubbs, *The Common Law Mind* (Baltimore: Johns Hopkins University Press, 2000), chs. 1, 3.

18. Evidence of this influence is available in F. Suarez, *On Laws and God the Lawgiver* [OL] (1612), G.L. Williams, A. Brown, J. Waldron, trans. (Oxford: Oxford University Press, 1944), Bk I, ch. 5, *passim.*, esp. para. 10.
19. See especially OL I. 5, and II.6.
20. H.L.A. Hart, *Essays on Bentham* (Oxford: Clarendon Press, 1982), ch. 10.
21. See, for example, Suarez, OL I.1 and Book I generally. Suarez, of course, here follows Aquinas, see *Summa Theologiae* [ST] 1a2ae 90 and following questions. The approach is also equally evident in Pufendorf. See S. Pufendorf, *On the Duty of Man and Citizen* [DMC] (1673), J. Tully, ed., M. Silverthorne, trans. (Cambridge: Cambridge University Press, 1991), Bk I, ch. 2, paras.1–2, 16; and S. Pufendorf, *On the Law of Nature and of Nations* [OLN] (1672), in *The Political Writings of Samuel Pufendorf*, C.L. Carr, ed., M.J. Seidler, trans. (Oxford: Oxford University Press, 1994), Bk I, ch. 6, esp. para. 18. Austin, too, adopts this method in the *Province*, where he sets out to lay the conceptual foundations of a theory of positive law. For this purpose he starts with a *general* concept of law which he insists applies equally to positive law, true or proper morality (divine law), and conventional (positive) morality. In this respect, Austin is thinking and writing as a typical natural lawyer. Central to this concept of law, he maintains, is the concept of command, which is key to the sciences of jurisprudence *and morals* (*Province*, p. 13).
22. See, e.g., Suarez, OL I.1.1–2, I.3.2–3, 8. At OL I.4.2 Suarez writes: "properly speaking, only those who have the use of intellect and reason are governed by law, or are capable of being so governed..." This is echoed (though surely not intentionally) by Austin, *Province*, p. 10: " A law...may be said to be a rule laid down for the guidance of an intelligent being by an intelligent being having power over him." Pufendorf maintains that law operates by creating and imposing *obligations*, but one is subject to law and legal obligation, he argues, only if (*inter alia*) (1) one is *free*—"has a will that can turn either way," (2) one has ability to understand one's self (and so can understand one's situation and one's action relative to it), and so (3) one is capable of making one's actions accord with a rule or norm. See OLN I.1.7, I.6.8, and DMC I.2.4.
23. Suarez is even willing to say, "for this law prohibits a given thing because that thing is evil; and therefore prior to the existence of the said law, there exists the obligation of avoiding such evil" (OL II.9.4). This comment is uncharacteristic of Suarez, who typically restricts the term "obligation" to that which is imposed by law (note however, that he says here that the obligation in question is an "intrinsic natural obligation). A more characteristic formulation of the point can be found at OL I.5.21. Here he admits (in

accord with his attempt to reconcile the intellectualist and voluntarist wings of the natural law tradition) that insofar as law directs us to that which is in fact good and necessary (for our well-being) law has a certain "moving force" the appreciation of which is due to the intellect. However, the "moving force" in law that "makes an action obligatory" lies in an act of will of the prince. Both passages underscore my point that for Suarez, a *special kind* of normativity characterizes law.

24. "One may succumb to the policeman's voice or bearing not from any considerations, but like the snake obeying its charmer." W.D. Falk, "Goading and Guiding," in Falk, *Ought, Reasons, and Morality* (Ithaca: Cornell University Press, 1986), p. 51. Falk says that such "direct pleading" is "the continuation of violence by other means. It is coercive in the sense of controlling others while bypassing, if not paralyzing, any voluntary contribution to their own behavior."
25. Suarez OL I.3.2; Pufendorf, OLN I.1.7 and I.6.8; Austin, *Province*, p. 10.
26. J. Raz, *Engaging Reason* (Oxford: Oxford University Press, 1999), p. 67.
27. See, e.g., Pufendorf, DMC 1.2.4; OLN I.4.2, and I.6.8.
28. This focus on *lex*, of course, is announced in the title of Suarez's major jurisprudential work, *De Legibus, Ac Deo Legislatore*, which he opens with a chapter defining "*lex*" followed by one in which he distinguishes *ius* from *lex* (OL I.1–2). See also Hobbes in DC, ch. 14.1–4; Pufendorf, OLN I.6.3 and Pufendorf *Elements of Universal Jurisprudence* [EJU] (1660), in *The Political Writings of Samuel Pufendorf*, C.L. Carr, ed., M.J. Seidler, trans. (Oxford: Oxford University Press, 1994), p. 58. See also Austin, *Province*, pp. 285–88 and n. 26.
29. Austin, *Province*, p. 288. Austin here (like Suarez, OL I.2.2, 4) reflects his training in Roman Law, especially Ulpian in the *Digest* I.1.1.
30. On this debate, see J. Finnis, *Natural Law and Natural Rights* (Oxford: Clarendon Press, 1980), ch. XI.8.
31. Finnis puts Aquinas's view this way: "The important thing is that the expressed *imperium*, the promulgated 'intention of the legislator', represents to the subject an intelligible determinate pattern of action, which, having been chosen by the lawgiver to be obligatory, can actually *be* obligatory in the eyes of a reasonable subject because the ruler's *imperium* can (for the sake of the common good) be reasonably treated by the subject as if it were his own *imperium*" (p. 341).
32. Law involves by its nature an act of will, says Suarez, because a "characteristic condition requisite for law...[consists in] moving and bringing of the subject to performance of an action..." (OL I.5.15). At OL II.6.22 he says that law-generated obligation is a certain kind of "moral moving," and the lawgiver moves another to act through an act of the will (OL I.6.15, II.6.1).
33. P. Railton, "Normative Force and Normative Freedom," in J. Dancy, ed., *Normativity* (Oxford: Blackwell, 2000), p. 7.
34. "God, in establishing law, does not impel one physically toward the act prescribed by law, but merely imposes an obligation which is of a moral nature and cannot thus be brought about" (OL I.5.7). At OL I.4.9 he says

that "the object of the efficacious will of the legislator" is "moral rather than physical..."

35. "[*O*]*bligatio est motio quaedam moralis ad agendum*" (OL II.6.22). I follow a reading suggested by Terry Irwin in his "Obligation, Rightness, and Natural Law," (unpublished ms), pp. 8–9.
36. Suarez's motivation was at least partly theological. He wanted to claim that God commands us to comply with natural law and His divine law, but if commands by their nature determine (in the sense of efficiently caused) their subject's behavior, then we could never obey God *freely*, since the will of an omnipotent God is literally irresistible. God's command would utterly eradicate our freedom.
37. In his *Elements of Universal Jurisprudence*, Pufendorf writes, "obligation throws a kind of moral bridle over our freedom of action, as it were, so that we cannot rightly proceed in any other direction than the one in which it leads; although the natural efficacy of no obligation so constrains the natural freedom of our will that it cannot in fact turn toward other things" (p. 50). See also OLN I.6.5.
38. OLN I.6.5; the phrase, "farther engage[s] the Person", is Basil Kennet's English rendering of the passage in *De jure naturae et gentium* (London, 1769) p. 58.
39. Suarez wrote at OL I.5.23 "law is that act of the prince which of itself and by its own force creates an obligation and binds the subject." See also Pufendorf, OLN I.1.4.
40. It is standard practice for writers in this tradition to distinguish law from advice or counsel. See Suarez, OL I.1.7–8 and esp. I.12.4. Pufendorf OLN, I.6.1; EJU, p. 58; Hobbes, DC, 14.1; *Leviathan*, ch.25, esp. pp. 302–3.
41. Hobbes, *Human Nature*, ch. XIII, para. 6, in Molesworth, ed., *The English Works of Thomas Hobbes*, vol. 4, pp. 74–75.
42. Pufendorf, OLN I.6.1; Hobbes, *Leviathan*, ch. 25, p. 303. Joseph Raz, of course, denies that peremptory reasons preclude consideration of excluded reasons, but only *action on* them (*Practical Reason and Norms*, Princeton: Princeton University Press, 1990, p. 184). However, for Hobbes, in view of the close connection he finds between deliberation and action, this is likely to appear to be a distinction without a difference.
43. Hobbes, DC, ch.14.2; Pufendorf, OLN I.6.2 and VII.4.9; EJU, pp. 58–59.
44. Hobbes, *Leviathan*, ch.14; Pufendorf, OLN VII.4.9 and EJU, p. 59.
45. This is especially clear in Pufendorf, see OLN I.6.11–12. At DMC I.2.5, he says "When a [superior] has signified his will, fear tempered by respect [*reverentia*] must arise in a man's mind [*animus*]—fear from power, respect from reflection on the reason which ought to induce one to accept his will even apart from fear." The latter reasons include "if [the superior] has conferred exceptional benefits on him" and "if it is evident that he wishes the other well and can look out for him better than he can for himself" (see also OLN I.6.9, 12).
46. This view also seems to have been held by Richard Cumberland. By definition, law includes sanctions, he argued, but the sanction does not generate

the obligation. Rather, it serves two other functions: (1) as a motivational supplement, and (2) as evidence of the sanctioned action's having been commanded. See R. Cumberland, *A Treatise of the Laws of Nature* (1672), ch. 5, para. xxii, trans. John Maxwell (London, 1727); in J. B. Schneewind, ed., *Moral Philosophy from Montaigne to Kant* (Cambridge: Cambridge University Press, 1990), vol. 1, pp. 151–52.

47. Herbert Fingarette develops this line of thought in his presidential address, "Punishment and Suffering," *Proceedings and Addresses of the American Philosophical Association*, vol. 50 (1977), pp. 499–525, esp. pp. 503–10.
48. Suarez, OL I.6, especially paras. 8–17; Austin, *Province*, pp. 18–24.
49. Hart (*Concept*, chs. 2–4), of course, exploited this strain in his critique of Austin's deployment of the model.
50. Suarez, OL I.6.12; see Hart, *Concept*, pp. 60–64.
51. Recall, Suarez thought that an act of judgment was necessary if a subject is to grasp the prince's command and bring it before his will (OL I.4.5).
52. See above, note 1. See also UC 70a. 3–6.
53. Bentham OLG, pp. 153–54. For a general discussion of this critique of common law theory, see G.J. Postema, *Bentham and the Common Law Tradition* (Oxford: Clarendon Press, 1986/1989), ch. 8.3.
54. The comments in the remainder of this section rest on an interpretation of Bentham's jurisprudence that is not uncontroversial. I will not attempt to defend it here. For a broader discussion and defense see *Bentham and the Common Law Tradition*, pp. 175–83, 275–78, 324–28, 368–73.
55. This view is common in the 17th century command tradition. See, e.g., Pufendorf, OLN I.6.14.
56. Bentham, *Works*, J. Bowring edition [Bowring], 11 vols. (Edinburgh, 1838–43), vol. 3, p. 161, and vol. 9, p. 12.
57. Hart, *Essays on Bentham*, p. 253.
58. Or so, at least, I have argued; see *Bentham and the Common Law Tradition*, ch. 5.
59. This contrast is a recurring theme in Bentham's work; see, e.g., Bowring, v. 6, p. 524 n. *, Bowring, v. 7, p. 563–64, and J. Bentham, *"Legislator of the World": Writings on Codification, Law and Education*, P. Schofield and J. Harris, eds. (Oxford: Clarendon Press, 1998), p. 249.
60. Hart, *Essays on Bentham*, ch. 10; J. Raz, *The Morality of Freedom* (Oxford: Clarendon Press, 1986), chs. 2–4.
61. S. Shapiro, "The Difference That Rules Make," in B. Bix, *Analyzing Law* (Oxford: Clarendon Press, 1998), pp. 33–62.

PHILOSOPHICAL ISSUES, 11
Social, Political, and Legal Philosophy, 2001

Criminal Justice and Legal Reparations as an Alternative to Punishment[1]

Geoffrey Sayre-McCord

I. Introduction

Consider a just society, with reasonable laws, fairly enforced by an appropriate authority. In this context, how should society respond to those legitimately determined to have broken the law?[2] Many have thought the right answer is: "with punishment."

In support of this answer, three sorts of justification for punishment are commonly offered. Some justifications appeal to the demands of justice and considerations of desert—to the criminal deserving punishment or to the victims or other members of society deserving state sanctioned retribution. Some justifications appeal instead to utility and especially to the prospect of deterrence—to the thought that the threat of punishment, or punishment itself, will work to prevent crime. Finally, some appeal to punishment's role in establishing, expressing, or affirming society's commitment to the (frequently moral) judgments embodied in the law.

Often enough one or another such justification is advanced by itself as both necessary and sufficient for determining when—and the extent to which—criminals may or must be punished. Yet they are also often combined in the attempt to fashion a theory that appeals to considerations of justice and desert as well as to the importance of deterrence and the role punishment can play in expressing moral disapproval and contributing to moral education.

My purpose in this paper is to argue that these familiar justifications of punishment, taken either individually or in combination, all (to the extent they are plausible) recommend a practice importantly different from punishment. I call the alternative Legal Reparations, and will, in the course of this paper, (i) distinguish it from punishment, (ii) sketch the institutional form it might take, and (iii) argue that the justifications traditionally offered in favor of punishment actually instead favor legal reparations. I won't spend a lot of time sorting through the variety of ways one might try to combine the three sorts of justifications but will instead focus on each kind considered alone. Nonetheless, my preferred mix of the three will, I suspect, become evident. Some such mix of all three considerations is, I think, essential to any defensible state response to violations of its laws. Only a practice that addresses considerations of all three kinds can be such as to secure the reasonable agreement of those who would be subject to the practice—and that is itself crucial to the practice being justified. I won't here defend this last claim. I mention it now only to acknowledge the role it will play—perhaps, in places, only surreptitiously—in the version of Legal Reparations I sketch.

II. Punishment and Legal Reparations: The contrast

Punishment, as Stanley Benn observed, is "inflicted on an offender because of an offense he has committed; it is deliberately imposed, not just the natural consequence of a person's action (like a hang-over), and the unpleasantness is essential to it, not an accidental accompaniment to some other treatment (like the pain of the dentist's drill)."[3] Similarly, H.L.A. Hart notes that punishment "must involve pain or other consequences normally considered unpleasant" and "must be for an offense against legal rules."[4] Along the same lines, Richard Wasserstrom emphasizes that "the point of the imposition of a deprivation when it is unmistakably a punishment is that it is being imposed because it is a deprivation, because the person upon whom it is being imposed should thereby be made to suffer and in that respect be worse off than before."[5] Punishment has at its core *the intentional infliction of pain or harm.*

It might be that the pain (or other unpleasantness) involved in punishment is thought important to inflict in its own right, or important to inflict in order to achieve some further end, or important to inflict in the context of respecting some broader concern. Whatever the justification is supposed to be, a response to an offense or violation counts *as punishment* only if it involves the intentional infliction of pain (or other unpleasantness). It is this aspect of punishment that especially raises moral concerns about the practice of punishing criminals.[6] The concerns, of course, might be met—that has been the point of various attempts to justify punishment. But they need to be met: the intentional infliction of pain requires justification.

Reparations, in contrast, aim not at inflicting pain (or harm) but at enforcing efforts at making amends for the offense. What is important to reparations is not that the offender feel pain or suffer some loss or harm but that he work to make amends for the offense he has committed. As a result, a system of legal reparations will resemble a system of restitution in emphasizing that committing a crime involves committing an offense against others that calls for acknowledgment and redress. Yet reparations is importantly different from restitution in that the latter views criminal justice as properly focused solely on the loss suffered by victims and demands only that the criminal compensate for that loss.[7] Although legal reparations recognizes the loss suffered by the victim as important, and important to address, it also sees in the crime an offense—an assault on the victim's rights—that is not properly acknowledged merely by repayment. In committing a crime where there is a victim, the criminal has not only imposed a cost on the victim, he has also acted offensively in a way that calls for making amends and not merely for repayment. Recognizing and responding to this aspect of crime is a crucial element of legal reparations and explains that system's emphasis on requiring efforts towards repair and not mere payment from the offender.

As Gerald Gaus notes, "wronging is not simply harming; consequently, undoing the harm does not undo the wrong. One cannot undo wrongs in the way one can repay debts."[8] To think compensating someone (even to the point where he is indifferent as between not suffering the crime and suffering but receiving the compensation) rights the wrong is to mistake the nature of offense. Gaus goes on to suggest that punishment might add to compensation what is needed in order to right the wrong and "restore the equality" the crime dislodged. Just why punishment should do the trick, though, is mysterious, to say the least.[9] It may be that as a matter of convention we accept someone having suffered punishment as absolving him or as an accepted equivalent of atonement. In these cases, however, the key to punishment's restorative role is the conventional arrangement (and the avenue it provides for securing reinstatement to good standing in society) not on the punishment itself. Something other than punishment could equally well serve as grounds for seeing someone as absolved or as an accepted equivalent of atonement. In fact, a system of legal reparations is built on the idea that the providing of one's own labor should serve this conventional role—not because a certain amount of labor cancels the harm and the wrong, but because in laboring oneself to cancel the harm (as opposed merely to paying compensation), one can be seen as (going through at least the motions of) making amends. The labor of the criminal, then, serves as a suitable conventional focus for addressing the offense while also working in fact (and not merely symbolically) towards both compensation and making amends.

A system of reparations, with its emphasis on the making of amends and repair, aims at restoring the situation in a way that allows the offender to be legitimately reinstated in society. To this extent, a system of reparations resembles in aim various treatment programs. Yet reparations rejects the idea, central to standard treatment proposals, that (in general) criminals should be seen as patients to be healed or threats to be changed; instead it recognizes criminals as (in most cases) agents rightly held responsible for their actions.[10] At the same time, though, it sees holding a person responsible as involving not the infliction of pain but the demand that he take responsibility by working (so far as he can) to make things right.

In thinking about the difference between a system of reparations and a system that puts treatment programs front and center, it is helpful to distinguish two sorts of rehabilitation. One sort of rehabilitation, the one aimed at by treatment programs, is a matter of the criminal being changed in ways that make him less likely to commit crimes. A different sort of rehabilitation, the one aimed at by reparations and approaches to punishment that see the criminal as (loosely speaking) "paying a debt," is a matter instead of re-establishing the criminal's entitlement to inhabit society.[11] Within a system of reparations, rehabilitation (in the second sense) is seen as involving the repair of the criminal breach by effort by the criminal.[12] The relevant repair, it is worth repeating, is not achieved merely by compensating the victim. Mere compensation, after all, might be secured in a number of ways that leave the criminal's standing vis-à-vis society unchanged, as, for instance, when the compensation is paid by some third party or by the criminal himself in a way that leaves the offense (even if not the harm) unaddressed. Whatever might effect the repair, and so the relevant rehabilitation, must do so by restoring the criminal's standing within society.

What is crucial to restoring the standing? I think there is no single substantive answer to this question. Society, in effect, needs to settle what it will, in practice, take as sufficient for rehabilitation. Various features of human psychology no doubt limit and shape what might be seen as appropriately addressing the breach an offense constitutes. Still, whatever limits there are evidently leave open a strikingly broad range of possibilities. No doubt, whatever is expected, by way of efforts at repair, should reflect the relative seriousness of the offenses, with the more serious offenses calling for more significant efforts. Yet what sort of efforts might be deemed appropriate, and how their significance might be measured, is a matter of convention. Some crimes, of course, will be so serious that no amount of effort will count as sufficient. In such cases, efforts at making amends can never be successful on their own and will need to be met with some sort of institutional forgiveness. But not all crimes will call for forgiveness once a perpetrator has made efforts to make amends. There can be a point at which the criminal has in fact paid his debt to society and is himself owed good standing. To bar him still is, I believe, to do him an injustice. What is it, then, that can repair the breach a crime introduces? The answer offered by reparations is: the criminal's effort towards repair—not because that effort is painful (though it may be), but because it addresses directly and positively the damage (the harm and the offense) done by the crime.

Legal reparations aim to enforce efforts at making amends for the offense committed, not to inflict pain for that offense. Still, any state response to crime—other than passive acquiescence—is bound to involve pain for the criminal, since it is bound often to rely on coercion. This does not mean, however, that a system of reparations is really one of punishment after all. Treatment programs and restitution schemes, no less than a system of legal reparations, will involve sometimes forcing people to do what they would rather not. Even so, there is an important moral difference between making someone act in a certain way, where so acting happens to be painful for them, and intentionally inflicting pain.

Punishment is in place only when the infliction of pain is part of the point of the practice.

Of course, knowingly causing pain requires justification, even when the pain caused is unintended. So a system of reparations, which will sometimes cause people pain, stands (as does punishment) in need of justification. The burden facing reparations, however, is reasonably thought to be different from and less than that facing a system of criminal punishment. If there is something right about the doctrine of double effect—so that intentionally inflicting pain or harm is worse in itself than merely knowingly causing pain or harm—then punishment (unlike reparations) stands on the wrong side of the contrast and requires special considerations in order to be justified, if it can be justified at all. And even if the difference between intending and merely knowingly causing pain is not morally significant in itself, the difference can make a huge difference in how much pain is actually produced. For there will likely be many situations in which a call for punishment will require the infliction of pain where a parallel call for reparations will require much less (if any).[13]

Systems of punishment and reparation alike can, and surely must, recognize a limit on how much pain might legitimately be produced in response to a given crime, so that both might reach such a limit and have to stop. Still, in aiming at the infliction of pain, a system of punishment is, one may suppose, more likely to reach that limit than will be a system that lacks that aim. This is even more likely if the system of reparations views the pain felt not just as a side effect, but as an unfortunate one that is reasonably alleviated so long as alleviating it does not work against the system's aims.[14]

The underlying idea of a system of reparations—that a person who commits an offense has a duty to make amends—seems to me appropriate not only for criminal offenses but more generally whenever someone violates a justified prohibition. My concern in this paper, however, is with the state's response to crime. In its institutional incarnation, as a part of a criminal justice system, reparations will, I am supposing, take on a structure that has the fruits of a criminal's efforts contribute to a state fund that victims can, in turn, call upon for at least partial compensation. Decisions as to what should be required of people for various offenses will be independent of the actual damages caused by particular instances of that kind of offense and will instead reflect an ordinal ranking of various kinds of offense in terms of their seriousness (though that ranking of seriousness will likely be sensitive to the usual damages offenses of the various kinds impose). Thus, barring extenuating circumstances and aggravating conditions, offenses of one kind will predictably be counted as more serious than others and will accordingly be met with a demand for greater effort at making amends. The effort, in turn, will (I am imagining) be measured in work time, so that in having committed an offense a criminal will be held accountable for working (to make amends) an appropriate amount of time. Thus labor (not punishment's pain) will serve as the common coin in which one "pays one's debt," with the market value of that labor paying into a victim compensation fund, so far as there is an excess over and above enforcement costs.

It is worth emphasizing that a system of legal reparations that responds to crime not with punishment but with demands for efforts at making amends is fully compatible with maintaining the distinction between criminal and civil actions. Civil procedures already, and I think appropriately, provide an avenue for victims to collect compensation for damages. The criminal procedures that would go with a system of reparations would not duplicate nor replace nor rely on these civil procedures. Their focus would not be on compensable damage but on offense and the demands that would be made of criminals would not be proportioned to the actual damages caused (as they are in civil cases) but to the nature of the offense committed (as they are in criminal cases). The efforts at making amends, not the monetary value of those efforts, are what matters in this context. Along with this difference in focus will go a variety of procedural differences concerning, say, burden of proof and the relevance of intent, that are already more or less in place now and that are crucial to the difference between criminal and civil cases. At the same time, though, to the extent the efforts demanded by a system of reparations do contribute positively to the state fund, extra resources will be available to address damages suffered.[15] And a significant advantage of such a system is that there is hope at least of compounding benefits a system of criminal justice might offer.

When the offenders are not dangerous, and are employed, the aims of a system of reparations might be well met by having them work in their current jobs, counting some proportion of their work time towards reparations (with the actual payments into the compensation fund being a function of their salaries), while those who are not dangerous but not gainfully employed would be put to work on public works projects. Those criminals who are dangerous would, I think legitimately, be incarcerated, not with the aim of inflicting pain but so as to ensure efforts towards reparations and, until reparations are made, to insulate them from society. In addition to the genuinely dangerous there are, of course, a variety of criminals who would not, absent supervision and enforcement, make reparations. So within a system of legal reparations there will no doubt need to be a variety of more or less restrictive housing arrangements (some surely being very similar to current prisons) and work options that might well be modeled on various alternative sentencing programs. In each case, the criminals would have their freedom limited not with the aim of inflicting pain (or some other harm) but rather on the grounds that an unwillingness to work towards making amends forfeits one's right to participate fully in society.[16]

When a person is willing but unable to work effectively, the focus of the system should be on effort, not effect, and it would be reasonable too to institute various training programs (e.g., that teach trades) that put offenders in a better position to have their efforts genuinely be effective and also improve their chances of contributing positively to society. Within a system of punishment, such proposals predictably run afoul of the objection that the training programs help rather than hurt the offenders, which is antithetical to the point of punishment. Within a system of reparations, no such objection gets traction, and the fact that these programs may help the offenders more effectively make amends counts in their favor. Indeed, across the board, with both dangerous and non-dangerous offenders, with those employed and those barely able to work, the focus of the institutional response to their crimes should be on their responsibility to make amends for their offense, not on making them suffer pain nor (for that matter) shame except as these are involved in or follow from holding them responsible for their crimes. That a system of reparations demands making amends and efforts at repair, and not shaming, is important, I think. It leaves room for someone to maintain his dignity, and insist that what he did was neither wrong nor properly the cause of shame, even as he acknowledges the offense and works to make amends.[17]

There are, of course, a range of obvious questions that need to be addressed concerning, for instance, victimless crimes and crimes that cause irreparable harm or involve unspeakable offense, as well as issues relating to the specification of appropriate sentences, equalizing burdens, and effectively speaking to victims' concerns. Before turning to these, however, I will survey the standard justifications for punishment and argue that, to the extent they are plausible, they all actually favor legal reparations over punishment as a way for society to address crime. I should emphasize that I will not be arguing that punishment is unjustified but that the various considerations that might successfully justify punishment recommend the alternative offered by a system of legal reparations.

III. The Familiar Justifications for Punishment

The familiar justifications of punishment fall into three groups, according to whether they appeal primarily to considerations of justice and desert,[18] or to utility and the prevention of crime,[19] or to the role of punishment in expressing moral condemnation and contributing to moral education.[20] The division is, of course, more than a little artificial; members of society might deserve to have institutions that work to prevent crime, and respecting constraints of justice might contribute significantly to overall utility, and both justice and utility might require mechanisms that forcefully condemn certain behavior and work effectively towards the moral education of actual and potential offenders.[21] Nonetheless, I will discuss them as if they were separate and independent.

A. Appeals to justice and desert

Often, arguments offered in defense of punishment take the proper focus of considerations of justice to be the criminal and what he deserves for having committed the crime. Sometimes, the thought is that in committing a crime the criminal has acted immorally and, because the immoral deserve to suffer, criminals deserve to suffer. Punishment is justified, then, because it involves giving the criminal what he deserves. As H.L.A. Hart puts the view, "the justification for punishing...is that the return of suffering for moral evil voluntarily done, is itself just or morally good."[22] If this is the argument, one might of course question the claim that those who commit crimes have *ipso facto* done something evil, or the claim that those who do something evil deserve to suffer, or the claim that those who deserve to suffer (because they have done evil) are rightly made to suffer *by the state*. I have my doubts on all three fronts, but here will simply assume that even if criminals are morally defective and therefore deserve to suffer, it is not the state's role to make them suffer for that reason.[23] I am not saying that a state never rightly makes someone suffer. Assuming the state's coercive power is sometimes justified it will almost surely sometimes justifiably coerce in circumstances where someone is thereby made to suffer. What seems mistaken is the suggestion that the justification of such coercion rests directly on the state's determination of moral defect. Making people suffer *because of their immoral acts* is not legitimately within the state's purview.[24] Moreover, to the extent one holds that those who act immorally deserve to suffer and that the state is properly involved in distributing that suffering in proportion to the immorality, such a distribution of suffering would it seems have to take into account not just how immoral the criminal is, but also how much he has already suffered.[25]

Other times, the thought is that punishing a criminal is a way of acknowledging him as a responsible agent and he deserves this acknowledgment (whatever he has done).[26] This line of thought does not depend on holding that the criminal is evil or immoral at all, but instead sees treating him a certain way, within a public system of justice, as part and parcel of recognizing his standing as a responsible agent. Here a system of reparations and a system of punishment can agree that a criminal actually deserves to be treated as a responsible agent—to do otherwise is to commit an offense against him. But agreeing on this is not yet to find grounds for punishing the criminal as opposed to responding to his crime in some other way, as long as the alternative constitutes a way of acknowledging his standing as a responsible agent. Indeed, it is a bit puzzling why anyone would think punishment *per se* is important to this acknowledgment, except incidentally as its legitimacy is seen as presupposing a finding to the effect that the criminal is responsible for the crime for which he is being punished. Of course this link to responsibility is maintained within a system of reparations that demands efforts toward making amends only from those who have been found to be responsible for the crime in question.

Still other times, a system of punishment is seen as justified to the extent, and on the grounds, that it would (under the appropriate circumstances) secure the consent of those subjected to it. Here the idea is often that people have a right to have their standing as moral agents recognized and that this is done properly only when one's treatment of them is such that they themselves would (under the appropriate circumstances) give their consent to it. Yet if a system of punishment might secure such consent, it seems pretty clear that a system that demanded reparations in place of punishment would likewise secure the relevant consent (and, likely, more easily). So, to the extent properly recognizing the moral standing of others involves subjecting them only to institutions that could, under the appropriate circumstances, secure their consent, reparations looks as if it would stand at least no worse than would punishment in giving the due recognition.

In any case, reparations, unlike punishment, finds a place for the thought that criminals—in addition to having a right to be treated as responsible agents—might also deserve the opportunity to make amends (a right that runs in parallel with the duty to make amends that reparations recognizes, which is in turn a duty that reflects the rights of those suffering the offense). A new injustice comes in (except perhaps in the most extreme cases) if a person who commits a crime is denied the opportunity to make amends. There are limits here—some crimes are so heinous that, in committing them, a person has forfeited this right—but most crimes surely don't fall into this category. And even those that do fall in this category might so fall more because the criminal has established himself as beyond the pale than because he would not have a right to make amends if he could take advantage of it. While I am somewhat ambivalent about seeing this as a right the criminal has, I think there is a point to the idea that people should be given the opportunity to "pay their debt to society" and to be free, as a result, of further recriminations. This idea is sometimes in play when people see undergoing punishment as a way of earning back one's place in society. There is, on this picture, a kind of rehabilitation to be sought, not a rehabilitation that depends on a reformation in the character of the criminal (as I noted above), but instead one that is accomplished by bringing the criminal back into society—by reinstating him.

So far the justifications discussed have concentrated on the idea that the criminal, for one reason or another, deserves to be punished. Other attempts to justify punishment by appeal to considerations of desert, however, see the proper focus as being on the victim and what he deserves as a victim. The general idea is that the victim has a right to have the criminal punished—perhaps as a way for the state to annul the crime, or as a way to right the wrong, or as a reaffirmation of the victim's standing. In each case, there is a serious question as to how punishment in particular is supposed to be crucial to meeting these aims. Why does making the criminal suffer annul his crime? How does the punishment right the wrong? In what way does it reaffirm the victim's standing? I ask not because I think punishment cannot possibly do these things, but because an explanation of how and why punishment might do them will reveal, I believe, that the difference between punishment (with its intentional infliction of pain) and reparations, is irrelevant to the explanation. This is because punishment, so far as I can see, serves these purposes only by taking on a conventionally established symbolic role. Punishment works to "annul a crime" or "right a wrong" or reaffirm a victim's standing not naturally, so to speak, but only in a context within which suffering the intentional infliction of pain or harm of the sort in question is accepted as having achieved these aims. Within the bounds set by general considerations of justice, precisely what can achieve these aims reflects a shared understanding of what to accept. What might serve as proper payment for offense, like what might serve as legal tender, is largely a matter of what people collectively are willing to recognize and treat as such.

If this is right, then to the extent punishment can reasonably be seen as annulling the crime, righting the wrong, or reaffirming the victim's standing, reparations can as well, as long as it can take on the crucial symbolic role. At the same time, I think, reparations can more effectively speak to the demand that the crime really be annulled (i.e., wiped out) and the wrong righted and the victim's rights reaffirmed, since it involves demanding of the criminal that he make efforts directly designed at accomplishing these ends. Here the system of reparations and a system of punishment can agree that a victim deserves to have the state enforce his rights where this might involve instituting efficient protections of it and reasserting them in contexts where they have been challenged or breached. But a system of reparations goes on to hold that he also deserves from the perpetrator of the crime effort to repair the situation and make amends for the offense.

It is reasonable, though, to see crime as an offense against not only particular victims (when there are victims) but also as an offense against society at large. As a result, some attempts to justify punishment give pride of place, in appealing to considerations of justice, either (i) to the idea that society as a whole has a right (say of self-protection) to punish the criminal for the violation of its rules[27] or (ii) to the idea that members of society deserve a fair distribution of social burdens which has been upset by the criminal (who, in committing a crime, shirks the burden of restraint that the law places on all).[28] Either way, punishment is justified on the grounds that law-abiding citizens have a certain claim of justice that requires allocating certain burdens (of suffering a threat or of self-restraint) to those who voluntarily break the law. Punishment is supposed to speak to burdens unjustly imposed or shirked by criminals by imposing new burdens on them and thereby establishing the balance of burdens demanded by fairness. Reparations too, though, can countenance shifting burdens in the name of justice. Yet it would do the shifting not by introducing a brand new burden—the pain of punishment—but by demanding that criminals (who have either imposed or shirked burdens) compensate others for the burdens even as it also acknowledges, and focuses on, the fact that in committing the crime they have done more and worse than simply imposing or dodging a burden—they have failed to treat others with the respect they are due. This aspect of their crimes calls not for the imposition of pain or some new burden, but rather an effort at reparations on the part of the criminals.

Putting aside the—I think indefensible—claim that punishment by the state is justified and demanded directly and simply by the immorality a criminal's acts exhibit, the various arguments for punishment that appeal to what the criminal, or the victim, or society at large, deserve all capture something important. Yet they all, also, mobilize considerations that are not essentially tied to punishment. In fact, it seems to me that a system of reparations clearly speaks to these considerations more directly and effectively than does punishment.

B. Appeals to utility and the prevention of crime

Of course appeals to justice and desert are often not the primary justifications offered for punishment, even if such considerations are often seen as constraining what sort of punishment might be justified by other considerations. Long ago, Protagoras argued that "he who desires to inflict rational punishment does not punish for the sake of a past wrong which cannot be undone; he has regard to the future and is desirous that the man who is punished, and he who sees him punished, may be deterred from doing wrong again."[29] Ever since, one of the main justifications for punishment has been found in its serving as an effective deterrent—thanks either to punishment effectively reducing recidivism or to the prospect of punishment working as a disincentive. This justification plays right to the core of punishment by claiming that the pain punishment intentionally inflicts keeps people from committing crimes they otherwise would commit.

There are of course familiar moral worries about this sort of justification that arise unless it is combined in some way with effective constraints on who might be liable to punishment and on just how much punishment might be administered.[30] Absent such constraints a direct appeal to the benefits one might secure by intentionally inflicting pain on people risks countenancing the 'punishment' of innocent people and the torturing of people, innocent or not, for minor as well as major crimes.

Yet even with appropriate constraints in place, the plausibility of a deterrence justification of punishment is seriously undermined by the evidence available—evidence that seems to show that the prospect of pain (and punishment in general) is an ineffective deterrent (at least as long as the punishment is not draconian), especially among those disposed to be criminals in the first place.[31] Witness the high recidivism rates among offenders who have been punished and the extraordinary failure of programs like Scared Straight that are aimed at making vivid the prospect of pain as a consequence of crime.[32]

Any justification of punishment that speaks to what motivates criminals needs to recognize that a great deal other than the prospect of pain is in play—including impulsiveness, perceived injustice, desire for excitement, apparent lack of better options, the need to establish one's standing, honor...[33] Threatening pain, as a system of punishment does, speaks to none of these, nor does it seem likely to have much impact on what, down the road, might come to motivate those who have been subjected to punishment. All it does is try to shift the balance of considerations by introducing one—the prospect of pain—that evidently does not figure very heavily when it comes to criminal behavior. Of course punishment can, under the rubric of inflicting harm, impose costs on criminals other than the costs of pain. Presumably a system of punishment that takes into account the extent to which criminals seem not to give significant weight to the prospect of pain would devise punishments that speak to depriving criminals of what they do value. Even then, though, evidence suggests that, to a large extent, long term and uncertain prospects of the imposition of a cost do not figure prominently in deterring crime.[34] Rather, the near term perceived certainty of some penalty or other—pretty much regardless of severity—appears to have a significantly greater deterrent effect. Indeed there is some evidence that increasing the severity of penalties actually increases crime rates.[35] The very fact that the severity of the penalty (given equal certainty) has at most little effect suggests that the importance of certainty of penalty is found not in its providing a cost (the imposition of which is central to punishment) but in something else. Plausibly, the relevant something else is, at least in part, its providing a clear message that the behavior is forbidden. This, however, is a message easily—and well—conveyed by a system of reparations.[36]

There is at least some additional evidence that what matters to deterrence is the message that the violation of the law is to be taken seriously. A number of studies suggest that police "cautions" as opposed to court appearances,[37] probation as opposed to conviction and fine,[38] and being discharged as opposed to being charged and fined,[39] all showed significant *increases* in subsequent criminality. When the authorities do not take the crime seriously, neither do the criminals. Yet there was no decrease in criminality when the serious responses were augmented by more severe penalties. It seems that once it is clear that the crime is being taken seriously, increasing the severity of the penalty has no positive impact on recidivism.[40] A reasonable hypothesis is that what is crucial, when it comes to an institutional response to crime, is that the significance of the offense be unambiguously conveyed. In any case, however much people think it a matter of common sense that punishment deters, the evidence shows fairly convincingly that the relationship between crime and the prospect of punishment is neither as simple nor as reliable as many would suppose.

C. Appeals to the expressive and educative role of punishment

That society must convey the significance of criminal offenses is one of the main ideas behind the suggestion that punishment is justified by its expressive or educative role. The thought is that a society can effectively mark its condemnation of certain behaviors, and thus conveys that they are wrong, only by backing prohibitions with threats of punishment. At the same time, society's willingness to follow through on the punishments and enforce citizens rights is a way of affirming both that the violation of the rights will not be tolerated and that the person whose rights were violated has standing in the community. To let violations go by, to offer only cautions or merely sentence someone to probation is to send the message that the violation, and by implication the person violated, is not to be taken very seriously. Punishment, so the argument goes, is society's way of not letting such things go by.[41]

I do think there is substantial evidence (cited above) that a light touch of the law will engender disregard both for it and for what it claims to protect. However, the evidence does not show that punishment is the best, let alone the only, way for society to indicate the significance it attaches to respecting the law. The expressive function of punishment, as important as it is, is pretty clearly a function that can be played by something other than punishment—and to better effect, I suspect. Indeed, to the extent there are grounds for thinking increasing the severity of penalties has no deterrent effect there is reason to think the important and effective message is not centrally conveyed by the punishment itself even when punishments are in place, but rather by society palpably taking the offense seriously. And conveying that the offense is to be taken seriously is something enforcing efforts at reparations would seemingly do effectively.

In addition to thinking punishment can play a crucial expressive role, when it comes to conveying condemnation, many have thought punishment works (either via the expressive role, or in some other way) to reform the criminal morally, to make him a better person. On this view, as Jean Hampton presents it, "there is a concrete moral *goal* which punishment should be designed to accomplish, and that goal includes the benefiting of the criminal himself. The state, as it punishes the lawbreaker, is trying to promote his moral personality..."[42] To the extent this goal is legitimately adopted by the state, the question remains as to whether punishment is the best way of achieving it. Hampton appeals to punishment's capacity to communicate a moral message in defending its educative role. And surely to the extent punishment does actually advance the cause, it is partly by being a means of effective communication. But, as I have already suggested, there is every reason to think that a system of reparations could play the same communicative role. Of course, punishment might also serve the goal of moral improvement in some other way. It might be, for instance, that by altering incentives for available actions, punishment works to change what people choose to do, and thus what habits (and so, character) they develop. Again, though, the evidence suggests that whatever impact punishment might have on incentives, it works poorly as a deterrent (and therefore cannot be working positively to change character by leading people away from crime). Most strikingly, it seems that increasing severity (which presumably increases disincentives) is often counter-productive. Still, if punishment does work to promote a criminal's "moral personality" either by getting him to act in certain ways or by forcing him to take responsibility for his actions, a system of reparations could justifiably claim the same advantages.

This has been, I realize, a whirlwind tour through what are, in point of fact, highly complex and subtle arguments. I have not even come close to doing them justice. My purpose, though, has not been to evaluate the arguments or to refine them to the point where I might fully endorse one or the other. The strategy has been, instead, to convey the extent to which arguments that are offered in defense of punishment regularly leave unexplored an important and attractive possibility—legal reparations. The quick discussion of the various familiar justifications of punishment are thus offered primarily as an invitation to those who find one or another attractive to ask whether reparations might actually speak to the morally legitimate purposes of the criminal law more effectively than does punishment.

No doubt just how attractive legal reparations proves to be depends not only on its answering to traditional justifications for punishment but on it addressing well problems that might seem its own alone to face. I will, in what follows, just briefly mention some of these apparent problems and suggest how a defender of legal reparations might speak to them.

IV. Some Worries

The system of reparations puts a lot of weight on the idea that in holding people responsible for what they do we should see them as owing not just compensation but amends—genuine efforts at repair—to others (victims and society at large, to the extent the laws are genuinely just). However, society is surely in no place to force people to make amends, since genuinely making amends is as much a matter of one's state of mind as one's actions. I think, as the worry suggests, that in breaking a just law a criminal undertakes a duty that no one else can force him to fulfill—that is the duty of acknowledging others as deserving better. This duty is most naturally met by sincere efforts to make amends for the offense constituted by the crime. And, as the worry highlights, sincere efforts are just the sort of thing no one can force another to make. Nonetheless, a society can arrange its institutions so as to acknowledge that this is what is in fact owed and can then work—within the bounds of respecting those involved, including the criminals—to encourage genuine respect of this debt and to enforce actual (if not always sincere) efforts at repair. The first aim is in large part met by pursuing the second. In enforcing efforts at repair—rather than simply inflicting pain—a system of reparations would be publicly and clearly acknowledging that something is owed to those against whom an offense has been committed. And that is, it seems to me, a proper primary focus for a criminal justice system—one that it can accomplish without being objectionably intrusive.

In concentrating on efforts at repair, however, it might seem that a system of reparations would find no grounds for responding to victimless crimes. How would a system of legal *reparations* legitimately see such crimes as within its purview? Well, even when crimes are "victimless," if they are crimes in a just society there is both a harm and an offense to society at large in their commission. The harm is at least the marginal costs each criminal adds to the criminal justice system. But the harm is often much more than that, since many "victimless" crimes are criminalized precisely because there is a real, albeit diffuse, harm caused by the act. Consideration of harm aside, an offense comes with any violation of a prohibition that society has reasonably deemed important enough to make a matter of law and the offense stands as grounds for a duty of reparations. I should emphasize, though, that acknowledging that an offense is involved in committing crimes is not the same as thinking committing the crimes are immoral. Sometimes one is morally justified in committing an offense. And this is true even when that justification has no standing as a legal justification or excuse. Whether or not a moral justification is present, however, a system of reparations will (I think appropriately) see the offense and whatever harm it causes (even if diffuse) as properly calling for efforts at repair on the part of the offender.

To go to the other extreme, where the victims are clear and both the harm and the offense are large, it might seem as well that a system of reparations would be at a loss. Some crimes (e.g. murder, rape, etc.) are such that it is out of place—perhaps even abhorrent—to talk of repair or making amends. These crimes involve offenses and harms so great, and of such a nature, that neither hope nor sense should be attached to the idea that the victim might be made whole. Any response to crime must recognize the distinctive standing of such offenses. Within a system of reparations this should be done, I believe, by seeing those who commit such crimes as having, through their actions, incurred debts that no amount of effort throughout the remainder of their lives will count as having made amends. They never have a legitimate claim to having earned reinstatement. Moreover, it is reasonable to see those who commit such crimes as having, through their actions, forfeited any right to liberty or control over their time (though not, I would say, their right to humane treatment nor their right to life).

Crimes of this sort—crimes for which a criminal will never be in a situation where he has a legitimate claim to have earned his reinstatement—highlight the role some form of institutional forgiveness will almost surely have to play in a system of criminal justice (whether it deploys punishment or demands reparations). Sometimes the proper response to people who have worked to make amends for a horrible offense is to forgive them. In such cases it would be a mistake to see the offenders as having a right to reinstatement thanks to their having made amends. But it would not necessarily be a mistake to see reinstatement as nonetheless justified or appropriate. The sort of institutional forgiveness this would involve is of course distinct from, but still related to, the forgiveness that may or may not be offered by victims of such crimes. The institutional forgiveness—conveyed, perhaps, by pardon—represents a collective choice by society concerning what should count as sufficient grounds for readmitting someone to full and equal status in society. Such a decision will no doubt have to be sensitive in some way to victims' attitudes. Presumably, though, considerations of fairness would require that the determination of pardons not be left solely to the discretion of the victims or the victims' families.[43]

Similarly, considerations of fairness would influence how an acceptable system of reparations would treat people who commit crimes that are very similar in intent but quite different in effect when it comes to the damages caused and offense taken. To the extent reparations focuses on damages and feelings of offense in determining efforts at repair, it seems the two cases will be treated very differently. Yet, to the extent the different effects are a matter of luck, so to speak, it seems as if fairness will require that the demands on each be the same. Of course, similar questions arise for systems of punishment where distinctions are drawn, say, between murder and attempted murder. Still, the grounds for marking differences might seem greatly magnified in a system that focuses on reparations, since every difference in damage might seem relevant to what burden should be imposed on the criminal. On the contrary, I believe exactly the same general issues of fairness arise whether the system in question is one of punishment or of reparations.[44] Either way, decisions need to be made concerning the extent to which the offensiveness of the act, as opposed to the harm or felt offense it happens to cause, is to determine society's institutional response to the crime. Whatever the balance, when actual effects are taken into account (as they are in the distinction between murder and attempted murder), differences due to luck will have an influence. It may well be, though, that while both are taken into account, some crimes are such that the offense so swamps the effects in significance that differences in the latter do not matter substantially to what reparations (or punishment) are deemed appropriate (and, perhaps, vice versa).

In any case, considerations of justice—specifically, concern to treat similar cases similarly—might allow what is demanded, by way of efforts at making amends, to be sensitive to the effects acts of the kind in question normally cause, but would require that those demands be insensitive to specific differences among particular cases. At the same time, though, a state compensation fund supported (at least in part) by fruits of the efforts at repair, could presumably pay out compensations that are highly sensitive to differences that are not taken into account in determining appropriate reparations. Payments from such a fund might, for instance, be sensitive to whether the victims in question have successfully secured compensation through other legal channels (e.g., civil action) or to how well off they are. Inevitably, too, the payments would be sensitive to the size of the fund, which in turn, will depend not only on the size of reparations paid in but on the society's willingness to tax itself (to provide insurance against suffering otherwise uncompensated harms). Decisions as to how to finance such a fund, and especially as to the extent to which it should depend upon those who owe reparations, turn on matters of social policy that go beyond and are, I think, tangential to, the question of whether demanding reparations, as opposed to punishing, is the appropriate response to crime. Interestingly, though, a system of reparations fits especially nicely with the independently attractive idea that victims of crime have a claim to compensation. And it fits well too with the general aim of designing social institutions so as to promote overall welfare since it organizes the response to crime around a concern to effect repair.

Any institutional response to crime—reparations no less than punishment—will have to face the challenge of those who pose an imminent threat. Sometimes the threat will be posed by those who have not yet committed a crime, other times by someone who has. Either way, to the extent the state is responding to the threat, and not to a crime for which the person has been convicted, the response should probably not be seen either as punishment or as enforcing efforts at repair. Nonetheless, if some sort of preventive detention or other preemptive reaction is sometimes justifiable in the context of a system of punishment, it seems it would likewise be justifiable, on the same grounds, in the context of a system of legal reparations.[45] As practically important, and morally complicated, as the issue may be, coming to terms with it will (I believe) not have significant implications for the choice between punishment and reparations.[46]

In contrast, the ubiquitous desire for revenge seems to call clearly for punishment rather than reparations. After all, punishment, but not reparations, can speak directly to the desire—by satisfying it. So one might see punishment as justified on the grounds that putting it into place both controls and satisfies a desire that otherwise would cause mayhem. James Fitzjames Stephen gives voice to this argument when he claims that, in addition to being an effective deterrent ("it prevents crime by terror"), the criminal law "regulates, sanctions, and provides a legitimate satisfaction for the passion of revenge; the criminal law stands to the passion of revenge in much the same relation as marriage to the sexual appetite."[47] Bentham advances a similar argument when he cites "vindictive satisfaction" as an important advantage of punishment.[48]

Thought of in these terms, as appeasing the desire for revenge, punishment's relevant advantages are simply unavailable to reparations. Only punishment provides this vindictive satisfaction and only punishment speaks directly to the desire for revenge by satisfying it. However, it is at least not clear that *satisfying* the desire is the best way of dealing with its presence. Indeed, there is reason to worry that public institutions of revenge actually encourage the desire by legitimizing it. In any case, it is clear that at least sometimes apologies, and efforts at making amends, and recognition of another's right to take offense, all work to extinguish (rather than satisfy) the desire for revenge. So it would be a mistake to assume that the desire simply cannot be addressed otherwise than by punishment (or revenge in some other form). Needless to say, it is reasonable to suppose that the more serious the offense—and especially the more directly the offense was an attack—the more likely the desire for revenge will remain. Surely what would work to eliminate the desire when it is provoked by minor offenses will not be sufficient when the offense is more significant. Yet it is a serious over-simplification to hold that what the more significant offenses call for is direct satisfaction of the desire for revenge rather than, say, more extensive efforts at making amends and other public acknowledgments of the significant nature of the offense.

Just how successfully a system of reparations might address the desire for revenge remains, it seems to me, an open question. But it is plausible to think victims and criminals and society as a whole might be better served if satisfying the desire for revenge were to be removed from center stage.

Against this suggestion, some will argue that the desire for revenge, and its appropriate satisfaction, are ineliminable features of a healthy moral community. On their view, to do without punishment "would be a sign," as John Cottingham puts it, "that the network of moral responses that defines civilized life had collapsed." [49] On this view, a proper appreciation of a crime is supposed to travel with a recognition that it calls for punishment. To do anything else, it is commonly suggested, is to fail to recognize the crime for the offense it is. I share the view that serious offenses are not properly ignored—that one should not simply let them go. Yet I wonder why reacting with punishment would seem the only appropriate response. Punishment, I suspect, will seem the only appropriate—and only appropriately serious—response to serious crime as long as people overlook the alternative a system of reparations offers. But that alternative, it seems to me, presents a framework within which society's response to serious crime can be given the necessary significance.

The plausibility of reparations as an appropriately serious response to serious offenses depends upon appreciating that the efforts it calls for can range in their significance and can be made proportional to the crime, so that more extensive efforts at repair are demanded of those who commit more serious crimes. At the same time, it is important to appreciate that a system of reparations imposes non-optional demands upon criminals. The demand for efforts at repair, the insistence that in committing a crime one acquires an obligation to make amends, is crucial to reparations' standing as an acknowledgment of the rights of all.

Of course, this very feature of reparations (which is so important to its respecting the seriousness of some offenses) makes it easy for people to miss the difference between such a system, on the one hand, and punishment, on the other. The fact that reparations are demanded and enforced, not optional, may lead some to think that in making the demands such a system would be actually, if only covertly, punishing those subject to it. No doubt, reparations, like any coercive response to crime (mandatory treatment programs no less than punishments), will inevitably sometimes impose costs, and be unwelcome.

Yet two things especially distinguish reparations from punishment. First, reparations in no way aims at causing the criminal pain or harm. It stands fully successful, on its own terms, whether or not someone subject to its demands welcomes the opportunity to make amends. A welcome punishment, in contrast, is no real punishment at all.[50] Second, reparations, unlike punishment, aim directly, and positively, at redressing crimes in a way that takes the victim into account. Unlike punishment, it naturally focuses attention on the fact that in committing a crime one is committing an offense against other members of society.

V. Conclusion

I have tried, in this paper, to describe and defend a system of legal reparations that might serve as a genuine, and genuinely attractive, alternative to the current practice of subjecting criminals to punishment.

I have not addressed the practical problems that might come with changing over from a system of punishment to one of reparations. I suspect, though, that the change might be effected without drama by gradually introducing alternative sentencing programs that embrace reparations (rather than punishment or treatment) as their underlying aim. Nor have I explored the practical complexities involved in the actual workings of a system of reparations. Most significantly, I have pretty much passed over the question of how appropriate reparations for specific offenses might be determined. There are, undeniably, serious issues here. Yet these problems have identical twins that stand as problems for any justifiable system of punishment. So they do not represent distinctive problems for a system of reparations. Moreover, by and large whatever solutions work in one system can (I believe) be fairly easily adapted to the other.

What I have done is argue that the most plausible justifications for punishment—whether they appeal to justice and desert, or to utility and deterrence, or to moral expression and education—all actually recommend a system of legal reparations. If this is right, then the best justifications of punishment are not justifications of punishment at all but are instead elements in a justification for an important alternative. This alternative, I maintain, has the signal advantage that, by enforcing efforts at making amends, it steers clear of the morally problematic practice of intentionally inflicting harm while publicly, clearly, and productively acknowledging crimes as offenses that call for redress.

NOTES

1. I have benefited from discussions of this material at University of Richmond, The Australian National University Law Program, the Research Triangle Ethics Circle, and the 1999 *Sociedad Filosofica Ibero Americana* (SOFIA) Conference on Legal and Political Philosophy, in Mazatlan, Mexico. I am especially grateful for comments from John Braithwaite, Valerie Braithwaite, Geoffrey Brennen, David Estlund, Claire Finkelstein, Don Garrett, Gerald Gaus, Geoff Goddu, Livia Guimaraes, Jim Hall, Tom Hill, Jr., Christopher Kutz, Loren Lomasky, Larry May, Joan McCord, Gerald Postema, and Peter Vallentyne.
2. For purposes of this paper, I bracket the problems that come with trying to decide what is required in order for a determination to be legitimate. What this (by assumption legitimate) determination comes to—whether a judgment of guilt, or of responsibility, or of efficient causation, will presumably both influence and be influenced by the institutional response to such determinations.
3. Stanley I. Benn, "Punishment," *The Encyclopedia of Philosophy* (Macmillan Publishing Co., 1967), Vol. 7 & 8, p. 29.
4. H.L.A. Hart, "Prolegomenon for the Principles of Punishment," Presidential Address to the Aristotelian Society, 1959; reprinted in his *Punishment and Responsibility* (Oxford: Clarendon Press, 1968).
5. Richard Wasserstrom, "Capital Punishment as Punishment: Some Theoretical Issues and Objections," *Midwest Studies in Philosophy*, 7 (1982), p. 476.
6. Although there is room to worry about subtle differences between unpleasantness, pain, deprivation, suffering, and harm, such differences won't, I think, have an impact on the argument that follows.
7. See Randy Barnett's "Restitution: A New Paradigm of Criminal Justice," *Ethics*, vol. 87 (July, 1977), pp. 279–301.
8. Gerald Gaus, "Does Compensation Restore Equality?" in John W. Chapman, ed., *Nomos XXXIII: Compensatory Justice.* (New York: New York University Press, 1991), pp. 45–81, p. 72.
9. Gaus mentions that even when compensation is accompanied by punishment there may be cases in which "the aggressor is not fully squared away with the victim." I am challenging the idea that the punishment in itself ever works to square things away, except in so far as society accepts a conventional arrangement whereby undergoing a certain amount of punishment is counted as sufficient.
10. Of course, some who commit crimes are genuinely not responsible for what they do. These people no doubt need to be dealt with in some other way—just how they should be dealt with will presumably turn on how dangerous they are and on whether they can, through treatment or education, become responsible agents.

11. Neither sort of rehabilitation need be primarily a matter of making the criminal a morally better person; but both are, of course, morally constrained, and insofar as they effect a minimal amount of moral decency in one's treatment of others there will be (potentially) a moral change involved.
12. Edgardo Rotman explores some of the complexities of the concept of rehabilitation in *Beyond Punishment* (New York: Greenwood Press, 1990).
13. Of course, it is possible that a little intentional infliction of pain might, over all, cause less pain than would acting always without that intention. Indeed, a claim to this effect underwrites the familiar utilitarian justification of punishment. The idea is that a system that steers clear of intentionally inflicting pain (as opposed merely to knowingly causing it) will, thanks to its not producing directly the extra amount of pain the intentions bring in, produce indirectly more pain by failing to deter criminal behavior. Obviously, this is at bottom an empirical issue, but the evidence, it seems to me, does not support the idea that the pain the system might introduce intentionally carries with it the sort of marginal benefit this argument supposes. I even suspect that the level of pain that would come with either punishment or reparations is likely to secure most of the deterrent effect there is and the extra pain intentionally inflicted serves more to raise a sense of injustice and resentment on the part of criminals than to deter them—and so may actually increase recidivism and crime in general. I cite some relevant (albeit not conclusive) evidence later in the paper, in the section concerning deterrence.
14. Whether a system of reparations should take this view, or should instead see the pain as neither here nor there, given that it accompanies an agent doing what he should, is something about which I am ambivalent.
15. Presumably, those who successfully collect civil damages will not also be eligible for support from the state funds and many who could not successfully collect using civil procedures might still have a claim on some state fund compensation.
16. In extreme cases, where a person has committed an especially heinous offense and is unwilling to work to make amends (presumably not an unusual combination), it might be legitimate to consider forcing such people to contribute in ways that don't require their willing participation. They might, I suppose, be coerced to participate in medical trials, assuming reasonable constraints are placed on what is being tested. Here the idea would be to substitute such criminals into trials that are currently approved as safe enough to allow participation by volunteers, though the criminals' participation would not be, in the cases in question, voluntary.
17. See John Braithwaite's *Crime, Shame, and Reintegration* (Cambridge: Cambridge University Press, 1989) for a discussion of responses to crime that rely on shaming.
18. See, for example, Immanuel Kant's *The Metaphysical Elements of Justice* (Indianapolis: Bobbs Merrill, 1965); Jeffrie Murphy's "Marxism and Retribution," in *Retribution, Justice, and Therapy* (Dordrecht: D. Reidel, 1979); and David E. Cooper's "Hegel's Theory of Punishment," in *Hegel's Political Philosophy*, edited by Z.A. Pelczynski (Cambridge: Cambridge University Press, 1971).

19. See, for a classic example, Jeremy Bentham's *An Introduction to the Principles of Morals and Legislation*, edited by J.H. Burns and H.L.A. Hart (London: Athlone Press, 1970).
20. See, for example, Joel Feinberg's "The Expressive Function of Punishment" in *Doing and Deserving* (Princeton: Princeton University Press, 1970), pp. 95–118; Herbert Morris's "A Paternalistic Theory of Punishment," *American Philosophical Quarterly* 18 (1981), pp. 263–71; and Jean Hampton's "The Moral Education Theory of Punishment," *Philosophy and Public Affairs* 13 (1984), pp. 208–38.
21. Most attempts to justify punishment mix these various considerations in some way or other, which seems only reasonable in that they all appear to capture something both relevant and important. John Rawls' "Two Concepts of Rules," *Philosophical Review* 64 (1955), pp. 3–32, is especially concerned with sorting out the mix, as are H.L.A. Hart's "Prolegomenon to the Principles of Punishment," *op. cit.* and Thomas Hill's "Kant on Punishment: A Coherent Mix of Deterrence and Retribution?" in *Respect, Pluralism, and Justice.* (Oxford: Oxford University Press, 2000), pp. 173–199.
22. *Punishment and Responsibility*, p. 231.
23. There are all sorts of reasons for rejecting this as the state's role, not least being that the state is in no position to determine how immoral people are over-all, and such a determination would presumably be necessary in order to settle how much punishment a particular person deserves. See Gertrude Ezorsky, "The Ethics of Punishment," in Gertrude Ezorsky (ed.) *Philosophical Perspectives on Punishment* (Albany: State University of New York Press, 1972), in which she argues that an appeal to a criminal's deserving punishment because of his moral defects would require balancing "all of his moral wrongs against the sufferings of his entire life" (p. xxvi) in order to determine whether, for instance, he has already suffered enough.
24. See Jeffrie Murphy, "Retributivism and the State's Interest in Punishment," in *NOMOS XXVII: Criminal Justice*, edited by J.R. Pennock and J. Chapman (New York: New York University Press, 1985), pp. 156–64.
25. At the same time, this view seems also to encourage the idea that the law should expand to cover all immorality or at least that all such immorality is properly within the domain of the state as it exercises its power to distribute suffering. See Gertrude Ezorsky's "The Ethics of Punishment," in *Philosophical Perspectives on Punishment, op. cit.*, pp. xxiv-xxvi.
26. See Herbert Morris's "Persons and Punishment," in *Punishment and Rehabilitation*, edited by Jeffrie Murphy (Belmont: Wadsworth Publishing Company, 1973), pp. 40–64.
27. See Phillip Montague's "Punishment and Societal Defense" in *Criminal Justice Ethics*, 2 (1983), pp. 30–36.
28. See Herbert Morris's "Punishment and Fairness," *The Monist*, 52 (1968), pp. 476–79.
29. Plato. *Protagoras*, 324b, translated by B. Jowett, revised by Martin Ostwald, 1956 (Indianapolis: Bobbs-Merrill, 1956), p. 22.
30. See H. L. A. Hart's "Prolegomenon to the Principles of Punishment," *op cit.*

31. See David Farrington, "Social, Psychological and Biological Influences on Juvenile Delinquency and Adult Crime," in *Explaining Criminal Behaviour*, edited by W. Buikhuisen and S.A. Mednick (New York: E.J. Brill, 1988), pp. 68–89; J.H. Satterfield, "Childhood Diagnostic and Neurophysiological Predictors of Teenage Arrest Rates: An Eight-year Prospective Study," in *The Causes of Crime: New Biological Approaches* edited by S.A. Mednick, T.E. Moffitt, and S.A. Stack (Cambridge: Cambridge University Press, 1987), pp. 146–167; J. Hinton, M. O'Neill, S. Hamilton, and M. Burke, "Psychophysiological Differentiation Between Psychopathic and Schizophrenic Abnormal Offenders," *British Journal of Social and Clinical Psychology*, 19 (1980), pp. 257–269; and *Deterrence and Incapacitation: Estimating the Effects of Criminal Sanctions on Crime Rates* edited by Alfred Blumstein, Jacqueline Cohen, and Daniel Nagin, (Washington, D.C.: National Academy of Sciences, 1978).
32. See A.C. Petrosino, C. Turpin-Petrosino, and J.O. Finckenauer "Well-meaning programs can have harmful effects! Lessons from experiments of programs such as Scared Straight." *Crime & Delinquency* 46 (2000), pp. 354–379; J.C. Buchner and M. Chesney-Lind, "Dramatic Cures for Juvenile Crime: An Evaluation of a Prisoner-run Delinquency Prevention Program," *Criminal Justice and Behavior*, 10 (1983), pp. 227–247; and R.V. Lewis, "Scared Straight–California Style," *Criminal Justice and Behavior*, 10 (1983), pp. 284–289.
33. See Joan McCord, "He Did It Because He Wanted To...," W. Osgood (ed.) *Nebraska Symposium on Motivation: Motivation and Delinquency* (Lincoln: University of Nebraska Press, 1997), pp. 1–43.
34. See T. E. Moffitt, "The Learning Theory Model of Punishment: Implications for Delinquency Deterrence," *Criminal Justice and Behavior*, 10 (1983), pp. 131–158.
35. See G. Antunes and A.L. Hunt, "The Impact of Certainty and Severity of Punishment on Levels of Crime in American States: An Extended Analysis," *Journal of Criminal Law and Criminology*, 64 (1973), pp. 489–493.
36. There are, of course, other possibilities. It may be, for instance, that certainty offsets an otherwise dramatic discount criminals might place on future costs.
37. David P. Farrington and T. Bennett, "Police Cautioning of Juveniles in London," *British Journal of Criminology*, 21 (1981), pp. 123–135.
38. D. Glaser and M.A. Gordon, "Profitable Penalties for Lower Level Courts," *Judicature*, 73 (1990), pp. 248–252.
39. David P. Farrington, S.G. Osborn, and D.J. West, "The Persistence of Labeling Effects," *British Journal of Criminology*, 18 (1978), pp. 277–284.
40. This fits nicely with the research concerning the impact of certainty to the extent low certainty is due to lack of enforcement or casual or inconsistent treatment of offenders that would convey the message that the offenses in question are not being taken very seriously.
41. For an account of punishment that emphasizes its expressive role, see Joel Feinberg's "The Expressive Function of Punishment," in his *Doing and Deserving* (Princeton: Princeton University Press, 1970), pp. 95–118; and

Robert Nozick's *Philosophical Explanations* (Cambridge: Harvard University Press, 1981), pp. 363–397.

42. "The Moral Education Theory of Punishment," in *Punishment* , edited by A.J. Simmons, M. Cohen, J. Cohen, and C. Beitz, (Princeton: Princeton University Press, 1995), pp. 112–142, p. 119. See also Herbert Morris' "A Paternalistic Theory of Punishment," *American Philosophical Quarterly*, 18 (1981), pp. 263–271; and R.A. Duff's *Trials and Punishments* (Cambridge: Cambridge University Press, 1986).
43. Within certain bounds, though, it may be both fair and reasonable to let decisions concerning institutional forgiveness be significantly influenced by the victims or their families.
44. These general issues are nicely raised by Thomas Nagel's "Moral Luck," in his *Mortal Questions* (Cambridge: Cambridge University Press, 1979), pp. 24–38.
45. It is worth noting that the very fact that we expect someone to commit a crime after having served his sentence often seems evidence that we think he has not genuinely made amends. (Sometimes, of course, recidivism is traceable not to a failure to regret an offense. It might, for instance, be due to people having, at least as they see it, counterbalancing reasons to offend again or to the acts being due to something for which the criminal is not fully culpable.) Still, the state cannot legitimately be in the business of determining genuine regret and should not be imposing sentences the limits of which are set by the state's being satisfied that the criminal regrets his actions. It is in society's interest as a whole to keep the state out of that arena and so to settle for sentences that constitute public and publicly enforceable efforts at making amends in proportion to the offense. It should steer clear of making actual regret the benchmark. Nonetheless, one hope of a system of reparations is that the focus on making amends rather than causing pain, and the insisting on people taking responsibility for their actions in the form of working to repair the damage they have done, is that in fact the practice will encourage genuine regret and repair, and not merely symbolic representations of those.
46. For an attempt to spell out when and why preventive detention and other preemptive strikes might be justified, see Norval Morris' "'Dangerousness' and Incapacitation," from *Record of the Association of the Bar of the City of New York*, 39 (1982), pp. 102–28. See also Andrew von Hirsch, *Past or Future Crimes* (New Brunswick: Rutgers University Press, 1985).
47. James Fitzjames Stephen, *A General View of the Criminal Law of England* (London: Macmillan, 1863), p. 99.
48. Jeremy Bentham, *An Introduction to the Principles of Morals and Legislation* Chapter 13, footnote 1, p. 158, *op. cit.*
49. John Cottingham, "Just Punishment," *Proceedings of the Aristotelian Society*, Supplementary Volume 61, (1987), pp. 41–55, p. 53.
50. More accurately, the fact that some punishment is welcome and not viewed as a burden will mean that, in an important respect, it has misfired.

PHILOSOPHICAL ISSUES, 11
Social, Political, and Legal Philosophy, 2001

Judicial Can't

Scott J. Shapiro

In the winter of 1988, nuns of the Missionaries of Charity were walking through the snow in the South Bronx in their saris and sandals to look for an abandoned building that they might convert into a homeless shelter. Mother Teresa, the Nobel Prize winner and head of the order, had agreed on the plan with Mayor Koch after visiting him in the hospital several years earlier. The nuns came to two fire-gutted buildings on 148th Street and, finding a Madonna among the ruble, thought that perhaps providence itself had ordained the mission. New York City offered the abandoned buildings at one dollar each, and the Missionaries of Charity set aside $500,000 for the reconstruction. The nuns developed a plan to provide temporary care for 64 homeless men in a communal setting that included a dining room and kitchen on the first floor, a lounge on the second floor, and small dormitory rooms on the third and fourth floors. The only unusual thing about the plan was that Missionaries of Charity, in addition to their vow of poverty, avoid the routine use of modern conveniences. There would be no dishwashers or other appliances; laundry would be done by hand. For New York City, the proposed homeless facility would be (literally) a godsend....

Providence, however, was no match for the law. New York's building code, they were told after almost two years, requires an elevator in every new or renovated multiple-story building. The Missionaries of Charity explained that because of their belief they would never use the elevator, which also would add upward of $100,000 to the cost. The nuns were told that the law could not be waived even if an elevator didn't make sense.

Mother Teresa gave up. She didn't want to devote much extra money to something that wouldn't really help the poor: According to her representative, "The Sisters felt they could use the money much more usefully for soup and sandwiches." In a polite letter to the city expressing their regrets, the Missionaries of Charity noted that the episode "served to educate us about the law and its many complexities."[1]

I. Rule-Think

A. THE LAW IS AN ASS

In his book *The Death of Common Sense*, Philip Howard uses the above anecdote as a chilling illustration of the currently dysfunctional state of the law. Howard's aim is to show the reader, by recounting a long string of similar mishaps, just how absurd the law has become. His has not been the only critical voice. The debate concerning the nature and scope of legal regulation has rarely played a greater role in public discussions. Once the province of the Right, the political Center now joins the chorus of those who rail against the supposed excesses of the regulatory state. Indeed, the media is saturated on a daily basis with such "horror" stories and these attacks have had their intended effect. Many have lost respect for the present system. They have become convinced that the law is composed of too many rules, a great percentage of which are either too rigid or lack sound rationale. American life is perceived to be both over-regulated and poorly regulated.

These complaints, however, are neither new nor likely to disappear. Perversity has always been the law's signature; as Dickens' Mr. Bumble famously observed, "The law is an ass." To be sure, the extent of the perversity fluctuates, the law being more absurd at some times than at others. But equally as certain, there will always be rules in a legal system which demand that people act in ways that seem to defy common sense.

What causes this apparently systemic perversity? The culprit, I suspect, is the practice which I will call "rule-think." One who engages in rule-think always looks, in the first instance, to a rule in order to determine whether a given action is justifiable. The rule-thinker doesn't consider whether the act is justifiable by virtue of its consequences; nor does he ask whether the action is intrinsically good or bad. When a rule prohibits an action, that action is deemed unjustifiable. But if a rule can be found which permits it, then that action suddenly becomes acceptable. In the curious "logic" of rule-think, the mere fact that a rule governs in any case is of paramount importance.

Bureaucrats, lawyers and judges often look foolish when they engage in rule-think. They don't appear to care about the questions that seem most relevant to those who are not steeped in their culture, i.e., they don't ask whether the public will be better off if others are allowed to engage in the activity under consideration. Rule-thinkers argue about whether Rule A, Rule B or Rule C actually governs in the given case. They scour legislative codes, administrative regulations and judicial opinions looking for some "loophole" which will justify the behavior they want to justify. And they all agree that an action is justified, even if completely absurd, if a rule can be produced which credibly sanctions that action.

Those who engage in rule-think can concede that sometimes they look foolish. But are they *really* foolish? In the Mother Teresa case, the Charity did not file suit in state court to compel the housing board to override the regulations. But if it had, would it have been rational for a judge to disregard the regulations?

Despite the ferocious pounding the American legal system has received in the last few years, everyone seems to be very comfortable with judicial rule-think. Indeed, a judge who took it upon herself to "correct" the regulations would be roundly criticized for the *ultra vires* act. Even the most vociferous conservative critics of the regulatory state do not advocate that judges should ignore duly enacted law. Their claim is that the regulatory state must be dismantled through proper legislative channels, by repealing certain law, passing others and shifting jurisdiction from larger entities, such as the federal government, to smaller more accountable ones, such as states and municipalities. In the meantime, however, "the law's the law."

The lack of any plausible opposition nevertheless should not stop us from examining the presuppositions of one of our most deeply entrenched practices. Indeed, it is fascinating that no one attacks the root cause of the law's perversity, i.e., judicial rule-think. Why don't the critics of the current system go "all the way" and declare judges who apply the law when doing so does more harm than good irrational? Put somewhat irreverently, if the law is an ass, what does that make judges?

An economist might try to rehabilitate judicial rationality by pointing to the sanctions that would befall judges should they fail to apply the appropriate regulations. These penalties would not be criminal because judges cannot be imprisoned or fined for disregarding statutes.[2] Rather, judges would suffer "reputational" costs because their rulings would surely be reversed on appeal and these "external negative incentives" would probably deter them from aiding, for example, the saintly nun.

This is all true, but our question just resurfaces at a higher level: why would an appeals court overrule an apparently reasonable decision by a lower court? It is futile to appeal to the public disapprobation which the higher court would face if it failed to reverse—one would of course then need to explain why we would criticize a court for acting reasonably. The attempt to explain rational obedience to legal rules by citing the costs of non-compliance is therefore hopeless—the meting out of penalties is an activity whose rationality itself must be justified.

These questions are rarely posed, I think, because the answers are thought to be so obvious. In a democratic system, the argument would go, there is a strict division of labor: popularly elected legislatures are supposed to "make" the laws and courts are supposed to "apply" them. For a judge to disregard a law is to substitute her own judgment for those of the people's representatives. We require judges to strictly follow the law because we don't trust them to act as we would want them to act. Judges, therefore, are rational to defer to the legislature because they recognize the importance of the democratic process.

Despite its initial plausibility, this explanation is surely misplaced here. The case of Mother Teresa is not one where the interests of the legislature and judge would have diverged. On the contrary, everyone involved desperately wanted these privately run homeless shelters to open. No one cared that these buildings lacked "useless" elevators.

It is therefore perverse to think that democratic principles are offended when judges do what we all want them to do. The Democracy Argument is appropriate in quite different contexts. Legislative supremacy is compromised when, for example, the judiciary refuses to enforce constitutional rules due to principled disagreements with the legislature. Judges usurp power whenever they decide individual cases as they see fit and willfully ignore the intended direction of statutes. However, in the Mother Teresa case, no similar conflict would have arisen. Why don't we then allow courts to disregard laws that lead to undeniably bad results?

It might be argued that judges should not be trusted with making these determinations. If judges were allowed to decide whether a result were "absurd" or "undeniably bad," they would abuse that discretion and end up thwarting the will of the people. There would be a strong temptation for judges with well-defined political views to claim that an outcome is in derogation of the legislature's intentions when they simply didn't like the legally mandated result.

It is unclear, however, why we should distrust judges here, but not with the many other tasks that judges are solely authorized to perform. Courts are charged, for example, with interpreting statutes and, indeed, must often appeal to legislative intent when deciding cases. Why are we not afraid that judicial activists will claim that they are interpreting the law and enacting the will of the people when they are actually trying to further their own ideological agendas? U.S. courts are also allowed to strike down statutes that fail to pass constitutional muster. Why is the determination that a piece of legislation is "unfair" (and hence violative of Substantive Due Process) or discriminates with respect to a "fundamental right" (and hence violative of Equal Protection) less prone to abuse than the assessment of whether a rule is "absurd" or not?

B. The Dilemma Stated

The separation of powers issue is, in reality, a red herring. The problem posed is not unique to judicial rule-think in modern democratic legal systems. Most rule-guided activities, whether the rules are legal, moral, social or personal, will face these types of questions.

The central dilemma concerning rules can be stated abstractly as follows: Consider any rule R and suppose that R requires an agent X to do A in circumstances C. When C obtains, either there is a better option than A available or there isn't. If there is a better option, then it would irrational for X to perform the inferior option A. On the other hand, if there is no better option, then it is rational for X to A, but not because A is required by R, but because rational agents should always pick options which have no better rivals. It, therefore, seems that rule-guided behavior can never be justified—if the rule gives the wrong result, then it is irrational to be guided by the rule; if the rule gives the right result, then the guidance of the rule is irrelevant.

As we can see, the question in the Mother Teresa case is merely another, albeit more sensationalistic, instantiation of this general dilemma. We wanted to know how it could be rational for judge to be guided by the housing rule requiring owners to install elevators in all renovated multi-story buildings. If disregarding the law were better than following it, then it would be irrational for the judge to affirm the board's ruling. If following the law were just as good as disregarding it, then it would be irrelevant that the rule requires the judge to deny Mother Teresa the occupancy certificate.

The Democracy Argument cannot solve this dilemma because democratic principles merely forbid judges from using their own beliefs and values in adjudication when they diverge from those of the legislature. But why is guidance by the housing regulations optimal *relative to the legislature's values*? If judges believe that there are strong reasons for them to evaluate options according to the beliefs and values of the legislature, then when disregarding the law is preferred according to those criteria, it would be irrational for the judge to follow the housing regulations. If, on the other hand, conforming to the law were optimal, it would be irrelevant that the legal rules require what is best from the legislature's perspective.

C. INSTRUMENTAL RATIONALITY

The dilemma about rules is very powerful because its assumptions are so weak. No presuppositions were made about the kinds of beliefs or values a rational person may or must have. Nor was any specific method of ranking options required. The only condition imposed on rational action was the prohibition against choosing an option that was judged to be inferior to another available option. This assumption should be completely uncontroversial. If the ultimate standard of rationality, whatever that may be, assesses option A to be better than option B, then it cannot counsel an agent to choose B over A. Let us call this the "Maximality" condition.[3]

> **Maximality**: An agent should never choose an option that compares unfavorably with another option.

Notice that no demand is made that rational agents choose the "best" option available. Such a condition would have been too strong. To be the "best," an option must be at least as good as all the other options. However, if some values are incommensurable, then no option may be the best or among the best. In such a case, a rational agent is permitted to choose any of those options that are not "bested," i.e., for which there is no comparably better option.

While the dilemma is very powerful, its scope should not be overexaggerated. The dilemma is not meant to challenge all rule-following activities. It is aimed, rather, at practices we might describe as "rule-guided" behavior. An agent is being "guided" by a rule when that agent takes the fact that the rule is applicable as a *conclusive reason* to follow it. It is possible, however, for someone to follow a rule but not be guided by it. For example, I am presently following the rule prohibiting murder because I am not now killing anyone or plotting to do so. I am not being guided by the rule against murder because I would not say that I am restraining myself from killing "because of the rule." I am not killing anyone because I have no inclination to do so. The dilemma does not touch cases like this, where the rule-following amounts to "mere conformity" to a rule.

Nor does the dilemma impugn all rule-guided behavior. Let me call rule-guided behavior "intrinsic" if an agent who is committed to it assigns a positive value to mere obedience to the rule. According to some theologies, religious observance should be viewed in this way. Given that the highest value is conformity to God's wishes, divine commands should be followed because, by doing so, one is conforming to the divine will.

Suppose Joel, who is an orthodox Jew, accords the religious injunction not to eat pork intrinsic value. Even though the forbearance from eating pork does maximize Joel's utility, it seems right to say that the rule "guided" his conduct. Not eating pork is optimal precisely because he assigns a positive value to obeying the rule.

Intrinsic rule-guidance dodges the dilemma because in such cases the rules are valued for their own sake. The rules are not means to greater ends that exist independently of the rules—the ends are simply to follow the rules. Therefore, such rules can be relevant to practical reasoning at the same time that agents who follow them are maximizing expected utility.

Clearly, the dilemma cuts at the rationality of "instrumental" rule-guidance.[4] The enigma surrounding rules is the apparent oddity of a rational agent citing a rule as a conclusive reason for his action and, in the same breath, admitting that he heeded the rule solely for the benefits it brings. If the agent assigns no value to obeying the rule as such, how can it have been so important in justifying his action? The only reasons for action are those that the rule is meant to serve. If the balance of the underlying reasons for action tilts towards conformity to the rule, then the fact that the rule applies does not matter in the least. And if the balance tipped the other way, the same thing is true: the fact that the rule applies does not matter in the least.

The dilemma, therefore, could be solved if none of the rules commonly followed were instrumental in nature. Such an idea, however, is simply preposterous. The rules of certain religions and possibly games aside, it is hard to imagine that the majority of rules are followed solely because we like following them. To be sure, some do find pleasure in following rules, but that is because following rules is instrumentally valuable. We prize the rules we follow because they enable us to achieve goals that we could not achieve otherwise, not because of their intrinsic worth. The claim is even more absurd in the Mother Teresa case. Surely only a very warped judge could derive that much pleasure from following the housing code in that situation. Most judges would truly regret having to do what they legally had to do, or so I would hope.

D. GODWIN BITES THE BULLET

The dilemma might sound familiar to those acquainted with the literature on utilitarianism, insofar as a slightly different version of the argument has been used by many to prove the alleged incoherence of rule-utilitarianism.[5] According to a rule-utilitarian moral theory, an act is justified if and only if it is required by a rule general conformity to which produces more human happiness than any other rule.[6] This is contrasted with act-utilitarianism which holds that an act is justified if and only if that act itself maximizes human happiness.[7]

The problem with rule-utilitarianism is that it is not clear how it can be a form of utilitarianism and not be act-utilitarianism. If an action required by a rule fails to maximize social utility, all things considered, then it seems immaterial that the rule is better than all other rules. What matters to a utilitarian is the maximization of human happiness and that's it. On the other hand, if the action required by the rule does maximize social utility, then the rule-utilitarian recommendation coincides with that of act-utilitarianism. Hence, it seems as if rule-utilitarianism is either act-utilitarianism or not utilitarianism.

This argument is simply seen to be an instance of our dilemma. It is run by substituting a specific standard of evaluation, namely, the maximization of human happiness, for our general standard of maximality. This should give those act utilitarians who accept the implications of this argument cause for concern. If the argument is valid, then most rule-guided behavior becomes suspect, not just moral rules.

Indeed, it is this type of reasoning that drove the act-utilitarian William Godwin to anarchism.[8] He claimed that no political authority could be morally legitimate: assume that before an authority issues an order to perform A, A is an act which the subject is already morally obligated to perform because it maximizes social utility. When the authority issues the order to A, the subject is still morally obligated to A. Hence, the order is redundant and has no independent normative force. "The nature of happiness and misery, pleasure and pain, is independent of positive institution. It is immutably true, that whatever tends to procure a balance of the former is to be desired, and whatever tends to procure a balance of the latter is to be rejected."[9]

Alternatively, assume that before the authority issues an order to A, the subject is morally forbidden to A because it does not tend to promote general happiness. The mere fact that the authority now commands the agent to A cannot make A morally permissible. "The most crowded forum, or the most venerable senate, cannot make one proposition a rule of justice that was not substantially so, previously to their decision."[10] Hence, the order is immoral and has no independent normative force. Godwin's conclusion: The mere fact that an authority has ordered one to act does not give anyone, or at least an act-utilitarian, a moral reason to obey. "To a rational being there can be but one rule of conduct, justice, and one mode of ascertaining that rule, the exercise of his understanding."[11]

If Godwin is right, then the act-utilitarian is in trouble. Act-utilitarians are in danger of throwing out the baby with the bath water: by using the dilemma to discredit rule-utilitarianism, they run the risk of impugning most rule-guided behavior. The utilitarian anarchist, of course, welcomes this conclusion. However, those act-utilitarians who hope to explain the role that rules can play in political, as well as personal, life have some explaining to do.

E. The Rule of Law

The standard response given by act utilitarians is to point out that the choice to follow rules can bring in its wake long-term benefits even though it might have short-term costs. One of the prime benefits that act-utilitarians tout for rule-guidance is predictability. Legal officials should stick to the rules because they enable the rest of us to anticipate their actions, thereby cutting down on the future's uncertainty and increasing personal autonomy. Jeremy Bentham, the prototypical and archetypal act-utilitarian, was a critic of the Common Law precisely because Common Law judges were permitted to overrule precedent.

> An old resolution made in the teeth of an old established rule is mischievous — on what account? In that it puts men's expectations universally to a fault, and shakes whatever confidence they may have had in the stability of any rules of Law, reasonable or not reasonable: that stability on which every thing that is valuable to a man depends. Beneficial be it in ever so high a degree to the party in whose favour it is made, the benefit it is of to him can never be so great as to outweigh the mischief it is of to the community at large. Make the best of it, it is general evil for the sake of partial good. It is what Lord Bacon calls setting the whole house on fire, in order to roast one man's egg.[12]

Bentham's position is obviously extreme. His concerns about the destabilizing effects of Common Law revision are certainly exaggerated, and his rigid policy of following judicial precedent decidedly impractical. His general point is nevertheless well-taken: judges must be cognizant of the fact that people rely on the rules of law and that disregarding them in particular cases frustrates settled expectations and breeds uncertainty and disappointment. Were the judge in the Mother Teresa case to disregard the housing regulations, it is possible that the net utility would have been negative: the short-term benefits of allowing two homeless shelters to open might be dwarfed by the destabilizing effects on the population as a whole.

A "qualified" judicial deference to legal rules is, therefore, not only consistent with act-utilitarianism but also demanded by it. The "qualification," of course, is that judges should defer to duly enacted law only as long as doing so maximizes utility. However, it is possible that deviating from the rules will increase social utility, even given the costs of decreased predictability. Then deference would be tantamount to irrational "rule-worship," the pathology of the rule-utilitarian. In fact, this is the position that Bentham eventually adopted later in his career. In his plans for a reconstructed court of Equity, Bentham allowed judges to ignore rules of law if doing so could maximize social utility. But he was quick to caution that there is a strong presumption against exercising that prerogative.[13]

One, of course, does not have to be a utilitarian to recognize the value of predictability. Many non-utilitarians believe that the Rule of Law is valuable precisely because the practice of following rules fosters predictability and engenders reliance. For example, Stephen Perry, who is a deontological Dworkinian, believes the normativity of rules in decision-making stems in part from integrity concerns: judges have an obligation to make present decision-making cohere with past decision-making. However, he also believes that fidelity to rules enhances predictability, fulfills expectations and promotes fairness. This gives judges strong moral reasons to pay deference to prior authoritative rulings.

> [A judge's] justification for deference [to precedent] is that her moral fallibility and the concomitant potential for unpredictability in her decision-making might create certain difficulties for other persons, in the form of uncertainty about how they should plan their lives, that can be at least partially rectified by instituting a practice of following precedents.[14]

The picture that emerges from this line of reasoning is that each adjudicatory occasion can be modeled as a decision between following a legal rule and departing from it. A judge should decide to apply a rule when the balance of reasons supports such a choice. Hence, following rules when they give locally suboptimal results can be justified as rational when the decision to follow a rule promotes certain values (i.e., predictability and fairness) and renders that option globally optimal. Yet, this model does not sanction the fetishizing of rules. Whenever the application of a rule would give globally suboptimal results (even if locally optimal), it is irrational for any agent to choose to apply such a rule in such a case.

Let me call this model the "Decision Model" for rules. Decision models are intuitively appealing because they appear to pay homage to the virtues of rules but temper that respect with a distaste for rule worship. This is probably why many commentators, including practicing judges, treat such accounts as fairly accurate descriptions of judicial behavior. For example, Justice Cardozo has written: "The rules and principles of case law have never been treated as final truths, but as working hypotheses, continually retested in those great laboratories of the law, the courts of justice. Every new case is an experiment; and if the accepted rule which seems applicable yields a result which is felt to be unjust, the rule is reconsidered."[15] However, Common Law judges should not be too quick to deviate from established doctrine. "It may not be modified at once, for the attempt to do absolute justice in every single case would make the development and maintenance of general rules impossible."

Likewise, the Realist Jerome Frank commented:

> The task of the judge, if well done, is no simple one. He must balance human interests and determine which of several opposing claims the law should favor in order to promote social well-being. As each case comes before him, he must weigh the claims of the parties. He must determine whether to fit a particular case into the terms of some old rule (either because they are working well, or because men acted in reliance upon them and he considers the protection of

such reliance socially valuable) or to "legislate" by revising and adjusting preexisting rules to the circumstances of the instant controversy. If these powers of the judiciary are unwisely exercised, the community will suffer.[16]

In this paper, I would like to argue that Decision models cannot rationalize the process we have called judicial rule-think. Judges who have the choice of whether to follow the law, and are believed to have that choice, could not rationally be guided by legal rules. For the benefits that are normally thought to follow from having judges reason in this manner, i.e. predictability and fairness, could not be had if those obligated to apply the law were known to be autonomous.

By contrast, I will claim that the limitations imposed by legal rules must be understood as constraints on action. A judge who presides over any dispute must be seen as having no choice whether he will apply the law or not. It is this commitment to the law, I will argue, which vindicates judicial rule-think and enables the Rule of Law to flourish.

II. Rules and Standards

Lawyers commonly distinguish between "rules" and "standards."[17] A rule is taken to be "bright-lined," which is to say that its application to concrete fact situations is fairly clear. An agent following a rule can usually do so in a relatively mechanical way, without having to engage in moral deliberations or balance policy considerations. Stock examples of rules include: "Don't drive over 55 MPH," "No dogs in the restaurant," and "The statute of limitation for medical malpractice cases is five years."

Standards, on the other hand, require some form of evaluative discretion in order to determine their applicability. Usually that discretion is moral in nature. Consider, for example, the negligence standard "Agents have a duty to act as a reasonable person would." In order to determine what a reasonable person would do in a given situation, agents must engage in ethical deliberations—they must see whether the risks being imposed on others are morally permissible given the circumstances. Often, however, the discretion to be exercised is directed towards some policy goal not necessarily moral in nature. Examples of these latter standards include Section 1 of the Sherman Act ("unreasonable restraints on trade"), the "probable cause" requirement for arrests and the "best interests of the child" analysis for custody determinations.

Employing standards to guide conduct has its advantages. First, since there is usually little difference between a standard's formulation and its justification, this type of direction is essentially purposive. Conduct is usually sanctioned by a given standard only if it furthers the standard's ends. Therefore, loopholes are rare and the ability of agents to subvert the law's intention is greatly limited.

Rules, by contrast, often lead to counter-purposive behavior. Perhaps the best examples of exploiting loopholes come from tax law. For instance, after the adoption of the Sixteenth Amendment, Congress relaxed certain depreciation rules for those owning family farms.[18] It was thought that most farmers are financially unsophisticated and would be disadvantaged with respect to more savvy business people. This rule, however, did not distinguish between those farmers who were financially sophisticated and those who were not. Many people who were fiscally adept decided to invest in farms so that they could take advantage of the liberalized depreciated schedules. The doctors and lawyers who invested in tax shelters undermined the law's aim by taking advantage of the formal nature of the tax code.

Second, guidance by standards allows agents to make situation-sensitive judgments. By calling for a large degree of discretion in implementation, agents are permitted to consider a wide range of factors in deciding whether conduct conforms to the standard. Rules, by contrast, lack this contextuality. They specify in advance those cases that are forbidden or permitted, independent of the normative setting. Rules, therefore, tend to be either under- or over-inclusive; under-inclusive when they fail to cover cases that should be covered, and over-inclusive when they cover cases that should not be covered. For example, the rule "No driving over 55 MPH" prohibits *all* drivers from exceeding 55 MPH. Excellent drivers are not allowed to speed even though they may drive safer at 75 MPH than poor drivers who drive at 45 MPH. The standard "Drive safely," on the other hand, would distinguish between these two cases. The excellent driver would be given license to drive over 55 MPH, while the poor driver would have to travel at a slower, more manageable pace.

This last example, however, also shows that the advantages of standards over rules will often be outweighed by its disadvantages. First, there is the administrative problem of monitoring compliance—police might not be able to tell whether a driver is good or not and, therefore, whether they are breaking the law. Even if this could be known, getting the information may be costly and not worth the effort. Second, using the standard "Drive safely" would greatly reduce consistency in enforcement. Different officials would have divergent conceptions of safety and would, therefore, apply the standard in conflicting ways. One driver might be allowed to drive 70 MPH on Tuesday and then get ticketed on Wednesday for driving at 50 MPH. Third, because of this lack of consistency, enforcement would be quite unpredictable. Motorists would not know whether police officers or municipal judges would rate them as good drivers or not. A driver, for example, might not be able to predict whether, on any given day, he would be ticketed for going at—what for him is—a "safe" speed. He might get ticketed for going 50 MPH, while another would be allowed to speed at 70 MPH.

In a traffic regime using the "Drive Safely" standard, motorists would have two basic responses. Some would be risk averse, and decide to drive slower than 55 MPH so as to avoid being fined erroneously. Others would believe that they were good drivers and drive faster than 55 MPH, confident that those enforcing the traffic laws would come to the same conclusion. This result would be favorable as long as the risk averse group consisted of poor drivers and the confident group was made up of skilled drivers. However, if this were not so, bad consequences could ensue. Some competent motorists would drive very slowly to work, while some inept drivers would race along causing many accidents. The marginal utility gained from allowing some good motorists to driver faster than 55 MPH might be offset by the marginal disutility of the accidents caused by poor motorists also driving at those speeds. Likewise, the marginal utility gained by having some poor motorists drive slower than 55 MPH might be outweighed by the marginal disutility of having a great many competent drivers travelling at a snail's pace.

Despite the under- and over-inclusiveness of the 55 MPH rule, its virtue consists in its "definiteness"—at least people subject to that rule know when they are going to get fined. Those who are risk averse can be confident that they will not be ticketed for riding at 55 MPH, while those who erroneously believe themselves to be excellent drivers will be deterred from driving at socially unacceptable speeds. The costs of the bright-line are often outweighed by its benefits.

The prevalence of rules in modern legal systems is, therefore, a response to a "signaling" problem: law-makers need to convey their will to both law-subjects and law-appliers in a manner understandable to all. The channels of communication, however, are not always clear. Because different people will use their judgments to arrive at different conclusions, it is often imperative that legislative formulations be relatively value-neutral. Coordination is often achieved by directives that are formal in nature—those who follow such rules need only employ their linguistic intuitions, rather than their moral ones.

It is not enough for legislatures to issue formal rules, however. These rules cannot just be suggested guidelines; legal officials must stick to them and refuse to apply their independent judgment concerning the balance of reasons. The law thus promises and threatens: it promises to allow or reward conduct conforming to the rules and it threatens to punish or not reward actions that deviate from the rules.

The law's promise to follow the rules is meant to reassure reasonable people that they will not get penalized erroneously for acting reasonably. Similarly, the law's threat to follow the rules is meant to deter unreasonable people from acting unreasonably. However, because the rules will tend to be under- and/or over-inclusive, the law's remedy will have very serious side-effects: it will end up promising that unreasonable conduct will be allowed or even rewarded if done within the provinces of the rules and threatening to punish or not reward deviations from the rules even though such behavior is eminently sensible and socially beneficial.

III. Threats and Promises

A. Problems

It might be comforting to think that the Rule of Law takes the form of a combination threat and promise. For threats and promises are familiar entities of practical reasoning. Threats are used to deter others from engaging in behavior that threateners wish would not take place and promises are used to reassure others that promisors will act in ways that promisees wish will take place. Although it may sometimes be both irrational and immoral to threaten or promise, it seems that there are certain situations where it is perfectly appropriate to do so.

Yet, as Thomas Schelling reminds us, the rationality of threatening and promising behavior ought not to be taken for granted. Consider threats. A threat involves the expression of an intention to act in the future in a costly manner, at a time when the action can no longer influence conduct. One follows through on a threat only when the threat has been ineffective! If the mugger says "Your money or your life" it is unclear why the victim would turn over his money. Why doesn't the victim reason as follows: "If he shoots me, then he will have to run away and thereby lose his chance at getting my money. Besides, he will be charged for murder if caught. Therefore, it would be irrational for him to carry out his threat." And knowing that the victim will not treat his threat as credible, it would seem irrational for the mugger to make the threat in the first place.

Applying this to the context of adjudication, we might wonder what is to be gained from ticketing an excellent driver for going 60 MPH? Once the threat has been made, there seems to be no reason why legal officials should carry them out when doing so involves a net moral loss.

Now consider promises. Promises are similar to threats in that they usually involve expressions of intentions to act in a costly manner in the future at a time when the action can longer affect conduct. Assume A promises B to mow B's lawn in exchange for the use of his lawnmower. As a matter of self-interest rationality, once A has used B's lawnmower, he should refuse to mow B's lawn. Of course, as a matter of self-interested rationality, B should not lend his lawnmower to A. Because B knows that if A has the choice he will not uphold his end of the bargain, B cannot rationally expect that his lawn will be mowed after A has used it.[19]

Again, applying this to adjudication, we might wonder why the IRS would reward professional syndicates who bought cattle simply to appropriate the tax deductions? It is true that the tax code allowed such benefits. And it is also true that having everyone believe that the IRS will follow congressional directives will greatly diminish anxieties and promote planning. However, once everyone has adjusted their behavior in light of these expectations, why follow through on these promises? Isn't it irrational for legal officials to permit unreasonable conduct to continue? And isn't it irrational for everyone to believe that legal officials will permit this behavior to take place if they, at the same time, believe that legal officials are rational?

While these problems arise chiefly with respect to rules, they can crop up even in cases where standards are involved. For example, reductions in child support awards are generally permitted only if the supporting parent can show that such changes would be in the best interests of the supported child or children. This restriction is thought justified by the need to deter the supporting parent from claiming changed circumstances in an effort to harass the supported parent. This standard works fine most of the time; however, it gives bad results when the supported parent uses the money chiefly for him- or herself. The supporting parent cannot get a reduction in payments even though the children are not receiving any of the money, given that the children's welfare would be unaffected by such a modification. The puzzle of judicial rule-think, therefore, applies to judicial standard-think as well, although the magnitude of the problem is much less severe.

B. Some Responses That Fail

It may seem as if there are two obvious responses to these challenges. First, if the law did not keep its promises, those who relied on them and expected their fulfillment would be treated unfairly. This inequity would often outbalance the bad consequences that would follow from the enforcement of the rules.

Second, fidelity to the law is a diachronic principle—it applies to continuous legal systems and its benefits can only be understood in such a context. If the law did not follow through on its stated intentions, people would stop believing the authorities and would adjust their behavior accordingly. Legal officials choose to stick to the rules because *in the long run* the costs of deviating from them are too high to bear. They recognize the need to cultivate and maintain a "reputation" for rule-adherence.

Yet, neither argument is persuasive. As for the fairness argument, why, it might be asked, is it unfair to frustrate a citizen's expectations? Because, according to the fairness argument, the citizen trusts that the law will fulfill his or her expectations. But why is it justified for the citizen to have such faith? The justification for such expectations cannot come from the fact that it would be unfair not to apply the law in their case. This reasoning is circular—one cannot establish the unfairness of legal officials' reneging on their promises by reference to the justified expectations of citizens and then justify these expectations by citing the unfairness of unsettling such expectations.

The Reputation Argument fares no better. In an effort to establish that authorities have reason to carry out their promises or threats in any given instance, the Reputation Argument contends that such behavior will have beneficial global effects. If the authorities carry out their stated intentions, this will lead the subjects to predict similar behavior in the future; likewise, for any reneging on the part of the authorities. However, in order for this argument to work, these theorists must first show that the subjects have reason to believe that like behavior will follow in the future—such an inference cannot simply be assumed.

However, in situations where common belief exists with regards to the rationality and morality of the participants, any attempt to show that present conduct can influence future expectations leads to an infinite regress. In order to demonstrate that the authorities have reason to follow through on their promises and threats in the present, the Reputation Argument must first establish that the authorities have reason to follow through on their promises and threats in the future. Believing that the authorities are rational, moral and autonomous, the only way the subjects will be persuaded that the authorities will apply the rules in the future is if it is rational to choose to do so at that time. But what reason can the authorities have in the future? Wouldn't it be irrational to be guided by the rules then as well?

Reapplying the Reputation Argument to the future case gets us nowhere: in order to show that the authorities have reason to follow through on their promises and threats in the future, the Reputation Argument must establish that the authorities have reason to follow through on their promises and threats in the future of that future. Yet, what reason can the authorities have to act that way in the future of that future? We can obviously repeat the Reputation Argument at this point, but the same problems will always reappear at the next iteration.

The problem with the Reputation Argument is its bootstrapping. It tries to establish present optimality by reference to future optimality. It can succeed, however, only if the claim that the authorities have reason to apply the law in the future can be independently sustained. Our puzzle arises precisely because we don't know what this independent justification could be. If we had it, we wouldn't need the Reputation Argument.

We might, at this point, opt for the solution that Schelling offered in *The Strategy of Conflict*: it may be rational for someone to try to convince another that he is irrational. The mugger, for example, if rational, will want to convince the victim that he is irrational and hence the victim will succumb to his threats. And in the long run, it may be rational to cultivate and maintain a reputation for irrationality.

To be sure, judges could persuade future litigants that they will apply the law in the future if they could convince them of their irrationality or immorality. It may be rational for criminals to act irrationally in order to get their victims to take their demands seriously. Yet, it would be very strange if this were the case for judges—do we really want to say that the Rule of Law essentially depends on the community believing that their legal officials are crazy or evil? We should hope that the dilemma can be solved without saying that the Rule of Law is sustained by our thinking that the judicial mind is essential an irrational one.

C. WHY COHERENCE IS NO HELP

Theorists who subscribe to the Decision Model might try to use a Dworkinian "coherence" argument to justify judicial rule-think. If a judge punishes one person for violating the rules, then he becomes obligated by the virtue of integrity to do so in future cases. Political morality requires that like cases be treated alike—legal officials must not make exceptions for some people and not others. As Dworkin would put it, legal officials are prohibited from instituting "checkerboard" solutions.[20]

This argument, however, clearly begs the question. Treating like cases alike does not mean that all similar cases must be treated in similar ways. The similarities must be *morally* relevant—integrity requires only that morally similar cases be treated in morally similar ways. We now ask the question: why is rule-conforming behavior a morally relevant category? Why, for example, should all those who drive over the speed limit be lumped into the same category? This is proper only if we can establish that adherence to the rules is, by itself, morally relevant and this has not yet been shown.

Indeed, integrity to the principles that underpin the rules would counsel judges to deviate from the law in such situations if they were unconstrained and believed to be so. After all, manifestly excellent drivers should not be punished merely because they exceed the speed limit. Given that they are driving safely, their activities are socially beneficial. Similarly, financially sophisticated farmers should be denied lucrative tax benefits, even though the rules require it. Insofar as the purpose of the rules is to help those who lack their fiscal acumen, their activities are socially unproductive.

One might argue that punishing excellent drivers for driving safely but over the speed limit is indeed supported by the principle of ensuring that motorists drive safely. For if judges allowed excellent drivers to go faster than the speed limit, this would encourage poorer drivers to do so and, hence, would increase the frequency of unsafe driving on the roads. Judges would then have a reason to apply these rules because such a practice coheres with the principles that underlie that area of the law.

Despite the seductive nature of this type of argument, we know it to be fallacious within the context of the Decision Model. Agents who are believed unconstrained and rational cannot deter activity when following through on their threats does more harm than good. Poor drivers who fancied themselves excellent drivers would rationally predict that rational and moral legal officials would not fine them for driving over the speed limit. From their perspective, to conform to the rules is to fail to act in accordance with the balance of reasons. A principle that nevertheless required judges to carry out their threats would be useless, and hence would not be deserving of respect.

IV. Commitment to the Law

A. Binding Oneself to the Rule of Recognition

According to the Decision Model, people who are guided by rules are free not to follow them if they so wish. Nevertheless, these people choose to follow the rules each time they deem the rules applicable. Each act of compliance with a rule implies choice.

If the Decision Model were true, then I believe that the dilemma would be a knock-down argument: if agents who are guided by rules actually have a choice to apply them when they deem them applicable, then it would be irrational to decide to apply the rules when doing so does more harm than good. Contrawise, if it is better for these agents to conform to the rules, then their applicability is normatively irrelevant.

I would like to suggest, by contrast, that we see rules as operating as constraints on action. An agent who adopts a rule is strategically interacting with another agent—his later self. The present self, by his decision to guide his actions by a rule, constrains his later self, precluding future choice behavior inconsistent with the rule. In this "game," the present self makes the first move and the future self will be barred from choosing contrary to such a rule if the present self's actions are successful. This *lack of choice* is precisely the point of having rules.

Adopting a rule is doing internally what Ulysses was able to do externally when he lashed himself to the mast.[21] It is to forgo later choice by the operation of the Will, but it is as real as using some precommitment mechanism. This view of rule-guided behavior might be called the "Constraint Model" where rules[22] are relevant to practical reasoning because, and only because, they affect feasibility. A rule, once adopted, is not a factor to be considered in future deliberation about whether to comply. Once adopted, the agent no longer deliberates about whether to comply. The rule-guided agent merely figures out what counts as implementation of the rule, not which action will maximize expected utility.

Notice that the dilemma dissolves once the Constraint Model is assumed: when conformity to a rule is suboptimal, it is not irrational for an agent to apply the rule. For, on this view, when an agent is committed to a rule, that agent has no choice but to apply the rule when she recognizes that it is applicable. Likewise, the optimality of conformity does not rob a rule of its normativity. Because rules affect the feasibility of non-conformity, they make conformity the best available option by default.

We might see a judge's relationship to the law in accordance with the Constraint Model. When a judge becomes a judge, she commits herself to apply the laws when she deems them applicable. She does this by committing herself to what H.L.A. Hart called a "rule of recognition."[23] This master rule specifies those features that a rule or standard must possess in order for the judge to be legally obligated to apply it in any given case. In the American legal system, for example, the rule of recognition requires judges to apply the rules and standards issued by federal, state and local legislatures, as well as those issued by courts of the same or higher jurisdiction.[24]

By committing to the legal system's rule of recognition, a judge will thus be constraining her future self to implement the rules that share these authoritative features. She will not be choosing to apply the rules when she deems them applicable—she will simply follow through on her earlier commitment. And given our previous discussions, it is easy to see why this constraint is rational to adopt. For the commitment enables the Rule of Law to flourish. When judges constrain themselves to apply the rules, people will be led to predict that they will follow through on the law's threat. Reliance would also be engendered by the constraint. It would be reasonable for future litigants to rely on judicial fulfillment of the law's promise by applying the rules regardless of consequences.

According to the Constraint Model, the inference from the belief that judges are committed to the law to the prediction that they will fulfill their commitment does not lead to an infinite regress. For if rule-guided behavior is not a form of decision-making, there is no need to explain the rationality of an instance of rule-guidance by reference to future consequences. It is rational for the committed judge to apply the law in any given instance because that is the only option available. To be sure, any instance of rule-guidance will enhance predictability and hence engender important positive benefits; however, it is crucial that enhancing predictability is not the reason for following through but rather the reason for adopting the commitment in the first place.

Even if the law is sometimes an ass, therefore, judges are not asses when they apply it in those cases. This is true regardless of whether applying the law actually does more harm than good in an individual case. For if judges are constrained to apply the law, they must apply it regardless of its consequences.[25]

It should be added that, in order for the law to be predictable, judges need not actually constrain their future selves. It is entirely possible that their commitment to the law is feigned and their choice to apply the law is always made in order to keep up this illusion. If so, we would find ourselves with a "conspiracy theory" of legal rules.

B. FORMALISM

It might be objected that I am making the "formalist" error, i.e., thinking that rules are maximally determinate, and that for every case they constrain how a judge must decide. However, language is open-textured, filled with vague and ambiguous terms and often very malleable. It is, therefore, naive to treat rules as constraining a judge in all cases.

Let me briefly explain why I think this objection is misdirected. Any theory of adjudication will be concerned with a variety of issues. One aspect of the theory will address the effects that legal rules have on the reasoning of judges: once judges deem that a rule is applicable, how does or how should rules affect their practical reasoning? My contention has been that rules are constraints on action.

A theory of adjudication will also be concerned with these assessments of applicability: how should judges arrive at such judgments? This is the central issue for the theory of interpretation. It may turn out that legal rules are much less determinate than is commonly thought. They may not constrain courts to judge them applicable in many cases that arise in litigation.

The question of whether judges are constrained by rules is, therefore, ambiguous. It can mean either: (1) Do rules constrain the actions of judges once judgments of applicability have been resolved? or (2) Do rules constrain judges in their assessments about whether they are applicable? I have been concerned exclusively with the former question.[26]

I do, therefore, believe that in some sense judges makes decisions in adjudication—in fact, judicial opinions are called "judicial decisions." The point, however, is that when they are guided by the law, these decisions are generally about whether the law is applicable, never whether to apply the law. Once these decisions of applicability are made, judges no longer make choices—they merely apply the law.

We can now see that the difference between a rule and a standard is not the difference between a principle that fetters and one that permits autonomous action. When a judge who guides her behavior by law finds that a standard is applicable, that judge is constrained to apply it just as she would a rule. The difference between these norms lies in the degree to which they constrain interpretation. A rule that prohibits the death penalty, for example, constrains a judge's assessment of the legality of using the electric chair more than a standard that prohibits cruel and unusual punishment. Under the first regime, no English speaker could sincerely permit death by electrocution; under the latter, knowledge of English is not enough to force a decision.

V. Feasibility

Because the dilemma is dissolved by arguing that rule-guided behavior is essentially compelled behavior—disregarding the rule is seen as "infeasible," as not being an option available to the agent—it is important that I say at least a few words about the concept of "feasibility" and "optionality" that I am employing. We will say that a course of action is a feasible option for an agent if and only if that agent has the ability to perform that action *for a reason*. A course of action is infeasible, therefore, whenever the agent cannot perform the action for a reason—that is, when that action is not a possible *intentional* action.

Now, if we were to speculate about the mechanisms by which rules render disobedience infeasible, two possibilities come to mind. First, adopting a rule might be the psychological counterpart of precommitment, where the agent is physically disabled from moving his body in certain ways. This physical disability would not be imposed by some external device, but would be generated from "within" by purely psychological means.

I am inclined to think that this approach is unpromising, at least if we attend to the phenomenology of rule-guided behavior. It does not normally seem as if commitment to rules induces physical paralysis. If John adopts a rule never to take another drink of alcohol in a bar, he does not think that somehow he will be physically precluded from ordering the drink. It is not as if he thinks that if he opens his mouth, he will not be able to utter the words "I'll have a beer" or if he does get a beer, his hand will be frozen in the down position. In this respect, he is unlike Ulysses: Ulysses can intend to break free of the rope and try to do so. Rule-guidance, on the other hand, seems more like a constraint on the will. If John really does try to drink alcohol, he will probably end up doing so.

I would like to suggest instead that rules normally prevent agents from "willing" disobedience to its demands, not by physically disabling the will's expression. How might these constraints on the will arise? First, the rule might prevent the agent from considering the reasons for disobeying the rule. The reasons for breaking the rule would, in other words, be "repressed" by the rule. This repression blocks the possibility of intentional action contrary to the rule—the agent, being unaware of reasons for breaking the rule, would be unable to break the rule for a reason. Second, the rule might disable the person's normal psychological inhibitions. An agent in the grip of a rule might no longer be able to withstand certain emotional pressures, such as guilt and shame, even though the agent would be aware of the important reasons for breaking the rule.

All of this is speculation, of course, but I do think it is plausible speculation. If one thinks about the abilities of the human mind, undoubtedly one of its powers is that of repression. We normally hide "reasons for action" from ourselves all the time. Awareness of all the reasons we had for acting one way rather than another would simply be too painful to bear. I am suggesting that when we follow rules, we harness this ability, at least sometimes, to repress certain facts and wishes from our practical reasoning. The most common expression indicative of this process is: "I have a rule against doing this so I am not even going to think about acting otherwise." By refusing to think about it, one guarantees that one cannot break one's rules for reasons.

Most of the time, however, we aren't even aware of repressing reasons for breaking our rules. We simply follow rules without any struggle or conflict, even in situations where if we thought about it, we would be deeply disturbed by our actions. They become almost like habits in that they can be executed virtually without thinking.

The ability to repress reasons is not one that everyone has nor do they have it to the same degree. Nor is the need to repress reasons as important in some people as in others, chiefly because all people do not monitor their actions with the same frequency. As control theorists say, some have longer "feedback loops." In situations where the need for rule-guidance is most acute, for example, in the military, people need to be trained to lengthen their feedback loops. Boot camp consists in training people to ignore their instincts, to react first rather than think. This is accomplished partly through the complete regimentation of life and partly through the compelled performance of absurd tasks like cleaning floors with toothbrushes. The easiest way to get people to repress reasons is, therefore, to stop them from prompting themselves for reasons in the first place.

As for disinhibition, it is well-known that people who act subject to orders can be made to act in monstrous ways. It is not that they don't realize what they are doing; rather, they seem to be unable to oppose the demands of the authority issuing the directives. In reporting on the results of his famous obedience experiments in the 1960's, Stanley Milgram vividly described this phenomenon (Recall that in these experiments, Milgram wanted to see how far ordinary people would go in hurting others when ordered by an authority to do so. The subjects were told that they were to participate in an experiment on learning and negative reinforcement. Whenever the supposed learner would make a mistake, the subject was directed by the leader of the experiment to administer an increasing series of electric shocks to punish the learner for the mistake. To Milgram's surprise, many of the subjects followed the leader's orders and administered what the subjects thought were extremely painful shocks. What was even more surprising is that the subjects often expressed great reservations about continuing with the experiment but followed through anyway because they were ordered to do so.) This is Milgram's description:

> Some people interpret the experimental situation as one in which the subject, in a highly rational manner, can weigh the conflicting values in the situation, process the factors according to some mental calculus, and base his actions on the outcome of this equation. Thus, the subject's predicament is reduced to a

> problem of rational decision making. This analysis ignores a crucial aspect of behavior illuminated by the experiments. Though many subjects make the intellectual decision that they should not give any more shocks to the learner, they are frequently unable to transform this conviction into actions. Viewing these subjects in the laboratory, one can sense their intense inner struggle to extricate themselves from the authority, while ill-defined but powerful bonds hold them at the shock generator. One subject tells the experimenter: "He can't stand it. I'm not going to kill that man in there. You hear him hollering in there. He's hollering. He can't stand it." Although at the verbal level the subject has resolved not to go on, he continues to act in accord with the experimenter's commands. Many subjects make tentative movements toward disobedience but then seem restrained, as if by a bond.[27]

Milgram hypothesized that by accepting the authority of another, one relinquishes the ability to inhibit actions in light of one's own values: "The inhibitory mechanisms which are vital when the individual element functions by itself become secondary to the need to cede control to the coordinating component." I am suggesting that rule-thinkers might be so disinhibited. In rule-guided behavior, we may lose the ability to act autonomously and it may be rationally and morally incumbent upon us to do so.

To be sure, this is all speculation and crude speculation at that. In some sense, it is irrelevant whether the mechanisms I have described are present in normal functioning humans. Strictly speaking, rules can serve the benefits they are meant to serve just in case we think, or it is part of our concept of a rule, that individuals have the ability to constrain their future selves. Whether judges can actually do such a thing is another matter. We might be wrong in our belief that the law, and rules in generally, can give rational agents reasons for action, but this belief is neither incoherent nor implausible.

VI. Hercules or Ulysses?

If the Constraint Model of rules is correct, then judges cannot be morally obligated to decide individual cases according to the balance of reasons. Nor can they be legally obligated to do so. For the balance of reasons absent constraint by rules would counsel judges to break the law. When a rational agent is unconstrained, she is required to maximize and therefore cannot be guided by rules at all. Deterrence and reassurance are impossible by unconstrained rational agents who are believed to be unconstrained and rational. The law works as a moral instrument precisely because judges are not free to apply the principles of morality to individual cases.

Dworkin names his ideal judge Hercules, for only Hercules has the ability to apply the principles of morality to construct a complete justification for the law for every court case.[28] I agree that an ideal judge would have to have great will power and energy. But much of her efforts would be spent on constraining her future self—something which takes great will power—rather than allowing herself the luxury to apply the principles of morality to every case. Perhaps "Ulysses" is a more appropriate role model for judges who are rational and commonly believed to be so.

NOTES

1. Philip K. Howard, *The Death of Common Sense* 1–2 (1994).
2. Except, of course, if they receive monetary compensation for doing so.
3. The term "maximality" is Amartya Sen's. *See* Amartya K. Sen, *Collective Choice and Social Welfare* 9–10 (1970). The Maximality Condition is explicitly endorsed by Hans Hertzberger (who calls it "Optimality") in Hans Hertzberger, "Ordinal Preference and Rational Choice," 41 *Econometrica* 187, 198–99 (1973). Isaac Levi has argued, however, that the Maximality Condition is both too liberal and too restrictive. *See* Isaac Levi, *Hard Choices* 90–95, (1986). Levi's criticisms of the Maximality Condition do not materially affect the discussion in the text.
4. This is not to say that intrinsic rule guidance is free from paradox. On the puzzles that arise in such cases, see my "Authority" in *Oxford Handbook of Jurisprudence and Philosophy of Law*, Jules L. Coleman and Scott J. Shapiro, eds. (Oxford: forthcoming).
5. See, e.g., David Lyons, *The Forms and Limits of Utilitarianism* (1965); David Lyons, "Utility and Rights," in *Theories of Rights* 110, 126 (J. Waldron ed., 1984); R.M. Hare, *Freedom and Reason* 130–6 (1963); John L. Mackie, *Ethics: Inventing Right and Wrong* 136–40 (1977).
6. John Austin is generally credited with being the first unambiguous advocate of rule utilitarianism. See John Austin, *The Province of Jurisprudence Determined* 47–48 (1954). See also Stephen Toulmin, *An Examination of the Place of Reason in Ethics* (1950); Kurt E.M. Baier, *The Moral Point of View* (1958); Marcus G. Singer, *Generalizations in Ethics* (1961); R.B. Brandt, "Some Merits of One Form of Rule Utilitarianism," 3 *University of Colorado Series in Phil.* 39 (1967).
7. See, e.g., G.E. Moore, *Ethics* 121 (1966); J.J.C. Smart, "Extreme and Restricted Utilitarianism," in *Theories of Ethics* 171 (Phillipa Foot ed., 1967).
8. See William Godwin, *Enquiry concerning Political Justice* 90–93 (K. Carter ed., 1971).
9. Id. at 91. Godwin does add that authorities may turn virtuous actions into

vicious ones by offering rewards. Such motivations destroy the selfless character of morally worthy behavior.

10. Id. at 88.
11. Id. at 90.
12. Jeremy Bentham, *A Fragment on Government* 19–20 (J.H. Burns and H.L.A. Hart eds., 1988).
13. See Gerald Postema, *Bentham and the Common Law Tradition* ch. 8 (1986).
14. See Stephen Perry, "Second-Order Reasons, Uncertainty and Legal Theory," 62 *S. Cal. L. Rev.* 913, 970 (1989). See also Michael S. Moore, "A Natural Law Theory of Interpretation" 58 *S. Cal. L. Rev.* 279, 387–88 (1985).
15. Benjamin N. Cardozo, *The Nature of the Judicial Process* 23 (1921) (quoting Munroe Smith).
16. Jerome Frank, *Law and the Modern Mind* 120–21 (1930).
17. See generally Louis Kaplow, "Rules vs. Standards: An Economic Analysis," 42 *Duke L.J.* 557 (1992); Duncan Kennedy, "Form and Substance in Private Law Adjudication," 89 *Harv. L. Rev.* 1685 (1976); Kathleen M. Sullivan, "Foreword: The Justices of Rules and Standards," 106 *Harv. L. Rev.* 22 (1992); Colin S. Diver, "The Optimal Precision of Administrative Rules," 95 *Yale L.J.* 65 (1983); Sunstein, "Problems with Rules," 83 *Cal. L. Rev.* 953, 964 (1995).
18. See Mark Kelman, *A Guide to Critical Legal Studies* 41 (1987).
19. Problems do not disappear when we switch to wholly-executory agreements. Even when neither side has complied, it would seem irrational for either party to live up to their end of the bargain, insofar as this will simply convert the agreement to a partially-executory one and then the problems we have seen in the text reemerge. If A performs first, it will not be rational for B to comply and hence not rational for A to believe that his complying will induce B to comply.
20. See Ronald Dworkin, supra note 2, at 178.
21. But see section V, infra, where I discuss an important disanalogy with Ulysses.
22. All the comments about rules are applicable to standards as well.
23. See H.L.A. Hart, *The Concept of Law* 92–107 (1961).
24. See Kent Greenawalt, "The Rule of Recognition and the Constitution," 85 *Mich. L. Rev.* 621 (1987).
25. It is true that judges are sometimes given the discretion to depart from rules in order to avoid harmful consequences. In these cases, however, it is best to consider avoiding harmful consequences as constituting exceptions to the rules.
26. While these two parts of the theory of adjudication are analytically distinct, they are nonetheless linked. If one thought that rules are maximally indeterminate—that, it is impossible to say whether a rule applies in any individual case—there would be no point in asking the second question of whether they constrain once those judgments are made.
27. Stanley Milgram, *Obedience to Authority* (1974), 148–49
28. See Ronald Dworkin, "Hard Cases," in *Taking Rights Seriously* 81, 105 (1977).

Contributors

Richard J. Arneson, Professor of Philosophy, University of California, San Diego

Marcia W. Baron, Professor of Philosophy, Indiana University

Ruth Chang, Assistant Professor of Philosophy, Rutgers University

Jules L. Coleman, Wesley Newcomb Hohfeld Professor of Jurisprudence, Yale Law School

Michael L. Corrado, Arch Allen Distinguished Professor of Law and Professor of Philosophy, The Law School, The University of North Carolina at Chapel Hill

Robert E. Goodin, Professor of Social & Political Theory and Philosophy, Research School of Social Sciences, The Australian National University

Russell Hardin, Professor of Politics, New York University, and Professor of Political Science, Stanford University

Douglas N. Husak, Professor of Philosophy and Law, Rutgers University

Jody S. Kraus, Professor of Law and E.J. Kelly Research Professor of Law, School of Law, University of Virginia

Christopher Kutz, Assistant Professor of Law, School of Law, University of California, Berkeley

Charles Larmore, Chester D. Tripp Professor in the Humanities and Professor of Philosophy, University of Chicago

Brian Leiter, Charles I. Francis Professor in Law, Professor of Philosophy, and Director of the Law & Philosophy Program, The University of Texas at Austin

Philip Pettit, Professor of Philosophy, Research School of Social Sciences, The Australian National University

Thomas W. Pogge, Associate Professor of Philosophy, Columbia University

Gerald J. Postema, Cary C. Boshamer Professor of Philosophy and Professor of Law, University of North Carolina at Chapel Hill

Geoffrey Sayre-McCord, Bowman and Gordon Gray Professor of Philosophy, University of North Carolina at Chapel Hill

David Schmidtz, Professor of Philosophy and joint Professor of Economics, University of Arizona

Scott J. Shapiro, Professor of Law, Benjamin N. Cardozo School of Law, Yeshiva University

A. John Simmons, Commonwealth Professor of Philosophy and Professor of Law, University of Virginia

Larry S. Temkin, Professor of Philosophy, Rutgers University

George C. Thomas III, Professor of Law, Rutgers University

Printed and bound by CPI Group (UK) Ltd, Croydon, CR0 4YY

16/09/2026

14963380-0001